# THE SCOTT FORESMAN

# Handbook

# for

# Writers

**EIGHTH EDITION**

**JOHN RUSZKIEWICZ**
University of Texas at Austin

**CHRISTY FRIEND**
University of South Carolina

**MAXINE HAIRSTON**
Late of University of Texas at Austin

**Prentice Hall**
Upper Saddle River   London   Singapore
Toronto   Tokyo   Sydney   Hong Kong   Mexico City

**Editorial Director:** Leah Jewell
**Executive Editor:** Paul Crockett
**Assistant Editor:** Melissa Casciano
**Editorial Assistant:** Megan Dubrowski
**Marketing Director:** Brandy Dawson
**Senior Marketing Manager:** Windley Morley
**Marketing Assistant:** Kimberly Caldwell
**Text Permission Specialist:** Kathleen Karcher
**Media Editor:** Christian Lee
**Editorial Development Editor-in-Chief:**
Rochelle Diogenes
**Development Editor:** Laura Olson
**VP/Director of Production and Manufacturing:**
Barbara Kittle
**Production Liason:** Maureen Benicasa
**Prepress & Manufacturing Manager:** Nick Sklitsis
**Prepress & Manufacturing Assistant Manager:**
Mary Ann Gloriande

**Creative Design Director:** Leslie Osher
**Art Director:** Nancy Wells
**Interior & Cover Art Design:** Ximena Tamvakopoulos
**Director, Image Resource Center:** Melinda Patelli
**Manager, Cover Visual Research and Permissions:**
Karen Sanatar
**Manager, Rights and Permissions:** Zina Arabia
**Manager, Visual Research:** Beth Brenzel
**Image Permission Coordinator:** Debbie Latronica
**Cover Art Director:** Leslie Osher
**Photo Researcher:** Kathy Ringrose
**Cover Illustration/Photo:** Philip Rostron/Masterfile
**Full-Service Project Management:** Cindy Miller,
GGS Book Services
**Composition:** GGS Book Services
**Printer/Binder:** Quebecor World Book Services
**Cover Printer:** Phoenix Color Corp.
**Text typeface:** 10/12 Garamond

This book includes 2009 MLA guidelines.

Credits and acknowledgments borrowed from other sources and reproduced, with permission, in this textbook appear on appropriate page within text (or on page 851).

Library of Congress Cataloging-in-Publication Data
Ruszkiewicz, John J., (date)
    The Scott Foresman handbook for writers / John Ruszkiewicz, Christy Friend, Maxine Hairston.—8th ed.
    p. cm.
    Maxine Hariston's name appears first on the earlier ed.
    Includes index.
    ISBN 0-205-73562-2
    1. English language—Rhetoric—Handbooks, manuals, etc. 2. English language—Grammar—Handbooks, manuals, etc. 3. Report writing—Handbooks, manuals, etc. I. Hairston, Maxine. II. Friend, Christy. III. Title.
    PE1408.H2968 2006
    808′.042—dc22
                                                        2006028707

10 9 8 7 6 5 4 3 2 1

# Prentice Hall
## is an imprint of

www.pearsonhighered.com

ISBN 10:    0-205-73562-2
ISBN 13: 978-0-205-73562-4

# Contents

iii

After a hiatus of several editions, Maxine Hairston decided to return to *The Scott Foresman Handbook for Writers* for the eighth edition, coordinating its revision plan and completing a draft of its first chapter before her death on July 22, 2005, at the age of 83. In a remarkable career, Maxine helped to improve the way writing was taught and elevated the status and morale of composition teachers nationally. She retired as professor emerita at the University of Texas at Austin in 1992, but continued to edit her much-admired textbooks, while earning a master's degree in history. Anyone who knew Maxine Hairston appreciated the vitality of her intellect, her absolute delight in learning, and her eternal goodwill and optimism. She was our mentor, colleague, and friend, and we dedicate this edition to her memory.

JR & CF

# Preface

When we published the first edition of *The Scott Foresman Handbook for Writers*, the tools of the trade were still legal pads and typewriters. Students used pens and note cards to record the information they'd found via library catalogs and dusty indexes. Revising a paper meant retyping it or mastering the niceties of correction fluid. Times have certainly changed.

But the guiding principles of *The Scott Foresman Handbook* haven't because they always made sense: ***anticipate the questions that student writers might have and answer them clearly, fully, and imaginatively***. The book has both grown and contracted over the years as the needs (and questions) of writers have evolved. Early editions introduced students to revising with a word processor; this version explains how to compose position papers and how to document sources culled from online library services. And precisely because this handbook has never been a one-trick pony built around one or another single dimension of a writer's work—whether it be *language, reading, technology,* or *visual learning*—it has remained a vital and authoritative guide for generations of students.

Each new edition has provided complete and remarkably up-to-date material about writing processes, argumentation, style, grammar, mechanics, and punctuation, offered in a friendly and accessible style. We've routinely broken new ground in anticipating how writers might respond to emerging technologies and theories. Earlier editions of *The Scott Foresman Handbook* led the field in addressing document design, visual rhetoric, online research, and service learning. As a result of our forward-looking philosophy, writers using *The Scott Foresman Handbook* have always been prepared for the opportunities they'd meet both in and well beyond the college classroom.

The eighth edition continues in that tradition.

## What's New

**Paperback version.** *The Scott Foresman Handbook* is now available in a limited paperback edition. If you are interested in adopting the paperback version of the text, please contact your local Prentice Hall Sales Representative.

**A trim new look designed for accessibility.** The eighth edition of *The Scott Foresman Handbook* is cleaner and more contemporary—designed for ease-of-use. A smaller size than past editions makes the text more comfortable for students to carry and keep open on a desktop. A sleeker design with plenty of white space makes key information easier to find. In many sections, checklists replace intimidating blocks of text, and the graphics throughout have been improved. More important, these cuts follow from a thorough appraisal of the content itself: whole sections of the book have been rearranged and revised to make chapters more efficient and readable and images more pertinent.

**An expanded and updated Part VIII: Documentation.** Many writers consult the documentation chapters of a handbook more than any other.

For that reason, *The Scott Foresman Handbook* has always given special attention to the organization and clarity of these materials. In the eighth edition, we continue this tradition with:

- **An entirely new design for documentation chapters.** The new chapters offer quick reference for writers in a hurry, and yet also provide extraordinarily detailed information about how to document every element of a source: author, title, secondary acknowledgements publication information, online access information, etc. The sensible visual design of these pages enables students to choose the level of detail they need, whether documenting a simple position paper or a full senior thesis or research project.

  It goes without saying that the documentation chapters offer an ample number of models for works cited or reference pages, both print and electronic. But the chapters also provide model in-text citations for each item as well, so students don't have to look in two places just to document one source.

  Because students now routinely have materials delivered via library subscription sources such as EBSCO, Gale, or LexisNexis, we cover such sources clearly and separately in our MLA and APA sections.

- **New student papers in both the MLA and APA styles.** These papers include a variety of print and electronic sources, show how to use and cite visuals, and provide annotations to help students with formatting and labeling. We hope, too, that the new papers treat topics that will resonate with and interest students.

- **Innovative guides to help students find information from a variety of sources.** New citation guides in "Chapter 49: How Do You Document a Research Paper?" show students exactly where to look up a source to find the information they will need to document it, whether it is a book, newspaper, magazine, scholarly journal, online database (from a library service), or Web site. These guides even display model MLA and APA citations derived from the sources pictured.

The documentation guides appear in a chapter that offers specific information about citation systems in a variety of fields and explains what source materials, in fact, ought to be documented.

- **A documentation directory on the inside-back cover.** The back-inside cover of the eighth edition includes an alphabetically organized directory to every type of citation for all the documentation styles covered in the book. It provides students with a quick way to find examples as they write their research papers. And, because of the unique way *The Scott Foresman Handbook* presents documentation (in-text notes and citation models are paired instead of separated), students will be able to find either type of example using these clear lists.

- **Expanded number of entries for all documentation styles.** The number of citation models for MLA, APA, and CMS documentation has increased, particularly in the "electronic sources" sections of these chapters.

**Thoroughly revised Part IV: Design and Shape of Writing.**

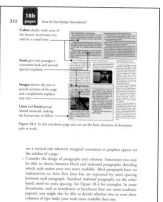

Reflecting continuing developments in writing and technology, our four chapters most concerned with document presentation and design are better focused and easier to follow. Chapter 18 "How Do You Design Documents?" now combines material from several previous chapters into a clear presentation on artful design. It features an especially practical new section on sizing, cropping, and modifying digital images.

Similarly, Chapter 21 "How Do You Design a Web Site?" has been recast to focus on the rhetorical aspects of presenting material online rather than on the technicalities of HTML and

Web servers. Students need concise advice about understanding audience, purpose, and page design these days more than instructions for simply getting online.

**Added visuals that include captions with questions to promote critical thinking.** Visuals have been an important feature of the past three editions of *The Scott Foresman Handbook*. In the eighth edition, we have purposefully increased the number of visuals to reflect the enhanced use of graphs, charts, and digital photographs in student writing. In addition, we've added an important element to most of the illustrations—their captions often include critical thinking questions or brief exercises, so that the visuals not only support the text, they also become part of the learning process and a starting point for discussion.

**Enhanced coverage of argument, including new material on analyzing visual arguments.** Because the reading and writing students do in college increasingly involves responding to or constructing arguments, we have expanded our coverage to two chapters. The first (Chapter 9 "How Do Written and Visual Arguments Work?") focuses on reading and critically analyzing arguments, including a detailed discussion of visual arguments. The second (Chapter 10 "How Do You Write Powerful Arguments?") offers comprehensive advice on composing written arguments and features a new, annotated student paper.

**A new section on writing a response paper.** Chapter 8 "How do You Think and Read Critically?" features a new section on writing a response paper, an assignment students encounter often in humanities and social science courses. This section provides practical advice and a student sample written in response to an article on gender and math aptitude.

**A new section on writing a personal statement.** "Chapter 6: How Do You Write in College?" now includes a section on writing a personal statement to help students applying for college scholarships, internships, or special programs of study. This section gives step-by-step guidelines and includes a sample statement from a student applying to a study-abroad program.

# What's Familiar

**A Respected, Proven Resource.** Although we've made many revisions to this new edition, the most important features of *The Scott Foresman Handbook* haven't changed. The handbook retains its authoritative discussion of the writing process, its full coverage of critical thinking and reading, argumentation, and academic writing; its engaging and thorough treatment of grammar, mechanics, and usage; its lively discussion of research; and its exhaustive treatment of documentation. Because we teach undergraduate writing courses year after year, we know that student writers need accurate, current information. We've applied this experience in the creation of *The Scott Foresman Handbook*.

**Serving Students Best.** Since its first edition, *The Scott Foresman Handbook* has aimed to help students achieve their goals as writers. So each chapter is framed around the questions students commonly ask about writing, rather than presenting rules and terminology out of context. As in past editions, we continue to tackle thorny issues such as evaluating electronic sources, plagiarism, and civil language. And, as in the past, we have refined every chapter of the book, reviewing each line with an eye to making our points sharper, clearer, or more engaging.

We pay special attention to the needs of ESL writers in Chapter 31: Is English a Second Language for You? and Chapter 32: Questions About Verbals (ESL). These chapters review common problems for ESL writers. As well, ESL tips appearing in these chapters offer advice from successful ESL writers on negotiating problematic areas of academic English.

Perhaps most important, we continue to address student writers in language that is both personal and encouraging. We recognize that writing is hard work and that even a volume as thick as this one only begins to address the complexities writers face in sharing their ideas. We are committed to the success of students.

## Supplements

The following supplements accompany *The Scott Foresman Handbook for Writers, 8/E*, to aid teaching and learning:

### For the Instructor

**Instructor's Resource Manual: Creating a Community of Writers** offers guidance to new and experienced instructors for teaching composition with the *Scott Foresman Handbook*. In addition, the manual provides an answer key for all exercises within the handbook.

All of the following supplements are provided to assist instructors.

- **mycomplab** ™ (<www.mycomplab.com>) offers a wealth of teaching resources, including:

  - **GradeTracker** helps instructors track student progress.

  - The **MyCompLab™ Faculty Teaching Guide** gives instructors strategies for using this valuable resource.

  - Online course-management versions of **MyCompLab™** are available in **CourseCompass**, **Blackboard**, and **WebCT** so instructors can manage their course in their preferred format.

  - **MyDropBox**, a leading online plagiarism detection service, assists interested instructors in tracking plagiarism.

- **Prentice Hall Resources for Writing**. A set of supplements for the instructor designed to support a variety of popular composition topics.

  - **Teaching Writing Across the Curriculum** by Art Young is written for college teachers in all disciplines and provides useful advice on teaching writing across the curriculum.

  - **Teaching Civic Literacy** by Cheryl Duffy offers advice on how to integrate civic literacy into the composition classroom.

- **Teaching Visual Rhetoric** by Susan Loudermilk provides an illustrated look at visual rhetoric and offers guidance on how to incorporate this topic into the classroom.

- **Teaching Writing for ESL Students** by Ruth Spack addresses various strategies that can be employed to teach writing to non-native speakers.

## For the Instructor and Student

**Open Access Companion Web site**—The companion Web site offers many resources to help students use their book and improve their writing. Students can use the site on their own (it is not password protected), or their instructor may direct them to portions of it as part of his or her course assignments.

The Companion Web site can be accessed at <www.prenhall.com/SFHandbook>. Click on *The Scott Foresman Handbook for Writers, 8/E,* cover or title to link to the Web site and access the following:

- More than a thousand electronic exercises helps students master various topics from basic grammar to research to ESL

- Our *Resources for Writing* section offers best practices related to the writing process

- The ***Research and Documentation tutorial*** provides a quick guide to writing a research paper and documenting sources.

- The ***Understanding Plagiarism* tutorial** helps students understand what plagiarism is and provides strategies for avoiding plagiarism

- Links to other Web sites provide help on key topics

- Instructor support, including PowerPoint presentations, Instructor's Manual, links to helpful Web sites and more, give instructor a head start when preparing their course

**MyCompLab™—Online writing support created by composition instructors for composition instructors and their students.** **MyCompLab™** (<www.mycomplab.com>), including an electronic and interactive version of *The Scott Foresman Handbook for Writers 8/E,* offers comprehensive online resources in grammar, writing, and research in one dynamic, accessible place:

- Grammar Resources include **ExerciseZone,** with more than three thousand self-grading practice questions on sentences and paragraphs; and **ESL ExerciseZone,** with more than seven hundred self-grading questions.

- Writing Resources include a hundred writing activities involving videos, images, and Web sites; guided assistance through the writing process, with worksheets and exercises; and an extensive collection of sample papers from across the disciplines.

- Research resources include **ResearchNavigator™,** which provides help with the research process, the *AutoCite* bibliography maker, and access to **ContentSelect™** by **EBSCO** host and the subject-search archive of **The New York Times;** and **Avoiding Plagiarism,** which offers tutorials in recognizing plagiarism, paraphrasing, documenting sources in MLA or APA style, and other topics.

**MyCompLab™** includes an intelligent system called **Grade Tracker** so students can track their work, communicate with instructors, and monitor their improvement.

Students using **MyCompLab™** will also benefit from Pearson's **English Tutor Center,** offering live help from qualified writing teachers.

And more . . . **MyCompLab™** includes even more resources to help students use the book and improve their writing. They can use the site on their own, or their instructor may direct them to portions of it as part of his or her course assignments.

- Downloadable checklists and other materials from the book

- More than a thousand electronic exercises

- Video tutorials that supplement the book's explanations

- Hundreds of links to other Web sites providing help on the book's topics

- Sample research papers from various academic disciplines
- Usage flashcards on tricky words and phrases

**Dictionary, Thesaurus, Writer's Guides, Workbooks, and Pocket Readers.** The following resources can be packaged with *The Scott Foresman Handbook for Writers, 8/E.* These valuable student resources provide additional depth on specialized topics that may only be touched upon in the text and allow you to customize the handbook to specific needs. Contact your local Prentice Hall representative for discount pricing information.

- *The New American Webster Handy College Dictionary*
- *The New American Roget's College Thesaurus*

- *Writer's Guide to Research and Documentation*
- *Writer's Guide to Oral Presentations and Writing in the Disciplines*
- *Writer's Guide to Document and Web Design*
- *Writer's Guide to Writing About Literature*
- *The Prentice Hall Grammar Workbook*
- *The Prentice Hall ESL Workbook*
- *Applying English to Your Career (Workbook)*

- *A Prentice Hall Pocket Reader: Argument*
- *A Prentice Hall Pocket Reader: Literature*
- *A Prentice Hall Pocket Reader: Patterns*
- *A Prentice Hall Pocket Reader: Themes*
- *A Prentice Hall Pocket Reader: Purposes*
- *A Prentice Hall Pocket Reader: Writing Across the Curriculum*
- *Papers Across the Curriculum*

## Acknowledgments

We are grateful to all the editors and staff at Prentice Hall who worked hard to make the eighth edition of *The Scott Foresman Handbook for Writers* as exciting and innovative as the first. In particular, we wish to thank Paul Crockett and Laura Olson. Paul kept his eye on every detail of the project, never faltering in his determination to produce a sophisticated and unusually handsome book. Laura brought her experience and good sense to every page she edited. She navigated the remarkable complications of assembling a full-sized, full-color handbook with a grace that made our work much easier.

We would also like to thank Daniel Seward for the substantial contribution he made to the shape and content of our entirely new documentation section. Our chapters are up-dated versions of the remarkably innovative chapters he wrote and designed for the third edition of *SF Writer*.

We are grateful to Brooke Rollins, who located many new examples, images, and student papers for this edition, and to Lindsay Green for providing general research assistance. We also thank student authors Jessica Carfolite, Jeremy Christiansen, Tallon Harding, and Maria Morozowich for allowing us to publish their work.

Finally, we thank all the instructors who have used *The Scott Foresman Handbook* throughout its many editions, especially the following reviewers whose comments enabled us to refine this new edition:

Wendy Allman, Baylor University; Susie Berardi-Rogers, Lamar Community College; Clark Draney, College of Southern Idaho; Diana Kaye Campbell, North Carolina Wesleyan College; Deborah Coxwell-Teague, Florida State University; Philip Gaines, Montana State University; Theresa Greenwood, Montana State University; Tim Gustafson, University of Minnesota; Gary Heba, Bowling Green State University; Cheri Hoeckley, Westmont College; Edis Kittrell, Montana State University; Charlotte Laughlin, McLennan Community College; Sandra Marshburn, West Virginia State University; Kelly Martin, Collin County Community College; Theresa McGarry, East Tennessee State University; Brett Millan, South Texas Community College; Paul Miller, Davidson College; Chere Peguesse, Valdosta

State University; Amy Phillips, Thompkins Cortland Community College; Melinda Reichelt, University of Toledo; Joyce Sloper, Linn Benton Community College; Jean Sorensen, Grayson County College; Greta Vollmer, Sonoma State University; Eric Waggoner, West Virginia Wesleyan College.

## Composition and Visual Argument in Practice

The part openers throughout *The Scott Foresman Handbook for Writers* display images by Bobby Haas, a Dallas investor who first discovered a talent for photography during a trip to Africa in 1994. He subsequently developed a remarkable second career, using his striking images of African peoples and landscapes to support conservation projects—contributions that won him a 2002 United Nations Environmental Programme award.

Haas now has five books to his credit, the most recent *Through the Eyes of the Gods: An Aerial Vision of Africa* (2005) published by National Geographic, the gold standard for nature photographers. We feature Haas's images in *The Scott Foresman Handbook* not only because they are arrestingly beautiful, but also because they make a powerful case for protecting Africa's native landscapes. They demonstrate the power of visual argument.

# PART I | Writing Processes

# 1

# What Does Writing Involve?

## 1a Why write?

Writing is not a mysterious activity at which only a talented few can succeed. Nor is it a purely academic skill that you will leave behind at graduation. On the contrary. In our information-based society, nearly everyone must write.

Through writing, people share what they know, debate issues, promote their beliefs, and advocate change. Whether you are drafting a letter to your senator, making a PowerPoint presentation at work, or reading an original poem at a local coffeehouse, writing gives you a public voice. Writing is also a rich medium for intellectual inquiry. Many people use writing to work through their ideas on an issue or to help organize complex material they learn in school or on the job. As the novelist E. M. Forster put it, "How do I know what I think until I see what I say?"

The ability to write has become even more important with the explosion of electronic media. People once could get along in school by writing papers that would be seen only by their teachers, or at work by writing an occasional memo to the boss. But today writers address wider audiences as part of a typical day's work. In school, you may communicate with classmates and instructors online—in fact, if you are taking distance education courses, email may be your primary mode of communication. Conferencing software and the Internet make it easy to communicate and access information worldwide.

Years ago, some futurists predicted that computers would make writing obsolete. How wrong they were! Now, more than ever, writing matters.

## 1b What does it take to write well?

The good news about writing is that with practice, nearly anyone can learn to do it well. Many people underestimate their potential as writers. Don't let these discouraging myths fool you:

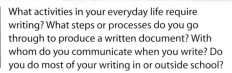
What activities in your everyday life require writing? What steps or processes do you go through to produce a written document? With whom do you communicate when you write? Do you do most of your writing in or outside school?

- **Myth:** *Good writers are born, not made.*
  **Fact:** People become good writers by working at it. If you want to write well, you can if you invest the time.
- **Myth:** *Good writers know what they want to say before they start writing.*
  **Fact:** Many good writers begin with only a general notion of what they want to say. They know that the process of writing can help them generate new ideas and rethink what they already know.
- **Myth:** *Good writers get it right the first time.*
  **Fact:** It's rare for even experienced writers to produce polished work on the first try. Like you, they usually work through several drafts.
- **Myth:** *Good writers work alone.*
  **Fact:** Writers rely on colleagues for ideas and help. Even if they do much of the actual composing alone, experienced writers ask editors and friends for help and suggestions.

- **Myth:** *Writing means putting words on a page—nothing more.*
  **Fact:** Most writers produce traditional texts such as letters and reports. However, composing such documents as proposals, presentations, and Web pages often includes working with images, graphics, and other visual and multimedia elements.
- **Myth:** *Only professional authors publish their work.*
  **Fact:** Computers make it easy to preserve and distribute documents. The writing you do in school or at work may reach large audiences via the Internet.

**EXERCISE 1.1** When you hear the term *writer*, what kind of person comes to mind? Many people reserve the terms *author* and *journalist* for those who make their living solely by writing. But can you think of other people who write frequently? What kinds of writing do they do? Discuss your answers with your classmates.

## 1c How does writing work?

It's tempting to believe that there's a secret formula for writing well and that if you could just discover it, your life would be much easier. Unfortunately, there's no foolproof way to turn an initial idea into a polished final text. However, researchers do agree that most people, when they write, follow general thinking patterns similar to those that occur in other creative activities. Chart 1.1 on page 5 lists these patterns as stages and describes some of the activities writers engage in during each.

Remember, though, that any formal diagram can only hint at what writers really do. A chart is a useful guide, but it can't show nuances in the process, nor can it differentiate among individual writers and varied writing situations. Some successful writers shift freely among the preparing, researching, planning, and revising stages as they work. Others delay major revisions until they have a first draft. Still others revise as they go along.

Writers must also adjust their work patterns to their purpose, their audience, and the specific demands of the project. An instant-messaging exchange among friends will require little planning or revision; yet a fifteen-page research paper may go through several cycles of researching, revising, and editing. So don't think of the writing process as a lockstep march from outlining to proofreading. It's a flexible network of choices and skills.

---

**Chart 1.1  Stages of Writing**

- **Preparing:** Read, brainstorm, browse online, and talk to people in order to decide what you want to write about and to generate ideas about it.

- **Researching:** Gather facts or examples from reading, conversations with others, field research, laboratory research, or your own experiences to support your ideas.

- **Planning:** Develop and organize your ideas further, perhaps preparing working lists, outlines, or sketches of visual elements.

- **Drafting:** Begin to put words (and images or other visual elements, if you're using them) onto a page or screen. Compose one or more drafts, rethinking and reshaping your materials as necessary.

- **Incubating:** Take time off to let your ideas simmer. New ideas may come to you after you've taken a break.

- **Revising:** Critically review what you have written and make any large-scale changes you need in topic, organization, content, design, or audience adaptation.

- **Editing:** Critically review your draft to make smaller-scale changes in style, clarity, and readability.

- **Proofreading:** Read carefully to rid your project of mechanical problems such as spelling, punctuation, and formatting errors.

---

**EXERCISE 1.2**  Think back to a piece of writing you were proud of—perhaps a letter to the editor that was published, a personal statement that won you a scholarship, or an *A* paper in a difficult class—and write a paragraph describing the preparation you put into it, how many times you revised it, and why you think it was successful.

**EXERCISE 1.3**  Write a paragraph or two candidly describing your most hectic writing experience, when you were most pressed to get a project done. What did you have to do to finish the project? Was it successful? Why or why not? What, if anything, would you do differently if you had the chance to do it again?

## 1d How do you define a writing situation?

Writing is a social activity, a way of interacting with others. Every time you write, you enter into a *writing situation* in which

- *You*
- Say *something*
- To *somebody*
- For some *purpose*

For each writing project you undertake, think carefully about your purpose, your audience, and how you want to come across to your readers. Probably no other single habit will do more to strengthen your writing.

## 1e How do you define your purpose(s) for writing?

When you begin a writing project, ask why you are writing in the first place. Do you need to show an instructor that you've mastered a difficult concept or reading assignment? Do you have an idea you care about and want others to care about too? Is there an ongoing debate you wish to enter? Of course, not everything you write must aim at a serious and lofty goal, but having a general purpose in mind will help you to focus and to decide what kinds of supporting materials you will need.

**◉ 1 Decide what you hope to accomplish.** Centuries ago, theorists of *rhetoric*—the art of persuasive communication—identified three basic purposes for writing:

- writing *to inform*, or writing that teaches readers new information;
- writing *to persuade*, or writing that convinces readers to believe or act in new ways;
- and writing *to entertain*, writing that diverts and engages readers.

Often you may want to achieve more than one of these goals within a single paper. To review a restaurant for a campus magazine, for example, your primary aim might be to *evaluate* the food and service, but you would also want to *persuade* readers to visit or avoid the restaurant and perhaps to *entertain* them as well. See Section 3c for specific methods of organizing projects to suit particular purposes.

Thinking about these purposes isn't just an exercise; it's a practical matter. When you don't know why you're writing, you'll find it difficult to produce a coherent paper. Sometimes you may not be completely sure of your purpose until you've explored the topic by writing a first draft. You may explore several angles on an idea as you figure out what you want to say. Eventually, though, you must articulate a purpose that satisfies both you and your readers. Use Checklist 1.1 to think about your goals.

---

**Checklist 1.1   Purpose**

1. If you are writing a paper for a course, what cues does the assignment provide about purpose? Target words like *explain, define, argue, evaluate*.

2. What do you want readers to get from your paper? Do you want to inform, persuade, or entertain them? If you have multiple goals, which is the most important?

3. What supporting materials will you draw on to achieve your goals? What research, examples, or personal experiences will you use?

4. How will you present material in your paper? Will you narrate, describe, compare and contrast, or argue, for example?

5. What form will the project take? Will you write a letter, a report, a Web page, or a research paper, for example? Will you incorporate images, tables, or other visual elements?

---

**● 2  Consider how other elements in the writing situation shape your purpose(s).** Although we discuss each aspect of the writing situation separately in this chapter, in practice it's difficult to consider any of these elements in isolation. For any project, your purpose(s) will help you define your audience, the form in which you present your ideas, and the impression you want to make. Suppose, for example, that you are angry about a proposal to stop offering evening courses at your college. If you want to convince people that these courses should continue, you have a choice of audiences. Here is where your purpose becomes important.

If you want direct action, you need to write to the person in charge of scheduling courses, perhaps the campus registrar. For this audience, your purpose might be to construct a calm, well-supported letter explaining the harmful effects of cancellation—graduation delays for working students who can attend class only in the evening, shrinking enrollment if angry evening students transfer to other local colleges, and so on. If, however, you want to get fellow students to join your cause, you might draft a petition and circulate it on a campus electronic mailing list.

## 1f How do you write for an audience?

Each time you write, think carefully about who your readers might be and how they will respond to the material you are writing about. Doing this can be a challenge. Sometimes writers have to contend with multiple and possibly conflicting audiences: men and women; young, middle-aged, and older people; liberals and conservatives; teacher and classmates. In other cases, identifying an audience at all seems nearly impossible. When you create a Web page, for example, literally anyone in the world who has access to the Internet might read it.

Learning how to appeal to an audience takes time and practice, but it is a skill that any writer can master. As you begin to think about your readers, consult Checklist 1.2. If within a single project you will reach several potential audiences, run through the checklist for each group.

---

### Checklist 1.2  Audience

1. Does the assignment specify a particular audience? If so, describe that audience. If not, whom do you visualize as the audience(s) for this project?

2. What do they already know about your subject? What kinds of information will they need you to provide?

3. What values and beliefs are important to them? To what kinds of examples and arguments are they likely to respond?

4. Will they feel most comfortable with a formal or more casual approach to the topic? What kind of formats, layouts, or visuals will appeal to them?

What qualities make musician Sheryl Crow an effective spokesperson for an advertising campaign promoting milk? If you were asked to design a new ad in this campaign, what spokesperson might you choose? Why? Visit <www.whymilk.com> and compare your choice to the celebrities featured in past "Got Milk" ads..

---

**Checklist 1.3   Presenting Yourself to Readers**

1. How can you show readers that you are knowledgeable about your subject? What research, reading, or personal experience will you draw upon?

2. How will you show readers that you are trustworthy? What will you do to present information accurately and fully?

3. How will you show readers that you are reasonable and fair? What tone will you adopt, and how will you talk about opposing views?

---

◉ **2 Present material fairly and honestly.** Readers believe writers whom they perceive as trustworthy, so you'll need to present material accurately and fairly in a writing project. Base your arguments on reputable sources, and be truthful about gaps or limitations in what you know. Suppose you're writing a paper arguing that day care negatively affects young children. You will need to acknowledge that some studies indicate that day care is not especially harmful. Otherwise, readers who have heard of such studies may think that you are trying to hide something.

You will also need to cite the sources of your information, to show that the materials you've consulted are reliable and authoritative. When readers see that you treat your subject honestly, they'll be more open to your ideas. See Chapters 45 through 48 for more about evaluating and documenting sources.

◉ **3 Use a civil tone.** Being polite to those who disagree with you may seem a bit naive given the hostile tone of much public discussion in our society. But don't be fooled—the loudest voices aren't always the ones that people end up listening to. You will project the most credible image when you treat different viewpoints fairly and generously. It's fine to disagree strongly with another's ideas. But confine your criticism to the issues rather than attack your opponent's worth as a human being. Avoid name-calling, inflammatory language, and ethnic or gender stereotypes. Not only will you sound more professional, but your fairness will lay the groundwork for ongoing conversation with readers who hold different views.

See Section 15d for more on avoiding bias in your language. For advice on addressing opposing views, see Section 10c.

**EXERCISE 1.6**   Select a subject that you know a lot about, and imagine that you have been asked to write about it for several different venues: a college research paper, a televised public-service announcement, and a letter for the editorial page of a local newspaper. How would each element of the writing situation—your purpose, your audience, and the image you want to project as a writer—affect the written product? Which task appeals to you the most?

# 2 How Do You Find and Explore a Topic?

## 2a How do you find a topic?

Sometimes you will start a writing project knowing exactly what you are going to write about—perhaps an instructor has assigned a specific paper topic, or you're writing in response to a particular issue or situation. When you don't have to find your topic, you can begin immediately to generate ideas, plan, and start a draft.

Occasionally, however, college instructors encourage students to choose their own topics, believing that students write better when they can investigate subjects that interest them. "Having a choice is great," you may say, "but how do I find a topic that both my readers and I will enjoy?"

**1 Think beyond broad, traditional topics.** College students sometimes think that they should always write about issues of earthshaking importance. Does this list look familiar?

| | | |
|---|---|---|
| Abortion | Terrorism | Global Warming |
| School Choice | Capital Punishment | Euthanasia |

These issues *are* important. And if you feel passionately enough about one of them to do the research that will add to the debate, then go for it. But because so much has been written about these issues, you risk bogging down in generalizations and clichés. If you do choose a well-worn topic, look for a new or local angle to investigate. For example, rather than writing a general paper on global climate change, you might explore the effects that recent tropical storms have had on your hometown's economy.

**2 Choose a topic in your world.** When you write about a subject with authority and passion, your readers will respond. So choose a topic that interests you, preferably one you know well. Brainstorm a list of possibilities:

activities you enjoy, interesting experiences you've had, or subjects that have always sparked your curiosity. For example, do you play bluegrass guitar, teach first-aid classes, or volunteer at a local hospice? Have you always wanted to study African art? Then decide which topic on your list best fits the particular writing assignment. Checklist 2.1 will help you to discover such topics.

You can also make a paper unique by spotlighting issues in your own community. For example, an assignment to research the civil rights movement for a history course could lead you to inquire about local concerns. Was your campus or community ever segregated? How did your city react to civil rights initiatives or legislation? Do contemporary concerns for women's or gay rights have roots in this earlier political movement? Any one of these issues would make a promising paper topic.

Because local topics connect to your everyday life, you're bound to have a strong interest in finding out more about them. You will find it easier to do original research, since expert sources—newspapers, community organizations, and local leaders—are close at hand. And you may discover opportunities to publish your writing on such topics outside the classroom, perhaps as a letter to the editor or to a public official.

---

### Checklist 2.1    To Find a Topic, Ask Yourself . . .

- **What three subjects do you enjoy reading about or are you curious about?** What magazines do you pick up? What kinds of books do you browse through? Which newspaper headlines catch your eye? If you could become an expert in one topic, what would it be?

- **What three subjects do you know the most about?** What topics could you discuss for half an hour without notes? What problems lead people to seek your advice or expertise? What could you teach someone else to do?

- **What three subjects do you enjoy arguing about most?** On what subjects can you hold your own with just about anyone? What opinions do you advocate most strongly?

- **What three issues in your community do you care about the most?** What issues affect you or people you know? For what causes do you volunteer? What opinions and ideas would you like to communicate to government officials or to the community at large?

⊚ **3 Browse in the library and online.** Look in the library catalog or in the directory of the Library of Congress (better known as the *Subject List*). Just the way a broad subject is broken down into headings and subheadings should suggest many topic possibilities. Consult such reference sources as specialized encyclopedias too. If you want to learn about endangered animal species in your state, for example, a glance at the *Encyclopedia of the Environment* might provide several topic ideas.

Even when you don't have a general subject area to direct your library search, try browsing in the new book section or through the op-ed and analysis pages of national publications like *The New York Times, The Wall Street Journal*, or *Slate* for current topics that spark your curiosity. You can also use an online search engine such as *Google* or *Yahoo!* to identify possible topics, but be careful. These tools often call up so many information sources that it's easy to become distracted or overwhelmed. A librarian at your campus library can help you direct your online research to reliable, manageable sources.

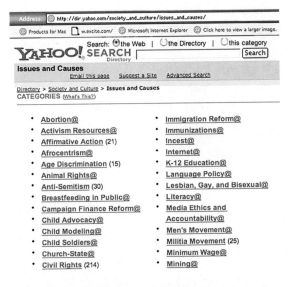

**Figure 2.1** *Yahoo's* "Issues and Causes" page offers dozens of general topic ideas and thousands of supporting links. You can find it under the "Society and Culture" heading in the *Yahoo!* directory.

● **4 Talk with others.** There's no reason to search for a topic in a vacuum. Discuss possibilities with everyone who has a connection to the project, including your instructor. He or she may be willing not only to suggest interesting areas, but also to steer you away from topics that won't work. Classmates working on the same assignment may also spark your imagination; talk with them outside of class or share ideas via email.

## 2b  How do you refine your topic?

Once you have found a promising topic, you'll probably need to narrow it down. If you don't focus your efforts, you may end up trying to cover more material than you can within the parameters of the project—for example, attempting to present a comprehensive account of the evolution versus intelligent design debate in a five-page paper. This kind of overreaching can result in a project long on generalities but short on lively details and thoroughly developed ideas.

● **1 Don't try to cover everything.** Remember that your time to develop a paper is limited. You can't discover all there is to know about a topic in a few weeks. Even if you could, you wouldn't be able to fit all that material into one paper. Narow your research to something manageable, an aspect of your topic that you will be able to discuss thoroughly. Any paper you write should contain only a portion of what you know about its subject.

If you needed to write a five-page paper about an issue in U.S. high schools, what might you choose as your focus and why? How narrow would your topic need to be? Discuss and compare your choice with a group of classmates, noting the range of possibilities. Then compare your group's choices with Tallon Harding's topic proposal, featured on pages 25–26.

**2 Make a tree diagram.** One way to narrow a topic is to create a tree diagram that divides it into smaller components. Make a chart on which you divide and subdivide your subject into smaller and smaller parts, each of which branches out like an inverted tree. The upside-down tree helps you see many potential areas within each division as well as the relationships among them.

Suppose you've become interested in writing about college student debt after watching your roommate run up several thousand dollars in credit card bills during a single semester. Your tree diagram might look something like this:

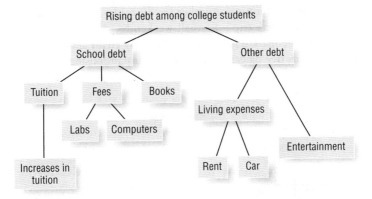

Now select the most promising branch from your first diagram and make a new diagram to refine that idea further.

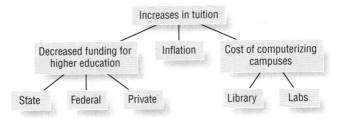

**3 Make an idea map.** Another way to narrow a topic is to make an idea map that shows patterns of related ideas worth exploring. In the middle of a blank sheet of paper, write down a phrase that describes your

**EXERCISE 2.1** Suppose you want to write a short paper for a composition course on one of the following subjects. Write down several promising subtopics that you might focus on; then use a tree diagram or an idea map to generate ideas about the subtopic that you find most interesting.

Illegal drug use

Scandals in professional sports

The popularity of cosmetic surgery

Organic foods

## 2c How do you explore and develop a topic?

You have a topic. What's next? Now you need to explore its implications, find supporting evidence, and fill in specific details. Experts on rhetoric use the term *invention* to describe the techniques writers use to generate subject matter for a paper.

Invention techniques can help you explore and develop a thesis. You can use these techniques at any point in your writing process. Return to them anytime you need to expand and develop your ideas.

**1 Freewrite about the topic.** Freewriting is writing nonstop for ten to fifteen minutes on a topic to explore what you already know and to discover areas you'd like to learn more about. Don't worry about grammar, spelling, or other niceties while you're freewriting—the point of freewriting is to generate ideas. Continue to write as long as ideas come, and don't cross out anything. Be alert for phrases and concepts that extend your thesis in promising directions.

**GOING PUBLIC** **Freewriting**

Here is an excerpt from a freewriting that student writer Tallon Harding did before writing the paper that appears on pages 69–75. Notice that she has not always capitalized, that she does-n't always write complete sentences, and that her style is informal. But also notice how many ideas even this short excerpt articulates.

I definitely want to write about how high schools are pushing students to take too many AP and other college level courses to the point that *they don't have time for a lot of the things young people are supposed to do in high school. The move towards college level education in the public high school system is becoming a big problem. Academics have become the main focus, what happened to rounding out the student? Sports and extracurricular activities get side-lined at the expense of the student. Too many AP and IB courses result in stress overload that many high schoolers are not prepared to face. Educators need to focus more on the needs of the students. High school students shouldn't work as hard as college students do, they have less time. . . .*

**2 Use the journalist's questions.** Beginning journalists are taught to keep six questions in mind when writing a news story.

| | | |
|---|---|---|
| Who? | What? | Where? |
| When? | Why? | How? |

Simple as they seem, these questions can help you be sure you have covered all the bases, especially when you are writing an informative paper (though not every question will apply to every topic).

**3 Look at your topic from different perspectives.** Classical rhetoricians used four broad questions to explore topics: questions of *fact, definition, value,* and *policy.* Originally designed to develop speeches for the law courts, these questions move from simple to more complex ways of examining an issue.

- Questions of **fact** involve things already known about your topic: What has already happened? What factual information is already available? What policies are already in place?
- Questions of **definition** interpret these facts and place them in a larger context: What category does your topic fit into? What laws or approaches apply?
- Questions of **value** ask you to make a judgment: Is the idea you're talking about a good thing or a bad thing? Is it ethical or unethical? Is it workable or unworkable?
- Questions of **policy** allow you to consider specific courses of action: What exactly should be done in response to the issue? Are old solutions working, or is a new approach needed?

You won't be able to answer all these questions in a single paper, but they are useful for comprehensively examining a topic. Below, for example, are ways a writer might use these questions to find material for a paper on whether the fashion industry's use of thin models in advertising indirectly encourages eating disorders among young women. Once you've run through all the questions, decide which one(s) you want to treat most fully in your paper. For example, an editorial on this topic might focus on the definitional question "How does our culture define 'beauty'?" A report, however, might gather information that answers the factual question "How many fashion ads feature unusually thin models?" For more on how these questions can help you construct a thesis statement, see Section 48a.

---

**Highlight  Looking at a Topic from Different Perspectives:**

### Fashion and Body Image Among Young Women

- **Questions about the facts:** To what extent do young women draw their beauty ideals from fashion ads? How many fashion ads feature unusually thin models? How many young women have eating disorders?

- **Questions about key definitions:** How does our culture define "beauty"? How preoccupied with thinness must one be to be defined as having an eating disorder?

- **Questions about values:** Is it ethical for fashion designers to display their clothes on models who are much thinner than most women can ever be? Is it sensible for the industry to produce clothing that doesn't look good on most people? Does the artistic value of fashion trends outweigh any harmful social effects they may cause?

- **Questions about policy:** What could the fashion industry do to promote a healthier ideal of beauty? How might young women be discouraged from trying to look like models?

**4 Write a zero draft.** Just start a draft. The very act of writing will often get the creative juices flowing and help you to organize your thoughts. Think of this first try as a "zero draft," a trial run that doesn't really count. Zero drafts are easy to write, and after they're complete, you can select the best material to use in your next draft. Try writing several zero drafts of a paper to test possible approaches to a topic.

**5 Read.** Look up your subject in the library or on the Internet and read. Read to find facts. Read to discover how other writers have approached topics like yours. Perhaps you want to write about a bicycle trip you took across the American Northwest. Look up some travel literature. Your eyes may be opened by the sheer variety of approaches available to record your adventures, everything from serious field accounts written by anthropologists to the rollicking narratives in travel magazines. Seeing others' work will suggest possibilities for your own.

You'll find detailed instructions for doing research in Chapters 44 through 46.

**6 Talk to others about your topic.** From the start, invite others to join in exploring your topic. Look for information about lectures, films, or community meetings where you might meet people interested in your work. And when you find such people, network with them to find more people and organizations tied to your subject.

Online newsgroups and electronic mailing lists offer instant access to an even wider network of contacts. Once you have a good sense of the issues you want to write about, consider posting to one of these forums a short description of your project and a request for input.

Classmates and friends are also useful resources. Utilize a class team or talk and email with classmates who share an interest in your topic. You'll find that as you start to explain your ideas to others, more ideas will come to you. You may see arguments you hadn't considered and learn about new examples or sources.

**7 Visit your campus writing center.** Many colleges and universities house writing centers designed to help students with their writing projects. Unfortunately, many students misperceive these facilities as emergency rooms that fix papers in trouble. In fact, the tutors and consultants who staff them are usually eager to help writers at every stage of the writing process— including finding a workable, challenging topic and focusing and narrowing their work. Chart 2.1 offers some tips for getting the most out of a writing center session.

---

**Chart 2.1    Getting Help at a Writing Center**

- Use a writing center at every stage of the writing process. The consultants there can help you find a topic, formulate a thesis, and evaluate a draft in progress.
- Don't treat a writing center as a one-stop fix-it shop. The consultants are there to help you become a better writer, not to edit your papers for you.
- Bring the assignment sheet with you to a writing-center appointment. The assignment may help a tutor better understand your paper.
- Bring to your session any comments you have received from your instructor or peer editors. Read the comments carefully yourself.
- Be on time for your appointment.
- Decide whether you want a report of the session sent to your instructor. Many writing centers will give you this option.

---

**EXERCISE 2.2**  Choose a current controversy in your neighborhood, campus, or city. (If no ideas come to mind, consult a local or campus newspaper.) Use the four categories outlined on page 22 to identify questions about facts, definitions, values, and policies regarding that issue. Which questions generate the most disagreement? Which ones could provide the focus for an interesting paper?

**EXERCISE 2.3**  Use any two of the techniques described in Section 2c to generate ideas about one of your writing projects in progress. Then discuss your experience with your classmates: Which strategy yielded the best ideas? Which are you likely to use again?

## 2d  How do you write a topic proposal?

Occasionally an instructor may ask you to write a preliminary proposal defining your topic and analyzing the writing situation for a paper. Even when it's not assigned, such a proposal can help you refine your ideas about your topic, audience, purpose, and tone early so that your decisions can guide your research and shape your first draft.

A topic proposal typically includes the elements listed in Checklist 2.2. Check with your instructor to find out if he or she has additional requirements.

---

**Checklist 2.2    Writing a Topic Proposal**

1. Identify your topic.
2. Articulate a working thesis statement, research question, hypothesis, or key issue that you plan to focus on in the paper (see Section 2b).
3. Indicate what kinds of supporting materials you will use (see Section 6a-3).
4. Briefly analyze your writing situation (see Section 1d).

---

**GOING PUBLIC    A Topic Proposal**

In the following sample proposal, first-year composition student Tallon Harding describes her plan for the paper shown in draft form on pages 69–75. The assignment asked her to write a researched argument on a topic relevant to her and her classmates. Harding begins by describing her topic and purpose, and then she identifies her audience. She ends by considering the kind of impression she wants to make on readers.

Although she has thought carefully about her topic, at this point in the process Harding is still refining and developing her ideas. She hasn't yet developed all the supporting points for her position or located her research materials, and her approach is less formal than her instructor will expect to see in the finished paper.

Tallon Harding

Topic Proposal, Essay #2

### Today's High Schools are Failing to Meet Student Needs

School has just let out but the library is packed. Each one of us is studying, working frantically to finish the next day's assignments. The Advanced Placement Tests will be given on Monday; therefore the pressure is almost unbearable. This scene is becoming common in high schools across the nation, as more and more students are being encouraged to enroll in college-type courses that are offered in the high school classroom. Do these kinds of courses help students prepare for the demands of college? Or are they robbing students of the well-rounded education that they will need to become mature and well-adjusted adults?

My paper will argue that a good, well-rounded high school education involves more than just academics and instruction in the basic courses. It also includes extracurricular activities that help students to mature both physically and socially. However, under the current system, many students have to eliminate extracurricular activities to account for the heavy course loads resulting from a doubled academic burden. I plan to discuss examples showing the sacrifices students make to keep up with heavy academic loads, and I will research to find statistics on the size of this problem. I will also briefly explore the reasons why schools are pushing students to overachieve, including the pressures caused by high-stakes testing and federal funding requirements.

My audience will be my classmates, many of whom, I anticipate, experienced a similar environment at their high schools and probably have a strong opinion on this issue. I hope to write a paper that will interest them and give strong support for my position.

# 3 How Do You Focus and Organize a Writing Project?

Now you have an interesting, workable topic for your writing project. You've thought carefully about it and gathered information about it. What's next? It's time to make some decisions about the shape the project will take.

## 3a How do you craft a thesis statement?

As you explore your topic, you will discover one or two issues that will shape your *thesis statement*. A *thesis* is a sentence (or sometimes two or three sentences) that explicitly identifies the point of a paper. Depending on the project, it may be a conclusion you draw as a result of doing research, your answer to a puzzling question about your topic, or a claim you will spend the rest of the paper explaining or supporting.

Try to construct a working thesis statement early in your writing process and use it as a framework for developing your first draft. By keeping your thesis in mind, you can be sure of covering all the important points.

● 1 **Make a strong point.** A thesis statement is more than just an observation; it is a strong, focused statement that might be questioned or challenged. It should offer a clearly stated analysis, critique, or position on your topic that readers will find new and significant.

> **INSIGNIFICANT**  The doughnuts in Jester cafeteria are terrible. Even if true, few readers will find this observation substantial enough to support an entire paper.

> **MORE SIGNIFICANT**  University administrators should investigate the impact a Krispy Kreme franchise might have on revenues for the Student Union.

**3a**
**thesis**   How Do You Focus and Organize a Writing Project?

28

| | |
|---|---|
| NOT DEBATABLE | Domestic violence harms families. Who's going to argue with this claim? |
| DEBATABLE | The state legislature should pass the current bill mandating harsher penalties for second-offense child abuse and spousal abuse convictions. |
| TOO GENERAL | Environmental groups and landowners disagree over many issues, including land use, species protection, and pollution regulations. You won't be able to research and thoroughly analyze more than one or two specific disagreements in a typical academic paper. |
| MORE SPECIFIC | The debate over whether wolves should still be protected as endangered species, now that wild populations are thriving in the Northwest, raises key questions about how to balance individuals' property rights with the long-term viability of the species. |

Once you've written a thesis, ask yourself how a member of your audience might react to it. If you can envision a polite yawn ("So what?") or a blank stare ("What's your point?"), revise your thesis, using the guidelines in Checklist 3.1.

---

**Checklist 3.1   What Makes a Strong Thesis?**

• Does it focus on a **substantive issue**, one that deserves readers' attention?

• Is it **debatable**? Could reasonable people disagree with it?

• Is it **current** and **relevant**? Will readers care about the issue it addresses?

• Is it **clearly stated**? Do you take a stand?

• Can it be **supported** with evidence from your research or personal experiences?

---

**EXERCISE 3.1**   Using the guidelines listed in Checklist 3.1, evaluate the following thesis statements. Revise the statements that don't seem effective to make them stronger.

1.  Why are more college students now graduating within four years? Perhaps they are more career oriented and better prepared for college, but the biggest reasons are probably financial.

2.  In today's environment of global conflict, many Americans wonder whether our military should restore the draft.

3.  Many drivers are so dangerous that they should not be allowed on the road.

4.  Movies such as *Lara Croft: Tomb Raider* and the *Mortal Kombat* series show the growing influence of video games.

**2 Preview the direction your paper will take.** Write a complete sentence or two that forecasts in some detail the ideas you expect to write about, in roughly the same order in which you plan to address them. Your thesis sentence(s) should be *succinct* yet *comprehensive*—that is, it should be short yet indicate the major points you want to make. Suppose you are writing an article for the business student newsletter on your campus. This thesis tells readers what to expect:

> When you start looking for a summer job or internship, think globally:
> in the past few years, many students on our campus have found
> lucrative and interesting positions with overseas corporations.

**3 Place your thesis effectively.** Don't assume that your thesis must be the first sentence of your paper, although it can be. Your decision about where to put your thesis depends on the writing situation: your audience, your purpose, and the position you want to take on the topic.

If you want to present information or arguments in a straightforward, no-nonsense fashion—as you should in an essay examination or a business letter—then state your thesis early. It may even be your first sentence. At other times you'll need to provide a context for your thesis, by defining key terms or giving background information. That's why, in academic papers, the thesis statement often appears at the end of the introductory paragraph.

In other situations, you may want to delay your thesis even more. If you're writing to explore a question rather than to present a settled opinion

**30**

**3a**
**thesis**    How Do You Focus and Organize a Writing Project?

on it, or if your thesis is controversial, you may want to present your evidence first and then lead readers gradually to your point. In the social sciences, writers often begin research reports by describing their methods and data and end with larger conclusions. In such cases, your thesis may not be stated until the last paragraph. Just remember, a delayed thesis doesn't give you license to write an unfocused paper—readers should understand what central ideas your paper will address from its very beginning.

⊘ **4 Revise your thesis as your project evolves.** Don't be surprised if your thesis shifts as you continue to explore, research, and plan your project. Most writers will revise a working thesis statement to make it more precise or to reflect changes in the paper's direction. Don't worry about such changes. This is the right time to be testing your preliminary ideas so that your final paper will be stronger. Learn from every part of the process, and don't be discouraged easily. Your final thesis may be nothing like what you imagined at the outset—and that's okay.

**GOING PUBLIC**    **An Opening Paragraph with Thesis Statement**

A thesis statement pulled out of context, like the previous examples in this chapter, can seem pretty bland. Fortunately, in a real paper, a thesis isn't solely responsible for shaping a reader's first impression. Notice how Tallon Harding positions her thesis statement in an opening paragraph designed to capture readers' interest. A full draft of this paper appears on pages 69–75.

> School has just let out but the library is packed with students. Each one of us is studying, working frantically to finish the next day's assignments. The Advanced Placement Tests will be given on Monday; the pressure is almost unbearable. A couple of years ago this spectacle would have confounded the average high school librarian, who would have been able to leave as soon as school let out. Recently, however, this scene has become commonplace. Due to a push by school officials

looking to receive government grants, students are increasingly pressured to enroll in college-level courses offered in the high school classroom. As part of a new "Steps to Prosperity" measure recently introduced by the South Carolina state legislature, many districts are even beginning to require students to declare a major as early as their sophomore year in high school (Landrum). Unfortunately, a good, well-rounded high school education involves more than just academic study. It must also include extracurricular activities that help students to grow socially, physically, and emotionally. As schools eliminate these broader elements in the quest to achieve higher and higher academic standards, they leave gaps in students' education and neglect important student needs.

## 3b How do you avoid plagiarism?

Early in the writing process, you must understand what constitutes plagiarism, particularly if you're writing papers for an instructor who expects you to use outside sources. Doesn't that require you to use someone else's material and ideas? Well, yes it does. The trick is knowing how to incorporate other people's ideas or research into your work while giving them full credit. Chapters 46 and 47 show you several strategies for acknowledging someone else's ideas or arguments in a way that gives the original source its due. The point is always to be up front about where you found the idea, quotation, or conclusion that you're incorporating into your work. You should make it possible for anyone who wants to clarify a point or get more information on your topic to go to the source and check it out.

If in previous years you've attended a school in which teachers expected you to memorize large quantities of material and then demonstrate your mastery of that material, it may seem natural to you to simply repeat information that you've gathered from your reading. You're likely to find, however, that's not what instructors want in most composition courses or in other liberal arts courses for which you write papers or create pages on the Web. Rather, those instructors want you to go beyond mastery of a body of material to synthesize, respond to, and evaluate its ideas and its arguments.

As a Web-wise student, you know what a wealth of information the Internet can provide on almost any writing topic. You can find anything from a psychological profile of Lady Macbeth, to directions for building a kayak, to an essay about the benefits of Pilates or yoga. You can also find commercial sites that will, for a price, provide you with a finished term paper on just about any topic of your choice. You may have friends who have bought such papers or have done a cut-and-paste job of piecing together a paper from Internet sources. Whatever process they chose, the project they turned in can only be called plagiarism. We want to convince you not to go there and to show you why.

When you take a process-centered writing course, you have a special opportunity to master a craft essential for doing well in college and, later on, in most professions—certainly in science, law, engineering, college teaching, public relations, and even in medicine and accounting. A skilled writer has an edge in getting what he or she wants in the everyday transactions of life, whether it's to persuade a business to sponsor a charity project, appeal a spike in your property tax, or construct an effective Web site for an organization you support. You don't want to miss an opportunity to acquire such a powerful tool.

## 3c How do you organize a writing project?

No matter how good your ideas are, if you don't organize them, readers will get lost and blame you. Coherent organization is the foundation of any writing project. If you are not sure how you want to organize a writing project, one of the best things you can do is find a model. Looking at a finished document will give you valuable clues about how readers may expect you to arrange your ideas. If you're writing a college paper, assess the assignment sheet carefully and ask your instructor for sample papers. In writing for a journal or magazine, look at past issues. If you're preparing a

How might you organize a description of your last summer job differently if you were composing (1) your resume, (2) a humorous personal narrative for a composition course, or (3) an interview segment for a documentary film on labor conditions in the industry? What would you talk about first? What points would you emphasize? In what order would you present them? What would you discuss in the most detail?

report at work, colleagues and supervisors can help you understand the structure and format your company prefers.

### ● 1 Consider an introduction-body-conclusion structure.    This basic pattern works for many kinds of projects. Lawyers, scientists, and writers in many academic fields favor this design because it suggests a logical movement from statement to proof.

- In the **introduction** you begin by telling your readers clearly and simply what topics your paper will cover.
- In the **body** of the paper you follow with examples and explanations for each of your main points.
- In your **conclusion** you tie your points together and leave readers with a sense of closure.

Another way of describing this basic structure is to call it a commitment and response pattern. That's because in the first section of the paper a writer promises to cover certain issues or address particular questions.

Papers that result from the basic introduction-body-conclusion pattern will usually take a simple shape.

## Basic Introduction-Body-Conclusion Pattern

| **Introduction** | I. First-year students need a rep. |
|---|---|
| *Present thesis . . .* | on the board of the student union. |
| ♦ *First argument* | II. Other years have representation |
| ◻ Support: examples, | A. All students need a voice |
| reasons, evidence, etc. | B. First-years have special needs |
| ♦ *Second argument* | III. First-years need to be welcomed |
| ◻ Support: examples, | A. Student union can be friendlier |
| reasons, evidence, etc. | B. Good to socialize outside dorms |
| ♦ *Other arguments . . .* | IV. Welcoming campus helps retention |
| **Conclusion** | V. An inviting student union can help |
| *Closing summary . . .* | first-years join campus communities. |

(Body)

Such papers can also incorporate significant variations. When you make a point or support an argument, for example, you must usually deal with opposing views; if you don't address them, the paper will seem to evade key questions. Counterarguments—discussions of opposing views—inevitably make the structure of the paper more complex. They can be addressed immediately, near the beginning of the paper, or they can be dealt with as they arise in the body of the piece. Just don't end with a counterargument; it will only weaken your case.

Here's how the basic model might look when counterarguments are added to the mix. (See Section 10c for more on handling different views in a paper.)

## Introduction-Body-Conclusion Pattern with Counterarguments

| **Introduction** | I. First-year students need a rep. |
|---|---|
| *Present thesis . . .* | on the board of the student union. |
| ♦ *First argument* | II. Other years have representation |
| ◻ Support . . . | A. First-years need a voice |
| ◻ Counterarguments | B. First-years may not understand |
| addressed by rebuttal | the system, but can learn it |
| ♦ *Second argument* | III. First-years need to be welcomed |
| ◻ Support . . . | A. Student union better than dorms |
| ◻ Counterarguments | B. Dorm rec-rooms are good but not |
| addressed by rebuttal | for meeting older students |
| ♦ *Other arguments . . .* | IV. Welcoming campus helps retention |
| **Conclusion** | V. An inviting student union can help |
| *Closing summary . . .* | first-years join campus communities. |

(Body)

**2 Consider a narrative or a process design.** When you narrate a story, you usually describe events in the order they occurred. The structure can be quite straightforward. A narrative can also be more complicated—for instance, by moving back in time as a movie does with flashbacks.

Narrative Pattern

| | |
|---|---|
| **Introduction**<br>*Present thesis . . .* | I. Our town's public buildings reflect the architectural styles of several different historical periods. |
| **Body**<br>◆ *First event*<br>◆ *Second event*<br>◆ *Third event*<br>◆ *Other events . . .* | II. Colonial town hall (1793)<br>III. Victorian courthouse (1846) and post office (1888)<br>IV. Art-deco library (1932) |
| **Conclusion**<br>*Closing summary . . .* | V. These buildings tell a story about our town's gradual development. |

A process pattern is essentially the same as a narrative pattern, but instead of telling a story you are explaining how something works. You list and describe each step in the process.

Process Pattern

| | |
|---|---|
| **Introduction**<br>*Present thesis . . .* | I. Winning a reality-TV game show requires patience and cunning. |
| **Body**<br>◆ *First step*<br>◆ *Second step*<br>◆ *Third step*<br>◆ *Other steps . . .* | II. First, display trustworthiness<br>III. Second, form a small coalition<br>IV. Third, lie low for a while<br>V. Last, betray coalition members |
| **Conclusion**<br>*Closing summary . . .* | VI. To win the big bucks, you need to remember it is only a game. |

Be careful to include all the necessary steps in the proper order. You can find good examples of process patterns in instructional and technical manuals.

**3 Consider a comparison-and-contrast structure.** In many kinds of papers you will have to examine different objects or ideas in relation to each other, especially when you are evaluating or arguing. In organizing such papers you can use one or two basic plans, either describing the things you are comparing one at a time (*subject by subject*) or describing them in an alternating sequence (*feature by feature*). We show both models on page 36.

## Comparison-and-Contrast Pattern: Subject by Subject

| | |
|---|---|
| **Introduction**<br><br>*Present thesis . . .* | I. Sport-utility vehicles, though currently more popular than family sedans, have environmental and safety drawbacks that should make potential buyers beware. |
| **Body**<br><br>♦ *First subject examined*<br>❑ First feature<br>❑ Second feature<br>❑ Other features . . .<br>♦ *Second subject*<br>❑ First feature<br>❑ Second feature<br>❑ Other features . . . | II. Pros and cons of SUVs<br>  A. Popularity<br>  B. Environmental impact<br>  C. Safety<br>III. Pros and cons of family sedans<br>  A. Popularity<br>  B. Environmental impact<br>  C. Safety |
| **Conclusion**<br><br>*Closing summary . . .* | IV. Buyers who value safety and the environment over style should bypass sport-utility vehicles in favor of traditional sedans. |

The subject-by-subject plan works best in short papers involving only a few comparisons; in such pieces readers don't have to recall a large quantity of information to make the necessary comparisons. When you're doing a longer paper, however, use the feature-by-feature pattern; otherwise, readers may lose track of the features you're comparing.

## Comparison-and-Contrast Pattern: Feature by Feature

| | |
|---|---|
| **Introduction**<br><br>*Present thesis . . .* | I. Sport-utility vehicles, though currently more popular than family sedans, have environmental and safety drawbacks that should make potential buyers beware. |
| **Body**<br><br>♦ *First feature examined*<br>❑ In first subject<br>❑ In second subject<br>♦ *Second feature*<br>❑ In first subject<br>❑ In second subject<br>♦ *Other features . . .*<br>❑ In first subject<br>❑ In second subject | II. Popularity<br>  A. Of sport-utility vehicles<br>  B. Of family sedans<br>III. Environmental impact<br>  A. Of sport-utility vehicles<br>  B. Of family sedans<br>IV. Safety<br>  A. Of sport-utility vehicles<br>  B. Of family sedans |
| **Conclusion**<br><br>*Closing summary . . .* | V. Buyers who value safety and the environment over style should bypass sport-utility vehicles in favor of traditional sedans. |

**4 Consider a division or classification structure.** These two ways of organizing a paper are quite different, though both involve creating categories to make material more manageable. A paper organized according to the principle of *division* breaks a topic into its components—its separate parts. A paper on the solar system might devote a section to each planet; a paper on a political candidate might describe her positions on several major issues in an order that seems appropriate.

## Division Pattern

| | |
|---|---|
| **Introduction**<br>*Present thesis . . .* | I. Candidate Everson's platform is based on four main issues. |
| **Body**<br>♦ *First division*<br>♦ *Second division*<br>♦ *Third division*<br>♦ *Other divisions . . .* | II. Crime prevention<br>III. Local tax rates<br>IV. Traffic control<br>V. Environment |
| **Conclusion**<br>*Closing summary . . .* | VI. Everson will devote the most resources to crime prevention. |

*Classification* involves breaking a large subject into categories according to some consistent and useful principle of division. Classification must follow rules that don't apply to division. First, classifications must be *exhaustive*: every member of the class must fit into a category. Any principle of division you use must also be *consistent*. You can't classify by more than one principle at a time—for example, if you group planets according to the number of moons they have *and* whether or not they have rings, you are not really classifying. Finally, classes *must not overlap*. That means you should be able to place an object in only one category.

## Classification Pattern

| | |
|---|---|
| **Introduction**<br>*Present thesis . . .* | I. This year's most popular bands represent many musical genres. |
| **Body**<br>♦ *First classification*<br>♦ *Second classification*<br>♦ *Third classification*<br>♦ *Other classifications . . .* | II. Modern rock<br>III. Reggae and ska<br>IV. Hip-hop and "new soul"<br>V. Folk, bluegrass, and country |
| **Conclusion**<br>*Closing summary . . .* | VI. Young music fans appreciate a variety of musical styles. |

Yet most systems of classification break down at one point or another, like the one in the model on the previous page. What do you do with performers who play more than one kind of music? Well, you can create yet another class (Latin-pop or folk-rock), or you can classify by the musician's major body of work. But you won't always be able to eliminate every exception.

● **5 Consider a cause-and-effect design.** This design is appropriate when you write a paper explaining why something has happened. The typical cause-and-effect paper moves from an explanation of some existing condition to an examination of its particular causes. In other words, you see what has happened and you want to know why.

### Cause-and-Effect Pattern

| | | |
|---|---|---|
| **Introduction**<br>*Present thesis . . .* | I. | Animated films have succeeded recently due to good writing. |
| **Body** ◆ *Effects explained* | II. | Animated films have made money and gained critical accolades |
| ◆ *Least important causes* | | |
| ◆ *More important causes* | III. | Because animation is better |
| ◆ *Most important cause* | IV. | Because scripts have broad appeal |
| **Conclusion**<br>*Closing summary . . .* | V. | Plots and dialogue of new animated films entertain both young & old. |

Typically you'll see more than one explanation for a given event, so a cause-and-effect paper may examine various causes, from the least important to the most important. You can begin your essay by identifying an effect and then go on to hypothesize about the causes, or you can start by listing a number of causes and then show how they contribute to a particular effect.

● **6 Consider a problem-and-solution pattern.** You can use this pattern effectively for papers in which you argue for change or propose an idea to settle a problem.

The first part of this pattern says, "We've got a problem and we've got to solve it—now." This part of the paper provides background information to demonstrate that the problem exists and is urgent.

The second part of the problem-and-solution pattern steers the reader through proposals for solving the problem. Since most of these ideas will be rejected (or furnish only a part of the recommended solution), the advantages and limitations of each are examined carefully. This section of the essay assures readers that no plausible approach has been ignored.

In the third part of this pattern you propose and defend one solution to the problem. You may then want to discuss the disadvantages and advantages of this proposal, highlighting the advantages. Readers need to feel that nothing is under wraps and that no hidden agendas guide your proposal. You can then conclude by explaining how the change can be put into place.

## Problem-and-Solution Pattern

| | |
|---|---|
| **Introduction** | I. All business school graduates should be required to take a course on professional ethics. |
| *Present thesis . . .* | |
| ♦ *Problem and need for solution established* | II. Public distrust following recent scandals is bad for business |
| ♦ *Rejected solutions* | III. Threat of punishment not enough |
| ▢ First rejected solution | A. May deter some illegal actions |
| • Advantages | B. But damage is done whether or |
| • Disadvantages | not crime is punished, and |
| ▢ Other rejects . . . | C. Unethical actions may be legal |
| ♦ *Proposed solution* | VI. Ethics class prevents problems |
| ▢ Feasibility | A. Easy to add a new requirement |
| ▢ Disadvantages | B. Some want fewer requirements |
| ▢ Advantages | C. Focus on ethics not legalities |
| ▢ Implementation | D. Principles addressed via debate |
| **Conclusion** | V. A discussion of principles will help graduates balance obligations to public, customers, & investors. |
| *Closing summary . . .* | |

(**Body** labels the middle section of the outline)

**⦿7 Use formatting and visual elements to reinforce your paper's organization.** When the assignment allows it, don't hesitate to use visual devices such as bulleted and numbered lists, headings, color, and images to help readers see at a glance how you've organized your project. For detailed advice on incorporating visual elements into a text, see Chapter 18.

**EXERCISE 3.2** Working with your classmates, consider what patterns you might use for writing about two of the topics listed below. Give reasons why you think those patterns would work well in each case.

> Where to eat out near campus
>
> The popularity of *The Simpsons*
>
> Safety problems in your community
>
> Whether the United States should reinstate the military draft

## 3d How do you outline a paper?

An outline can help you keep a writing project on track, whether you are following one of the patterns described in Section 3c or following one of your own. But a blueprint for your essay doesn't have to be a formal, full-sentence outline. Experiment with several techniques until you find out what works best for you.

**● 1 Try a working list.** The working list is the most flexible of all outlining devices. Start by jotting down the key points you want to make, leaving plenty of room under each major idea. Then, working from a brainstorming list or perhaps from freewriting on the subject, select subpoints to fit under these major headings. This strategy works best as a preliminary planning technique because it allows you to add examples and points under the main ideas they support as they occur to you.

**EXAMPLE 3.1**    **Working List: Should People be Allowed to Own Exotic Pets?**

**Why the issue of owning exotic pets is getting attention**

- Internet makes it easy to purchase exotic wildlife
- International animal trade a multibillion-dollar business *(quote John's roommate?)*
- More people interested in owning wild animals

- Few states have strict laws limiting who can *(recent Times article: 5,000–7,000 pet tigers in U.S. alone)* own exotic snakes, big cats, tropical birds, and other wildlife as pets

- Recent safety problems *(give examples: neighbor's escaped boa constrictor, North Carolina case of tiger cubs roaming suburban neighborhood)*
- Animal welfare agencies are calling for stricter rules

**Arguments for owning exotic pets**

- Many owners responsible, take good care of animals
- Some take homeless or rescued animals that no one else wants *(Animal Finders Guide site)*
- Individual property rights

**Why stricter limits on ownership should be imposed nationwide**

- Would ensure that people don't buy dangerous animals on a whim, then get tired of them
- Could prevent neglect and abuse of pets by requiring owners to educate themselves *(Florida case)*
- Would still allow reputable wildlife preserves and parks to operate

When you think you have enough material, look over your list and decide which points you want to treat first and how you can arrange the others. Then start writing and, as you work, refer to your list to check that you are staying on track. Add and delete items as you need to—nothing in a working list is untouchable.

### ● 2 Make an informal (scratch) outline.

Many writers like working from careful plans but dislike the formality and restrictions of formal outlines. For them the informal or scratch outline—which arranges points into categories and subcategories—provides a happy medium.

A scratch outline should begin with a thesis that states your claim or main idea. Then decide what major points you'll use to support that thesis. For each major point you'll need subpoints that support, explain, or illustrate the main point. However, your statement of points and subpoints can be quite loose since the conventions of the full-sentence outline need not be followed. Here's a sample scratch outline on reviving family dinners, following a cause-and-effect pattern of the sort described in Section 3c-5. Note that the scratch outline is considerably fuller than the working list; thus it provides more organizational guidance.

**EXAMPLE 3.2** **Scratch Outline Format**

| | |
|---|---|
| **Working Title** | **Who Should Be Able to Own Exotic Pets?** |
| **Working Thesis Statement** | **Thesis:** Lawmakers should pass stricter laws governing who can own exotic wildlife and under what conditions, since the increasing popularity of such pets has created problems with irresponsible owners, neighborhood safety, and unwanted animals. |
| **Main point 1** | 1. Exotic pets have become increasingly popular in the United States during the past few years. |
| Supporting reasons and evidence for 1 | • The Internet has made it easy to buy exotic animals from other nations.<br>• Statistics: international pet trade now a multibillion-dollar business.<br>• Few states strictly limit ownership of these pets.<br>• Ordinary people are increasingly owning such pets: my next-door neighbor, tiger cubs in NC suburbs |
| **Main point 2** | 2. Many exotic pet owners endorse lax ownership requirements. |

Supporting reasons and
evidence for 2

- Most owners are responsible and
  caring.
- Many owners are caring for homeless or
  rescued animals (*Animal Finders Guide*
  site).
- Law-abiding citizens should be able to
  choose their pets.

**Main point 3**

3. However, stricter ownership requirements
   are needed to prevent serious problems.

Supporting reasons and
evidence for 3

- These can prevent owners from
  buying exotic wildlife on a whim (give
  examples of abandoned animals).
- Requirements can ensure that owners
  are educated enough to properly care
  for animals.
- Requirements can insist on safety
  precautions so that animals do not
  become a neighborhood threat.

**3 Make a formal (sentence) outline.** A formal outline is a fairly
complex structure that compels you to think rigorously about how the ideas
in a piece of writing will fit together. (That's why instructors sometimes
require them.) If your major points really aren't compatible or parallel, a formal outline will expose the problems. When your supporting evidence is
thin or inconsistent, those flaws may show up too.

In a formal sentence outline you state every point in a complete sentence, and you make sentences within each grouping parallel, according to
the format in Chart 3.1 on page 44. As you read through the chart, imagine
how you would convert the preceding scratch outline into the fuller structure of a formal outline.

---

**Chart 3.1    Framework of a Formal Outline**

**Title:** Start by stating the working title of your paper.
**Thesis:** State your thesis fully as a complete sentence.
I. State the first major point in a complete sentence.
   A. Give the first subpoint for I.
      1. This example, evidence, or subpoint develops subpoint A.
      2. This example, evidence, or subpoint develops subpoint A.
   B. Give the second subpoint for I.
      1. This example, evidence, or subpoint develops subpoint B.
      2. This example, evidence, or subpoint develops subpoint B.
      3. This example, evidence, or subpoint develops subpoint B.
   C. Give the third subpoint for I (and so on).
II. State the second major point in a sentence parallel in structure to the
first major point (and so on).

---

**4 Outline on a computer.** What makes outlining on a computer preferable to doing the job on paper is the ease with which an on-screen outline can be expanded, contracted, rearranged, and otherwise altered. Rather than constraining ideas, a computer outline encourages a writer to be flexible because adding and rearranging ideas is as easy as moving the cursor and pressing a few keys.

**EXERCISE 3.3** Make a working list or scratch outline for a paper you're currently working on. When you are done, make a formal outline of the same project. What additions and changes did you make to construct the formal outline? Which outline will you find most helpful when you sit down to begin your first draft? Why?

## 3e How do you choose a title?

It may seem odd to choose a title while you are still planning and organizing a project. But titles are surprisingly important. Readers want and expect them. In fact, they may be annoyed if they don't find one that helps them anticipate what they will be reading—so craft your title carefully, keeping these tips in mind.

- **Choose a working title early in the process** (one you can change as the work progresses) that will keep you on track as you move through the planning and drafting stages of your project. Check your working title periodically to be sure it still fits the paper and make adjustments if necessary.
- **Be sure your title accurately reflects the content of your paper.** No cute titles, please. It's essential that your title let readers know what your paper is really about.
- **Try a two-part title** if you have your heart set on a clever phrase that's not particularly descriptive. Start with the unconventional phrase and follow it with a colon. The second part of the title, after the colon, should clarify exactly what the paper is about, as in "Short Guy, Big Ego: A Psychological Analysis of Napoleon's Military Strategy."

**EXERCISE 3.4** Which of these titles seem as if they'd be good predictors of content in a paper? Why?

1. iPods and Identity: How Push Technology Led to a Cultural Revolution

2. The Growing Trend of Hybrid Cars

3. College Students and Religion

4. What's in a Name?

5. Politics in the Hollywood Western

# 4 How Do You Write a Draft?

## 4a How do you start a draft?

Even professional writers sometimes feel anxious as they sit and stare at a blank page or computer screen. Beginnings *are* hard, but remember that a first draft doesn't have to be perfect. It's simply a place to start. In this section we offer suggestions to help you through the drafting process—so that you can stop worrying, take the plunge, and *start writing*.

In what writing environments do you produce your best work? What resources and tools help you to write? Make a conscious effort to re-create these conditions each time you begin a draft.

**● 1 Find a place to write and gather the things you'll need.** If you can, find a spot away from friends, family, and noise, where you won't be distracted. Collect your materials—laptop, computer disks or jump drive, notes, source materials, and a copy of the assignment—and lay them out where you can see them. In making preparations like these, you're not procrastinating; you're creating a working environment.

**2 Keep the ideas coming.** Try not to agonize over the first few sentences. Treat your first paragraph as a device to get rolling. Write three or four sentences nonstop to build momentum, no matter how imperfect they may be. You may be surprised at how quickly words begin to flow once you've warmed up to your topic.

Remember, too, that you don't have to write the opening paragraph first. You can always begin with whatever section of the paper seems easiest to write and come back to the introduction later. See Section 13a for more on writing opening paragraphs.

**3 Don't criticize yourself or edit prematurely.** As you work on a first draft, cut yourself some slack. Good writing develops over time—you can't expect something to be perfectly polished when you first start working on it.

Don't fiddle with problems of mechanics, formatting, or style in your early drafts. You can go back and fix difficulties with spelling, punctuation, parallelism, word choice, and the like *after* you've gotten your ideas down on paper. If you bog down in details of form too early, you may lose your momentum for writing, letting your brightest ideas fade. Don't play it too safe in a first draft. Push yourself to grapple with difficult ideas, try an unfamiliar organizational pattern, or experiment with a more interesting style.

**4 Set your own pace.** When you're not sure what pace best suits you, try writing quickly at first. If you hit a snag or can't produce the specific phrase or example you need, skip the troublesome spot and move on. Above all, keep writing. A draft in hand, even a sketchy one, will give you a sense of accomplishment and material to develop and refine.

**5 Get feedback from other writers.** Brainstorm, share ideas, compare findings, and test out arguments with fellow writers. Your classmates and colleagues can serve as important audiences for your first draft and help keep you motivated. Many college writers also visit a campus writing center to get feedback as they develop a paper draft.

In Section 4e you'll find tips for approaching collaborative writing projects. See Section 5d for advice on helping another writer revise a draft.

● **6 Draft on a computer.** Even before you begin a draft, use your computer to accumulate and store material for your paper. Start a file that records your initial notes for a project days or weeks before the deadline. Bookmark online sources and download copies of relevant articles and images.

With a computer it's also easy to experiment with major changes without losing the work you've already done. Save alternate versions of your draft until you decide which one you want to use. You can also try out different formats and visual elements at this stage. See Chapter 18 for more on working with formatting, graphics, and images in your writing.

## 4b How do you keep a draft on track?

When you begin a draft, you will probably have a thesis and a general organizational plan in mind. You will have gathered the resources you plan to use in the paper (articles, Web sites, statistics) and perhaps developed an outline. But the real work of writing a draft doesn't start until you begin putting words onto a screen. Only then can you see precisely how your plan may have to be altered. You will need to be both focused and flexible: focused enough to guide readers through your ideas and flexible enough to shift strategies when necessary.

● **1 Highlight key ideas.** Keep your thesis and main points in mind as you compose the draft. One way to do this is to summarize your thesis up front, in the first paragraph. Beginning with key points gives readers a notion of what to expect; then you can follow with supporting material. Even if you choose to ease your readers into your thesis by opening the paper with background information or an attention-getting anecdote (see Section 13a), you still need to keep your main point in mind so that the opening doesn't wander too far astray.

Continue to highlight main ideas throughout the draft. Use phrases like these to snap readers to attention.

> The main points of disagreement are . . .
>
> The chief issue, however, is . . .
>
> Here is the crucial question.

Constructions that express your own thoughts about the topic or that draw attention to contrasting viewpoints can also help you stay focused.

> I propose that . . .
>
> Other researchers say . . .
>
> Critics of this view have argued . . .

Even cues as simple as *first, second,* and *third* can help readers follow the structure of your paper. For more guidance on using transitional words and phrases, see Section 14b.

**● 2 Keep the amount you write about each point roughly proportionate to its importance in the paper.** Be careful not to write a lopsided draft that misleads readers. Your introduction paragraph shouldn't take up half the paper. If your thesis promises to develop a new solution to a problem yet neglects it until the last paragraph, you haven't fulfilled that promise. Should you find yourself writing at length on a minor point, or quoting at length from one source while neglecting others, step back and return to your central argument.

However, although you should respect the principle of proportion, don't be too stingy with words and ideas in a first draft. You'll discover in editing that it is easier to prune material you don't like than it is to fill in where your ideas are thin. Don't stray too far from your thesis, but do capture any fresh thoughts that emerge as you write. The same is true of examples, illustrations, facts, figures, and details: if they don't work, you can always cut them later or find a better place in the draft to use them.

**● 3 Allow yourself enough time to draw conclusions.** Conclusions are important, so don't skimp on the final paragraphs. The ending often determines what impression readers will take from your piece.

When you approach the end of a draft, take time to reread what you have written. Then consider what remains to be done: What are the larger implications of the ideas you've discussed? What do you want readers to know, believe, or do? What loose ends need to be tied up? Let these concerns shape your concluding paragraph(s). If you have time, try out several endings and choose the one that you think best fits your audience and purpose. See Section 13b for more on closing paragraphs.

**GOING PUBLIC** **A Drafting Journal**

 Student writer Tallon Harding recorded in a writer's journal the steps she went through in drafting "Overwhelmed and Overworked: How Today's High Schools Fail to Meet Students' Needs," which she wrote for a first-year writing course (see the full draft on pages 69–75). In what ways does her process reflect the suggestions made in this chapter? How does her drafting strategy match and differ from your own? During her drafting process, who might Tallon talk to about her paper? Which of her strategies, if any, might you try next time you write a paper?

—When I got the assignment, two weeks before the draft was due, I knew almost right away what topic I wanted to write about—the fact that high schools push students so hard to do college-level work before graduation. I started by doing freewriting to explore my general argument and my own experiences with the topic.

—Next, I made a scratch outline of main points and allotted myself about a week to complete the draft, with the first two days entirely devoted to research. I searched the campus library's online resources and found sources that provided evidence to back up my arguments and new information that helped me to better develop my thesis—I also found sources that disagreed with my viewpoint and had to figure out how to address these in the paper.

—The next day, I began to form my rough draft, using my outline as a guide along with the information that I had gathered in my research. There were several times when I was unable to focus on my paper, and during these instances I would go for a quick run to clear my head. When

I returned, I was able to pick up where I had left off and complete the thought that had eluded me.

—In this way, over several days, I wrote most of my paper, working on one or two paragraphs at a time, taking breaks in between each one. Within four or five days I had completed my rough draft, at which point I took a day off, completing the assignments in my other courses.

—After twenty-four hours had passed, I returned to my paper and read it over. With a fresh mind, grammatical and structural mistakes were more obvious, and I was able to edit and proofread my work. I did this again on the following day, correcting smaller errors and fine-tuning my wording until I was satisfied and ready to give the draft to my instructor for feedback.

## 4c When should you take a break?

In the middle of a writing project you may suddenly find yourself stumped. You gaze at your computer screen or look at a blank page, but nothing happens. No ideas come. Such a lull can be stressful, especially when a deadline looms. But don't panic; you may simply need to kick back and let your thoughts *incubate*.

Incubation is an interval during which a writer stops composing for a time to let ideas germinate or develop. You can't force or rush incubation; you can only be ready to grab a new idea when it surfaces. When possible, start a writing project well before its deadline, since you may need several incubation periods. For authors who work consistently, such rest periods are absolutely necessary. When they've written themselves out for the day, they know it's fruitless to sit at the desk any longer.

The breaks writers take between writing the first, second, and even third drafts of a paper can be productive. But shorter incubation periods help too. When you are stuck for a word or can't think of the example you need to illustrate a point, get away from the desk long enough to do an errand or chat with someone. Even such a brief pause can trigger an insight.

Don't use incubation as an excuse to procrastinate, however. If you're still having problems with a project after a few hours (or a weekend) of rest, get back to work anyway. Review your notes or outlines; consult your research;

reread what you've already written; try focusing on a new section of the paper. Most important, just write!

## 4d How do you know when you have a solid draft?

Although you'll usually have a chance to revise and polish before the final product is due, don't settle for a first draft that's incomplete or rushed—especially if you plan to ask others to read and comment on it. How do you know when you've made a solid effort? Ask yourself the questions in Checklist 4.1.

---

**Checklist 4.1   Knowing When You Have a Solid Draft**

1. **Have you made a good-faith effort?** Be sure you've invested substantial time and thought in your paper. If you haven't, you're passing up the opportunity to get useful feedback while the project is still in progress.

2. **Is it a *complete* draft?** Have you stated a thesis, developed it with supporting arguments and examples, and finished with a defensible conclusion? Have you included any charts, tables, or images that will appear in the final project? A few paragraphs don't qualify as a working draft. Nor does a carefully written opening followed by an outline of what the rest of the paper will cover.

3. **Is the draft readable?** You can't expect instructors, classmates, or colleagues to respond carefully to a paper that's hard to read.

   • Double-space your draft, leaving ample margins all the way around the page for comments.

   • Be sure that your printer or photocopier has made dark, legible copies.

   • If you must handwrite a draft, *print* in ink on every other line.

   • Print or write on one side of the paper only and number your pages.

---

**EXERCISE 4.1** Evaluate a draft you have recently written against the three criteria in Checklist 4.1. Does your paper meet the standards? If not, what changes would you have to make to remedy the problems?

# 4e How do you work on a draft collaboratively?

Being able to write as part of a group is an important skill in college, in business, and in many community settings. It's always a relief to share the workload, and collaboration often produces better ideas than a single individual could. But pundits don't joke about the ineffectiveness of committees for no reason. Without a shared focus and careful planning, collaborative writing projects can become frustrating exercises.

The kind of collaborative drafting we discuss in this section is different from the work of peer revision groups that meet to help individual writers improve an already written draft. For more on peer revision, see Section 5d.

**1 Decide on shared goals.** Suppose your instructor has asked you and several classmates to develop a promotional Web site for a local historical museum as part of a service-learning project. Before you begin work, you'd need to come to a consensus on what you want to accomplish:

- Do you want to construct a primarily informational site where readers can find the museum's address, hours of operation, admission fees, and upcoming exhibits?
- Will your site also try to persuade readers to serve as volunteer tour leaders or to donate funds?
- Will your Web site be technically sophisticated or very basic?

Of course, you may not be able to sharply define a group project in a first meeting. You may need to brainstorm or do background research. If group members have conflicting ideas, you'll need to negotiate these differences.

**2 Consider dividing the project into individual sections.** You may find it efficient to ask group members to research and compose a section of the project individually, and then schedule a group meeting to combine and edit the sections into a single document. Students working on the museum Web site might ask one writer to take responsibility for constructing an informational home page, another to compose pages on current exhibits, and another to create a list of external links to other Web sites of interest to museum patrons.

When you compose a group project in this way, set aside plenty of time to pull the pieces together. You'll need to eliminate overlap, address gaps in your coverage, and revise for consistency. The finished product shouldn't read like several short pieces awkwardly cobbled together.

Splitting a document into individually authored parts is the quickest way to complete a group writing assignment. However, this approach doesn't work well for texts that aren't easily separated into components or for a document that must represent the shared perspective of a group.

**● 3 Consider writing the document collaboratively.** Collaborative drafting—a method in which the entire group writes a document together—can yield impressive results. The advantage of this method is that several ideas and viewpoints are often better than one: you'll have diverse input and ideas at every point in the composing process.

The primary disadvantage is the amount of time required. You'll need to schedule plenty of group meetings or frequent email exchanges to write and discuss the text in progress. If you choose this method, ask one person to be in charge of maintaining the draft in progress and recording new text and ideas.

**● 4 Address disagreements promptly.** Some college students resist group projects because they've had bad experiences with classmates who monopolized a project or neglected their responsibilities.

To prevent such problems, work out a schedule of meetings and deadlines that everyone can agree on and distribute copies to each group member. If one writer fails to abide by the agreement, raise the issue in your next meeting. You may need to ask your instructor to help if the problem persists.

Other difficulties arise when group members disagree about the direction a project is taking. Suppose that in a persuasive paper for an English composition course, some members of a group want to create a multimedia presentation on the health risks of body piercing whereas the rest want to write a traditional report. If you can't settle on an approach that satisfies everyone, consult your instructor. He or she may allow you to compose two smaller subprojects or to incorporate a statement of minority views into your document.

The Declaration of Independence is one of the most famous and influential collaboratively drafted documents. How do you think the document might have turned out if the signers had split up the work and written different sections individually? What elements of their writing situation might have inspired them to work as a group?

# 5 How Do You Revise, Edit, and Proofread?

Why make a fuss distinguishing among terms as similar as *revising, editing,* and *proofreading*? It's because revising, editing, and proofreading are different phases of the writing process, each of which involves thinking about a different aspect of the paper.

| Chart 5.1 | Revising, Editing, Proofreading |
| --- | --- |

| | Focus on |
| --- | --- |
| **Revision** (early draft) | Purpose, audience, content organization |
| **Editing** (later draft) | Style, emphasis, tone |
| **Proofreading** (final draft) | Mechanics, format |

When you **revise** your draft, don't think in terms of *fixing* or *correcting* your writing—that's not really what you are doing. You are *shaping a work in progress*, reviewing what you have written, and looking for ways to improve it. You may get new ideas and shift the focus of the paper; you may cut, expand, and reorganize. At this point you are making large-scale changes.

When you **edit** a paper, you are less concerned with the big issues. Instead, you turn your attention to *clarity, style,* and *tone.* You may rewrite sentences you find awkward or correct problems with parallelism and repetition. Your goal is to create sentences and paragraphs that present your ideas effectively. These are small-scale changes.

When you **proofread** a paper, you go back over it line by line to *correct typographical errors, check for omissions, verify details,* and *eliminate inconsistencies.* This is the fix-it stage, when you're preparing the paper to appear in public. Postpone proofreading until the end of a project. Otherwise, you may waste time repairing sentences that later might be revised or deleted.

Although being able to distinguish among revising, editing, and proofreading is important (especially when your instructor has asked you to do one of these steps), the writing process is often more fluid and complicated than a three-part system. Sometimes, for example, you may not want to wait until the proofreading stage to fix a misspelled word or to insert a comma where you know one is needed, expecially if you find that these small problems distract you from the higher-level revisions you're trying to focus on. It's okay to combine revision, editing, and proofreading if that's what works for you.

## 5a What does revising involve?

When you revise a draft, don't try to work through it paragraph by paragraph, making changes as you go. Large-scale issues of content and rhetorical strategy that affect every paragraph must be addressed before you can polish individual sentences. At this point, reconsider everything you have written. Don't tinker. THINK BIG!

Prototypes of possible future vehicles often appear at auto shows to test consumer reactions. In response, manufacturers then modify the product's design, just as you might revise a draft of a paper after showing it to readers. Think about the last few papers you wrote. Did you make changes in response to readers' suggestions? What kinds of changes did you make? Whose suggestions did you find most useful, and why?

**1 Read your draft thoughtfully.** Begin by printing out a copy of your first draft and reading it from start to finish. Review the assignment and any feedback you have received. Ask yourself how you feel about the draft. What's good that you definitely want to keep? Where does it seem weak? Ideally you should appraise your draft several days (or at least several hours) after you have completed it so that you can read it more objectively.

When you dislike what you've written, editors have found little to praise, or you just need a fresh start, consider writing an entirely new draft. Creating a new draft may seem discouraging, but starting from scratch may be easier than repairing a draft that just won't work. Often an unsuccessful version points a writer toward what he or she really wanted to write.

● **2 Refine the focus of the paper.** Once you've determined that your draft is workable, be sure that it makes and develops a central point. If the draft makes a lot of general statements without supporting and developing them, you have a problem with focus. Check your examples and supporting material. Have you relied mostly on common knowledge? If so, your draft may lack the credibility that comes from specific information.

Check also to see that your draft stays on track. Your introduction and thesis will evoke certain expectations in your readers. As you revise, rein in discussions that wander, and then tie up any loose ends.

---

**Checklist 5.1     Revising for Focus**

- Have you taken on a larger topic than you can handle?
- Are you generalizing instead of stating a specific claim or thesis?
- Do you support your main ideas with evidence and examples?
- Does your conclusion agree with your opening?

---

See Section 2b for more on focusing a topic and Section 3a for advice on creating and refining a thesis.

**EXERCISE 5.1**   Using a working draft of one of your papers, try "paragraph mapping" to help you revise for focus. For each paragraph in your paper, write a short paragraph title, a paragraph thesis, and a list of your supporting points. Did you have trouble coming up with a title or a thesis for each paragraph? If so, this section of the paper probably isn't focused enough.

**● 3 Consider your purpose.** Ask yourself whether someone reading your draft would understand what you're trying to achieve. Decide exactly what you want to accomplish and be sure that your intentions are evident to yourself and to your readers.

---

**Checklist 5.2    Revising for Purpose**

• Do you clearly state in the first paragraph or two what you plan to do?

• Does the draft develop all the main points you intended to make?

• After reading the draft, will most readers be able to summarize your main idea?

---

See Section 1e for more on refining your purpose.

**● 4 Examine your paper's proportions.** *Proportion* means the distribution and balance of ideas. You should develop your ideas in relation to their importance.

---

**Checklist 5.3    Revising for Proportion**

• Are the parts of the paper out of balance? For example, have you gone into too much detail at the beginning and then skimped on the rest?

• Can your readers tell what points are most important by the amount of attention you've given to them?

• Does the conclusion do justice to the ideas it summarizes?

---

**● 5 Check for adaptation to audience.** Sometimes a first draft is *writer-centered*; that is, the writer has concentrated on expressing his or her ideas without thinking much about the audience. Such an approach can be productive in a first draft, but a major goal of revising should be to change *writer-centered* writing to *reader-centered* writing. Put yourself in the place of your readers.

---

**Checklist 5.4 Revising for Audience**

- Do you spend too much time discussing material that most of your readers already know?

- Do you answer important questions that readers might have about your topic?

- Do you define all the concepts and terms your readers need to know?

- Do you use language your readers will understand?

---

See Checklist 1.2 on audience (page 8) for more advice.

**6 Check the organization.** A well-organized project has a plan and a clear direction. Readers can move from the beginning to the end without getting lost. To revise the structure of a draft, you'll need a printed copy because organizational problems can be hard to detect on a screen.

---

**Checklist 5.5 Revising for Organization**

- Does your paper state a clear thesis or claim? Does it then develop key points related to that thesis?

- Does the development of your points follow a pattern readers will recognize?

- Do the transitions move readers sensibly from point to point?

- Would the paper work better if you moved some paragraphs around?

---

See Section 3c for more on organization and Section 14b for more on making smooth transitions between ideas.

**7 Evaluate your design and check images and graphics.** Now that you have a complete draft, you can assess how well the document is working visually: Have you used an appropriate format for the writing situation? Are the pages readable? Are sections logically arranged? Check any tables, charts, and images. Are they substantive, accurate, and legible? For more information about revising design elements, consult Chapter 18.

**●8 Check the content of the paper.** When you revise, you may need to add information to give your paper more substance.

---

**Checklist 5.6 Revising for Content**

- Do you fully explain and support each main idea?
- Do you need to add specific information and concrete examples that will make your case stronger? Do you need to do more research?
- Do you cite reliable, credible sources to back up your ideas?
- Does the title of your paper reflect its content?

---

If the content of your draft seems thin, return to the library or to other sources. See Chapters 44 and 45 for more on doing research.

**●9 Revise from a printed copy.** Whether you are revising, editing, or proofreading, you'll probably work best from a hard copy of your paper. Problems that seem all but invisible on a screen (weak organization, sprawling paragraphs, poor transitions, repeated words) show up more clearly in print.

**EXERCISE 5.2** Apply the criteria for large-scale revision described in Section 5a to a draft you have written.

## 5b What does editing involve?

Revision has given you a more focused, better-organized, more interesting draft. Now you're ready to *edit*, that is, to make the small-scale changes that you put on hold while you were revising. Now is the time to use the handbook to check on style (Part III), grammar and usage (Part V), and mechanics (Part VI).

The "deleted scenes" included in DVD versions of most popular movies—such as the scene represented in this still from *Pirates of the Caribbean* (Dir. Gore Verbinski, 2003)— give us clues about how filmmakers approach editing choices in their work. View the deleted scenes from a movie you like. What can you infer about why this material was cut? Do the director's choices suggest strategies that you might apply to your writing?

**1  Make your language concrete and specific.** Language is *concrete* when it describes things as they are perceived by the senses: colors, textures, sizes, sounds, actions. Language is *specific* when it names particular people, places, and things.

Although generalizations and abstract terms are appropriate in some writing situations, readers usually need vivid descriptions that bring concepts to life. As you edit, add people to your discussions, illustrate generalizations with examples, and supply your readers with facts and images. Give your writing texture. See Chapter 17 for more on adding detail and variety to your writing.

**2  Strive for a readable style.**  Look at your word choices. Do you achieve the right level of formality for the writing situation? Do you balance technical terms with everyday language? Are your subjects specific? Do your verbs express powerful actions? Are your word choices vivid and accurate?

Different writing styles are appropriate in different settings. When in doubt about what kind of language you should use in a piece, take a look at similar pieces others have written. For example, if you are writing a textbook review for an education course, look at similar reviews in education journals to see whether their authors use contractions and first-person pronouns, or whether more formal constructions are the rule. See Chapters 15 through 17 for more advice on style.

**3 Be sure that your tone is appropriate.**  Avoid polarizing or hostile language that will alienate your readers. Replace name-calling stereotypes (such as "traitor" to describe someone who disagrees with the president or

"Religious Right fanatic" to describe a member of an evangelical church) with more accurate and objective descriptions.

Nor should a reasoned argument rely on intensely emotional language ("this greedy, evil policy is disgusting . . ."). Although a well-timed expression of feeling can move readers, your personal anger shouldn't become the focus of an argument.

● **4 Cut wordiness.** Many writers produce wordy first drafts. In subsequent drafts, however, it's time to cut. Go after sprawling verb phrases ("make an evaluation" → "evaluate"), redundancies ("initial start-up" → "start"), and strings of prepositional phrases ("in the bottle on the shelf in the refrigerator" → "in the bottle on the refrigerator shelf"). Be ruthless. You can often cut up to a fourth of your prose without losing anything (see Section 17c).

● **5 Test your transitions.** *Transitions* are words and phrases that connect sentences, paragraphs, and whole passages of writing. When transitions are faulty, a paper will seem choppy and disconnected. Read your draft aloud. Improve the places where you pause, stumble, and detect gaps. Often you'll just need to add a word or phrase such as *on the other hand, however,* or *finally.* In some cases you'll have to rearrange whole sections to put ideas in a more coherent order. See Chapters 12 and 14 for additional suggestions.

● **6 Polish the introduction and the conclusion.** The introduction of a draft merits special attention, but don't edit the first paragraph until you know precisely how your paper is going to come out. Then you can make sure that the introduction is accurate and interesting.

The conclusion also warrants special care, but don't fuss with it until you have the main part of the paper under control. Then work out a strong ending that pulls the paper together and leaves your readers satisfied. For more specific suggestions on how to improve introductory and concluding paragraphs, see Chapter 13.

● **7 Use a computer grammar or style checker very carefully.** For all their cleverness, grammar and style checkers identify problems in a draft chiefly by counting items. They can't assess context. And it is usually context that determines, for example, whether expletives or repetitions are appropriate. If you have access to a style checker, use it, but don't assume that it can create a polished paper for you.

● **8 Refine your layout and design.** Now is the time to fine-tune and polish your document's design. For example, would adding color or changing font size make the project more readable? Do you need to adjust the position of images or tables? Do the different parts of your paper look consistent? See Chapter 18 for more detailed advice on design issues.

---

**Checklist 5.7   Editing**

• Is your language sharp—concrete and specific?

• Are sentences readable and clear?

• Have you eliminated unnecessary wordiness?

• Is your tone appropriate for the purpose and audience?

• Are your transitions effective?

• Are your opening and closing paragraphs polished and clear?

• Are format and visual elements appropriate and effective?

---

**EXAMPLE 5.1   Edited Sentences from Student Papers**

Here are some sentences from student papers that have been improved by judicious editing. Notice that the changes do not greatly alter the sentences' meaning.

ORIGINAL

*wordy*                    *awkward passive construction*

At some point or another, the experience of peers pressuring one to

engage in binge drinking is a dilemma that most college students will

have to face.

EDITED

At some point, most college students face peer pressure to engage

in binge drinking.

ORIGINAL

*wordy*

The companies ~~and products~~ that advertise in ~~women's~~ fashion

magazines know that most young women in the United States want to be

*awkward*     *unclear reference*                *vague*

beautiful (and) alluring (and) design their ads to reflect (this).

EDITED

The companies who advertise in fashion magazines know that

young women in the United States want to be beautiful and alluring, so

they design their ads to reflect these qualities.

---

**EXERCISE 5.3** Apply the criteria for editing listed in Checklist 5.7 to a draft you are working on. Give your paper all the attention to detail it deserves. And don't back away from making changes where they are necessary.

## 5c What does proofreading involve?

Like checking your appearance in the mirror before an important meeting, *proofreading* provides a final measure of quality control. The more you care about the impression a paper makes, the more important it is *not* to neglect this last step.

Use Parts III, V, and VI of the handbook to check punctuation, usage, and the conventions of edited American English.

● **1 Check your weakest areas.** If you are a poor speller, consult a dictionary frequently. If you are inclined to put commas where they're not needed, check to be sure they don't interrupt the flow of ideas. And see that you have used the correct forms of troublesome words such as *its/it's, your/you're, there/their/they're.*

**2 Check for inconsistencies.** Have you switched your point of view in ways that might be confusing—for example, addressing readers initially as *you* and later referring to them as *we* or *they*? Do you use contractions in some parts of the paper but avoid them in others? Are headings in boldface on some pages and italics on other pages? Is the tone consistent throughout (not casual in some places and formal in others)?

**3 Check punctuation.** Look for comma splices—places where a pair of independent clauses are mistakenly joined with a comma instead of a semicolon. Take a moment to review all semicolons. See that proper nouns and adjectives (*England, African*) and *I* are capitalized. Check that quotation marks and parentheses are in pairs (see Chapters 38 and 39).

**4 Check for typographical errors.** Look especially for transposed letters, dropped endings, faulty word division, and omitted apostrophes.

**5 Check the format of your paper.** Number your pages, italicize or underline titles of sources as needed, put other titles between quotation marks (see Chapters 38 and 41), and clip your pages together. Be sure that you've cited outside sources appropriately and listed them in your bibliography (see Chapters 46 and 49 through 52). Set the margins correctly and review the page breaks.

**EXERCISE 5.4** Proofread a writing project you've recently completed, looking at all five of the areas discussed in Section 5c. Which problems do you spot most often? How do you think you might avoid them in future projects?

## 5d How do you help another writer revise, edit, and proofread?

Many writing instructors ask students to help each other in the revising, editing, and proofreading phase. (For advice on interpreting your instructor's comments on your paper, see Section 6a-7.) Meeting in small groups, writers read copies of each other's drafts and respond to them. Sometimes called *peer revision*, this method allows each writer in the class to receive feedback from one or more readers. Even if you don't have the chance to participate in a formal peer editing session, try to get several readers' reactions to your work in progress.

It takes skill to respond to another person's writing critically and honestly. When you do so, remember that you aren't taking the place of the writing teacher: you're an editor, not a grader. You can help a fellow writer most by showing an interest in what he or she has written, asking questions, giving encouragement, and making constructive suggestions.

Similarly, use peers' criticism of your own drafts constructively, listening closely and selecting the comments that best suit your goals for the project. This section provides tips to help you get the most out of a revision session.

**1 Read the writer's draft straight through once.** Get a feel for the big issues before worrying about details of mechanics and usage. Do you understand what the writer is trying to achieve? Could you summarize the point of the paper? Do you find it informative, persuasive, or interesting? First impressions are important; if you don't think the draft works, try to explain why.

**2 Read the paper a second time.** Use the guidelines in Checklist 5.8 on page 68 to help you formulate specific responses. It's important that you say more than "I really like your paper" or "A few of your points are confusing." Explain *what* you like about it, such as well-researched facts or colorful turns of phrase. Show *where* you believe the paper needs development. At this stage keep your focus on large-scale issues, not on misspellings or editing problems to be dealt with later.

**3 Make marginal comments.** Jot comments in the margins of the draft as you read it the second time. Editorial comments should be genuine queries or pointed observations, not stinging criticisms. Even when you're pointing out a weakness in a paper, use a courteous and supportive tone, not a sarcastic or unkind one. Be as specific as you can about your reaction to the paper, and let the writer know where something is working well.

**4 Write a general response to the paper.** After you have carefully read and annotated the paper, write a thoughtful note at the end summarizing your reactions. Begin by saying what you think the paper has accomplished. That way the writer knows whether the paper has achieved at least part of what he or she hoped. Conclude your note with suggestions for revision, stressing what you believe the writer's priorities might be.

---

### Checklist 5.8 Responding to a Draft

- What do you like most about the paper?

- How well does the paper achieve its purpose?

- How well does the writer tailor the piece to the audience? What suggestions might you make for better adapting the paper for its intended readers?

- What suggestions can you make about focusing the topic? Should the focus be narrower? Does the paper need a sharper thesis?

- Does the writer come across as credible? What suggestions can you make that might add greater authority to the paper?

- What questions does the paper raise? What additional information, discussion, or examples would you like to have?

- How effectively does the writer use language? Are sentences clear and readable? How appropriate is the tone? Do you notice recurring problems with grammar, usage, or mechanics?

- What general comments do you have for the writer?

---

**GOING PUBLIC**    **Draft with Peer Comments**

Here is a draft of a paper by first-year composition student Tallon Harding. The assignment asked her to write a researched argument on a topic relevant to her and her classmates. It is a fine draft in many respects, focused and thoughtful. It uses personal experience and clearly articulated claims to catch readers' attention, drawing them into the argument. The draft also incorporates source materials effectively.

The draft also has some weaknesses. To get at them, we've reproduced some marginal comments and a concluding memo that is a composite of comments written by several of Tallon's peers, including undergraduate student writer Todd Lucas. Notice that most of these comments target large issues for revision rather than editing and mechanical problems.

Note, too, that Harding's draft cites and documents sources in MLA Style, the system used for most academic writing in the humanities. You'll find more information about MLA Style in Chapter 50.

Tallon Harding

Professor Rollins

English 101

Paper #2

30 October 2005

Overwhelmed and Overworked: How Today's High Schools

Fail to Meet Students' Needs

School let out an hour ago but the library is packed with students. Each of us is working frantically to finish the next day's assignments. The Advanced Placement Tests will be given on Monday and we all need the weekend to study; the pressure is almost unbearable. A couple of years ago this spectacle—an evening not much different from most during my senior year—would have confounded the average high school librarian, who would have been able to leave as soon as school let out. Recently, however, such scenes have become commonplace. Due to a push by school officials looking to receive government grants, students are increasingly being pressured to enroll in college-level courses offered in the high school classroom. As part of a new "Steps to Prosperity" measure recently introduced by the South Carolina state legislature, some districts in our state

*Good point— a lot of high schools are pushing this now.*

*Can you give more information about this program?*

are even beginning to require students to declare a major as early as their sophomore year in high school (Landrum). What these ambitious administrators forget is that a good, well-rounded high school education should involve more than just academic study. It must also include extracurricular activities that help students to grow socially and physically, to become well-rounded citizens. As schools neglect these qualitative dimensions in their quest to achieve higher and higher academic standards, they leave gaps in students' education and neglect important student needs.

College-level courses, such as the Advanced Placement (AP) and International Baccalaureate (IB) Programs, were originally developed for high school students as a means to better prepare them for the rigorous demands of a postsecondary education. It was hoped that the most gifted, organized students would be able to take classes that would help them bypass introductory college courses and allow them to dive into more challenging ones upon entering college. In recent years, however, government grants have been made available to states that had high participation rates in these courses (Educationmoney.com). As a consequence, many school officials now push as many students as possible to enroll in AP and IB classes, with less regard for the student's qualifications or level of preparedness. This has left a number of students struggling to pass, when they would do better in a lower-level class. Similarly, the brighter students, for whom the courses were designed, have ended up packing their schedules with advanced courses and in turn overworking themselves.

*Say more about these grants.*

The number of students becoming involved in college-level courses has increased tremendously in the past few years. According to the College Board, sponsor of the Advanced Placement Program, the number of administered AP exams has more than doubled since 1990, reaching an astonishing 1,270,000 exams taken last year (High). The media has greeted these numbers with praise and applause, congratulating the nation's school districts for a job well done. Less attention has been paid to the number of students actually passing the exam, however. The national passing rate on all AP exams taken in 1989 was 69 percent, yet in 2000 that number had fallen to 64 percent (Advanced), which means that 36 percent of the students enrolled in the program were unqualified and unprepared for the exam. These numbers show that as the number of students taking college-level courses has increased, the percentage passing them has shrunk.

*Is a drop of 5% dramatic?*

Unfortunately, as participation in challenging academic programs grows, some students are forced to drop extracurricular activities to make time for studying. This leaves students with only a narrow portion of the high school education that they are entitled to receiving. For example, high school student Jenni Deming, a talented dancer, reported in a personal interview, "I quit ballet training right after the beginning of ninth grade, because I couldn't figure out how to fit in daily dance classes along with the three or four hours of nightly homework I had in my Honors courses." Other students, such as Marisa Astiz, who was featured in a recent news article on high school student stress, find themselves running from one academic activity to another, with little time to make friends and even less sleep (Strauss). In fact, with the use of so many college-level courses and the introduction of high school majors, secondary education is becoming more and more like college. The average college student spends the majority of his or her day studying and is not as involved in the community as one might hope. This description is increasingly expanding to include the typical high school student as well. However, the high school student's situation is even more difficult: The typical college student spends a smaller portion of her day in the classroom and usually will only enroll in five classes a semester, whereas high school students spend almost eight hours a day in school and take up to seven classes a semester.

*Are extra-curriculars more important than studying?*

Today's high school students are being cheated out of a well-rounded education by being pushed into overly challenging college-level courses. They are no longer free to participate in a wide variety of activities that would help them to grow as a person, but are instead skipping that part of their education and basically starting college four years early. The personal cost of focusing too hard, too soon can be tremendous. A survey study of first-year college students found that rising numbers of students arrive at college already suffering from depression and stress-related disorders (Strauss) A recent article in the *San Francisco Chronicle* reports that increasing numbers of overachieving students now burn out before they even get to college, deciding to take one or more years off to pursue

*If these students are over-achievers, they might be stressed out anyway.*

interests that they did not have time to enjoy in high school (Strauss). Perhaps these students are guilty of being too ambitious, but they are not solely to blame, since many educators and parents are the ones pushing them to overachieve.

Instead of focusing on grant money and enrollment numbers, school officials need to reevaluate the impact these courses are having on students. Simply studying the recent AP scores would show them that this new form of academics is doing more harm than good. Instead of packing their schedule with Advanced Placement and International Baccalaureate classes, students need to take one or two in order to be able to focus their attention on them, and yet still be able to have time for other activities. High school is a critical point in young people's lives, and without both the academics and extracurricular activities, they are not able to establish the strong and well-evolved character that they otherwise would be able to develop. A good high school education should include both of these things, and many schools today simply do not meet these criteria.

Works Cited

"84.330 Advanced Placement Program." *EducationMoney.com*.
American Resource Discoveries, n.d. Web. 15 Sept.
2003.

"Advanced Placement Results." *Beverly Hills High School*.
Beverly Hills High School, 25 Aug. 2003. Web. 22 Sept.
2003..

Deming, Jenni. Personal interview. 14 Oct. 2005.

"High School: The Shifting Mission." *Education Week*.
Editorial Projects in Education, 25 Apr. 2001. Web. 16
Sept. 2003..

Landrum, Cindy. "State Wants High School Students to Have
Majors." *GreenvilleOnline.com*. The Greenville News,
4 Feb. 2003. Web. 16 Sept. 2003.

Strauss, Valerie. "Students Are Taking Time Out Over
Stress." *SF Gate*. Hearst Communications, 23 Oct. 2005.
Web. 2 Nov. 2005.

**GOING PUBLIC**   **Peer Comments**

Dear Tallon,

I think your paper is interesting and persuasive. Almost anyone who
has graduated from high school in the past few years is familiar with
your topic, and they will sympathize with your feeling that students
are being pushed so hard academically that they don't have time to do

anything else. The examples you give of the students who have had to sacrifice to keep up with their studies are powerful.

Your opening contains good background information to show why schools are pressuring students, especially the statistics about the AP exam. Consider adding more specific facts about the government grant programs. I wasn't familiar with them. I also wasn't sure whether this is the only cause of the problem. Parents sometimes insist that their child be in the best courses regardless of ability, and teachers may want the prestige of teaching advanced courses. Even students can feel competitive with their peers.

I think you also need to say more about why academics shouldn't be the most important priority for schools. I see your point about the importance of maintaining a balance, but that might not sound practical for all readers. Most students know that they have to have good test scores and grades to get into a good college. No one gets admitted to college based on being a "well rounded" person. Give a little more importance to academics in your argument, because otherwise it might come across as too idealistic.

I marked a couple of confusing places, but overall, I believe that with a little more revision, this will be a good paper.

Todd

# PART II | Writing for Academic and Public Forums

# 6

# How Do You Write in College?

## 6a How do you write a successful academic paper?

As a college student, you can count on having to write. That's a fact of life, regardless of your major. Academic writing is not necessarily tricky, but it differs from high school writing because college instructors have unique requirements in mind. Although expectations vary from subject to subject, most instructors will expect you to approach topics with a critical eye, to justify your ideas with logical reasons and evidence, and to cite the sources of your information. Once you understand these responsibilities, you can address academic audiences with confidence.

**1 Review the assignment.** When instructors assign a writing project, they usually have specific expectations in mind: a certain approach to a topic, certain kinds of research, a set number of pages, and a particular due date.

Before you get too far into a project, ask yourself these practical questions: How much research will you have to do? What special materials will you need? How much time do you have? Some books may not be immediately available, or the library may not carry the periodical you want. If you need to do interviews, allot time to contact people and keep appointments. And if the paper is due in the same week as two papers for other courses, start extra early.

**2 Don't take on too much in a writing project.** When you make a claim in a paper, you've staked out a piece of territory: you've asserted what you believe and drawn lines around it, and now you have to defend it. You don't want to find out when you're halfway through that your claims are overextended, so stake out a topic that you can manage. Then you'll have a chance to think and write about it in detail. See Section 2b for advice on how to narrow a topic.

**⊕3 Support your claims with logical reasons and sufficient evidence.**
Unless you're doing an informal assignment such as a journal entry, it's usually not enough in a college course to claim on the basis of personal feelings or popular opinion that something is true or that something should

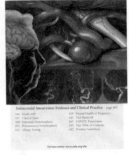

Popular and academic publications often report on similar topics, such as diet and health, but they usually support their claims quite differently. How do you think the kinds of information and arguments provided in the two cover articles above might differ? Which would you be most likely to consult in writing a paper for a course? Would the kind of course (e.g., an English course versus a biology course) affect your decision? Why or why not?

be done. Instructors want students to support their claims with reasons and evidence appropriate for academic writing.

In a college paper, your supporting materials should come from reliable, recent sources, and you should be able to produce enough of them to show that you're knowledgeable about the topic. This means doing research. Depending on the paper you're writing, you might look for the following kinds of data:

- Historical documents
- Research findings
- Eyewitness accounts
- Analyses written by experts on the subject
- Statistics

You'll find such evidence in reference sources, scholarly books and articles, government archives, and publications produced by professional organizations.

However, some arguments and evidence are more appropriate to some writing tasks than to others. If you are writing a paper for a history class, historical documents and secondary sources written by historians will be the most relevant. A profile article for a journalism course might draw primarily on material collected in personal interviews with your subject. See Sections 44b through 44d for more on finding and selecting academic sources.

**GOING PUBLIC**   **Writing an Annotated Bibliography**

An instructor may ask you to turn in an *annotated bibliography* that briefly describes and evaluates the sources you plan to use in a paper. This excerpt from student writer Matt Valentine's annotated bibliography assesses some of the materials he discovered in researching a paper about the Holocaust, which he wrote for a composition course. Note the breadth and variety of his sources. Do you think he's chosen materials that his instructor will find valid and reliable?

Matt Valentine

Dr. Friend

Topics in Writing

12 November 2006

Annotated Bibliography for "The Rhetoric of Atrocity:

Nazi Propaganda and the Holocaust"

American Jewish Committee. *The Jews in Nazi Germany: A Handbook of Facts Regarding Their Present Situation.* 1935. New York: Fertig, 1982. Print. This republished book gives perspectives held by American Jews in the years preceding the Holocaust.

Eltin, Richard A., ed. *Art, Culture and Media Under the Third Reich.* Chicago: U of Chicago P, 2002. Print. This book, which contains scholarly essays by historians, deals with how propaganda in the form of art and mass media influenced the development of anti-Semitic sentiments in Germany leading to the Holocaust. Also, some essays discuss artists who were exiled from Germany because their art resisted Hitler's views.

Keegan, John. "Code of Silence." *New York Times* 25 Nov. 1996: A13. Print. This news article reports on the release of government records suggesting that officials of the Allied forces were aware of the Holocaust death camps but chose to keep the information away from the public and not to act upon it.

Meyer, Walter. Personal interview. 24 Nov. 2006. First a member of the Hitler Youth and later a concentration camp prisoner, Dr. Meyer talks about propaganda, attitudes in urban Germany and in the camps, and the reactions of the Allied occupation forces after the war.

Spiegelman, Art. *Maus II: A Survivor's Tale.* New York: Pantheon, 1997. Print. This best-selling, Pulitzer Prize-winning graphic novel tells the story of one survivor's experience of the Holocaust.

---

Be aware that some instructors will ask for bibliographic entries that are longer and more in-depth than the ones Matt composed. Check with your instructor if you have questions about the content and length of your annotations. For examples of longer annotated bibliography entries, visit the Cornell University Library's site *How to Prepare an Annotated Bibliography,* at <http://www.library.cornell.edu/olinuris/ref/research/skill28.htm#what>.

**⊘4 Document your sources.** When you cite statistics or research, your instructor will want to know where you got your data. And if you use *any* material that someone else thought of or wrote first, you're obligated to give that source credit. If you don't, you're committing plagiarism. (See Section 46c for more about plagiarism.)

Documenting sources takes time, but it's an essential part of college writing. It's not difficult to do once you know where to look for guidelines. Sections 49a and 49c offer comprehensive information on documenting sources.

● 5 **Follow research and writing conventions appropriate to your subject area.** The guidelines we discuss in this chapter apply generally to the writing you'll do in any course, but be aware that some expectations differ from subject area to subject area. Suppose that you want to write a paper on alcoholism. Imagine the various forms it might take in different courses: In a creative writing course you might craft a poem about a character's struggle with recovery. In a sociology course you might write a case study based on interviews with a member of Alcoholics Anonymous. In a biology course you might collect and report on data about the physical effects of alcohol on laboratory rats. All three projects would require critical thought, research, and the ability to construct a clear argument. Their differences grow out of the different *goals* and *approaches* valued in each discipline—the humanities, the social sciences, and the natural sciences.

- **Goals:** What kinds of topics and questions interest scholars in this discipline? What do they want to find out?
- **Methods:** How do scholars in a particular discipline go about finding out what they want to know? Do they test hypotheses systematically and empirically? Do they critically interpret texts and other artifacts?
- **Evidence:** What kinds of materials do scholars in a subject area typically use to support their arguments—numerical data, historical artifacts, quotations from literary or philosophical texts?
- **Genres:** What kinds of documents do scholars in a field typically produce—lab reports, critical analyses, case studies, personal commentaries? What organizational and stylistic conventions are typical?
- **Documentation:** What system do scholars in the field use for citing and documenting sources?

The chart on pages 83–84 lists some basic characteristics of research and writing in the humanities, social sciences, and natural sciences. Keep these in mind as you approach your writing in your various courses, and ask your instructor when you're unsure about what rules apply.

**Highlight   Writing in Different Academic Disciplines**

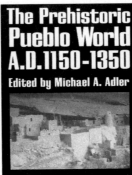

| HUMANITIES | SOCIAL SCIENCES | NATURAL SCIENCES |
|---|---|---|
| **Subject areas** | | |
| Literature, philosophy, history, classics | Sociology, psychology, anthropology, social work, education | Astronomy, botany, chemistry, physics, zoology |
| **Purposes** | | |
| To study how people use language or other symbols to interpret experience | To study how people create and live within social systems | To study the structure and workings of the physical world |
| **Methods** | | |
| Close reading and analysis of texts | Fieldwork and other observational research; statistical analysis of data | The scientific method, experimental testing of hypotheses |
| **Sources** | | |
| Literary, philosophical, and historical works and critical commentaries on them | Data collected from interviews, surveys, field observations; previous research by other scholars | Data collected through systematic observation in controlled settings |

*(Continued)*

## Writing in Different Academic Disciplines *(Continued)*

| HUMANITIES | SOCIAL SCIENCES | NATURAL SCIENCES |
| --- | --- | --- |
| **Formats** | | |
| Critical and interpretive essays, book reviews, personal and reflective pieces, creative writing | Field notes, case studies, research reports, reviews of research | Lab reports, research reports, summaries of research, process analyses |
| **Documentation** | | |
| Usually MLA | Usually APA | Often CSE |

**◉6 Submit professional-looking work.** When you turn in a paper, you send your instructor a message about the kind of student you are. Even if your instructors have been lenient about usage or punctuation errors when they read your drafts or haven't issued special warnings about grammatical correctness, they care about such details in the final product. If your paper looks good, it will make a good first impression.

Before you submit an essay for a grade, proofread for faulty punctuation, agreement errors, and spelling. Get a second opinion from a friend. Consult the grammar and usage portions of this book and run your computer's spell checker. Then check to see that your paper complies with any formatting instructions included in the assignment: Has the instructor specified MLA or APA style? a particular font size? single or double spacing? See Section 5c for advice on proofreading and Chapters 50 through 52 for help with particular formats.

Instructors don't like to get papers they can barely read. Word-process all writing projects, double spaced, with numbered pages. Be sure your printer produces quality output. Fasten pages together with a staple or paper clips.

If the assignment allows it, you may want to experiment with layout, images, and other visual elements to create an even more attractive finished product. Chapter 18 provides comprehensive advice on document design.

**◉7 Understand how your writing will be evaluated.** Much of the writing you do in college will be evaluated and graded. Commenting and grading policies differ from institution to institution and from instructor to instructor. But in most courses, you should seek out the following information before you submit a writing project for a grade. Find out

- what the grading standards are in your course and in your school. What specific qualities does *A, B,* or *C* work have? What does *A, B,* or *C* work represent: *Excellent, Superior, Average?*
- how the grade in the course or the particular assignment will be calculated.
- what counts toward the grade. Will outlines, notes, or drafts be evaluated? What role will class participation, quizzes, or peer editing play?
- what the revision policy—if any—in a writing course will be.

Your instructor will often provide this information in a course syllabus or assignment sheet; if you have questions, ask.

In most college courses, your instructor will also provide you with periodic feedback, in the form of grades or written comments, to tell you how well your writing matches his or her standards. Not all instructors provide written comments, but most are willing to meet with you to talk about your work.

However, grading is not a one-way street; as a college student, you have the responsibility to

- recognize that grading standards in college courses are generally more stringent than those in high school courses.
- assume that your instructor is acting in good faith in evaluating your work.
- pay attention to instructions, to grading criteria, and to instructor comments on your work.
- pursue grading inquiries reasonably and responsibly.

Most important, recognize that you can learn from the evaluation process if you approach it as a tool for improving your writing.

---

### Checklist 6.1 Writing for College Assignments

When you write an academic paper, remember to

- Assess the assignment carefully.

- Limit your thesis to one that you can adequately cover and support.

- Support your claims with reasons and evidence.

*(Continued)*

**Writing for College Assignments**   *(Continued)*

• Follow conventions appropriate for the subject area.

• Document your sources.

• Hand in only carefully edited, proofread, professional-looking papers.

**EXERCISE 6.1**   Here are several claims from undergraduate writing assignments. For each claim, suggest specific kinds of supporting evidence you think the writer's instructor would find appropriate and convincing.

1. *From a research project for a social work course:* For children who come from abusive families, high-quality institutional care is a better option than programs that try to reform the parents in an effort to keep the family together.

2. *From a research paper for a first-year writing course:* Professional athletes are poor role models because so many of them engage in unsportsmanlike or illegal behavior, on and off the playing field.

3. *From an essay exam for an ethics course:* Circuses are unethical because they exploit animals purely for entertainment.

4. *From a research review for a human biology course:* A growing body of data suggests that asthma has a strong genetic component.

**EXERCISE 6.2**   Evaluate a paper you've recently written for a college course against Checklist 6.1 on pages 85–86. Then ask yourself these questions: Does your paper meet the standards? Where does it fall short? If you could write the paper over again, to which item on the list would you pay the most attention? Why?

## 6b How do you write on essay examinations?

If you're like many writers, you'll do most of your writing outside the classroom—in your room, the library, or another familiar and relatively comfortable setting. However, every college writer should also know how to compose under pressure. Researchers estimate that up to half the writing you do during college will occur on exams. After you leave school, you'll find that many jobs require the ability to write quickly and efficiently. Journalists must create news stories on tight deadlines. Engineers and other technical workers frequently write on-the-spot progress reports. And teachers, lawyers, police officers, and social workers must pass licensing examinations. Unfortunately, many writers resign themselves to failure at this kind of writing, believing, "I freeze under pressure."

Don't give up before you start. You *can* write well in an exam setting if you understand the unique skills involved and work to master them.

### ● 1 Know the material.

Preparation is half the battle in an essay exam. Lay the foundation for success by attending class regularly, keeping up with required readings, and participating actively in class discussions.

But simply absorbing the material is not enough. You also need to organize and think critically about what you know. Look for clues in course lectures and readings about what ideas and examples are important (*Three basic arguments for . . . ; A central figure in . . .*). Summarize important theories and concepts in your own words to be sure that you understand them. Review your notes periodically and ask yourself how new material fits with the old. When you have questions, speak up.

If your teacher often asks students to express their views on course material or apply it to new situations, you can bet that he or she will include these kinds of questions on the exam. Prepare yourself by rehearsing your views about key points in the lecture and readings: Do you agree? Do you disagree? What approaches or theories make the most sense to you?

To practice applying your knowledge, imagine how the material you're studying might relate to a current event or controversy. For example, that article you read in your U.S. history course about the debates between the Federalists and the Anti-Federalists in the Revolutionary period might help you understand what's at issue in a contemporary Supreme Court decision about states' rights. See Chapter 8 for detailed advice on getting the most out of your reading.

### ● 2 Find out as much as you can about the exam.

Because an exam may cover hundreds or even thousands of pages of material, focus your preparation on those portions most likely to appear on the exam. Ask your instructor for details: How many questions will the test include? What kinds of questions? What topics will be emphasized? Will you get to choose from several questions? Knowing some parameters will help guide your study: for instance, if the test consists of four short essays, you won't have time to list many examples or details, so you should concentrate on learning main ideas.

If your instructor provides copies of exams from previous semesters, seize the opportunity. An old exam can help you anticipate what kinds of items will appear, and you can use it for a practice run. If your instructor does not offer sample exams, many schools maintain test files that archive exams from a variety of courses.

### 3 Use your study time intelligently.

This advice may seem obvious, but it's true. An exam requires you to quickly pull together what you know—so you'll need to be in top academic form. Forgo extreme studying techniques, such as cramming or pulling all-nighters, that leave you exhausted at the time of the test. Instead, spend your time practicing the thinking and writing skills that exam essays require. Make scratch outlines of important theories or arguments you think are likely to be covered, along with one or two key examples or details, and use these as the basis for your review.

Classmates can be another valuable resource. If you enjoy working collaboratively, form a study group. Meet before the exam to compare notes, puzzle out gaps in your knowledge, and practice explaining key points to each other. But don't substitute group meetings for individual study. Allow yourself plenty of time to go over group insights and integrate them with your own knowledge.

### 4 Devise strategies for coping with pressure.

Many writers have trouble adapting their writing process to an inflexible test environment. But don't panic. You can anticipate certain difficulties and decide beforehand how you will deal with them.

First, eliminate unnecessary stress. Get a good night's sleep, eat a healthful meal, and keep anxiety-producing cramming to a minimum. Gather all your materials—examination booklets, pens, calculator, and notes or books when the instructor allows them—well in advance. Arrive a few minutes early, but not too early; sitting in an empty classroom for too long may make you nervous.

Plan also to head off specific problems that can occur during an exam: if you haven't had much experience writing under pressure, time yourself on practice questions beforehand. If you panic when you see an unfamiliar question, work on the easiest items first, then come back to the more challenging ones. If you fall apart when time runs short, give yourself a safety net by outlining each response before you start writing, so you can attach the outline to any unfinished response. And if you will write the exam on a computer, save frequently so that you don't lose something important.

⏺ **5 Figure out what the question is asking you to do.** Analyze each exam question carefully before you begin writing. Start by locating all the key terms—usually nouns or noun phrases—that *identify* or *limit* the subject: "Discuss the *major components* of *Plato's educational ideal* as elaborated in *The Republic*"; "Explain *four kinds of confounding* that can occur in *observational research*." Next, underline key verbs that tell you what to do with the topic: *analyze, compare, discuss, explain, trace.* Each of these instructions means something a bit different, as Chart 6.1 on pages 90–92 shows.

Finally, cross out any material that does not seem relevant to the question. Instructors sometimes begin an exam with a quotation, an example, or an introductory discussion that serves primarily to clarify the main question. In this rather daunting example from a British literature course, for instance, the core question is stated only in the last sentence.

> Since the beginning of the semester, we have seen thinkers such as Freud, Marx, and Nietzsche describe the philosophical contradictions that inhabit the twentieth century. *Choose one major text we have read this semester and trace the ways that work describes contradictions in private, public, or intellectual activities.*

Here the references to Freud, Marx, and Nietzsche only introduce the idea of "contradiction," the focus of the main question. To answer this question, you don't need to comment on any of these thinkers; you just have to explain how contradiction shows up in one of the literary texts you studied for the class.

**EXERCISE 6.3** Identify key terms in an examination question from a course you are taking or from a standardized test for college admission, job certification, or another purpose. What specific topics does the question stake out? Which verbs tell you what to do with those topics? Make a scratch outline showing how you would address these components of the question in your response.

● 6 **Budget your time.** Keep the amount of time you spend on each question roughly proportionate to its importance. If you squander most of your time on a single question, you may jeopardize your chance for a good grade. Here is a simple way to figure out how to allocate your time: Divide the number of points each question is worth by the number of points on the whole exam. The result equals the percentage of time you should devote to that question. For example, suppose you have a fifty-point question on a one-hour test that is worth two hundred total points. You should probably spend about fifteen minutes, or 25 percent of the hour, on that response.

If you run out of time in the middle of a response, resist the temptation to steal time set aside for other questions. Instead, jot a note to your instructor explaining that you ran out of time, and attach your outline. Many instructors will give partial credit for outlined responses.

---

**Chart 6.1  Common Exam Terms**

**Analyze:** Break an argument or a concept into parts and explain the relationships among them; evaluate or explain your interpretation or judgment.

> Analyze the effects of ketosis on the digestive system.

**Apply:** Take a concept, formula, or theory and adapt it to another situation.

> Apply Bernard's elements of sound executive management to President Ronald Reagan's management practices during his first term.

**Argue, prove:** Take a position on an issue and provide reasons and evidence to support that position.

> Argue whether or not you believe it is possible to run government agencies like private sector businesses.

*(Continued)*

**Common Exam Terms** *(Continued)*

**Compare:** Point out similarities between two or more concepts, theories, or situations.

> Compare the educational philosophies of Dewey and Rousseau. How did each conceptualize the learner, the function of education, and the role of the teacher?

**Contrast:** Point out differences between two or more concepts, theories, or situations.

> Contrast the imagery in Yeats's "The Second Coming" and Hardy's "The Darkling Thrush."

**Critique, evaluate:** Make and support a judgment about the worth of an idea, theory, or proposal, accounting for both strengths and weaknesses.

> Evaluate the effectiveness of medication versus behavioral therapy in the treatment of hyperactivity disorder in children.

**Define:** State a clear, precise meaning for a concept or object, and perhaps give an illustrative example.

> Define the three measures of central tendency (mean, median, mode); then explain which would provide the most accurate gauge of annual income in a given community.

**Discuss, explain:** Offer a comprehensive presentation and analysis of important ideas relating to a topic, supported with examples and evidence. These questions usually require detailed responses.

> Discuss the Ebonics controversy, drawing on the research we have studied this semester to clarify key points of difference.

**Enumerate, list:** Name a series of ideas, elements, or related objects one by one, perhaps giving a brief explanation of each.

> List Jean Piaget's stages of moral development, and give an example of how moral choices are negotiated at each stage.

*(Continued)*

**Common Exam Terms** *(Continued)*

**Review, summarize:** Briefly lay out the main points of a larger theory or argument.

> Summarize the definitions of legal discrimination presented in the decisions *Sweatt v. Painter* and *Hopwood v. The University of Texas.*

**Trace:** Explain chronologically a series of events or the development of a trend or idea.

> Trace the pathway of a nerve impulse from stimulus to response.

**7 Make a plan.** To pack as much writing as possible into the allocated time, take five minutes or so to map out your answer. If the question asks for independent argument or analysis, brainstorm or freewrite to generate ideas. If the question asks you to synthesize course material, try an idea map that organizes information under key categories. (See Section 2c for more on prewriting techniques.)

Use these initial ideas as the foundation for a list or scratch outline of the full response. Whatever format you choose, it should include your thesis, main supporting ideas, and important examples. Once your outline is in place, you are ready to begin the actual writing. See Sections 3c and 3d for more on organizing and outlining an essay.

**8 Understand what a good response looks like.** Although no single approach can guarantee you perfect marks on every test you take, most college instructors want a tightly organized response that contains the following elements.

- **A clear thesis statement** in the first paragraph or, better yet as the first sentence.
- **Logical organization** with a single key idea developed in each paragraph and with clear transitions between points.
- **Adequate support and evidence** for each point, drawn from course readings and lectures.

- **Your own views or analysis** when the question asks for them. Remember, though, to justify your ideas with evidence and support.
- **A conclusion** that ties together main points and summarizes their importance, even if you have time for only a sentence or two.
- **Clear prose** free of major grammatical and mechanical errors.

Finally, before you set aside a lot of time for editing and proofreading, ask your instructor how he or she deals with grammatical and mechanical problems. Many teachers don't penalize minor mistakes unless they hinder the clarity of your argument, but others are sticklers for correctness.

**GOING PUBLIC** **Framing a Successful Examination Essay**

Undergraduate writer Jena Gentry encountered this question on the midterm for a U.S. history course: "Discuss some important causes of the Great Crash of 1929. How did Presidents Hoover and Roosevelt try to deal with the resulting Great Depression? How successful were they?" Note how the opening paragraph of her response, excerpted here, summarizes basic concepts and forecasts the direction of her argument.

> The economic boom of the 1920s had a dramatic impact on the U.S. economy. While corporate profits were large, they weren't being recycled into the consumer market, but rather invested into an inflated stock market whose prices were continually increasing. The terrible result—the Great Crash of 1929—came as a result of four main causes: the saturation of the consumer market, a rigid price structure and speculative market, an unequal distribution of wealth, and Republican public policies that favored the rich. Two presidents, Hoover and Roosevelt, tried to deliver Americans out of the subsequent Great Depression. However, Hoover believed that the government should stay out of the economy, and his modest program

of legislation didn't do much. Roosevelt's ambitious New Deal was more successful, bringing many Americans a measure of relief, recovery, and reform.

The rest of Gentry's essay contains eight paragraphs: one devoted to each cause of the Great Crash, one discussing Hoover's efforts to deal with the Depression, two explaining and evaluating Roosevelt's New Deal, and a brief conclusion.

## 6c How do you write for electronic forums in a college course?

Many college courses now use Web sites and email to do things traditionally done on paper. For example, your instructor may ask you to respond to reading assignments on a class discussion board, to conduct peer editing workshops via email, or to participate in online chat sessions. The guidelines for academic writing discussed in Sections 6a and 6b generally apply to any writing you do in a course, but online genres also have unique conventions and expectations. See Section 19a for examples of and guidelines for composing email messages and Section 19f for advice on composing messages for online forums.

Most important, keep your audience and purpose in mind. Although you might adopt a chatty tone and forgo standard spelling or capitalization when you instant-message your best friend, class-related communication should be much more formal. Use civil language and observe standard grammatical and mechanical conventions. Find out what your instructor's expectations are and abide by them. For example, is the class discussion board a place to post specific assignments, or a forum for open-ended discussion? Does your instructor prefer that students email only in emergencies, or does he welcome questions, inquiries about upcoming assignments, and general comments? Does she allow students to turn in work via email, or does she want printed documents? Observing these courtesies will help you to make the most of these forums for writing, which are now standard in many academic, professional, and social communities.

# 6d How do you write a personal statement?

When you apply for a college scholarship, internship, or special program of study, you may be asked to write a personal statement. This kind of essay allows you to give a selection committee a more complete view of your qualifications than an application form or transcript can provide. In it, you can tell a narrative about your experiences, interests, and goals. You can provide additional details about your academic and personal achievements. Such a statement also allows a committee to evaluate your writing skills. In short, it gives readers a sense of you as a person—as well as a student.

**1 Follow instructions carefully.** Although requirements for personal statements vary, you will usually be asked to compose a brief essay (no more than one to two pages, double spaced) that falls into one of two categories:

- **A general, comprehensive personal statement** is open ended, allowing you considerable freedom to choose which experiences and qualities you wish to discuss. This type of statement is often required for general medical school and law school application forms. For example, applicants for a Rhodes Scholarship are asked to provide "a signed short statement describing the applicant's academic and other interests." The University of Texas at Austin Law School instructs applicants, "Your personal statement should give the admissions council insight into your character and experience."
- **A personal statement that responds to specific questions** is often required for scholarship applications, applications for business, graduate school, and other specific programs such as study abroad or teacher certification programs. Questions are typically tailored to the particular nature of the award or program. For instance, the University of South Carolina Study Abroad application has five essay prompts, including "Describe how you anticipate dealing with adjustments to unfamiliar surroundings, cultural differences, and separation from family and friends."

Before you begin writing, review the instructions carefully and tailor your essay(s) to fit them. Be sure that your response addresses *all* questions asked and that you adhere carefully to any length and formatting requirements. And if you are applying for several awards or programs, avoid the temptation to use exactly the same statement for every application.

**● 2 Provide a vivid, focused narrative.** Personal statements are often read by committees who have hundreds, maybe even thousands, of applications to review. They'll have little patience for an essay that rambles off-topic or that provides a scattered list of disparate accomplishments. Instead, they'll look for a response that provides a focused, vivid picture of *you*—one that tells them exactly what makes you an excellent applicant. Here are some tips.

- **Find a specific "angle,"** theme, or thesis and organize your statement around it. You won't be able to tell readers every detail about your qualifications, so focus on one controlling idea that informs the introduction, body, and conclusion of your statement. When Maria Morozowich wrote the study abroad application excerpted on the facing page, for example, she chose to focus on how her experiences growing up in a multicultural family have shaped her educational and career goals.
- **Start with a compelling introduction.** An opening that gets right to the point and uses precise, vivid language will stand out more than a statement that begins with predictable generalities.
- **Provide plenty of supporting details.** Don't say that you would make an excellent teacher or literary scholar unless you can back up your claim with specific reasons and details. Your claim should be the result of specific qualifications or experiences that you develop in your statement. Your stated goal should emerge as the logical, supported conclusion to your argument.

**● 3 Be yourself.** Remember that your statement should tell readers something about you that they can't learn from examining your transcripts or reading a form. Allow your particular background, experiences, and personality to emerge. Now is the time to talk about how a church mission trip to Costa Rica sparked your interest in wildlife preservation law, or how your experience assisting a professor with research on children's language development strengthened your desire to become a pediatrician. Your statement should also be reflective; it should show that you have thought carefully about your experiences and have developed a clear perspective on what you hope to do in the future.

**⊘4 Edit and proofread carefully.** Your finished statement should be as polished as you can make it. Ask for suggestions from friends, colleagues, instructors, or the staff of a campus writing center. Tighten wordy passages and replace clichés and technical jargon with concrete, vivid prose. Correct any errors in grammar, mechanics, and punctuation—and check for typos one last time before you submit your statement.

**GOING PUBLIC**   **A Personal Statement**

This sample comes from a study abroad application submitted by college junior Maria Morozowich. Her response, though short and focused, still manages to give a strong description of how her personal experiences will make her a good candidate to study in Europe.

> Having grown up in a family that blends Ukrainian and American traditions, I have long appreciated and valued cultural differences. My grandmother came to the United States from the Ukraine after World War II, and she never learned to speak English fluently. Despite the language barrier between us, we have always had a close relationship that emphasizes family and cultural traditions: from her, I learned how to cook Ukrainian foods, do traditional Ukrainian embroidery, and understand and speak some basic Ukrainian. I would not be the same person had I not had this opportunity to blend Ukrainian and American traditions. These positive experiences, I believe, will help me to be open and adaptable to the traditions and practices of my host culture as I study abroad. My respect for what other cultures can teach me make me a good fit for this program.

# 7 How Do You Write for the Public?

## 7a How do you write outside the classroom?

Knowing how to write an effective academic paper is crucial to your success in college. However, college writers must also adapt their writing to settings outside the classroom. Writing instructors at many universities now require students to compose documents for nonprofit groups, to publish pieces in local media, or to post their writing to the Web, in addition to writing traditional papers. You may write letters to friends or elected officials, applications for jobs or scholarships, publicity materials for campus groups, or editorials for local publications. What do all these tasks have in common? They are all *public* statements of one kind or another.

Yet what impresses readers in one setting may offend them in another, just as the same joke might get a big laugh at a family dinner but raise eyebrows at a church banquet. When you adapt your writing to different situations, think about what those readers expect and what seems appropriate under the circumstances.

◉1 **Learn to spot opportunities for public writing.** Writing can be a powerful way to make your views heard and to get things done. But not all situations lend themselves equally well to it. Before you undertake a public writing project, ask yourself these questions.

- **Is writing the most effective response to this situation?** Suppose that your neighbor's dog has just bitten the mail carrier. Would it be more effective to write a letter to your neighbor warning her to keep her dog inside or to simply pry the dog off the mail carrier's ankle? The answer is obvious (at least, we know which answer the mail carrier would prefer). However, if you believe that your neighbor's dog is part of a larger problem caused by lax leash laws in your city, that problem might be addressed by sending an email to the city council members or circulating a citizen petition.

- **Is there an audience who cares (or can be persuaded to care) about your message?** Each year thousands of preteens write love letters to pop idols such as Lindsay Lohan and Ashton Kutcher. Are such letters examples of effective public writing? No, because no matter how passionately the writers feel about their arguments, neither the stars to whom the letters are directed nor any other audience beyond the individual writer has strong feelings about the letters' topic. On the other hand, a group of students might successfully write to request that Kutcher make an appearance at a school fund-raiser.
- **Is the timing right?** Public writing is most effective if it appears when an issue is relevant to readers. Your boss doesn't want to read your memo calling for longer employee lunch breaks during the busiest workday of the year; nor does a newspaper editor want to print a letter responding to a column that appeared three months ago (though she might print responses submitted within a week).

Writing is challenging—too much so to be wasted where it's unlikely to have an impact. When you choose to write, choose the setting and the timing carefully to make sure that every word counts.

When Hurricane Katrina displaced thousands of New Orleans–area residents in September 2005, student and community groups from all over the United States wanted to get involved. In what ways did people from your campus or community respond to this event? Which of these efforts involved writing? What purposes and audiences did the writing serve? Can you cite examples of writing related to this event that were especially effective or ineffective? Discuss your answers with your classmates.

**2 Research your readers' expectations.** When you write in a public setting—especially a setting new to you—don't automatically fall back on familiar academic conventions. The kind of writing your instructors reward in college will not always be received with enthusiasm in other forums.

Before you begin any project for an unfamiliar audience or situation, find out what is expected.

- What genres and topics are typical for this forum?
- What are the typical length, style, and tone of documents published in this setting?
- What kinds of arguments and evidence do writers typically draw on?
- What are the expectations for formatting and for citing sources?

Many publications make submission guidelines available to prospective writers. If these are not available, seek out models. If you're entering an essay to win a scholarship, request a copy of the previous year's winning essay. If you hope to publish an article in a local music magazine, skim previous issues to get a feel for the kinds of topics and stories it prints. (Chapter 19 contains models of several kinds of academic and nonacademic writing projects.)

Also call on colleagues, instructors, friends, or the staff of your university writing center for advice and feedback. When you're unsure, it's better to head off a potential mistake than to recover from one that appears in print.

**3 Understand the unique benefits and risks of public writing.** Although you may feel anxious when you turn in a course paper, your instructor and classmates are a relatively private audience. Slips in logic or punctuation won't usually damage anything other than your grade, and you can generally experiment with new ideas without fear of offending your instructor. But when you write for larger public audiences, responses may be more direct and less predictable. If you write an email message to your office electronic mailing list criticizing the company scheduling policy, your boss, unlike your writing instructor, may take your complaints personally—and may be less sympathetic the next time you ask for a night off.

For this reason, it's especially important to consider the impression you hope to make on readers when you undertake a public writing project. Knowing that your ideas have reached and affected others is precisely what makes public writing so rewarding. But be prepared: *Before* you publish or mail your piece, think through the possible responses your writing might elicit. When you've anticipated these consequences, you can decide how you want to address them.

For instance, when student writer Jesse Faleris wrote the letter advocating gun control that appears on pages 102–103—a letter he submitted to National Rifle Association (NRA) leadership at their annual convention— he faced a tricky rhetorical situation. As a longtime member of the organization, he understood their entrenched resistance to gun control measures of any kind and knew that such arguments would have to be carefully presented in order to be heard. He solved this problem by prefacing his arguments with a statement of his commitment to gun ownership rights and to the organization's general goals. He recognized that his letter might nonetheless evoke negative responses, but he felt that the argument was important enough to justify the risk. (See Section 1g for more on creating a positive impression on readers.)

● **4 Be professional.** You'll be taken seriously as a writer if you submit attractive, polished, and carefully edited and proofread documents. That rule applies to virtually every writing situation. See Section 5c for more on this topic.

GOING PUBLIC  **Shaping an Argument for a Public Audience**

As you read this letter that student writer Jesse Faleris addressed to NRA leaders, note how he carefully tailors his argument to his audience. Consider, too, the ways in which his letter differs from an academic research paper on gun control.

Jesse M. Faleris
3321 Edisto Street
Columbia, SC 29207

January 15, 2005

National Rifle Association of America
11250 Waples Mill Road
Fairfax, VA 22030

To Fellow Members of the National Rifle Association:

I am greatly concerned about the current escalation of gun legislation and how our organization's position may affect the rights of American citizens to own firearms. Unfortunately, I believe that our organization's current philosophy of "Guns do not kill—people do" is no longer an effective stance, and that if the Second Amendment is to survive future abolition legislation, our organization must transform its image.

Before I continue with my suggestions, let me offer a summary of my background. I am a military careerist with ten years' United States armed forces active duty service. I am the son of an accomplished gunsmith who is actively involved in Canadian firearms legislation. I have four years' experience in military public relations, and I am currently a public relations and law philosophy student at the University of South Carolina. I am the coach of the USC ROTC pistol team. Most importantly, I am a gun owner and an advocate of all Americans' right to bear arms.

It is this last concern that prompts me to write to you today. The primary mission of our organization is to protect Americans' rights to own and use firearms for sport as well as self-defense. But currently the majority of our literature and activities focus narrowly on opposing all attempts at firearms legislation. I understand why the NRA maintains the firm stance on the Second Amendment that "the right of the people to keep and bear arms, shall not be infringed," but a firm philosophical position does not solve social problems any more than misdirected legislation does. This is because the general public simply no longer accepts our "guns don't kill" logic. In the midst of heightened awareness to hate crimes and random violence, the handgun is quickly becoming the social icon of America's violence problem. Polls from the Gallup Organization, the Associated Press, and others reveal that upwards of 75 percent of Americans favor further gun legislation.

For these reasons, the NRA must drop our current antilegislation attitude in favor of a "responsible gun owner" platform. We must demand that not only our members, but also the gun owners outside our membership and the firearm manufacturers actively advance responsible gun ownership, even if this means new legislation. As gun owners, we must take responsibility to safeguard our firearms against use by irresponsible persons with the following steps.

- *We must protect unsupervised minors from access to firearms.* Yes, trigger locks! If used, trigger locks are a responsible means of regulating who uses a firearm. Again, I understand the NRA's fear that any infringement will lead to abolition, but if we look at Canada as an example we may find voluntary compliance unrealistic.

- *The manufacturers must contribute to safeguarding the public from firearm products.* Including trigger locks with the purchase of new firearms is a necessity. Providing additional trigger locks for existing guns at manufacturers' cost is reasonable and would be recognized as a positive and responsible response to consumer America's concerns.

- *Finally, we must work with legislators, particularly those supportive of gun owners, to draft and introduce effective and responsible gun legislation.* This legislation should focus on criminal use of guns. We must find a way to keep criminals from using guns, without limiting the law-abiding citizens' right to keep and bear arms.

As a linchpin between gun owners, Congress, and gun manufacturers, the NRA possesses the influence to arbitrate these responsible proposals. These are our guns, our streets, our children and our legislatures— let us take responsible action to safeguard all we hold precious.

I hope that my honest intentions are clear. I do not want to lose my rights, nor my children's, nor my grandchildren's rights to keep and bear arms. I am convinced that the NRA wants to protect our rights in a changing social atmosphere. What I hope is that we can reshape our tactics in order to effect positive changes in the average American's beliefs about gun ownership.

Respectfully,

Jesse M. Faleris

**EXERCISE 7.1** Here is a list of four public writing projects completed by undergraduate students. For each project answer these questions: How do you think the piece differs from an academic treatment of the same topic? What kinds of adjustments do you think the writer made for audience, purpose, and setting? Discuss your responses with classmates.

1. An article on aging and nutrition for a nursing-home newsletter.

2. A proposal directed at the city arts commission requesting funding for Diversity Week activities sponsored by a local cultural organization.

3. An informational Web site that rates local landlords and apartment complexes according to the number of renters' complaints filed against them.

4. A review of the latest Adam Sandler film for the local paper.

## 7b How do you write in service-learning courses?

Although much of the writing you do in college will never leave the class-room, an increasing number of composition courses nationwide now incorporate one or more *service-learning projects*—projects that ask students to engage in community work as part of an academic course. Service learning can take many shapes. Some service-learning courses ask students to draw on their service experiences to write traditional academic papers and assignments. In other courses, students apply what they learn in a course by writing "real" documents for community agencies or groups. Composition students at Carnegie Mellon University, for example, work with inner-city teenagers to produce newsletters and videos that explore the young people's views on drug use, curfews, violence, and gender issues. (For more examples, visit Campus Compact, a national alliance of colleges and universities committed to community service, at <http://www.compact.org>.)

If you're taking a writing class that includes a service-learning component, you'll learn more about organizations in your community and the work they do. You'll gain experience working collaboratively with others, and you'll make contacts that may help you find future volunteer opportunities or a job.

Perhaps most important, you'll have a chance to test your research and writing skills on real audiences. However, because they combine several audiences, purposes, and sets of expectations, service-learning projects pose special challenges. This section offers general guidance for dealing with these and introduces you to Ray McManus, a student writer who completed a service-learning project at the University of South Carolina.

**● 1 Understand the dual purpose of service learning.** Service-learning projects differ from the volunteer work that you may have done outside school, even if that work has involved writing. Service learning always involves an academic dimension—your instructor asks you to work in the community not just because it's a civic-minded thing to do but so that you can also explore concepts and strategies that you're learning in the course. In service-learning projects, both the service and the academic dimensions of the course are equally important: one reinforces the other.

When you begin a service-learning course, ask yourself:

- How does my work in the community reflect, reinforce, or call into question the material I'm learning in class?
- How does the material I'm learning in class help me to effectively approach the work I'm doing in the community?

Ray McManus, the student writer whose work is featured throughout this section, engaged in a service-learning project as part of a course on teaching writing. The project, in which he and other students designed and led poetry workshops for teenagers at the local public library, had both practical and academic components. On the one hand, his experiences with the workshops allowed him and his classmates to test approaches to teaching poetry that they'd studied in class. On the other, the workshops gave Ray, who hopes to become a teacher of creative writing, valuable practical experience in his major field.

**● 2 Be aware of the different audiences your writing may address.** The dual purpose of service learning means that at times, you may write for two different audiences—your instructor and the community readers of any document you produce. Sometimes you'll write for both audiences simultaneously. Be aware of their differences and tailor your work accordingly, since the expectations in one setting are likely to differ from those in another. If you have questions about what's expected, don't hesitate to ask.

In Ray McManus's project, for example, he composed some documents to turn in to his professor, some that were seen only by library staff and patrons, and others that were directed to both audiences:

- **Work produced for his instructor** included an annotated bibliography of resources on children's poetry, lesson plans for the poetry workshops, reflective journal entries, and a final research paper.
- **Work produced for the library staff and patrons** included collaboratively written publicity flyers, a newspaper press release, and a thank-you letter to the library director.
- **Work produced for both audiences** included the lesson plans, materials, and activities for the poetry workshops.

**3 Find out how your work will be evaluated.** The fact that you must write for several audiences sometimes makes it hard to figure out whether you're doing a good job with a service-learning project. For example, what if your instructor expects you to write very detailed lesson plans for tutoring sessions in an adult literacy program, when most tutors in the program take a more relaxed approach to planning by jotting down just a sentence or two?

When you encounter different sets of expectations, you'll feel more confident if you know how your work will be evaluated: Which pieces of your writing will your instructor grade? Will he or she evaluate them according to academic criteria? Will the community members you work with judge some or all of your writing? If so, what criteria will they use, and will they determine part of your course grade? Once you know these parameters, you can adjust your work accordingly. See Section 6a-7 for more on how writing is evaluated.

**4 Be willing to learn and to collaborate.** Certainly a key goal of service-learning programs is to make university students' energy and talents available to others in the community. But remember that anytime you enter a new writing situation, *you're* the novice. Be ready to learn from the people you work with and to collaborate productively with them.

When Ray McManus and his classmates began designing poetry workshops for local teenagers, they had had plenty of experience with writing poetry and had researched ways to engage teenagers in learning about it. But when it was time to craft publicity materials for the sessions, they knew little about how to reach young people likely to attend. Ray and his partners needed the expertise of library staff who had advertised previous youth programs and who had contacts with local teachers. They also needed the library's publication office to translate their ideas into an eye-catching format. The flyer that resulted from this collaboration is featured below.

**GOING PUBLIC**    **Collaboration and Service Learning**

Here's the publicity flyer that resulted from the collaborative efforts of Ray McManus and numerous library staff. Do you think the flyer is effective? Why or why not?

# 8 How Do You Read and Think Critically?

Each day you are bombarded with messages that try to influence you—that urge you to buy a particular brand of shoes, to support a certain charitable organization, to vote for one candidate rather than another, and to see the latest blockbuster film. Dealing with these competing messages requires that you examine ideas, ask questions, challenge arguments, and decide which viewpoints are worth accepting—in other words, that you think *critically*. Much of the information you absorb in college will be obsolete in a few years, but the critical and analytical skills you develop will serve you the rest of your life.

In college, a crucial element of critical thinking involves learning to read critically, because much of what you write and think about is in response to what you read.

## 8a How do you read to understand complex material?

College reading assignments pose special challenges. In high school, teachers may cover a textbook chapter in a week; in college, instructors often assign several chapters in the same amount of time, along with supplementary readings from scholarly journals, literary texts, and other sources. College assignments may also address more abstract ideas and use more complicated language. Whereas you may be accomplished at reading sources that summarize and analyze issues *for* you—as high school textbooks or popular magazines do—in college you'll often have to weigh issues or interpret data on your own.

But the classroom isn't the only place you'll encounter difficult texts. You'll also sift through competing viewpoints and complex material when you research campaign issues before voting, or when you draft a report at work or follow news coverage of a local event. To navigate these texts, you'll need to be an active, engaged reader.

**● 1 Preview the text.** Just as you can navigate an unfamiliar city more easily when you have a map, you'll find it easier to read an unfamiliar text if you first scope out its features.

- **Genre.** What kind of document is it? an introductory textbook? a Web log (blog)? a literary work? a scholarly article? Different genres have different purposes and audiences, which you should keep in mind as you read.
- **Title.** What does the title tell you about the piece's content and purpose?
- **Organization.** If you're reading a printed text, are there headings or subheadings? If you're reading a Web site, are major sections listed in the left-hand frame or on a home page? What do these divisions suggest about the text?
- **Sources.** Inspect the bibliography and index. What do the sources listed there tell you about the kinds of information the writer will draw on?
- **Point of view.** Is the author's point of view known and relevant? What are the interests and biases of the publisher or the sponsoring institution? Does the text purport to be objective, or does it present itself as subjective and personal?

Before reading a text, determine your goals: Are you skimming to see if it's relevant to a paper you're writing? Are you mainly interested in major concepts and arguments, or do you need to know details? Do you want to develop your own opinions on the subject? These goals should influence how much time you spend reading and which strategies you use.

**● 2 Look up unfamiliar terms and concepts.** Understanding difficult material is easier if you have the relevant background knowledge. When you preview a text, circle major terms, concepts, or topics that sound unfamiliar. For instance, you'll feel completely at sea reading an article about the African diaspora if you don't know what *diaspora* means and your knowledge of the continent is limited to vague memories from eighth-grade social studies. A look at a dictionary and an encyclopedia entry on Africa will put you on more solid ground.

Even if you have some general knowledge about a topic, keep a dictionary at hand while you read so that you can clarify confusing references as they crop up.

**3 Slow down.** Read slowly and reread two or three times to fully grasp a complex argument or explanation. Some experts advise reading everything twice: the first time just to understand what the writer is saying, the second to focus on your own reactions and opinions. Whatever your strategy, don't rush.

**4 Annotate the text to clarify and respond to its content.** Critical reading involves more than passively absorbing words on a page. It's an active process. One way to read actively is to annotate—that is, attach notes, comments, and questions directly to the text, either by writing on a printed source (or a photocopy of it) or by using the commenting features of your word-processing program.

If you're not accustomed to taking notes on your reading, here are some useful strategies.

- **Content notes.** Most college students highlight key passages in their texts. But if you want to get the most from your reading, don't stop there. When you arrive at an important point or get tangled in a difficult passage, translate it into your own words to clarify its meaning.
- **Context notes.** Notes can also help you follow a text's structure. At crucial transitions, jot down a key word or two that explains where the argument is going or how a new point fits in: "Opposing argument," "Previous theories," "Example 3," for instance.
- **Response notes.** Don't just accept what a reading says; talk back. Does a proposal excite or anger you? Write "Yes!" or "Bad logic." If the text raises questions, write them down: "But what about the innocent victims?" or "Does this argument follow?" Carrying on this kind of dialogue with your reading develops your own perspective on the issues raised.

The box on pages 111–112 shows how one reader used these three strategies to annotate the opening passage of an opinion piece she read while researching a paper on women in math and science professions. She made response notes in the left-hand margin and content and context notes in the right-hand margin; notice how these notes help her follow a fairly complicated argument.

When you're working on a project that involves research, it's especially important to take notes. Your annotations identify ideas and information worth returning to, highlight passages you want to quote in your paper, and, more important, help you synthesize and engage in dialogue with the authors and texts you are encountering. See Chapters 46 and 47 for more on incorporating material you've read into a research paper.

---

**Highlight** **Sample Annotations**

Caryl Rivers

## The Persistence of Gender Myths in Math

By Rosalind Chait Barnett and Caryl Rivers

(*Education Week*, October 13, 2004)

*# of women in science is decreasing—they are asking whether teachers can help reverse this trend*

Should we be worried that young girls are not pursuing math-related careers at the same rate as young men? After all, in our technological era, many of tomorrow's well-paying jobs will require competence at mathematics. But today, women make up only 19 percent of the science, engineering, and technology workforce. In 1998, only 16 percent of computer science degrees were awarded to women, down from nearly 40 percent in 1984, and the downward trend continued in 2003.

Can teachers have a role in changing this picture? Or would they just be going up against innate biological differences in a (futile) attempt at social engineering?

*look up*

Some argue that girls don't have the right brain structures to be good at math. Cambridge University Psychologist Simon Baron-Cohen, the author of *The Essential Difference*, goes so far as to say that men have "systematizing brains" well-suited for the hard sciences. Women, in contrast, have "empathizing brains," designed for caretaking and mothering. And the best-selling author Michael Gurian (*The Wonder of Boys*) says that only 20 percent of girls have the right brain structure for performing well at math.

*Possible cause #1: girls' brains not suited for math*

*fact or his opinion? when published?*

*(Continued)*

**Sample Annotations** *(Continued)*

It is indeed the case that men far outnumber women in math-related fields. But is this evidence for innate male superiority? The answer is no. New research finds few sex differences in the math abilities of boys and girls. In 2001, sociologists Erin Leahey and Guang Guo of the University of North Carolina at Chapel Hill looked at some 20,000 math scores of students between the ages of 4 and 18 and found no differences of any magnitude, even in areas that are supposedly male domains, such as reasoning skills and geometry. The finding astonished the researchers, who said, "Based on prior literature . . . we expected large gender differences to emerge as early as junior high school, but our results do not confirm this." And a meta-analysis of SAT scores for some 3 million students found that girls and boys performed virtually identically in math.

*new study w/opposite finding*

**5 Adapt your reading process to online settings.** Although most critical reading strategies apply to both print and online environments, electronic texts pose special challenges. Experts on reading have even coined a new term—*screen literacy*—to describe the skills readers need to navigate online texts.

Online texts are less stable and more loosely structured than printed texts. Reading a Web site or blog, for example, you may scroll through long passages without page markers, follow complicated series of links, or encounter audio and visual elements. The content or format of the text may change periodically. These features can make it hard to find your place within a text and to return to important material.

The boundaries that separate one online text from another are also blurred. In researching a paper for your American literature class, for example, you may wonder whether a link to biographical information on the poet Walt Whitman that's embedded in an online text of *Leaves of Grass* is a part of that text or a separate text.

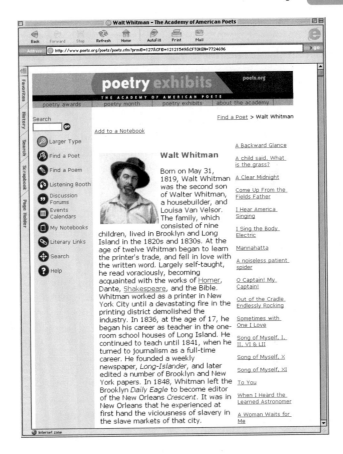

These differences mean that you should adjust your reading process when you read online. Here are some strategies that experts recommend:

- Be selective about what you choose to read. Skim and peck to find the most relevant items.
- Approach reading with your own agenda rather than always following the author's preferred path through a text.
- Pay as much attention to visual elements as you do to the words in a text. (See Section 9b for more on this topic.)

You'll also need to develop strategies for keeping track of the material you find online: When you want to read an online text carefully or return to it later, download and print it. Having the document in hand will help you follow the arguments and see how components of the text work together. (Be sure to record the date you found the text; if you use the source in your paper, you'll need the date for the "Works Cited" page.) Use your browser's "bookmark" feature to mark sites that you refer to frequently, so that you don't lose them. You can "bookmark" all sites or pages relevant to a project, arranging the items in folders that reflect its overall structure, one folder for each major section or theme. If a site is likely to change frequently, download and save material that you want to return to.

Finally, online texts support different methods of responding to your reading. You can use the annotation features of many word-processing programs to record your reactions to files you download onto your computer. (But be careful to clearly separate your comments from the original text.) Web pages can also be marked with comments. It's even possible to annotate bookmarks you've created to remind yourself why a particular site or page is important. (See Section 45b for more advice on organizing research materials and Chapters 46 and 47 for advice on incorporating research into a writing project.)

**EXERCISE 8.1** Use the three note-taking strategies described in Section 8a-4 to annotate a reading assignment in one of your courses. How do these strategies compare to your typical approach to reading? Which strategy did you find most helpful, and why?

**EXERCISE 8.2** Find and read a text that is published in both print and online versions. Possibilities include magazines (like *Newsweek* and *Newsweek.MSNBC.com*, shown on the facing page), informational materials about a nonprofit organization or political candidate, and university documents. Which version do you find more difficult to read? Why? How did your reading process differ in the two settings? Discuss your answers with a group of classmates.

## 8b How do you think critically about your reading?

Critical thinking is only an extended and focused version of the kind of thinking we all do every day when we set out to solve problems: we gather evidence, we examine options, we look at advantages and disadvantages, and we weigh others' opinions for possible bias.

● 1 **Read as a believer and as a doubter.** You'll get the most from your reading if you approach it with an open mind. Try to learn something, even from perspectives contrary to your own. An excellent way to engage with your reading is to play what the writing expert Peter Elbow calls the "believing and doubting game." This approach asks you to read and respond to a piece twice, each time adopting a dramatically different attitude.

To play the "believing" half of the game, read the piece with as much generosity as you can muster. Try to see what makes the argument so compelling to the writer, and look for claims, examples, or beliefs that seem reasonable or persuasive. Keying in on strengths may keep you from rejecting the writer's arguments prematurely. Write a paragraph exploring whatever seems most worth believing in the piece.

Then read the piece a second time as a "doubter." Scrutinize every statement for gaps, exaggerations, errors, and faulty reasoning. Ferret out any problems you can see in the writer's perspective, even if you agree with it. Again, summarize your conclusions in a paragraph. Finding weaknesses will prevent you from accepting the argument too readily.

Here's how one writer played the "believing and doubting game" with the excerpt from the article on gender myths in math in Section 8a-4.

believing     The study showing that boys and girls have similar math
              test scores is powerful. If both boys and girls show about
              the same ability level, but more girls are opting out of math
              and science, then something cultural must be going on. I do
              think it's true that parents and teachers tend to assume
              that smart boys will be good at math and science; gifted
              girls may not be actively discouraged from these areas, but
              they usually aren't encouraged as strongly.

doubting      I'm not sure that culture is all to blame. Women have been
              successful at breaking into so many of the professions
              historically dominated by men—think of how many lawyers,
              doctors, and professors are women—despite the
              stereotypes. If women aren't going into sciences and math
              in similar numbers, is it realistic to blame it all on the
              culture? The authors never really refute the idea that
              maybe girls just don't like math as much as boys do, even
              if they are very intelligent and have the aptitude for it.

**2 Assess the writer's qualifications.** Check the author's qualifications for everything you read. Does the writer have expertise in or personal experience with the topic? Does he or she demonstrate adequate knowledge? You might find, in reading a debate about sexist lyrics in hip-hop, that some of the loudest calls for censorship come from writers who admit they have never listened to the music. A lack of expert qualifications doesn't necessarily invalidate a writer's arguments, but it should make you examine them with extra care. See Section 45a-3 for more on evaluating a writer's credentials. Section 45a-4 tells how to evaluate the credibility of different kinds of publications.

**3 Look carefully at the evidence presented.** A strong argument must back up its claims. When you read an argument, size up its supporting evidence.

- **How much evidence does the writer present?** Does the amount of support seem substantial enough, or does the writer rely on just one or two examples?
- **Where does the evidence come from?** Is it recent, or is it so old that it may no longer be accurate? Does it seem trustworthy, or does the writer rely on dubious sources?
- **Is the evidence fairly and fully presented?** Do you suspect that the writer has manipulated information in order to make his or her case look better?

Guard against the tendency to gravitate toward arguments that confirm your own beliefs and to avoid those that don't. Try to find arguments written by women and men, liberals and conservatives, and supporters as well as opponents of a proposal. See Section 9a for more on evaluating the evidence presented in an argument.

**4 Assess whether the writer's claims go beyond what the evidence actually supports.** Does the writer draw conclusions that go beyond what his or her support warrants? For instance, some safety experts once made claims about the safety of air bags based on crash-test data calculated for crash dummies the size of adult men. These claims didn't hold true for children and small women. Faced with dozens of fatalities attributed to injuries caused by air bags, those experts admitted that their original claims went beyond what the data had established.

Although overstating one's claims doesn't usually result in such tragic consequences, you should question any argument that stretches its conclusions too far.

**5 Look for what's *not* there: the unstated assumptions, beliefs, and values that underlie the argument.** Does the writer take for granted certain knowledge or beliefs? If what someone takes for granted in an argument can reasonably be disputed, then you should challenge the author's claims.

Consider the assumptions made in this sentence, taken from an article advocating the legalization of drugs.

> The violence brought about by the black market in drugs is attributable in large part to the fact that we have chosen to make criminals out of people who have a disease.

The statement makes two assumptions: (1) People who buy and sell drugs do so primarily because they suffer from a sickness—addiction—beyond their control. (2) It's wrong to criminalize behavior that results from illness. Both assumptions may well be true, but without further explanation and support, a reader might question them on the following grounds: (1) Drug offenders may engage in illegal behavior not because they're sick but for profit, for entertainment, as a response to peer pressure, or because they can't find legal work. (2) Even if drug abuse results from illness, so do many other crimes punishable by law; we don't legalize drunk driving just because many drunk drivers are alcoholics.

See Section 9a on how to spot and evaluate hidden assumptions in an argument.

**6 Note any contradictions.** Look for places where pieces of an argument don't fit together. Suppose a political candidate advocates mandatory prison sentences for first-time drug offenders yet dismisses as "immature behavior" her own use of alcohol and other drugs as a teenager. One should question why the candidate excuses for herself behavior that she condemns in others.

**7 Examine the writer's word choices to identify underlying biases.** Everyone has biases—it's unavoidable. It's only natural that writers who want to convince others use language that favors their own point of view. But critical reading requires that you be sensitive to such biases so that you aren't unwittingly swayed by them.

Being a critical reader doesn't mean you have to distrust everything you read. But you should be alert when writers overload their prose with what rhetoricians call "god terms" (words such as *democratic, responsible, natural, fair*) or "devil terms" (words such as *destructive, fanatic, immoral, selfish*). See Chapter 15 for a more detailed discussion of biased language.

**⊚8 Be skeptical of simple solutions to complex problems, and resist black-and-white thinking.** Be wary of quick, easy answers to difficult problems. Most serious issues are complex—there is seldom one "right solution."

Consider the complex issue of affirmative action in college admissions and the calls from many sectors that schools judge prospective students on merit rather than taking racial, ethnic, and economic background into account. Here are a few of the questions that complicate this solution.

- What, exactly, constitutes "merit"? Test scores and grades? Special talent in a single area, such as music or sports? Character? If all these factors count, how should each be weighed?
- Should students who come from educationally disadvantaged backgrounds be judged by the same standards as more privileged students?
- Do some measures of merit favor certain groups of students over others? For example, using high school class rankings as an admissions criterion may work against students who graduate from elite high schools with many high-achieving students.
- Do schools have a responsibility to make up for past discrimination against particular groups? If so, what should this obligation entail?

Any solution to a problem, however perfect it may seem, has consequences. As you read an argument, look for evidence that the writer has neglected to consider the long-term implications of his or her position.

**EXERCISE 8.3**  Read an editorial in today's news twice, playing the "believing and doubting game" described in Section 8b-1. Which did you find more challenging, reading as a believer or reading as a doubter? Why? Did you notice anything using this method that you might not have noticed if you had read the piece just once?

## 8c How do you write a response paper?

When you are enrolled in a small class, particularly in such subjects as history, psychology, government, or literature, your instructor may ask you to react critically to reading assignments by turning in (or posting to a class discussion board) short response papers. Such papers often combine critical reading and argument; you read the assignment material carefully and with a critical eye, and then react to it with an opinion, a question, a challenge, or an expansion of some point. Instructors who assign such papers often set a strict limit of one or two double-spaced pages—500 words. Thus it's important to compose responses that are succinct and to the point.

So what's involved in writing such a paper? Well, there are no universal formulas, but we can make some suggestions. First, instructors almost certainly don't want just a summary. They *do* want to know that you've understood the piece and can recount its central points, of course. But they also want to see that you've engaged with the reading: thought critically about what the author said, put the piece into some kind of context, reacted to it, argued with it, or perhaps enlarged on some point in it. They'll be really pleased to learn something from you, get a fresh insight or slant on what has become old information for them. Second, your instructor probably doesn't expect you to do research for such a paper, particularly if it's just one assignment of many for the course. If you do bring in an outside opinion, whether from a magazine, book, or Web site, of course you should acknowledge the source. But for the most part you'll want to refer primarily to the reading itself, citing ideas or passages that illustrate the point you're making.

The following sections outline some specific strategies for writing a response paper. These suggestions cover only a few of the possibilities that response papers offer for doing fresh thinking about the rich reading material you'll encounter in your college courses, but they may help you get started if this kind of assignment is new to you. Such assignments give you an opportunity to inject some of your own ideas into a course and set up a productive dialogue with your instructor or with other students if you're posting the response to a class discussion board. They also provide useful practice in focusing and tightening your writing; you have to organize your thinking to develop a cogent and thoughtful response in just one or two pages.

**1 Begin with a (brief) summary.** Begin your response paper by identifying the author and title of the piece you're responding to and giving a brief overview of its main arguments. In doing so, you'll demonstrate that you read the piece carefully and understood it. Be careful, however, not to devote more than a few sentences to summarizing. Most instructors will want you to spend the majority of your response commenting on the reading—not rehashing it.

**2 Challenge an author's assertions.** Don't assume that a book or article an instructor assigns is beyond criticism. If you encounter a statement that seems incorrect and you can give your reasons, have the confidence to challenge it. For instance, the book *The Great War and Modern Memory* by Paul Fussell is often required reading in courses on twentieth-century European history. In it, Fussell reflects on the effect that World War I had on the writers and intellectuals of the early twentieth century. In Fussell's view, it was a miserable and ultimately pointless war in which millions of young men on both sides died and European economies were shattered.

But Fussell gets himself out on a limb when he says, "What we call gross dichotomizing (we/them thinking) is traceable, it would seem, to the Great War." At this point, a careful reader might skid to a stop and ask, "What are you saying? That kind of black/white, insider/outsider mentality has been around forever. Look at tribal mentality, whether among Africans, Arabs, American Indians, or the Boston Irish in the nineteenth century. It's the we/them view that made the ancient Greeks call anyone who wasn't a Greek a barbarian. It's also the attitude behind centuries of anti-Semitism that culminated in the Holocaust." You're quite warranted in making this kind of commonsense response even to a distinguished author when you think that he or she has lapsed into careless thinking.

**3 Expand on an idea introduced in a book or article that gives you new insights into an important issue.** Sometimes you're lucky enough to be assigned a reading that throws new light on a subject about which you already know something or about which you have strong feelings. For example, in an introductory course in child development, you might read "What Makes a Perfect Parent?" an essay from economist Steven D. Levitt and Stephen J. Dubner's 2006 book *Freakonomics*. In it, Levitt and Dubner present statistics suggesting that "what parents *do*" in raising their children may matter less than most people think. For example, reading to one's children, being a stay-home parent, and limiting television viewing— all conventionally thought to increase children's chances of educational success—in fact have no measurable effect. On the other hand, "who parents *are*"—well-educated versus uneducated, affluent versus poor, younger or older when they have children—correlates strongly with a child's later level of success. Given these data, the authors ask whether parenting technique matters as much as previously thought. Their argument shakes up familiar assumptions about how to foster healthy development in young children.

You could respond to this fresh look at the role of parenting in a number of ways. For instance, you could ask whether Levitt and Dubner's findings suggest a parallel to the activities of day-care providers and teachers: Do these caregivers' activities have a similarly negligible effect? Does it really matter whether a preschool teacher reads to her charges or plops them in front of the TV? Or you might consider the policy implications of the findings: If parenting techniques are relatively unimportant, should the resources now spent on parenting education programs be diverted to other efforts? New interpretations like Levitt and Dubner's are rich with possibilities.

**⊘4 Analyze and evaluate a writer's argument.** Look at the central claim an author makes and how he or she supports it. Do the data seem sound and unbiased? Does the argument seem oversimplified? If so, what's missing? Could there be another, equally useful way to interpret the material being discussed?

**GOING PUBLIC**  **Responding to a Reading**

Sometimes you can grant some of the writer's conclusions but dispute others and show alternative views. That's what student writer Ashley Hamm does in the following sample paper, in which she responds to the editorial on gender myths and math reprinted on page 111–112.

Ashley L. Hamm

Response Paper #1

Dr. Friend

13 January 2006

Rosalind Chair Barnett and Caryl Rivers's article "The Persistence of Gender Myths in Math" explores theories to explain the difference in mathematical achievement between males and females, questioning the notion of innate male superiority. The authors first discuss biological and psychological theories which suggest that women are not naturally inclined to choose the math or science fields because of their nurturing instinct; this instinct, some experts say, leads girls to pursue people-oriented fields such as history, medicine, or journalism. Cultural influence is examined, and the authors conclude that this is the true reason for the gender differences. The authors contend that the idea of innate male superiority is so deeply ingrained in our society that females assume it to be true, and, therefore, choose to pursue other fields of study; they suggest that even teachers are guilty of perpetuating this stereotype and should undertake special efforts to encourage girls to excel in math.

Barnett and Rivers's argument for cultural influence is both strong and valid, particularly the notion of teachers' own acceptance of the "male = math connection." However, the authors could have included stronger examples to further show the prevalence and transmission of these cultural attitudes. For example, the authors could have explored how men and women are portrayed in the media; it is much more

It's important to identify the work under review in the response paper. Some writers forget this detail.

Ashley begins with a brief summary of the piece, demonstrating that she has read carefully.

Now the paper discusses two contributing causes—media and parents' occupations—that the authors did not consider.

common to see a man portraying a scientist, engineer, or computer specialist, just as it is unsettlingly common to see women portraying fashion experts, housewives, and social workers. Is life imitating art or is art imitating life? Either way, the stereotype is perpetuated.

It is also important to understand student background, another factor that the authors do not discuss. Because children often emulate their parents (especially the same-sex parent), we should consider the occupation of a gifted student's parents. If a young girl's mother is an engineer, will she accept the stereotype and turn to a career in the humanities—or will she be more likely to see a technical field as a viable option? The same question could be asked about a boy whose father is an artist or a social worker—will his career choice be influenced more by stereotypes or by his father's example? While the authors' arguments are generally valid, they lack specificity and regard for the full range of variables.

My experience coincides with these points. My parents each only have a high school education, and, as the curriculum has changed dramatically over the decades, they were unable to help me in math or science after the sixth grade; however, they were able to help me in English and history. Did this affect my decision to major in English? Perhaps. My aptitude for math and science is lacking compared to my peers who grew up with parents in fields requiring advanced knowledge of math or science. In turn, these were also students whose aptitude in the humanities was lacking. My "talent" for literature was not

Here the paper brings in personal experience to demonstrate the importance of parents' backgrounds.

decided by my gender; had I been raised by accountants or engineers, I probably would have excelled in these subjects. The differences are clearly cultural, but all aspects and influences must be thoroughly examined before the stereotype can be fully understood and before it can be expelled.

The paper ends with a general assessment of the arguments made in the article.

# 9 How Do Written and Visual Arguments Work?

## 9a What is an argument?

In college, many of the documents you read and compose will make *arguments*—that is, try to persuade an audience to accept a general claim, using *logical reasoning* supported by facts, examples, statistics, or other kinds of *evidence*. Arguments take many different forms and serve different purposes. If you write a paper opposing euthanasia for a composition course, that's an argument. If you email your instructor to convince her that the paper merits a *B* rather than a *C,* that's an argument too. So is a poster urging students to get free flu shots at the campus clinic or a bumper sticker promoting environmental conservation. This chapter introduces you to some basic structures and strategies for understanding how arguments work, so that you can more critically assess the ones you encounter. For advice on using these strategies to compose your own arguments, see Chapter 10.

**1 Know the difference between genuine arguments and other kinds of disagreements.** In everyday life, people use the term *argument* to refer to any disagreement. But rhetoricians use the term in a more specialized way, to mean a discussion of an issue with two qualities:

1. People might reasonably disagree about it.
2. There are *reasonable* grounds for supporting one viewpoint over another.

An assertion that no one would dispute is not an argument. Statements such as "A broken leg is painful" and "If you drop that chair, it will hit the ground" can be immediately proved, so there's no need to argue about whether they're true.

Disputes about subjective personal tastes aren't arguments either. It's possible to disagree about whether vanilla ice cream is tastier than chocolate and whether Brad Pitt is more handsome than Tom Cruise, but it's impossible to come up with support that most people would regard as reliable to prove one opinion more valid than the other. One *could* logically argue that vanilla ice cream is more popular than chocolate and that Brad Pitt has a narrower range as an actor than Tom Cruise. Statistics on ice cream sales and flavor preference polls could support the former argument, and examples from particular films and quotations from reviews and experts on acting could build a case for the latter.

Finally, a statement is not an argument when it seeks to persuade with threats, emotional manipulation, or trickery rather than with reasoning. An employer who persuades workers to sign up for weekend shifts by hinting that their annual raises depend on it is using threat, not argument. A campaign advertisement that depicts a candidate alongside cooing babies is appealing to viewers' emotions, not their intelligence. Although writers who use these techniques may present them as though they were arguments, don't be fooled. Arguments draw on different strategies entirely.

Though the t-shirt slogans pictured here seem to threaten readers, both address serious public issues. The "Vote or Die!" shirt was part of a larger public relations campaign spearheaded by Sean "P. Diddy" Combs to encourage citizens aged 18 to 30 to participate in the 2004 election. The shirt on the right is available on <http://www.thoseshirts.com>, a Web site that caters to politically conservative tastes. Do you think either of these images implies a reasoned argument? If so, what is being argued? If not, what would need to be added for you to consider the slogan an argument?

**2 Understand an argument as a claim supported by reasons and evidence.** British philosopher Stephen Toulmin has developed a useful model for understanding how arguments are structured. (Note: We follow the Toulmin model throughout this chapter because it is a commonly used way of understanding argument, but your instructor or classmates may use different terminology to refer to the basic parts of an argument. Ask your instructor to clarify any confusion you may have about these terms.)

The Toulmin model says that every argument begins by making a general assertion—a *claim*—and then produces one or more grounds for supporting that claim. Support for a claim may include *reasons* (smaller assertions that often begin with the word *because*) and *evidence* (relevant examples, facts, statistics, or experts' statements).

Here's a simple way of outlining how an argument is put together.

**Argument = Claim + Reason(s) and Evidence**

An editorial in a campus newspaper, for example, might make the following argument proposing a mandatory grade penalty for students who skip classes.

CLAIM
: Our university should adopt an attendance policy imposing automatic grade penalties on students who miss a substantial number of classes.

REASON
: (Because) Students who miss class frequently do not truly learn the material, even if they manage to do well on tests and assignments.

EVIDENCE
: **1.** A recent study found that college students who wrote and talked frequently about course material retained more knowledge after four years than those who did not.

**2.** My ex-roommate missed so many accounting classes that she had to rely on friends' notes and cramming to pass the final exam. She did not really learn the material and is now struggling in all her business courses.

Many written arguments open with a paragraph that leads to a claim stated in a thesis statement, then develop the supporting reason(s) and evidence in subsequent paragraphs. But not all arguments follow this

VISITOR WARNING
FLORIDA RESIDENTS CAN
USE DEADLY FORCE

Florida law now allows
people to shoot to kill
if they feel threatened.

PLEASE BE
CAREFUL

The Brady Campaign to
Prevent Gun Violence
www.shootfirstlaw.org

> Consider this bumper sticker created by the Brady Campaign to Prevent Gun Violence. What claim(s) does the bumper sticker make? Is(Are) the claim(s) directly stated or implied? What reasons or evidence does the sticker present to support the claim(s)?

pattern. In some cases, the actual claim doesn't appear until nearly the end of the argument. And in some cases, the claim may be implicit—never directly stated in the piece. Many visual arguments leave it to the audience to give shape to the claim, though the point the author is making is obvious.

**● 3 Recognize that arguments rest on unstated beliefs, or warrants.** Simply laying out a claim and some kind of support isn't enough to make a solid argument. For example, the argument "Mina should do well in college because she's tall" would convince no one. A thinking person would respond, "That's an unwarranted conclusion. Being tall has nothing to do with excelling in school." Obviously some ways of connecting claims with reasons and evidence are more persuasive than others.

Toulmin uses the term *warrant* to describe the justification—the general belief, rule, or principle—that links together the claim and its support in an argument. A persuasive argument must rest on warrants that readers find satisfactory, or readers will reject it.

Sometimes a warrant is so self-evidently true that it's left unstated. The writer assumes that once the claim and its support are presented, readers will supply and accept the warrant on their own: "Mina should do well in college because she made straight *A*'s in high school." The writer doesn't need to state and support the warrant—that making straight *A*'s is a good

**Parts of an Argument**

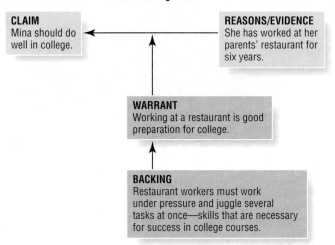

**CLAIM**
Mina should do well in college.

**REASONS/EVIDENCE**
She has worked at her parents' restaurant for six years.

**WARRANT**
Working at a restaurant is good preparation for college.

**BACKING**
Restaurant workers must work under pressure and juggle several tasks at once—skills that are necessary for success in college courses.

**Figure 9.1**

indicator of success in college—because just about everybody believes this connection is "warranted," or justified.

But sometimes an argument rests on a warrant that not all readers will agree with. Consider this statement: "Mina should do well in college because she has worked at her parents' restaurant for six years." Although the connection may seem reasonable to some readers, others might need convincing. The writer needs to state the warrant and provide some explanation and support for it. Reasons and evidence used to support the warrant in an argument are called *backing*. Figure 9.1 above shows how the argument would look with warrant and backing.

**EXERCISE 9.1** Each argument below contains a claim and supporting reasons or evidence. Supply the unstated warrant(s) that link each claim to its data, and then evaluate the warrant. Do you find the warrant convincing? Why or why not? We've done the first one for you.

ARGUMENT      *Claim:* The federal government should spend more money on cutting-edge cancer research.

*Reason/evidence:* Studies show that the treatments developed in this kind of research save lives.

**RESPONSE** *Warrant:* The government should fund programs that save lives.

*Analysis:* This warrant is fairly convincing. However, it's possible that the government doesn't have enough money to fund *every* program that might save lives. What if a program is very expensive but will save only a few lives? This argument needs some support to show that cancer research is more worthy of funding than other potentially life-saving research.

1. *Claim:* Dr. Olson is an excellent literature professor.

   *Reason/evidence:* She truly knows her subject matter; she has published nine books on British poetry and is recognized as a leading expert on William Wordsworth.

2. *Claim:* Local governments should not use tax money to subsidize the construction of professional sports stadiums.

   *Reason/evidence:* Only a small portion of the population attends professional sporting events. Some people simply don't like sports, others don't have the time to attend games regularly, and many simply can't afford to pay $30 to $50 for a single ticket.

3. *Claim:* The push to legislate higher fuel efficiency standards for cars is misguided.

   *Reason/evidence:* New federal mandates for gas mileage will create a financial hardship for consumers, since the automakers will have to add to the price of new cars the cost of researching and manufacturing more efficient engines.

**4 Recognize that many claims include a qualifier that clarifies the limited circumstances in which that claim holds true.** Because most claims aren't true in every single case, many arguments include a limiting phrase or statement called a *qualifier—probably, in most cases, primarily in suburban areas*, for example. The argument proposing a campus attendance policy laid out in Section 9a-2 would overstate its case if it claimed that *all* students should be penalized for missing classes. Students who become seriously ill or experience a family emergency are obvious exceptions. A more solid statement of this argument would add what Toulmin calls a *qualifier*: "*Except in cases of serious illness or emergency*, students absent for a substantial number of classes should incur a mandatory grade penalty."

**EXERCISE 9.2** Working with a group of classmates, analyze the following argument taken from a magazine article reviewing recent perspectives on women, welfare, and work. Identify the statements that come after each number as claim, reason, evidence, warrant, backing, or qualifier. You may use some terms more than once and others not at all.

There are two [. . .] big reasons why [1] the responsible choice for a low-income single mother might be welfare rather than work. [2] Welfare provides health insurance for her children, and most low-wage jobs don't. [3] And welfare, however miserly, provides security that most jobs don't—at least before [welfare reform laws passed in] 1997. [4] In the jobs available to many low-skilled or unskilled women, such as fast food or home health care, workers can never be sure of getting enough hours to make enough money while they have a job, and they are always subject to firing or layoffs. [5] When insecurity doesn't just mean a little less of something but the possibility of starvation or homelessness, the rational risk-benefit calculation counsels taking the secure but less rewarding option.
—Deborah Stone, "Work and the Moral Woman"

## 9b How do you critically interpret visual arguments?

Many of the arguments you encounter every day come through media that consist substantially or almost entirely of images. When you watch a music video, scroll through a Web site, or tune in to the evening news, you take in information so quickly that you have little time to critically reflect on it. But it's important to remember that, like written arguments, arguments made in visual media are carefully constructed to appeal to readers, and you should read them as critically as you would any other text.

Increasingly, even traditional types of written documents such as articles, books, and reports assert their claims in conjunction with images. We cannot begin to catalog the many different kinds of visual arguments. However, this section will help you become aware of some basic ways in which visuals persuade, so that you can sharpen your critical viewing skills.

**1 Understand how visual arguments work.** The nonprofit Center for Media Literacy (<http://www.medialit.org>) suggests the following starting points for critically approaching arguments presented on film, television, or other media that work primarily through images:

- **Remember that, like written arguments, arguments composed partly or entirely with visual images are purposefully constructed for a particular audience and purpose.** In a single television news story, for example, a team of people filmed footage, interviewed sources, wrote a reporter's script, and combined selections from all that raw material into a carefully produced package. Viewers never see what the film crew *didn't* shoot, what the story would have been like if different material had been selected, or what portions of film the producer edited out. Because visual texts are the products of human choices, they generally reflect their creators' values, viewpoints, and biases.
- **Be aware that visual arguments come in many genres, each of which operates according to its own conventions.** Think how different your expectations are when you see national news events discussed on an Internet news site, a late-night talk show, a political poster, and a documentary film. These different formats govern how information can be presented.
- **Recognize that many visual arguments are open ended; they may be interpreted differently by different viewers.** Parents often say that they can't make any sense of the music videos their teenaged children watch; it's all just noise and disconnected images, they complain. On the other hand, adults who watch the Disney cartoons they loved as kids often catch cultural references or jokes that eluded them when they were younger. Creators of visual arguments rely on these differences when they try to reach several audiences at once.

**2 Pay close attention to visual design and layout.** As in written arguments, whatever is front and center will get the most attention in a visual argument. Ask yourself how the arrangement of information directs your attention as you move through a text.

- **What ideas or information is emphasized?** What material takes up the most space? What catches your eye? Many design devices are used to highlight information, from traditional headings and boxes to pull quotes, sidebars, colors, unusual type fonts, shading, pop-ups, animation, and even aural signals in electronic media. Examine the placement of photographs or other images on a page: How do these images shape your perception of the argument? Also examine the layout and placement of graphs, tables, and other visual representations of information. To what data and patterns do these devices draw your attention? (See Section 18d for more on how graphs and tables work.)
- **What ideas or information does the writer downplay?** What information is buried in the middle of the text or set in small print? How does the size or cropping of images influence what you see? What is left out?
- **What formatting and organizational devices are used?** Look for patterns. For example, writers use similarly sized headings to indicate that topics are at comparable levels of importance or generality in an argument. Or they might use recurring colors in a PowerPoint presentation to help viewers understand where they are in an argument. How do such devices affect your perception of the argument?

**3 Evaluate images critically.** Pictures trigger impressions that are stronger and more immediate than those most writers can convey with words. And because images can be so powerful, it pays to view them with caution. Ask yourself these questions.

- **How, if at all, does the picture reinforce or add to the written information?** Is the image helpful, or is it only decoration? For example, you've probably seen personal Web pages that make distracting use of flashy graphics—multicolored backgrounds, blinking lights, animated characters—that don't relate clearly to the content.

- **What emotions, values, or beliefs does the image appeal to?** Is this appeal relevant and fair? For example, this photograph of a soldier holding a child might be an evocative image, but its effectiveness as evidence supporting a claim depends upon how well the argument can move readers beyond their initial emotional reactions (which might be positive or negative, depending on the audience) to consider the significance of the facts displayed by, or left out of, the picture itself.

- **What does the image reveal about the writer's opinions or biases?** If a televised story on successful local entrepreneurs included only pictures of men, you might wonder whether the story slights women business owners.

- **Does the image exaggerate or distort the information?** This might happen if an advertisement for a summer study abroad program featured only photos showing luxury accommodations, when in fact most participants stay with local residents in modest homes.

**EXERCISE 9.3** Examine the posters at right, which were created by the National Institute on Drug Abuse as part of an anti-steroid-abuse campaign (<http://www.steroidabuse.gov>). How does each employ layout, graphics, and images to emphasize and deemphasize certain information or to influence readers? Discuss your findings with a group of classmates. How effective do you believe campaigns such as this one are in changing the behavior of their target audience? If you believe this campaign is ineffective, discuss why.

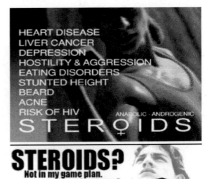

**EXERCISE 9.4** Keeping in mind the principles discussed in Section 9b-1, view a television commercial, public service announcement, print advertisement, commercial Web page, or political poster with a critical eye. What features do you notice that you hadn't noticed before? Do you enjoy the text more or less than you would have had you watched it less critically? Why or why not? Bring your answers to class for discussion.

---

**Highlight    Analyzing an Advertisement**

Writing a critical analysis of an advertisement or other visual argument is a common assignment in composition courses. Here is a professional example of an ad analysis, written by Seth Stevenson for the April 24, 2006 edition of *Slate* magazine. (To see more examples of Stevenson's "Ad Report Card" columns, visit <www.slate.com>.) In this piece, Stevenson critically assesses the effectiveness of a recent Dunkin' Donuts commercial, looking closely at the visual devices the ad's producers use to create an appealing image for their product. As you read the essay, ask yourself, what specific features of the commercial does Stevenson draw on to support his analysis? Do you agree with his assessment of the commercial and its target audience? In what ways would this piece differ from an academic papaer on the same topic?

Coffeeholics A Dunkin' Donuts ad for an addict nation.
By Seth Stevenson
Posted Monday, April 24, 2006, at 6:29 AM ET

The Spot: *In one long take, the camera snakes through the bustling center of a small town, catching various blue-collar types in the midst of busy workdays. House painters, furniture movers, postal workers, tow-truck drivers—all of them are seen bopping around with various* Dunkin' Donuts *products in hand. Meanwhile, a singer on the soundtrack shouts, "Doing things is what I like to do!" The ad closes with a new slogan flashing on screen: "America Runs on Dunkin'."*

*(Continued)*

## Analyzing an Advertisement *(Continued)*

Dunkin' Donuts is spreading its wings. The chain is expanding nationwide and plans to triple in size within the next 10 years. According to a Dunkin' press release, this new ad campaign "marks the most significant repositioning effort in the company's 55-year history." A big part of the goal here is to introduce the brand to Americans not yet familiar with it.

Having grown up in Massachusetts—home to Dunkin' headquarters—I'm plenty familiar with the brand already. Just last week, I got a breakfast sandwich at the Dunkin' (or, as [people around here] somewhat inexplicably call it, the "D&D") around the corner from my mother's house in Brookline. (By the way, that particular franchise is completely kosher. Seriously. No sausage on your breakfast sandwich—even if you ask nicely.)

To me, the iconic Dunkin' campaign will always be the one in which that sad-sack fellow with the moustache says, "Time to make the donuts." But donuts are no longer Dunkin's bread and butter (or bread and lard, as the case may be). Coffee is by far the chain's biggest seller now. According to *Business Week*, beverages account for 63 percent of Dunkin' sales, while donuts make up only 17 percent. Which means that Dunkin' is competing less with Krispy Kreme than with Starbucks.

Of course, it's not exactly competing with Starbucks, either. The Starbucks consumer sees his latte as a gourmet indulgence; the Dunkin' guy views his cuppa joe as necessary fuel. The brands' relative price points reflect this, as do their store interiors. John Gilbert, Dunkin' Donuts' vice president of marketing, has been quoted as saying, "We're not about music and WiFi and couches and fireplaces." What they're about is low prices, quick service, and unpretentious reliability.

So, how do you capture those qualities in an ad without creating an image so boring and unsexy that it turns off customers? The gold standard for blue-collar cool of late has been Target, which managed to transform itself from schlocky to hip on the strength of a clever ad campaign. I think the keys to Target's success are twofold. 1) They choose interesting music (they've used songs from Devo, Cornershop, and Sir Mix-a-Lot); and 2) They shy away from showing actual Target stores. Taking us into a store, with its aisles of garbage cans and discount dry goods, would just remind us about the underlying schlockiness. Instead, Target recontextualizes the

*(Continued)*

## Analyzing an Advertisement *(Continued)*

products it sells inside a colorful, bouncy world of the campaign's own invention.

This flagship "Things I Like To Do" ad from the Dunkin' campaign is pretty straightforward: It suggests that a Dunkin' break helps average Americans power through their busy lives. But it follows Target's lead in not showing an actual Dunkin' franchise. And the music creates an arch sensibility, turning the spot into a sunny ode to caffeine addiction. (Sample lyric: "I'm slightly more productive now than previous because/ I'm slightly more efficient than I previously was.") Nerd rockers (and native Massholes) They Might Be Giants provide the theme song here and contribute several other songs to the Dunkin' campaign. The band is known for catchy hooks, quirky rhymes, and an often cloying sensibility. Sounds just right for a career in jingle writing!

Hill Holliday*, the ad agency behind the campaign, has been running a blog about the ads and what went into them. Here you can see a few other spots from the campaign. Each relies on an oddball They Might Be Giants tune and illustrates an everyday moment. The lyrics inject a bit of whimsy and knowingness into these familiar scenes, lifting the average Joe's workaday existence into a funnier, cooler realm. Some sample lines from the tunes: "Get your 8-year-old out of the tree. He got up there quite a ways" (as we see a mom sip her Latte Lite and then hoist herself up into the branches); "The backs of my legs, sticking to the pleather" (as we watch people drinking Dunkin' iced coffee in an effort to mitigate that post-beach cling to their car seats).

One Hill Holliday blog entry about the jingle from the flagship ad muses: "Doing things is what we like to do. Why do I think millions of people are about to have that line going through their heads on a regular basis?" Funny, I've always wondered how ad execs feel when they inflict some insipid catchphrase or jingle on us. I'm sure there's pride, but is there also a modicum of guilt involved? I hope?

Grade: A. The ads are very watchable, and I think the campaign nails the brand image Dunkin' is striving for. Down-to-earth, value-oriented, but still fun and just a tiny bit hip. As for that new slogan, America Runs on Dunkin'? Given the calorie counts on some of those donuts and flavored coffee items, it might be more accurate to go with America Waddles on Dunkin'. But I guess that doesn't scan quite as well.

# 9c How can you recognize and avoid fallacies?

*Fallacies* are shoddy imitations of well-reasoned arguments—flashy short-cuts that look good at first but turn out to be based on dubious assumptions and careless generalizations. Learning to detect and debunk them is an important part of understanding how arguments work. Here are ten kinds of fallacy you're likely to encounter frequently.

● **1 Avoid argument to the person (in Latin, *ad hominem*).** This fallacy makes a personal attack on an opponent rather than focusing on the issue under discussion. Ad hominem arguments become smear tactics when a speaker or a writer attacks an opponent's personality or personal life. Here is an example.

> A legislator argues that those who oppose amending the U.S. constitution to prohibit flag burning are traitors who don't love their country and probably sympathize with anti-American terrorist groups.

The speaker who resorts to such abusive rhetoric may well be avoiding the real issues, such as whether such an amendment is necessary or practical.

But don't confuse the ad hominem fallacy with relevant questions about credibility. It's perfectly legitimate to question a writer whose qualifications or motives are dubious, as long as those considerations are relevant to the issues being discussed.

● **2 Avoid circular reasoning.** This fallacy—also called *begging the question*—happens when instead of supporting a claim, the writer simply restates the claim in different words. Take this faulty argument:

> The death penalty is wrong because the state should not have the power to end a criminal's life.

But that's exactly what the death penalty is—state-sanctioned execution. Unless the writer goes on to explain *why* it's wrong to end a criminal's life and provides supporting data, this claim begs the question.

**3 Avoid hasty generalizations.** This fallacy involves drawing conclusions from too little evidence.

> It's not safe to swim at the beach because there were two shark attacks at Myrtle Beach last month and another attack last week in Miami Beach.

Shark attacks at two beaches do not provide sufficient evidence on which to base a broad claim about the safety of beaches all over the United States. Be careful about making claims that use absolute terms such as *always, never, everyone, no one, all,* and *none.* When you're talking about human events, absolutes are seldom accurate, so cover yourself by using such qualifiers as *some, in most cases,* and *many.* And as a reader and a listener, you should always be skeptical about arguments that overstate their claims in this way. (See Section 10a-4 for more about qualifiers.)

**4 Avoid false cause arguments (in Latin, *post hoc, ergo propter hoc,* or "after this, therefore because of this").** These arguments incorporate the faulty assumption that because one event follows another, the first event caused the second. Consider this statement.

> In the years since the highway speed limit was raised to 70 miles per hour, the annual number of traffic fatalities in our state has doubled. Clearly, the higher speed limit is causing unnecessary deaths.

Too many factors enter into changes in traffic fatality numbers for such a conclusion to be legitimate. Increased numbers of drivers on the road, altered traffic patterns due to new construction, an increase in the number of large trucks or other dangerous vehicles on the road, changes in how law enforcement monitors and enforces speeding or reckless driving—any of these factors might have influenced the number of fatal accidents. Without evidence *directly* linking the speed limit to traffic fatalities, one cannot reasonably infer a causal relationship.

**5 Avoid either/or arguments (also called *false dilemma* or the *fallacy of insufficient options*).** This type of faulty reasoning states an argument in terms that imply that one must choose between only two options—right/wrong, good/bad, moral/immoral, and so forth. This is another form of simplistic reasoning that glosses over complex issues and instead attacks the opposition.

> If we allow that factory to come into town, we are dooming ourselves and our children to a lifetime of breathing filthy air.

Many other options are available between the extremes of no factory and filthy air; one might be to require the factory to install scrubbers to clean its emissions.

The loaded rhetorical question that allows for only one acceptable answer is another form of the either/or argument.

> Are we going to increase the number of police officers in this city, or are we going to abandon it to gangs and drug dealers?

When an arguer tries to force a false dilemma on you, your best response is to challenge your opponent's polarized thinking immediately and point out other alternatives to his or her oversimplified view.

**●6 Avoid red herrings.** This tactic involves diverting the audience's attention from the main issue by bringing up an irrelevant point. (The phrase refers to the practice of dragging a strong-smelling smoked herring across a trail to confuse hunting dogs and send them in the wrong direction.) For example, an elected official might complain:

> While it may be true that my press secretary accepted bribes, my administration is just being targeted by hostile media.

The charges of press bias might be true, but the attitude of the media has no bearing on the official's misbehavior.

**●7 Avoid slippery slopes.** This fallacy occurs when a writer assumes that taking an initial action will automatically set in motion an unstoppable chain of events. You'll encounter slippery slopes most often when writers are promoting or opposing a particular course of action. For instance, a politician who supports funding a new complex to house agencies dealing with homelessness might argue that when homeless people have easy access to services under one roof, they will be able to get the help they need, find jobs, gain confidence, and become productive citizens. Perhaps so, but without explanation and evidence to support each link in that chain, these predictions have no real foundation, and you shouldn't readily accept them.

**8 Avoid false analogies.** These are comparisons that do not hold true or prove misleading. Analogies can be useful in helping readers understand abstract or elusive ideas and concepts—for instance, a writer might clarify how the turbocharger in an automobile works by comparing it to a windmill. Sometimes, however, writers create a false analogy in which the comparison drawn simply won't hold up. For example:

> A corporation couldn't operate without the leadership of a CEO to set priorities and make the big decisions. A family operates the same way: one spouse must be the head of the household, or chaos will result.

Certainly a business and a household share superficial similarities, but the two entities have different functions, involve different kinds of interpersonal relationships, and operate according to different value systems (profit and efficiency vs. nurturance and loyalty). To assume that what holds true in one environment should hold true in the other is an unwarranted logical leap.

Pay attention to the analogies you encounter in arguments. Are the similarities between the things being compared strong enough to warrant the conclusions being drawn? If they're not, reject the analogy.

**9 Avoid non sequitur.** Latin for "it does not follow," this fallacy occurs when writers draw on irrelevant evidence or reasons to support a claim. Non sequitur is similar to the red herring fallacy, but whereas red herrings are designed to distract a reader from the central argument, non sequitur asks readers to accept the irrelevant material as proof. Here are two examples.

> That candidate would be an excellent governor—after all, he comes from one of the wealthiest, most well-established families in the state.

I'm sure that it can't be a top-notch university. It's in a rundown area of the city, surrounded by housing projects and abandoned warehouses.

What do wealth and family connections have to do with a candidate's qualifications to govern? About as much as being in a bad neighborhood has to do with the quality of a university: that is to say, little.

**10 Avoid bandwagon appeal.** This tactic argues that a product or course of action must be worthwhile because it is popular. Youngsters who try to persuade their parents that they must have a particular brand of jacket or a new video game because "everybody has them" are using bandwagon tactics. As millions of parents have pointed out, popularity doesn't necessarily guarantee merit.

---

### Checklist 9.1    Ten Common Fallacies

1. **Argument to the person (ad hominem):** attacking the person instead of focusing on the issues.
2. **Circular reasoning:** restating instead of proving a claim.
3. **Hasty generalization:** drawing conclusions from scanty evidence.
4. **False cause:** presuming that if *B* follows *A*, *A* caused *B*.
5. **Either/or:** suggesting that only two choices are possible when in fact there may be several.
6. **Red herring:** bringing in an irrelevant issue to deflect attention from the main point.
7. **Slippery slope:** assuming that one event will set off an unstoppable chain reaction.
8. **False analogy:** making a comparison between things that are too dissimilar for the comparison to be useful.
9. **Non sequitur:** drawing a conclusion from irrelevant data.
10. **Bandwagon:** claiming that widespread popularity makes an object or idea valuable.

**EXERCISE 9.5** Work with other students in a group to spot the fallacies in these arguments. In some instances you may find more than one.

1. Two kinds of students go to college: the kind who are truly interested in learning and those who simply want to get a diploma with as little effort as possible so that they can graduate and get a job. Our university should only admit the first type.

2. Everyone knows that the next decade will be a poor time to go into medicine because government regulation is ruining the profession.

3. The great peasant rebellions in the Middle Ages happened because the rulers taxed the peasants to the limit to pay for foreign wars and neglected conditions in their own countries; the United States can expect similar uprisings if it doesn't drastically cut its defense budget and invest in domestic social programs.

4. As a legislator, I can't get too upset about the proposed tuition raise when every time I drive by our state university I get caught in a traffic jam of students in their new SUVs and convertibles.

# 10 How Do You Write Powerful Arguments?

## 10a How do you construct a solid written argument?

Making a claim and supporting it with reasons and evidence seems like a natural process, since most of us engage in informal arguments nearly every day. But it is not a process to take for granted, especially when you're asked to prepare a formal written argument in school or for a job. In college, you'll be asked to write persuasive papers that include strong theses and carefully chosen support, and this writing will have to take your purpose into account even as it appeals to a specific audience.

Being able to engage in formal argument is essential because it allows you not only to develop but also to demonstrate your knowledge of the topics you study. In fact, formal argument is one of the most important elements that distinguishes college-level writing from the high school essays that merely summarize existing research. Because of the importance of argument in educational and professional settings, you'll want to know how to present your cases effectively and memorably. This chapter walks you through a general process for constructing a formal written argument, using the Toulmin model and terminology outlined in Chapter 9.

**1 Clarify your claim.** First, figure out what you want readers to take from your piece: Do you want them to look at some issue in a new way? Do you want them to be aware of a problem they hadn't noticed before? To adopt a particular viewpoint? To take action? Your answer is your claim.

Suppose that, after reading in a child development course some studies of the influence of media violence on children, you decide to write a course paper arguing that parents should be cautious about allowing their children to play the video games marketed to young people, since many of them encourage players to participate in realistic portrayals of violent acts. That assertion is your claim, the one set forth in Figure 10.1 (see page 149). In many academic papers, your major claim(s) will be stated early, as a thesis statement.

(For more detailed advice about discovering and narrowing a topic and developing a thesis statement, see Sections 2a, 2b, and 3a.)

● **2 Generate strong reasons to support your claim.** Often these supporting reasons will grow out of the reading and research you do on the topic. However, rhetoricians have also identified several general categories of reasons that you can consider when trying to find serious arguments in favor of your position. When you need help finding good reasons for a paper, you can use these categories as brainstorming devices:

- **Argue for the greater good;** *or* **argue for the lesser evil.** More often than not, readers will see merit on both sides of a hot issue; after all, contradictory proposals can offer different yet legitimate benefits. When that's so, you may want your proposals to be perceived as the *greater* good or the *lesser* evil.

- **Argue from fairness and equality.** Perhaps the most dependable line of argument in America today is the appeal to fairness. The argument is hard to challenge because it invokes a key concept of democracy: equal treatment. In almost any situation, if your research shows that people have been treated unfairly, you will find supporters for your case.

- **Argue for the long-term good;** *or* **argue for the short-term good.** When what you are proposing in your argument will have slow or deferred benefits, urge readers to appreciate the "big picture." A long-term benefit can almost always be portrayed as more substantial and more judicious than an immediate one. On the other hand, your evidence may support immediate action. In such a case you might stress the "critical" status of the current situation and carefully list factors contributing to an imminent crisis.

- **Argue for the benefit of greater numbers;** *or* **argue the special case.** When your research suggests a course of action that would help a majority of people, you can apply the weight of numbers to your argument, pleading for the common good. It is somewhat harder to argue the case of a smaller group. The key then is to ask individual members of the majority to imagine themselves in the position of those in the minority.

- **Argue from self-interest;** *or* **argue against self-interest.** Unless readers understand their stake in a case, they aren't likely to act. So explain exactly how readers might benefit from your position and its consequences; be as specific as possible, and cite real advantages when you can. Quite often, however, writers have to urge readers to look beyond self-interest—to act for the good of their institutions, posterity, the nation, or the world community.

- **Argue from the consensus of experts;** *or* **argue against the consensus of experts.** When your research can show that major authorities in a field support your position, you should have a case worth making. However, there is no reason to be dismayed when your research puts you at odds with most experts in a given field. After all, experts in a field often have a stake in the status quo, and they will resist change. That resistance is worth pointing out, especially when you have hard data to back up your claims.

- **Argue from precedent;** *or* **argue against precedent.** If something has been done in the past and has been accepted as either legal or traditional, it becomes a defense for similar actions in the present. When the precedents of a given case weigh against your argument, you need information to suggest that they might be outdated or that they do not apply in the current situation.

- **Argue from feasibility.** It's important to show that any proposal you might argue for is workable, not a pie-in-the-sky idea. And the burden of proof is on you, so gather the figures, furnish the plans, provide examples of comparable projects undertaken elsewhere. Of course, your research may suggest just the opposite—that the project can't be managed or is based on wildly implausible projections. If so, change it.

- **Argue the consequences: where does the argument lead?** Be sure that readers appreciate the implications of your argument. If your findings suggest that a small problem now may only get worse, explain why and how. If necessary, construct a worst-case scenario to show what might reasonably happen if current trends go unchecked.

In planning your argument opposing violent video games for children, for example, you might choose to focus on the *consensus of experts* that exposure to violent media builds violent attitudes and behavior and on promoting the *long-term benefits* of raising children who are empathic and compassionate.

● **3 Gather supporting evidence.** Check the library catalog for books, periodical articles, research reports, and government documents on the topic. Search the Internet. For expert testimony, consider setting up an interview with a professor who specializes in child development, or visit a blog that discusses children's entertainment or video gaming. You should also seek out firsthand evidence by closely examining the games themselves. Borrow or rent several of the most popular—*Grand Theft Auto 3, Doom, Mortal Kombat*—and take notes on the role-playing elements in each.

Depending on the audience for your paper, you might also explore more personal and anecdotal kinds of support—for example, a description of your shock at seeing your two young nephews engrossed in a game of *Mortal Kombat* at a recent family gathering. You could also ask friends whether their children or younger siblings play such games.

As you gather evidence, cast a wide net. You may not include everything you find in the finished paper, but new evidence may help you adjust a claim that is overstated or misguided. It can also suggest supporting reasons that hadn't initially occurred to you. For example, you may discover examples of convicted violent offenders who were addicted to video games as teenagers—a point you can then add to your argument. For more information about finding sources, see Chapter 44.

● **4 Evaluate your evidence.** Check that your supporting materials are appropriate to the writing situation. In writing a paper for a course, concentrate on scholarly research and theories. If you're writing an article for a PTA newsletter, you might balance academic sources with real-life anecdotes that will catch busy parents' interest. Wherever your evidence comes from, it should meet certain basic requirements.

- **Timeliness.** Are the statistics, information, and examples you use recent, or are they so old that they may no longer be accurate?
- **Comprehensiveness.** Do you have enough support for your claim, or are you making generalizations based on one or two examples?
- **Credibility.** Do you draw your evidence from sources that both you and your readers trust?

For a detailed discussion of how to evaluate source materials, see Chapter 45.

**⏣ 5 Identify the warrants, or beliefs, that underlie your argument and consider whether readers will accept them.** If you suspect that readers may doubt or disagree with any of your assumptions, be prepared to explain and support them.

This step is especially important when you're writing for a hostile or unfamiliar audience. In a paper on video games, consider whether some readers might question your warrant that simulating violent acts harms children. Readers who play such games might believe they are cathartic and do no real damage. Here's where the research studies from your child development course fit in: since they establish a causal link between violent media and behavioral problems, you can cite them as *backing* for your warrant.

Figure 10.1 shows how the fully developed argument might look.

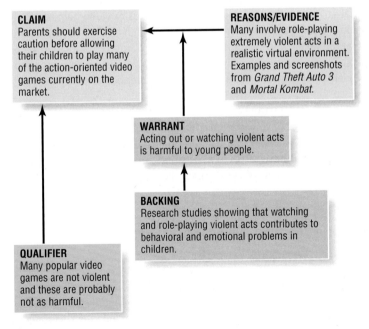

**CLAIM**
Parents should exercise caution before allowing their children to play many of the action-oriented video games currently on the market.

**REASONS/EVIDENCE**
Many involve role-playing extremely violent acts in a realistic virtual environment. Examples and screenshots from *Grand Theft Auto 3* and *Mortal Kombat*.

**WARRANT**
Acting out or watching violent acts is harmful to young people.

**BACKING**
Research studies showing that watching and role-playing violent acts contributes to behavioral and emotional problems in children.

**QUALIFIER**
Many popular video games are not violent and these are probably not as harmful.

**Figure 10.1**

**EXERCISE 10.1** Review the lines of argument discussed in Section 10a-2, then brainstorm as many reasons as you can think of that could be used in a paper that advocates limiting young people's access to video games. Which reasons do you think are the most persuasive? Which, if any, would you recommend that the writer whose argument is featured in Figure 10.1 include in her paper? Explain your answer. Finally, brainstorm a similar list of reasons to support the claim that access to violent video games does *not* harm children.

**EXERCISE 10.2** Construct a diagram similar to the one presented in Figure 10.1 to outline a claim, reasons, evidence, warrant, backing, and qualifiers for a course paper you're working on. Then answer these questions: How helpful did you find these terms in generating persuasive material for your argument? Which portions of the diagram did you find most challenging to complete? Why?

## 10b How do you write an argument that appeals to readers?

Some people see an argument as a sort of verbal war in which enemies line up on opposing sides of an issue, each with the goal of demolishing the other side. Yet remember that you won't persuade people by making them angry.

You'll only make them stick to their positions more stubbornly. For this reason, we suggest that you think of argument not as a battle but as a persuasive dialogue. In a dialogue, both sides exchange ideas as they search for the best stance on an issue. In this section, we offer tips for writing an argument that appeals to and respects readers—even those who may not initially agree with you.

**1 Be credible.** Be certain that the way you present yourself in your project—your *ethos*—is that of a person readers can respect and trust. People are more likely to listen to what you have to say if you present yourself as believable, knowledgeable, thoughtful, and fair. If you treat your readers as informed equals who are open to rational persuasion, they'll be more likely to listen sympathetically. You don't persuade people by making them angry.

To this end, you'll want to use civil and inclusive language. Slurs, name-calling, and negative stereotyping may impress a small audience that already shares your feelings. But the wider audience of people you don't know will probably think you are simplistic and small-minded if you use terms such as *bleeding-heart liberal* or *right-wing nut case* in an argument.

You'll also want to be sure that your language is directed at your actual audience, not above them or below them. You want readers to identify with you, and they won't do that if you are either too technical for them to understand or too simplistic to be taken seriously.

**2 Draw on shared beliefs and values.** Even if you're addressing readers whose position is completely opposed to your own, search for common ground. Any shared belief, no matter how general, may serve as a warrant on which you can build an argument those readers will find reasonable. For instance, both proponents and opponents of gun-control legislation value public safety, though they have different ideas about how to achieve it, and both supporters and opponents of school vouchers are concerned about the quality of public education. An argument that begins from these common beliefs may not change anyone's mind immediately. But it probably will get a fair hearing, and it may initiate a civil exchange of ideas. And that's what public argument is all about. (See Section 15c for more on building consensus with readers.)

● **3 Handle information honestly.** It may be tempting to construct an argument by using only sources that favor your argument or to cite information selectively—leaving out data or trends or incidents that don't support your case. In the long run, such an argument won't go down well with critical readers. They'll ask just the sorts of questions about your claims and supporting evidence that may undermine your work:

- Are the claims supported by evidence from reliable and authoritative sources?
- Are the claims supported by evidence from a variety of sources?
- Has evidence been fairly—not selectively—reported?
- Is enough evidence presented to support the claims?
- Has evidence been accurately documented?

You should be able to answer *yes* to every question.

No argument is ever watertight. However, when you are dealing with complex and significant issues, readers want to be informed and enlightened, not bamboozled. Remember, too, that checking out factual claims and assertions is relatively easy these days. A whole generation of bloggers now keep the national media on their toes by constantly assessing their claims and evidence. Critical readers may do the same with your work.

● **4 Quote fairly from your sources.** Citing authorities is a powerful way of supporting an argument. But you must quote responsibly and fairly, presenting the words of any source just as the author intended them, so far as you can tell. You shouldn't trim or embellish a quotation to make it sound more in accord with your positions. Nor should you quote unfairly those who disagree with you, leaving out words or contextual information that might make a difference in the sense. In September 2005, *New York Times* reporter Louise Story caused a journalistic flap when she quoted Yale student Angie Ku as saying that she did not think it was unfair that women generally take on most of the responsibility for raising their children.

> "I accept things how they are," she said. "I don't mind the status quo. I don't see why I have to go against it."
> —Angie Ku, quoted in "Many Women at Elite Colleges Set Career Path to Motherhood" by Louise Story, *New York Times Online* 20 Sept. 2005.

Although she did not deny having made the comment, Ku charged that Story had distorted her position on the issue. She pointed out that Story had selectively printed only a few sentences from a lengthy series of interviews, leaving out her comments regarding the obstacles women face and the importance of women's right to choose from a range of career and family options. In leaving out this contextual information, Ku believed, Story painted an unfair picture. In response to Ku and to similar complaints about her presentation of source material, Story issued a response three days later that more carefully explained how she had compiled and presented students' words in the article. You don't want to be subject to similar complaints when you make an argument.

**5 Use emotional appeals sparingly.** Just as your credibility or personal *ethos* plays a role in making an argument work, your ability to generate emotions in your readers can also play a part. In many academic and public forums, overtly emotional arguments don't play well. They are seen as sentimental or manipulative. So you need to deal with emotions carefully, understanding that many arguments do generate feelings such as anger, fear, sympathy, envy, or jealousy. You can raise such feelings with just a few hot-button phrases.

Consider the power of calls to patriotism, for example, in many political arguments, or how easy it is to pit students against administrators or politicians against ordinary citizens simply by contrasting their power. There is a role for feelings in arguments, but an emotion should not be evoked as a substitute for reasonable claims or a preponderance of evidence. Rather, emotions should complement a case supported by good reasons and solid evidence.

**EXERCISE 10.3** Check all the quotations used in a paper you've written for a course against their original sources. Do you see any problems in how you present information or quoted material? If so, use the guidelines in Section 10b to remedy these problems.

## 10c How do you effectively address other viewpoints?

If you're going to write about controversial issues, you can't simply pretend that your position is the only one. You'll need to acknowledge that other arguments exist, or readers will think that you haven't done your homework. It is equally important that you learn to describe other positions accurately and respectfully. In doing so you enhance your own credibility.

**● 1 Present opposing arguments fairly.** Logicians use the term *straw man fallacy* to describe the misleading practice of summarizing another position in an oversimplified way that makes it easy to knock down. The following statement, from a billboard promoting school vouchers, uses this tactic:

> Care about the children more than the teachers' unions. Put parents in charge of education.

People oppose school vouchers for many reasons, including a desire to put available resources into the public schools attended by most children and the practical difficulties of ensuring that a voucher program would be available to the neediest students. Although many of these concerns are shared by the leadership of teachers' unions, to suggest that opposition to vouchers is solely motivated by a desire to preserve union privileges over children's learning is simplistic and unjustified. When you compose an argument, summarize opponents' reasoning fully and generously, or readers will perceive you as unfair.

**● 2 Consider refuting an opposing argument.** Once you've acknowledged other viewpoints, what do you do with them? Don't just let them sit there; readers want to know how they affect the strength of your argument. One option is to *refute* an opposing position—that is, to disprove the argument by pointing out its weaknesses or fallacies. It's possible to critique an argument on several grounds.

- **Question the claim.** Is it overstated? Is it insufficiently supported? (See Section 8b-5 for more on how to spot a flawed claim.)
- **Question the evidence.** Does the evidence come from reliable sources? Is there enough of it? Is it recent enough to be accurate? (Sections 8b-4 and 45a contain guidelines for evaluating evidence.)
- **Question the warrants and backing.** Does the argument rest on beliefs, values, or assumptions that you think are invalid? Does the writer need to justify and support those assumptions? (See Section 9a for more on warrants and backing.)

When you've identified problems in one or more of these areas, point them out and call on readers to reject the argument.

**3 Consider making concessions to another position.** Often you won't be able to reject an opposing argument completely; most reasoned arguments do have some merit. In such cases you'll do well to concede that some of your opponent's points are valid and then argue that under the circumstances you believe yours are stronger. When you do this, you not only seem fair-minded but you avoid backing yourself into an untenable position.

One community organizer successfully used this strategy when she convinced the city council to grant her a permit to locate a homeless shelter across the street from a popular playground.

> I agree with you that safety concerns often make it inappropriate to locate shelters in areas frequented by children. The people served by homeless shelters are often troubled and difficult to monitor. However, the shelter I am proposing is different, because it will serve only mothers with small children who have been recommended by churches and social service agencies as good candidates for job training. These mothers will pose little danger to the neighborhood and their children will make good use of the playground.

By admitting that the city council's concerns are valid in many situations, she established valuable common ground with her audience. In addition, she freed herself from having to argue about the safety of homeless shelters in general, allowing her to focus on the special features of her particular shelter.

**GOING PUBLIC**   **An Annotated Argument Paper**

Lauren Schultz wrote the paper excerpted below in response to a class assignment that asked her to argue a position on an issue she felt strongly about. Her paper is documented using MLA style. As you read, assess how effectively she articulates and supports her position. How does she attempt to create common ground between her position and that of others? Is she fair?

Lauren Schultz

Professor Ruszkiewicz

Rhetoric 368C

18 March 2006

Native American Mascots: Time to Go

For over fifty years, the Native American (Native) community in the United States has fought against the use of sports mascots demeaning to its people. Professional teams that currently have Native mascots include the Washington Redskins, Atlanta Braves, Kansas City Chiefs, and Cleveland Indians. College teams with Native mascots include the Florida State University Seminoles and the University of Illinois Fighting Illini. In October 1991, Native rights activists formed the National Coalition on Racism in Sports and Media in reaction against such mascots. The issue heated up again in August 2005, when the National College Athletic Association (NCAA) published a ruling that will bar college teams from using "hostile and demeaning" mascots in postseason bowl games beginning this year—a ruling that

> Term "Native" defined in a special sense for the paper.

specifically mentioned twelve schools, including Florida State and Illinois ("NCAA Bans"). Officials at Florida State are fighting the ruling, and many sports fans nationwide see the push to get rid of the mascots as misguided. Many non-Native Americans (non-Natives) consider such mascots as well-meaning portrayals of Native culture, focusing on positive values such as honor and bravery. However, such non-Native perspectives are often superficial and insensitive. In fact, the misuse of Native imagery in sports mascots is racially offensive because it promotes stereotypes of Native peoples, dehumanizes them, and falsely defines Native cultures. These mascots should be retired by all sports teams, professional, college, and high school alike.

> The claim for the argument, stated with three supporting reasons.

Native mascots such as the Cleveland Indians' Chief Wahoo depict Natives stereotypically and disrespectfully. (See fig. 1.) In "The Form of Native Stereotyping," Native opinion leaders claim that 45% of "anti-Indian sentiment is due to such media stereotypes. The recurring features of these mascots

> The first reason to oppose the mascots, focusing on stereotypes.

Fig. 1. Cleveland Indians mascot Chief Wahoo.

include red skin, scant dress, adornments (feathers, makeup), and weaponry (arrows, hatchets).

> The remainder of this paragraph provides evidence of stereotyping.

Collectively, the features of the Native stereotype reflect the demeaning seventeenth-century term "noble savage," coined by British poet John Dryden. Despite the modifier "noble," the term "savage" implies inferiority. Native mascots present non-Native cultures as homogeneous and primitive societies. Modern Native rights activists such as Dr. Cornel Pewewardy of the University of Kansas claim that such stereotypes are not only insulting but harmful because they are damaging to the self-identity, self-concept, and self-esteem of Native peoples.

> Citation of an expert to strengthen the argument.

Indian mascots also possess the power to dehumanize Native Americans. Their exaggerated features strip away the uniqueness and civility of individual people and underscore the relationship of non-Native oppressor to Native victim. In "The Harm of Native Stereotyping," Dr. David P. Rider suggests that Native mascots are especially dehumanizing because "negative images and attitudes" serve to assuage the guilt of the white majority while "[justifying] further exploitation." In other words, objectifying Natives collectively denigrates their status in the eyes of non-Natives and makes it easier to accept the genocide they suffered as well as ongoing oppression and discrimination.

> A second reason to oppose mascots, focusing on dehumanization.

> A possible slippery slope fallacy here. (See Section 9c.)

It is true that some mascots focus on the tribal image of the Native warrior, a highly respected figure. The mascot of the Florida State Seminoles depicts a Native warrior in profile who appears with closed eyes and mouth open, as if in mid-chant, thick stripes of paint on his cheeks and nose. (See fig. 2.)

> This paragraph summarizes opposing views.

Fig. 2. The Florida State University Seminoles mascot.

Similar Native mascots are also common in American high schools, where values such as honor, good sportsmanship, and pride surround the image. For example, Mirabeau B. Lamar High School in Houston, Texas, my <u>alma mater</u>, proudly supports its "Redskin" mascot. Even the Cleveland Indians' brick-red, toothy Chief Wahoo may possess an honorable origin. The name "Indians" supposedly honors player Louis Sockalexis of the Penobscot tribe, the first major league Native player. Sockalexis played from 1897 to 1899 for the former Cleveland Spiders, and Cleveland fans selected the new name "Indians" by a newspaper vote in his honor. However, *CNN Sports Illustrated* suggests that owner Charles W. Somers may have influenced the results of the vote. Still, it is at least arguable that certain mascots depict the positive attributes of Natives, thus promoting an appreciation for the unity and strength of Native culture.

Yet even if that is so, Native people are still being trivialized for the sake of sporting events. In an article for *Educators Resources*, Dr. Cornel Pewewardy states that the manipulation of any aspect of a culture by an outsider is the

> This sentence concedes to some points in the previous paragraph, then offers a rebuttal, which the rest of this paragraph develops.

ultimate "power and control" that one ethnic group can assert over another. When the predominantly non-Native sports industry presents its distorted images of Natives, it is exerting power over the Native identity. In addition, because foreign cultures cannot understand the full meaning of Native culture, they often make a mockery of deeply meaningful ceremonies, traditions, and dress. Non-Natives who claim to honor Natives through any mascot, crude or not, distort years of tradition and beauty that are inaccessible to outsiders.

Because stereotypes harm and dehumanize Native culture, the presence of Native mascots in United States sports is ultimately racially and culturally offensive. In addition, the continuing resistance of schools, the sports industry, and fans to retiring these derogatory mascots shows disrespect for the wishes of Natives. The Civil Rights Movement of the 1970s provided a forum for Natives to voice their disapproval of "Indian" mascots. Yet even when Natives openly spoke out against them, they have been largely ignored. (See fig. 3.)

Fig. 3. Protestor Sonny Hensley holds an anti-mascot button at a 2003 powwow sponsored by Ohio Center for Native American Affairs.

According to *Washington Post* columnist Courtland
Milloy, the continued insistence by major sports organizations
that it is not harmful to use Native mascots is best
characterized as a delusion: "To them, making a mascot out of
a people that were nearly exterminated on their homeland is
the ultimate show of respect." This lack of response has led
Native groups in recent years to file lawsuits against
professional baseball franchises and university teams under
the 1974 Civil Rights Act. Fear of such lawsuits may have
helped to bring about the NCAA's controversial ruling. But
even this ruling is a small victory—it applies only to
postseason games and only to college teams. In most settings,
the mascots still endure. Perhaps Barbara Munson of the
Oneida Nation best describes the ethical situation:
unintentional harm becomes intentional when people discover
their errors and continue in their behavior nevertheless.

Works Cited

Bellecourt, Vernon. "Wahoo-Chant-Chop: Bad Medicine for
        Cleveland and Atlanta Baseball?" *National Coalition on
        Racism in Sports and Media*. American Indian
        Movement, 27 Oct. 1999. Web. 13 Mar. 2003.

"Chief Wahoo." *Official Site of the Cleveland Indians*. MLB
        Advanced Media, n.d. Web. 19 Jan. 2006.

"The Harm of Native Stereotyping: Facts and Evidence."
        *Peace Party*. Blue Corn Comics, 2002. Web. 4 Feb. 2003.

Milloy, Courtland. "Indian Mascots Disrespect Us All."
        *The Washington Post*. Washington Post Co., 14 Nov. 2005.
        Web. 19 Jan. 2006.

Munson, Barbara. "Not for Sport: A Native American Activist Calls for
an End to 'Indian' Team Mascots." *Teaching Tolerance*. Southern
Poverty Law Center, 1 Nov. 1998. Web. 19 Jan. 2006.

"NCAA Bans Postseason Indian Mascots." *Teaching Tolerance*.
Southern Poverty Law Center, 5 Aug. 2005. Web. 19 Jan. 2006.

Pewewardy, Dr. Cornel. "Why Educators Can't Ignore Indian Mascots."
*American Indian Sports Team Mascots: Educators' Resources*.
American Indian Sports Team Mascots, 1998. Web. 4 Feb. 2003.

"Seminole Mascot." *Seminoles.com*. CBS Interactive, n.d. Web. 19 Jan.
2006.

Simons, Mike. "Protest Against Using Symbols of American Indians as
Mascots, Columbus, Ohio." *gettyimages*. Getty Images, 1 Jan.
2003. Web. 12 Oct. 2006.

"What's in a Name? Research Leads Indians to Alter History of
Nickname." *CNN Sports Illustrated*. Sports Illustrated. 18 Jan. 2000.
Web. 13 Mar. 2003.

Young, Joanne. "Lincoln Public Schools." *Lincoln Journal Star*. Lincoln
Journal Star, 2002. Web. 4 Feb 2003.

# 11 How Do You Write About Literature?

A literary or popular culture analysis is a common assignment in most English courses, even in composition classes. But requirements and critical approaches range from close readings of individual texts to wide-ranging confrontations with issues of politics, gender, and culture. So how you write about works of literature or popular culture (movies, plays, music, television) may depend as much on how you are taught as on what you read or view. You may be asked to simply summarize a play, a film, or a television commercial, or you might be asked to write your personal response to one of these texts. When you're writing sustained arguments

Writing a literary or popular culture analysis differs from simply summarizing or reacting to what you see in a text. Look carefully at these two stills from the 2005 film *King Kong*. First, describe your initial reactions: How does the first image, which closely frames Kong and Ann Darrow, make you feel about the two characters? What do you think is happening here? Now, take a more analytical approach to the image. What visual elements can you identify in the frame, and how do they work to elicit the emotions you initially described? What happens in the second image when the camera zooms out?

about literature and popular culture, however, summary or response is rarely enough. In many cases you'll have to analyze these texts—to take them apart critically and to comment on how the different elements work together.

What is the point of writing about literature or pop culture? It can be to heighten your appreciation for literary works, to demonstrate your ability to support a thesis about a literary or pop culture text, to explore how readers respond to texts, to enhance your skill at interpretation, to expand your knowledge of a particular era or literary movement, or to heighten your sensitivity to other cultures. It can also be a creative activity—a way to go public with your writing.

## 11a What elements should you look for when you read literature?

There are dozens of ways to read, think about, and analyze literature and pop culture, and all of these approaches begin with a basic assumption: *the work must be read closely, often more than once.* Whether you are studying a short story, a poem, or a movie, you will have to read—or watch—that work carefully to be able to write about it authoritatively.

Many readers, however, initially feel intimidated by literature. Unfamiliar with literary forms and techniques, they may feel unprepared to analyze and comment on a text. Or, more commonly, they may worry about "getting it"—about coming away with a poem or short story's "right" meaning. One way to deal with these concerns is to try to see literature as an accessible, if often challenging, form of creative communication. Once you spend some time with the text you are reading, the pressure to "get it" should start to fade. Try to read the text the first time without any goals or expectations—simply enjoy it for the piece of art that it is. On subsequent readings, you can start to study the work, looking carefully at its structure, imagery, or other formal features (see Checklist 11.1 for more on literary elements.) Keep a reading journal, a notebook in which you can jot down reactions, questions, and ideas as you read.

Checklist 11.1 summarizes some basic elements that are integral to literary works. (Some of these—diction, tone, and figurative language among them—are not exclusive to literature; they matter in many kinds of writing.) Recognizing these elements can help you to formulate a topic, develop a thesis statement, and find supporting evidence for a paper.

---

### Checklist 11.1 Basic Literary Elements

- **Plot:** Plot refers to the writer's arrangement of events in a story and the reasons behind that arrangement. Plot can be presented in a number of ways, including chronologically and by using flashbacks.

- **Setting:** The setting establishes the world in which the characters live and act, including time, place, and social and cultural contexts.

- **Character:** Writers create characters to make readers care about what is happening or to reinforce symbols or themes in a text.

- **Theme:** The theme of the work is, to put it simply, what the work is *about* (its main concept), as opposed to what *happens* in it (see the discussion of plot, above). A writer will often use a theme to pull together several other elements of the work. Some common themes are *jealousy, ambition, hypocrisy,* and *prejudice.*

- **Point of view:** Point of view focuses on who is telling the story (the narrator or speaker) and how it is told. Narrators can speak in the first, second (rarely), or third person. Some narrators are *omniscient* (able to tell us what is going on in the minds of characters), whereas others are *objective* (able to tell us only what the characters say and do.) Some are involved in the plot, and others are mere observers.

- **Diction (word choices):** As you read, assume that every word was chosen carefully. Look up any words you don't understand. Dictionaries provide the literal meanings of words, their *denotations*; also be aware of possible *connotations*, or emotional associations and meanings. In addition, look for *ambiguity*, or the possibility of two or more meanings, in a writer's diction.

*(Continued)*

**Basic Literary Elements** *(Continued)*

- **Figurative language:** A figure of speech is a deviation from the literal meaning of a word or phrase. Writers use figurative language to challenge, inspire, or connect with readers, or simply to stretch their creative wings. *Metaphor* and *simile* are probably the most common figures of speech; others include *oxymoron, personification, hyperbole, synecdoche*, and *metonymy*. (Explanations of these terms and other figures of speech usually can be found in the glossaries at the back of literature textbooks.)

- **Imagery:** Writers use concrete language to make readers see what they are seeing, to hear, smell, taste, and feel. As you read, be aware of how the writer uses words to speak to your senses.

- **Symbols:** It can be easy to confuse symbols with metaphors. A metaphor is a comparison of two unlike objects or concepts, whereas a symbol is one thing that stands for another. The dove, for example, can be a symbol for peace, just as the heart is a common symbol for love. A symbol's context will often suggest its meaning.

- **Sound and rhythm:** Because of the musical nature of their work, poets are especially concerned with the sound and rhythm, or *meter*, of words in a text. Common devices that involve sound include *onomatopoeia* (the sound of the word suggesting its meaning) and *alliteration* (the repetition of the same consonant sounds at the start of words near each other in a text.)

- **Tone:** Tone is the mood or feeling the writer creates about the subject matter of a text. The tone might be serious or comical, angry or sad, optimistic or pessimistic, for example. Once you have an idea about the tone of a piece, ask yourself how the writer achieves it—through imagery, descriptive details, diction, or symbols, for instance.

- **Visual, dramatic, or cinematic elements:** Media such as film and television are primarily visual and thus involve specialized technical elements—shots, scenes, camera angles, lighting, and so on. When you undertake a writing project that focuses on a visual or multimedia text, your instructor may explain relevant terminology and elements in class. If you're unsure, ask which devices he or she expects you to be familiar with.

## 11b What approaches can you use to write about literature?

When you begin a literary analysis, have a general strategy in mind. The following approaches are common; you can often choose one or two of these as the framework for your paper.

**●1 Perform a close reading.** A "close reading" of a text carefully explains the meaning and possible interpretations of a selected passage, sometimes line by line (or, in the case of film, shot by shot or scene by scene). In a close reading, you ordinarily consider how the language of a work makes readers entertain specific ideas and images. If a work includes visual images, you may examine how they interact with elements of a written text. Sally Shelton's paper, which appears at the end of this chapter, offers close readings of several passages in a poem. (Also see Section 8a on how to read critically.)

**●2 Analyze key themes in a work.** Reading a work carefully, you might discover certain key themes. In examining a theme, show how the various parts of a work convey their meanings to readers. In this introduction to an essay exam for an American literature course, the student writer identifies a central theme—human selfishness—in Jonathan Swift's *Gulliver's Travels*.

> In *Gulliver's Travels*, Gulliver's sea voyages expose him to the best and worst aspects of human civilization. Through Gulliver's eyes, readers come to share Swift's perception that no matter how good people's intentions, their innate selfishness corrupts the social institutions they construct. All the societies Gulliver visits give evidence of this theme, but we see the problem especially clearly in his descriptions of Lilliput and Brobdingnag.

**●3 Analyze plot or structure.** You may study the way a work of literature is put together and consider why a writer chooses a particular arrangement of ideas or plot.

Here is an excerpt from a student's analysis of a subplot of Christopher Marlowe's play *Dr. Faustus*.

> There are two distinct plots in *Dr. Faustus*. The main plot chronicles Faustus's bargain with the devil and fall into damnation, while the subplot shows the humorous adventures of Faustus's servant Wagner during the same period. Although at first the two plots may seem unrelated, the subplot serves three important functions in the play. It serves the practical purpose of creating a break between the main plot's scenes; it provides comic relief from the tragic tone of the play; and finally, the subplot reinforces the play's moral message.

**4 Analyze character or setting.** You may study the behavior of characters in a novel, poem, play, or short story to understand their motivations and the ways in which different characters relate to each other. Or you can explore how a writer creates characters through description, action, reaction, and dialogue and embodies them with specific themes and ideas. The following paragraph from an essay by student writer Joshua Michael French offers a close reading of the central character in Herman Melville's short story "Bartleby the Scrivener":

> By denying his responsibilities and avoiding conflict with the narrator of the story, Bartleby displays his central character trait: alienation. The narrator calls the scrivener into his office to ask him a few simple questions and even offers Bartleby his friendship, but there is no emotional response. Instead, Bartleby stares blankly and refuses the narrator's advances as usual. The narrator notes that Bartleby "[keeps] his glance fixed upon [his] bust of Cicero" (122) instead of looking directly at him. Even when the narrator comments, "I feel friendly towards you" (122), there is no response from Bartleby. His lack of connection with others is absolute.

Similarly, you might study an artist's creation of a setting to figure out how the environment of a work (where things happen in a novel, short story, or play) affects what happens in the plot or to the characters. Settings can also be analyzed as the exterior representations of characters' inner being or as manifestations of cultural values.

**5 Analyze the text as an example of a particular genre.** You can study a particular work by evaluating its form—tragedy, comic novel, sonnet, detective story, epic, situation comedy, film noir, and so on. Compare the work to other literary pieces of that genre, looking for similarities and differences and perhaps comment on the relative quality of the achievement.

The *Lord of the Rings* series, from which this still is taken (*The Return of the King*, 2003), is among the most critically successful fantasy films ever made. If you have seen one or more films in the series, what is your opinion of the films' quality? What features, if any, do you believe set them apart from other films of this genre? If you haven't seen the *Lord of the Rings*, think of another film that you believe is an excellent or interesting example of its genre, and summarize the elements that you believe make it noteworthy.

**6 Explore a historical or cultural analysis.** You can study a literary work as it reflects the society that produced it or as it was accepted or rejected by that society when it was published. Or you can study the way historical information makes a literary work from an earlier time clearer to a reader today.

You can similarly explore how a work of art embodies the culture that produced it. That is, what assumptions about the beliefs and values of a society can be found in the literary work? Such analysis may reveal how certain groups gained or maintained power through the manipulation of literary myths or symbols.

This etching depicts the famous orphanage scene from Charles Dickens's novel *Oliver Twist*, in which young Oliver pleads for a second helping of gruel. What might a scene such as this one suggest about life in Victorian England? If you are familiar with this novel, what other scenes and details can you recall that reinforce or complicate the impression given in this scene? If you were asked to write a historical analysis of the novel, what might you look for in the text to develop your analysis?

**●7 Analyze a work from the perspective of gender.** You might examine how a literary work portrays women or men and defines their roles in society. Feminist analyses in particular have greatly influenced the reading of literary works in the last generation, though such interpretations vary as much as any other form of criticism. Many feminist critics explore the way literary works embody relationships of power between men and women. Sally Shelton's paper, which appears on pages 179–182, is an example of this kind of analysis.

**●8 Examine the biography of the author or the author's creative process.** Such analyses may be related to cultural and political studies, but they may also focus on the individual psychology of a writer. Similarly, you might learn all you can about the way a particular work was created. You might examine the sources, notes, influences, manuscripts, and revised texts behind a finished book, poem, or film. Or you might compare different versions of the same work. In the following example, taken from the introduction of a paper written for a composition course, student writer Kathryn R. Samra draws on information about author Langston Hughes's life to interpret "Theme for English B," a poem about being the only black person in a literature class.

Known for his ability to mix popular culture and radical politics with poetry and a few jazzy beats, Langston Hughes became a prominent figure of the Harlem Renaissance. Born in 1902, Hughes lived during a time when African Americans were finally able to express the types of music and literature that were a part of their cultural history. And when he died at the age of 65, it was at the pinnacle of the civil rights movement, when African Americans were beginning to be treated as equals. Most of Hughes's poetry reflects this point in his life. His poem "Theme for English B," although not written as a protest poem, demonstrates how he felt as a black person growing up in Harlem.

**9 Edit a text or produce a literary Web site.** One type of literary work increasingly common in college settings is the production of literary journals or, more recently, Web sites that focus on cultural ideas and themes. Introducing new works is an important creative responsibility that requires the careful selection and editing of texts—an important way of going public with writing. Whether in print or on the Web, you can present and comment on new works or edit older, neglected texts in the public domain. For an example of an undergraduate literary journal published online, see *Aurora*, published at Eastern Kentucky University (<http://studentweb.eku.edu/aurora/>).

## 11c What sources can you use in writing essays about literature?

The resources available to you as you begin a literary analysis can seem overwhelming. But many of them will in fact make your work easier, more authoritative, and more interesting.

**1 Understand the primary texts you are reading.** In working with literary and cultural texts, you may first need to establish certain basic facts about them. Are you reading (or viewing) a first edition of a work or a revised version, an edited version, a translation, or, in the case of a film, a later "director's cut" that differs from the version shown in theaters? Each of these considerations may have a bearing on your subsequent analysis. Evaluate any publication information you find in the prefaces or front matter of works of literature to discover when they were written, by whom they were published, how they might have been transmitted to readers, and how they may have changed over the years. In general, the older a work, the more complicated (and fascinating) its publication history might be. But even more recent texts deserve your attention. The techniques of positioning that you apply to research materials (see Section 45b) can be modified to work with literary and cultural texts before you analyze them.

**2 Consult secondary sources on literary subjects.** To locate secondary sources on literary topics, begin with the following indexes and bibliographies available in a library reference room.

> *Essay and General Literature Index*
>
> *MLA International Bibliography*
>
> *New Cambridge Bibliography of English Literature*
>
> *Year's Work in English Studies*

Many other useful reference works and Web sites are available; see Checklist 11.2.

---

**Checklist 11.2 Reference Works for Literary Analyses**

**PRINTED TEXTS**

Aaronson, Charles S. *International Motion Picture and Television Almanac.* New York: Quigley Publications, 1930- . Annual.

Beacham, Walton, ed. *Research Guide to Biography and Criticism.* Washington, DC: Research, 1990.

Bloom, Harold. *American Women Fiction Writers, 1900–1960.* 3 vols. Philadelphia: Chelsea, 1997–1999.

Crystal, David. *The Cambridge Encyclopedia of Language.* 2nd ed. New York: Cambridge UP, 1997.

*(Continued)*

**Reference Works for Literary Analyses** *(Continued)*

Drabble, Margaret, ed. *The Oxford Companion to English Literature.* 6th. ed.
2nd rev. Oxford: Oxford UP, 2006.

*Encyclopedia of World Literature in the Twentieth Century.* 3rd ed. Farmington
Hills: St. James, 1999.

Evans, Gareth L., and Barbara Evans. *The Shakespeare Companion.* New York:
Scribner's, 1978.

Gates, Henry Louis, Jr., et al. *The Norton Anthology of African American Literature.*
2nd ed. New York: Norton, 2004.

Gilbert, Sandra M., and Susan Gubar. *The Norton Anthology of Literature by
Women: The Traditions in English.* 3rd ed. New York: Norton, 2007.

Harmon, William, and C. Hugh Holman. *A Handbook to Literature.* 10th ed. New
York: Prentice, 2005.

Harner, James L. *Literary Research Guide: A Guide to Reference Sources for the Study
of Literature in English and Related Topics.* 3rd ed. New York: MLA, 1998.

Hart, James D., ed. *The Oxford Companion to American Literature.* 6th ed. New
York: Oxford UP, 1995.

Hayward, Susan. *Key Concepts in Cinema Studies.* 2nd ed. London; New York:
Routledge, 2000.

Howatson, M. C. *The Oxford Companion to Classical Literature.* Rev. ed. New York:
Oxford UP, 2006.

Modern Language Association. *MLA Handbook for Writers of Research Papers.*
7th ed. New York: MLA, 2009.

Sage, Lorna. *The Cambridge Guide to Women's Writing in English.* Cambridge:
Cambridge UP, 1999.

Sampson, George. *The Concise Cambridge History of English Literature.* 3rd ed.
Cambridge: Cambridge UP, 1972.

**WEB RESOURCES**

*The Complete Works of William Shakespeare.* <http://the-tech.mit.edu/
Shakespeare>.

*(Continued)*

**Reference Works for Literary Analyses** *(Continued)*

*The English Server.* <http://eserver.org>.

*Literary Resources on the Net.* <http://andromeda.rutgers.edu/~jlynch/Lit>.

*MLA on the Web.* <http://www.mla.org>.

*The On-Line Books Page.* <http://digital.library.upenn.edu/books>.

*The Browne Popular Culture Library.* <http://www.bgsu.edu/colleges/library/pcl/pcl.html>.

University of Virginia Library Electronic Text Center. <http://etext.lib.virginia.edu>.

*Voice of the Shuttle.* <http://vos.ucsb.edu/shuttle/english.html>.

*Yahoo! Arts: Humanities: Literature.* <http://www.yahoo.com/Arts/Humanities/Literature>.

# 11d How do you develop a literary project?

How you develop a literary paper or project will depend on your course assignment and your own purpose. In some courses you'll be asked to do a close reading of an individual poem, novel, or short story; in others you may be expected to contribute to a Web site that places artists or works in their historical or political contexts. Here we assume that you are most likely to write a paper with a thesis—but the principles we discuss will apply to other projects as well.

**1 Begin by reading carefully.** The evidence you'll need to write a thoughtful, well-organized analysis may come from within the literary work itself and from outside readings and secondary sources. Your initial goal is to find a point worth making, an assertion you can prove with convincing evidence.

To find your point, begin by *positioning* the work (or works) and then reading and *annotating* them carefully (see Sections 8a and 45b).

Assigned to read Shakespeare's *Macbeth*, you might position the work by doing a little background reading (see Section 11b). You'd quickly learn that

*Macbeth* is a tragedy written by the most famous of English playwrights around 1605–06, though not published until 1623. An unusually brief tragedy, *Macbeth* may have been designed expressly to please the English monarch James I, who was fascinated by witches and whose legendary ancestor appears in the play.

Yet you should also read with an open mind, being certain to savor the literary experience. Do, however, annotate texts in some way to record your immediate responses. You might simply ask yourself a series of questions.

- What issues engage me immediately as I read the work?
- What puzzles or surprises me?
- What characters or literary devices seem most striking or original?
- What upsets me or seems most contrary to my own values and traditions?

Make a list of such queries as you read, and reexamine them when you have finished. At this point you might stimulate your thinking both by considering specific ways of approaching a literary text (see Sections 11b and 11c) and by using one of the techniques we describe for finding and focusing ideas, particularly brainstorming and idea mapping (see Sections 2a and 2b).

**2 Develop a thesis about the literary work(s) you are studying.** Begin with questions you are eager to explore in depth, a research query or hypothesis generated perhaps by your reading of secondary sources or by your discussions with classmates. When you've put your question into words, test its energy. Is the answer to your inquiry so obvious that it isn't likely to interest or surprise anyone?

- Is Shakespeare's *Macbeth* a great play?

If so, discard the issue. Try another. Look for a surprising, even startling question—one whose answer you don't necessarily know. Test that question on classmates or your instructor.

- Could Shakespeare's *Macbeth* actually be a comedy?
- What role do the lower classes play in a dynastic struggle like the one depicted in *Macbeth*?
- Are the witches really the physical embodiment of Macbeth's own mind?

When you have found your question, turn it into a claim—your preliminary thesis statement.

- Shakespeare's *Macbeth* is really a comedy.
- The welfare of the lower classes seems to have been ignored in dynastic struggles like those depicted in *Macbeth*.
- The witches in *Macbeth* are a physical representation of the state of Macbeth's mind.

**⬤3 Read the work(s) again with your thesis firmly in mind.**
Look for characters, incidents, descriptions, speeches, dialogue, or images that support or refute your thesis. Take careful notes. If you are using your own text, highlight significant passages in the work. When you are done, evaluate the evidence you have gathered from a close reading. Then modify or qualify your thesis to reflect what you have learned or discovered. In most cases, your thesis will be more specific and more limited after you have gathered and assessed your evidence.

- The many unexpected comic moments in *Macbeth* emphasize how disordered the world becomes for murderers like Macbeth and his wife.

When necessary, return to secondary sources or other literary works to supplement and extend your analysis. Play with ideas, relationships, implications, and possibilities. Don't hesitate to question conventional views of a work or to bring your own experiences to bear on the act of reading and interpreting literature. Be sure also to keep accurate bibliographic information for your Works Cited page. (See Chapter 43 on planning a research project.)

**⬤4 Use scratch outlines to guide the first draft.** Try out several organization plans for the paper (see Section 3c), and then choose the one you find most solid or most challenging. Here's how a scratch outline for a paper on comic elements in *Macbeth* might look.

<u>Thesis</u>: Comic moments in <u>Macbeth</u> emphasize how disordered the world becomes for the Macbeths after they murder the king.

I. Comic moments after the murder of King Duncan

II. Comedy at the feast for Banquo

III. Comedy in the sleepwalking scene

IV. Conclusion

When you have a structure, write a complete first draft. Stay open to new ideas and refinements of your original thesis, but try not to wander off into a biography of the author or a discussion of the historical period unless such material relates directly to your thesis. If you do wander, consider whether the digression in your draft might be the topic you *really* want to write about.

Avoid the draft that simply paraphrases the plot of a literary work. Equally ineffective is a paper that merely praises its author for a job well done. Avoid extremely impressionistic judgments: "I feel that Hemingway must have been a good American." And don't expect to find a moral in every literary work, or turn your analysis into a search for "hidden meanings." Respond honestly to what you are reading—not the way you think your teacher expects you to. (For full examples of literary papers, see Sally Shelton's essay on pages 179–182 and the paper demonstrating Chicago Manual documentation style in Chapter 52.)

**5 Follow the conventions of literary analysis.** One of those conventions is to introduce most direct quotations. Don't just insert a quotation from a literary work or a critic into your paper without identifying it and explaining its significance. And be sure quotations fit into the grammar of your sentences.

> **The doctor in *Macbeth* warns the gentlewoman,** "You have known what you should not" (5.1.46–47).

> **Commenting on the play, Frank Kermode observes that** "*Macbeth* has extraordinary energy; it represents a fierce engagement between the mind and its guilt" (1311).

In shaping the paper, you may want to follow the conventions of the MLA research paper or the *Chicago Manual of Style* paper (see Chapters 50 and 52). Check with your instructor to find out which form he or she prefers.

---

**Checklist 11.3**    **Conventions in a Literary Paper**

- **Use the present tense to refer to events occurring in a literary work:** Hester Prynne *wears* a scarlet letter, Hamlet *kills* Polonius.

- **Identify passages of short poems by line numbers:** (*"Journey of the Magi,"* lines 21–31). Avoid the abbreviations *l.* or *ll.* for *line* or *lines* because they are sometimes confused with roman numerals; spell out the words. See Section 40d-4 for advice on punctuating lines of poetry that appear within a paper.

- **Provide act and scene divisions (and line numbers as necessary) for passages from plays.** Act and scene numbers are now usually given in Arabic numerals, although Roman numerals are still common and acceptable: *Ham.* 4.5.179–85 or *Ham.* IV.v.179–86. The titles of Shakespeare's works are commonly abbreviated in citations: *Mac.* 1.2; *Oth.* 2.2. Check to see which form your instructor prefers.

- **Provide a date of publication in parentheses after your first mention of a literary work:** Before publishing *Beloved* (1987), Toni Morrison had written. . . .

- **Use technical terms accurately.** Spell the names of characters correctly. Take special care with matters of grammar and mechanics.

---

**GOING PUBLIC**    **A Literary Analysis Paper**

In the following literary analysis, "Queen Jane Approximately" (a clever allusion to a song by Bob Dylan), Sally Shelton from the University of South Carolina does a close reading of a poem by Sharon Olds, "The One Girl at the Boys' Party." She approaches the work from a feminist perspective, examining the interplay of gender roles between one young girl and a group of boys. Shelton supports her analysis by carefully citing passages from the poem, which we have reprinted in its entirety.

The One Girl at the Boys' Party
By Sharon Olds

| | |
|---|---|
| When I take my girl to the swimming party | 1 |
| I set her down among the boys. They tower and | 2 |
| bristle, she stands there smooth and sleek, | 3 |
| her math scores unfolding in the air around her. | 4 |
| They will strip to their suits, her body hard and | 5 |
| indivisible as a prime number, | 6 |
| they'll plunge in the deep end, she'll subtract | 7 |
| her height from ten feet, divide it into | 8 |
| hundreds of gallons of water, the numbers | 9 |
| bouncing in her mind like molecules of chlorine | 10 |
| in the bright blue pool. When they climb out, | 11 |
| her ponytail will hang its pencil lead | 12 |
| down her back, her narrow silk suit | 13 |
| with hamburgers and french fries printed on it | 14 |
| will glisten in the brilliant air, and they will | 15 |
| see her sweet face, solemn and | 16 |
| sealed, a factor of one, and she will | 17 |
| see their eyes, two each, | 18 |
| their legs, two each, and the curves of their sexes, | 19 |
| one each, and in her head she'll be doing her | 20 |
| wild multiplying, as the drops | 21 |
| sparkle and fall to the power of a thousand from her body. | 22 |

Sally Shelton

Professor Moore

English 102

21 April 2006

### Queen Jane Approximately

Sharon Olds's "The One Girl at the Boys' Party" examines the
tense competition between the sexes. The poem illustrates the innate
vulnerability of men while portraying females as winning attention

and respect they rightfully deserve. Olds achieves these insights by examining the isolation of a young girl at a party of boys. She infuses the situation with ironies and repeated images that probe themes of gender, sexuality, and domination.

The poem deceives the reader initially by putting the youths in typical gender roles. The speaker takes her daughter (1) to a party where she "set[s] her down among the boys" (2) like a toy or doll for their amusement. She is placed within a situation where she must prove herself. The boys, in turn, "tower and / bristle" (2-3) at the intrusion. While she is being "set down," the boys move like a gang, intimidating and, perhaps, angry. Yet suddenly, the attention of the poem shifts from the girl to the boys as the young woman quickly and nonchalantly asserts her dominance over them.

The contrast between the girl and the group of boys is established early in the poem. While the boys "tower and bristle," the lone girl "stands there smooth and sleek" (3), firmly placed, establishing her ground, unabated in her delicate sensuality, and controlling the air about her. It is in this "brilliant air" (15) that her "math scores" (4) begin to unfold. References to mathematics throughout the poem illustrate how the young girl, and perhaps the speaker of the poem, have conquered the situation already. They have figured the boys out through methodical and meticulous calculations.

To complete the reversal of gender roles, the boys, who were the first to dominate in the poem, assume a subordinate and effeminate role. As if to expose themselves as sensual and enticing beings, "[t]hey will strip to their suits" (5), leaving themselves vulnerable (she can count the "curves of their sexes" [19]) and hoping that the girl will "strip" to her vulnerability as well. The girl, however, remains in control, "her body hard and / indivisible as a prime number" (5-6). The pool of males will forever attempt to figure her out, but she has solved them. She stands before the boys in the pool, with "the numbers / bouncing in her mind" (9-10), her calculations racing. She, who was initially perceived as an intrusion, has now silently attracted the curiosity of the boys.

Now that the girl's presence has consumed the scene, the boys become enchanted by her sensuality. The infinite "molecules of chlorine" (10) that comprise the girl's intelligence intoxicate the boys, who have by now succumbed to the innocent appeal of "the bright blue pool" (11). Sexual desires come into play: her tomboyish ponytail catches their gaze. Although it "hang[s] its pencil lead" (12), a phallic symbol with piercing connotations, the boys still allow their gaze to follow the ponytail "down her back" (13). Then they notice the girl's figure, more "smooth and sleek" (3) than before, in "her narrow silk suit" (13) with the mouth-watering "hamburgers and french fries printed on it" (14) that "glisten in the brilliant air" (15). Lastly, they notice her face, "sweet," "solemn," and "sealed" (16-17). No longer an object to discard, the girl becomes for the boys an embodiment of a desire that will never be satiated.

Again, the speaker widens the schism between the girl and the youths. It began with the girl doing all the observing and calculating, but soon the boys catch on. Threatened by her ability to strip them, they "plunge in the deep end" (7), hoping to hide their vulnerability while attempting to entice the girl. The act of plunging is risky and the boys nearly drown in their attempts to impress her. Defeated and weakened, they have to "climb out" (11), and they discover how badly they are getting beaten. Then they enter the game, the observed becoming the observers. While the boys "see her sweet face . . . a factor of one", the girl outnumbers them when she "see[s] their eyes, two each,/their legs, two each, and the curves of their sexes, / one each". She sheds some power when she lets her "drops / sparkle and fall", but they will never gain a hold on her because she will forever "be doing her / wild multiplying". The boys cannot enumerate her "to the power of a thousand" (22), so her "power" controls and overwhelms them. She has reduced these once towering and bristling boys to vulnerable, starstruck subordinates by daring them to plunge into the deep end of womanhood.

Through the character of the girl, the speaker offers insight into how women encompass an infinite power and elegance that men miscalculate and misunderstand. The girl triumphs while the boys sink into her deep intelligence, stamina, and sensuality. In the game of relationships, here staged as a pool party, there are those who tower, those who plunge, and those who calculate.

Work Cited

Olds, Sharon. "The One Girl at the Boys' Party." *The Dead and the Living*. New York: Knopf, 1984. Print.

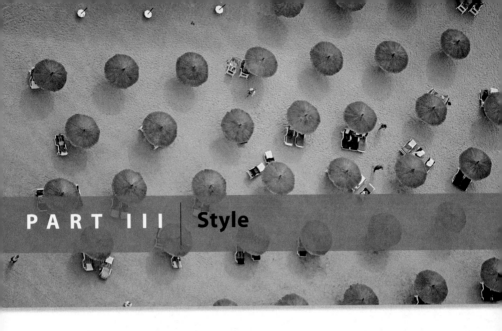

# PART III | Style

# 12 What Makes Paragraphs Work?

Imagine how you'd feel if you opened a newspaper and saw pages filled with a single, unbroken stretch of print. You'd probably think, "I'll never be able to keep this straight"—and you'd be right. When writers organize material into paragraph form, treating a single idea in each paragraph and connecting the paragraphs to each other, readers can follow the material more easily. Paragraphing also makes a text look visually inviting, drawing readers in and encouraging them to read on.

How do the paragraph breaks, images, and headlines help readers to navigate the array of information on this newspaper front page? How would the effect differ if all the text were presented in a single, unbroken stretch?

## 12a How do you construct unified paragraphs?

When we say that a paragraph is *unified*, we mean that it makes a single point and develops it, without detours into irrelevant or tangential information.

● 1 **Find a focus and stick with it.** In a unified paragraph, you can follow the author's thinking because he or she concentrates on a single idea. Here's a professional example about golf:

Here, primarily, is what's wrong with Phil Mickelson, Sergio Garcia, David Duval, Justin Leonard, Jesper Parnevik, Lee Westwood, Darren Clarke, Jim Furyk and a handful of others: They were born at the wrong time. They were born too close to Tiger Woods, the same way Charles Barkley, Patrick Ewing, Karl Malone and John Stockton were born at the wrong time, too close to Michael Jordan. That's all they were guilty of, being in the wrong place at the wrong time for pretty much the duration of their careers.

—Michael Wilbon, "It's Just Tiger's Time"

Suppose, however, that this writer had written his first sentence and then gone off in another direction, jotting down sentences as they occurred to him. The paragraph might have turned out like this:

Here, primarily, is what's wrong with Phil Mickelson, Sergio Garcia, David Duval, Justin Leonard, Jesper Parnevik, Lee Westwood, Darren Clarke, Jim Furyk and a handful of others: They were born at the wrong time. Since Tiger Woods has come along, everything in golf has changed. There are more fans watching the game on TV, and Woods is becoming one of the world's best-known people because of all his endorsement deals. Some courses are even changing their layouts to try to "Tiger-proof" them.

Now the paragraph lacks unity because the writer opens with a statement and then, instead of expanding on it or following through with connected examples, jumps into several new subjects.

When you begin a paragraph, first ask yourself, "What point am I trying to make?" and then check your draft periodically to be sure you haven't strayed from your purpose.

**● 2 Anchor your paragraph with a topic sentence.** One way to keep a paragraph focused is to use a *topic sentence* that states your main idea clearly and directly. The topic sentence doesn't have to be the first one in the paragraph, although it often is, particularly in academic writing.

**Sleep has become another casualty of modern life.** According to sleep researchers, studies point to a "sleep deficit" among Americans, a majority of whom are currently getting between 60 and 90 minutes less a night than they should for optimum health and performance. The number of people showing up at sleep disorder clinics with serious problems has skyrocketed in the last decade. Shift work, long working hours, the growth of a global economy (with its attendant continent-hopping and twenty-four-hour business culture), and the accelerating pace of life have all contributed to sleep deprivation. If you need an alarm clock, the experts warn, you're probably sleeping too little.

—Juliet Schor, *The Overworked American*

A writer can also lead up to a topic sentence (or topic sentences), first giving readers details that build their interest and then summarizing the content in one sentence.

In 1938, near the end of a decade of monumental turmoil, the year's number-one newsmaker was not Franklin Delano Roosevelt, Hitler, or Mussolini. It wasn't Pope Pius XI, nor was it Lou Gehrig, Howard Hughes, or Clark Gable. **The subject of the most newspaper column inches in 1938 wasn't even a person. It was an undersized, crooked-legged racehorse named Seabiscuit.**

—Laura Hillenbrand, *Seabiscuit: An American Legend*

Not all paragraphs have topic sentences, nor do they need them, since writers can unify paragraphs in a number of ways. But they work especially well to anchor and control the flow of ideas in academic writing. By reading from one topic sentence to the next in the paragraphs that make up your paper, you can usually tell if you're developing your thesis as you have planned. For more on organizing a draft around a thesis, see Section 3c.

## ● 3 Use internal transitions to unify your paragraphs.

Even when you have a clear focus, the connections among sentences or ideas in a paragraph may not always be immediately apparent to readers. In such cases, you'll need to incorporate *internal transitions*—words and phrases that act like traffic signals to move readers from one point in an argument or explanation to another.

Consider this paragraph from a student draft. It is focused on a single issue—the rise of cheating on campus—but the first version seems choppy because it lacks internal transitions.

**WEAK TRANSITIONS**

Cheating has become frighteningly common. My roommate brought her mother to campus to complain when she failed Spanish for copying her term paper from a Web site. My English professor reported two students in my English literature class to the dean for allowing a high school teacher to write a paper for them. The Academic Affairs office reported that academic misconduct is up by 30 percent over last year. What is happening on our campus? Parents and teachers once instilled in students the value of doing one's own work instead of cheating.

**INTERNAL TRANSITIONS ADDED**

Cheating is becoming frighteningly common **on our campus**. **Last week** my roommate brought her mother to campus to complain when she failed Spanish for copying her term paper from a Web site. **Earlier this semester**, my English literature professor reported two students to the dean for allowing a high school teacher to write a paper for them. **These cases are not unusual, campus officials say.** The Academic Affairs office reported **last week** that academic dishonesty cases are up by 30 percent over last year. What is happening on our campus? Parents and teachers **used to** instill in students the value of work; **now** many are encouraging them to **cheat**.

To incorporate internal transitions into a paragraph you've written, try these strategies:

- **Use transition words** such as *first, next, however,* and *in addition* to show the relationships among sentences and ideas. See Section 14b-1 for a list of such words.
- **Repeat key words or phrases** to tie related sentences together. The paragraph above, for example, repeats the terms *dishonesty* and *cheating* to connect the examples of cheating on campus. See Section 14b-2 for more on using repetition.
- **Use parallel phrases**—phrases that begin with the same word or that share the same grammatical structure—to emphasize connections among similar examples or related pieces of information. For more on using parallel structure to unify a paragraph, see Section 14b-5.

See Chapter 14 for a detailed discussion of transitions.

**EXERCISE 12.1** Identify the strategies the writer has used to unify the following paragraph: Is there a topic sentence? Do you see transition words, repetition, or parallel structures? Then discuss whether and how these devices helped you follow the writer's ideas.

> Day 1 set the tone for our really heavy driving days: We stopped only for gasoline and bathroom breaks, which usually coincided after 350 to 400 miles. We averaged about 70 mph for at least 14 hours. We ate what we had in the car or what we could get from travel plazas and gas stations. We didn't run the air conditioning, though we never talked about why. We didn't listen to the radio much because we had the windows down and could barely hear. We discussed—in shouts—whatever popped into our heads: "What just hit the windshield?" "Did you see what was growing in that bathroom?" "Kansas doesn't look so flat at night." "If there is a hell, do you think I-70 is it?" We slept in cheap motels because we were too tired to pitch a tent by the time we stopped. We thought we would get farther than we did.
>
> —Lee Bauknight, "Two for the Road"

**EXERCISE 12.2** Examine critically one or two paragraphs of a draft you're currently working on: Do the paragraphs seem adequately unified? What unifying strategies have you used? Can you think of others that might be useful?

## 12b How can you organize paragraphs?

Why do specific organizational patterns recur in writing? Perhaps these patterns emerge because they resemble typical ways of thinking. Whatever their origins, the paragraph patterns discussed in this section are common, and writers looking for a way to begin a draft can profit by trying them.

● **1 Illustration.** A paragraph of illustration begins with a general statement or claim and develops it with supporting details, evidence, or examples. In an argument paper, writers often follow a general claim with one or more pieces of supporting evidence.

> For more than 40 states, the days of traditional multiple-choice tests that required teachers to set aside real learning and teach test-taking

skills are fading. Today's tests often include open-ended questions, demand writing samples, and require students to show, honestly and accurately, what they know. The new tests ask students to solve complex mathematics problems and explain solutions, to critically examine literary techniques and articulate their thinking in written essays. That's a far cry from drills in information regurgitation. On the recent New York state test for 11th-graders, 92 percent passed the new, tougher test in English language arts. This kind of testing leads to better teaching. It also tells elected officials and educators where they ought to direct resources and efforts.

—Louis V. Gerstner, Jr., "High Marks for Standardized Tests"

**2 Question and answer.** Asking and answering a question is another way to organize a paragraph.

How good are graphic novels, really? Are these truly what our great-grandchildren will be reading, instead of books without pictures? Hard to say. Some of them are much better than others, obviously, but this is true of books of any kind. And the form is better suited to certain themes and kinds of expression than others. One thing the graphic novel can do particularly well, for example, is depict the passage of time, slow or fast or both at once—something the traditional novel can approximate only with empty space. The graphic novel can make the familiar look new. The autobiographical hero of Craig Thompson's *Blankets*, a guilt-ridden teenager falling in love for the first time, would be insufferably predictable in a prose narrative; here, he has an innocent sweetness.

—Charles McGrath, "Not Funnies"

**3 Narration or process.** One way to develop a paragraph is to relate events or the steps of a process in chronological order. This pattern is obviously appropriate for writing personal or historical accounts, but you can also use it effectively to describe a scientific or technical process.

The clanking from within the giant white magnetic resonance imaging (MRI) scanner sounds like somebody banging a wrench on a radiator. "Tommy," a healthy 8-year-old, is halfway inside the machine's

round chamber, and his little white-sweat-socked feet keep time with the noise. A mirror on a plastic cage around his head will allow him to see images and video. During the next 45 minutes, Dr. Golijeh Golarai, a researcher at Stanford University, will ask Tommy to hold his feet still as she directs a computer to flash pictures at him, including faces of African American men, landscapes, faces of white men, then scrambled faces in a cubist redux. When the boy thinks he sees the same image twice, he pushes a button. The machine is tracking the blood in his brain as it flows to the neurons he is using to perform the assigned task.
  —Joan O'C. Hamilton, "Journey to the Center of the Mind"

● **4 Definition.** Paragraphs of definition often work well in the first part of a report or article that explains or argues. They help to establish the meaning of important terms the author is going to use.

From kids and people my own age I picked up *Pachuco*. *Pachuco* (the language of the zoot suiters) is a language of rebellion, both against Standard Spanish and Standard English. It is a secret language. Adults of the culture and outsiders cannot understand it. It is made up of slang words from both English and Spanish. *Ruca* means girl or woman, *vato* means guy or dude, *chale* means no, *simón* means yes, *churo* is sure, talk is *periquiar*, *pigionear* means petting, *que gacho* means how nerdy, *ponte águila* means watch out, death is called *la pelona*. Through lack of practice and not having others who can speak it, I've lost most of the *Pachuco* tongue.
  —Gloria Anzaldúa, "How to Tame a Wild Tongue"

● **5 Classification.** A classification paragraph that divides a subject into the categories to be discussed can work well as the opening paragraph of a paper or a section of a paper. Used this way, it helps to unify the essay by forecasting its organization. ·

In fact, over the past two decades, there have been essentially two forces contributing new words to the language: rap music and business consultants. One gave us "dis," "props," and "for shizzle"; the other gave us "proactive," "synergy," and "agent of change."
  —Adam Sternbergh, "Got Bub All Up in the Hizzle, Yo!"

**●6 Comparison and contrast.** A paragraph can also be built on a comparison-and-contrast pattern. The following example, taken from a report on homeless youth in New York City, sets up a comparison in the first sentence.

> While urban nomads and the city's traditional homeless youth often share a history of physical or sexual abuse, the two groups differ in many respects. Typically, New York's population of runaways and homeless youths is heavily minority and includes both girls and boys. By contrast, urban nomads tend to be white and largely male, with backgrounds that are typically working-class and occasionally middle-class. Many are children from homes where a parent's remarriage has produced family conflicts. Others are simply bored.
>
> — Alison Stateman, "Postcards from the Edge"

**●7 Cause and effect.** Cause-and-effect paragraphs can proceed in two ways: they can mention the effect first and then describe the causes, or they can start by giving causes and close with the effect. We illustrate both patterns here.

**CAUSE TO EFFECT**

Once overhunted, white-tailed deer have returned in such explosive numbers that they're ravaging forestland and besieging rural and even suburban communities. The animals cause car accidents, carry ticks that can transmit infectious diseases to people, chew up landscaping, and otherwise make pests of themselves, albeit sometimes strikingly graceful ones.

—Anne Broache, "Oh Deer!"

**EFFECT FOLLOWED BY CAUSES**

Why do so many citizens of the world's oldest democracy not vote when they can, at a time when the struggle for democracy in Europe and throughout the rest of the world has reached its most crucial and inspiring level since 1848? Partly, it's an administrative problem—the disappearance of the old party-machine and ward system, whose last vestige was Mayor Daley. Whatever its abuses, it got people street by street, household by household, to the ballot boxes. Its patronage system did help tie American people, especially blue-collar and lower middle-class ones, to the belief that they as citizens had some role to play in the running of their country from the bottom up, ward by ward. It reinforced the sense of participatory democracy.

—Robert Hughes, *The Culture of Complaint*

● **8 Analogy.** An **analogy** is an extended comparison. One especially good use of analogy is to help readers understand a concept by showing a resemblance between a familiar idea and an unfamiliar one.

Short-order cooking is like driving a car: anyone can do it up to a certain speed. The difference between an amateur and a crack professional isn't so much a matter of specific skills as of consistency and timing. Most diner kitchens are fairly forgiving places. You can break a yolk or two, lose track of an order, or overcook an omelette and start again without getting swamped. But as the pace increases those tolerances disappear. At the Tropical Breeze, a single mistake can throw an entire sequence out of kilter, so that every dish is either cold or overdone. A cook of robotic efficiency, moving steadily from task to task, suddenly slips a cog and becomes Lucy in the chocolate factory, stuffing candies into her mouth as they pile up on the assembly line.

—Burkhard Bilger, "The Egg Men"

**EXERCISE 12.3** Use the paragraph patterns discussed and illustrated in Sections 12b-1 through 12b-8 to write paragraphs for two of the following situations.

1. Summarize the arguments on one side of a local controversy you feel strongly about—for example, a new city ordinance, an upcoming election, or a controversial public event or program.

2. Explain how to operate a machine you use regularly—for instance, a PalmPilot, a jet ski, an iPod, or a coffeemaker.

3. Set up a classification of your relatives at a family get-together, the students in your major, the CDs in your personal collection, or the passengers you encounter every day on a bus or subway.

# 12c How can you create polished paragraphs?

A paragraph that's merely focused and well organized is like a family sedan: it gets your readers where they need to go, but the ride may lack pizzazz. If you want readers to enjoy and respond strongly to your writing, then craft paragraphs that are stylish and engaging as well as clear.

**◑ 1 Revise for variety.** Good paragraphs offer readers a mix of general statements and vivid details. This sort of variety keeps readers interested. Variety also helps to communicate your ideas: details help to illustrate abstract concepts that readers might otherwise find difficult, and general statements tie together details that might initially seem unrelated. Here is a writer clarifying a hard-to-grasp, abstract concept by helping us to picture it very specifically.

> The distinction between Newton and Einstein's ideas about gravitation has sometimes been illustrated by picturing **a little boy playing marbles in a city lot. The ground is very uneven, ridged with bumps and hollows. An observer in an office ten stories above the street would not be able to see these irregularities in the ground. Noticing that the marbles appear to avoid some sections of the ground and move toward other sections**, he might assume a "force" is operating which repels the marbles from certain spots and attracts them toward others. But **another observer on the ground would instantly perceive that the path of the marbles is simply governed by the curvature of the field**.
>
> —Lincoln Barnett, *The Universe and Dr. Einstein*

**EXERCISE 12.4** Imagine that you are writing a magazine article that includes one of the following paragraphs. Revise the paragraph, incorporating specific details, examples, or other material to add variety.

1. "Reality shows" dominate weekly television programming in the United States. There are more shows of this type each season, and their ratings are increasing. These shows often depict real people in physically dangerous or emotionally charged situations.

2. College and university officials see binge drinking as a serious problem on campuses nationwide. Recent studies have documented its widespread occurrence across different demographic groups and different types of schools.

●**2 Revise for economy.** Well-crafted paragraphs move readers smoothly from point to point without bogging down in unnecessary verbiage or repetition. When you revise a paragraph, you'll often have to gut whole phrases or sentences when they contribute little to your meaning. (See Section 17c for more advice on streamlining sentences.)

**INFLATED FIRST DRAFT**

~~Bicycles are a major form of transportation in many Third World countries because they are inexpensive and easy to maintain.~~ Nowhere are they more important than they are in China, where one can see masses of them on the streets in every city. ~~Probably no one knows how many bicycles there are in China, nor does there seem to be any way of finding out.~~ Virtually everyone seems to ride them—well-dressed businessmen with their briefcases strapped to the frame; a husband with his wife riding behind him and their child on the handlebars; women of all ages, some even in long, narrow dresses; and college students carrying their schoolbooks on their backs. The newly arrived American cyclist ~~in Beijing or Shanghai,~~ however, would be astonished ~~not only~~ to see ~~the great numbers of bicycles, but to see what kinds of bicycles the Chinese ride and~~ how many other uses, besides simply riding, the Chinese have been able to figure out for bicycles.

**REVISED FOR ECONOMY**

Although bicycles are a major form of transportation in all Asian countries, nowhere are they more important than in China, where one can see masses of them on the streets in every city. Virtually everyone seems to ride—well-dressed businessmen with their briefcases strapped to the frame; a husband with his wife behind him and their child on the handlebars; women of all ages, some even in long, narrow dresses; and college students carrying their books on their backs. The newly arrived American cyclist, however, would be astonished to see how many other uses, besides simply riding, the Chinese have for their bicycles.

**EXERCISE 12.5** Streamline and strengthen this paragraph from a student's first draft by trimming in places that seem wordy. You may need to cut or revise words, phrases, or whole sentences. Compare and contrast your revised version with a classmate's version.

> There are many different scholarly views concerning Alexander the Great's ultimate goal in relation to his military pursuits. Some historians consider Alexander to have been a power-hungry tyrant without whom the world would have been better off. Others see Alexander as the great unifier of humankind, one who attempted to bring together many cultures in one coherent empire. Others view him as the ultimate pragmatist—not necessarily having any preplanned goals and aspirations of conquering the world, but merely a king who made the very best of his existing circumstances. Some believe that Alexander's accomplishments were not great at all, but that most of what was written concerning Alexander is basically just a mixture of legend and myth. Others feel his achievements stand as monuments in human history to the enormous capability of the human spirit and will.

## 12d How can you improve paragraph appearance?

Writers need to think about how their work is going to look in print. If readers see a long stretch of text unbroken by paragraphs, white space, headings, dialogue, or images, most assume that the material will be hard to read. Your readers are much more likely to take a friendly attitude toward a piece when they can see that your paragraphs are fairly short. How short is a "fairly short" paragraph? Probably no more than seven or eight sentences—and in many cases, even fewer.

● **1 Break up long paragraphs that look hard to read.** You shouldn't chop up paragraphs arbitrarily just to make your paper look inviting; a paragraph is supposed to develop an idea, and it usually takes several sentences to do that. After you write a paragraph and reread it, use the items in Checklist 12.1 on page 196 to help you spot places to divide it.

---

**Checklist 12.1  Places to Break Up a Long Paragraph**

- **Shifts in time.** Look for spots where you have written words such as *at that time, then*, or *afterward* or have given other time signals.

- **Shifts in place.** Look for spots where you have written *another place* or *on the other side* or have used words that point to places.

- **Shifts in direction.** Look for spots where you have written *on the other hand, nevertheless*, or *however* or have otherwise indicated contrast.

- **Shifts in emphasis or focus.** Look for spots where you have shifted to a new point, perhaps using words such as *another, in addition*, or *not only*.

---

But don't break an entire paper into one- or two-sentence paragraphs. It's true that long paragraphs intimidate readers; however, too many short ones can distract them or make them feel the material is trivial. Extremely short paragraphs are best saved for special effects.

**2 Use short paragraphs for effect.** Don't be afraid to use one- or two-sentence paragraphs occasionally, but do so deliberately and to achieve a specific effect. Sometimes you may want to insert a very short paragraph to make a transition between two longer paragraphs. At other times you can use brevity for dramatic emphasis, as Natalie Angier has done in the passage below.

Ah, romance. Can any sight be as sweet as a pair of mallard ducks gliding gracefully across a pond, male by female, seemingly inseparable? Or, better yet, two trumpeter swans, the legendary symbols of eternal love, each ivory neck one half of a single heart, souls of a feather staying coupled together for life?

**Coupled for life—with just a bit of adultery, cuckoldry, and gang rape on the side.**

Alas for sentiment and the greeting card industry, it turns out that, in the animal kingdom, there is almost no such thing as monogamy. As a wealth of recent findings makes clear as a crocodile tear, even creatures long assumed to have faithful tendencies and to need a strong pair bond to rear their young are in fact perfidious brutes.

—Natalie Angier, "Mating for Life?"

**●3 Adapt paragraph length to your writing situation.** Finally, then, how long should a paragraph be? The answer, as you might expect, depends on your writing situation—your purpose, your audience, and your medium.

Intraguild Predation Among Larval Treehole Mosquitoes, *Aedes albopictus, Ae. aegypti,* and *Ae. triseriatus* (Diptera: Culicidae), in Laboratory Microcosms

J. S. EDGERLY,[1] M. S. WILLEY,[2] AND T. LIVDAHL[2]

J. Med. Entomol. 36(3): 394–399 (1999)

ABSTRACT  We compared the tendency for 4th-instar larvae to prey on newly hatched larvae, and the vulnerability of these 1st instars to such predation for *Aedes triseriatus* (Say), *Ae. aegypti* (L.), and *Ae. albopictus* (Skuse), all container-breeding mosquitoes. The latter 2 species were introduced to North America and are now sympatric with *Ae. triseriatus,* a native species in eastern North America. Our experiment also enabled the assessment of species-specific influences of food supplements and spatial heterogeneity on predatory behavior. *Ae. triseriatus* was substantially more predatory and less susceptible to attack than the other 2 species. These differences were amplified in food deprived and spatially simple conditions, indicating that *Ae. triseriatus* predatory behavior may have important retarding effects on the colonization of occupied treehole habitats by *Ae. albopictus. Ae. aegypti* and *Ae. albopictus* were similar in imposing little (*Ae. aegypti*) or almost no (*Ae. albopictus*) predation on 1st instars and in being susceptible to predation by *Ae. triseriatus.* The general lack of species-specific differences between *Ae. aegypti* and *Ae. albopictus* indicates that intraspecific predation is not a likely explanation for the rapid displacement of *Ae. aegypti* by *Ae. albopictus* in domestic containers in the southeastern United States

KEY WORDS  *Aedes albopictus, Aedes aegypti, Aedes triseriatus,* invasive exotic, cannibalism, mosquitoes

*Aedes albopictus* (Skuse), a container-inhabiting mosquito recently introduced from Asia, has spread throughout southeastern and midwestern North America. Its range in the United States has expanded quickly from 1985 when it was first recorded (Sprenger and Wuithiranyagool 1986) to include 25 states, including New Jersey (Crans et al. 1996) and Chicago to the north, Texas to the west, and Florida to the south (O'Meara et al. 1992, 1995; Jamieson et al. 1994; Nasci 1995; Richardson et al 1995). The ongoing colonization by this species has provided an excellent opportunity for ecologists to observe a mosquito invading habitats already occupied by ecologically similar species, particularly its congeners, *Aedes albopictus* has displaced a previously introduced, resident *Africanus mosquito, Aedes aegypti* (L.), in some habitats in Florida (O'Meara et al. 1992) and apparently is in the process of displacing *Ae. aegypti* in South Carolina (Richardson et al. 1995) and Louisiana (Nasci 1995). In contrast, Lounibos et al. (1997) found that *Ae. albopictus* has not displaced the native treehole mosquito, *Aedes triseriatus* (Say), in natural treeholes in Florida.

Temperature extremes may limit the northern extent of the United States population of *Ae. albopictus* (Nawrocki and Hawley 1987, Hanson and Craig 1995),

[1] Department of Biology, Santa Clara University, Santa Clara, CA 95053.
[2] Department of Biology, Clark University, Worcester, MA 01610.

which appears to have originated from a temperate zone population in Japan (Hawley et al. 1987). The biological factors that might promote or restrict range expansion have been less tractable. Numerous biological mechanisms promoting colonization by *Ae. albopictus* have been investigated, including mating interference (Black et al. 1989), competitive displacement by larvae (Barrera 1996, Black et al. 1989, Ho et al. 1989, Livdahl and Willey 1991, Novak et al. 1993, Juliano 1998), oviposition site preferences (Black et al. 1989, Titus 1996), parasitic protozoan parasitism (Fukuda et al. 1997, Juliano 1998), and egg hatch inhibition imposed by larvae (Edgerly et al. 1993).

To further our understanding of potentially significant behavioral interactions in *Aedes,* we investigated the role that intraguild predation might play in successful colonization by *Ae. albopictus.* Facultative predation may occur among *Aedes* larvae, and such predation might contribute to the displacement of *Ae. aegypti* from container habitats by *Ae. albopictus.* Differential predation may contribute to a slow rate of colonization of natural treeholes by *Ae. albopictus* when they are occupied by *Ae. triseriatus,* despite prevalence of *Ae. albopictus* in nearby domestic habitats. Although their food is predominantly microorganisms and detritus (Merritt et al. 1992), both *Ae. aegypti* (MacGregor 1915) and *Ae. triseriatus* (Koenekoop and Livdahl 1996) are capable of cannibalism: 4th instars consume 1st-instar conspecifics in the laboratory. The ecological significance of canni-

**Consider long paragraphs when**

- You are developing complex ideas in detail.
- Your audience is experienced and skillful.
- You are writing in a genre, such as the academic essay, in which longer paragraphs are the norm.
- Readers are patient and seeking information.

**Consider short paragraphs when**

- Readers are impatient or are skimming for content.
- Readers are inexperienced or unfamiliar with the topic.
- You are writing in a genre, such as a newspaper editorial, in which short paragraphs are the norm.
- Readers are reading online.

**EXERCISE 12.6** Analyze the writing situation for the scientific article excerpt and the "Mosquito Control Pro" Web page pictured on page 197. Who is the intended audience and what might their expectations be? What can you deduce about the writer's purpose?

**EXERCISE 12.7** Review a paper draft you're currently working on, paying attention to paragraph lengths. What patterns do you notice? Do you see places where paragraphs could be combined, divided, or reorganized to better fit the writing situation? If so, make the changes.

# 13 How Do You Craft Opening and Closing Paragraphs?

## 13a What makes an opening paragraph effective?

Like the lead of a front-page newspaper story, the first paragraph of any document you write must do four things:

- Get your readers' attention and interest them in reading more.
- Introduce your main idea.

Almost everyone in the United States can recite the opening lines from *Star Wars* ("A long time ago, in a galaxy far, far away . . .") and Abraham Lincoln's "Gettysburg Address" ("Four score and seven years ago our fathers brought forth . . ."). Why do you think these introductions are so memorable? How does each catch attention, suggest content, and set a particular tone? Which of the strategies used in these opening lines, or in other memorable opening lines, might you try in writing a paper?

- Signal to readers what direction your paper will take.
- Set the tone of your project.

These are important functions, and that's why first paragraphs can be difficult to write—but it's also why they're worth your time and attention.

Different kinds of writing call for different opening paragraphs. For certain kinds of writing—laboratory reports, grant proposals, business letters—readers expect specific kinds of opening paragraphs. In such cases, find out what the typical pattern is and use it. In other kinds of writing, such as newspaper articles, critical analyses, personal experience papers, and opinion pieces, you have more freedom and can try various approaches. We list several possibilities below.

**1 Begin with a narrative.** An attention-getting narrative or anecdote catches readers' attention and sparks their interest in the topic. The following opening paragraph from a magazine article pulls readers into a terrifying experience and makes us want to know more about what caused it.

> Like most Peace Corps volunteers, Martin Giannini embarked on his mission full of high hopes and enthusiasm. His assignment in Togo promised to be the adventure of a lifetime. It certainly was—but not the kind he expected. Giannini's African adventure ended in a padded room in a Chicago psych ward. "I was totally loony," admits Giannini. "It felt like I was in some 'X-Files' episode with instructions being planted in my brain. I tried to escape, but couldn't get past the four guards." What led Giannini, a healthy young man with no history of mental illness, to take on a battalion of guards in a psychiatric hospital? A drug, say his doctors. An antimalaria drug the Peace Corps recommended.
> —Dennis Lewon, "Malaria's Not-So-Magic Bullet"

You may occasionally want to begin a paper with two or three short anecdotes rather than a single, longer one. This variation works well to show that your topic touches upon several issues or situations.

**2 Begin with a description.** In this example from an article on exotic Southern cuisine, John T. Edge creates a vivid picture of the region he's writing about and sets a tone of cautious fascination.

It's just past four on a Thursday afternoon in June at Jesse's Place, a country juke seventeen miles south of the Mississippi line and three miles west of Amite, Louisiana. The air conditioner hacks and spits forth torrents of arctic air, but the heat of summer can't be kept at bay. It seeps around the splintered doorjambs and settles in, transforming the squat particleboard-plastered roadhouse into a sauna. Slowly, the dank barroom fills with grease-smeared mechanics from the truck stop up the road and farmers straight from the fields, the soles of their brogans thick with dirt clods. A few weary souls make their way over from the nearby sawmill, the kind of place where more than one worker has muscled a log into the chipper and drawn back a nub. I sit alone at the bar, one empty bottle of Bud in front of me, a second bottle in my hand. I drain the beer, order a third, and stare down at the pink juice spreading outward from a crumpled foil pouch and onto the dull, black vinyl bar.

I'm not leaving until I eat this thing, I tell myself.

—John T. Edge, "I'm Not Leaving Until I Eat This Thing"

**● 3 Begin with a question or a series of questions.** A provocative question raises readers' expectations about what is to come.

Should we be worried that young girls are not pursuing math-related careers at the same rate as young men? After all, in our technological era, many of tomorrow's well-paying jobs will require competence at mathematics. But today, women make up only 19 percent of the science, engineering, and technology workforce. In 1998, only 16 percent of computer science degrees were awarded to women, down from nearly 40 percent in 1984, and the downward trend continued in 2003.

—Rosalind Chait Barnett and Caryl Rivers,
"The Persistence of Gender Myths in Math"

**● 4 Start with your thesis.** Sometimes you will do best to open your essay by simply telling your readers exactly what you are going to write about. Such openings work well for many papers you write in college courses, for reports you might have to write on the job, and for many other kinds of factual, informative prose. Here's a good example from a student essay that evaluates the effectiveness of spanking.

It is unfortunate that the new spanking advocates get so much attention in the popular press, since their arguments are so poorly supported. These crusaders draw on personal anecdotes and "experts" of dubious credibility to glorify physical punishment and to blame non-spanking parents for everything from school shootings to violent rap lyrics. Yet even a cursory look at the scientific research in this area confirms that kids who are spanked are more—not less—likely to misbehave, turn to criminal behavior, or suffer from mental problems. How we choose to treat our nation's children is a serious matter. We must make these decisions based on the best information available, not on the dire predictions of a few extremists.

See Section 3a for more on constructing a thesis statement and incorporating it into a writing project.

**EXERCISE 13.1** Choose from the strategies discussed above and write two versions of an opening paragraph for one of the following essay titles. Then join with classmates who have chosen to write on the same title and read your paragraphs aloud. Discuss which ones seem to work well and why.

1. The American Medical Establishment as Seen Through *Scrubs, ER*, and *House*

2. What It Means to Live Below the Poverty Level: A Case Study

3. Why You Should Vote in the Next Election

4. Is Steroid Use a Major Problem in Professional Sports?

**EXERCISE 13.2** Reread student author Tallon Harding's essay in Chapter 5 (pages 69–75). What strategy does she use in her introductory paragraph? Do you think this was a wise choice? If so, why? What other strategies might Tallon have chosen given the topic of her paper? Once you've settled on another approach that would work well, try your hand at writing this version of the essay's opening paragraph.

# 13b What makes a closing paragraph effective?

Closing paragraphs can be hard to write because it's often difficult to come to a satisfying conclusion that doesn't fall back on clichés. The only direct advice we can give is that your closing paragraph should wind up your paper in a way that makes readers feel that you have tied up the loose ends—that you have fulfilled the commitment you made in the opening paragraph. You don't want your readers asking "And so?" when they finish, or looking on the back of the page for something they may have missed.

There are no simple prescriptions for achieving that important goal. However, we suggest five general strategies you can use, alone or in combination, as seems appropriate for your rhetorical situation.

● **1 Summarize the main points you have made.** Often you'll want to bring your paper to a close by reemphasizing your main points. (But don't repeat the very same words you have already used, or your ending may sound redundant or forced.) In this example, student writer Jeremy Christiansen reviews key points about school resegregation.

America continues to see a growing trend towards public-school resegregation, a problem that was not discovered until recent studies were conducted to test the successes of *Brown v. the Board of Education* after 50 years. The findings were startling, since they suggest that what was once known as the most important court decision of the 20th century may have been a failure. American ideals espouse diversity and equal opportunities for all. School resegregation not only discourages diversity but limits opportunities for minorities and whites alike. We will not have true equality in educational opportunities until we find a way to create racially, ethnically, and economically integrated public schools. Unfortunately, further attempts to desegregate, though necessary, will likely spark even more controversy, which may last 50 more years.

● **2 Make a recommendation when one is appropriate.** Such a recommendation should grow out of the issue you have been discussing. This strategy brings a paper to a positive ending and closes the topic. Here is a conclusion from a piece that explores the cognitive benefits of watching television.

Kids and grown-ups each can learn from their increasingly shared obsessions. Too often we imagine the blurring of kid and grown-up cultures as a series of violations: the 9-year-olds who have to have nipple brooches explained to them thanks to Janet Jackson; the middle-aged guy who can't wait to get home to his Xbox. But this demographic blur has a commendable side that we don't acknowledge enough. The kids are forced to think like grown-ups: analyzing complex social networks, managing resources, tracking subtle narrative intertwinings, recognizing long-term patterns. The grown-ups, in turn, get to learn from the kids: decoding each new technological wave, parsing the interfaces and discovering the intellectual rewards of play. Parents should see this as an opportunity, not a crisis. Smart culture is no longer something you force your kids to ingest, like green vegetables. It's something you share.
—Steven Johnson, "Watching TV Makes You Smarter"

● **3 Link the end to the beginning.** One excellent way to end a writing project is to tie your conclusion back to your beginning, framing and unifying your paper. Notice how skillfully Gary Engel uses this strategy in an article analyzing the cultural significance of Superman.

**OPENING PARAGRAPH**

When I was young I spent a lot of time arguing with myself about who would win in a fight between John Wayne and Superman. On days when I wore my cowboy hat and cap guns, I knew the Duke would win because of his pronounced superiority in the all-important matter of swagger. There were days, though, when a frayed army blanket tied cape-fashion around my neck signaled a young man's need to believe there could be no end to the potency of his being. Then the Man of Steel was the odds-on favorite to knock the Duke for a cosmic loop. My greatest childhood problem was that the question could never be resolved because no such battle could ever take place. I mean, how would a fight start between the only two Americans who never started anything, who always fought only to defend their rights and the American way?

**CLOSING PARAGRAPH**

In the last analysis, Superman is like nothing so much as an American boy's fantasy of a messiah. He is the male, heroic match for the Statue of Liberty, come like an immigrant from heaven to deliver humankind by sacrificing himself in the service of others. He protects the weak and defends truth and justice and all the other moral virtues inherent in the Judeo-Christian tradition, remaining ever vigilant and ever chaste. What purer or stronger vision could there possibly be for a child? Now that I put my mind to it, I see that John Wayne never had a chance.

Gary Engel, "What Makes Superman So Darned American?"

**4 Point to directions for future research or action, or identify unresolved questions.** Concluding paragraphs that suggest these sorts of connections are especially common in academic research projects.

Reading the arguments about assisted suicide reminded me of a line from Bertolt Brecht's *The Three-Penny Opera*: "First feed the face, and then talk right and wrong." As a general rule, that statement itself is wrong, of course, but it can serve as a salutary warning. First, provide decent health care for the living; then, we can have a proper debate about the moral problems of death and dying.

—Michael Walzer, "Feed the Face"

**5 Stop when you're finished.** Probably the most important thing to remember about closing a paper or essay is not to overdo your conclusion. If you have covered all your points and are reasonably satisfied with what you've said, quit. Don't bore your reader by tacking on a needless recapitulation or adding a paragraph of platitudes.

**EXERCISE 13.3** Exchange drafts with two or three other students who are working on the same assignment. Each person should read the closing paragraphs of the other papers. Working in a group, identify the strategies each writer has used to bring his or her paper to a conclusion; discuss how well they work, and suggest alternative possibilities.

**EXERCISE 13.4** Look once again at student author Tallon Harding's essay on pages 69–75, this time noting her strategy for concluding the paper. How well do you think she summarizes her main points? Does she link the end of her paper to the beginning, or point to directions for future actions? How might you improve this concluding paragraph?

# 14 How Do You Manage Transitions?

Skilled writers work hard to help their readers move easily through a piece of writing. They know that readers won't stick around long if they have trouble following an argument or the thread of a narrative. The best unifying device for any piece of writing is *organizational*; that is, it comes from an underlying pattern that moves the reader along smoothly. You'll find examples of such patterns in Sections 3c (for whole papers) and 12b (for paragraphs).

But even when your paper follows a clear pattern, you sometimes need to tighten your writing by using *transitions*, those words and phrases that act like hooks, links, and directional signals to keep readers moving from point to point within a paragraph, and from one paragraph to another.

## 14a How do you spot problems with transitions?

When you're revising, check for places where your readers might find your writing choppy or abrupt, and revise accordingly. Look for these trouble spots.

**◑ 1 Check for paragraphs made up of short, simple sentences that seem disconnected.** Effective paragraphs follow what writing experts call the "old-new contract"—they advance an argument or idea by linking each piece of new information to something that's gone before, so that the connections are immediately clear to readers. When a writer neglects to link old and new information, a paragraph may read more like a random series of observations than a coherent discussion.

> **WEAK TRANSITIONS**
> Some Americans live in affluent suburbs or university communities. It's easy to get the impression that the American population is healthy. Joggers and bicycle riders are everywhere. Many restaurants feature low-fat

entrees. Many Americans are unhealthy. Thirty percent are seriously overweight. Alcoholism is a problem and many teenagers smoke. Obesity among children is increasing.

Here is a revised version, with some sentences combined and others connected (transitional words are boldfaced).

**BETTER**

If one lives in an affluent suburb or near a university, it's easy to get the impression that the American population is healthy. In **such** places, joggers **and** bicycle riders are everywhere, and restaurants feature low-fat entrees. The truth is, **however**, that many Americans are not healthy. Thirty percent are seriously overweight, alcoholism is a problem, **and** an increasing number of teenagers smoke. **Moreover**, obesity among children is increasing.

●**2 Check for sentences that begin with vague references such as** *it is, there are***, and** *there is***.** Often sentences that begin with these phrases (called *expletives*) are poorly connected to each other because it's hard to tell who or what the subject is. For example:

**WEAK TRANSITIONS**

It is a truism that good manners are like skeleton keys. There are few doors they will not open. Some people think that good manners are pretentious. They are a way of condescending to people. That is a misunderstanding. The real purpose of manners is to make social situations comfortable and to put the people you are with at ease. Manners are also practical to have. There are many companies that insist that their executives have good manners. Some business schools include a course on manners in their curricula.

Here is the paragraph reworked with better sentence openings and stronger connections. Transitional terms are boldfaced.

**BETTER**

Good manners, like skeleton keys, will open almost any door. **Although** some people think that good manners are pretentious and condescending, that's a misunderstanding. **On the contrary**, manners exist to make social situations comfortable by putting everyone at ease. **Moreover**, manners are a practical asset in the job market. Many companies insist on well-mannered executives, **which** has prompted some business schools to include a course on manners in their curricula.

For suggestions on revising to eliminate expletive phrases, see Section 17c-6.

**● 3 Check for gaps between paragraphs.** Sometimes major gaps appear between paragraphs, and readers get temporarily lost. Suppose that you encountered the following two paragraphs in a personal essay. You'd probably have trouble figuring out how the second paragraph relates to the first.

> When I arrived here four years ago, I found that the skills I had learned in order to survive in Sudan were useless. I knew how to catch a rabbit, challenge a hyena or climb a coconut palm, but I had never turned on a light, used a telephone or driven a car.
>
> Within a month I understood how to work most modern conveniences and started my first job as a courtesy clerk and stocker at Ralph's grocery store in San Diego. Things like mangoes, chard and yams were familiar, but when customers asked about Cheerios or Ajax, it was as though my years of learning English in the refugee camp were worthless.

Here's the original passage as it appeared in Alephonsion Deng's essay, which appeared in *Newsweek* magazine. The linking sentence is boldfaced.

> When I arrived here four years ago, I found that the skills I had learned in order to survive in Sudan were useless. I knew how to catch a rabbit, challenge a hyena or climb a coconut palm, but I had never turned on a light, used a telephone or driven a car.
>
> **Luckily, the International Rescue Committee provided us with classes and mentors to teach us basics about computers, job interviews and Western social customs.** Within a month I understood how to work most modern conveniences and started my first job as a courtesy clerk and stocker at Ralph's grocery store in San Diego. Things like mangoes, chard and yams were familiar, but when customers asked

about Cheerios or Ajax, it was as though my years of learning English in the refugee camp were worthless.

—Alephonsion Deng, "I Have Had to Learn to Live With Peace"

Links between paragraphs can take several forms; Section 14b explains these in more detail.

# **14b** How can you strengthen transitions?

If you want to use transitions successfully, remember the old-new contract: Each sentence or paragraph should contain a seed out of which the next sentence or paragraph can grow. Always include a hint, a reference, a hook, or a repetition that helps the reader link what you're saying with what has come before and what lies ahead.

**● 1 Use common transition words to connect ideas.** You can make your paragraphs tighter and more focused by using transition words to tie sentences together.

- **Pointer words,** such as *first, second, next,* and *last,* set up a path for readers to follow by indicating shifts in time or place.

  One student, a nonsmoker, argued eloquently before the committee that there are many reasons to oppose a campus-wide ban on smoking. **First,** such a policy penalizes an activity that, though obnoxious, is not illegal. **Second,** enforcement of the policy might encourage insidious intrusions on the privacy of students in their dormitory rooms and faculty in their offices. **Last,** a ban on smoking might set an unfortunate precedent, leading to the elimination of other activities certain groups regard as offensive or harmful: drinking alcohol, eating fatty foods, dancing, listening to rock music, or even driving a car.

- **Relationship words,** such as *however, therefore,* and *yet,* show similarity, opposition, addition, or other connections between ideas.

  Opinion at the hearing had generally favored the proposal to abolish smoking on campus. **However,** the student's arguments made some proponents waver as they considered the wider implications of their actions. What would happen, **for example**, if one group on campus, citing statistics on heart disease, demanded a campus-wide ban on fast foods? The ban on smoking would provide grounds for such a restriction.

As these examples show, transition words are not neutral; each one gives readers a different signal about where your argument is going. When you're in doubt about which term to choose, check Chart 14.1 below.

---

**Chart 14.1    Common Transition Words and Phrases**

**TO SHOW SIMILARITY**
likewise
like
similarly
in the same way
just as

**TO SHOW CONTRAST**
however
instead
nevertheless
although
in spite of
on the other hand
not only
but
rather

**TO SHOW ACCUMULATION**
moreover
in addition to
for example
and
for instance

**TO SHOW CONSEQUENCE**
hence
consequently
so
therefore
as a result of
thus

**TO SHOW CAUSATION**
because
since

**TO SHOW A SEQUENCE**
next
subsequently
after
finally
first, second, third

● **2 Repeat a key term throughout a paragraph to establish a central idea.** Using one or two key words or phrases several times in a paragraph can tie it together effectively.

**REPEATED WORDS BOLDFACED**

The new black middle class came of age in the 1960s during an unprecedented American **economic boom** and in the hub of a thriving **mass culture**. The **economic boom** made luxury goods and convenient services available to large numbers of hard-working Americans for the first time. American **mass culture** presented models of the good life principally in terms of conspicuous consumption and hedonistic indulgence. It is important to note that even the intensely political struggles of the sixties presupposed a perennial **economic boom** and posited models of the good life projected by U.S. **mass culture**. Long-term financial self-denial and sexual asceticism was never at the center of a political agenda in the sixties.

—Cornel West, *Race Matters*

● **3 Use the demonstrative pronouns *this, that, these, those,* and *such* to tie ideas together.** Each boldfaced word in the following example hooks directly into the previous sentence.

**DEMONSTRATIVE TERMS BOLDFACED**

Making a movie is a collaborative endeavor, and scriptwriters point **this** out frequently. Occasionally a screenplay will survive the transfer from paper to film intact, but **that** is the exception rather than the rule. Typically, producers, directors, actors, and agents all have a say in the final product. Coping with **such** high-handed meddling is often difficult for young writers, and **those** who cannot compromise rarely stay in the business for long.

● **4 Use relative pronouns to show links between ideas.** *Who, which, where,* and *that* are powerful words that link a descriptive or informative statement to something that has preceded it. Relative pronouns can be especially helpful when you need to combine several short, choppy sentences into one. Notice how the boldfaced pronouns in the following paragraph serve as links to previous ideas.

**RELATIVE PRONOUNS BOLDFACED**

Emma's first few weeks at the conservatory were exhausting but exhilarating. It was a place **that** challenged her, one **where** she could meet talented people **who** shared her passion for dance. The competition among the students was friendly but intense, **which** only increased her determination to practice and learn.

**5 Use parallelism to link ideas.** You can create tightly focused paragraphs by writing a series of sentences that incorporate parallel phrases.

**PARALLEL PHRASES BOLDFACED**

I spent my two days at Disneyland taking rides. **I took** a bobsled through the Matterhorn and a submarine under the Polar Ice Cap and a rocket jet to the Cosmic Vapor Curtain. **I took** Peter Pan's Flight, Mr. Toad's Wild Ride, Alice's Scary Adventures, and Pinocchio's Daring Journey. **I took** a steamboat and a jungle boat. **I took** the Big Thunder Mountain Railroad to coyote country and the Splash Mountain roller coaster to Critter Country. **I took** a "Pirates of the Caribbean" ride (black cats and buried treasure) and a "Haunted Mansion" ride (creaking hinges and ghostly laughter). **I took** monorails and Skyways and Autopias and People Movers. More precisely, those rides **took** me: up and down and around sudden corners and over rooftops, and all I had to do was sit back and let whatever conveyance I was sitting in do the driving.

—William Zinsser, *American Places*

Zinsser holds the details of his paragraph together by using a parallel pattern that begins every sentence with the phrase "I took"; then, when he reverses the phrase to "More precisely, those rides **took** me," he wraps up his paragraph with a final unifying touch.

**6 Use a semicolon to link two closely related statements.** The semicolon signals a tight connection that says, "These groups of words go together." Often a semicolon can connect parts of a sentence more effectively than *and* or *also*. For more details about the semicolon, see Section 37a.

**CONNECTING SEMICOLONS HIGHLIGHTED**

The sculptor Ilya Karensky no longer has to endure his neighbors' contempt for his work; now he has to put up with their insincere and inept praise. Ilya knows perfectly well that what his neighbors admire most about his work is the amount of money for which it now sells; they like the sculptures themselves no better than they did before.

**7 Consider using headings or other visual markers as transitions.** In some kinds of documents, writers may use visual signals as well as—or sometimes instead of—words to help readers follow an argument.

Business and technical writers commonly use headings and subheadings to separate sections of a document so that readers can see where one idea ends and another begins. Résumés often use headings such as "Education," "Experience," "Awards," and "References" so that readers can locate relevant information. Brochures, flyers, and instructional manuals employ graphics, images, and color to mark divisions or to tie together related material. On the Web, writers create hyperlinks to connect documents.

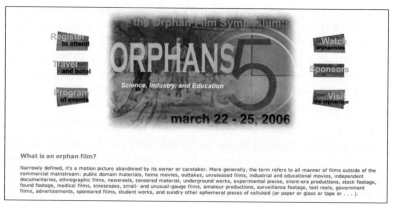

Examine this Web page designed by Laura Kissel and Dan Strieble for an annual film festival at the University of South Carolina. How do the designers use color, fonts, headings, lists, hyperlinks, or other visual elements to help readers navigate the information on this page? What elements link similar ideas? Which elements show relationships among ideas? How effectively do you think these visual elements work? What changes might you suggest?

When you incorporate visual transitions into a writing project, ask whether the particular strategy is appropriate for the situation. Graphics and color fonts aren't always welcome in academic papers, and a flyer or short essay might not need headings. If you're not sure, look at models to see the kinds of transitions other writers have used in similar situations.

Also be sure that a particular transition gives readers the right signal. For example, a heading indicates a new topic, but it doesn't necessarily show readers how one topic relates to another. You'll often need to supplement visual devices with traditional linking words and phrases.

For more information about integrating visual elements into a text, see Chapter 18. For examples of documents that incorporate visual elements, see the model documents in Chapter 19.

**EXERCISE 14.1** Read the following two paragraphs and diagnose the transition problems you find between the paragraphs and within each one. Where do you have trouble following the writer's line of thought? Why? Then revise the paragraphs to improve the transitions, drawing on at least two of the strategies described in this section.

There is nowhere to park on campus. The parking situation is impossible for first-year students. My roommate missed her first college class because she could not find a parking spot. I have received three parking tickets already this semester. Some people say that freshmen should not be allowed to drive to campus. First-year students are required to live in the dorms. The dorm I live in is 15 minutes away from all my classes. I can't walk to them. I have to drive.

There are only a few parking garages and many underutilized grassy areas on campus. There is a large green space on either side of the engineering complex that is not being used. The courtyard in front of the library is always empty. The fountain attracts litter. Why can't the university use some grassy areas for parking garages? The university could use some money from parking tickets to pay for new parking. The shuttle bus system could be used to transport students from remote parking areas onto campus.

**EXERCISE 14.2** Use one or more of the transitional devices discussed in this section to strengthen connections between new and old information in a writing project you're currently working on.

# 15 What Kinds of Language Can You Use?

Many people assume that *what* we say is more important than *how* we say it. "Just get to the point," we often hear. "Say what you mean." But even small nuances in the tone, vocabulary, connotation, and formality of your writing can powerfully affect readers. These kinds of language choices—often called *stylistic choices*—are the focus of this chapter.

## 15a How formal should your writing be?

Different writing situations call for different levels of formality. Imagine what would happen if you responded to a casual party invitation with a business memo, or if you began a graduation speech with a rendition of your favorite pop song. In either case, you'd be using a style inappropriate to the situation—and your audience would quickly let you know it.

How do you strike the right level of formality in a particular writing situation? When you know your readers well or are writing a familiar kind of assignment, these choices may come almost intuitively. When you don't, you will need to analyze your purpose and audience carefully so that you can make good language choices.

Chart 15.1 identifies a range of styles, classifying them as formal, informal, and casual, and lists typical kinds of documents that use each. But you should view these styles as points on a continuum rather than hard-and-fast categories. In practice, different writers approach documents in different ways, and even the same writer may shift between formal and less formal language within a single text.

● 1 **Choose formal language for academic writing and for situations when you don't know your audience well.** In most college courses, instructors will expect you to write in a relatively formal style (unless the assignment designates a writing situation in which informality

## Chart 15.1    Levels of Formality

| FORMAL | INFORMAL | CASUAL |
|---|---|---|
| Compound and complex sentence structures; longer sentences | Variety of standard sentence types in agent/action style | Shorter sentences; minor sentences and fragments |
| Abstract and technical language; precise vocabulary: *the attenuation of patriotic sentimentalism* | Mix of abstract and concrete terms; direct language: *the weakening of patriotic feeling* | Concrete language; slang and colloquial terms: *nixing the flag waving* |
| Impersonal tone; infrequent use of *I* or *you* | Occasionally and comfortably personal; some use of *I* and *you* | Aggressively personal; frequent use of *I* and *you* |
| Few contractions, if any | Familiar use of contractions where easy and natural | Contractions without guilt |
| Serious or professional tone and subject matter | Moderate variations of tone and subject | Wide tone and sometimes unexpected shifts in tone and topic—sometimes light and satirical |
| Careful control of imagery and analogy | Conscious and frequent use of figurative language | Deliberate, frequent use of contemporary comparisons and idioms |
| Standard formats or templates for presentation | Increasingly supported with images and design elements | Aggressive melding of words, images, and graphics |
| Scholarly books and articles; technical reports; academic papers and projects; job application letters; legal and some business correspondence; some speeches | Newspapers and editorials; general interest magazines; newsletters; popular books; political discourse; some business letters; professional email; .com and .org Web sites; oral presentations | Special interest magazines; personal email; personal letters; listserv communications; personal Web sites |

is appropriate—for instance, a reading-response journal or a pop quiz.) Academic papers require that you discuss serious subject matter in a thoughtful, well-informed manner and that you maintain some critical distance from your audience. The following excerpt from a book written by a well-known historian effectively demonstrates some key elements of a formal style:

The women who assembled as delegates at Seneca Falls had demanded equality of opportunity for men and women in affairs of state, church, and family. Elizabeth Cady Stanton, the organizing force and intelligence behind this historic conclave, was an advanced and innovative thinker on women's issues, who understood the complex sources of sexual subordination and, in addition to the vote for women, advocated domestic reforms including the right of women to affirm their sexuality if they chose to do so, or contrarily, to refuse sexual relations altogether when necessary to avoid pregnancy. Stanton also supported cooperative child rearing, rights to property, child custody, and divorce. Though venerated within her own small circle, she came to be viewed by more traditional supporters as a source of potential controversy and embarrassment.

—Ellen Chesler, *Women of Valor*

Chesler's tone is authoritative and she uses high-level vocabulary and complex sentences with confidence. She projects the image of a careful, knowledgeable scholar—exactly the kind of persona readers expect in academic writing.

**● 2 Choose informal language when you feel comfortable with your audience and want a more relaxed tone.** Writers who choose an informal style usually do so because, although their topics may be serious, they don't want to sound solemn or impersonal. They want their readers to feel as if they're in a conversation. Writers use informal language in many different kinds of documents. Here's just one example, taken from an article on high school football published in the popular magazine *Texas Monthly*.

But even if change is afoot, Texas high school football remains one of the few institutions that distinguishes us from the rest of the universe. We have more players, coaches, band members, cheerleaders, and pep squads than anyone else. We send more of our boys to college and the pros than any other state (more than three hundred signed letters of intent to play for Division I schools last year alone). Our fans are more fanatical. Our parents are more passionate. So believe the hype: we're Number One.

—Joe Nick Patoski et al., "Three Cheers for High School Football"

In this vividly descriptive paragraph, Patoski and his co-authors mix high-level and low-level vocabulary: *distinguishes, institution,* and *fanatical* contrast with the colloquial *our boys* and *hype*. They also mix concrete and abstract language, vary the sentence length, and use the first-person *we* to draw readers in.

**● 3 Choose casual language for personal writing and for audiences you know very well.** Although it's unlikely you'd choose this style for an academic assignment, you might want to use it if you were posting an entry to your personal blog or writing for a small group of friends or insiders. Columnists often use casual language because they want their readers to feel like insiders. This example comes from a column in the *Cleveland Free Times*, an alternative weekly published in print and online (the column is about the staff's attempts to stop swearing).

> For years we were the cussingest office it would ever be your misfortune to hear. We turned the air blue, with f-bombs exploding everywhere. Male and female workers alike swore more than a bunch of drunken sailors on shore leave (indeed, a bunch of drunken sailors on shore leave once came by the office and were absolutely appalled).
>
> —Eric Broder, *Cleveland Free Times*

Broder's fast-paced, conversational style—infused with sarcasm and humor—suits the *Free Times*, a publication that deliberately sets itself apart from mainstream media.

Writers also choose casual language for intensely personal writing like autobiographical essays, letters, or journals. This example comes from a published diary by a first-year teacher.

> October 5, my birthday. Terrible thing. Somebody stole the Columbus comic book. I said, "Whoever did it, just put it back," but nobody did. So after school I took the whole library down and shoved it in the closet and locked it. The kids noticed right away the next morning.
>
> "I told you if you stole from me, I'd take it all back. I'm not a liar."
>
> "That's not fair," one girl complained. "We didn't all steal the book!" [. . .] I passed out the reading textbooks. The children complained noisily. "You're getting what the rest of the school gets," I reminded them. "I don't see what's the problem."
>
> God, kid! Give me back the stupid book and let me teach you the best way I know how!
>
> —Esme Raji Codell, *Educating Esme*

Codell's choppy sentences, emotional language, and realistic dialogue create a sense of intimacy with her readers. Such a colloquial account wouldn't be appropriate for a research article or an academic paper, but it's effective here.

**EXERCISE 15.1** What level of formality do you think would be appropriate for writing in these situations? In each case, consider what impression you might want to make and how much distance you would want to maintain from readers. Give reasons for your choice.

1. A letter to a representative or senator asking to be considered for a summer internship in his or her office.

2. A brochure recruiting volunteers to work on a house being constructed by Habitat for Humanity.

3. A column in your weekly church newsletter that recounts noteworthy activities by members of the church.

4. An email to your calculus instructor.

# 15b How emotionally charged should your language be?

Words affect people strongly, and even subtle differences in meaning can have dramatic effects. If they didn't, it would make no difference whether a teacher called your six-year-old "a highly imaginative child" or "a big liar." And we wouldn't see national debates over hate speech legislation and "political correctness" on college campuses.

It's simply because words are so powerful that writers must understand the kinds of emotional associations words carry and then use them appropriately. And what's appropriate will depend on your writing situation.

**● 1 Understand how denotation and connotation work.** **Denotation** is the literal meaning of a word, the object or concept that it refers to. For instance, the denotative meaning of *puppy* is *young dog*. **Connotation** refers to the positive or negative emotional associations that go along with a word. Connotatively, *puppy* suggests cuteness, playfulness, and warmth. Even when words have similar denotative meanings, their connotations may differ greatly. Consider these examples.

**Highlight   Similar Denotations, Different Connotations**

POSITIVE – – – – – – – – ► NEUTRAL – – – – – – – – ► NEGATIVE

| | | | | |
|---|---|---|---|---|
| urge | remind | nag | browbeat | drive insane |
| lithe | slender | thin | skinny | scrawny |

What different words and phrases can be used to denote "homeless person"? Make a list of as many synonyms as you can. Then arrange the words along a continuum moving from the most positive, to neutral, to the most negative connotations. How might readers' impressions of the individual in the photo change depending on which words or phrases you chose to describe him? In which writing situations might each word or phrase on your list be appropriate or inappropriate? Effective or ineffective? Accurate or inaccurate?

Writers need to be concerned about denotation—that is, you should choose words that precisely convey the idea you're trying to express (don't say *puppy* if you really mean *young wolf*). But choosing words with appropriate connotations is a trickier challenge. Connotative meanings elicit stronger responses from readers. And because they have to do with the contexts in which particular words are used, they also shift more frequently and vary more from audience to audience. For these reasons it's usually not a good idea to simply lift words out of a thesaurus and place them into your writing.

**● 2 Choose mostly neutral language for informative research, academic papers, case studies, and reports.** When you're writing a piece that's primarily informative, your readers usually expect you to give them a neutral report on the topic, as anthropologist Michael Moffett does in the following excerpt from his study examining how undergraduate students choose their majors.

> The top ten majors and all the rest [. . .] fell into a gradient of status in general student opinion, one that was based on three criteria. First, how good was the occupation to which a given subject presumably led? Second, and closely related, how difficult was that subject at Rutgers? And third, much less important, how much social good did the occupation or profession in question accomplish?
> —Michael Moffett, "How College Students Choose Their Majors"

Although Moffett probably has opinions about what criteria students should use to pick a major, his purpose here is to report what the students he interviewed for this study thought about the issue. He thus uses neutral, descriptive language, focusing not on his feelings about the topic but on communicating his data.

**● 3 Avoid strongly connotative language when you are writing newsletters, press releases, or informative brochures.** The audience for these documents might expect a writer to put a positive spin on the information he or she is presenting, but they don't want to be showered with emotional language. Consider this paragraph from a brochure describing a student tutoring program called Helping One Student To

Succeed (HOSTS). Words and phrases with positive connotations are boldfaced.

> At Zavala Elementary School, teachers select second- and third-grade students to attend the HOSTS program for four half-hour periods each week. Mentors come once a week to meet with students in a **cheerful, book-lined classroom** for 30 minutes. The students and their mentors read together, talk about books, learn study skills, and practice writing. **They also become friends.**

This is not strictly neutral language. But the connotation doesn't distract from the information or give the impression that the writer is selling something.

**● 4 Use connotative language appropriately in arguments, reviews, editorials, and opinion pieces.** Connotative language sometimes works well when you want to express strong feelings of approval or disapproval. Here are two examples, one that uses language with moderately strong connotations, and one that's more emotionally charged. The first example is from the conclusion of Roger Ebert's review of the movie classic *Casablanca*. It comes from his Web page, *Ebert's Great Movies*, at <http://www.suntimes.com/>. Again, strongly connotative words and phrases are boldfaced.

> Seeing the film over and over again, year after year, I find it **never grows over-familiar**. It plays like a **favorite** musical album; **the more I know it, the more I like it**. The black-and-white cinematography **has not aged** as color would. The dialogue is so spare and cynical it **has not grown old-fashioned**. Much of the emotional effect of *Casablanca* is achieved by indirection; as we leave the theater, we are **absolutely convinced** that the only thing keeping the world from going crazy is that the problems of three little people do after all amount to more than a hill of beans.
>
> —Roger Ebert, *Casablanca*

Ebert uses connotative language effectively here. His praise is moderate but warm, and he supports his claims with details from the film. Such a review is a suitable model for an evaluative piece you might write for a class or a local paper.

Our second passage, taken from an editorial column in an online political newsletter, uses much stronger language (the column advocates home schooling). Again, strongly connotative terms are boldfaced.

> Why have we put our children into educational **prisons** called public schools? What **crimes** have they committed? Why do we **condemn** almost 45 million **innocent** children to this **punishment**? Do I exaggerate by calling these schools "prisons?" Well, let's compare prisons and public schools. [. . .]
>
> School authorities **force** millions of children to sit in **boxes called classrooms** with 20 other children-**inmates** for six to eight hours a day, five days a week, for up to ten years. The children must obey the adult education **wardens** (teachers and principals), who they may **fear** or dislike. They must study subjects they may **hate** or that **bore** them to **death**.
>
> —Joel Turtel, "Public School Prisons"

One encounters this kind of heavy-handed language fairly often on the editorial pages of newspapers, in political campaign literature, in blogs, and on television and radio talk shows. Vehement language is sometimes appropriate in these settings, where writers voice strong positions on important questions.

Yet writers take risks when they choose such charged language. Turtel's piece is so laden with extreme terms ("prisons," "children-inmates," "hate") that it's likely to turn many readers off. Emotionally charged writing is best left for audiences you know well or for settings where readers expect it. This means that it's rarely appropriate for academic writing. (See Section 6a for detailed advice about what instructors expect in academic papers.)

**EXERCISE 15.2** Find a syndicated newspaper column such as those written by George Will, William Safire, Molly Ivins, or William Raspberry. Underline words and phrases with strong negative or positive connotations. Then find a news story from the same paper. Discuss the differences in how the two pieces handle connotative language.

# 15c How do you choose reader-friendly language?

Have you ever suffered through a lecture that went completely over your head? Or stopped reading an editorial halfway through because the writer made assumptions that insulted you? Or fallen asleep while reading a particularly dull textbook? Writers who don't think sufficiently about their audiences sometimes find that their language alienates the readers they want to reach. This is why it's important that you choose your words carefully when you write. Draw readers into your discussion; don't shut them out.

**1 Choose language familiar to your readers.** When you're drafting or revising a piece of writing, ask yourself whether your readers will be comfortable with the vocabulary you're using. There are times when a difficult or technical term *is* appropriate—when it draws a subtle distinction or describes a complex phenomenon that simpler words can't capture. But writers sometimes wrongly assume that they need to impress readers by choosing formal and highly complicated language. Here's an example from an academic paper.

> **UNNECESSARILY DIFFICULT LANGUAGE**
> Scholarly authorities hold a myriad of viewpoints with regard to the ongoing disputation involving the major prescription drug companies' ethical obligation to manufacture minimally profitable pharmaceuticals that ameliorate the world's major diseases.

> **REVISED**
> Scholars disagree on whether big drug companies have a moral obligation to manufacture low-profit drugs to treat the world's major diseases.

See how much more readable the second sentence is? Even when you're writing in a relatively formal style, you'll reach more readers by choosing familiar words when you can. (See Section 17c for tips on reworking inflated sentences.)

**2 Balance abstract and concrete language.** **Abstract words** are general; they refer to ideas, concepts, and categories that we can't perceive directly through our five senses—words such as *justice, charm, culture, life.*

**Concrete words** do just the opposite; they name specific people and things that we can see, hear, taste, smell, or touch—*Johnny Depp, lopsided grin, turquoise bracelet, my pet poodle.* Of course, most words are neither wholly abstract nor concrete. They exist on a continuum between the two extremes, and writers must decide what level of specificity seems most appropriate for their purpose.

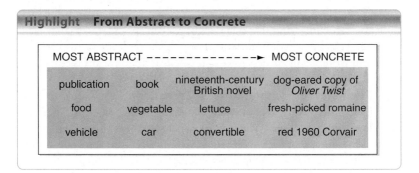

**Highlight   From Abstract to Concrete**

MOST ABSTRACT – – – – – – – – – – –▶ MOST CONCRETE

| | | | |
|---|---|---|---|
| publication | book | nineteenth-century British novel | dog-eared copy of *Oliver Twist* |
| food | vegetable | lettuce | fresh-picked romaine |
| vehicle | car | convertible | red 1960 Corvair |

Passages laden with too many abstractions can be intimidating and hard to follow. Yet if writing contains nothing but specifics, readers may not see the main point amid all the details. That's why skilled writers strive for an effective mix of both. Exactly what ratio of abstract to concrete language you use in a particular text will depend on your writing situation. For more on balancing concrete and abstract language, see Sections 17b-1 (sentences) and 12c-1 (paragraphs).

● **3 Limit your use of jargon.** The specialized insider language of professional groups is called jargon. Physicians, for instance, use the terms *hypertension* and *idiopathic*, whereas graphic artists use the terms *pixel* and *color separation.* When you're writing for a group of specialists, these technical terms are a necessary part of your vocabulary, as in the following passage from an article in *Guitar Player Magazine.* Jargon words are boldfaced.

Your guitar's **passive tone control** is a potent **sound-sculpting** tool—at least when it's correctly matched to your **pickups, stompboxes, amp**, and playing style. But if you find yourself ignoring your guitar's

**tone knobs**, it's probably because you hate the **flabby sounds** that result from twisting them counterclockwise.

—Andy Ellis, "Stellartone Tonestyler"

But you'll shut out readers if you use this kind of jargon when you're writing for an audience that includes nonspecialists. When you need to use a specialized term for a general audience, define it the first time you use it and then give an example. For example, an article on guitars for nonspecialists would need to clarify that "stompboxes" are pedals that electric guitar players use to create special sound effects such as echoes and tonal distortion.

● **4  Avoid clichés.** Clichés are expressions that were once fresh and vivid but which have been so overused that they've lost their impact: *dead giveaway, better late than never, powers that be, brought back to reality, back to basics*, and so on. It's easy for phrases such as these to slip into an early draft of a project, but as you edit, replace them with more lively language.

● **5  Use a civil tone for public writing.** Treat your audience—even those who disagree with you—with respect. Most readers will be put off by an author who sounds arrogant and contemptuous. Consider the following passage.

The existence of a literature presupposes a literate and coherent public that has both the time to read and a need to take seriously the works of the literary imagination. I'm not sure whether the United States ever had such a public; certainly it hasn't had one for the last thirty years. What we have instead is an opening-night crowd, astonished by celebrity and opulent spectacle, tolerating only those authors who present themselves as freaks and wonders and offer the scandal of their lives as proof of their art.

—Lewis Lapham, "Notebook"

Lapham is a longtime social critic who has been writing his grumpy column for *Harper's* for years. Undoubtedly the caustic tone—characterized by name-calling, sarcasm, and sweeping condemnations—appeals to some people, particularly those who already agree with the author. But many readers may feel insulted and quit reading.

If you want readers to pay attention to your concerns, begin with the assumption that your readers are intelligent and that each of you is able to understand the other's point of view. Avoid name-calling and blanket generalizations. Instead of making pronouncements, qualify your claims using words and phrases such as *One solution is . . . , in many cases, often, usually.* (For more on building credibility in your writing, see Section 1g. For advice on handling different viewpoints, consult Section 10c.)

**EXERCISE 15.3**  Revise one of the passages below to achieve a more effective balance between abstract and concrete language. You may need to add sentences and revise existing sentences. Discuss your revisions with a group of classmates.

1.  Never buy a pet from a pet shop without first checking to see where the establishment gets its animals. Many stores buy their stock from unregulated "puppy mills," where large numbers of animals are raised in terrible conditions. Buyers may end up with a sick or mentally damaged pet.

2.  During the month of February, twelve students were mugged at knifepoint in the main student parking garage. In April, a woman barricaded herself in the garage elevator to escape an assailant. In June, two cars parked on the top level of the garage had their windshields smashed. My roommate is even afraid to park her car on campus.

**EXERCISE 15.4**  Revise the following paragraph to create a more civil tone. Assume that you're writing to readers of your campus newspaper.

Apparently the university "doesn't have the funds" this year to renovate the dorms on campus. Whatever. It's tough for me to believe that there's a money shortage when every time I pass by the president's house he's having another fancy party for his rich donor friends. Everyone knows that all the administrators do is go to parties, make a speech every now and then, and draw fat salaries. What a scam! They don't care about the students; they just care about lining their wallets. If they had to live in our dorms, I bet we'd see some upgrades pretty fast.

# 15d How do you avoid stereotyped language?

Biased language isn't always bad. Slanted but colorful writing regularly enlivens articles in popular books, humorous pieces in magazines, and the editorial pages of any newspaper. When you write papers in college, in business, or in most community settings, however, you have a different kind of audience. Now you're writing to inform or persuade readers whom you don't know well, and you don't want to offend them by lapsing into language that excludes a part of your audience or suggests that you think in stereotypes.

No matter who their audience may be, responsible writers avoid language that stigmatizes or demeans particular groups. Language that attributes to individuals negative associations based on gender, race or ethnicity, religion, profession, or class is always out of place in public writing.

**● 1 Avoid sexist language.** Over the past four decades, women's activists have made most of us more aware of how profoundly language shapes attitudes and reinforces traditional gender roles. To keep sexist blunders out of your writing, consider these guidelines.

- **Avoid using *he* and *him* as all-purpose pronouns to refer to people in general.** Use *he or she* or *him or her.* Using plurals will often solve the problem of sexist pronouns.

| WHY WRITE . . . | WHEN YOU COULD WRITE . . . |
|---|---|
| Every executive expects *his* bonus. | Every executive expects *a* bonus. Executives expect *their* bonuses. Every executive expects *his or her* bonus. |

- **Avoid using the word *man* as a catchall term to refer to all people or all members of a group.**

| WHY WRITE . . . | WHEN YOU COULD WRITE . . . |
|---|---|
| the *man* who wants to be an astronaut | *anyone* who wants to be an astronaut |
| *men* who do their own auto repairs | *car owners* who do their own repairs |

- **Avoid implying that professions or roles are primarily for men or for women.**

| WHY WRITE . . . | WHEN YOU COULD WRITE . . . |
|---|---|
| *men* who hope to become professional basketball players | *young people* who hope to become professional basketball players |
| stay-at-home *mothers* | stay-at-home *parents* |
| police*man* | police officer |
| business*men* | business executives |

- **When possible, find out what name a married woman wants to go by and honor that choice.** Here are the possibilities.

| | |
|---|---|
| woman's first and last names | Olga Perez |
| woman's first and last names + husband's last name | Olga Perez Marciano |
| woman's first name + hyphenated last name | Olga Perez-Marciano |
| woman's first name + husband's last name | Olga Marciano |
| title + husband's full name | Mrs. Ralph Marciano |

Many women, single or married, prefer the title *Ms.* to *Miss* or *Mrs.* When you're not sure, *Ms.* is the best choice.

- **Avoid implying that men and women behave in stereotypical ways.** Don't suggest that women are generally talkative and overly emotional or that most men are sports-minded and sloppy. Avoid sexist descriptions such as "a slim blonde" or "a petite brunette" unless you make the same kind of comments about men. Finally, the generic term *woman* (or *women*) is more appropriate than *lady* or *girl.*

**EXERCISE 15.5** Rewrite the following sentences to eliminate sexist language or implications.

1. Women in their forties and fifties who want to look their best often consider cosmetic surgery.

2. Today even a high school physics teacher should know his chaos theory, or he'll look out of date to his students.

3. Businesswomen often worry about leaving their children in day care while they work long hours to get ahead.

4. The blonde lady running for Congress in my district has been a county judge for many years.

● **2 Avoid language that suggests racial or ethnic bias.** In many writing situations, you simply don't need to mention race or national origin—it's not relevant. However, when issues of race or nationality are central to your discussion, these guidelines may be helpful.

- **Be specific and accurate in your descriptions.** For example, *Asian* may be too broad to be meaningful; *Filipino, Japanese, Chinese, Korean*, and *East Indian* are more specific. Likewise, rather than use *Hispanic*, use *Cuban, Puerto Rican, Mexican*, as appropriate. The term *Latino* (or *Latina*), used to refer broadly to people of Latin American descent, is widely accepted.

  When you refer to individuals whose forebears came from another country but who were themselves born in the United States, combine the term with *American*: for example, *Japanese American*. *Native American* is preferable to *Indian*; *Inuit* is now preferred to *Eskimo*.

  When you're writing about individuals' religious affiliations, be similarly specific; generalizations such as *Eastern sects* and *Christian conservatives* are vague and inaccurate. It's better to specify a particular religion or denomination (*Sunni Muslims, Orthodox Jews, Southern Baptists*) or to name a particular religious group (*Promise Keepers, Campus Crusade for Christ*).

- **Use terminology preferred by the people you're writing about, insofar as you know their preferences.** If you're not sure, adopt the terminology you see in major newspapers and magazines. For example, preferred usage in these media seems to have shifted from *black* to *African American*.

- **Be careful not to allow ethnic, national, or religious stereotypes to sneak into your writing.** Might one infer from your language that you think of Jews as rich financiers? Is there a hint that someone with an Italian surname has underworld connections? Check your writing for such biases.

**EXERCISE 15.6** Almost everyone has had some experience with the difficult issue of ethnic labels and names. Working with fellow students, make a list of all the ethnic groups represented in your composition class, writing on the board the terms preferred by members of each definable group. Discuss those preferences and a writer's responsibility to know and use them.

**EXERCISE 15.7** Consider which of these sentences might be inappropriate in an academic paper. Which seem acceptable? Why? Revise those that aren't appropriate.

1. Jewish director-producer Steven Spielberg traces his interest in filmmaking back to his childhood, when he recorded family occasions with his parents' movie camera.

2. Negro baseball players formed their own leagues in the early 1900s.

3. Indians, Eskimos, and other primitive groups are often portrayed sympathetically in the movies.

4. Unlike most American teenagers, Asian students are hardworking, academically oriented, and respectful of authority figures.

● **3 Avoid stereotypes about age, physical condition, and sexual orientation.** A responsible writer strives to treat all groups and individuals fairly and with respect. These guidelines may be helpful.

- **For people in their sixties or older, use specific designations such as** *middle sixties* **or** *early eighties* **rather than** *elderly, senior citizens,* **or** *old people.* Don't slip into patronizing remarks such as "For a 75-year-old man, he's remarkably alert."

- **Reserve the terms** *boys, girls, children,* **and** *kids* **for people under age twelve.** *Kids* is appropriate only in casual writing. *Teens* and *youths* are fine for high school students. *College kids* is patronizing as well as inaccurate: almost half of all U.S. college students now are over 25.

- **Be as specific as possible when you refer to people's disabilities or illnesses, and avoid language that implies pity—for example,** *crippled* **and** *victim.* In general, mention the individual first and his or her handicap or illness second—"a person with AIDS" or "my cousin who is autistic." Terms such as *disabled* and *hearing-impaired* are generally acceptable. Once again, it's useful to know with what terms the individuals themselves feel comfortable.

- **Mention a person's sexual orientation only when it is relevant to the issue under discussion, and then use specific, nonjudgmental terminology.** Many people whose sexual orientation is toward their own gender are comfortable with the adjective *homosexual* to refer to both men and women but less comfortable with the noun, *a homosexual.* You may use the terms *gay* and *lesbian* when you want to be more specific. Although some groups of gay rights advocates use the word *queer* in their literature, that term is inappropriate coming from someone outside such a group. The use of the word *gay* as an all-purpose pejorative is also offensive.

**EXERCISE 15.8** Working in a group, decide which of these sentences have hints of offensive bias (some of them are certainly arguable). Which might be acceptable in some circumstances? How could you change those that are not?

1. Barney Frank, who is almost the only open homosexual in the U.S. Congress, represents a district in Massachusetts.

2. Although Betty Friedan is over 70, she still writes extensively and travels widely.

3. The hospice is looking for volunteers to help AIDS victims with household tasks and grocery shopping.

**4 Avoid language that derides people's professions or implies unflattering class distinctions.** In serious writing, don't use *shrink* for psychiatrist or *cop* for police officer. Also avoid terms that have negative class connotations, such as *preppie, yuppie, soccer mom, welfare mother, redneck,* and *dropout.* Terms such as *ghetto* and *lower class* are demeaning; instead, use *low income.*

**5 Use good judgment and keep your sense of humor when you edit for bias.** Don't sanitize your writing to the point that it becomes deadly dull. Every day we read columnists or listen to commentators who

Humor is not always civil. Satirical items such as this one posted on *The Onion* (<http://www.theonion.com>) push the envelope, hoping to arouse and, sometimes, even offend readers. Do you find this graphic funny? Why or why not? Which words and phrases would be inappropriate for academic or professional writing? In what situations might you "push the envelope" in your own writing?

| Leading Ways To Reduce Gas Use | |
| --- | --- |
| Getting drunk at home | $17\frac{9}{10}$ % |
| Repealing the federal Mandatory Car Ownership Act of 1953 | $39\frac{9}{10}$ % |
| No longer leaving car running while parked overnight | $19\frac{9}{10}$ % |
| Invading unsuspecting wind-powered nation of Holland | $25\frac{9}{10}$ % |

Reprinted with permission of THE ONION. © 2005, by ONION, INC. www.theonion.com

use biased language to spoof, satirize, persuade, or praise, and they do it very well. It's unrealistic to say you should never use biased or exaggerated language to convey a mood, create an image, or make sardonic comments. Like a professional writer, however, you should make it your goal to be so attuned to your readers that you can write for them with respect, awareness, and good taste—and still have fun with language.

**EXERCISE 15.9** Which of these sentences might alienate a reader sensitive to bias? Which ones should be changed? Why or why not? What changes would you suggest?

1. The cops used poor judgment about gathering evidence at the crime scene.

2. Welfare mothers have become the target of budget-conscious legislators who believe that hardworking taxpayers shouldn't have to support people who won't work.

3. That organization is known for attracting sorority girls and fraternity guys.

4. It's amazing that Jason became a successful lawyer, since he grew up in the inner-city ghetto, surrounded by poverty and despair.

● **6 Check that photos or other visual images in a document don't suggest harmful stereotypes.** Because images often affect readers more immediately than words do, select photos and other visuals as carefully as you choose your words—if not more so. Are you writing an illustrated history of jazz for your music history course? Be sure to include photos of African American, white, and Latino musicians. Are you composing a brochure to publicize a campus organization whose members include nontraditional students? Make sure that your cover photo doesn't include only 18-year-olds. Visual elements and text should work together to create a fair, accurate picture of the subject at hand.

## **15e** How do you handle language varieties?

If you're like most people in the United States, you know several varieties of English, each shaped by your cultural heritage, your region, and your exposure to other languages. Linguists call these varieties of English **dialects**. Dialects of English—which include southern dialect, northeastern dialect, African American Vernacular English (AAVE), standard English, and many others—differ from each other in vocabulary, pronunciation, and grammar. Their features can be quite distinctive.

One dialect of English, sometimes referred to as **edited American English**, or **standard English**, is the language used in most academic, business, and public writing. It's the variety taught in most schools and emphasized in this book. If a regional dialect you use in other settings differs from this "standard," you may have difficulties when some of its features appear in your writing. You can use this handbook and other resources, such as your campus writing center, to edit out those features.

Learning to use a standard dialect for certain writing situations doesn't mean that you have to abandon all others. It means only that you have to cultivate some flexibility so that you can switch back and forth among different ways of speaking as the situation demands. But all educated people need to be able to use the standard written dialect of the United States, edited American English, so they can communicate on an equal footing with the millions of others who use it.

In addition to the various dialects of English, many languages are spoken in the United States. If you speak English as your second language (ESL), you'll find information in Chapters 31 through 33, in addition to the information at the end of this chapter, to help you with the challenges of writing in a new language.

In certain writing situations, it may be effective for writers to mix different dialects or languages, as this home page for *BarrioRBK* (a Web site sponsored by the Reebok shoe company to promote its products to young Latinos <www.rbk.com/us/barrio/>) illustrates. Notice how the site mixes English and Spanish to appeal to a specific audience. Do you ever use a mix of dialects or languages in your writing? What language varieties would you include if you were asked to create a site similar to *BarrioRBK*, aimed at a group you belong to?

**●1 Recognize the uses and importance of dialects.** Regional and nonstandard dialects are important and useful to the groups that speak them. A dialect helps to hold a group together and to give it a sense of community and identity. Dialects thus should be appreciated and protected for private communication among individuals within a particular community. Usually such communication is spoken.

Here is how the writer James Lee Burke represents the Cajun dialect of southern Louisiana in a novel.

> She had put my three-legged raccoon, Tripod, on his chain. [. . .] She pulled him up in the air by his chain. His body danced and curled as if he were being garroted.
> "Clarise, don't do that."
> "Ask him what he done, him," she said. "Go look my wash basket. Go look your shirts. They blue yesterday. They brown now. So smell, you."
> "I'll take him down to the dock."

"Tell Batiste not to bring him back, no. [. . .] He come in my house again, you gonna see him cooking with the sweet potato."

—James Lee Burke, *Black Cherry Blues*

**● 2 Acknowledge the limitations of dialect and use it appropriately in your writing.** When regional or nonstandard dialects show up in *public writing*—and that is what most of the writing you do in college and your profession will be—they can be misinterpreted. Some vocabulary within a dialect may not be understood by those outside it. Certain grammatical forms that are completely natural and logical within a dialect community may be regarded as nonstandard by other users of the language. Letting a private dialect enter your writing, then, is not "wrong"—but it may be inappropriate for the writing situation.

When can you use a nonstandard dialect in your writing? First, you can use it in your private life among friends, family, or others who share the dialect, either in conversation or in letters or email. Second, you might use it in a first, discovery draft when you're trying to get your ideas down and don't want to slow your thinking by worrying about the conventions of standard English. (You can edit out or translate inappropriate dialect features in a future draft.) Finally, you might use dialect in an anecdote you are adding to a paper to illustrate a point, or you could incorporate it into dialogue that is an essential part of a personal narrative. Here's an example from a professional writer.

Two years ago, when I started writing this paper, trying to bring order out of chaos, my ten-year-old daughter was suffering from an acute attack of boredom. [. . .] Patiently I explained that I was working on something special and needed peace and quiet, and I suggested that she paint, read, or work with her computer. None of these interested her. Finally, she pulled up a chair to my desk and watched me, now and then heaving long, loud sighs. [. . .] I lost my patience. "Looka here, Allie," I said, "you too old for this kinda carryin' on. I done told you this is important. You wronger than dirt to be in here haggin' me like this and you know it."

—Barbara Mellix, "From Outside, In"

Except for these instances, however, spoken dialect generally doesn't fit into the kind of public writing you'll be doing in college, in business, or in community work.

● **3 Use languages other than English sparingly.** If you speak a language other than English, you might use it in your writing for the same reasons that you'd use a nonstandard dialect of English. You might use it in your private life to communicate among friends or family or to explore and develop ideas before beginning a writing project.

You might also use another language to reproduce a speaker's exact words or to create an authentic atmosphere in a description or narrative. Finally, it's appropriate to include non-English words that can't easily be translated into English, as the essayist Judith Ortiz Cofer does in the following example.

> Even the home movie cannot fill in the sensory details such a gathering [a family New Year's Eve party] left imprinted in a child's brain. The thick sweetness of women's perfumes mixing with the ever-present smells of food cooking in the kitchen: meat and plantain *pasteles,* as well as the ubiquitous rice dish made special with pigeon peas—*gandules*—and seasoned with previous *sofrito* sent up from the Island by somebody's mother or smuggled in by a recent traveler.
>
> —Judith Ortiz Cofer, "Silent Dancing"

As with dialect, words and phrases from different languages should be used in public writing only to achieve a particular effect—otherwise you'll risk confusing readers. And if the meaning of a word or phrase isn't apparent from the context, it's wise to provide an English translation, as Cofer does above.

# 16 How Do You Construct Effective Sentences?

## 16a How are sentences structured?

Traditional terms used to describe the architecture of sentences—*clauses, phrases, subordination, coordination, parallelism*—can make writing sentences seem complicated. But even the most complex sentences are based on a few comprehensible structures and principles. We cover these elements in this chapter.

We know, of course, that you'll rarely think about particular sentence structures when you compose. Few writers—if any—work that way. But even while dashing off a draft, you'll be more confident when you've developed a feel for the way sentences function, an instinct for how the parts fit together.

**◑ 1 Understand sentence patterns.** Sentences are tough to define. A **sentence** can be described as a group of words that expresses an idea and that is punctuated as an independent unit. All sentences have a **subject** (the doer of an action) and a **predicate** (the action done). Beginning with this assumption, you'll find that just five patterns can describe the framework of many sentences you write. In recognizing these patterns and their variations, you take a step toward controlling the shape of your sentences.

1. **Subject + verb (intransitive).** This is the simplest sentence pattern, the one with the fewest parts. Like all sentences, it includes a *subject*, the doer of an action; and a *verb*, the action performed. But in this pattern the verb is *intransitive*—that is, it doesn't need an object to complete its meaning.

| Subject | Verb (intransitive) |
|---|---|
| The lawyer | fainted. |
| The floodwaters | receded. |
| All the children | smiled at once. |

**EXERCISE 16.1** Compose three sentences that follow the subject–intransitive verb pattern. Underline the intransitive verb in each sentence.

2. **Subject + verb (transitive) + direct object.** This sentence pattern adds a third element to the subject and verb: an *object*, which identifies to what or to whom an action has been done. Objects can be words, phrases, or clauses. The pattern requires a transitive verb that conveys its action to an object.

| Subject | Verb (transitive) | Object |
|---|---|---|
| The lawyer | accepted | the case. |
| The heavy rains | destroyed | the levee. |
| Some of the children | were reading | books. |

Note that the subject–verb–object pattern illustrates the *active voice*, in which the subject performs the action described by the transitive verb. But when that action is performed by the object, you have a *passive construction* (see Section 23e).

The case was accepted by the lawyer.

The levee was destroyed by heavy rains.

The books were being read by some of the children.

Only transitive verbs can be involved in passive constructions because they require an object that can become a subject. Intransitive verbs don't take objects.

A transitive verb and its object must fit together logically. In the following example, the verb *intimidate* cannot logically convey its action to the object *enthusiasm*. *Enthusiasm* might be *undermined, dampened,* or *eroded,* but we don't usually speak of it as *intimidated.*

| FAULTY | The negative attitudes of the senior staff *intimidated* the **enthusiasm** of the volunteers. |
|---|---|
| REVISED | The negative attitudes of the senior staff *dampened* the **enthusiasm** of the volunteers. |

**EXERCISE 16.2** Write three sentences that follow the subject–verb–object pattern. Underline the object. Be sure the verb is in the active voice.

**EXERCISE 16.3** Revise any of the following sentences in which the bold-faced verb cannot logically convey its action to its object. First try to explain the problem with the original verb; then change the verb, not the object.

1. At her parents' request, Margery **interrogated** her sister Kyla's low grades at college.

2. Kyla **blasphemed** her instructor's methods of teaching history.

3. Her chemistry teacher **obliged** difficult lab reports every week.

4. Worst of all, her English teacher persistently **admonished** the clarity of her writing.

3. **Subject + verb (linking) + subject complement.** Linking verbs, which are often forms of *to be*, connect a subject to a subject complement, that is, to a word or phrase that extends or completes the meaning of a subject or renames it in some way. Among the common linking verbs are *to seem, to appear, to feel,* and *to become.*

| Subject | Linking verb | Subject complement |
|---------|--------------|--------------------|
| The lawyer | became | a federal judge. |
| The storms | seemed | endless. |
| The children | are | happy. |

A complement should be compatible with its subject. When it is not, the sentence is illogical, sometimes subtly so.

FAULTY COMPLEMENT **Prejudice** is unacceptable **behavior** in this club.

The problem is that *prejudice* is not behavior; it's an attitude. So the sentence has to be modified to reflect this difference.

REVISED **Prejudiced behavior** is unacceptable in this club.

For the same reason, it's wrong to use *when* as a complement.

> **WRONG**    **Plagiarism** is **when** a writer doesn't credit her source.

*When* is an adverb; *plagiarism* is a noun. *Plagiarism* has to be a concept or an idea, so it cannot be *when*.

> **RIGHT**    **Plagiarism** is the **failure** to credit a source.

**EXERCISE 16.4**  In the following sentences, indicate whether the bold-faced words are objects or complements.

1. Halloween may be the oddest **holiday** of the year.

2. The roots of Halloween are deeply **religious**.

3. But Halloween celebrations today seem quite **secular**.

4. Children and adults wear **costumes** and pull **pranks**.

**EXERCISE 16.5**  Write three sentences that follow the subject–verb–subject complement pattern. Underline the subject complement. Try to vary your linking verbs.

**EXERCISE 16.6**  Revise any of the following sentences in which the subject complement cannot work logically with its subject. First explain the problem with the original complement; then change the complement, not the subject. The complement is boldfaced.

1. Photography is an excellent **fun**.

2. Revising every paper in this class four times seems **exorbitant**.

3. Gerald felt **unconscionable** after arriving too late to say farewell.

4. Philosophy is **when** you read Plato and Aristotle.

4. **Subject + verb (transitive) + indirect object + direct object.** An **indirect object** explains for whom or to what an action is done or directed. As you can see in this pattern, indirect objects ordinarily precede direct objects.

| Subject | Verb (transitive) | Indirect object | Direct object |
|---------|-------------------|-----------------|---------------|
| The lawyer | found | the clerk | a job. |
| The storms | brought | local farmers | needed rain. |
| The children | told | their parents | stories. |

If you have trouble understanding what an indirect object does in a sentence, turn it into the object of a prepositional phrase.

The lawyer found a job **for the clerk**.
The storms brought needed rain **to local farmers**.
The children told stories **to their parents**.

**EXERCISE 16.7** In the following sentences, circle the indirect objects and underline the objects.

1. The placement office finds students jobs after college.

2. Did you send Rosa, Peg, Lester, and Davida the same email message?

3. Give Daisy more cookies.

4. The distinguished senator gives proponents of the National Endowment for the Arts headaches.

**EXERCISE 16.8** Write three sentences that follow the subject–verb–indirect object–direct object pattern. Circle the indirect object and underline the direct object.

5. **Subject + verb (transitive) + direct object + object complement.** Just as a subject complement modifies or explains a subject, an **object complement** does the same for the object of a sentence.

## 16a
### sent How Do You Construct Effective Sentences?

| Subject | Verb (transitive) | Direct object | Object complement |
|---------|-------------------|---------------|-------------------|
| The lawyer | called | the verdict | surprising. |
| The flood | caught | the town | napping. |
| The children | found | their spinach | vile. |

**EXERCISE 16.9** In the following sentences, underline the direct objects and circle the object complements.

1. Most men find football entertaining.

2. Thoroughbred horses often turn their wealthy owners poor.

3. Our careful preparation makes us lucky.

4. The mayor called the federal court decision against the city ordinance unfortunate.

**EXERCISE 16.10** Write three sentences that follow the subject–verb–direct object–object complement pattern. Underline the direct object and circle the subject complement.

**● 2 Understand compound subjects, verbs, and objects.** You can develop sentences simply by expanding their subjects, verbs, or objects to include all the ideas you need to express. Such modifications are usually routine, but some writers do have problems punctuating the resulting sentences.

**Compound subjects.** Two subjects attached to the same verb are usually connected by the conjunction *and* or *or*. No comma is needed between these compound subjects.

> **Lawyers and judges** attended the seminar.

> **Storms or fires** ravage California each year.

When a third subject is added, the items are separated by commas (see Section 36c-2).

> **Storms, fires, and earthquakes** ravage California each year.

Subjects can also be expanded by expressions such as *neither . . . nor* and *either . . . or*, which are called **correlatives**.

> **Neither the judge nor the lawyer** attended the seminar.

> **Either fires or earthquakes** strike California each year.

**Compound verbs.**   Single subjects can perform more than one action. When they do, the verbs attached to them are compound. Like nouns, verbs can be joined by *and, or*, or correlatives such as *either . . . or*. No comma should be used between two verbs that form a compound verb.

> The judge **confused and angered** the prosecutor.

> The earthquake **damaged or destroyed** many homes.

> Children **either like or hate** spinach.

When a third verb is added, the items are separated by commas.

> The judge **confused, angered, and embarrassed** the prosecutor.

Compound verbs can each take separate objects, expanding the sentence structure even more.

> The judge **confused** *the jury* **and angered** *the prosecutor.*

> The earthquake **damaged** *roads* **and destroyed** *homes.*

**Compound objects.**   A verb may also have more than one object. Two objects attached to the same verb are usually connected by the conjunction *and* or *or*. No comma is needed between two objects; commas are required for three or more objects.

> Lawyers attended **the seminar and the dinner**.

> Forest fires ravage **California, Arizona, New Mexico, or Colorado** every year.

Objects can also be connected with correlatives.

> Forest fires ravage **either California or New Mexico** every year.

Many variations of these elements are possible. But don't pile up more compound expressions than readers can handle easily. Sentences should always be readable.

**TOO MANY COMPOUNDS**

Both lawyers and judges attended the after-lunch seminars and discussion groups; broke for drinks, cocktails, and coffee in the late afternoon; returned for a film, a professional roundtable, and a business session; and then either went out to dinner or retired to their hotels.

**REVISED FOR CLARITY**

Both lawyers and judges attended the after-lunch seminars and discussion groups. **They** broke for drinks, cocktails, and coffee in the late afternoon **and then** returned for a film, a professional roundtable, and a business session. **Afterward**, they either went out to dinner or retired to their hotels.

# 16b What do modifiers do?

**Modifiers** are words, phrases, or clauses that expand what we know about subjects, verbs, or other sentence elements, including other modifiers and complete sentences. In fact, it would be hard to compose sentences without them. Even simple modifiers change the texture of sentences, while more complex modifiers increase your options for shaping sentences.

● **1 Use adjectives to modify nouns and pronouns.** Adjectives describe and help to explain nouns and pronouns by specifying *how many, which size, what color, what condition, which one*, and so on. Single adjectives are usually placed before the terms they modify.

The **angry** judge scowled at the **nervous** witness.

But adjectives often work in groups. Adjectives in a group are called **coordinate adjectives** when each one works on its own, describing different and unrelated aspects of a noun or pronoun.

the **undistinguished, tired-looking** lawyer

our cat, **shedding and overweight**

Placed before a noun or pronoun, coordinate adjectives can be linked either by conjunctions (usually *and*) or by commas. The order of the adjectives doesn't affect their meaning.

> The **angry, perspiring** judge scowled at the **balding and nervous** witness.

> The **perspiring, angry** judge scowled at the **nervous and balding** witness.

> The **tired and underpaid** jurors listened to a **tedious and awkward** interrogation.

> The **underpaid and tired** jurors listened to an **awkward and tedious** interrogation.

Coordinate adjectives may also follow the words they modify, giving variety to sentence rhythms.

> The judge, **angry and perspiring**, scowled at the witness, **balding and nervous**.

For a stylish variation, you can also move coordinate adjectives ahead of an article (*the*) at the beginning of a sentence.

> **Tired, bored, and underpaid**, the jurors listened to an endless interrogation.

Not all clusters of adjectives are coordinate. Often groups of adjectives must follow a specific sequence to make sense. Changing their sequence produces expressions that are not *idiomatic*; that is, they don't sound right to a native English speaker.

| | |
|---|---|
| **NOT IDIOMATIC** | the wooden heavy gavel |
| **IDIOMATIC** | the heavy wooden gavel |
| **NOT IDIOMATIC** | a woolen green sweater |
| **IDIOMATIC** | a green woolen sweater |
| **NOT IDIOMATIC** | the American first satellite |
| **IDIOMATIC** | the first American satellite |

Adjectives in such groupings—which often include numbers—are not separated by commas.

> The judge wielded a **heavy wooden** gavel.

The **first American** satellite was Explorer I.

The police rescued **two lucky** kayakers.

Adjectives (along with adverbs and nouns) can also form *compound* or *unit modifiers*, groups of words linked by hyphens that modify a noun (see Section 40c-5). The individual words in compound modifiers need each other; they often wouldn't make sense standing alone in front of a noun.

A **well-known** case would provide a **high-impact** precedent.

The **wine-dark** sea surged in the moonlight.

Finally, adjectives play an important role as subject complements and object complements (see Section 16a-1), modifying words to which they are joined by linking verbs.

The judge's decision seemed **eccentric**.

The children were **sleepy**.

The press called the jury **inept**.

**EXERCISE 16.11** Rewrite each of the following sentences so that the adjectives in parentheses modify an appropriate noun or pronoun. Place the adjectives before or after the word they modify, and punctuate them correctly (for example, be sure to add hyphens to unit modifiers and to separate coordinate adjectives with commas or the conjunction *and* as necessary).

1. The elm trees once common throughout North America have disappeared, victims of disease. (*towering; graceful; Dutch elm*)

2. This infection destroys the vascular system of the elm, causing trees to become husks in a few short weeks. (*fungal; relentless; mature; thriving; leafless*)

3. Few parks in the United States can match the diversity of New York's Central Park, with its zoo, gardens and fields, ponds and lakes, and museum. (*great urban; sizable; pleasant; glistening; world class*)

4. Bankers, show people, and street people alike jostle shoulders and shopping bags in this oasis. (*wealthy; glittering; down on their luck; refreshing; urban*)

**● 2** **Use adverbs to modify verbs, adjectives, and other adverbs.** Adverbs in sentences explain *how, when, where,* and *to what degree* things happen.

**ADVERBS THAT MODIFY VERBS**

The prosecutor *spoke* **eloquently** to the jury.

**Immediately**, the defense attorney *replied.*

The jury *tried* **hard** to follow their summaries.

**ADVERBS THAT MODIFY ADJECTIVES**

Tornadoes seem **freakishly** *unpredictable.*

Tornado chasing remains **quite** *popular.*

**ADVERBS THAT MODIFY OTHER ADVERBS**

The reading program has improved **very** *considerably.*

**Less** *easily* appreciated is a new interest in music at the school.

Adverbs increase your options in constructing sentences because they typically can be put in more places than adjectives, enabling you to experiment with sentence structure and rhythm. All three versions of the following sentence convey the same information, but they do so in subtly different ways.

The news reporter **passionately and repeatedly** defended the integrity of her story.

**Passionately and repeatedly**, the news reporter defended the integrity of her story.

The news reporter defended the integrity of her story **passionately and repeatedly**.

But this very flexibility causes significant problems. Be sure to review Section 30f on the appropriate placement of adverbs, especially *only.*

**EXERCISE 16.12** Rewrite the following sentences so that each adverb in parentheses modifies an appropriate verb, adjective, or adverb. Notice which adverbs work best in one position only and which can be relocated more freely in a sentence.

1. The elm trees once common throughout North America have disappeared, victims of disease. (*sadly; quite; almost; completely*)

2. This lethal infection destroys the vascular system of the elm, causing trees to become husks in a few short weeks. (*nearly; always; completely*)

3. Annoyed, the senator replied to the reporter in an angry tone. (*visibly; unusually*)

4. We left the photo shop poorer but better equipped for difficult telephoto shots. (*considerably; much; extremely*)

**● 3 Understand that nouns can operate as modifiers.** In some sentences you may find words that look like nouns but act like adjectives, modifying other words. Don't be confused: nouns often work as modifiers.

> We ordered the **sausage** plate and a **vegetable** sampler.
>
> The **instrument** cluster glowed red at night.

Proper nouns can serve as modifiers too.

> The choir was preparing for the **Christmas** service.
>
> We ordered a **New York** strip steak.

**EXERCISE 16.13** In the following sentences, underline any nouns that function as modifiers. Discuss disputed cases with colleagues.

1. The Atlanta Braves, Washington Redskins, and Cleveland Indians are sports teams whose names occasionally stir controversy among Native American political interest groups.

2. Car insurance is getting so expensive in urban areas that many college students have to rely on the city bus.

3. Ike signed up for the yoga class because his doctor told him that doing the cobra stretch and the sun salutation would strengthen his injured back muscles.

4. At Martha's Fourth of July party, the Vienna sausage didn't sit well with the Boston cream pie and strawberry ice cream.

**● 4 Understand that verbals can operate as modifiers.**
Especially common as modifiers are participles—words such as *dazzling, frightening, broken*. Because participles are based on verbs, they give energy and snap to sentences.

> The waiter brought a **sizzling** steak on a **steaming** bed of rice.
>
> The margaritas arrived **frozen**, not on the rocks.
>
> The officer, **smiling**, wrote us a $100 ticket.
>
> **Trembling**, I opened the **creaking** door.

For more about participle and infinitive phrases, see Section 16c-2.

**EXERCISE 16.14** In the following sentences, underline any participles that function as modifiers. Discuss disputed cases with colleagues.

1. I. M. Pei is one of America's most original and inspiring architects.

2. Born in Guangzhou, China, in 1916, Pei came to the United States in 1935 and became a naturalized citizen in 1954.

3. Pei is responsible for some of the most startling and admired buildings of our era.

4. Pei's work includes the glittering and much debated pyramid that now serves as the main entrance to the Louvre, one of the leading museums in the world.

5. Yet Pei can also count among his commissions Cleveland's Rock and Roll Hall of Fame, a daring work poised on the shores of Lake Erie.

# 16c What are phrases?

Technically, a **phrase** is a group of related words without a subject and a finite verb, but this definition is hard to follow. It's probably more helpful to appreciate phrases in action, doing their part to give shape to sentences.

● **1 Understand prepositional phrases.** Among the more mundane of sentence elements, a *prepositional phrase* consists of a preposition and its object, either a noun or a pronoun. The object can be modified.

| Preposition | Modifier (optional) | Object(s) |
|---|---|---|
| to | | Jeff and me |
| in | your own | words |
| beyond | the farthest | mountain |

It's easy to generate examples of prepositional phrases: *off the sofa, on the hard drive, across the miles, under the spreading chestnut tree, over the far horizon, from me, for her.* Just try writing a paragraph without using prepositional phrases and you'll appreciate how essential they are to establishing relationships within sentences. Don't, however, mistake prepositional phrases with *to* (*to Starbucks, to Lila*) for infinitives or infinitive phrases, which include a verb form (*to see, to watch the stars, to be happy*). For more on prepositions and infinitives, see Section 24a-1.

The power of prepositional phrases resides in their flexibility and simplicity. Moving a prepositional phrase into an unexpected slot gets it noticed. Consider what happens to the first sentence in this paragraph when its prepositional phrase is repositioned.

ORIGINAL    The power of prepositional phrases resides in their flexibility and simplicity.

PREPOSITIONAL  In their flexibility and simplicity, the power of
PHRASE MOVED  prepositional phrases resides.

The sentence sounds just different (some might say awkward) enough to cause readers to pause—which may or may not be the effect you wish to achieve. And that's the point: where you put prepositional phrases can influence readers enough to make a difference. For additional discussion, see Section 17c-7.

**EXERCISE 16.15** Study the following passages and discuss the effect of relocating the boldfaced prepositional phrases within the speeches. How would the style of the passage be changed—if at all?

1. **Upon this battle** depends the survival of Christian civilization. **Upon it** depends our own British life, and the long continuity of our institutions and our Empire. The whole fury and might of the enemy must very soon be turned **on us**. Hitler knows he will have to break us in this island or lose the war.

   —Winston Churchill

2. **With malice toward none, with charity for all, with firmness in the right**, let us strive on to finish the work we are in, to bind up the nation's wounds, to care for him who shall have borne the battle and for his widow and his orphan, to do all which may achieve and cherish a just and lasting peace among ourselves and with all nations.

   —Abraham Lincoln

## ● **2** Appreciate the versatility of verbals and verbal phrases.

Verbals are verb forms that can act as nouns, adjectives, or adverbs (see Chapter 24). Verbals can stand alone, or they can form phrases by taking objects, complements, or modifiers.

|  | Verbal | Verbal phrase |
|---|---|---|
| **Infinitive** | to serve | to serve the sick |
|  | to prevent | to prevent forest fires |
| **Gerund** | serving | serving the sick [is] |
|  | preventing | preventing forest fires [is] |
| **Participle** | serving | serving without complaint, |
|  | prevented | prevented from helping, |

Verbals and verb phrases that act as nouns can serve as subjects or direct objects. As modifiers, verbals can function as adverbs or adjectives. Although verbals may seem complicated, you'll recognize the roles they play in sentences.

**Verbals as subjects.**    Both infinitives and gerunds can act as subjects in sentences. On their own, they don't look much different from other subjects.

> **INFINITIVE AS SUBJECT**
>
> **To serve** was the doctor's ambition.
>
> **GERUND AS SUBJECT**
>
> **Serving** was the doctor's ambition.

But when they expand into phrases, they can be harder to recognize. Yet they remain subjects and can be either simple or compound.

> **INFINITIVE PHRASES AS SUBJECTS**
>
> **To serve the sick** was the doctor's ambition.
>
> **To serve the sick and to comfort the afflicted** were the doctor's ambitions.
>
> **GERUND PHRASES AS SUBJECTS**
>
> **Serving the sick** was the doctor's ambition.
>
> **Serving the sick and comforting the afflicted** were the doctor's ambitions.

**Verbals as objects.**    Both infinitives and gerunds can act as objects in sentences. On their own, they don't look much different from other objects.

> **INFINITIVE AS DIRECT OBJECT**
>
> The lawyer loved **to object**.
>
> **GERUND AS DIRECT OBJECT**
>
> The lawyer loved **objecting**.

As phrases, verbals can seem complicated in their role as direct objects. Yet they play that role like any other noun, simple or compound.

> **INFINITIVE PHRASES AS DIRECT OBJECTS**
>
> The lawyer chose **to object to the motion**.
>
> The lawyer chose **to object to the motion and to move for a mistrial**.

**GERUND PHRASES AS DIRECT OBJECTS**

The lawyer loved **objecting to the prosecutor's motions**.

The lawyer loved **objecting to the prosecutor's motions and winning concessions from the judge**.

**Verbals as complements.**   Both infinitives and gerunds can act as complements in sentences.

**INFINITIVE AS SUBJECT COMPLEMENT**

To know Rebecca was **to love her**.

**GERUND AS OBJECT COMPLEMENT**

The IRS caught Elmo **cheating on his taxes**.

**Verbals as adjectives.**   You'll frequently want to use participles and participle phrases to modify nouns and pronouns in your sentences.

**PARTICIPLES AS ADJECTIVES**

**Frowning**, the instructor stopped her lecture.

The **suspended** fraternity appealed to the dean.

**PARTICIPLE PHRASES AS ADJECTIVES**

**Frowning at us**, the instructor stopped her lecture.

The fraternity, **suspended for underage drinking**, appealed to the dean.

We kept close to the trail, **not knowing the terrain well**.

Notice the freedom you have in placing participle phrases. You do want to be certain, however, that readers can have no doubt what a particular phrase modifies.

Infinitives, too, can function as adjectives, although it can be difficult to perceive the infinitive in this role as a modifier, providing details.

**INFINITIVES AS ADJECTIVES**

The manager had many items **to purchase**. modifies *items*

Reasons **to stay** were few. modifies *reasons*

**INFINITIVE PHRASES AS ADJECTIVES**

The manager had many items **to purchase for the grand opening**.
modifies *items*

Reasons **to stay calm** were few. modifies *reasons*

**Verbals as adverbs.** Infinitives and infinitive phrases can act like adverbs, answering such questions as *why, how, to what degree*, and so on.

**INFINITIVES AS ADVERBS**

Difficult **to please**, Martha rarely enjoyed movies. modifies *difficult*

The sedan seemed built **to last**. modifies *built*

**INFINITIVE PHRASES AS ADVERBS**

The gardener dug a trench **to stop the spread of oak wilt**. modifies *dug*

The Senate recessed **to give its members a summer vacation**.
modifies *recessed*

The pilot found it impossible **to see the runway in the fog**.
modifies *impossible*

**EXERCISE 16.16** Underline all verbals in the following sentences and then indicate whether they function as subjects, objects, complements, adjectives, or adverbs.

1. Waving at the crowd, the winner of the marathon took a victory lap.

2. The waiter certainly seemed eager to please us.

3. The salesperson enjoyed demonstrating the self-closing door on the minivan.

4. Harriet bought an awning to reduce the light streaming through her bay windows.

5. To cherish the weak and the dying was Mother Teresa's mission in life.

● **3 Understand absolute phrases. Absolutes** are versatile phrases that modify whole sentences rather than individual words. They are constructed from participles or infinitives. When absolute phrases are based on participles, they always include a subject and may include modifiers and other elements.

Our representatives will, **time permitting**, read the entire petition to the city council.

**The supply craft having docked**, the astronauts on the *International Space Station* were ready for their space walk.

Our plane arrived early, **the winds having been favorable**.

When the participle is a form of *to be*, it can often be omitted for a more economical or elegant expression.

**The winds [being] favorable**, our plane arrived early.

Absolutes based on infinitives don't require a noun or pronoun.

**To speak frankly**, we are facing the gravest crisis in the history of this company.

Your buzz cut, **to be honest**, would look better on a coconut.

Because absolutes are not attached to particular words, you can place them exactly where they work best in a sentence. Absolutes can add sophistication to your sentences. They are worth trying.

**EXERCISE 16.17** Turn the phrases in parentheses into absolutes and incorporate them into the full sentences preceding them.

> **EXAMPLE** The senator's amendment to the tax bill would fund a worthless pork barrel project. (*to put it bluntly*)
>
> **REVISION** The senator's amendment to the tax bill would, to put it bluntly, fund a worthless pork barrel project.

1. Many newspaper reporters don't know beans about their beats. (*to speak candidly*)

2. We should be able to take the launch to the island. (*the weather having cleared*)

3. Johnson became a viable candidate for governor again. (*the tide of public opinion having turned*)

4. Work in the electronic classrooms had to stop for the day. (*the entire network down*)

**● 4 Appreciate appositive phrases.** An **appositive** is a noun or noun phrase that restates or expands the meaning of the words it modifies. Think of appositives as variations on a theme, a second way of naming nouns and giving them more texture. Appositives are placed immediately after the words they modify and are usually surrounded by commas (see Section 36b-2).

> Napoleon, the **Emperor of France**, crowned himself.
>
> Death Valley, **the largest national park in the continental United States**, blooms with wildflowers in the spring.

Appositives are also routinely introduced by words or phrases such as *or, as, for example, such as*, and *in other words.*

> Dachshunds, **or wiener dogs**, are growing in popularity.
>
> Katharine Hepburn's best movies, **including *The African Queen* and *The Philadelphia Story***, are classics of American cinema.

Most appositives are interchangeable with the words they modify: delete those modified terms and the sentence still makes sense.

**APPOSITIVES AS MODIFIERS**

> Abraham Lincoln, **the first Republican President**, presided over the Civil War.
>
> Halloween, **All Hallows' Eve**, comes two days before All Souls' Day, **also known as the Day of the Dead**.

**MODIFIED TERMS REPLACED BY APPOSITIVES**

> **The first Republican President** presided over the Civil War.
>
> **All Hallows' Eve** comes two days before **the Day of the Dead**.

Some appositives—often proper nouns—can't be deleted without blurring the meaning of a sentence. These appositives are not surrounded by commas (see Section 36b-2).

> Bob Dylan's masterpiece ***Blonde on Blonde*** is a double album.
>
> Nixon **the diplomat** is more respected by historians than Nixon **the politician**.

**EXERCISE 16.18** Turn the phrase(s) in parentheses into appositives and incorporate them into the full sentences preceding them. Be sure to use the right punctuation.

EXAMPLE   Sally Ride served on the presidential commission that investigated the 1986 explosion of the space shuttle. (*America's first woman astronaut*; Challenger)

REVISION   Sally Ride, America's first woman astronaut, served on the presidential commission that investigated the explosion of the space shuttle *Challenger*.

1. Rudolph Giuliani first gained prominence as a federal prosecutor. (*107th mayor of New York City*)

2. In Anasazi architecture, a prominent feature is the kiva. (*a covered circular enclosure sunk in the ground and used for religious ceremonies and community meetings*)

3. The technique called pure fresco produces enduring images such as those on the ceiling of the Sistine Chapel. (*painting with plaster stained with pigment; Michelangelo's masterpiece*)

4. The gizzard of a bird is thick with muscles for grinding food. (*a part of the digestive system*)

5. Shakespeare's masterpiece includes three witches. (Macbeth; *the Weird Sisters*)

# 16d What do clauses do in sentences?

**Clauses** are groups of related words that have subjects and verbs. As such, they are the framework for most sentences, the parts to which other modifying words and phrases are attached. The four basic sentence types (*simple, compound, complex,* and *compound-complex*) are based on some combination of independent and dependent clauses (see Section 16e).

● **1 Understand independent clauses.** An **independent clause** can stand alone as a complete sentence. Most independent clauses have an identifiable subject and a predicate (that is, a verb plus its auxiliaries and modifiers). Sometimes a subject is understood and is not stated in the clause.

| Subject | Predicate |
|---------|-----------|
| The house | burned. |
| The dreams we had | came true today. |
| The children | caught colds. |
| [You] | Come here at once. |

**EXERCISE 16.19** Circle the subject and underline the predicate in the following independent clauses. If the subject is understood, write the word *understood* as the subject in parentheses after the sentence.

1. The wood on the deck warped after only one summer.

2. Jeremy has been trying to reach you all day.

3. Attend the rally this afternoon.

4. Keeping focused on schoolwork is hard on weekends.

5. Be careful.

● **2 Understand dependent clauses.** A **dependent clause** is one that cannot stand alone as a complete sentence. Many dependent clauses that have identifiable subjects and predicates are introduced by subordinating conjunctions—words such as *although, because, if, until, when, whenever, while*—that place the dependent clause in relationship to another independent clause.

| Subordinating conjunction | Subject | Predicate |
|---------------------------|---------|-----------|
| When | the house | burned . . . |
| If | the dreams we had | came true today . . . |
| Because | the children | caught colds . . . |

Dependent clauses can have various functions in a sentence. Easiest to understand are those that act as adjectives or adverbs. Slightly more intricate are dependent clauses that act as nouns (and serve as subjects, objects, or complements). Note that all dependent clauses must work with independent clauses to create complete sentences.

**Adjective clauses.**   **Adjective clauses**, also known as *relative clauses*, attach themselves to nouns or pronouns using one of the relative pronouns: *who, whom, whomever, whose, that, which.*

> Actress Gwyneth Paltrow, **who was born in Los Angeles**, moved to New York when she was 11 years old.
>
> Venus is the planet **that shines brightest in the sky**.

The adverbs *when* and *where* can introduce adjective clauses when the resulting clauses modify nouns, not verbs.

> The immigrants settled in those California cities **where jobs were plentiful**. clause modifies the noun *cities*, not the verb *settled*
>
> We enjoy the winter **when the snow falls**.
> clause modifies the noun *winter*, not the verb *enjoy*

Adjective clauses are surrounded by commas when they are considered nonessential—that is, when they can be removed from a sentence without destroying its coherence. When clauses are essential to the meaning of a sentence, they are not surrounded by commas (see Section 36d-5).

One caution about adjective clauses: sentences sometimes derail when a writer mistakes an adjective clause for a main clause.

> **INCORRECT**    Talks with North Korea **which** may create a situation favorable to the emergence of a middle class that will push for democratization.
>
> **REVISED**    Talks with North Korea may create a situation favorable to the emergence of a middle class that will push for democratization.

**EXERCISE 16.20** Add an adjective clause to each of the following sentences at the point indicated. Remember that adjective clauses are usually introduced by *who, whom, whomever, whose, that*, or *which*. An adjective clause may also begin with *where* or *when* if it modifies a noun, not a verb.

1. All the students in class who . . . said they supported the Democratic party's proposals.

2. But everyone in the class who . . . opposed the Democrats' policies.

3. Companies that . . . are prospering more today than firms that. . . .

4. The original *Star Wars* trilogy, which . . . , has been joined by a new series of films in the saga.

5. Teens prefer to congregate in places where. . . .

**Adverb clauses.** **Adverb clauses** work just like adverbs, modifying verbs, adjectives, and other adverbs. They are easy to spot since they are introduced by one of the many subordinating conjunctions, words such as *after, although, as, before, if, since, though, until, when,* and *while.*

> Lillian left **before the hail fell.** modifies the verb *left*
>
> The bookcase was not as heavy **as we had expected.**
> modifies the adjective *heavy*
>
> Hubert spoke haltingly **whenever a girl looked him in the eye.**
> modifies the adverb *haltingly*

Sometimes an adverb or subordinate clause seems to modify an entire sentence or a group of words.

> **Although the stock market plunged**, investors had high hopes for a quick recovery.

As subordinate clauses, adverb clauses play a notable role in crafting powerful sentences. For much more about subordination, see Section 16g.

**EXERCISE 16.21** Add an adverb clause to each of the following sentences at the point indicated. Remember that adverb clauses are introduced by subordinating conjunctions such as *although, before, since, unless,* and many others.

1. Even though . . . , Americans vote in record low numbers.

2. Many young people put little faith in the social security system since. . . .

**3.** If . . . the polar ice caps will melt and the level of the oceans will rise.

**4.** Although they . . . , surprising numbers of children still smoke.

**Noun clauses.**   Whole clauses that act as nouns are quite common. Such clauses act as subjects or objects, not as modifiers.

> **How a computer works** is beyond my understanding.
> noun clause as subject

> The FAA report did not explain **why the jets collided**.
> noun clause as direct object

> The employment agency found **whoever applied** a job.
> noun clause as indirect object

> You may speak to **whomever you wish**.
> noun clause as object of a preposition

Because noun clauses are distinctive structures, they can work beautifully in parallel constructions (see Section 16h), as this passage from Abraham Lincoln's Gettysburg Address illustrates.

> The world will little note, nor long remember, **what we say here**; but it can never forget **what they did here**.

**EXERCISE 16.22** Underline all the noun clauses in the following sentences. Then explain the function of each clause, as either a subject or an object.

**1.** What politicians say often matters much less than how they say it.

**2.** Whoever sent a letter of condolence should receive a prompt reply from us.

**3.** Why so many people care so much about celebrities is beyond my comprehension.

**4.** Someone had better explain how the dogs got loose.

# 16e What types of sentences can you write?

Although you'll rarely revise sentences just to make a *simple* sentence *compound* or a *compound* sentence *complex*, recognizing these terms will make it easier for you to diagnose problems in your sentences and to talk about them with peer editors. The most familiar sentence types are all built from just two basic components: independent clauses and subordinate clauses (see Section 16d).

**SIMPLE SENTENCE**
one independent clause
**Windows rattled.**

**COMPOUND SENTENCE**
independent clause + independent clause
**Windows rattled** and **doors shook.**

**COMPLEX SENTENCE**
dependent clause(s) + one independent clause
*As the storm blew*, **windows rattled.**

**COMPOUND-COMPLEX SENTENCE**
dependent clause(s) + two or more independent clauses
*As the storm blew*, **windows rattled** and **doors shook.**

● **1** Use simple sentences to express ideas clearly and directly.
Simple sentences can attract the attention of readers with the power of their single independent clauses.

> Jesus wept.

> I come to bury Caesar, not to praise him.

But don't assume that simple sentences will necessarily be short or without ornament.

> NASA, the federal agency in charge of space exploration, has no current plans for a moon base or for human missions to Mars and Venus, the planets closest to earth in both size and distance.

As you can see, simple sentences can be expanded by compounding or modifying their subjects, verbs, or objects.

| | |
|---|---|
| ORIGINAL SENTENCE | Extreme sports worry parents. |
| VERB EXPANDED | Extreme sports **have captured the attention of a fascinated media but worry many parents**. |
| OBJECT EXPANDED | Extreme sports worry **police, health-care workers, and many parents**. |
| EXPANDED SENTENCE | Increasingly popular among teenagers, extreme sports such as BMX biking, bungee jumping, and skateboarding have captured the attention of a fascinated media but worry police, health-care workers, and many parents. |

Despite its increased length, the final sentence still has only one independent clause and no dependent clauses, so it remains a simple sentence.

**EXERCISE 16.23** Working in small groups, expand the following simple sentences by compounding subjects, objects, and verbs and adding modifying words and phrases as necessary. You may replace a general term (*aircraft*) with particular examples (*helicopters, jets, gliders*). But do not add either full independent or dependent clauses. Make sure the final versions remain simple sentences.

| | |
|---|---|
| EXAMPLE | Bugs scare people. |
| EXPANDED | Tiny spiders, harmless caterpillars, and frail mantises sometimes terrify or even paralyze full-grown adults, from PhDs in physics to NFL linebackers. |

1. Pets enrich our lives.

2. The sciences challenge our assumptions.

3. Many activities can damage our health.

**● 2 Use compound and complex sentences to express relationships between clauses.** These relationships involve *coordination* when independent clauses are joined to other independent clauses.

The rain fell for days, **but** the city's reservoirs were not filled.

Our fuel pump failed, **so** we were stranded on the expressway.

They involve *subordination* when dependent clauses are joined to independent clauses.

> **Although** the rain fell for days, the city's reservoirs were not filled.

> **Because** our fuel pump failed, we were stranded on the expressway.

To write effective sentences, you need to handle both coordination (see Section 16f) and subordination (see Section 16g) confidently.

# 16f How does coordination build sentences?

When you coordinate two or more independent clauses, you connect or associate ideas. Independent clauses can stand on their own grammatically, but they grow richer when they enter into coordinate relationships. These relationships can be established in several ways: with *coordinating conjunctions*; with various *correlative constructions*; with semicolons, colons, and dashes; and with *conjunctive adverbs*.

**●1 Use coordinating conjunctions to join independent clauses.** The **coordinating conjunctions** are *and, or, nor, for, but, yet*, and *so*. They express fundamental relationships between ideas: similarity, addition, or sequence (*and*); exception, difference, or contrast (*or, nor, but, yet*); and process or causality (*for, so*). Commas ordinarily precede coordinating conjunctions between clauses (see Section 36c-1).

> The solemn service ended, **and** we went home immediately. sequence

> SAT scores in math rose nationally, **but** verbal scores dropped. contrast

Different coordinating conjunctions give readers different signals, so select them carefully. Many writers habitually choose *and* even when another conjunction might express a relationship more precisely.

| VAGUE | The statue's hair is carved in early archaic style, **and** its feet show traits of late archaic sculpture. |
| MORE PRECISE | The statue's hair is carved in early archaic style, **yet** its feet show traits of late archaic sculpture. |

VAGUE    Michelangelo's Sistine Chapel ceiling is among the greatest works of Renaissance art, **and** conservators approached the task of cleaning it with great caution.

MORE PRECISE    Michelangelo's Sistine Chapel ceiling is among the greatest works of Renaissance art, **so** conservators approached the task of cleaning it with great caution.

Coordinating conjunctions are also useful for combining sentences that are short, choppy, or repetitive. Linking sentences this way can produce more readable and mature writing.

CHOPPY AND    We liked the features of the computer. It was too expen-
REPETITIVE    sive for our budgets. We thought it looked complicated.

COMBINED    We liked the features of the computer, **but** it was too expensive for our budgets **and** looked complicated.

Relying too much on coordinating conjunctions (especially *and*) to link ideas can be stylistically dangerous. A string of clauses linked by *and*s quickly grows tedious and should be revised, often by making some clauses subordinate (see Section 16g).

TOO MANY    The French physician Nostradamus was active in fight-
ANDS    ing the plague in the sixteenth century **and** he grew so interested in astrology that he wrote a book of prophecies called *Centuries* **and** it has fascinated readers ever since.

REVISED    The French physician Nostradamus, active in fighting the plague in the sixteenth century, grew so interested in astrology that he wrote a book of prophecies called *Centuries* which has fascinated readers ever since.

**EXERCISE 16.24** Use coordinating conjunctions (*and, or, nor, for, but, yet, so*) to create compound sentences by linking the following pairs of independent clauses. Be sure to punctuate the sentences correctly.

1. The stock market finally rose. Investors remained nervous.

2. Citizens' groups invest time and money on get-out-the-vote campaigns. Many voters still skip general elections.

3. Vitamin C is good for colds. Vitamin E keeps the skin in good condition.

4. Most Americans get their news from television. News anchors are powerful people.

5. Tough drunk-driving laws are fair. There is no reason to tolerate inebriated drivers on the highway.

**● 2 Use correlative constructions to join independent clauses.**
**Correlatives** are conjunctions that work in pairs, expressions such as *if . . . then, either . . . or, just as . . . so*, and *not only . . . but also*. Like coordinating conjunctions, correlatives can be used to form compound sentences that ask readers to examine two ideas side by side.

> **Just as** Napoleon faced defeat in Russia, **so** Hitler saw his dreams of conquest evaporate at the siege of Leningrad.

> **Not only** is Captain Janeway a better leader than Kirk, **but** she is **also** a more interesting human being.

**EXERCISE 16.25** Create compound sentences by finishing the correlative construction begun for you. Be sure that the sentence you produce is a compound sentence, one with two independent clauses. Punctuate the sentence correctly.

1. If I agree to read *War and Peace* by the end of the summer, then you . . .

2. Either the new owners of the former Soviet Union's nuclear weapons will safeguard these deadly stockpiles, or . . .

3. Just as eating too much fat contributes to poor physical health, so . . .

4. Not only does the First Amendment protect speech, but it also . . .

**● 3 Use semicolons, colons, and dashes to link independent clauses.** Semicolons usually join independent clauses roughly balanced in importance and closely associated in meaning.

> We expected chaos; we found catastrophe.

> The eyes of the nation were suddenly on the Supreme Court; the nine justices could not ignore the weight of public opinion.

Colons are more directive than semicolons. They imply that the second independent clause explains, exemplifies, or expands on the first.

> There was a lesson in the indictment: even small acts have consequences.

Like colons, dashes can function as conjunctions, connecting clauses with verve and energy. Some writers and editors, however, object to dashes used this way.

> Expect George Ratliff's new film to cause controversy—the theme is bold and provocative.
>
> The cathedral of Notre Dame was restored in the nineteenth century—its facade had suffered damage during the French Revolution.

See Chapters 37 and 40 for more on semicolons, colons, and dashes.

**EXERCISE 16.26** Use a semicolon, a colon, or a dash to link the following independent clauses. Be prepared to explain why you chose each form of linkage.

1. Don't feel sorry for the spare and thorny plants you see in a desert. They don't want or need more water.

2. Barren stalks, wicked thorns, and waxy spines are their adaptations to a harsh environment. Such features conserve water or protect the plants from desert animals and birds.

3. Spring rains can create an astonishing desert spectacle. Cacti and other plants explode into colorful bloom.

4. Many animals call the desert home, too, from tiny lizards to scrawny coyotes. They are just as well adapted as the plants.

● **4 Use conjunctive adverbs with semicolons to join independent clauses.** **Conjunctive adverbs** are words such as *consequently, however, moreover, nevertheless, similarly,* and *therefore*. Like any adverb, they can appear at various places in a sentence. But often the adverb follows a semicolon, illuminating the relationship between clauses and holding our attention.

> Members of the zoning board appreciated the developer's arguments; **however**, they rejected her rezoning request.

> The muffler was leaking dangerous fumes; **moreover**, the brake linings were growing thin.

The comma that typically follows a conjunctive adverb in these constructions also gives weight to the word or phrase.

Note that it is the semicolon, not the adverb, that actually links the independent clauses. That connection becomes more obvious when the conjunctive adverb is moved.

> Members of the zoning board appreciated the developer's arguments; they rejected her rezoning request, **however**.

> The muffler was leaking dangerous fumes; the brake linings, **moreover**, were growing thin.

The punctuation surrounding conjunctive adverbs can be confusing. See Section 37a-3 for more details.

**EXERCISE 16.27** Use a semicolon and the conjunctive adverb in parentheses to link the following independent clauses. To gain practice punctuating this tricky construction, use the form illustrated in the example—with the semicolon followed immediately by the conjunctive adverb, followed by a comma.

EXAMPLE   The aircraft lost an engine in flight. It landed safely. (*however*)

REVISED   The aircraft lost an engine in flight; however, it landed safely.

1. Ordinary books are still more convenient than most computerized texts. They employ a technology that doesn't go out of date as quickly—paper. (*moreover*)

2. Most people would save money by using public transportation. They elect to use their private automobiles for daily commuting. (*nevertheless*)

3. American colonists resented England's interference in their political and commercial lives. The thirteen colonies decided to fight for independence. (*therefore*)

4. German and Japanese automakers discovered that they could build quality products cheaper in North America than at home. Foreign computer manufacturers decided to build silicon-chip plants in the United States. (*similarly*)

5. Many cities have been unable to meet air-quality standards. Tougher air-pollution measures have been imposed on their factories and drivers. (*consequently*)

**EXERCISE 16.28** Build coordinate sentences by combining the following independent clauses. You may use coordinating conjunctions, correlatives, conjunctive adverbs, semicolons, or colons. Be sure to get the punctuation right.

> EXAMPLE      Pencils were invented in the sixteenth century. Erasers were not added to them until 1858.
>
> COORDINATION      Pencils were invented in the sixteenth century; however, erasers were not added to them until 1858.

1. Today, French Impressionist paintings are favorites among art lovers. The public loudly rejected them at their debut in the nineteenth century.

2. Painters such as Renoir and Monet wanted art to depict life. They painted common scenes and ordinary people.

3. Many critics of the time were disturbed by the Impressionists' banal subjects. They thought the Impressionists' paintings themselves looked crude and unfinished.

4. The official Salon refused to hang the Impressionists' works. The painters were forced to exhibit independently.

5. The Impressionists refused to abandon their examination of modern life. They refused to change their style to please the critics.

# 16g How does subordination build sentences?

Use subordination to create complex or compound-complex sentences. Subordinating conjunctions provide the link between main ideas (independent clauses) and secondary ones (dependent or subordinate clauses). Subordination can be achieved with the aid of relative pronouns or subordinating conjunctions. The relative pronouns are *that, what, whatever, which, who, whom, whomever,* and *whose.*

Subordinating conjunctions are more numerous and suggest a wide variety of relationships; see Chart 16.1 below. For more on subordinating conjunctions, see Section 16d-2.

| Chart 16.1 Subordinating Conjunctions | | |
|---|---|---|
| after | in order that | unless |
| although | now that | until |
| as | once | when |
| as if | provided | whenever |
| as though | rather than | where |
| because | since | whereas |
| before | so that | wherever |
| even if | than | whether |
| even though | that | which |
| if | though | while |
| if only | till | |

A subordinating conjunction or a relative pronoun turns an independent clause into a dependent clause that cannot stand alone as a sentence.

INDEPENDENT    I wrote the paper.

DEPENDENT    **While** I wrote the paper . . .

DEPENDENT    The paper **that** I wrote . . .

**● 1** **Use subordination to clarify relationships between clauses.** Like most tools for building sentences, subordination provides options for stating and clarifying thoughts. So it's probably misleading to regard the independent clause in a subordinate construction as always more important or more weighty than the dependent clause. In fact, the clauses work together to establish a complex relationship—of time, causality, consequence, contingency, contrast, and so on.

**USING SUBORDINATION TO EXPLAIN *WHO* OR *WHAT***

VAGUE      The *Morte D'Arthur* includes stories about the knights of the Round Table. It was the work of Sir Thomas Malory.

CLEARER      The *Morte D'Arthur*, **which** was the work of Sir Thomas Malory, includes stories about the knights of the Round Table.

**USING SUBORDINATION TO EXPLAIN *UNDER WHAT CONDITIONS***

VAGUE      Many people go into debt. Credit is easy to get.

CLEARER      **If** credit is easy to get, many people go into debt.

**USING SUBORDINATION TO CLARIFY *CAUSALITY***

VAGUE      The film enjoyed a brisk summer box office. It won an Academy Award last March.

CLEARER      The film enjoyed a brisk summer box office **because** it won an Academy Award last March.

**USING SUBORDINATION TO HIGHLIGHT *CONTRAST***

VAGUE      Members of Congress often campaign for a balanced budget. Most of them jealously protect projects in their own districts from cuts in federal spending.

CLEARER      **Although** members of Congress often campaign for a balanced budget, most of them jealously protect projects in their own districts from cuts in federal spending.

**● 2** Use subordination to shift the emphasis of sentences.
Generally readers will focus on ideas in your independent clauses. Compare the following sentences, both equally good but with slightly different emphases due to changes in subordination.

> **Although** the Supreme Court usually declares efforts to limit the First Amendment unconstitutional, Congress regularly acts to ban forms of speech most citizens find offensive.

> The Supreme Court usually declares efforts to limit the First Amendment unconstitutional, **even though** Congress regularly acts to ban forms of speech most people find offensive.

The first sentence directs readers to consider the efforts of Congress to rein in the First Amendment; the second sentence gives more emphasis to the Supreme Court. The differences are small but significant. Notice the same kind of shift in focus in the following pair of sentences.

> Jared had never walked a picket line, **even though** he had been a staunch union member for twenty years.

> **Even though** Jared had never walked a picket line, he had been a staunch union member for twenty years.

**● 3** Use subordination to expand sentences. You can often use subordination to combine simple clauses into more graceful or powerful sentences.

| | |
|---|---|
| CHOPPY | The running back had an ankle injury. He chalked up a hundred-yard afternoon. He had been laid off for two months too. |
| SUBORDINATED | **Although** he had endured an ankle injury and a two-month layoff, the running back chalked up a hundred-yard afternoon. |
| CHOPPY | Spectators at the air show were watching in horror. An ultralight aircraft struggled down the runway. It was built of Kevlar and carbon fiber. It hit a stand of trees and disintegrated in a plume of smoke and fire. |
| SUBORDINATED | **While** spectators at the air show watched in horror, an ultralight aircraft built of Kevlar and carbon fiber |

struggled down the runway **until** it hit a stand of trees and disintegrated in a plume of smoke and fire.

● **4 Use subordinate clauses sensibly.** If you pile more than two or three subordinate clauses into one sentence, you may confuse readers. Be sure readers can keep up with all the relationships you establish between clauses. If you suspect they can't, simplify those relationships, perhaps by breaking one long complex sentence into several simpler sentences.

| | |
|---|---|
| TOO MUCH SUBORDINATION | **Although** their book *Chicken Soup for the Soul,* **which** spawned a hugely successful series, **which** has sold millions of copies, was turned down 33 times **while** they tried to find a publisher, Jack Canfield and Mark Victor Hansen did not quit, **which** suggests the importance of persistence. |
| REVISED | Persistence counts. Jack Canfield and Mark Victor Hansen never gave up, **even though** their *Chicken Soup for the Soul,* the first in a string of best-sellers, was turned down by 33 publishers. |
| TOO MUCH SUBORDINATION | An assumption **that** is held by many people in certain cultures, **that** people **who** have college degrees should never have to work with their hands, is often a deterrent to capable young people in those cultures **who** seek nontraditional careers. |
| REVISED | Many people in certain cultures assume **that** college-educated people should never work with their hands. This attitude often, however, deters capable young people from seeking nontraditional careers. |

**EXERCISE 16.29** Join the following pairs of sentences by making one of the independent clauses subordinate.

1. The original books of Babylonia and Assyria were collections of inscribed clay tablets stored in labeled containers too heavy for one person to move. We think of books as portable, bound volumes.

2. Clay tablets had many drawbacks. They remained the most convenient medium for recording information until the Egyptians developed papyrus around 3000 BC.

3. Egyptian books were lighter than clay tablets but still awkward to carry or read. A single papyrus book comprised several large, unwieldy scrolls.

**EXERCISE 16.30**  Join the following pairs of sentences by making one of the independent clauses subordinate.

1. Japan was a powerful and thriving nation early in the seventeenth century. Its leaders pursued a policy of isolation from the rest of the world.

2. This policy lasted for more than two centuries. Commodore Matthew Perry of the United States forced Japan to open itself to trade in 1854.

3. Many Japanese resented the presence of Europeans and Americans. They attacked both the foreigners and the rulers called shoguns who had yielded to foreign military pressure.

4. A rebellion in 1867 deposed the shogun. The Japanese emperor was restored to power.

# 16h How does parallelism work?

Sentences are easier to read when closely related ideas within them follow similar language patterns. Subjects, objects, verbs, modifiers, phrases, and clauses can be structured to show such a relationship, called **parallelism**.

| | |
|---|---|
| PARALLEL WORDS | The venerable principal spoke **clearly, eloquently**, and **invariably**. |
| PARALLEL PHRASES | **Praised by critics, embraced by common readers**, the novel became a best-seller. |
| PARALLEL CLAUSES | **It was the best of times, it was the worst of times**. |

Items are parallel when they share common grammatical structures.

clearly,
eloquently,
invariably

| praised | by | critics, |
| embraced | by | common readers, |

| It | was | the | best | of | times, |
| it | was | the | worst | of | times |

The famous opening clauses from Dickens's *A Tale of Two Cities* are exactly parallel. Longer expressions generally show more variation in their parallel terms, especially in the modifiers.

● **1 Recognize sentence patterns that require parallel construction.** When words or phrases come in pairs or triplets, they usually need to be parallel. That is, each element must have the same form: a noun or noun phrase, an adjective or adjective phrase, an adverb or adverbial phrase.

| NOUNS/NOUN PHRASES | **Optimism in outlook** and **egotism in behavior**— those are essential qualities for a leader. |
| ADJECTIVES | The best physicians are **patient, thorough**, and **compassionate**. |
| ADVERBS | The lawyers presented their case **passionately** and **persuasively**. |

The elements of this Navaho rug in the Chinle style are roughly parallel. The rug is by Irene Harvey.

Items in a list should also be parallel.

| LIST ITEMS | The school board's objectives are clear: **to hire** the best teachers, **to create** successful classrooms, **to serve** the needs of all families, and **to prepare** students for the future. |

**●2 Use parallelism in comparisons and contrasts.** Sometimes parallelism adds a stylistic touch, as in the following example. The first version, though acceptable, is not as stylish as the revised and parallel version.

| | |
|---|---|
| NOT PARALLEL | Pope was a poet of the mind; Byron wrote for the heart. |
| PARALLEL | Pope was a poet of the mind, Byron a bard for the heart. |

Parallelism is required in comparisons following *as* or *than.*

| | |
|---|---|
| NOT PARALLEL | The city council is *as* likely **to adopt the measure** *as* **vetoing it**. |
| PARALLEL | The city council is *as* likely **to adopt the measure** *as* **to veto it**. |
| NOT PARALLEL | **Smiling** takes fewer muscles *than* **to frown**. |
| PARALLEL | **Smiling** takes fewer muscles *than* **frowning**. |

**●3 Recognize expressions that signal the need for parallel structure.** These include the following correlative constructions: *not only . . . but also, either . . . or, neither . . . nor, both . . . and, on the one hand . . . on the other hand.*

As Franklin once remarked, *either* **we hang together** *or* **we hang separately**.

A musician's manager sees to it that the performer is *neither* **overworked onstage** *nor* **undervalued in wages**.

We spoke *not only* **to the President** *but also* **to the Speaker of the House**.

*On the one hand,* **interest rates might be tightened;** *on the other hand,* **prices might be increased**.

**●4 Use parallelism to show a progression of ideas.** You can set up parallel structures within sentences or entire paragraphs. These structures make ideas easier to follow.

Jane Brody, the *New York Times* health writer, says, "Regular exercise comes closer to being a fountain of youth than anything modern medicine can offer." **Exercise halves** the risk of heart disease and stroke, **lowers** the chance of colon cancer, and **reduces** the likelihood of osteoporosis. **It lessens** the chances of developing diabetes and **strengthens** the immune system. **Exercise** even **helps** people overcome depression.

**5 Use parallelism for emphasis.** Readers really take note when patterns are repeated in longer clauses. By using parallelism of this kind, you will get their attention.

If welfare reform works, **the genuinely needy will** be protected and assisted, **the less conscientious will** be motivated to find work, and **the average taxpayer will** see federal dollars spent more wisely.

You can also use parallelism to express an idea cleverly. Parallelism offers patterns of language perfect for setting up a joke or underscoring sarcasm.

People who serve as their own lawyers in court have *either* **a fool for a client** *or* **a judge for a brother.**

Sentences and paragraphs can be both more economical and more powerful when you set their related ideas in parallel patterns. When revising a passage, look for opportunities to use parallelism.

**6 Correct faulty parallelism.** It is easy for parallel constructions to go off track. When an item doesn't follow the pattern of language already established in a sentence, it lacks parallelism and disrupts the flow of the sentence. To correct faulty parallelism, first identify the items that ought to be parallel; then choose one of the items (usually the first) as the pattern; and finally revise the remaining items to fit that pattern. Review these examples to see how they have been revised to achieve parallelism.

| | |
|---|---|
| NOT PARALLEL | Criminals are imprisoned for two reasons: **to punish them** and **for the protection of law-abiding citizens.** |
| PARALLEL | Criminals are imprisoned for two reasons: **to punish them** and **to protect law-abiding citizens.** |

| | |
|---|---|
| NOT PARALLEL | When you open a new computer program, it's easy to **feel overwhelmed by the interface, frustrated by the vague documentation**, and **not know what to do next**. |
| PARALLEL | When you open a new computer program, it's easy to feel<br><br>**overwhelmed by the interface,**<br>**frustrated by the vague documentation,** and<br>**confused about what to do next**. |

Sometimes you'll have to decide how much of a parallel structure to repeat. You may want to reproduce a structure in its entirety for emphasis, or you might omit a repeated item for economy.

| | |
|---|---|
| EMPHASIS | We expect you **to** arrive on time, **to** bring an ID, **to** have three sharpened pencils, and **to** follow instructions. |
| ECONOMY | We expect you to arrive on time, present an ID, have three sharpened pencils, and follow instructions. |

The difference can be striking. Consider what happens when we remove the artful repetition from a famous speech by Winston Churchill that is a model of parallel structure.

| | |
|---|---|
| EMPHASIS | **We shall fight** on the beaches, **we shall fight** on the landing grounds, **we shall fight** in the fields and in the streets, **we shall fight** in the hills; we shall never surrender. |
| ECONOMY | We shall fight on the beaches and landing grounds and in the fields, streets, and hills; we shall never surrender. |

No simple style rule can be given for structuring a parallel sentence. But you don't want to be inconsistent within a single sentence, both including and omitting an element that is part of a parallel structure.

| | |
|---|---|
| WRONG | The education bill is expected **to fund** literacy programs for another year, **give** teachers more autonomy in the classroom, **to authorize** a dozen new charter schools, and **make** honors courses more widely available. |

The words signaling the parallel structure are inconsistent. Either all the items must be expressed as infinitives (*to fund, to give, to authorize, to make*) or only the first item should include *to*.

> REVISED    The education bill is expected **to fund** literacy programs for another year, **to give** teachers more autonomy in the classroom, **to authorize** a dozen new charter schools, and **to make** honors courses more widely available.

**EXERCISE 16.31** Write a sentence with good parallel structure that incorporates the elements given below. Here is how one example might work.

> SUBJECT    A football coach: three actions during a game
> SAMPLE SENTENCE    Controlling his temper as well as he could, the coach paced the sidelines, gnashed his teeth, and tried not to cry during the 66-to-3 drubbing.

1. A shy guy: three actions before asking for a date

2. A senator: two actions in delivering a speech

3. A teacher: three actions in calming a noisy class

4. A schnauzer: three actions to get a cookie

**EXERCISE 16.32** Read these sentences and decide which ones have faulty parallel structures. Then revise those in which you find inconsistent or faulty patterns.

1. On opening night at the new Tex-Mex restaurant, the manager called the servers together to be sure they understood all the items on the menu, could pronounce *fajitas*, and that they would remember to ask, "Salt or no salt?" when customers ordered margaritas.

2. Offering the best Southwestern cuisine and to serve the hottest salsa were the restaurant's two goals.

3. But customers soon made it clear that they also expected real barbecue on the menu, so the manager added slow-cooked beef ribs smothered in

sauce, hefty racks of pork ribs dripping with fat, and there was smoked sausage on the menu too that was juicy and hot.

4. Servers had to explain to tourists that one was supposed to eat beef ribs with one's fingers, wrap one's own fajitas, and to bite into jalapeños very carefully.

# 16i  How do you craft balanced sentences?

Effective balanced sentences merge the best attributes of coordination and parallelism (see Sections 16f and 16h). In a **balanced sentence**, a coordinating conjunction links two or more independent clauses that are roughly parallel in structure. The result is a sentence so intentionally designed and rhythmic that it draws special attention to its subject. For that reason, balanced sentences are often memorable and quotable.

And so, my fellow Americans, ask not what your country can do for you; ask what you can do for your country.
—John F. Kennedy, Inaugural Address

We live here and they live there. We black and they white. They got things and we ain't. They do things and we can't. It's just like living in jail.
—Richard Wright, *Native Son*

In your writing you might find balanced sentences effective for openings and closings, where you want readers to remember a major point. But they may seem out of place in lighter, more colloquial writing.

In crafting a balanced sentence, you'll almost always begin with two independent clauses joined to make a compound sentence (see Section 16f). Then you can sharpen the relationship between the clauses by making them reasonably parallel. You may need to revise both clauses quite heavily.

| COMPOUND | New programs to end adult illiteracy may be costly, **but** the alternative is continued support of even more expensive welfare programs. |
|---|---|
| BALANCED | New adult literacy programs may be costly, **but** current welfare programs are costlier still. |
| COMPOUND | Most people involved in education and business take computers for granted, **yet** that doesn't mean these people really understand what computers do. |
| BALANCED | Most people in business and education take computers for granted; few understand what computers do. |

**EXERCISE 16.33** Complete the following sentences in ways that make them balanced.

1. If Alfred Hitchcock is the master of suspense, then . . .

2. Politics makes strange bedfellows, and . . .

3. If all the world is really a stage, then . . .

4. In theory, college seems the surest pathway to economic security; in practice, . . .

5. When the going gets tough, the tough get going, but when . . .

# **16j** How do you craft cumulative sentences?

The intricate architecture of balanced sentences (see Section 16i) can make them seem formal and even old-fashioned. A structure perhaps better suited to contemporary writing, which tends to be informal, is the **cumulative sentence** in which an independent clause is followed by a series of modifiers, sometimes simple, sometimes quite complex.

The apprehensive mood was shot through with shafts of gaiety, as a black sky is streaked with lightning.
—Maya Angelou, "Champion of the World"

She [Georgia O'Keeffe] is simply hard, **a straight shooter, a woman clean of received wisdom and open to what she sees**.

—Joan Didion, "Georgia O'Keeffe"

In writing a cumulative sentence, you add on to an original thought, expanding and enriching it by attaching modifying words, phrases, and clauses. The effect is artful but also easy and natural. In our daily speech we often state an idea and then explain or embellish it; cumulative sentences can convey the same informality.

Dusty? Of course, it's dusty—this is Utah. But it's good dust, **good red Utahn dust, rich in iron, rich in irony**.

—Edward Abbey, *Desert Solitaire*

But then they danced down the street like dingledodies, and I shambled after as I've been doing all my life after people who interest me, because the only people for me are the mad ones, **the ones who are mad to live, mad to talk, mad to be saved, desirous of everything at the same time, the ones who never yawn or say a commonplace thing, but burn, burn, burn like fabulous roman candles exploding like spiders across the stars and in the middle you see the centerlight pop and everybody goes "Awww!"**

—Jack Kerouac, *On the Road*

Crafting effective cumulative sentences takes practice, but the habit of addition is easy to acquire and especially useful in writing descriptive and narrative passages. Almost any of the modifying phrases and clauses described in Sections 16b through 16d can be attached gracefully to the ends of clauses.

**● 1 Attach adjectives and adverbs.** Either as individual words or as complete phrases, these modifiers play an important role in shaping cumulative sentences.

It was a handsome sedan, **black as shimmering oil, deeply chromed, and sleek as a rocket**.

The storm pounded the coast **so relentlessly that residents wondered whether the skies would ever clear again**.

● **2 Attach prepositional phrases.** You can place prepositional phrases (see Section 16c-1) at the ends of sentences to describe or modify nouns or pronouns within the sentence.

The church was all white plaster and gilt, **like a wedding cake in the public square**.

When the object of a closing prepositional phrase is artfully compounded, the effect can be memorable. In the following example, dust is described as settling *upon* a rich variety of plants.

A veil of dust floats above the sneaky, snaky old road from here to the highway, drifting gently downward to settle **upon the blades of the yucca, the mustard yellow rabbitbrush, the petals of the asters and autumn sunflowers, the umbrella-shaped clumps of blooming buckwheat**.

—Edward Abbey, *Desert Solitaire*

● **3 Attach appositives and free modifiers.** You can conclude cumulative sentences with modifiers that rename someone or something within the body of a sentence. These modifiers act like appositives (see Section 16c-4), but they may be separated in distance from the noun or pronoun they embellish. Here are two such *free modifiers* from Bob Costas's eulogy for baseball legend Mickey Mantle.

And more than that, he [Mickey Mantle] was a presence in our lives—**a fragile hero to whom we had an emotional attachment so strong and lasting that it defied logic**.

He got love—**love for what he had been; love for what he made us feel; love for the humanity and sweetness that was always there mixed in with the flaws and all the pain that wracked his body and his soul**.

—Bob Costas, *Eulogy for Mickey Mantle*

Notice the way these modifiers are introduced by dashes. Notice, too, that the modifying phrase itself can be quite complex and much longer than the original independent clause.

● **4 Attach clauses.** You can experiment with both relative and subordinate clauses (see Section 16d) at the ends of sentences, compounding them and keeping them roughly parallel.

> Mother Teresa was a woman **who gave her life to the poor and gained the admiration of the world for her service**.

> The astronaut argued that Americans need to return to the moon **because our scientific explorations there have only begun and because we need a training ground for more ambitious planetary expeditions**.

As the lengthy example on page 284 from Jack Kerouac demonstrates, you can combine different kinds of modifiers to extend a sentence considerably.

> The Kennedys had a spark and Jack Kennedy had grown into a handsome man, **a male swan rising out of the Billy the Kid version of an Irish duckling he had been when he was a young senator**.
> —Stanley Crouch, "Blues for Jackie"

**EXERCISE 16.34** Combine the following short sentences into one longer cumulative sentence.

> EXAMPLE    Virginia adopted the dog. It was a friendly pup with skinny legs. It had a silly grin.

> COMBINED   Virginia adopted the dog, a friendly pup with skinny legs and a silly grin.

1. Caesar was my friend. He had been faithful to me. He had been just to me.

2. Dr. Kalinowski recommended that her patient take up racquetball. It would ease his nerves. It would quicken his reflexes. It would tone his muscles. The muscles had grown flaccid from years of easy living.

3. The members of the jury filed into the courtroom. The members of the jury looked sullen and unhappy. They looked as if they'd eaten cactus for lunch.

4. The reviewer thought the book was a disappointment. It did not summarize the current state of knowledge. It did not advance research in the field.

# 17 How Do You Write Stylish Sentences?

Good sentences must be carefully and grammatically constructed, but there's more to writing well than simple correctness. Successful writing uses words much as successful advertisements use color and images—to create powerful effects on an audience. Think about the highly successful advertising campaign for the Apple iPod. Of course, the iPod needed to be technically and mechanically sound in order for consumers to buy it, but it became the best-selling product of its kind partly because Apple created a hip, modern image with which consumers could identify.

Just as there's more to the iPod than its ability to store and play songs, there's more to effective writing than crafting competent sentences. To affect readers powerfully, you'll want to compose sentences that are varied, rhythmic, rich in detail, and sometimes even memorable. This chapter discusses various ways to give your sentences that subtle yet powerful quality called *style*.

Examine closely this advertisement for the Apple iPod. What words would you use to describe the product's "style"? How do the colors, images, and words in the still work together to create this style? Would the product seem just as appealing if the ad featured only a listing of the iPod's technical features? Now, think about your writing. What words would you use to describe your typical writing style? Straightforward? Ornate? Informal? In what writing situations is your typical writing style most effective? In what situations does it work less well?

# 17a What are agent/action sentences?

You can build readable sentences by using an agent/action pattern. In agent/action sentences, clear subjects (agents) perform strong actions.

agent/action

The **pilot** *ejected.*

agent/action

My **grandmother** *makes* hand-sewn quilts.

Agent/action sentences are highly readable because they answer these important questions.

- What's happening?
- Who's doing it (and to what or to whom)?

**● 1 Whenever you can, make persons or things the subjects of your sentences and clauses.** Readers take more interest in what you're writing if people are involved. And they usually are—most issues touch on human lives, one way or another.

| | |
|---|---|
| **WITHOUT PEOPLE** | Although the federally funded student loan program has made education accessible to a low-income population, the increasing default rate among that population has had a significant effect on the program. |
| **WITH PEOPLE** | Hundreds of thousands of **young people** have been able to go to college because of federally funded student loans, but **students** who have defaulted on their loans may be jeopardizing the program for **others**. |

When you can, start your sentences with references to people.

**EXERCISE 17.1** Recast these sentences in agent/action patterns that show more clearly who is doing what to whom. Break the sentences into shorter ones if you like.

1. Raising $3 million to renovate the drama facilities on campus was the goal of Lincoln Brown, the new college president.

2. The experience of playing Horatio in a college production of *Hamlet* had been influential in convincing President Brown of the value of the performing arts.

3. Helping President Brown to convince wealthy donors that restoring and expanding the old theater was a good idea was a small group of actors, all of them alumni of the school.

4. An unexpected donation of $1 million made by a prominent local banker who had once played Hamlet gave the actors and President Brown reason to celebrate.

● **2 Don't overload the subjects of sentences.** Readers will get lost if you bury subjects under abstract words and phrases. When revising, you may have to recover the central idea of a particularly difficult or murky sentence. Ask yourself, "What is its key word or concept?" Make that key word the subject. In the following sentence, the main idea is buried in an opening noun phrase twenty-four words long.

> OVERLOADED
> SUBJECT
>
> **The encouragement of total reliance on the federally sponsored student loan program for medical students from low-income families to pay their way through school** causes many young doctors to begin their careers deeply in debt.

What is this sentence about? Many readers would say "young doctors." See what happens when the sentence is revised to focus on them.

> REVISED
>
> **Many young doctors from low-income families** begin their careers deeply in debt because they have relied totally on federal student loans to pay their way through medical school.

**EXERCISE 17.2** Rewrite the following sentences to simplify their overcrowded openings.

1. Among those who are unhappy about the lack of morality and standards in the television shows coming from Hollywood today and who would

like to see pressure on producers for more responsible programming are activists from remarkably different political groups.

2. The elimination of hurtful gender, racial, and ethnic stereotypes, particularly from situation comedies, where they are sometimes a key element of the humor, is a key demand of political groups on the left.

3. TV's almost complete disregard of the role religion plays in the daily lives of most ordinary people, evident in the fact that so few sitcom characters ever go to church or pray, irritates groups on the political right.

4. Raising the specter of censorship and equating every attack on Hollywood to an assault on the First Amendment has been the quick response of many television producers to criticism of their products.

● **3 Choose verbs that convey strong actions.** Strung-out verb phrases such as *give consideration to* and *make acknowledgment of* slow down your writing. Get rid of them; focus on the action. Ask, "What's happening?" and try to express that action in a single lively verb.

| | |
|---|---|
| DULL VERB | Some groups who **are in opposition to** the death penalty **believe that there is doubt about** its morality. |
| STRONGER VERB | Some groups who **oppose** the death penalty **doubt** its morality. |

Identifying the action may also help you spot the real agent in a sentence, as in this example.

| | |
|---|---|
| DULL VERB | American society **has** long **had** a fascination with celebrities. |
| STRONGER VERB | Celebrities **have** long **fascinated** Americans. |

**EXERCISE 17.3** Rewrite the following sentences to pinpoint their centers of action and to make their verbs stronger.

1. The fears of many prospective students over age 30 are understandable to college counselors.

2.  Many such students are apprehensive about seeing textbooks, syllabi, and assignments for the first time in a decade or more.

3.  In many schools, counselors have proceeded to establish special groups or programs for older students so that their feelings of dislocation and discomfort will be relieved.

4.  The sobering realization among those responsible for demographic studies of colleges is that older students may hold the key to financial solvency for many institutions.

● **4 Make sure subjects can do what their verbs demand.** Verbs describe actions that subjects perform: *butter melts; scholars read.* In most cases, you know when you've written nonsense: *butter reads; scholars melt.* But as sentences grow longer, you can sometimes lose the logical connection between subjects and predicates, a problem described as **faulty predication**.

| | |
|---|---|
| FAULTY PREDICATION | The narrative **structure** of Aretha Franklin's song **begins** as a child and continues through her adult life. |

Can *narrative structures begin as children*? Unlikely. The writer is probably thinking either of a character in the song or of Aretha Franklin, the singer. The sentence has to be revised.

| | |
|---|---|
| REVISED | In Aretha Franklin's song, the narrative **structure follows** the life of a character from childhood to adulthood. |

Notice how heavily the sentence had to be revised to make it work. Just swapping one verb for another often won't solve the problem.

**EXERCISE 17.4** Revise any of the following sentences in which the subject cannot logically perform the action described by the verb. Try to explain what is wrong with the original verb choices, which are boldfaced.

1.  Hundreds of miles from any city or large airport, Big Bend National Park in Texas **endeavors** an experience of pristine isolation unlike that of busier parks such as Yellowstone.

2.  The park **comprehends** mountain, desert, and riparian environments.

3. Although coyotes, road runners, and javelinas are common, a few lucky visitors also **apprehend** mountain lions and bears.

4. Other national parks can **profess** more spectacular landmarks than Big Bend, but few **entertain** a more remarkable outdoor experience.

**● 5 Replace *to be* verbs whenever possible.** Though the verbs *is*, *are*, and their variants are often unavoidable, they're not as interesting as verbs that do things. When you use action verbs instead of *to be* verbs, you bring your readers into the action of the sentence immediately.

| | |
|---|---|
| **DULL VERBS** | It **is** the tendency of adolescents **to be more concerned** about the opinion of others in their age group than they **are** about the values parents are trying to instill in them. |
| **ACTION VERBS** | Adolescents **crave** the approval of their peers and often **resist** their parents' values. |

**EXERCISE 17.5** Replace the *to be* forms in these sentences with active and more lively verbs. The original verbs are boldfaced. (It may help if you make the agent a person or a concrete object.)

1. There **was** an inclination to protest among restaurateurs when the city decided to increase the number of health inspectors.

2. It **had been** the determination of city officials, however, that many restaurants **were** not in a state of compliance with local health ordinances.

3. The occurrence of rodent droppings in pantries and the storage of meat at incorrect temperatures **were** also matters of concern to several TV reporters.

4. It was the hope of both politicians and restaurateurs that there **would be** a quick solution to this embarrassing problem.

**● 6 Reduce the number of passive verbs.** Passive verb constructions (see Section 23e) often make sentences harder to read. It's easy to spot a sentence with a passive verb: the subject doesn't perform the action, the action is *done* to the subject. In effect, the object switches to the subject position, as in the following sentences.

> subj.      action
> *Madison* **was selected** by Representative Barton for an appointment to the Air Force Academy.

> subj.      action
> *The candidate* **had been nominated** for the academic honor by several teachers.

Passive verbs are always constructed with some form of *be* plus the past participle. (See Section 23b for an explanation of what a past participle is.)

> *be* + past participle
> The latest budget bill **has been vetoed** by the President.

> *be* + past participle
> The veto **was provoked** by a stubborn House of Representatives.

Notice that not every sentence with a form of the verb *to be* is passive, especially when *be* is used as a linking verb.

> The President **was** unhappy that members of the House of Representatives **had seemed** unwilling to fund new projects.

Nor is every sentence with a past participle passive. Perfect tenses, for example, also use the past participle. (See Section 23a-3 for an explanation of perfect tenses.) Here's an active verb in the past perfect tense.

> Congress **had funded** such projects in previous years.

To identify a passive verb form, look for *both* the past participle and a form of *be.*

> The projects **had been supported** by previous Congresses when they **had been proposed** by other presidents.

When you have identified a passive form, locate the word that actually performs the action in the sentence and make it the subject.

> subj.  performer of action
> **ORIGINAL PASSIVE** *Madison* **was selected** by Representative Barton for an appointment to the Air Force Academy.

REVISED ACTIVE
$\overset{\text{subj.}}{\textit{Representative Barton}}$ $\overset{\text{action}}{\textbf{selected}}$ Madison for an appointment to the Air Force Academy.

But not every passive verb can or should be made active. Sometimes you don't know who or what performs an action.

Hazardous road conditions **have been predicted**.

Our flight **has been canceled**.

**EXERCISE 17.6** Identify the passive verbs in the following sentences and then rewrite those that might be improved by changing passive verbs to active verbs.

**1.** The writing of research papers is traditionally dreaded by students everywhere.

**2.** The negative attitudes can be changed by writers themselves if the assignments are regarded by them as opportunities to explore and improve their communities.

**3.** When conventional topics are chosen by researchers, apathy is likely to be experienced by them and their readers alike.

**4.** But if writers are encouraged to choose topics in their communities that can be explored through books, articles, fieldwork, interviews, and online investigations, a better project will be produced.

# 17b How can you achieve clarity?

When something is well written, a careful reader can move along steadily without backtracking to puzzle over its meaning. You can work toward this goal by using a number of strategies.

● **1 Use specific details.** Writing that uses a lot of abstract language is often harder to understand and less pleasurable to read than writing that states ideas more specifically. Abstract terms such as *health-care provider system, positive learning environment,* and *two-wheeled vehicle* are usually harder to grasp than concrete terms such as *hospital, classroom*, and *Harley*. Of course you have to use abstract words sometimes; it's impossible to discuss big ideas without them. But the more you use specific details, the clearer your sentences will be.

An especially effective way to add texture to sentences is to *downshift*—that is, to state a general idea and then provide more and more details. The resulting sentences will be clear and interesting.

> Toi Soldier was a magnificent black Arabian stallion, **a sculpture in ebony, his eyes large and dark, his graceful head held high on an arched neck**. He was a competitor in any Arabian horse show, **equally poised in equitation classes or under harness**.

Downshifting is the principle behind many cumulative sentences (see Section 16j).

**EXERCISE 17.7** Working in a group, develop one of the following sentences into a brief paragraph by downshifting. Each subsequent sentence should add more detail to the original statement.

1. Colleges could do more to get students involved in their communities.

2. It's not surprising that so few Americans speak a foreign language.

3. The commercialization of sports has changed more than just professional athletics.

● **2 State ideas positively.** Negative statements can be surprisingly hard to read. When you can, turn negative statements into positive ones. Your writing will seem more confident and may be more economical.

DIFFICULT   Do we have the right **not to be victims** of street crime?

CLEARER   Do we have the right **to be safe** from street crime?

DIFFICULT   It is **not unlikely** that I will attend the conference.

CLEARER   **I will probably** attend the conference.

**EXERCISE 17.8** Revise the following sentences to restate negative ideas more positively or clearly where such a change makes for a better sentence. Not all sentences may need revision.

1. It would not be awful if you never turn in a paper late.

2. Would it ever not be inappropriate not to say "Hello" to an ex-spouse?

3. What do I think of your new leopard-skin pillbox hat? Why, it's not unattractive.

● **3** **"Chunk" your writing.** Consider breaking lengthy sentences into more manageable pieces or creating a list to present unusually complex information. People can comprehend only so much material at one time.

**TOO LONG**

Citing an instance in which a 16-year-old student was working 48 hours a week at Burger King in order to pay for a new car and simultaneously trying to attend high school full time, New York educators have recently proposed legislation that prohibits high school students from working more than 3 hours on a school night, limits the total time they can work in a week to 17 hours when school is in session, and fines employers who violate these regulations as much as $2,000.

In many respects this long sentence is admirable. It uses parallelism to keep a complex array of information in order. Yet most readers would probably like to see its information broken into more digestible chunks.

**REVISED**

Educators in New York have recently proposed legislation that prohibits high school students from working more than 3 hours on a school night. In support of the proposal, they cite the example of a 16-year-old student working 48 hours a week at Burger King in order to pay for a new car while simultaneously trying to attend high school full time. The proposed law would limit the total time students can work in a week to 17 hours when school is in session and would fine employers who violate these regulations as much as $2,000.

Another efficient way to cut very specific or technical information to manageable size is to create a list. Lists give readers a sense of order and direction. Which of the following passages do you find more readable?

To get started with your new computer, unpack it, saving the Styrofoam packing; position it away from sources of heat; plug the keyboard, mouse, and printer into the designated ports on the back of the machine; and, finally, attach the power cord to the computer and plug it in.

To get started with your new computer:
1. **Unpack** it, saving the Styrofoam packing.
2. **Position** your computer away from sources of heat.
3. **Plug** the keyboard, mouse, and printer into the designated ports on the back of the machine.
4. **Attach** the power cord to the computer and plug it in.

Notice that all the items in the list are parallel (see Section 16h).

**EXERCISE 17.9** Make the following sentences more readable by breaking them into manageable chunks.

1. Parents are often ambivalent about having their high school–aged children work because almost inevitably it causes a conflict between the demands of schoolwork and extracurricular activities (such as sports, civic clubs, debate teams, band) and the expectations of employers, a balance many high schoolers are simply not mature enough to handle on their own, often choosing the immediate material goods furnished by a job over the less obvious benefits afforded by a good education.

2. Many parents, however, aware of the limitations of their own training in school, may believe that it is no more important to learn square roots, the capitals of Asian countries, or the metrics of Chaucer's poetry than it is to discover how tough it is to deal with customers, show up on time, manage other workers, or pay taxes, experiences that an after-school job will quickly give most teenagers, whose images of work are badly distorted by films and television.

● **4 Use charts and graphs to present quantitative information.** Readers grasp numbers and statistics much more quickly when they see them presented visually. See Section 18d for more on how charts and graphs work and for advice on incorporating them into your writing.

# 17c How can you write more economically?

For those who aspire to be good writers, the war against "clutter" never ends. Clutter consists of clichés, strung-out phrases, pointless repetitions, and over-stuffed descriptions. But wait until you have a first draft before you start trimming your prose. Many writers overstuff a first draft because they want to get all their ideas down. That's fine: it *is* easier to cut material than to create more.

**●1 Condense sprawling phrases.** Some long-winded expressions slow a reader's way into a sentence, especially at the beginning.

| WHY WRITE . . . | WHEN YOU COULD WRITE . . . |
| --- | --- |
| in the event that | if |
| in light of the fact that | since |
| on the grounds that | because |
| regardless of the fact that | although |
| on the occasion of | when |
| in today's society | now |
| it is clear that | clearly |
| on an everyday basis | routinely |
| with regard/respect to | for |

We are so accustomed to these familiar but wordy expressions that we don't notice how little they convey.

WORDY    **At this point in time**, the committee hasn't convened.

REVISED    The committee hasn't convened **yet**.

**EXERCISE 17.10** Revise the following sentences to eliminate the sprawling, wordy, or clichéd opening phrase.

1. On the occasion of the newspaper's seventy-fifth anniversary, the governor visited the editorial offices.

2. Regardless of the fact that I have revised the speech three times, I still don't like my conclusion.

3. In the modern American society in which we live today, many people still attend church regularly.

4. By virtue of the fact that flood insurance rates are so high, many people go uninsured, risking their property.

● **2 Cut nominalizations.** **Nominalizations** are nouns made by adding endings to verbs and adjectives. The resulting words tend to be long and abstract. Worse, nominalizations are often grafted onto terms that are themselves recent coinages of dubious merit.

| WORD | NOMINALIZATION |
|---|---|
| connect | connect**ivity** |
| customize | customi**zation** |
| historicize | historici**zation** |
| utilize | utili**zation** |
| prioritize | prioriti**zation** |
| victimize | victimi**zation** |

Unfortunately, writers in college, business, and government sometimes think that readers will be more impressed by prose laden with these grand abstractions. Here's a parody of a "bureaucratic" style.

The **utilization** of appropriate **documentation** will achieve a **maximization** of **accountability**, assuring a **prioritization** and ultimate **finalization** of our budgetary requisitions.

Writing loaded down with nominalizations tires readers and obscures meaning; avoid such verbiage.

**EXERCISE 17.11** Revise the following sentences to reduce nominalizations that make the prose wordy.

1. The registrar's note is a clarification of the school's admissions policy.

2. It is a matter of substantial disputation among sociologists whether the gentrification of urban neighborhoods is a beneficial process to inner-city residents.

3. The utilization of creative writing in more and more elementary language arts classes is an indication that many teachers are feeling dissatisfaction with older, more rigid approaches to language instruction.

4. The systems analyst convinced us that the connectivity and interchangeability of our equipment gave our new computer system enhanced potential.

● **3 Condense long verb phrases to focus on the action.** To show tense and mood, verb phrases need auxiliaries and helping verbs: I *could have* gone; she *will be* writing. But many verb phrases are strung out by unnecessary clutter.

| WHY WRITE . . . | WHEN YOU COULD WRITE . . . |
| --- | --- |
| give consideration to | consider |
| make acknowledgment of | acknowledge |
| have doubts about | doubt |
| is reflective of | reflects |
| has an understanding of | understands |
| put the emphasis on | emphasize |

Similarly, don't clutter active verbs with expressions such as *start to, manage to,* and *proceed to.*

| CLUTTERED VERBS | Malls and supermarkets **always manage to irritate me** when they **start to display** Christmas paraphernalia immediately after Halloween. |
| --- | --- |
| REVISED | Malls and supermarkets **irritate me** when they **display** Christmas paraphernalia immediately after Halloween. |

**EXERCISE 17.12** Revise the following sentences to condense long verb phrases into more active expressions.

1. Many people are of the opinion that the federal government has grown too large.

2. An almost equal number of people hold the conviction that many citizens have need of services provided by federal programs.

3. This difference in public opinion is indicative of the dilemma faced by many politicians today.

4. Their constituents often are not in favor of paying for exactly the services that they have expectations of getting.

## ● 4 Eliminate doublings and redundancies.

*Doublings* are expressions in which two words say exactly the same thing. One word can usually be cut.

| | |
|---|---|
| trim ~~and slim~~ | ~~proper and~~ fitting |
| ready ~~and able~~ | willing ~~and eager~~ |

*Redundancies* are expressions in which a concept is repeated unnecessarily. A redundancy compels a reader to encounter the same idea twice.

Our entire society has been corrupted by ~~the evil of~~ commercialism.

Mother's holiday feast on the table was surrounded by our family ~~sitting around it~~.

One might argue, in some cases, that doublings subtly expand the intended meaning. But they usually don't.

Thanksgiving fosters a sense of belonging ~~and togetherness~~.

I am of two worlds, which are forever at odds ~~with each other~~.

Many habitual expressions are in fact redundant.

| WHY WRITE . . . | WHEN YOU COULD WRITE . . . |
|---|---|
| trading activity was heavy | trading was heavy |
| of a confidential nature | confidential |
| her area of specialization | her specialty |
| blue in color | blue |

Avoid the repetition of major words in a sentence—unless there are good reasons to emphasize particular terms.

REPETITIOUS    When college **friends come** together, you'll inevitably find some **friends** who **come** from the same background.

REVISED    When college **friends come** together, you'll inevitably find some who share the same background.

**EXERCISE 17.13**  Rewrite the following sentences to reduce redundancy and wordiness.

1. I realized that if I were ever to reach law school, I would have to increase my competitiveness in the skill of written prose composition.

2. *Ellen* to me is a daytime talk type of television show.

3. Many traits characterize a truly excellent student adviser, and one of the more important qualities, if not the most important quality, is a lively personality.

⦿ **5 Eliminate surplus intensifiers.** An adverb that functions as an **intensifier** should add weight or power to an expression. You waste its energy when you use it carelessly.

| WHY WRITE . . . | WHEN YOU COULD WRITE . . . |
|---|---|
| We're **completely** finished. | We're finished. |
| It's an **awful** tragedy. | It's a tragedy. |
| I'm **totally** exhausted. | I'm exhausted. |
| That's **absolutely** pointless. | That's pointless. |
| The work is **basically** done. | The work is done. |

**EXERCISE 17.14**  Review the intensifiers in the following passage and cut any words or phrases you regard as unnecessary.

The Grand Canyon is a quite unique geological treasure in northwestern Arizona, basically formed by the relentless power of the Colorado River cutting a gorge for many, many eons through solid rock. Standing at the edge of the canyon is a totally awesome experience. The canyon walls drop far into the depths, thousands of feet, a seriously deep drop, exposing very different layers of limestone, sandstone, and volcanic rock. These really magnificent canyons recede into the distance like ancient castles, an absolutely remarkable panorama of color and shadow.

**● 6 Cut down on expletive constructions.** **Expletives** are short expressions such as *it was, there are,* and *this is* that function like starting blocks for pushing into a sentence or clause. For example:

**It was** a dark and stormy night.

**There were** five of us huddled in the basement.

**There are** too many gopher holes on this golf course!

**It is** a proud day for Bluefield State College.

Some expletives are unavoidable. But using them habitually to open your sentences will make your prose tiresome. In many cases, sentences will be stronger without the expletives.

| | |
|---|---|
| **WITH EXPLETIVE** | Even though **it is** the oldest manufacturer of automobiles, Mercedes-Benz remains innovative. |
| **EXPLETIVE CUT** | The oldest manufacturer of automobiles, Mercedes-Benz remains innovative. |

| **WHY WRITE . . .** | **WHEN YOU COULD WRITE . . .** |
|---|---|
| There is a desire for | We want |
| There are reasons for | For several reasons |
| There was an expectation | They expected |
| It is clear that | Clearly |
| It is to be hoped | We hope |

**EXERCISE 17.15** Revise the following sentences to eliminate unnecessary expletive constructions.

1. There are many different ways to fulfill the science requirement at most colleges.

2. It is usually the case that liberal arts majors benefit from science courses that are geared to the history of the field.

3. Taking a course in the hard sciences is a challenge, and it should be taken seriously.

**4.** This is a point that many science teachers make early in a term, but it is a concept that many students don't grasp until after their first examination.

**◑7 Cut the number of prepositional phrases.** Stylistically, prepositional phrases are capable of dignity and grandeur, thanks to their clarity and simplicity.

> **In the beginning**, God created heaven and earth.

> . . . and that government **of the people, by the people, for the people**, shall not perish from the earth.

But that very simplicity can also grow tedious if you pack too many prepositional phrases of similar length and tempo into one sentence.

| | |
|---|---|
| **TOO MANY PREPOSITIONS** | **In** late summer **on** the road **from** our town **into** the country, we expected to find raspberries in the fields near the highway by the recent construction. |
| **REVISED** | We expected to find late summer raspberries **on** the country road, **near** the recent construction. |

Also avoid strings of prepositional phrases that congeal around abstract nouns, making sentences thick and hard to read. In the example, the abstract nouns are boldfaced and prepositional phrases are underlined.

| | |
|---|---|
| **WORDY** | The current **proliferation** of credit cards among college students is the result of extensive **marketing** by banking **institutions** who see college students in terms of their future **affluence**. |

Revise a cluttered sentence by looking for the center of action: *who* is doing *what* to *whom?*

| | |
|---|---|
| **REVISED** | Banks today are marketing credit cards to college students because they see them as affluent future customers. |

For more on prepositional phrases, see Section 16c-1.

**EXERCISE 17.16** Revise the following sentences to reduce the number of prepositional phrases where they make the sentences awkward or monotonous. Some sentences may require extensive revision.

1. J.R.R. Tolkien was the author of one of the most popular series of fantasy novels about the battle between good and evil forces in the distant past of the fictional world of Middle Earth.

2. Tolkien's series *The Lord of the Rings* focuses on the adventures of a genial hobbit by the name of Frodo Baggins and his sidekick by the name of Sam who, along with Frodo, becomes involved in the race to destroy a ring of magical but evil power.

3. The novels cover a long period of time, focusing on the colossal struggle for the magical ring and for the future of Middle Earth that goes on between Frodo and his allies and the forces of Sauron, the leader of the forces of evil.

4. In his love of adventure, his fascination with tales of heroism, and his faith in the redemptive power of friendship, Tolkien resembled his much loved characters.

● **8 Cut relative pronouns (*that, which, who, whom*) when you can do it without changing the meaning of a sentence.** Relative pronouns introduce many modifying clauses (see Section 16d-2). You can often cut them for economy.

| | |
|---|---|
| WORDY | The book **that I had quoted** was missing. |
| REVISED | The book **I had quoted** was missing. |

**EXERCISE 17.17** Rewrite these sentences to practice eliminating relative pronouns (*that, which, who, whom*) that might be contributing to wordiness. Retain any such pronouns you regard as necessary for clarity.

1. Some of the people who might be willing to endure a little less environmental consciousness are parents of children whom environmental education programs have turned into Green Police.

2. Second graders who used to read Dr. Seuss stories suddenly can't wait to locate "Tips to Save Our Planet" in the daily newspaper, which carries dozens of slick, unrecyclable inserts.

3. Full of moral superiority, youngsters who can barely read are circulating petitions that condemn industries that are polluting the air.

4. Shrewd are the parents who steer their children's activist impulses in productive directions by asking them to read supermarket labels and to find the items that are marked "Recyclable."

**9 Condense sentences into clauses and clauses into phrases or words.** Often one forceful word can do the work of several. Say more with less.

| | |
|---|---|
| ORIGINAL | Queen Elizabeth I was a complex and sensuous woman. She seemed to love many men, yet she never came close to marrying any of her suitors. |
| CONDENSED | Complex and sensuous, Queen Elizabeth I seemed to love men, yet she never came close to marrying. |
| ORIGINAL | Thanksgiving is a time for all of us to be together for the simple purpose of enjoying each other's company. |
| CONDENSED | Thanksgiving is a time for us to be together, enjoying each other's company. |

**EXERCISE 17.18** Rewrite the following sentences to reduce clutter by substituting single words for wordy phrases. Rearrange the sentences as necessary.

1. In the event that you are in proximity to Greene County this weekend, you should not miss the opportunity to visit the autumn Concours d'Elegance, an annual exhibit of classic cars.

2. There is the possibility that you may have the chance to touch and feel many quite unusual and different vehicles, from dowdy Edsels with gearshift buttons in the middle of their steering wheels to tiny Corvairs with air-cooled engines under louvered deck lids at the back.

3. However, don't expect to make an inspection of the more unique makes and the basically timeless art of such prestigious automakers as Bugatti, Duesenberg, or Hispano-Suiza.

4. Regardless of the fact that Greene County's show is a small show, you can take great satisfaction in examining quite handsome old Hudsons, Nashes, Jaguars, and Corvettes that are tended by owners who are willing and eager to talk about them at great length.

## 17d How can you achieve sentence variety?

Your readers will quickly be bored if all your sentences are of the same type and pattern. Write sentences that move easily and maturely, conveying readers from point to point with appropriate clarity and emphasis. You can't do this without offering some variety.

**●1 Vary sentence types.** The familiar sentence types discussed in Section 16e offer you a range of possibilities. Simple sentences attract the attention of readers with their economy and punch. Compound sentences put ideas of equal weight side by side. Complex sentences give you a means to state ideas subtly and richly. Varying these sentence types will keep your readers engaged.

**●2 Vary sentence patterns.** The five standard sentence patterns in English (see Section 16a) are reliable but dull when repeated over and over. Variations can add style. Consider inverting the usual word order.

**Gone** is the opportunity to win this month's lottery.

**Intelligent, cultured, and politically shrewd** was Eleanor of Aquitaine, a twelfth-century liberated woman.

Or play with the way a sentence opens.

ORIGINAL    The punk-rock protest songs of the early 1980s were the musicians' way of expressing their criticism of the political establishment.

VARIATION 1    To express their criticism of the political establishment, punk-rock musicians of the early 1980s wrote protest songs.

VARIATION 2    In the early 1980s, punk-rock musicians wrote protest songs as a way of expressing their criticism of the political establishment.

The variations are not necessarily better than the original. They're just different, and they demonstrate the options you have in crafting sentences.

Another way to vary the shape of sentences is to put interesting details into modifying clauses or phrases at different points in a sentence.

AT THE BEGINNING    **Convinced that he could not master rhetoric until he knew Greek**, Thomas began studying the language when he was 40.

IN THE MIDDLE    Li Po, **one of the greatest of the Chinese poets**, drowned when he fell out of a boat while trying to kiss the reflection of the moon in the water.

AT THE END    Sixteenth-century Aztec youths played a complex game called *ollamalitzli*, **which some anthropologists believe to have been the forerunner of modern basketball**.

**EXERCISE 17.19** The following sentences all begin approximately in the same way. Rewrite them to vary the pattern. Treat the four sentences as a single paragraph; you may not need to change all the sentences.

EXAMPLE    Directors and producers have adapted Shakespeare's plays to contemporary tastes in every age and era.

REVISED    In every age and era, directors and producers have adapted Shakespeare's plays to contemporary tastes.

1.  Directors and producers learned to move Shakespeare from the stage to the screen in the twentieth century.

2.  Filmmakers first had to adapt dramas to fit the new medium of film; early Shakespeare movies from the silent era looked much like stage plays presented before a camera.

3. Directors quickly realized that actors on the big screen had to restrain their traditional facial expressions and exaggerated stage gestures.

4. Directors and producers have since produced many Shakespeare films that adapt the dress, music, style, and attitudes of particular decades.

**EXERCISE 17.20** To each of the following sentences, add at least one modifying phrase or clause. Vary your placement of the modifiers.

1. Three books stand out in my mind as the ones I would recommend to a friend.

2. Johnny Cash is best known for his song "Folsom Prison Blues."

3. The Super Bowl occurs in January.

4. Reform of the IRS rarely gets far in Congress.

**3 Vary sentence length.** Readers like a balance between long and short sentences. If you've produced a cluster of short sentences, your writing may seem choppy. If you write only medium-length sentences, your prose may seem monotonous. Give readers a break; vary the rhythm.

Here is a paragraph that is tedious chiefly because all the sentences are nearly the same moderate length.

**ORIGINAL**

Our impressions of people are frequently based on our interpretation of their body language. We notice whether or not someone meets our gaze, fidgets constantly, or gestures when speaking. We use our observations to deduce personality traits such as arrogance, submissiveness, or trustworthiness. Most of us are confident of our ability to judge personality by reading body language. We reason that these skills must be highly developed since we rely on them regularly. Recent research confirms that most people can read emotion and gauge social skills from nonverbal signals. However, the same research suggests that they just as consistently fumble or misinterpret cues to more subtle personality traits.

A more lively revised version not only varies the length of sentences but uses varied sentence types.

**REVISED FOR VARIETY**

Our impressions of people are frequently based on our interpretation of their body language. Does someone meet our gaze or turn away? Does he fidget? Does she gesture? From nonverbal cues such as these we draw our conclusions: this person is arrogant, that one is trustworthy. Most of us are confident of our ability to judge personality from nonverbal cues—after all, we've been doing it all our lives. But how accurate are we really? Not very, it turns out. Recent research reveals that although most people can read emotion and gauge social skills correctly, they consistently fumble or misinterpret nonverbal cues to more subtle personality traits.

An occasional short sentence works well even in academic and professional writing—where the tendency is to avoid the quick jab. The fact is that short sentences catch the attention of readers. Mixed with longer sentences, they can mark a writer as direct and confident, able to make a bold claim or a clear statement.

**EXERCISE 17.21** The sentences in the following paragraph are monotonously brief. Combine some of these short sentences and edit as necessary to produce a more readable passage. Compare your version to others written by classmates.

The National Air and Space Museum is in Washington, D.C. It is located on the Mall near the Hirshhorn Museum and Sculpture Garden. The Air and Space Museum is one of the capital's most popular attractions. It presents the artifacts of aviation history. It presents these artifacts in a creative manner. The museum houses a replica of the Wright brothers' first plane. Lindbergh's plane hangs from the ceiling. The plane carried him across the Atlantic to Paris in 1927. It was a solo flight. Also in the museum are planes from World War II and a full-size lunar landing module. Every manner of flying machine is represented in the museum. There are dirigibles and zeppelins. There are fighter planes, passenger planes, and space capsules. There are helicopters and balloons. There is even a remarkable movie projected onto a large screen. The screen towers six stories.

# 17e How do you use figurative language?

Writers who make an impact on their readers are often those with a gift for finding the image that lasts, the analogy that clarifies, the metaphor that makes a concept come alive. Probably no writer finds it easy to learn to use figurative language. It is a talent developed over time through careful reading and self-conscious experimentation. Stay alert for the way authors use figures of speech such as analogy and metaphor, and have the courage to experiment in your own writing.

**●1 Look for fresh images that will strike your reader's imagination.** Such images can often be found by paying close attention to the world you can see and feel, as this writer did.

I went to high school at J. W. Sexton in Lansing, Michigan, **a Depression-era brick fortress that sat across the street from a Fisher Body auto assembly plant.** The plant was blocks long on each side and wrapped in **a skin of corrugated steel** painted a **shade of green somewhere between the Statue of Liberty and mold.** It loomed so near the high school that on football Fridays, when the Big Reds butted heads in Memorial Stadium, night-shift workers stood on balconies and watched the game.

—Ted Kleine, "Living the Lansing Dream"

To create powerful images, sometimes all you have to do is turn general terms into more particular ones.

| | |
|---|---|
| GENERAL TERMS | While striking baseball players drove off in **their fancy sports cars**, the **newly created unemployed** at ballparks struggled to **find work**. |
| SPECIFIC IMAGES | While striking baseball players drove off in **Porsches and Jaguars**, the **peanut vendors and grounds crews** at ballparks found themselves **in unemployment lines**. |

**●2 Use similes and metaphors to dramatize ideas. Similes** are comparisons that use *as* or *like*. Here are two examples.

As another fire season approaches, **anxiety about fires in the West is building as inexorably as piles of dead wood** on the forest floor.
— Ted Williams, "Only You Can Postpone Forest Fires"

Life in China was for millennia **like a lethal board game in which a blind destiny threw the dice, and to land on the wrong square at the wrong moment** could mean sudden ruin and repulsive death.
— Dennis Bloodworth, *The Chinese Looking Glass*

**Metaphors** are direct comparisons, without the use of *as* or *like*. Here are two examples.

Better watch out or **the pendulum of medical dogma** will bash your head in. **It swings back and forth** far more often than most people realize, and with far more velocity.
— Sherwin B. Nuland, "Medical Fads: Bran, Midwives, and Leeches"

The **geological time scale is a layer cake** of odd names, learned by generations of grumbling students with mnemonics either too insipid or too salacious for publication: Cambrian, Ordovician, Silurian, Devonian.
— Stephen Jay Gould, "The Power of Narrative"

A word of advice: don't mix metaphors. What's a mixed metaphor? It's a comparison that is either inconsistent or illogical because it begins with one image and ends with another.

Don't count your **chickens** until the **tide** comes in.

The Internet marketing **ship has sailed**, and companies that have failed to establish a presence on the Web are already **circling the wagons**.

**EXERCISE 17.22** Complete the following clauses by creating metaphors or similes.

1. The kitchen smelled awful, like a _____ that had _____.

2. Like a _____, the mayor protested over and over that she was innocent of taking illegal campaign contributions.

3. At the end of summer break, I'm usually a _____.

4. My seat in coach for the six-hour flight felt like a _____.

# 17f How do you develop and hone your writing style?

Writing stylish sentences takes a lot of practice. In fact, for many centuries, "style exercises"—short assignments that asked students to experiment with different ways of phrasing ideas—were a central component of any writing course. Even today, many professional authors attribute their success to frequent stylistic practice. Here are two tried-and-true exercises to try. Practiced regularly, each will enrich your stylistic repertoire.

● **1 Practice phrasing ideas in many different ways.** The more sentence patterns you master, the more aware you will be of your options when you compose a piece for a particular purpose and audience. To increase your repertoire, experiment with composing different kinds of sentences—the more possibilities you can generate, the better. Even small changes in word order, tone, or grammatical structure can make a big difference to readers. Consider, for example, these varied ways of saying, "I'd like to receive an A in English." Which do you like best? Which do you think are most effective?

Would you consider giving me an A, Professor Hairston?

Few students have worked as diligently for an A as I have.

I'll be devastated if I get anything other than an A.

What grade do I want in this course? Here's a hint: it's the first letter of the alphabet.

An A would make my day.

I'll settle for nothing less than the highest grade.

**EXERCISE 17.23** Try writing ten different sentences that express one of the following ideas.

1. Writing well takes constant practice.

2. College life requires many adjustments.

3. May I borrow $100?

**● 2 Imitate the sentence patterns used in writing you admire.**
Which writers' prose do you find especially persuasive, elegant, or compelling? In a notebook, collect passages you admire, paying careful attention to how each is constructed. Then try your hand at producing a similar sentence (on a different topic), trying to emulate the structure, figurative language, and tone of the original. Doing this imitation exercise regularly will help you to cultivate new sentence patterns, ones that you can later incorporate into your own writing. Here are two examples.

> **ORIGINAL PASSAGE**
> Now we are engaged in a great civil war, testing whether that nation, or any nation so conceived and so dedicated, can long endure.
> —Abraham Lincoln, "The Gettysburg Address"

> **IMITATION**
> Today Greg is scheduled to take the big chemistry exam, meaning that his scholarship, like any scholarship based on grades and on effort, may soon disappear.

> **ORIGINAL PASSAGE**
> The cheetah may be a gorgeous Maserati among mammals, able to spring at speeds approaching seventy miles an hour, yet it has not been able to run away from its many miseries.
> —Natalie Angier, "Chasing Cheetahs"

> **IMITATION**
> My roommate may be a virtual Einstein in the classroom, quick to solve equations involving dozens of cryptic symbols, but he has never learned to operate the dishwasher.

**EXERCISE 17.24** Imitate the following passages, trying to emulate the sentence patterns and figurative language used in each.

1. The lights were on in the car, so while we ran between trees I couldn't see anything except my own face and a woman across the aisle with a hat sitting right on top of her head, with a broken feather in it, but when we ran out of the trees I could see the twilight again, that quality of light

as if time really had stopped for awhile, with the sun hanging just under the horizon, and then we passed the marquee where the old man had been eating out of the sack, and the road was going on under the twilight, into twilight and the sense of water peaceful and swift beyond.

—William Faulkner, *The Sound and the Fury*

2. Rumors flew in unplanned and shifting patterns, like flocks of geese disturbed to the air by dogs.

—Elise Blackwell, *Hunger*

3. Let us not seek to satisfy our thirst for freedom by drinking from the cup of bitterness and hatred. We must forever conduct our struggle on the high plane of dignity and discipline.

—Martin Luther King, Jr., "I Have a Dream"

4. A stylistically interesting sentence of your choice.

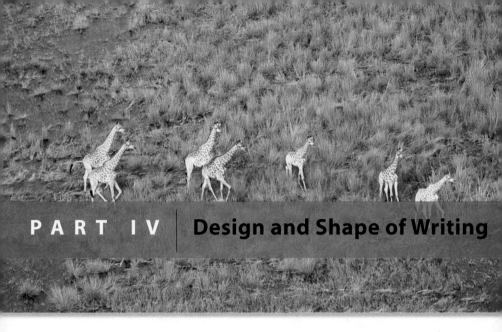

# PART IV | Design and Shape of Writing

# 18 How Do You Design Documents?

Today, computers and digital media are reshaping the look of writing by providing remarkable design opportunities to anyone with the patience to explore these tools. Even academic writers need not think solely in terms of black-and-white words on plain paper any more. Instead, you can shape the design of your projects to fit the needs of your audiences. But appreciating visual design is not a simple matter of adding pictures to a conventional text; rather, it involves understanding how all the physical elements of "texts" in any media work together to reach audiences.

Yet even when you know how you want a document to look, creating that look is a separate matter. This chapter offers pointers for working with specific design elements and avoiding common pitfalls of document design.

With a personal computer and a color printer, writers can publish on their desktops in minutes what historically has taken elaborate equipment and long hours of labor. The lithograph press illustrated here shows how many hands were once involved in producing a professionally printed document.

## 18a How do you design documents with a computer?

You'll most likely use a computer when you create a document with strong visual elements, whether the final product will appear on paper or on a screen. But although most writers use computers, few use them to their full advantage as tools for design.

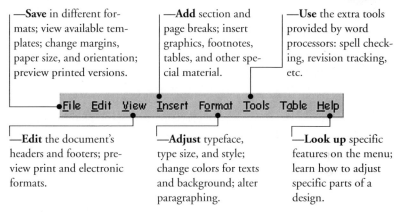

—**Save** in different formats; view available templates; change margins, paper size, and orientation; preview printed versions.

—**Add** section and page breaks; insert graphics, footnotes, tables, and other special material.

—**Use** the extra tools provided by word processors: spell checking, revision tracking, etc.

—**Edit** the document's headers and footers; preview print and electronic formats.

—**Adjust** typeface, type size, and style; change colors for texts and background; alter paragraphing.

—**Look up** specific features on the menu; learn how to adjust specific parts of a design.

**Figure 18.1** Learn the basic features of your word processor through its menu.

**1 Explore the design features of your word processor.** Word-processing programs support a variety of print and electronic formats, and they often have sophisticated options for enhancing visual style. You can easily insert pictures and graphics, add tables, create multiple columns, enhance text with colors and decorations, save texts in online formats (such as HTML), and do much, much more. To explore such features, consult the user's manual or help files for the program and try some hands-on experimentation (see Figure 18.1).

**2 Consider using other kinds of software.** Although you can do a lot with word processors alone, other types of software, such as those listed in Chart 18.1, offer additional design options.

| Chart 18.1 **Design Software** | |
|---|---|
| **SOFTWARE** | **WHAT IT CAN CREATE** |
| **Spreadsheet software** (e.g., Excel, Lotus 1-2-3) | Complex tables, graphs, statistical reports |
| **Drawing software** (e.g., Adobe Illustrator) | Simple images, charts, decorated text |

*(Continued)*

**Design Software** *(Continued)*

| | |
|---|---|
| **Image editors** | Digitized photos, complex images |
| (e.g., iPhoto, PhotoShop) | |
| **Presentation software** | Slide shows and handouts |
| (e.g., PowerPoint, Keynote) | |
| **HTML editors** | Web pages of varying complexity |
| (e.g., Dreamweaver, FrontPage) | |
| **Sound and video editors** | Digitized music and film clips |
| (e.g., iMovie, Garage Band) | |
| **Page layout software** | Posters, brochures, letterheads, pamphlets |
| (e.g., PageMaker, Quark) | |

**EXERCISE 18.1** If you have never used the graphic capabilities of your word processor, consult its "Help" features (searching the boldfaced terms) to learn how to do the following:

- **Insert a picture** into a text file, then **resize** it.
- Place a **horizontal line** on a page.
- Draw an **arrowhead** on a page.
- Create a **text box** on a page and then **color** the **text**.

> Make the text in your box blue.

## 18b How do you lay out pages?

For many projects, you'll receive specific guidelines for page size, margin width, paragraphing, alignment, and so on. Follow them exactly. But when you have flexibility, take advantage of it by shaping the layout of your document to suit your purposes.

● **1 Choose a manageable size and orientation.** When you are working with a page size other than the standard 8.5 × 11″ (as you might when designing a poster or pamphlet), the size of your pages may affect the

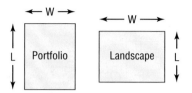

**Figure 18.2** Portfolio (or portrait) layouts are longer than they are wide. In landscape layouts, width is greater than length.

amount of material you can put on each. Large pages give you more surface area, but they can be difficult to manipulate: for example, they don't work well for extended blocks of text because readers must concentrate on a relatively small area of a wide surface. Similarly, large electronic pages may require too much scrolling.

Orientation—the direction material faces on the page—also affects readers. The most common orientation is *portfolio*, shown in Figure 18.2. Portfolio orientation (also sometimes called *portrait*) works well with most formats because it presents the main text in one medium-sized column. *Landscape* orientation is generally reserved for graphic material too wide for portfolio orientation.

**2 Break material into readable units.** This is especially important with layouts that require large blocks of text, which many readers find unappealing.

- In documents such as pamphlets and newsletters, use colors, fonts, boxes, borders, background shading, and images to chunk information to make it more readable (see Figure 18.3 on page 322). In others—such as research papers or résumés—use headings to break the information into helpful sections.
- Insert horizontal lines or rules to mark the beginning of new sections in a document; rules might also distinguish secondary material from the central content of a page—for instance, you'll see rules separating footnotes or running heads from the main text on a page. You might even

**Colors** clearly mark areas of the layout, accentuate text, and set a casual tone.

**Fonts** give text passages a consistent look and provide special emphasis.

**Images** attract the eyes to special sections of the page and complement explanatory text.

**Lines** and **boxes** group related material, making the layout easy to follow.

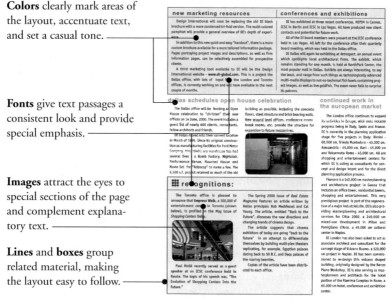

**new marketing resources**

Design International will soon be replacing the old DI black brochure with a more condensed tri-fold version. The multi-colored pamphlet will provide a general overview of DI's depth of experience.

In addition to this new quick and easy "handout", there is a more custom brochure available for a more tailored information package. Pages portraying project images and descriptions, as well as firm information pages, can be selectively assembled for prospective clients.

A third marketing tool available to DI will be the Design International website - **www.di-global.com**. This is a project the Dallas office, with lots of input from the London and Toronto offices, is currently working on and will have available in the next couple of months.

**conferences and exhibitions**

DI has exhibited at three recent conferences, MIPIM in Cannes, ICSC in Berlin and ICSC in Las Vegas. All have produced new client contacts and potential for future work.

All of the DI board members were present at the ICSC conference held in Las Vegas. All left for the conference after their quarterly board meeting, which was held in the Dallas office.

DI Dallas will again be exhibiting at Retrospect, an annual event which spotlights local architectural firms. The exhibit, which remains standing for one month, is held at NorthPark Center, the most popular mall in Dallas. Exhibits are always interesting, to say the least, and range from such things as technologically advanced multi-media displays to not-so-technical fish bowls containing project images, as well as live goldfish. The event never fails to surprise its patrons.

**dallas schedules open house celebration**

The Dallas office will be hosting an Open House celebration to "christen" their new offices on 14 June, 2000. The event includes a guest list of nearly 600 clients, consultants, fellow architects and friends.

DI Dallas moved into their current location in March of 1999. Since its original construction as manufacturing facilities for Ford Motor Company, this 1940's era warehouse has had several lives as a Bomb Factory, Nightclub, Performance Venue, Haunted House and Movie Set for "Robocop" to name a few. The 9,500 s.f. project retained as much of the old building as possible, including the concrete floors, steel structure and brick bearing walls. New ground level offices, conference rooms break rooms, etc. provide the structure for expansion to future mezzanines.

**continued work in the european market**

The London office continues to expand its activities in Europe, with most notable progress being in Italy, Spain and France. DI is currently in the planning application stage for five projects in Italy: Rimini - 60,000 sm, Trieste Montedoro - 45,000 sm, Alessandria - 45,000 sm, Bari - 45,000 sm and Valcanmuta Rome - 45,000 sm. All are shopping and entertainment centers for which DI is acting as consultants for concept and design intent and for the direct planning application process.

Fiumara is a 140,000 sm masterplanning and architecture project in Genoa that includes an office tower, residential towers, shopping and entertainment. This very prestigious project is part of the regeneration of a major industrial site. DI is also providing masterplanning and architectural services for Citta 2000, a 240,000 sm mixed-use development in Milan and Pomigliano d'Arco, a 45,000 sm cultural center in Naples.

DI London has also been asked to act as associate architect and consultant for the concept stage of Vulcano Buono, a 120,000 sm project in Naples. DI has been commissioned to re-design this volcano shaped building, originally designed by the Renzo Piano Workshop. DI is also serving as masterplanners and architects for the hotel portion of the Fiorina Complex in Rome, a 60,000 sm hotel, conference and exhibition center.

**⊞ recognitions:**

The Toronto office is pleased to announce that Empress Walk, a 300,000 sf entertainment center in Toronto (shown below), is profiled in the May issue of *Shopping Centers Today*.

Paul Mollé recently served as a guest speaker at an ICSC conference held in Russia. The topic of his speech was, "The Evolution of Shopping Centers Into the Future."

The Spring 2000 issue of *Real Estate Magazine* features an article written by Dallas principals Bob Meckfessel and Cal Young. The article, entitled "Back to the Future", discusses the new directions and changing trends of cinema design.

The article suggests that cinema exhibitors of today are going "back to the future" in an attempt to differentiate themselves by building multi-plex theaters replicating, for example, Egyptian palaces dating back to 50 B.C. and Deco palaces of the roaring twenties.

Copies of the article have been distributed to each office.

**Figure 18.3** In this newsletter page you can see the basic elements of document style at work.

see a vertical rule wherever marginal comments or graphics appear on the sidebar of a page.

- Consider the design of paragraphs and columns. Sometimes you may be able to choose between block and indented paragraphs, deciding which style makes your text more readable. *Block paragraphs* have no indentation on their first lines but are separated by extra spacing between each paragraph. Standard *indented paragraphs*, on the other hand, need no extra spacing. See Figure 18.4 for examples. In some documents, such as newsletters or brochures (but not most academic papers), you might also be able to decide whether two or even three columns of type make your work more readable than one.

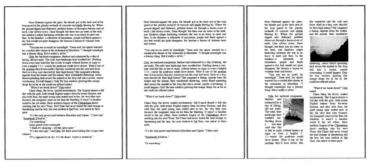

**Figure 18.4** Indented paragraphs (left) follow one after another, without spacing between them. In academic papers, the indention is 5 spaces or 1/2″ and the right-hand margin is not "justified" (that is, aligned straight against the right margin. Block paragraphs (middle) are not indented, and so they must be separated by spaces. They usually look better if justified, right and left, as shown. Multiple columns (right) may be more readable than a single column for newsletters or other professional documents. Paragraphs are usually indented only two or three spaces, spaces may be left to divide sections, and a page might easily incorporate images of various sizes.

● **3 Arrange material according to relevance.** Readers of English tend to move from the upper left corner of a page to the lower right. So put important lead-ins, such as titles and informative images, at the top of a page and less interesting but necessary material toward the bottom. Here are specific suggestions.

- Place the most important material in one or more columns spanning the body of the page (but be aware that columns wider than six or seven inches can be difficult for readers to follow).
- Move supplementary material, such as comments and brief notes, toward the side and bottom margins.
- Group related pieces of material (explanatory text and illustrations, for example) near each other. Bullets indicate that the items listed are related.
- Distinguish special material by indenting, framing, or screening it. Slight adjustments to typeface, type size, type style, and colors can make material easier to read, as Figure 18.5 illustrates.

**Figure 18.5** Although the formatting in the document on the left is generally effective, the revision on the right has enhanced the arrangement with colors, images, multiple type styles, and simple graphics. The original would be fine for an internal policy statement; the revision is more appropriate for a customer information packet. Note these changes: (1) Display text has been highlighted with color. (2) The first list uses stylized bullets and background screen for contrast; the second list has portrait photos instead of bullets, is set in two columns, and uses boldface to emphasize each name. (3) The margin has been colored and widened to hem in the main content of the page.

- In headers, add navigational details such as current section titles (also called *running heads*), page numbers, and information about the writer.
- In footers, place routine but necessary information such as contact addresses, page numbers, organizational information, and credits (in cases where the writer's organization is emphasized more than the writer).

**● 4 Align material to direct readers' eyes down and across the page.** Left alignment is usually the most readable layout for extended passages of text, but images and graphics often work well with center or right alignment. Right-aligned images are effective when they are "wrapped" by left-aligned text—that is, when the lines of text appear on the same horizontal lines used by the image (see Figure 21.3 on page 384). Center alignment is better for images not wrapped by text, since left or right alignment leaves too much white space in the body of the page.

**Subsections.** By highlighting topics within a larger section, subsections help readers follow your discussion.

### Reviews from Center Stage

**Lame indeed.**

The recent popularity of boy-band parody Wounded Duck isn't all that surprising. What is surprising is the ability of surly fans to endure the tiresome antics for an hour-long set. How many times can you watch the elaborately choreographed dancers flub their moves before it gets old?

Okay, I'll admit to guffawing through the first three songs—but once you get the gist of the show, there isn't much more to see. My advice—should the Duck fly into town opening for another band—show up ten minutes before the headliners, get a few laughs, and then listen to some real music.

**How old school is too old school?**

Before Friday, I thought I had an answer to this question. DJ Crusty's energetic set showed that digging up musical fossils isn't all about giving rock legends cameos in your music video. There are still treasures to be found—treasures encased in wax. Crusty's ability to synthesize diverse flavors of vinyl into addictive compounds explains why he has crossed over from the club set into the mainstream.

**Lists.** It's often awkward to form a series of regular, repetitive statements into a paragraph. Try a list instead. Use numbered lists when information needs to be presented in a strict order.

### Festival 2006: Survivor's Guide

The spring rains and crowds can sometimes put a damper on your ability to enjoy the music. Never fear! We've provided a list of suggestions to make the best of your aural outing.

♪ Take your own water bottles. You'll have to wait in line for even the basics once inside.

♪ A waterproof mat is also a good idea. The ground gets pretty muddy, especially by the final days.

♪ Bring plenty of your own toilet tissue. Supplies in the portable facilities run low after just a few hours.

♪ If you're planning on attending more than one day, earplugs will keep your hearing from going dull.

♪ A hooded raincoat can keep you dry during the early afternoon showers.

♪ If you plan on heading for the mosh pit, ignore all of the above and just bring elbow pads.

**Tables.** Tables work well for presenting more structured information, especially (but not exclusively) statistical data, which can also be turned into graphs (see Section 18d). You can also use tables to display categories of information and complicated lists.

| Festival 2006: Daily Venue Schedules | | | | |
|---|---|---|---|---|
| | Center Stage | East Stage | West Stage | Welcome Stage |
| **Wed.** | Classic Rock | World Beat | Punk | Polka |
| **Th.** | Funk and Soul | Swing | Reggae and Ska | Metal Mania |
| **Fri.** | Rock and Pop | Blues | Hip-hop and R & B | Local Grab Bag |
| **Sat.** | Rock and Pop | Jazz | Country | DJ Showcase |
| **Sun.** | International Folk | Classical | Gospel | Amateur Contest |

**Frames.** When you want to set material apart from the main text, place it in a *frame* or a box, which you can create with lines and/or changes in background color.

**About the Festival (cont.)**

The annual festival began in 1982 as a relatively small, "y'all come" event. There was only one stage in the town square at that time. Those first few years didn't attract much national attention, but the music was rich with a variety of local flavors—from rock to jazz to punk to (we're not ashamed to admit) disco.

1987: Going National
A big break came for the festival in 1987, when national, independent label Snub Pop agreed to host a second stage. Before long, other national labels were seeing the festival as an opportunity to promote otherwise unknown bands.

The menu of bands was interesting enough to attract music lovers from all over the state. Eventually, the small festival grew to include most types of American music, until, last year, we finally added a fourth venue, allowing us to accommodate more and more international genres as well.

You can also use alignment to make readers pause at important points, as Figure 18.6 illustrates. Page designers will use this technique to make section openings stand out by centering or right-aligning headings within a left-aligned body of text. Use this method of emphasis carefully; too many disruptions can make pages seem choppy.

● **5 Use white space to avoid clutter.** White space reduces clutter by separating material into readable units. Here are common ways of creating white space.

- Leave ample margins at the top and sides of your pages.
- Surround titles, graphics, and frames with unused space.

<table>
<tr><td>

### Rules for Hiking in the Park

**Don't go off the trail.** The animal habitats in the park are extremely fragile. While we encourage people to enjoy the natural benefits provided inside, in order to maintain the survival of the fauna and flora, visitors must restrict themselves to clearly marked trails.

**Don't take anything out of the park.** Just as we don't want visitors leaving their marks, we don't want them removing what might be necessary parts of a fragile ecology.

**Don't feed the animals.** Wild animals can become dependent upon humans, if they expect to be fed. Once in the habit of receiving handouts they can become aggressive when refused—then they must be removed.

**Report violations of these rules.** It's your park. When other visitors violate these rules, they are destroying public property.

</td><td>

### Rules for Hiking in the Park

#### Don't go off the trail.
The animal habitats in the park are extremely fragile. While we encourage people to enjoy the natural benefits provided inside, in order to maintain the survival of the fauna and flora, visitors must restrict themselves to clearly marked trails.

#### Don't take anything out of the park.
Just as we don't want visitors leaving their marks, we don't want them removing what might be necessary parts of a fragile ecology.

#### Don't feed the animals.
Wild animals can become dependent upon humans, if they expect to be fed. Once in the habit of receiving handouts they can become aggressive when refused—then they must be removed.

#### Report violations of these rules.
It's your park. When other visitors violate these rules, they are destroying public property.

</td></tr>
</table>

**Figure 18.6**  The subsection headings are clearly emphasized in both pages, but the center alignment in the page on the right makes them stand out even more. But this alignment of the headings doesn't lead as smoothly into the main text. Readers might find the poster on the left more attractive.

- Double-space between paragraphs.
- Indent special blocks of material.
- Allow adequate space between columns in multicolumn documents.

● **6 Revise for readability, impact, and flow.**  When you've created a page layout or template, evaluate how well format and style work together. Can readers move through the document easily and intuitively? Do its immediate impact and lasting impressions serve your writing goals? Even if your first draft seems relatively successful, chances are you'll need to revise to enhance readability, impact, and flow.

- **Add meaningful contrasts to improve readability.** Imagine the nightmare of reading a twenty-page document with no paragraphing or sentence punctuation to show where ideas begin and end. Readers might have a similar reaction—though not so drastic—to pages that contain a great deal of material in a plain format or style. Variations in color, font size, and font style help readers more clearly identify points of special interest and transitions.

- **Enhance contrasts where appropriate.** To strengthen the impact of your document, increase the contrast among design elements. Bright colors, extra-large fonts, and vivid images all attract readers' eyes. Keep in mind, however, that such striking features can make it difficult for a reader to focus on the surrounding material. Splashy, subtle, or something in between—the choice is yours.
- **Group related material to improve flow.** When readers' eyes dance around the page, they can't easily focus on a single point. Help readers navigate smoothly by grouping related material—explanatory text, graphics, images, tables. Emphasize groupings by framing material in boxes or using a common background color.
- **Position material strategically for balance.** Too much material in one area makes it difficult for readers to focus. Too much space between material disrupts flow. Use white space strategically to show places where readers might pause as they move toward a new thought—but don't create such a wide gap that they don't know which way to go.

**EXERCISE 18.2** Copy enough text into a word-processing file to fill at least one single-spaced page. (You might use material you have written yourself earlier.) Then use your word-processing software to manipulate it in various ways such as those described below, producing four visually different pages. Then decide for what sorts of documents a page in each of the four styles you have created might be appropriate.

- Double spaced, courier font, single column, indented paragraphs, portfolio orientation, one-inch margins all around, no images
- Single spaced, New York font, single column, block paragraphs, right justified, portfolio orientation, one-inch margins all around, no images, headings as appropriate
- Single spaced, Times New Roman font, two columns, indented paragraphs (indented just two or three spaces), right justified, portrait orientation, one-inch margins all around, one or more images

- Single spaced, Helvetica font, three or more columns, block paragraphs, landscape orientation, appropriate margins, two or more small images with text wrapping around them, some material framed or highlighted

## 18c  How do you choose type?

*Typefaces* (or *fonts*) and *type styles* have their own personalities. A thick, heavy typeface like **Helvetica Black** speaks loudly and commands attention; a script font like *Mistral* conveys a delicate, artistic mood. Type styles, such as **boldface**, *italic*, and SMALL CAPS, serve more practical purposes, enhancing words and phrases to make them stand out. Finally, you can adjust *type size* (usually measured in *points*) to enhance your document's style and readability.

● **1** **Select a suitable typeface.** What typeface you choose depends on your purpose and format. Some fonts read better in print than on a computer screen. Other fonts are decorative—not designed for extended passages of text. Fortunately, fonts have been divided into families that share certain characteristics.

- **Serif fonts.** Serifs are the little lines, or "feet," that appear at the bottom or top of the main strokes in a letter. Two common serif fonts are `Courier` and **Bookman**. Serif fonts are highly readable for print documents.
- **Sans serif fonts.** Sans serif fonts—letters without the little feet—have a clean, avant-garde look. Two common sans serif fonts are Arial and Helvetica. Sans serif fonts are generally the best choices for material to be read on an electronic, faxed, or photocopied page.
- **Decorative or ornamental fonts.** Decorative fonts have a lot of personality—they can be elegant, jazzy, authoritative, comical. But they aren't always easy to read in long passages of text. Save these fonts for where you want to create a special effect. Many options will be available on your word processor, from **OldTown** to *OPIS Camella Handscript* to *Vivaldi*.
- **Symbol fonts.** Special characters, called *dingbats*, allow you to add simple graphic ornaments to your documents. To find out what you have

available, select a font with "symbol" or "ding" in its title and start typing characters, or choose the "Insert Symbol" command in your word processor. You'll see small graphics suitable for various purposes, as shown in Chart 18.2.

---

**Chart 18.2   Symbol Fonts ("Dingbats")**

| | |
|---|---|
| Stylized bullets | ▶ ◊ ☞ ✓ ❶ |
| Explanatory diagrams | 🗀 💾 ⇒ 📄 ↑ 🖃 |
| Business-related text | © ® ™ ％ ¢ £ ¥ |
| Technical writing | θ ∠ ⊆ π √ Ω Σ ♭ ♯ |
| Informative symbols | ♂ ♀ ? − |

---

**● 2 Use type styles strategically.** Type styles that differ from plain text will draw readers' attention. But use them sparingly, or they'll lose their impact. Chart 18.3 shows common type styles and suggestions for using each.

---

**Chart 18.3   Type Styles**

| TYPE STYLE | COMMON USES |
|---|---|
| **Boldface** | Strong emphasis, headings |
| *Italic* | Highlights, special/foreign words, book titles |
| <u>Underline</u> | Emphasis, headings, book titles |
| Superscript and subscript | Footnotes, endnotes, technical notation |
| ~~Strikethrough~~ | Revisions in drafts |
| SMALL CAPS | Subtle emphasis, strong highlights, headings |
| Shadow, Emboss, <u>Wave</u> | Decorative emphasis, highlights, headings |

---

**● 3 Adjust type size for readability.** Medium type sizes (usually 10 or 12 points) work best for the main body of text. Extended passages in large type can be difficult to read. Reserve larger type for headings and titles. "Fine print," on the other hand, isn't always bad. Use smaller type to downplay less important material in margins, headers, and footers.

Here are a few final cautions.

- Electronic documents may look strange if the fonts you use aren't installed on your readers' computers.
- Changing the font face may change the height and length of lines.
- Serif fonts can be difficult to read on computer screens.
- Certain font styles and colors (such as blue underlining) may have special meaning in Web pages and other hyperlinked documents.

## 18d How do you use charts, tables, and graphs?

When you present information through charts, graphs, and tables, you draw pictures for readers. These pictures help readers grasp a complex body of data that could be hard to absorb through words alone. Imagine, for example, that you wanted to illustrate the cost of student housing in your area. If you created a fact sheet that used a bar graph to show the price ranges for one-bedroom, one-bath apartments in four areas close to your college, you would do a service for students on a budget looking for a small place.

Charts, graphs, and tables present information in different ways. This section explains how each works.

● 1 **A pie chart shows how the parts of a whole are distributed.** A pie chart is a simple graphic that shows percentages (the slices) of a total (the whole pie). The example in Figure 18.8 on page 333 presents basic information about how property tax revenues are spent in Indiana. Using this chart, you could answer various questions: How much of the state's revenue goes to city and county governments? Do schools receive a substantial share? And so on.

But pie charts can't tell readers everything. Since pie charts generally can't include more than six or seven slices without becoming visually confusing, you wouldn't use them to create fine distinctions. Writers often collapse several smaller categories into a single "slice." For example, you can't tell from

**Bar graphs** show comparative values.

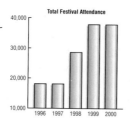

**Pie charts** show portions of a whole.

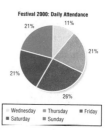

**Line graphs** show trends and changes across time.

**Area graphs** show portions of a whole as comparative trends.

**Organizational charts** show hierarchical relationships.

**Flow charts** show procedural relationships.

**Timelines** show sequential relationships.

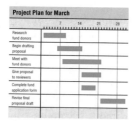

**Diagrams** illustrate textual descriptions.

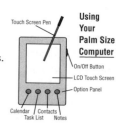

**Figure 18.7** Graphs, charts, and graphs come in many forms. Use them to add information—not decoration—to a project.

Figure 18.8 exactly which county and city services (police, water, roads) are funded by the property tax.

You can draw pie charts with drawing tools in your word processor or let software such as *Excel* create them for you. Be sure that the slices are clearly labeled, that colors used are visually distinctive, and that your labeled percentages of the pie don't exceed 100. You can vary the design of a basic pie chart, as shown in Figure 18.9. But be sure that any variation remains clear to readers.

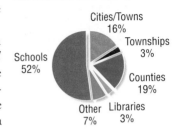

**Who Receives the Property Tax?**

Cities/Towns 16%
Townships 3%
Schools 52%
Counties 19%
Libraries 3%
Other 7%

**Figure 18.8**

**●2 A bar graph shows the relationship between two variables.** It does this by charting the data for one variable along a horizontal scale and the data for the other variable along a vertical scale, using vertical bars to depict data in one or more categories. In Figure 18.10, different parts of the world (Africa, Latin America, etc.) are shown on the horizontal axis; numerical data are represented by the vertical bars. By depicting this information visually, the graph dramatizes how reserves of natural gas compare worldwide.

Bar graphs can give more information than pie charts. They can show not only general trends, but also subtle distinctions within categories of data. For example, each bar in Figure 18.10 could be divided into two or three subcategories, perhaps using different colors for different countries in each region or for urban versus rural areas. Once again, you can draw bar graphs by hand or with electronic tools. You want to be certain that readers can

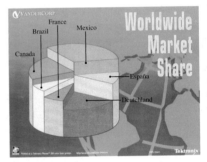

**Figure 18.9**

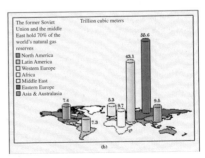

**Figure 18.10**

quickly grasp the relationships you are plotting, so be certain that your labels are clear and colors show sufficient contrast.

**● 3 Line graphs also show relationships but depict trends more emphatically.** Like bar graphs, line graphs chart the relationship between two variables, one depicted along the horizontal axis and one along the vertical axis. The sharply declining line in Figure 18.11 makes a strong impact on readers, who will immediately grasp the sense of what they're seeing—in this case suggesting a steep decline in unemployment between 1992 and 1999.

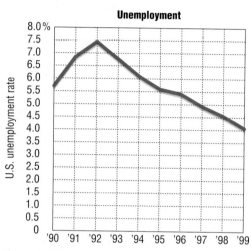

**Figure 18.11**

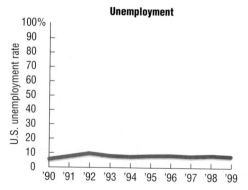

**Figure 18.12**

But you must be careful not to use the impact of a line chart to mislead readers. Figures 18.11 and 18.12 present exactly the same data on unemployment rates in the United States, but Figure 18.11 appears to show a sharp drop in the national rate during the 1990s, whereas Figure 18.12 makes the decrease look insignificant by plotting it on a grid that shows the full range of rates, from 0 to 100 percent of the population. The creators of the graphs may have had different reasons for plotting the charts as they have, either emphasizing or minimizing the significance of the change in employment rates. But consider also that a reader using Figure 18.11 could more accurately determine the exact unemployment rates from 1990 to 1999 than someone using Figure 18.12.

When you create a line graph, be sure that you depict a relationship fairly and precisely, clearly labeling the graph itself and the two axes and making the entire visual easy to interpret. It should present a quick overview of a relationship, yet also furnish the data points a reader might need.

**● 4 Tables organize categories of information into vertical columns and horizontal rows that show relationships.** You can create tables to provide more detailed information than graphs or charts, but they're visually less appealing because readers must look more carefully, analyze data for themselves, and draw their own conclusions.

To create a table, think of how you might array the data most clearly. Provide a heading that identifies the data being given, then break down the data into useful categories. Even word processors typically have a feature to help you to design tables once you know how many columns and rows you need to present—though database programs are far more efficient with large amounts of data. Table 18.1 on page 336 presents information from the U.S. Department of Education about academic degrees earned in the United States in a single year, breaking down the data by gender, race, and ethnicity. Using this table, you could discover which groups are graduating with which number of academic degrees. With a little math, you could also calculate the proportions.

**● 5 Ensure the accuracy of your charts, graphs, and tables.** You should approach visual representations of data with a critical eye. Numbers *themselves* don't lie, but you can present them in misleading or confusing ways.

When you create a chart, graph, or table, try to imagine how a reader might *misread* it. In particular, look for missing labels and quantities (Is the item marked in percentages, lbs, meters, mpg, etc.?). Be sure to check how the colors will look in the final format. Orange and red might look distinct in the pie chart you create on your computer screen, but they might merge in a printed document.

Checklist 18.1 on page 336 will help you detect problems that commonly appear in visual representations of information.

**Table 18.1** **College Degrees Conferred in 2001–2 by Racial and Ethnic Group**

Related data:
- Earned Degrees: Conferred, 2001–2
- Degrees Awarded by Type of Institution, 2001–2

| | | U.S. Citizens and Resident Aliens | | | | | |
|---|---|---|---|---|---|---|---|
| | Total | American Indian | Asian | Black | Hispanic | White | Nonresident Aliens |
| **Associate** | | | | | | | |
| Men | 238,109 | 2,306 | 13,259 | 22,800 | 23,963 | 170,627 | 5,154 |
| Women | 357,024 | 4,524 | 17,688 | 44,537 | 36,040 | 247,112 | 7,123 |
| Total | 595,133 | 6,830 | 30,947 | 67,337 | 60,003 | 417,739 | 12,277 |
| **Bachelor's** | | | | | | | |
| Men | 549,816 | 3,625 | 37,666 | 39,194 | 32,953 | 414,885 | 21,493 |
| Women | 742,084 | 5,540 | 45,435 | 77,430 | 50,016 | 543,700 | 19,963 |
| Total | 1,291,900 | 9,165 | 83,101 | 116,624 | 82,969 | 958,585 | 41,456 |
| **Master's** | | | | | | | |
| Men | 199,120 | 994 | 11,749 | 11,796 | 8,431 | 128,770 | 37,380 |
| Women | 282,998 | 1,632 | 13,665 | 28,577 | 13,956 | 198,865 | 26,303 |
| Total | 482,118 | 2,626 | 25,414 | 40,373 | 22,387 | 327,635 | 63,683 |
| **Doctorate** | | | | | | | |
| Men | 23,708 | 67 | 1,240 | 921 | 649 | 13,334 | 7,497 |
| Women | 20,452 | 113 | 1,077 | 1,476 | 783 | 13,571 | 3,432 |
| Total | 44,160 | 180 | 2,317 | 2,397 | 1,432 | 26,905 | 10,929 |
| **Professional** | | | | | | | |
| Men | 42,507 | 292 | 4,613 | 2,223 | 2,045 | 32,224 | 1,110 |
| Women | 38,191 | 289 | 4,971 | 3,588 | 1,920 | 26,650 | 773 |
| Total | 80,698 | 581 | 9,584 | 5,811 | 3,965 | 58,874 | 1,883 |

Source: U.S. Department of Education

---

**Checklist 18.1** **Evaluating Charts, Graphs, and Tables**

When you create a chart, a graph, or a table, ask yourself . . .

- Are the data up to date?

- Have you labeled all the important elements so that readers can interpret numbers, percentages, and headings? Provide a legend if necessary to explain terms or unfamiliar abbreviations.

- What is the source of your data? Is that source credible?

- Have you argued for no more than the data can actually prove?

- Have you presented the data fairly and without distortion?

For more information on how numbers are used in charts, graphs, and tables, and for useful definitions of common statistical terms, consult Robert Niles's *Statistics Every Writer Should Know* at <http://www.robertniles.com/stats>.

**EXERCISE 18.3** Imagine that you want to give an oral presentation that uses data on academic degrees. Read Table 18.1 with this focus in mind. Working with another student, decide what information from the table would be most useful for your talk and how you might supplement the information you find there with other statistics. Share your findings with the class.

**EXERCISE 18.4** Pick up a copy of *USA Today, Time, Newsweek,* or another popular publication that uses charts, graphs, and tables to present information. See if you can find an example that you think presents data in an inaccurate, oversimplified, or misleading way. Bring your example to class for discussion.

# 18e How do you use images and photographs?

According to the maxim, a picture is worth a thousand words. Used thoughtfully, it can be worth even more; used poorly, much less. Effective graphics in a project take planning and editing. The tips in this section will help you use images to enhance and complement the text of your document.

### ● 1 Enliven writing with photos and illustrations.

Some ideas and emotions are difficult to express in words. Photos and illustrations (such as cartoons, drawings, engravings) let you show readers—at a glance—aspects of your subject that would otherwise need lengthy description. But be sure that photos and illustrations reinforce important points and do not mislead readers.

Many options exist for acquiring photos and illustrations to use in a document. You can purchase digitized photos on the Web (some are even free) or on CDs, usually with certain copyright restrictions. You can create your own with a digital camera, or you can translate existing photos or illustrations into electronic formats with a scanner.

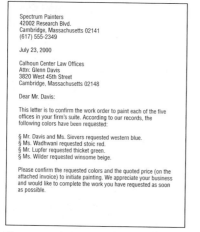
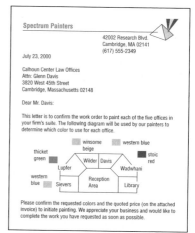

**Figure 18.13**  Even a standard business letter (left) can be made more effective with the addition of images (right): (1) A horizontal rule helps distinguish the letterhead from the main content. (2) A graphic logo creates a professional persona. (3) An explanatory diagram helps to clarify written instructions.

For a minimal cost, you can buy disks or CDs that have thousands of clip art images. Clip art collections may not furnish you with sophisticated images, but they can be useful when you need graphics for posters, brochures, newsletters, and other low-cost publications.

● **2 Edit your images.** In most projects today, you'll likely use digital images and photographs, which can be easily cropped, edited, and improved to look good on a page or screen. You can use software as sophisticated as *Adobe Photoshop* or tools included with your computer, such as *iPhoto* or *Picture Man*, to edit images you download or take yourself. Even word processors enable you to resize and position images you import into documents. Check out the software available to you and then explore how it works. You'll master the basic features quickly.

One caution: the power you have to alter digital images also brings with it the responsibility to make changes ethically. So respect the copyrights of any graphics you don't own or create and get appropriate permissions whenever

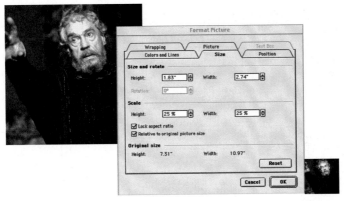

**Figure 18.14** One way to change the size of a picture on a word processor is by typing the dimensions you want into a format box and clicking "OK." Sizing by dimension enables you to make different images all the same size if that's what you need on a page.

your use of images requires them. Do not modify an image in ways that might alter its original content (for example, by cropping people out of a photograph).

**Sizing images.** After you import an image into a document, you can change its size, usually just by pulling a corner or typing a size in a control box. In reports and research papers, an image should be no larger than it needs to be to be effective and "readable." In electronic projects, smaller images are also quicker to download than larger ones and take up less digital space. Use bigger images in those projects that need their impact—such as brochures or posters. Note that changing the size of an image can affect its quality and sharpness. At some point, an enlarged digital image will become grainy or even begin to show the edges of its pixels. But it's unlikely that you would require so large an image for most conventional projects.

**Cropping images.** Use editing tools to focus on those parts of an image your project needs. Simple cropping tools allow you to select exactly which part of a digital image to use. You can usually constrain the cropping to be sure that you maintain familiar proportions, such as square, 4 × 6, or 8 × 10 in landscape or portrait orientations.

**Figure 18.15** A cropping tool is used to select one part of a photograph and to reshape its proportions from rectangular to square. One caution: the image of the chipmunk here would lose sharpness as it is enlarged. Is anything else lost in this particular image?

**Placing images.** Software tools ordinarily allow you not only to place an image where you want it on a page (left, right, center), but to wrap

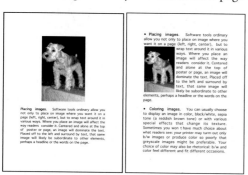

**Figure 18.16** A format box in a word processor will enable you not only to place a photograph exactly where you need it, but to wrap text around it in a variety of ways. Which of the two page designs do you prefer and why?

text around it in various ways. Where you place an image will affect the way readers consider it. Centered and alone at the top of a poster or page, an image will dominate the text. Placed off to the left and surrounded by text, that same image will likely be subordinate to other elements, perhaps a headline or the words on the page.

**Coloring images.** You can usually choose to display an image in color, black and white, sepia tone (a reddish-brown tone), or with various special effects that change its texture. Sometimes you won't have much choice about what readers see: your printer may turn out only black-and-white images or produce color so poorly that grayscale images might be preferable. Your choice of color may also be rhetorical: black and white and color feel different and fit different occasions.

**Figure 18.17** Note how this image changes in character as it moves from its original full color into black and white, sepia, and finally a special effect. How might you describe the differences?

**Modifying images.** Your digital images can usually be improved if their colors are off or the images are too dark or light. Use the available editing tools to improve the color balance (to get flesh tones right, for example), to add or flatten contrast, to brighten or darken the image, to deepen or moderate the color (called "saturation"), and so on. Tinker with these tools until you get an image you feel is "right." But when you'll be making

**Figure 18.18** Software is used here to make the flesh tones in this image look more natural. Why do you think flesh tones are typically used to adjust the colors in a photograph?

major changes, work with a *duplicate* of your original image just in case you want to return to your original image.

**EXERCISE 18.5** Download a news photograph from the Web and then crop it in a way that substantially alters its content or focus. Print out your altered images and discuss them with classmates, exploring the implications of such changes.

## 18f  How do you work with color?

You'll need to match your use of color to your writing situation. For instance, color may not be appropriate in academic papers but necessary to attract readers to brochures, newsletters, and Web pages. Once you've decided to use color, there are many factors to consider.

● **1 Select a readable color scheme.** Designers create color schemes to orchestrate the interaction of multiple tones and hues within a layout, all to achieve specific effects, from adding emphasis to setting a mood. They do so by assigning specific colors to various elements on a page (headings, rules, frames, borders, graphics). The most important decisions in any scheme are what color to use for background and what color for type. To be readable, these colors must contrast but not clash. Bright colors must be used sparingly, since they can tire the eyes. Readable color combinations include dark blue on beige, black on orange, brick red on blue, white on blue-green, and, of course, black on white.

● **2 Create a mood for your document.** Different colors evoke different emotions. Bright colors have a bold effect, even when applied sparingly. Soft colors, on the other hand, may need to cover an entire page to have a noticeable impact. Combinations make a difference too. Some combinations—for example, purple and orange or yellow and black—are bold; they shout for attention. Others—shades of blue combined with ivory—are subtle. Some colors just seem to clash—pink and bright green, for instance, and purple and yellow. But tastes in color vary greatly, and one can't say flatly that certain colors should never be combined.

**● 3 Use color to highlight or soften elements of your layout.**
Colors, because of their wide range of effects, give you more control over the impact created by other features of your layout. Once you've decided to go beyond black and white, you'll have many more options for emphasizing or downplaying text and images. A bold heading can be made less striking, for example, by changing the color from black to a softer blue or gray. Plain text in the body of a paragraph can be made more striking by changing it to red.

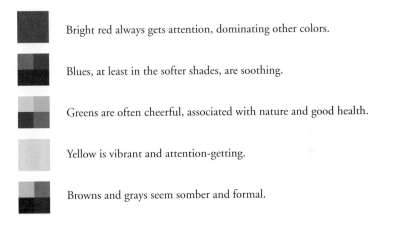

Bright red always gets attention, dominating other colors.

Blues, at least in the softer shades, are soothing.

Greens are often cheerful, associated with nature and good health.

Yellow is vibrant and attention-getting.

Browns and grays seem somber and formal.

# 19 How Do You Create Professional and Business Documents?

If you bristle at the specifications for lab reports and research papers, you might be surprised to learn that institutions and businesses have no less stringent expectations for their documents. In this chapter, we examine some of the formats, both print and electronic, you are likely to encounter today, both in school and out. You'll find model documents illustrating a variety of print and electronic formats. Where possible, we show examples of documents in both media.

Each example is accompanied by a discussion of the purpose and the common uses of the format, a checklist alerting you to conventions of that format, and an explanation of the document's basic parts. Although each of the formats presented in this chapter has its own checklist, Checklists 19.1 and 19.2 provide general guidelines for presenting documents in print and on screen. And of course you should proofread every document carefully.

---

### Checklist 19.1 Typical Print Documents

- Use standard letterhead paper ($8\frac{1}{2}'' \times 11''$).

- Use portfolio orientation unless you plan to fold the document or you need extra room for graphics and images.

- Leave at least a one-inch margin on all sides. If you plan to bind the document, add more space on the bound edge.

- Use double or single-and-a-half spacing unless otherwise specified, especially with small type. Single spacing is used in letters or sometimes in long documents to cut printing costs.

- Use headers and/or footers with running titles and page numbers for multi-page documents.

---

**Checklist 19.2    Typical Onscreen Documents**

- Make sure your audience has the right software to view the document format you're using.

- Short, single-spaced block paragraphs are most common for onscreen documents.

- Use sans serif typefaces and avoid long stretches of bold, underlined, or italicized text.

- If you have hypertext links, test them to make sure they work.

---

# 19a Email

Over the last few years, instructors and employers have come to expect students and workers to conduct business through email. In the writing class, you may be asked to submit assignments as file attachments or to collaborate with fellow students through online messages. In workplaces, email has replaced printed memos (see Section 19e) for everyday correspondence, and it has become an important means of communicating cheaply across long distances.

Although email is used to communicate for many purposes, all email includes a few basic elements. The sample message on page 346, composed by Arnold Peale for his English composition class, illustrates basic parts of an email message. Keep in mind that the onscreen look of messages will differ according to your *email client*, the program you use to read and write messages. Take some time to explore your email client's features.

**EXERCISE 19.1**   From your email files, select one that you find especially unreadable perhaps because it is too long, presents too much information, avoids paragraphing, or just seems cluttered. Copy the body of the email into another email file (being careful not to set an address) and then revise both its content and visual style as necessary to make it a more effective document.

EMAIL MESSAGE

The **message header** includes all necessary delivery information. (See below.)

A **salutation** may be optional in very informal messages, but most others should include a greeting of some kind.

The **body** can include block paragraphs, lists, and subsections set off by dashed lines or extra spacing.

The **closing** and **signature** will depend on the formality of the message. For professional messages, include your title and organization.

---

## Checklist 19.3   Email

- Use short block paragraphs; long paragraphs are difficult to read on screen. Double-space between paragraphs but don't indent.

- Avoid "Reply All" when responding to messages received. Respond to everyone on an email list only when you think all will be interested in your comments.

- Make sure attached files are in a format your audience can view and that you have scanned them for viruses.

- If you use a common signature for all your messages, make sure the text of the signature is suitable for both professional and personal audiences; otherwise edit the signature when the occasion calls for it.

- Avoid lengthy emails in business situations. Keep the message focused.

**EMAIL HEADER**

The **To** line includes one or more email addresses for recipients. Remember that addresses must be completely accurate.

The **From** line will usually be filled out by your email program with your name and address. If you have more than one email account, you may be asked to specify which one will be used to send the message.

```
     To: emilyjackson@mail.um.net
   From: Arnold Peale <apeale@mail.um.net>
Subject: Web project requirements
     Cc: jasonc@mail.um.net; betho@mail.um.net
    Bcc:
<-Attachments:
```

The **Attachments** line will include the file names of electronic documents you would like to send along with your message. Email clients vary in how they ask you to specify your attachments.

The **Subject** line includes a short phrase about the topic of your message—make sure it is relevant to your recipients.

**Cc** lines can be used to send other individuals copies of the message. (See also Section 19e.)

# 19b Business letters

When you write a business letter, remember that it may become part of a permanent file documenting your request or complaint. Make the letter as complete and accurate as possible so that the recipient(s) can act on it quickly. The letters on pages 348 and 349 were written by a student at Bowling Green State University to the Office of the Registrar asking for action to clear up a bureaucratic mistake. The letters were successful. After receiving the complaint, the registrar sent an email message to the student, promising to watch over his loan account personally for the remainder of his stay at Bowling Green.

BUSINESS LETTER IN FULL BLOCK FORMAT

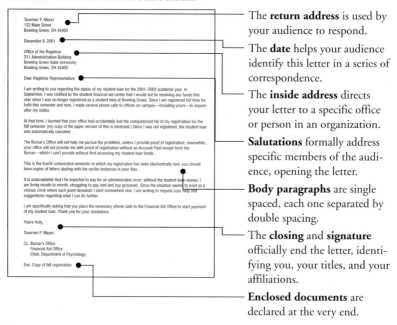

Taverner P. Meyer
122 Main Street
Bowling Green, OH 43403

December 8, 2001

Office of the Registrar
211 Administration Building
Bowling Green State University
Bowling Green, OH 43403

Dear Registrar Representative:

I am writing to you regarding the status of my student loan for the 2001–2002 academic year. In September, I was notified by the student financial aid center that I would not be receiving any funds this year since I was no longer registered as a student here at Bowling Green. Since I am registered full time for both this semester and next, I made several phone calls to offices on campus—including yours—to inquire after my status.

At that time, I learned that your office had accidentally lost the computerized file of my registration for the fall semester (my copy of the paper version of this is enclosed.) Since I was not registered, the student loan was automatically canceled.

The Bursar's Office will not help me pursue the problems, unless I provide proof of registration; meanwhile, your office will not provide me with proof of registration without an Account Paid receipt from the Bursar—which I can't provide without first accessing my student-loan funds.

This is the fourth consecutive semester in which my registration has been electronically lost; you should have copies of letters dealing with the earlier instances in your files.

It is unacceptable that I be expected to pay for an administrative error; without the student-loan money, I am living month to month, struggling to pay rent and buy groceries. Since the situation seems to exist as a vicious circle where each point demands I start somewhere else, I am writing to request your help and suggestions regarding what I can do further.

I am specifically asking that you place the necessary phone calls to the Financial Aid Office to start payment of my student loan. Thank you for your assistance.

Yours truly,

Taverner P. Meyer

Cc: Bursar's Office
      Financial Aid Office
      Chair, Department of Psychology

Enc: Copy of fall registration

The **return address** is used by your audience to respond.

The **date** helps your audience identify this letter in a series of correspondence.

The **inside address** directs your letter to a specific office or person in an organization.

**Salutations** formally address specific members of the audience, opening the letter.

**Body paragraphs** are single spaced, each one separated by double spacing.

The **closing** and **signature** officially end the letter, identifying you, your titles, and your affiliations.

**Enclosed documents** are declared at the very end.

---

## Checklist 19.4   Business Letters

- Choose a *full block, modified block,* or *indented block* letter format. (Indented block differs from modified block only in that its body paragraphs are indented: see example on page 349.)

- Single-space paragraphs and addresses in the letter; double-space between the return address, date, inside address, salutations, body paragraphs, and closing.

- Use one-inch margins on all sides.

- When using letterhead paper, you don't need to repeat the return address as long as the stationery includes all necessary contact information.

*(Continued)*

**BUSINESS LETTER IN MODIFIED BLOCK FORMAT**

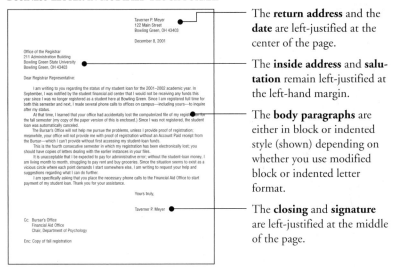

The **return address** and the **date** are left-justified at the center of the page.

The **inside address** and **salutation** remain left-justified at the left-hand margin.

The **body paragraphs** are either in block or indented style (shown) depending on whether you use modified block or indented letter format.

The **closing** and **signature** are left-justified at the middle of the page.

---

**Business Letters** *(Continued)*

- Make the inside address as specific as possible so that the letter will go directly to its intended audience.

- Place a colon after the salutation.

- In the body, be brief but state all pertinent facts, including names and dates. Keep your letter to one page if you can.

- Make your diction and style fairly formal, unless you already have established a casual tone with the addressee.

- Follow your closing with a comma, four blank lines, your name, and your professional title; sign in the space created by the blank lines.

- After the closing and signature, note any copies of the letter you have sent and any attached documents you have enclosed with the letter.

- Proofread your letter carefully and keep a copy for your records.

# 19c Letters of application

A letter of application (sometimes called a "cover letter") is an especially important form of business communication. The same advice and guidelines apply to it as to a business letter. In a letter of application, however, you have the extra challenge of presenting yourself favorably without seeming to brag. Use the application letter to draw attention to the reasons an employer should consider you for a job or an interview.

On the next page you'll find two examples of Chad Polatty's letter of application for a Web programming position, one of them formatted as a printed document, the other as email. The salutation, the body paragraphs, and the closing are the same in both examples. The only major differences between the two are in how Chad reaches the job recruiter, how the recruiter contacts him for further information, and the formatting of attached documents, such as résumés and references.

---

**Checklist 19.5   Letter of Application**

- Follow the basic formatting guidelines for a business letter (see Checklist 19.4) or email (see Checklist 19.3), depending on the medium you use to correspond.

- State the position for which you are applying. Follow up with a summary of your qualifications for the position. Focus on those qualifications that best suit the job in question; the résumé will cover the rest.

- Focus on how you might meet the organization's needs and on what you could accomplish *for the organization*—not on what you hope to get from the position.

- Show some knowledge about the organization or company to which you are applying, but offer praise only in order to show why you're interested in working for that employer.

- Maintain a polite and respectful—but confident—tone.

- Remember that your letter of application may have a long life. If you're hired, it will become part of your personnel record. If you're not hired, it may go into a file of applicants for later consideration.

## LETTER OF APPLICATION IN BLOCK FORMAT

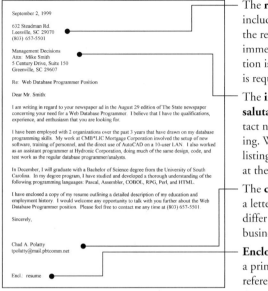

September 2, 1999

632 Steadman Rd.
Leesville, SC 29070
(803) 657-5501

Management Decisions
Attn: Mike Smith
5 Century Drive, Suite 150
Greenville, SC 29607

Re: Web Database Programmer Position

Dear Mr. Smith:

I am writing in regard to your newspaper ad in the August 29 edition of The State newspaper concerning your need for a Web Database Programmer. I believe that I have the qualifications, experience, and enthusiasm that you are looking for.

I have been employed with 2 organizations over the past 3 years that have drawn on my database programming skills. My work at CMB*LIC Mortgage Corporation involved the setup of new software, training of personnel, and the direct use of AutoCAD on a 10-user LAN. I also worked as an assistant programmer at Hydronic Corporation, doing much of the same design, code, and test work as the regular database programmer/analysts.

In December, I will graduate with a Bachelor of Science degree from the University of South Carolina. In my degree program, I have studied and developed a thorough understanding of the following programming languages: Pascal, Assembler, COBOL, RPG, Perl, and HTML.

I have enclosed a copy of my resume outlining a detailed description of my education and employment history. I would welcome any opportunity to talk with you further about the Web Database Programmer position. Please feel free to contact me any time at (803) 657-5501.

Sincerely,

Chad A. Polatty
tpolatty@mail.pbtcomm.net

Encl.: resume

The **return address** should include a telephone number so the recruiter can contact you immediately if more information is needed or an interview is requested.

The **inside address** and **salutation** will match the contact name given in the job listing. When not responding to a listing, locate a contact name at the company's hiring office.

The **closing** and **signature** in a letter of application do not differ from those in standard business letters.

**Enclosures** will often include a printed résumé and a list of references.

## LETTER OF APPLICATION IN EMAIL FORMAT

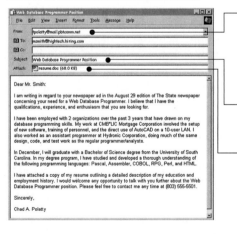

**Email addresses** replace postal addresses in the heading of the message. Postal addresses and telephone numbers can appear in the body of the letter if needed.

The **subject line** should announce the position for which you are applying.

**File attachments** are used instead of enclosures. Make sure to use common or requested electronic formats.

**EXERCISE 19.2** In the classified section of your student or local newspaper, locate an ad for a job for which you might be qualified. Then compose an application letter for that position. Assume that your résumé (see Section 19d) would accompany the cover letter. Present yourself confidently and plausibly in the application. Use one of the formats for a business letter shown in Section 19b.

# 19d Résumés

Your résumé is a concise and honest outline of your academic and employment history, designed to give a prospective employer a quick but thorough overview of your qualifications. (During your career, you will also likely compile a CV—short for Curriculum Vitae—which is a fuller record of professional experiences and accomplishments. At the beginning of your career, your résumé and CV might not differ much in length.)

Take great care in assembling your résumé. Once in the hands of a recruiter, your list of achievements and skills will be used to decide whether an employer will contact you for an interview. If you are eventually hired, it may also become a part of your employment record. For that reason, be sure to describe your career accurately, claiming only achievements and qualifications you can document.

You can enhance your qualifications, however, by demonstrating competence in your field. Learn the language of your profession and use the appropriate terms to describe your on-the-job training and course work. Remember, however, that you need to be comfortable with these terms—chances are you'll be expected to use them in an interview.

Consider, too, recent trends in how employers find job candidates and store information about them. Recruiters not only search for résumés on the Web, but also maintain databases of digitized résumés. Most recruiters collect these résumés as electronic submissions, but some save scanned versions of print résumés. As a database entry, your résumé will receive a serious look only if it can be found through keyword searches—all the more reason for you to become fluent with the language spoken by others in your profession.

Because résumés are so important, and because they've changed somewhat in recent years, we provide three examples after Checklist 19.6. The first is a printed résumé listing the qualifications of Danny Gomez, a student at the University of Texas at Austin. The second is an email, text-only version of Danny's résumé, as is sometimes requested when recruiters want you to enter the document in a database. Finally, on page 357, we present a Web résumé created by Jay O'Brien, a student at Shepherd College in West Virginia.

---

### Checklist 19.6 Résumés

- At the top of your résumé, give your name as you would like to be recognized in a professional setting.

- Provide up-to-date contact information so that a prospective employer can reach you for interviews.

- Before you list your skills, state your objective. This section may be omitted when your employment goals are explained in an accompanying cover letter. Some résumé guides now consider the objective line optional.

- Create a categorized list of your academic degrees and awards, professional certifications, previous jobs, technical skills, and relevant course work.

- Arrange this list according to how effective the categories and qualifications you have listed will be for attaining the desired job.

- Educational achievements usually go first. List year, degree, and institution, as well as scholastic honors won.

- If the prospective job requires specialized skills (computer skills, technical procedures), list those with which you have the most familiarity, assuming an interviewer might ask about them.

- List your work experience. Besides mentioning employers and time periods, state your responsibilities and achievements in succinct but specific terms. Account for all periods longer than a few months.

- List course work only when it explains how you attained skills outside your work experience. List nonwork, nonacademic activities and achievements only if you think an employer might consider them relevant assets.

*(Continued)*

**Résumés** *(Continued)*

• You cannot be required to mention age, gender, race, religious or sexual preference, political affiliation, or marital status.

• When requested, include a list of references (all of whom you have checked with beforehand) or indicate a placement service with your complete dossier. This list can usually be submitted as a separate, attached document.

## Highlight  Designing Your Résumé

Technology has upped the ante on preparing résumés. These days, even candidates for entry-level jobs are expected to present efficient, handsomely prepared documents. Although many people now use professional writing services to create their paper and electronic résumés for them, you can still design your own if you know how to use a computer and are willing to study effective models.

You can find many examples of effective résumés on the Web just by typing "resume" into a search engine such as <Google.com> and then exploring the sites of various professional writing services, most of which offer numerous sample documents. (You may even decide to hire one of these services.)

You will discover that effective résumés come in many shapes and formats, but all of them make it easy for readers to find key information. You may be surprised by how much information some model résumés squeeze onto just one or two pages, especially for job candidates seeking upper-level positions. Early in your career, you won't have so many credentials to present, but do pay attention to how these résumés work. They demonstrate how to array complex information clearly by using bullets, lines, columns, white space, and type fonts and styles effectively.

Electronic résumés need to be designed with equal care. If you are posting a résumé on a Web site, remember that a reader will encounter it only one screen at a time. The opening screen, therefore, might include links to other items farther down the page: Computer Skills, Work Experience, References. It is appropriate, too, to include Web links to

*(Continued)*

**Designing Your Résumé** *(Continued)*

job-related materials (such as writing samples, teaching materials, or photographs) that would not ordinarily appear on a résumé itself. Since electronic résumés are often scanned, you might even want to add a keyword section at the end of the document listing terms that an employer might be expecting in a particular job search.

Despite a move toward electronic production of résumés, most on-screen documents remain relatively simple and clean, especially for entry-level positions. You don't need brassy colors or stunning graphics if your credentials speak for themselves. Professional résumés rarely include personal photographs or headshots because they invite potential employers to make judgments about matters they should not (or legally cannot) consider: age, gender, race, appearance. So don't include a personal photograph on a résumé unless there is a very specific and legitimate reason to do so.

PRINT RÉSUMÉ EMPHASIZING EDUCATION AND EXPERIENCE

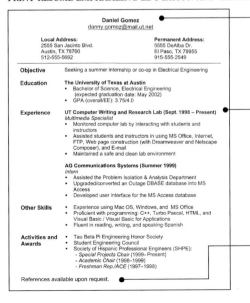

The **header** includes your name and contact information. Most students include a **local address** where they can be contacted at school as well as a **permanent address**.

The **body** includes a list of your qualifications divided into categories. Use different type styles to highlight information that employers might find most interesting, such as the names of companies you've worked for or your school.

The **footer** will often include the phrase "References available upon request."

RÉSUMÉ FORMATTED AS TEXT-ONLY EMAIL MESSAGE

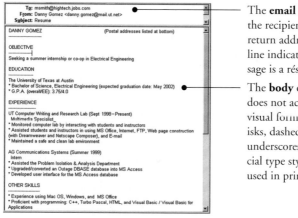

The **email header** will include the recipient's address, your return address, and a subject line indicating that the message is a résumé.

The **body** of a text-only email does not accept most types of visual formatting. Use asterisks, dashed lines, all caps, and underscores to replace the special type styles and graphics used in print or Web résumés.

**EXERCISE 19.3** If you don't have a résumé already, follow the guidelines in this section to assemble one of no more than two pages, listing your academic and job experiences, as well as other necessary material, including your contact information. Then experiment with the design of your new or existing résumé by creating two acceptable versions that differ visually. You may also rearrange the content to emphasize different qualifications or job interests.

## 19e Professional memos

Organizations use memos to communicate internally. Memos therefore omit some of the formalities used in business letters to be sent outside the organization: formal salutations and closings, for example, aren't usually required. But memos do maintain a professional tone, and they contain information needed for keeping records of business interactions.

Email (see Section 19a) is the online cousin of the memo. Indeed, many institutions now communicate almost entirely by email and such communications must therefore include the kind of specific information about subjects, readers, times, dates, and places that enables them later to serve as

**ONLINE RÉSUMÉ**

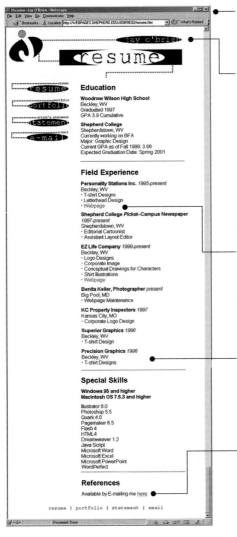

The **page title** includes your name and the word *résumé*, so that the page can be found by WWW search engines.

Jay O'Brien omits conventional **contact information** such as his postal address and current phone numbers on his Web résumé. He expects employers to reach him via an email link. However, it might be wise to offer a postal address, phone number, and full email address so employers who print out your résumé will still be able to reach you.

**Links** to other Web pages can help you better demonstrate your goals and qualifications. Jay O'Brien provides a link to an online portfolio of his work—something a print résumé doesn't accommodate.

The **body** can go beyond a single page—but make sure headings are easy to read, so someone browsing your résumé can quickly identify the highlights of your qualifications.

Your **list of references** should never be posted on the Web. Instead, ask interested employers to request references by email.

**PRINTED MEMO**

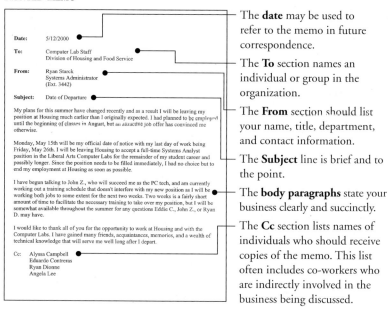

The **date** may be used to refer to the memo in future correspondence.

The **To** section names an individual or group in the organization.

The **From** section should list your name, title, department, and contact information.

The **Subject** line is brief and to the point.

The **body paragraphs** state your business clearly and succinctly.

The **Cc** section lists names of individuals who should receive copies of the memo. This list often includes co-workers who are indirectly involved in the business being discussed.

**EMAIL MEMO**

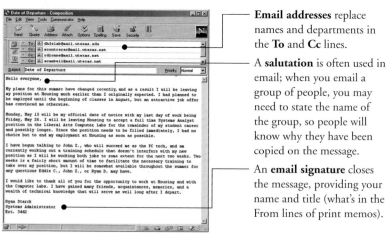

**Email addresses** replace names and departments in the To and Cc lines.

A **salutation** is often used in email; when you email a group of people, you may need to state the name of the group, so people will know why they have been copied on the message.

An **email signature** closes the message, providing your name and title (what's in the From lines of print memos).

useful records. Assume that any professional emails you write might later become a public document.

Opposite you'll find, in print and electronic formats, a memo written by Ryan Starck, then a student employee at the University of Texas at Austin. Although the topic of the memo is one you'll rarely use—a farewell message to fellow staff members—the format and tone Starck adopts reflect the professional yet collegial nature of most work environments.

---

**Checklist 19.7 Memos and Professional Email**

- Follow your organization's standard layout, which will usually include a date, a "To" section, a "From" section, and a subject line.

- Use block paragraphing and a one-inch margin (for print memos).

- In the subject line, enter a phrase that explains the relevance and importance of your message.

- Most printed memos don't have salutations because the intended audience is named in the "To" section. An email message sent to more than one person, however, might require a group salutation.

---

**EXERCISE 19.4** Write a fairly formal business memo (paper or email) to the members of a specific group or local organization to which you belong. In the memo raise a delicate issue in a professional way. You might, for example, request that club members who aren't current on their dues pay up immediately or lose their privileges or ask that officers in the club no longer abuse the group's travel funds or long-distance accounts. Keep the memo brief—less than one page or screen—but be sure to include enough information for the memo to serve as a record later.

# 19f Messages to online forums

Besides email, other forms of online communication sometimes walk a line between professional and personal interactions. Their subjects may be serious, related to the business or intellectual interests of their participants, but the communication is typically informal and not always part of a permanent record—though the messages in many groups are archived. Online forums generally consist of dated postings (messages submitted by discussion participants) and threads (lines of discussion focused on a particular topic). Web forums and newsgroups are two formats of online discussion that display threads and postings hierarchically, according to topic. The sample Web forum on the facing page shows a series of threads about a reading for a composition class. Email lists are another common type of online forum. Readers and writers participate by subscribing to the list, which allows them to receive new postings in their email inbox, and by sending messages to the list's email address. Whichever format you use, keep in mind the common conventions for participating in online discussions—conventions often referred to as "netiquette."

---

### Checklist 19.8  Messages to Online Forums

- Read a number of messages in the forum before you send your own. Get a feel for the tone and interests of other participants.

- Avoid posting personal attacks, or *flames*, to authors of messages disagreeing with you. Flame wars make productive discussion nearly impossible.

- Avoid starting off-topic threads—sometimes called *spamming*. Forums differ in how they treat spam, but expect some people to become annoyed if you regularly send irrelevant messages.

- Don't respond to the entire forum when you really want to respond to just one participant. Avoid this problem by making sure your "To" address doesn't match the address of the forum itself.

- When replying to a thread, remove all text from the previous message that doesn't relate to your response. Don't expect readers to scroll through screens of other people's writing to find your ten-line response.

**WEB MESSAGE FORUM**

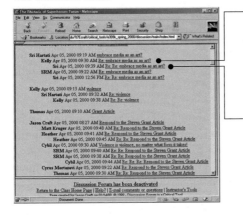

**Threads** appear as an initial message (starting at the left-hand margin) followed by a series of responses. Each response is attached to the message it most immediately addresses.

**Responses** are listed as linked text indicated by "Re:" and followed by the subject line of the initial message in the thread. Click on the link to read the message. Some forums allow respondents to create their own subject lines.

**WEB FORUM RESPONSE FORM**

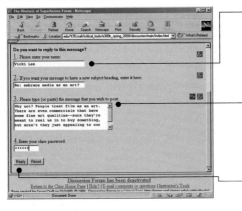

Enter the **name** you would like to appear with your posting. Some forums allow anonymous postings; others, such as class forums, require your real name.

Enter your **message** in plain text format. Some forums allow you to use HTML codes to enhance the appearance of the message.

Click the "**Reply**" button (or "Submit") to add your message to the thread. This forum happens to require a password to participate.

# 19g Newsletters

A newsletter gives an organization a way to keep in touch with its members. With a desktop publishing program or an up-to-date word-processing program, newsletters are relatively easy to create. The model newsletter on the next two pages, created by members of an English students' honor society at the Metropolitan State College of Denver, contains six pages, of which we reproduce the first and the third. Although the newsletter includes some enhanced visual features, the students kept production costs down by limiting the layout to two colors and using black-and-white images—a modest but effective decision for print documents having wide circulation. Online newsletters can, without extra expense, include more colors and images, assuming you have the time to create a more elaborate design.

---

**Checklist 19.9   Newsletters**

- Select the size of paper and the method of binding, and determine the number of pages you will have to work with. Choose a margin width that allows for binding or folding.

- Determine whether you'll use images and how many colors you want to show. Colorful designs are more costly.

- Decide whether you'll use multi-column pages. More columns usually mean more planning, but multiple columns can use space more efficiently.

- Map out each page with two goals in mind: (1) showcasing the most important articles and (2) preventing your reader from having to jump from page to page to read a single article.

- For your masthead, use a distinctive font that reflects the spirit of the organization represented by the newsletter.

- Adjust headlines according to their importance, but maintain a consistent font size and style throughout the body of the articles.

- Write short paragraphs to avoid long, unbroken stretches of print, especially when you're using narrow columns.

FRONT PAGE OF A NEWSLETTER

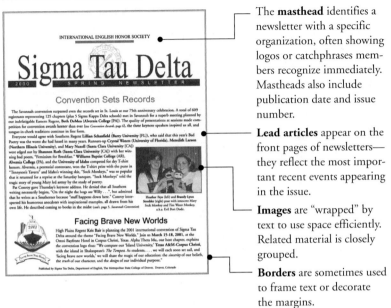

The **masthead** identifies a newsletter with a specific organization, often showing logos or catchphrases members recognize immediately. Mastheads also include publication date and issue number.

**Lead articles** appear on the front pages of newsletters—they reflect the most important recent events appearing in the issue.

**Images** are "wrapped" by text to use space efficiently. Related material is closely grouped.

**Borders** are sometimes used to frame text or decorate the margins.

**EXERCISE 19.5** Working with several other people, design a one- or two-page newsletter for an invented group—a political, social, or religious organization; a fan club for a local sports team; a techie group; and so on. (Better, create a newsletter for a real group or parody an existing newsletter.) Decide on the stories and features you should cover and then design an appealing newsletter—with at least one illustration or graphic. You may design the newsletter entirely on your own or, with instructor approval, base your newsletter on one of the templates typically offered in word-processing programs. (In *Microsoft Word*, for example, begin by selecting "Project Gallery" under the "File" menu.)

PAGE **3** OF A NEWSLETTER

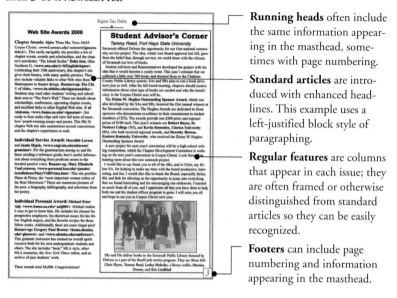

**Running heads** often include the same information appearing in the masthead, sometimes with page numbering.

**Standard articles** are introduced with enhanced headlines. This example uses a left-justified block style of paragraphing.

**Regular features** are columns that appear in each issue; they are often framed or otherwise distinguished from standard articles so they can be easily recognized.

**Footers** can include page numbering and information appearing in the masthead.

# 19h Brochures

Brochures can provide information about an organization and its activities easily and, depending on the elaborateness of your design, inexpensively. Brochures generally answer a few basic questions—who? what? why? when? where?—and they share the common goal of stimulating interest. Ideally, a brochure you create will provide enough information to capture your audience's attention and show readers where to find further details.

More expensive brochures are used by organizations that want to project a high-profile image, especially for recruiting new members. The brochure shown at right, designed by Brooke Rollins, a student employee at the University of South Carolina's College of Engineering, includes images, colors, stylized fonts, and an unusual square page layout—all features that drive up the costs of production. If your organization doesn't have a generous production budget, you might create a simple, elegant brochure that points readers to an organizational Web site—which is cheaper to develop than a printed brochure.

### Checklist 19.10   Brochures

- Decide on the purpose of the brochure. Is it to introduce your organization? to talk about events or activities? Think about how you want your audience to respond to the brochure, and choose content accordingly.

- Plan the layout of the brochure carefully, keeping in mind how it will fold and how both sides will look. If the brochure is to be mailed, leave one panel blank for the address.

- Sketch out, or storyboard, each panel to visualize how you'll lay out information in the brochure.

- If possible, make each panel of the brochure a self-contained unit so that each section will still make sense when read in its folded state.

- Limit the amount of information to what readers can absorb in a few minutes, but tell them how they can learn more. Provide contact information: a postal or email address, Web site, or phone number.

**FRONT PANEL OF A BROCHURE**

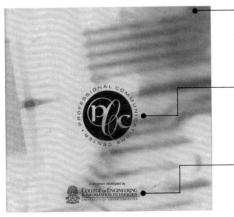

Use **graphics** and **colors** to attract the eyes of readers. Keep in mind that most brochures must compete for attention.

The **logo** for the organization should appear on the front panel. This logo begins building a persona that the following panels will develop.

Show **addresses** and **contact** information so that readers get a clear idea of the organization's affiliations and institutional relationships.

**INSIDE PANELS OF A BROCHURE**

Each **panel** includes a main heading with related passages of text. Panels have consistent layouts so readers can easily see the central points.

**Headings** are set apart from other text using inverted background and foreground colors. Provocative, eye-catching phrases draw readers in.

**Contact** information and the organizational **logo** reappear on the end panel, reminding readers that further details are available if they are interested.

**Images** have been carefully selected to portray themes and activities related to the organization. Here the images form a collage extending across all panels.

**Paragraphs** focus on the highlights of the organization, especially those that will seem most intriguing to the target audience.

**EXERCISE 19.6** Working with several other people, design a two-sided, three-panel brochure that explains some service or feature of your campus or local community. Decide on the elements you might cover and design appealing pages—with appropriate illustrations and graphics. You may design the brochure entirely on your own or, if your instructor approves, begin with one of the brochure templates typically offered in word-processing programs. (In *Microsoft Word*, for example, begin by selecting "Project Gallery" under the "File" menu.)

## Chart 19.1 Model Academic Documents

Academic writing projects, too, have design requirements formulated by associations of scholars and professionals in their respective fields. These standards are described in detail in the following chapters. Ask your instructor which style you should follow.

Modern Language Association (MLA) style, used in the humanities: Chapter 50
American Psychological Association (APA) style, used in the social sciences: Chapter 51
*Chicago Manual of Style* (CMS) style, used in the humanities: Chapter 52

For samples of different kinds of academic projects, see these examples featured elsewhere in this book.

| | |
|---|---|
| Topic proposal | page 26 |
| Annotated bibliography | pages 80–81 |
| Essay exam (excerpt) | page 93 |
| Personal statement (excerpt) | page 97 |
| Literary analysis papers | pages 178–179 |
| Research papers—MLA style | pages 68–74, 156–162, 733–746 |
| Research paper—APA style | pages 779–796 |

# 20 How Do You Design an Oral Presentation?

An instructor may ask you to prepare an oral presentation as a way of preparing you for a responsibility common in jobs and professions—designing a speech, sales talk, or group session of some kind. You may feel uncomfortable when presenting material before crowds (many people are), but public speaking is a valuable skill that can be learned with practice, particularly in the friendly environment a classroom provides.

Effective presentations call for many of the same qualities found in good writing—coherent organization, a highly developed sense of audience, an appreciation for audio and visual elements, and memorable examples and illustrations. In addition, they often require attention to such performance skills as voice, tone, pacing, and gestures. The sections that follow offer advice on all these elements.

## 20a What are the basics of an effective oral presentation?

Technology has transformed presentations so much that speakers sometimes forget that not every oral presentation must involve *PowerPoint*, an LCD projector, and a screen. Such tools are useful, but they should serve the overall purpose of the presentation, not overwhelm it. You still have to know what your subject is, how to organize your presentation, and how to deliver it appropriately for your audience.

**●1 Choose your topic and structure carefully.** When you have the option, speak on a subject you want to learn more about yourself. Or talk about something you already know well enough to seem like an expert. Look for subjects that connect your academic interests to real-world applications. For example, in a class on marketing, you might present facts about a famous (or infamous) political ad campaign. Choosing a topic that is specific and, if possible, local will also make it easier to find or create attractive multimedia elements, including photographs, video clips, and audio clips.

**●2 Decide on an overall organization.** In most reports, you'll want to give listeners a sense of your organization early in a presentation. A historical report might follow a chronological organization; an evaluative presentation, a comparison-and-contrast plan; and an argument, a claim-and-evidence design (see Chapters 3, 9, and 10).

In the introduction, explain who you are and what you intend to cover—or use a title screen to provide relevant information, including, when appropriate, a date and your institutional information. You can then follow up with a slide like the one shown in Figure 20.1 to preview the structure of the entire presentation. Openings can also include some humor to loosen up an audience and to help the speaker connect with listeners.

**Figure 20.1** A *PowerPoint* slide can briefly outline your oral report. Each bulleted point on this slide would become a major section of the report.

Plan the body of the talk carefully. To visualize and refine the relationships among your major ideas, consider preparing slides or overheads of your key points—but be careful not to read from your slides. In *PowerPoint*, for example, you can then use the "Slide Sorter" feature to try different sequences, as shown in Figure 20.2 on page 370. Once you are under way, punctuate your oral presentation with clear

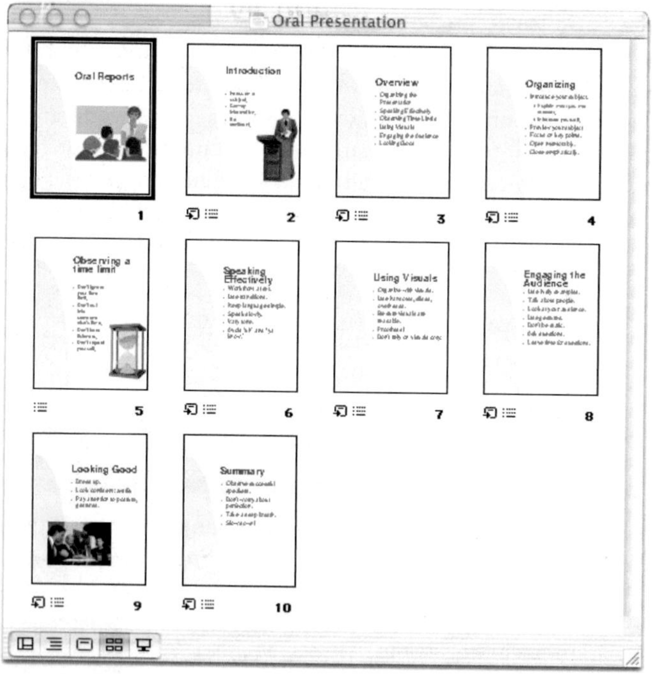

**Figure 20.2** With "Slide Sorter" selected, you can review thumbnails of all the slides you have created for a presentation and rearrange them as necessary.

transitions. You can simply number your major points ("I am going to explore three major reasons . . .") or make your transitions very explicit ("Now that I have covered *X,* I will explain . . ."). Remind readers occasionally what your main idea is and, in a longer report, summarize the points you have made in each section (without being tedious). Signal clearly, too, when you are nearing the end. Even a transition as bare-bones as "In conclusion . . ." works just fine. Any end-of-the-presentation summary should be direct, brief, and compelling. If you are using overheads or slides, your summary should fit on a single screen. Give listeners something compelling to think about.

● **3 Adapt your presentation to your audience.** Find out as much as you can about your audience as you prepare your talk. Make educated guesses about what they want to know, how formal or informal they expect the presentation to be, and what will interest them. Some groups will appreciate dynamic presentations that involve them in activities and encourage their participation throughout the session. But on other occasions, you might be expected to deliver a straight lecture without audience involvement until a question-and-audience period at the end. Do all you can to learn what your audience (or your instructor) wants, needs, and expects.

Naturally, you can respond to an audience as you deliver your report. You'll see and hear reactions immediately in smiles, furrowed brows, coughs, groans, and, maybe, applause. Interpret this feedback carefully and—as much as possible—adapt your material to the responses you are receiving.

---

**Checklist 20.1    Reaching and Responding to an Audience**

- Dress well to show respect for your audience. No ripped jeans or baseball caps!
- Don't bury your nose in your notes or hold them in front of your face.
- Don't rock back and forth at the podium.
- Don't punctuate every phrase with "like," "um," or "ya know."
- Know your material well enough to talk to an audience rather than read to it.
- Learn to interpret facial expressions and body language.
- Maintain eye contact with members of the audience and smile occasionally.
- Don't belabor points that an audience clearly gets.
- Backtrack when an audience seems confused.

---

Try to leave time at the end of your presentation for questions and then handle them with good humor. Occasionally, someone in your audience may ask a "hostile" question. Don't respond in kind. Your audience will respect you more if you respond to the challenge coolly and politely and then move on.

**● 4 Think of your presentation as a performance.** You'll need all your resources to connect with people, including your voice, gestures, and physical presence. Learn to vary the tone and intensity of your voice: raise or lower it to underscore key points; use pauses to mark shifts in topic. Above all, avoid speaking so swiftly that you garble your words. Inexperienced speakers sometimes start out fine, but begin to speak faster and faster (and softer and softer) until they become almost unintelligible. An oral report is not a race. Take a deep breath every so often and slow down.

If you discover that you have too much material to cover in the allotted time, edit your material as you go. Skip some details or examples rather than rush through the presentation or intrude into another speaker's time. Keep a discreet eye on the clock or keep a wristwatch on the podium. If no length is assigned to your talk, remember the rule of any good performance: leave the audience asking for more.

Be sure to convey some enthusiasm for your subject. Don't freeze up before an audience; instead, use your body. A shrug, a nod, a casual turn, a sweep of the arm, even a scratch of the head can all be used to reinforce a point. If appropriate, move away from the podium and change position during the speech a few times. Compel your listeners to refocus their attention. But don't pace—shifts of position should seem purposeful.

Above all, practice the full report aloud several times, complete with the equipment you intend to use. Don't imagine how you'll act—speak the words just as you intend to say them; flip through your slides, overheads, or posters; and be sure to time yourself. As much as possible, get familiar with the podium, lectern, microphone, screen, and other equipment. Practice at least once in the place you will deliver the presentation—with some sort of audience (perhaps a friend or classmate willing to give you honest feedback). If that's not possible, at least scope out the room or auditorium beforehand so you know what to expect. A group presentation should be choreographed so that all participants know their parts. Leave nothing to chance. And always anticipate the failure of equipment. Be ready to deliver a professional presentation even if the bulb in the projector burns out or there's no chalk for the board.

> **e-Tips** For advice on overcoming anxiety about speaking in public and additional information about improving your oral delivery skills, visit <http://toastmasters.org/pdfs/top10.pdf>. Or check with your campus writing center to see whether they offer online tutorials or workshops on public speaking.

**EXERCISE 20.1** Write a page or two describing an unsuccessful presentation or lecture you have recently attended. Be sure to list specific problems in the presentation and how they might have been fixed.

**EXERCISE 20.2** Choose a paper you have written recently for any course—it might be a history report or even a chemistry lab experiment—and imagine how you would adapt it as an oral presentation for a specific audience *other than your classmates*. (You might consider a group of sixth graders or a community group.) What visual or aural components might you use? Describe the presentation in a paragraph or two.

## 20b How do you manage the technology of a presentation?

Audiences today have high expectations for oral presentations because various tools—including computers, LCD projectors, and presentation software such as *PowerPoint* and *Keynote*—have made it easy to create absorbing multimedia events. But bells and whistles alone don't impress people. They want professional presentations that use appropriate tools to make memorable points.

**● 1 Choose the appropriate tools, props, and supplements for your report.** Don't use more equipment than you require, and never introduce a special effect just because you know how to create it. For many presentations, all the technology you may need is a podium, your lecture notes, and a flip chart. But even simple tools need to be used well. If you write on a chalkboard or flip chart, do so clearly, boldly, and quickly. Reduce full sentences to key words and phrases, if possible.

Plan ahead for all types of equipment you require. And do whatever you can to practice with that equipment and, especially, to anticipate problems. LCD projectors, for example, have notoriously difficult controls. Even figuring how to turn down the lights can be a problem in some situations. The more you work through ahead of time, the smoother your presentation will be.

**● 2 Create tables, charts, graphs, and other visual texts.** Charts, graphs, and other illustrations can often make a point better than words can. For instance, pie charts do an excellent job of explaining percentages whereas graphs plot trends nicely. (See Section 18d for more on using such visual texts.)

You can create professional-looking charts and graphs on your computer and then turn them into transparencies or slides. Or you can simply draw the items yourself on poster paper and display them on an easel. Just be sure whatever you present is large and clear enough to be read at a distance. Use fonts that are bold and thick. Don't clutter your illustrative materials: too much detail will make an item hard to read and interpret.

Show the same discretion with photographs. Images should be large enough to see from a distance and relatively simple. Be sure you give credit sources for any photos you display, and use only as many visual items as you need: an oral report shouldn't become a slide show. Most experts suggest that you should *not* display visual items continuously while you talk because viewers will pay more attention to the images than to you. So present such items only briefly.

**● 3 Use video and sound sensibly.** A video should not dominate your presentation or substitute for your own words and explanations. Be sure you know how to operate any video equipment. Turn the machine on when you need it and off when you are done. Otherwise audiences will stare at the glowing screen instead of looking at you.

You may also need to include audio materials in a presentation. Audiences may benefit from hearing President John F. Kennedy or Ronald Reagan at the Berlin Wall or the voice of Bessie Smith. Be sure you have speakers on your audio equipment powerful enough to project sound clearly to the back of the space you are using. Keep the audio portions of a presentation short. Such materials should serve as lively illustrations and examples, not tedious interludes.

● **4** **Use presentation software sensibly.** Presentation software such as *PowerPoint* or *Keynote* has become the default method of doing an oral report in many business, professional, and academic situations. Such software is easy to use, easy to learn, and full of many tempting options, as you can see in Figure 20.3. Choose wisely and you can create a set of slides that complements your presentation perfectly.

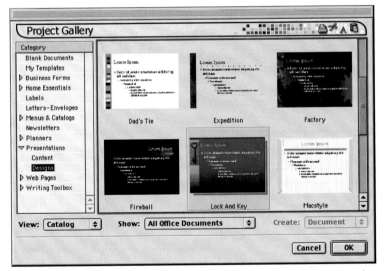

**Figure 20.3** In the *PowerPoint* "Project Gallery," you can select design templates for your presentation slides or create designs of your own.

The best advice is to *keep it simple*. All your slides should share a common style, so it makes sense to consider one of the design templates offered by the software. For academic presentations, look for the cleanest page and then select a cool palette of colors. Save the eye-dazzlers for informal situations.

Once you have established a basic style for your pages, you will have options for choosing your page layouts. Again, you can use templates provided by *PowerPoint* and then modify them to suit your materials. (Just select "Slide Layout" from the "Format" menu for your options.) Or you can arrange the pages on your own. In either case, design slides that are simple in appearance and content. You shouldn't read extensively from the screen or show slides with so much "content" that your audience finds you unnecessary. Figures 20.4 and 20.5 show some useful and distracting versions of slides.

Keep the transitions between your slides uncomplicated. In most cases, a quiet dissolve or fade adds a fine touch to the movement from slide to slide. No special effect should draw attention to itself—unless your intention is comic (and sometimes it may be). Be certain, too, that viewers can see and hear whatever you are showing—especially if you load a video into a slide. The audio quality of video clips can be especially disappointing.

Finally, edit your slides carefully. *PowerPoint* runs a spelling check as you compose your items. Be especially careful with the spelling of proper nouns

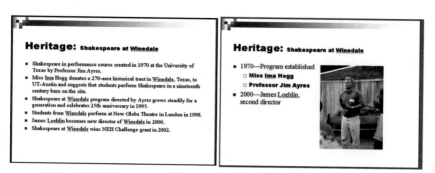

**Figure 20.4**  Too many words on screen will distract and irritate audiences. The slide on the left is too wordy; the slide on the right works better because it supports rather than dominates the presentation.

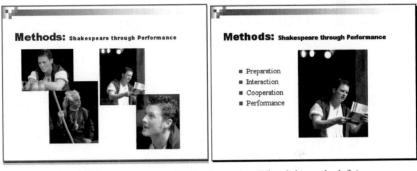

**Figure 20.5** Too many pictures can also be distracting. The slide on the left is handsome, but it doesn't make a clear point about methods for teaching Shakespeare through performance. The slide on the right—with a single image of actor Lawrence Kern—explains what methods the speaker intends to cover.

and adjectives. Spelling *Jane Austen* as *Jean Austin* on a dozen slides will destroy your credibility. Remember that your slide will receive the full and critical attention of your audience, so you don't want them catching gaffes in your facts, mechanics, or design.

**EXERCISE 20.3** Working in a group, use presentation software to design five-minute explanations of how to use presentation software effectively. Be creative and imaginative, given that everyone in the class is working on the same assignment. Vote on the best presentation, using the guidelines in Section 20b as criteria of evaluation.

# 21 How Do You Design a Web Site?

Web sites, perhaps more than any other documents, have made writers realize how important visual design is today. An entire design vocabulary has evolved—perhaps *exploded* is a better description—for Web sites in just the past decade. Early sites were simple and text-heavy, usually blocks of prose with occasional images and links. Today, Web pages are as diverse as any type of document.

We will leave it to your instructor, campus technology programs, Web-building software (such as *Dreamweaver*), or how-to books to lead you through the technical aspects of creating a Web page or site. Or you can check out the extensive material on Web design at the World Wide Web Consortium (W3C) at <http://www.w3.org/2002/03/tutorials>. Here, what we can offer are some suggestions for organizing and presenting your ideas in this environment.

Our basic advice for crafting Web pages doesn't differ from what we would recommend for designing any type of document: Thinking rhetorically, you must decide how to present

- the information you hope to convey
- to the audiences you expect to reach
- for the purposes you have in mind.

## 21a How do you structure your Web project?

Typically, you will begin by deciding whether the content, purpose, and readers of your project will be best served by a site with a single scrolling Web page or by a multi-page site. One scrolling page will work best if you have a limited amount of information to present—as in a personal home page, a résumé, or a very brief report. If you have more than two or three screens of information or if your material breaks easily into sections, consider creating a set of pages connected by links. The fact is that most online readers don't like to scroll much beyond a few screens.

A project with many dimensions may, in fact, require a site with multiple pages, and that usually requires more planning than a single-page site if readers are to navigate the pages easily and intuitively. Such a site will also require a home page as the entry into the site. But material deeper in the project may be connected to that home page in different ways—again depending on your purpose and subject. Three common patterns for linking pages are a **hierarchy**, a **sequence**, and a **hub** (see Chart 21.1 on page 380).

Besides creating links on your site that reflect the structure of your content, you'll also make links directly between pages or to other sites on the Internet. As you build your site, keep these suggestions in mind.

- Make sure all your pages link to your site's home page so readers are never lost.
- Don't create "dead ends" that require endless clicking on the "Back" button to return to your navigational menus.
- When you link to Web pages outside your site, make it clear to readers that they are being taken somewhere else.
- As your site grows, consider providing a *site map*, a special page that outlines the organization of your material.
- Use hypertext links to cross-reference material you discuss on a number of pages.
- Gather material you refer to often into a central resource, such as a glossary, to which other pages can easily link.

**EXERCISE 21.1** Examine the multi-page Web sites you commonly read. Which of the three basic Web structures—hierarchical, sequential, or hub—seems to be most common? Why might that be so, given the content of the sites you have reviewed? Which structure do you find least often? Can you speculate why that might be so?

**EXERCISE 21.2** Most blogs are single-page sites, but the blog page itself serves as a sort of home page, providing links to many other blog sites or to sites that explore related ideas. How would you classify the structure of the blogs you read?

## Chart 21.1   Common Multi-page Formats for Web Sites

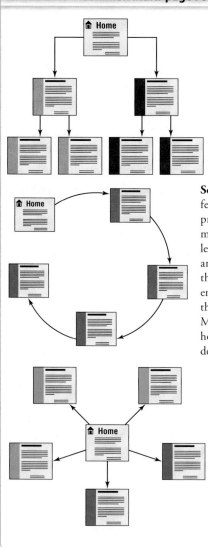

A **hierarchical** pattern organizes pages into increasingly more specific groupings. Readers find material by starting with general categories (topics, areas, units) and working their way down to more specific information. This structure is regularly used by large organizations (such as colleges and corporations), since their units and activities are already organized this way.

**Sequential** sites present readers with fewer options. If you are offering a proposal argument, your site might move readers step by step from problem to solution, with each stage of the argument building on material from the preceding screen. Readers are encouraged to click "Next Page" rather than select from a menu of options. Make sure to provide links back to the home page so readers won't reach a dead end.

A **hub** structure encourages exploration. Here the home page links to related pages that neither require a specific order of reading nor fit into hierarchical groups. You might use a hub design to catalog items—say, all the native plants in a particular wetlands area. Readers could browse each item, going back and forth from the home page. You might also provide direct links to related pages on the hub.

# 21b How do you design your pages?

The design of Web pages matters a lot to people. You can learn about the range of opinion on the subject just by entering "bad web design" or even "good web design" in a search engine. Or browse the archives of <http://www.webpagesthatsuck.com>, a site that has been active since 1996—which makes it a classic by Internet standards. You won't be surprised by what you discover. Good Web design doesn't differ radically from the principles outlined in Chapter 18. And yet the medium *is* challenging, in no small part because it offers you so many potent design options—in color, sound, and movement.

● **1 Look for good models of Web page design.** You've likely been reading the Web for years. But when you begin to create your own pages, you'll become much more aware of the choices site designers make to present information. Pay attention to sites that you find both attractive and easy to use and consider adopting some of their features. Ask yourself what devices make a site work. How does the page or site identify itself and its content? How does it arrange, separate, and highlight information? How does it use color and images? How does it help readers navigate the page or the entire site?

Web design has evolved rapidly. But while sites still vary enormously, you likely recognize that Web genres such as online newspapers, blogs, commercial sites, government sites, and so on each have their own styles and conventions. You can pattern any site you build after such models, depending on what you are creating (see Checklist 21.1).

---

**Checklist 21.1   Common Genres of Web Pages and Sites**

- Institutional Web sites
- Personal home pages and online résumés
- Online periodicals and newspapers
- Online essays and reports

*(Continued)*

**Common Genres of Web Pages and Sites**  *(Continued)*

- Blogs

- Frequently asked questions (FAQ) pages

- Online directories and informational listings

- Search pages and database listings

Understand that Web design remains in flux, with some site designers eager to exploit the multimedia potential of the electronic screen (check out the animation on the *Rolling Stone Magazine* or MTV sites), whereas others prefer a simpler, less frenetic screen experience (see the Web portal for your own college or its library, for instance). You should probably strive for simplicity and clarity until you are confident in your Web design capabilities.

**Figure 21.1** Your first Web pages are likely to be *much* simpler than sites for the Smithsonian Institution (left) or the *New York Times* (center). But you can study and borrow the devices they use—columns, shading, headings, boxes, and so on—for arranging their wealth of information. Even a simpler site such as the blog Instapundit (right) can teach a lesson about separating major text from other sorts of information, including ads and links to other bloggers. Which of these three pages most attracts your attention? Why?

**Figure 21.2** The home pages for popular search sites *Google* and *Yahoo!* represent different design philosophies. *Google's* opener is cool and uncluttered, but requires la second page to present additional options and services. *Yahoo!'s* highly kinetic home page offers more information but may feel busy to some viewers. If you were designing a search site, what approach might you take today?

● **2 Follow the principles of good design.** Novice designers tend to use too many fonts, too much color, and too obvious special effects in their initial pages. But that was true even for talented designers in the early days of the Web. Today, you see less flash on most sites—except perhaps in advertisements, which still do what they can to catch your eye. Your own pages should be carefully reviewed from a user's perspective and then refined for balance and clarity (see Figures 21.3 and 21.4 on page 384).

Keep your visual style consistent. You don't want your readers to have to adjust to a new style every time they turn a page. Although the content will differ, the layout of each page should follow a shared design motif. Professional document designers use tools called style sheets to guarantee consistency across a number of pages. Style sheets, which are now available in many word processors and Web browsers, specify the look of pages and passages in a section or an entire document. If your composing software doesn't provide style sheets, you can check the consistency of your design by skimming the layout of each page.

Finally, pay attention to the words on your site. Web sites may contain less written matter than you'd find in printed sources. But online prose needs to be just as clear and grammatical as any other professional writing. Remember, too, that what you post on a Web page is very public. So proofread carefully

**Figure 21.3** The Web page on the right has improved the original on the left just by making a few alignment and spacing changes: (1) The page was changed from center alignment to left alignment. (2) The photograph was right-aligned so that the text could wrap around it, eliminating the need for scrolling and preventing an orphaned heading above the photo. (3) Extra space was added above and within the navigation bar, reducing the clutter of images and text.

**Figure 21.4** The Web page on the right is clearer and more readable than the original on the left: (1) The heading is reduced and changed to the same typeface as the rest of the page. (2) The column headings have a lighter color to contrast with the dark background. (3) The row headings are boldfaced to distinguish them from the numbers in the body of the table. (4) Subtle background coloring added to odd-year rows makes each series of numbers easier to follow. (5) The "Note" text appears in plain style, since an extended text in italics and boldface is difficult to read.

and edit to eliminate wordiness (see Section 17c). Because reading on screen is more tiring than reading print, make every word count.

---

**Checklist 21.2**

**Web site do's . . .**

- Be sure readers can easily identify any links on your page.
- Place navigation buttons where readers can find them easily.
- Group like information together.
- List important site information on any home page: institution, date, safe contact information (though not your personal email, phone number, or address).
- If possible, test your pages on different systems and platforms (PCs, Macs, CRTs, flat panel monitors) to be sure that designs and colors work.

**and don'ts**

- Don't design pages that require left-to-right scrolling.
- Don't underline any words or phrases that aren't links—because readers will think they are.
- Don't expect readers to scroll down more than a few pages, except for archived material.
- Don't use color combinations for text and backgrounds that you haven't tested for readability.
- Avoid using all caps, too much boldfaced type, or anything that flashes, blinks, or pulses.

---

**EXERCISE 21.3**  You can find entertaining and useful advice about Web design at <http://www.webpagesthatsuck.com>, itself (and by the designer's own admission) not always the best-looking or easiest-to-navigate place on the Web. Browse this site long enough to find some useful principles for Web site design. Then apply those criteria of evaluation either to one of your favorite Web sites or to a project of your own design. Write a page that explains what you have discovered about the site.

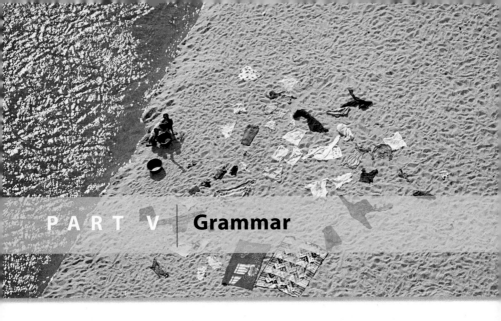

# PART V | Grammar

# 22  Questions About Subject-Verb Agreement?

When subjects and verbs don't agree, careful readers notice. Yet the rules for agreement can seem complicated. They merit your attention, especially when you are editing a draft.

## 22a  Agreement: Is the subject singular or plural?

A verb may change its form, depending on whether its subject is singular or plural. The verb is then said to *agree in number* with its subject. Following are guidelines to help you be confident about subject-verb agreement.

Subjects and verbs usually agree more readily than politicians.

1 **Understand how subject-verb agreement works.** With verbs in the present tense, agreement in number is relatively simple: most subjects take the base form of the verb. The base form is the word produced when *to* is placed before the verb: to *wait*; to *go*.

| | |
|---|---|
| First person, singular, present tense: | I predict. |
| | I go. |
| Second person, singular, present tense: | You predict. |
| | You go. |
| First person, plural, present tense: | We predict. |
| | We go. |
| Second person, plural, present tense: | You predict. |
| | You go. |
| Third person, plural, present tense: | They predict. |
| | They go. |

The single notable exception to this pattern occurs with third person singular subjects (for example, *he, she, it, Irene*). A regular verb in the present tense needs an *-s* or *-es* ending.

| | |
|---|---|
| Third person, singular, present tense: | She predict**s**. |
| | Irene predict**s**. |
| | He go**es**. |

So to choose a correct verb form in the third person (present tense), you must know whether the subject of a sentence is singular or plural. The choice of the verb form can be fairly easy when a subject is clearly either singular or plural.

sing. subj.
*The weather channel* **predicts** storms today.

plural subj.
*Meteorologists* **predict** storms today.

sing. subj.
*He* **goes** to Oklahoma City today.

plural subj.
*The teachers* **go** to Oklahoma City today.

Agreement is also required with irregular verbs such as *to be* and *to have* in a variety of tenses. (See Section 23b.)

**SINGULAR SUBJECTS**

*The weather forecast* **is** clear for today.

*The weather forecast* **was** clear for today.

*The weather forecast* **has been** accurate for some time.

**PLURAL SUBJECTS**

*The weather forecasts* **are** clear for today.

*The weather forecasts* **were** clear for today.

*The weather forecasts* **have been** accurate for some time.

**EXERCISE 22.1**  Decide which verb in boldface is correct.

1. The most violent of all storms, tornadoes (**occur/occurs**) more often in the United States than in any other country.

2. The rotational winds sometimes (**exceed/exceeds**) 500 miles per hour in the vortex of a tornado.

3. Dust devils (**is/are**) less ferocious vortices of warm air.

4. Rising heat currents (**cause/causes**) dust devils.

5. A tornado over water (**has/have**) many of the same characteristics as one over land.

⦿2 **In most cases, treat subjects joined by *and* as plural.**  Joining two subjects this way creates a *compound subject* that takes a verb without an -*s* or -*es* ending (in third person, present).

subj. + subj.            verb
*Storm chasers and journalists* alike **seek** great videos of destructive storms.

subj. + subj.            verb
*The press and storm chasers* alike **risk** their lives to get close to twisters.

subj. + subj.                  verb
*Meteorologists and the Office of Public Safety* **fear** that storm chasers often underestimate the magnitude of tornadoes.

However, some subjects joined by *and* clearly describe a single thing or idea. Treat such expressions as singular.

> subj.    verb
> *Peace and quiet* **is** rare in tornado alley during spring months.

> subj.    verb
> *Rock and roll* **is** usually as noisy as a thunderclap.

Similarly, when a compound subject connected by *and* is modified by *every* or *each*, the verb takes a singular form.

> subj. + subj.    verb
> *Every wall cloud and supercell* **holds** the potential for a tornado.

> subj. + subj.    verb
> *Each spring and each fall* **brings** the threat of more storms.

However, when *each* follows a compound subject, usage varies.

> *The meteorologist and the storm chaser* each **have** their reasons for studying the weather.

> *The meteorologist and the storm chaser* each **has** his or her story to tell.

**3** **Understand that subjects joined to other nouns by phrases such as *along with, as well as*, or *together with* are not considered compound.** So the verb agrees only with the subject, which may be either singular or plural.

> sing. subj.                    plural noun    verb
> *The National Weather Service*, as well as many *police officers*, **wishes** amateurs wouldn't chase severe storms in their vehicles.

> plural subj.              sing. noun    verb
> Many *amateurs*, along with the *press*, **chase** storms in the American heartland.

When singular subjects followed by expressions such as *along with, as well as*, or *together with* sound awkward with singular verbs, use *and* to connect the potential subjects and then modify the verb, as shown in the following example.

| SLIGHTLY AWKWARD | *The National Weather Service*, as well as *local storm chasers*, **considers** tornadoes unlikely today. |
| BETTER | *The National Weather Service and local storm chasers* **consider** tornadoes unlikely today. |

⊘**4 When subjects are joined by *or, neither . . . nor*, or *either . . . or*, be sure the verb (or its auxiliary) agrees with the subject closer to it.** In these examples the arrows point to the subjects nearer the verbs.

*plural*                                              *sing.*
*Neither police officers nor the National Weather Service* **is** able to prevent people from tracking dangerous storms.

          *sing.*                    *plural*
*Either severe lightning or powerful bouts of hail* **mark** the development of a supercell.

                *sing.*        *plural*
**Does** *the danger or the thrills of chasing storms* attract people to the "sport"?

              *plural*                          *sing.*
**Do** *the thrills of chasing storms or the danger* attract people to the "sport"?

The rule holds when one or both of the subjects joined by *or, either . . . or*, or *neither . . . nor* are pronouns: the verb agrees with the nearer subject.

Neither *she* nor *we* **admit** to fear of thunder.

Neither *we* nor *she* **admits** to fear of thunder.

If a construction seems especially awkward, it can be revised—usually by making the verb plural or rewriting the sentence.

| AWKWARD | Neither *you* nor *I* **am** bothered by lightning. |
| BETTER | Neither *I* nor *you* **are** bothered by lightning. |
| BETTER | *We* **are** not bothered by lightning. |

⊘**5 When the subject of a sentence is a phrase or a clause, examine the subject closely.** Many such constructions will be singular, though they may seem plural.

**SINGULAR SUBJECTS**

*Chasing tornadoes* **involves** risk.

*That George survived the storms that tore through three Oklahoma counties* **is** remarkable.

However, phrases and clauses can form compound subjects, requiring appropriate verb forms.

**COMPOUND SUBJECTS**

*Locating a waterspout and taking photographs of it* **are** his chief ambitions.

*That the skies are darkening and that the wind is rising* **concern** us.

**EXERCISE 22.2** Decide which verb in boldface is correct.

1. Storms of all types (**continue/continues**) to intrigue people.

2. The storm chaser, like other thrill seekers, (**learn/learns**) to minimize the dangers of the hunt.

3. It's unlikely that either the dangers or the boredom of storm chasing (**is/are**) going to discourage the dedicated amateur.

4. The meteorologist and the storm chaser (**know/knows**) that neither ferocious tornadoes nor the less violent waterspout (**is/are**) predictable.

5. That the last ten years have seen an increase in the numbers of storm chasers (**is/are**) certain.

## 22b Agreement: Is the subject an indefinite pronoun?

Words such as *each, none, everybody, everyone*, and *any* are called **indefinite pronouns** because they do not refer to a particular person, thing, or group. Sometimes it's hard to tell whether an indefinite pronoun is singular or plural, so you may have trouble choosing a verb that agrees with it in number.

**◉1 Determine whether an indefinite pronoun is singular, plural, or variable.** Consult the chart below (or a dictionary) to find out. Then select an appropriate verb form.

---

**Chart 22.1   Indefinite Pronouns**

| SINGULAR | VARIABLE (SINGULAR OR PLURAL) | PLURAL |
|----------|-------------------------------|--------|
| anybody | all | few |
| anyone | any | many |
| anything | either | several |
| each | more | |
| everybody | most | |
| everyone | neither | |
| everything | none | |
| nobody | some | |
| no one | | |
| nothing | | |
| somebody | | |
| someone | | |
| something | | |

---

**◉2 Be careful when indefinite pronouns are modified.** If a pronoun is always singular, it remains singular even if it is modified by a phrase with a plural noun in it. For example, *each* is usually singular in college usage, even when followed by a prepositional phrase (though this convention is often not observed in speech or casual usage).

> subj.            verb
> *Each* of the whales **makes** unique sounds.

> subj.            verb
> *Each* of the animals **has** a personality.

When the indefinite pronoun varies in number (words such as *all, most, none, some*), the noun in the prepositional phrase determines whether the pronoun (and consequently the verb) is singular or plural.

**NOUN IN PREPOSITIONAL PHRASE IS SINGULAR**

*Some* of the research **is** contradictory.

**NOUN IN PREPOSITIONAL PHRASE IS PLURAL**

*Some* of the younger whales **are** playful.

If the indefinite pronoun is more clearly plural, so is the verb.

indef. pron.                                    verb
A *few* in the scientific community **wonder** if the whale will survive.

indef. pron.          verb
*Many* very much **hope** so.

**EXERCISE 22.3** Decide which verb in boldface would be correct in academic writing.

1. Most of New York's immigrants (**is/are**) now non-European.

2. Everybody (**seem/seems**) to have something to contribute.

3. Nobody in the city (**run/runs**) politics anymore.

4. Everybody (**expect/expects**) a piece of the pie.

5. None of the candidates (**is/are**) qualified.

6. All of the groups in the city (**want/wants**) to be heard.

## 22c Agreement: Is the subject a collective noun?

Nouns that name a group are called **collective**: *team, choir, band, orchestra, jury, committee, faculty, family*. Some collective nouns may be either singular or plural, depending on how you regard them. Here is a sentence with the subject (the collective noun *family*) treated as singular.

The *Begay family* **expects** that *its* restaurant will benefit from a recent increase in Arizona tourism.

Here's the same sentence with the subject taken as plural.

The *Begay family* **expect** that *their* restaurant will benefit from a recent increase in Arizona tourism.

Both versions are acceptable.

To be sure verbs and collective nouns agree, decide whether a collective noun used as a subject acts as a single unit (the *jury*) or as separate individuals or parts (the twelve members of the *jury*). Then be consistent with your usage throughout a project, making the verb and any pronouns agree in number with the subject.

| | |
|---|---|
| SINGULAR | The *jury* **expects** its verdict to be controversial. |
| PLURAL | The *jury* **agree** not to discuss their verdict with the press. |
| SINGULAR | The *choir* **expects** to choose a variety of hymns and chants. |
| PLURAL | The *choir* **raise** their voices in song. |

Usually your sentences will be smoother if you treat collective nouns as singular subjects.

Chart 22.2 on the next page should help you manage collective nouns.

**EXERCISE 22.4** Decide whether the collective subjects in the following sentences are being treated as singular or plural. Then select the appropriate verb form for academic writing.

1. The research team (**reports/report**) to Captain Picard that its data (**is/are**) not subject to interpretation.

2. The starship crew (**is/are**) eager to resolve their differences.

3. Ten years (**has/have**) passed since the last intergalactic crisis.

4. A number of weapons still (**needs/need**) to be brought online, but the chief engineer reports that the actual number of inoperative systems (**is/are**) small.

5. The jury (**is/are**) still out as to whether a committee of Federation officials (**intends/intend**) to authorize action against the Klingons.

### Chart 22.2  Collective Nouns

| SUBJECT | GUIDELINE | EXAMPLES |
|---|---|---|
| Measurements | Singular as a unit; plural as individual components. | *Five miles* is a long walk. *Five more miles* are ahead. *Six months* is the wait. *Six months* have passed. |
| Numbers | Singular in expressions of division and subtraction. Singular or plural in expressions of multiplication and addition. | *Four* divided by *two* is two. *Four* minus *two* leaves two. *Two* times *two* is/are four. *Two* plus *two* is/are four. |
| Words ending in -*ics* | School subjects are usually singular. Other -*ics* words vary; check a dictionary. | *Physics* is a tough major. *Economics* is a useful minor. *Linguistics* is popular. His *tactics* are shrewd. *Athletics* are expensive. *Ethics* is a noble study. Her *ethics* are questionable. *Politics* is fun. Francie's *politics* are radical. |
| *data* | Plural in formal writing; often singular in informal writing. | The *data* are reliable. The *data* is reliable. |
| *number* | Singular if preceded by *the*; plural if preceded by *a*. | The *number* has grown. A *number* have left. |
| *public* | Singular as a unit; plural as individual people. | The *public* is satisfied. The *public* are here in great numbers. |

## 22d Agreement: Is the subject separated from its verb?

A verb agrees with its subject only, not with any nouns in modifying phrases or clauses that come between the subject and verb. So when editing for subject-verb agreement, first identify the subject in a sentence or clause and determine whether it is singular or plural; then choose the appropriate verb form. In the following sentence, for example, a singular subject (*power*) is modified by a prepositional phrase that contains a plural noun (*tornadoes*). But the subject remains singular, and it takes the appropriate verb form (*proves*).

>      sing. subj.                plural noun      verb
> The *power* of Midwestern tornadoes often **proves** deadly.

The principle is the same for plural subjects modified by phrases or clauses with singular nouns. The subject remains plural.

> plural subj.                  sing. noun   verb
> *Storms* that come late in the spring **are** sometimes unusually violent.

Be especially careful with lengthy or complicated modifiers. In the example that follows, the singular subject and verb are separated by ten words. But the plural nouns *mammals* and *humans* in the modifying phrase have no bearing on subject-verb agreement.

>         subj.                            modifying phrase
> The *killer whale*, <u>the most widely distributed of all mammals, excepting</u>
>               verb
> <u>only humans,</u> **demonstrates** highly complex social behavior.

**EXERCISE 22.5** Choose the correct verb for academic writing.

1. Most politicians, regardless of their party or ideology, (**embrace/embraces**) the idea that every child should be able to read by the end of third grade.

2. Almost everyone (**agree/agrees**) with this laudable goal.

3. Still, children's ability to learn how to read (**depend/depends**) on a combination of psychological, physical, and social factors.

4. Moreover, many children from low-income families, in both rural and urban environments, (**need/needs**) intensive tutoring because they are not ready to learn when they arrive in kindergarten.

5. The HOSTS tutoring program, which has had great success in helping children to start reading, (**require/requires**) as many as fifty volunteers in a small elementary school, and such volunteers can be hard to find.

## 22e Agreement: Is the subject hard to identify?

Occasionally you may simply lose track of a subject because the structure of a sentence is complicated or unusual. Just remember the rule: Keep your eye on the subject.

**1 Don't lose track of your subject when a sentence or clause begins with *here* or *there*.** In such cases, the verb still agrees with the subject—which usually trails after it.

**SINGULAR SUBJECTS**

Here **is** a surprising *turn* of events.

There **is** a *reason* for the commotion.

**PLURAL SUBJECTS**

Here **are** my *tickets*.

There **are** already *calls* for the police chief's resignation.

**2 Don't be misled by linking verbs.** Common linking verbs are *to be, to seem, to appear, to feel, to taste, to look*, and *to become*. They connect subjects to words that extend or complete their meaning.

The mayor's deputy **was** a severe critic of the police chief.

Many citizens **feel** betrayed.

A linking verb agrees with its subject even when a singular subject is linked to a plural noun.

> subj.                                                     l. v.   plural noun
> Good *evidence* of the power of television **is** its effects on political careers.

> subj.                                 l. v.                  plural noun
> The *key* to a candidate's success **is** television appearances.

The same is true when a linking verb connects a plural subject to a singular noun, but such sentences sound normal and don't ordinarily raise questions of agreement.

> plural subj.   l. v.   sing. noun
> The many new *patrol officers* **are** a tribute to Chief Carey's budget ingenuity.

⦿3 **Don't be misled by inverted sentence order.** A sentence is considered inverted when some portion of the verb precedes the subject. Inverted sentence structures occur most often in questions.

> verb              subj.        verb
> **Was** their *motive* **to gain** political advantage?

>                                                                     verb
> Among those requesting Chief Carey's resignation **were** many
> subj.
> *political activists.*

⦿4 **Don't mistake singular expressions for plural ones.** Singular terms such as *series, segment, portion, fragment,* and *part* usually remain singular even when modified by plural words.

A *series* of questions **is** posed by a reporter.

A substantial *portion* of many political talk shows **is** devoted to panel discussions.

The word *majority,* however, does not follow this guideline; it can be either singular or plural, depending on its use in a sentence. In this sentence, *majority* is treated as singular.

The *majority* **rules.**

Yet it can also function as a plural noun.

The *majority* of critics **want** Chief Carey's head on a platter.

**Fine Tuning** One of the subtlest subject-verb agreement problems occurs within clauses that include the phrase *one of those who*. In college English, the verb in such a clause is plural—even though it looks as if it should be singular.

Carey is one of those people who never **seem** [not **seems**] dispirited.

The verb is plural because its subject is plural. To understand the situation more clearly, rearrange the sentence this way.

Of those people *who* never **seem** dispirited, Carey is one.

Now watch what happens if you add the word *only* to the mix.

Carey is the only one of the city officials who **seems** eternally optimistic.

Why is the verb singular here? The subject of the verb *seems* is still the pronoun *who*, but its antecedent is now the singular pronoun *one*, not the plural *officials*. Again, it helps to rearrange the sentence to see who is doing what to whom.

Of the city officials, Carey is the only one who **seems** eternally optimistic.

**EXERCISE 22.6** Choose the correct verb.

1. The mayor of the town (**strides/stride**) to the microphone.

2. Among grumbles from the reporters, the crowd (**take/takes**) their seats.

3. (**Does/Do**) the mayor's decision to fire Carey surprise anyone after the last election?

4. The city council president claims that she is one of those people who (**objects/object**) most strongly to politics taking precedence over community unity.

5. But she knows she's not the only one who (**wants/want**) a nationally admired park system.

# 23

# Questions About Verb Tense, Voice, and Mood?

Perhaps the complexity of verbs first dawned on you when you tried to learn a foreign language. Suddenly, you had to pay attention to all the details

you took for granted when you used verbs in your native tongue. Understanding **tense**, **voice**, and **mood** mattered. In this chapter, we focus on such general properties of verbs, especially as they affect writers. For more technical descriptions of the ways verbs work, you may want to consult Chapter 32, "Questions About Verbs (ESL)?"—even if you've been speaking and writing English for most of your life.

Photographer Eadweard Muybridge (1830–1904) used stop-action photography to study the motion of people and animals: The horse will gallop; the horse gallops; the horse is galloping; the horse has galloped. For more Muybridge images, look for him at <http://www.masters-of-photography.com>.

## 23a How do you choose verb tenses?

**Tense** is that quality of a verb that expresses time. Tense is expressed through changes in verb forms and verb endings (*see, saw, seeing; work, worked*) and through the use of auxiliaries—what you may know as *helping verbs* (*had* seen, *will have* seen; *had* worked, *had been* working). Most native speakers of English handle basic past, present, and future tenses easily. But as a writer, you'll want to be confident about using all the tenses—for example, the more subtle perfect and progressive tenses.

● 1 **Know the tenses and what they do.** Tense depends, in part, on *voice*. Verbs that take direct objects—that is, transitive verbs—can be either in **active** or in **passive voice**. They are in active voice when the subject in the sentence actually does what the verb describes.

> subj.    action
> *Professor Gates* **invited** the press to the lecture.

They are in passive voice when the action described by the verb is done *to* the subject.

> subj.    action
> *The press* **was invited** by Professor Gates to the lecture.

Chart 23.1 outlines the shape and function of English tenses—past, present, and future—in the *active voice*. (See also more detailed treatment of verb tenses in Chapter 32, "Questions About Verbs [ESL].")

| Chart 23.1 | Verb Tenses in the Active Voice | |
|---|---|---|
| **WHAT IT IS CALLED** | **WHAT IT LOOKS LIKE** | **WHAT IT DOES** |
| Past | **I answered** quickly. | Shows what happened at a particular time in the past. |
| Past progressive | **I was answering** the question when the phone rang. **I was waiting** days for the call. | Shows one action in the past interrupted by a second; or shows an action in the past that has has continued for some time |
| Present perfect | **I have answered** that question often. **I have expected** it for a long time. | Shows something that has happened one or more times in the past; or expresses a condition that extends from the past to the present. |
| Past perfect | **I had answered** the question twice already when the phone rang. | Shows what had already happened before another event, also in a past tense, occurred. |

*(Continued)*

**Verb Tenses in the Active Voice** *(Continued)*

| | | |
|---|---|---|
| Present | **I answer** when I must. | Shows what happens or can happen now. |
| Present progressive | **I am answering** now. | Shows what is happening now. |
| Future | **I will answer** tomorrow. | Shows what may happen in the future. |
| Future progressive | **I will be answering** the phones all day. | Shows something that will continue to happen in the future. |
| Future perfect | **I will have answered** all the charges before you see me again. | Shows what will have happened by some particular time in the future. |
| Future perfect progressive | **I will have been answering** the charges for three hours by the time you arrive at noon. **I will have been working** at the company for thirty years on my next birthday. | Shows a continuing future action that precedes some other event also in the future; or expresses a condition that extends from the past to the future. |

Verbs usually look even more complicated when they are in the passive voice, as shown in the following chart.

**Chart 23.2  Verb Tenses in the Passive Voice**

| WHAT IT IS CALLED | WHAT IT LOOKS LIKE |
|---|---|
| Past | **No Chinese cars were exported** to the United States prior to 2006. |
| Past progressive | **Chinese cars were being exported** to other countries, however. |

*(Continued)*

**Verb Tenses in the Passive Voice**   *(Continued)*

| | |
|---|---|
| Present perfect | **Chinese cars have been exported** for years to Asia and Africa. |
| Past perfect | **Cars had been exported** from China rarely in the past. |
| Present | **Some cars are exported** today from China to the Middle East. |
| Present progressive | **More cars are being exported** by China today than a decade ago. |
| Future | **Many more Chinese cars will be exported** in years to come. |
| Future perfect | **Million of Chinese cars will have been exported** by the next decade. |

As you can see above, many tenses require **auxiliary verbs** such as *will, do, be,* and *have.* These auxiliary or helping verbs combine with other verbs to show relationships of tense, voice, and mood. Other auxiliary verbs, such as *can, could, may, might, should, ought,* and *must,* help to indicate possibility, necessity, permission, desire, capability, and so on. These verbs are called **modal auxiliaries**.

> Rosalind **can** write well.
>
> Audrey **might** write well.
>
> Marco **should** write well.

**2 Use the present tense appropriately.** The present tense has several special roles.

It may be used to introduce the words of authors you are quoting or citing, whether living or dead.

> Lincoln **defines** conservatism as "adherence to the old and tried, against the new and untried."
>
> Rice **argues** that democracy is necessary for long-term peace in the Middle East.

Use present tense when you are describing the action in literary works or quoting from them.

> Hester Prynne **wears** a scarlet letter.
>
> The doctor in *Macbeth* **warns** a gentlewoman, "You have known what you should not" (5.1.46–47).

Use present tense to make a general statement of fact or to express scientific truths.

> Oak trees **lose** their leaves in winter.
>
> Einstein **argues** that the principle of relativity **applies** to all physical phenomena.

Use present tense, too, to describe habitual action.

> We **get up** at five in the morning.
>
> People today **watch** television more than they **read**.

## ◉3 Use perfect tenses appropriately.

Because perfect tenses can look intimidating, some writers avoid them. But the result can be sentences a little less precise than they might be.

| | |
|---|---|
| **VAGUE** | Audrey **asked** Kyle to the concert when she learned that Jason wanted to take her. simple past |
| **PRECISE** | Audrey **had asked** Kyle to the concert when she learned that Jason wanted to take her. past perfect |

Perfect tenses enable you to show exactly how one event stands in relationship to another in time. Learn to use these forms; they make a difference.

| | |
|---|---|
| **SIMPLE PAST** | She already **quit** her job even before she knew that she **failed** the polygraph. |
| **PAST PERFECT** | She **had** already **quit** her job even before she knew that she **had failed** the polygraph. |

**EXERCISE 23.1** For each verb in parentheses, furnish the tense indicated. Use active voice unless passive is specified.

1. In Shakespeare's tragedy *Macbeth*, three witches tell Macbeth that someday he (**rule**—future) Scotland.

2. Macbeth then explains to his wife, the ambitious Lady Macbeth, what the witches (**promise**—past perfect) him earlier that day: the Scottish crown.

3. Lady Macbeth, even more ambitious than her husband, immediately (**devise**—present) a plot to murder King Duncan that very night and then (**convince**—present) her husband to do the horrid deed.

4. But even though the plot succeeds and Macbeth becomes king, the new ruler fears that he (**challenge**—future, passive voice) by other ambitious men.

5. Macbeth is finally slain by Macduff, whose wife and children (**slaughter**—past, passive voice) earlier in the play at Macbeth's orders.

## 23b How do regular and irregular verbs differ?

All verb tenses are built from three basic forms, which are called the *principal parts of a verb*. The three principal parts of the verb are these.

- **Infinitive** (or **present**): This is the base or simple form of a verb, what it looks like when preceded by the word *to*: *to walk; to choose; to go.*
- **Past:** This is the simplest form of a verb to show action that has already occurred: *walked; chose; went.*
- **Past participle:** This is the form a verb takes when it is accompanied by an auxiliary verb to show a more complicated past tense: *had* **walked**; *will have* **gone**; *would have* **chosen**; *was* **hanged**; *might have* **broken**. It is the form of the verb you will use to create verb phrases.

In English, most verbs are **regular**, which means that they form their past tense and past participles simply by adding *-d* or *-ed* to their infinitive (or present) forms. Here are the three principal parts of some regular verbs.

| INFINITIVE | PAST | PAST PARTICIPLE |
|---|---|---|
| talk | talk**ed** | talk**ed** |
| coincide | coincide**d** | coincide**d** |
| advertise | advertise**d** | advertise**d** |

A good many common English verbs, however, are **irregular**. *Irregular* means that they form their past tenses or past participles in nonstandard ways—that is, not by adding a *-d* or *-ed* to the present form. In fact, irregular verbs change their forms in many ways.

| INFINITIVE | PAST | PAST PARTICIPLE |
|---|---|---|
| choose | chose | chosen |
| go | went | gone |

A few irregular verbs even have the same form for all three principal parts.

| INFINITIVE | PAST | PAST PARTICIPLE |
|---|---|---|
| burst | burst | burst |
| set | set | set |

Some of the most important used verbs in English are irregular, for example, *to have* and *to be*.

There are no rules for determining the shape of irregular forms. To be sure you're using the correct verb form, consult a dictionary or check the following chart of irregular verbs. The list of troublesome irregular English verbs gives you three forms: (1) the infinitive, (2) the simple past tense, and (3) the past participle.

When in doubt, your safest bet is to check the list, because studies show that errors in verb form irritate readers a great deal.

| Chart 23.3 | **Irregular Verbs** | |
|---|---|---|
| INFINITIVE | PAST | PAST PARTICIPLE |
| arise | arose | arisen |
| be | was, were | been |
| | | *(Continued)* |

**Irregular Verbs**   *(Continued)*

| | | |
|---|---|---|
| bear (carry) | bore | borne |
| bear (give birth) | bore | borne, born |
| become | became | become |
| begin | began | begun |
| bite | bit | bitten, bit |
| blow | blew | blown |
| break | broke | broken |
| bring | brought | brought |
| burst | burst | burst |
| buy | bought | bought |
| catch | caught | caught |
| choose | chose | chosen |
| cling | clung | clung |
| come | came | come |
| creep | crept | crept |
| dig | dug | dug |
| dive | dived, dove | dived |
| do | did | done |
| draw | drew | drawn |
| dream | dreamed, dreamt | dreamed, dreamt |
| drink | drank | drunk |
| drive | drove | driven |
| eat | ate | eaten |
| fall | fell | fallen |
| find | found | found |
| fly | flew | flown |
| forget | forgot | forgotten |
| forgive | forgave | forgiven |
| freeze | froze | frozen |
| get | got | got, gotten |
| give | gave | given |
| go | went | gone |

*(Continued)*

**Irregular Verbs** *(Continued)*

| | | |
|---|---|---|
| grow | grew | grown |
| hang (an object) | hung | hung |
| hang (a person) | hanged, hung | hanged, hung |
| have | had | had |
| know | knew | known |
| lay (to place) | laid | laid |
| lead | led | led |
| leave | left | left |
| lend | lent | lent |
| lie (to recline) | lay | lain |
| light | lit, lighted | lit, lighted |
| lose | lost | lost |
| pay | paid | paid |
| plead | pleaded, pled | pleaded, pled |
| prove | proved | proved, proven |
| ride | rode | ridden |
| ring | rang, rung | rung |
| rise | rose | risen |
| run | ran | run |
| say | said | said |
| see | saw | seen |
| set | set | set |
| shake | shook | shaken |
| shine | shone, shined | shone, shined |
| show | showed | shown, showed |
| shrink | shrank, shrunk | shrunk |
| sing | sang, sung | sung |
| sink | sank, sunk | sunk |
| sit | sat | sat |
| speak | spoke | spoken |
| spring | sprang, sprung | sprung |
| stand | stood | stood |

*(Continued)*

**Irregular Verbs** *(Continued)*

| | | |
|---|---|---|
| steal | stole | stolen |
| sting | stung | stung |
| swear | swore | sworn |
| swim | swam | swum |
| swing | swung | swung |
| take | took | taken |
| tear | tore | torn |
| throw | threw | thrown |
| wake | woke, waked | woken, waked |
| wear | wore | worn |
| wring | wrung | wrung |
| write | write | written |

The glossary at the end of this handbook treats in greater detail various troublesome verbs, including some listed above. Check the entries for *can/may, get/got/gotten, lie/lay, set/sit,* and so on.

**EXERCISE 23.2** Replace the verb forms in parentheses with appropriate tenses. You may need to use a variety of verb forms (and auxiliaries), including passive and progressive forms. Treat all five sentences as part of a single paragraph. Consult the chart of irregular verbs on pages 408–411 for help with some of the verb forms.

1. Isambard Brunel (**design**) his ship the *Great Eastern* to be the largest vessel on the seas when it (**launch**) in 1857 in London.

2. Almost 700 feet long, the ship—originally named *Leviathan*—(**weigh**) more than 20,000 tons and (**power**) by a screw, paddle wheels, and sails.

3. Designed originally to be a luxurious passenger ship, the *Great Eastern* (**attain**) its greatest fame only after it (**refit**) to stretch the first transatlantic telegraph cable from England to Newfoundland.

4. In the summer of 1865, the *Great Eastern* (**lay**) cable for many difficult days when the thick line (**snap**) two-thirds of the way to Newfoundland. Nine days (**spend**) trying to recover the cable, but it never (**find**).

5. Many people (**be**) skeptical that the *Great Eastern*, a jinxed ship, (**succeed**) in stretching a cable across the Atlantic, but it finally (**do**) so in 1866.

## 23c Problems with tense in parallel constructions?

Parallelism is an arrangement that gives related words, clauses, and phrases a similar pattern, making it easier for readers to see relationships between the parallel expressions. For example, the verbs in the following sentence are parallel: The college band *played* out of tune, *marched* out of step, and yet somehow *maintained* its dignity.

But when verbs sharing the same subject don't also show the same tense and form, the result can be *faulty parallelism*. In the following example, the verbs describing a lawyer's action shift from past tense to past progressive tense without a good reason. The verbs lack parallelism.

**LACK OF PARALLELISM**

      subj.   verb                                            verb

The *lawyer* **explained** the options to her client and **was recommending** a plea of guilty.

The sentence reads more smoothly when the verbs are revised to show the same tense and form.

**REVISED FOR PARALLELISM**

      subj.   verb                                            verb

The *lawyer* **explained** the options to her client and **recommended** a plea of guilty.

Changes in verb tense within a sentence are appropriate, however, when they indicate obvious shifts in time.

> Currently, the lawyer **is defending** an accused murderer and soon **will be defending** a bigamist.

For much more on parallelism, see Section 16h.

**EXERCISE 23.3** Correct any problems with parallelism that the verbs in boldface are causing. Modify the tenses as needed to achieve parallelism.

1. In the middle of the nineteenth century, young French painters **were rejecting** the stilted traditions of academic art, **found** new methods and new subjects, and **would establish** the school of art one critic derided as "Impressionism."

2. The new artists **outraged** all the establishment critics and also **were challenging** all the expectations of Paris gallery owners.

3. Traditionalists thought that painters should **work** indoors, **depict** traditional subjects, and **be using** a balanced style that hid their brushwork.

4. But the youthful Impressionists, including artists like Monet, Degas, and Renoir, soon **were taking** their easels outdoors to the streets of Paris or to public gardens, **laying** on their colors thick and self-consciously, and **had been choosing** scenes from ordinary life to depict.

5. Now these revolutionary artists and their works **are regarded** as classics on their own and **being studied** and **are collected** by an artistic establishment they **are rocking** from its foundations a century ago.

## 23d Questions about tense consistency in longer passages?

In paragraphs or longer passages of writing, avoid shifting from tense to tense (for instance, from *past* to *present*) unless clarity and good sense require the moves. Choose a time frame and stick with it. The following paragraph shows what can happen when verb forms shift inappropriately.

At the dawn of the nuclear era in the 1950s, many horror movies **featured** monsters spawned by atomic explosions or bizarre scientific experiments. For two decades, audiences **flock** to movies with such titles as *Godzilla, Them, Tarantula,* and *The Fly.* Theater screens **come** alive with gigantic lobsters, ants, birds, and lizards, which **spent** their time attacking London, Tokyo, and Washington while scientists **look** for ways to kill them.

The passage sounds confusing because it jumps between two possible time frames. Making the tenses consistent makes the passage more readable. Here it is in the past tense.

At the dawn of the nuclear era in the 1950s, many horror movies **featured** monsters spawned by atomic explosions or bizarre scientific experiments. For two decades, audiences **flocked** to movies with such titles as *Godzilla, Them, Tarantula,* and *The Fly.* Theater screens **came** alive with gigantic lobsters, ants, birds, and lizards, which **spent** their time attacking London, Tokyo, and Washington while scientists **looked** for ways to kill them.

It can also be revised to feature the present tense.

At the dawn of the nuclear era in the 1950s, many horror movies **feature** monsters spawned by atomic explosions or bizarre scientific experiments. For two decades, audiences **flock** to movies with such titles as *Godzilla, Them, Tarantula,* and *The Fly.* Theater screens **come** alive with gigantic lobsters, ants, birds, and lizards, which **spend** their time attacking London, Tokyo, and Washington while scientists **look** for ways to kill them.

**EXERCISE 23.4** Revise the following paragraph to make the tenses of the boldfaced verbs more consistent. You may find it helpful to emphasize the present tense throughout the passage—but not every verb ought to be in the present. (Specific events in a literary work are usually described in present tense: After Macbeth *kills* King Duncan, he *seizes* the throne.)

(1) *Macbeth*, one of Shakespeare's shortest dramas, **depicts** rebellion, conspiracy, and murder most foul. (2) The smoke of battle **has** barely

cleared when Macbeth **encountered** three witches who **promise** him the throne of Scotland. (3) Almost immediately, his wife **persuades** him—against his good conscience—to act, and he quickly **has murdered** King Duncan while the old man **sleeps**. (4) But Macbeth himself **will sleep** no more; his conscience **gives** him no rest for the remainder of the play. (5) Only in the fourth act **did** the pace slow, but then the action **rose** again in the fifth toward a bloody conclusion.

## 23e Do you understand active and passive voice?

*Voice* is a characteristic of verbs that is easier to illustrate than to define. Verbs that take objects (called transitive verbs) can be either in **active** or in **passive voice**. They are in active voice when the subject in the sentence actually does what the verb describes.

> subj        action
> *Barbara* **managed** the account.

They are in passive voice when the action described by the verb is done *to* the subject.

> subj.         action
> The *account* **was managed** by Barbara.

Passive verbs are useful constructions when *who* did an action is either unknown or less important than *to whom it was done*. A passive verb puts the *victim* (so to speak) right up front in the sentence where it gets attention. Passive verbs also work well in scientific writing when you want to focus on the process itself.

> *Serena Williams* **was featured** on ESPN.

> *Serena Williams* **was interviewed** by several reporters.

> *The beaker* **was heated** for three minutes.

The passive is also customary in many expressions where a writer or speaker chooses to be vague about assigning responsibility.

Flight 107 **has been canceled**.

The check **was lost** in the mail.

When you need passives, use them. But most of the time you can make your sentences livelier by changing passive constructions to active ones. In a sentence with an active verb, it is often easier to tell who is doing what to whom. For advice on revising sentences to eliminate weak passive verbs, see Section 17a-6.

**EXERCISE 23.5** Identify all the passive verbs in the following sentences; then revise those passive verbs that might be better stated in the active voice. Some sentences may require no revision.

1. Even opponents of chemical pesticides sometimes use poisons after they have been bitten by fire ants, aggressive and vicious insects spreading throughout the southern United States.

2. These tiny creatures have been given by nature a fierce sting, and they usually attack en masse.

3. Gardeners are hampered in their work by the mounds erected by the ants.

4. By the time a careless gardener discovers a mound, a hand or foot has likely been bitten by numerous ants.

5. The injured appendage feels as if it has been attacked by a swarm of bees.

## 23f What is the subjunctive mood and how do you use it?

As a grammatical term, **mood** indicates how you intend a statement to be taken. Are you making a direct statement of fact? Then the mood of the statement will be **indicative** ("I enjoy reading science fiction"). Are you giving a command or making a request? If so, the mood becomes **imperative** ("Watch out for flying objects!" "Give me that book, please.").

When, however, you express a wish or hope, make a suggestion, or describe a *possible* (rather than actual) situation, you may need to use the

**subjunctive** mood. You signal a shift to the subjunctive simply by altering the form of the verb. For example, in *if* clauses that express a wish, hope, or desire, you would use the subjunctive verb form *were* instead of the more common indicative form *was*.

> *If* George **were** [not **was**] in charge, we'd be in good hands.
>
> *If* she **were** [not **was**] to accept their contract, she would begin work on September 1.
>
> *If* I **were** [not **was**] a rich man, I'd be no happier than I am now.

Rare in English, the subjunctive is still expected in some situations and can be tricky. So you need to understand what the subjunctive looks like and when to employ it.

**◉1 Recognize the subjunctive forms of verbs.** For all verbs, the present subjunctive is simply the base form of the verb—that is, the present infinitive form without *to*.

| VERB | PRESENT SUBJUNCTIVE |
|------|---------------------|
| to be | be |
| to give | give |
| to send | send |
| to bless | bless |

The base form is used even in the third person singular, where you might ordinarily expect a verb to take another form.

> It is essential that *Fernando* **have** [not **has**] his lines memorized by tomorrow.
>
> Albertina insisted that *Travis* **be** [not **is**] on time for their dinner at her mother's.

For all verbs except *be*, the past subjunctive is the same as the simple past tense.

| VERB | PAST SUBJUNCTIVE |
|------|------------------|
| to give | gave |
| to send | sent |
| to bless | blessed |

For *be*, the past subjunctive is always *were*. This is true even in the first and third person singular, where you might expect the form to be *was*.

> I wish *I* **were** [not **was**] the director.
>
> Suppose *you* **were** the director.
>
> I wish *she* **were** [not **was**] the director.

⏺**2 Recognize occasions for the subjunctive.** In addition to appearing in clauses that express wishes and desires, the subjunctive is also used in *that* clauses following verbs that make demands, requests, recommendations, or motions. These forms can seem legalistic and formal, but they are appropriate.

> The presiding officer asked <u>that everyone **be** silent</u>.
>
> I ask only <u>that you **be** courteous to the speaker</u>.
>
> The president asked <u>that everyone **show** courage</u>.

Some common expressions also require the subjunctive.

> **Be** that as it may . . .
>
> **Come** what may . . .
>
> As it **were** . . .
>
> Peace **be** with you.

**EXERCISE 23.6** In the following sentences, underline any verbs in the subjunctive mood.

1. It is essential that we be at the airport at 2:00 p.m. today.

2. I wish I were less susceptible to telephone solicitors!

3. Far be it from me to criticize your writing!

4. Come what may, the show must go on.

5. If Madison were to arrive early, what would happen to our plans?

6. It is essential that you take over as the supervisor.

# 24 Questions About Verbals?

## 24a What are verbals?

Verbals lead a double life: they look like verb forms but act like other parts of speech—nouns, adjectives, adverbs. Like verbs, verbals can express time (present, past), take objects, and form phrases. Though you may not recognize the three types of verbals by their names—*infinitives, participles*, and *gerunds*—you use them all the time. (See also Section 33a.)

**1 Understand infinitives.** You can identify an **infinitive** by looking for the word *to* preceding the base form of a verb: *to seek, to find*. Infinitives also take other forms to show time and voice: *to be seeking, to have found, to have been found*. Infinitives sometimes act as nouns, adjectives, and adverbs.

| | |
|---|---|
| **INFINITIVE AS NOUN** | **To work** in outer space is not easy. |
| | subject of the sentence |
| **INFINITIVE AS ADJECTIVE** | Astronauts have many procedures **to learn**. |
| | modifies the noun *procedure* |
| **INFINITIVE AS ADVERB** | NASA compromised **to fund** the International Space Station. modifies the verb *compromised* |

An infinitive can also serve as an *absolute*—that is, a phrase, standing alone, that modifies an entire sentence.

> **To make** a long story short, the current space station is smaller than it might have been.

In some sentence constructions, the characteristic marker of the infinitive, *to*, is deleted.

> Space station crews perform exercises to help them [**to**] **deal** with the consequences of weightlessness.

**419**

**2 Understand participles.** A **participle** is a verb form that acts as a modifier. The present participle ends with *-ing*. For regular verbs, the past participle ends with *-ed*; for irregular verbs, the form of the past participle varies. Participles take various forms, depending on whether the verb they are derived from is regular or irregular. Following are the participle forms of two verbs.

---

**Chart 24.1   Forms of the Participle**

| | |
|---|---|
| *perform* (a regular verb) | PARTICIPLES |
| **Present, active:** | performing |
| **Present, passive:** | being performed |
| **Past, active:** | performed |
| **Past, passive:** | having been performed |
| | |
| *write* (an irregular verb) | PARTICIPLES |
| **Present, active:** | writing |
| **Present, passive:** | being written |
| **Past, active:** | written |
| **Past, passive:** | having been written |

---

(For the forms of some irregular past participles, check the list of irregular verbs on pages 408-411.)

As modifiers, participles may be single words. In the following example, the participle *waving* modifies *astronaut*.

> **Waving**, the astronaut turned a cartwheel in the space station for the television audience.

But participles often take objects, complements, and modifiers to form verbal phrases. Such phrases play an important role in structuring sentences.

> <u>**Clutching** a camera</u>, the astronaut moved toward a galley window.

> The designers of the station, <u>**knowing** they had to work within budget constraints</u>, used their ingenuity to solve many problems.

Like an infinitive, a participle can also serve as an *absolute*—that is, a phrase, standing alone, that modifies an entire sentence.

> All things **considered**, the International Space Station is a remarkable if troubled project.

**● 3 Understand gerunds.** A **gerund** is a verb form that acts as a noun: *smiling, flying, walking.* Because most gerunds end in *-ing*, they look exactly like the present participle.

| | |
|---|---|
| GERUND | **Daring** is a quality moviegoers admire in heroes. |
| PARTICIPLE | Almost all passengers, however, would prefer not to have a **daring** cab driver. |

The important difference is that gerunds function as nouns, whereas participles act as modifiers. In the following sentences, for example, *snoring* functions as a noun (and gerund) in the first sentence and a modifier (and participle) in the second.

| | |
|---|---|
| GERUND | We recognized Marta's **waving**. |
| PARTICIPLE | We recognized Marta **waving**. |

Gerunds usually appear in the present tense, but they can take other forms. In the following example, the gerund is in the past tense (and passive voice) and acts as the subject of the sentence.

> **Having been treated** unfairly by the news media has angered directors of the program.

Here the gerund is in the present tense and passive voice.

> **Being asked** to design a mission to Mars is an opportunity NASA anticipates.

Gerunds have many functions.

| | |
|---|---|
| GERUND AS SUBJECT | **Keeping** within current budget restraints poses a problem for NASA. |
| GERUND AS OBJECT | Some NASA engineers prefer **flying** space missions without crews. |

| | |
|---|---|
| **GERUND AS APPOSITIVE** | Others argue that NASA needs to cultivate its great talent, **executing** daring missions. |

<table>
<tr><td></td><td>subj.</td><td>comp.</td></tr>
</table>

| | |
|---|---|
| **GERUNDS AS SUBJECT** **AND COMPLEMENT** | **Exploring** the heavens is **fulfilling** the dreams of humankind. |

**EXERCISE 24.1** Identify the boldfaced words or phrases as infinitives, participles, or gerunds.

1. **Regretting** compromises in the original design, engineers have refined the shuttle after the *Challenger* and *Columbia* disasters.

2. The mainstream media questioned both NASA's **engineering** and its **handling** of the shuttle program.

3. **To be** fair, NASA's safety record in the **challenging** task of space exploration has been defensible.

4. **Costing** even more than the space shuttle, the International Space Station may not prove viable much longer.

5. **To make** budget matters more complicated, NASA is **exploring** the possibility of a return to the moon.

## 24b How do verbals cause sentence fragments?

A verbal phrase that stands alone can create a sentence fragment—that is, a clause without a complete subject or verb. Fragments are considered errors in academic and professional writing.

> The Secretary of Homeland Security declined to be interviewed on CNN. **Having been ambushed in the recent past by an unfriendly reporter.**

Verbals alone cannot act as verbs in sentences. In fact, verbals are even described as **nonfinite** (that is, "unfinished") verbs. A complete sentence requires a **finite** verb, which is a verb that changes form to indicate person, number, and tense.

| | |
|---|---|
| NONFINITE VERB—INFINITIVE | **To have found** success . . . |
| FINITE VERB | **I have found** success. |
| NONFINITE VERB—PARTICIPLE | The comedian **performing** the bit . . . |
| FINITE VERB | The comedian **performs** the bit. |
| NONFINITE VERB—GERUND | **Directing** a play . . . |
| FINITE VERB | She **directed** the play. |

Verbal phrases are accepted in much informal writing. You'll see such fragments often in magazine articles and in advertising copy.

> Harold loved playing comedy clubs—every bit of it. **Telling political jokes. Making satirical comments.** It made life worthwhile.

But in academic writing, fragments should usually be revised. For help on recasting such fragments, see Section 35a.

## 24c What is a split infinitive?

An infinitive interrupted by an adverb is considered split.

> to **boldly** go       to **really** try       to **actually** see

Some writers believe that constructions such as these are incorrect, a point disputed by grammarians. Split infinitives are such common expressions in English that most writers use them without apology. Here are guidelines to help you through this minor, but still touchy, matter.

**◉1 Check whether any words separate the *to* in an infinitive from its verb.** If a sentence sounds awkward because a word or phrase splits an infinitive, move the interrupter.

| | |
|---|---|
| SPLIT INFINITIVE | Harold's intention as a stand-up comic was **to**, as best he could, **make** people laugh at themselves. |
| REVISED | Harold's intention as a stand-up comic was **to make** people laugh at themselves, as best he could. |

**2 Revise any split infinitives that cause modification problems.** In the following sentence, for example, *only* seems to modify *mock* when it should refer to *the crudest aspects*.

| CONFUSING | Harold intended **to** only **mock** the crudest aspects of human behavior. |
|---|---|
| CLEARER | Harold intended **to mock** only the crudest aspects of human behavior. |

Consider, too, whether a word dividing an infinitive is needed at all. Where the interrupting word is a weak intensifier that adds nothing to a sentence (*really, actually, basically*), cut it.

| WEAK INTENSIFIER | Harold found it especially easy **to** basically **demolish** the pretensions of politicians. |
|---|---|
| INTENSIFIER CUT | Harold found it especially easy **to demolish** the pretensions of politicians. |

**3 Consider whether a split infinitive is acceptable.** In most situations, split infinitives are neither awkward nor confusing, so revising them won't improve a sentence.

| SPLIT INFINITIVE | Words fail **to** adequately **describe** the cluelessness of some public figures. |
|---|---|
| REVISED | Words fail **to describe** adequately the cluelessness of some public figures. |

In academic and business writing, it's probably best to keep *to* and the verb together because some readers still object strongly to split infinitives.

**EXERCISE 24.2** Find the split infinitives in the following sentences and revise them. Decide which revisions are necessary, which optional. Be prepared to defend your decisions.

1. In his comic monologue, Harold decided to candidly describe his own inept campaign for city council.

2. Harold usually didn't allow his personal life to too much color his comedy routines.

3. But to really appreciate how absurd politics could be, a person had to basically run for office himself.

4. Harold quickly discovered that it wasn't easy to persuade contributors to only support the best candidate.

5. To actually succeed in politics, Harold learned that a candidate had to really understand human nature.

# 25

# Questions About Plurals, Possessives, and Articles?

---

## 25a How are nouns made plural?

Plurals can be tricky. Most plurals in English are formed by adding *-s* or *-es* to the singular forms of nouns.

> demonstration → demonstration**s**
> picture → picture**s**
> dish → dish**es**

However, substantial numbers of words are simply irregular. You could not reliably predict what their plurals would be if you didn't know them.

> **IRREGULAR**
> man → m**e**n
> ox → ox**en**
> mouse → m**i**c**e**
> fungus → fung**i** (or fungus**es**)

Plurals may vary, too, according to how a word is used. You might find maple *leaves* on your driveway but several Toronto Maple *Leafs* on the cover of *Sports Illustrated*.

● 1 **Check the dictionary for the plural form of a noun.** Most up-to-date college dictionaries provide the plurals of all troublesome words. If your dictionary does not give a plural for a particular noun, assume that it forms its plural with *-s* or *-es*.

You may eliminate some trips to the dictionary by referring to the following guidelines for forming plurals. But the list is complicated and full of exceptions, so keep that dictionary handy.

**2 Use *-es* when the plural adds a syllable to the pronunciation of the noun.** This is usually the case when a word ends in a soft *ch, sh, s, ss, x,* or *zz.* (If the noun already ends in *-e,* you add only *-s.*)

dish → dish**es**
glass → glass**es**
bus → bus**es** or bus**ses**
buzz → buzz**es**

**3 Add *-s* to form a plural when a noun ends in *-o* and a vowel precedes the *-o;* add *-es* when a noun ends in *-o* and a consonant precedes the *-o.*** This guideline has exceptions. A few words ending in *-o* have two acceptable plural forms.

| VOWEL BEFORE *-O* (ADD *-S*) | CONSONANT BEFORE *-O* (ADD *-ES*) |
|---|---|
| studio → studio**s** | hero → hero**es** |
| rodeo → rodeo**s** | tomato → tomato**es** |

**4 Add *-s* to form a plural when a noun ends in *-y* and a vowel precedes the *y.*** When a consonant precedes the *y,* change the *y* to an *i* and add *-es.*

| VOWEL PRECEDES *-Y* (ADD *-S*) | CONSONANT PRECEDES *-Y* (CHANGE *-Y* TO *-IES*) |
|---|---|
| attorney → attorney**s** | foundry → foundr**ies** |
| Monday → Monday**s** | candy → cand**ies** |

An exception to this rule occurs with proper nouns. They usually retain the *-y* and simply add *-s.*

| PROPER NAMES ENDING IN *-Y* (ADD *-S*) | EXCEPTIONS TO THE EXCEPTION (CHANGE *-Y* TO *-IES*) |
|---|---|
| Germany → Germany**s** | Rocky Mountains → Rock**ies** |
| Nestrosky → Nestrosky**s** | Smoky Mountains → Smok**ies** |

**5 Check the plural of nouns ending in *-f* or *-fe.*** Some form plurals by adding *-s,* some change *-f* to *-ves,* and some have two acceptable plural forms.

| **ADD -*S* TO FORM PLURAL** | **CHANGE -*F* TO -*VES* IN PLURAL** |
|---|---|
| chief → chie**fs** | leaf → lea**ves** |
| belief → belie**fs** | knife → kni**ves** |

**TWO ACCEPTABLE FORMS**
elf → el**fs**/el**ves**
scarf → scar**fs**/scar**ves**

### ⦿6 Check the plural of certain nouns that derive from other languages.

analysis → analys**es**        medium → medi**a**
criterion → criteri**a**        syllabus → syllab**i**

### ⦿7 Check the plural of compound words. In most compounds, pluralize the last word.

dishcloth → dishcloth**s**
housewife → housewi**ves**

But pluralize the first word in a compound when it is the important term. This is often the case in hyphenated expressions.

attorney general → attorney**s** general
father-in-law → father**s**-in-law
passerby → passer**s**by

Words that end with -*ful* add -*s* to the end of the whole word, not to the syllable before -*ful*.

handful**s** [not hand*s*ful]
tablespoonful**s** [not tablespoon*s*ful]

### ⦿8 Check the plural of letters, abbreviations, acronyms, and numbers. These constructions usually form their plurals by adding -*s*.

the SAT**s**
all CEO**s**
the 2000**s**
four Ph.D.**s**

Use *-'s* only where adding *-s* without the apostrophe might cause a misreading.

> three *e*'**s** and two *y*'**s**

**⊚9 Use plurals consistently within a passage.** For example, if the subject of a clause is plural, be sure that words related to it are appropriately plural. In the following example, *mind* and *job* should be plural because the subject *leaders* is plural.

| | |
|---|---|
| INCONSISTENT | **Leaders** able to make up their **mind** usually hold on to their **job**. |
| REVISED | **Leaders** able to make up their **minds** usually hold on to their **jobs**. |

**EXERCISE 25.1** Form the plurals of the following words. Use the guidelines above or a dictionary as necessary.

| | | |
|---|---|---|
| basis | gas | soliloquy |
| duo | loaf | zero |
| tooth | alkali | mongoose |
| alumnus | datum | heir apparent |
| moose | Oreo | court-martial |

## 25b Questions about possessives?

A noun or pronoun takes a possessive form to show ownership or some similar relationship: *Rita's, the students', the governor's approval, the day's labor, the city's destruction, hers, his, theirs.* Possession can also be signaled by the pronoun *of: the pride of Brooklyn, the flagship of the company, the signature of the author.* Note that there is disagreement about how to form some possessives, especially of words that end with "s." Our guidelines generally follow MLA principles, but you may want to check the style guide used in your own field or major (see Chapter 49). Although you may occasionally see the apostrophe omitted in signs—*mens room, Macys*—in academic writing don't omit an apostrophe that shows the possessive.

**1 Add an apostrophe + -s to singular nouns and to plural nouns that do not end in -s.**

| SINGULAR NOUNS | PLURALS NOT ENDING IN -S |
|---|---|
| dog's life | geese's behavior |
| that man's opinion | women's attitude |
| the NCAA's ruling | children's imaginations |
| the boss's daughter | mice's tails |

**2 Add an apostrophe + -s to singular proper nouns.**

SINGULAR NOUNS
America's shores
C. S. Lewis's novels
Alexis's career goals
Zeus's power
Descartes's *Discourse on Method*
Jesus's words

**3 Add an apostrophe (but not an s) to plural nouns that end in -s.**

hostesses' job          senators' chambers
students' opinion       Smiths' home

**4 Show possession only at the end of compound or hyphenated words.**

president-elect's decision
father-in-law's Cadillac
the United States Post Office's efficiency

**5 Show possession only once when two nouns share ownership.**

Marge and Homer's family
Smith-Fallows and Luu's project

But when ownership is separate, each noun shows possession.

> Marge's and Homer's educations
> Smith-Fallow s' and Luu's offices

**●6  Use an apostrophe + -s to form the possessive of living things and titled works; use of with nonliving things.**  Follow this guideline sensibly. Many common expressions violate the convention, and many writers simply ignore it.

| TAKE APOSTROPHE + -s | TAKE OF |
|---|---|
| the dog's bone | the size **of** the bone |
| Professor Granchi's taxes | the bite **of** taxes |
| *Time's* cover | the timeliness **of** the cover |

Use *of* whenever an apostrophe + -s seems awkward or ridiculous.

**RIDICULOUS**   The **student** sitting next to Peg's opinion was radical.

**REVISED**   The opinion **of the student** sitting next to Peg was radical.

In a few situations, English allows a double possessive, consisting of both -'s and *of.*

> That idea **of** Mariah's didn't win support, although an earlier one did.
> An opinion **of** Lane's soon spurred another argument.

**●7  Do not use an apostrophe with personal pronouns.** Personal pronouns don't take an apostrophe to show ownership: *my, your, her, his, our, their, its.* The forms *it's* and *who's* are contractions for *it is* and *who is* and shouldn't be confused with the possessive pronouns *its* and *whose* (see Section 28c).

> **It's** an idea that has **its** opponents alarmed.
> **Who's** to say **whose** opinion is right?

Indefinite pronouns—such as *anybody, each one, everybody*—do form their possessives regularly: *anybody's, each one's, everybody's.* For more about possessive pronouns, see Section 28b.

**EXERCISE 25.2** Decide whether the forms boldfaced in these sentences are correct. Revise any that you believe are faulty.

1. That claim **of her's** may be right.

2. **James'** belief was that the main concern **of most citizens'** was a thriving economy.

3. **Society's** problems today are not as great as they were in the **1900s'**; each generation benefits from its **parent's** sacrifices while tackling **it's** own problems.

4. **Its** a shame that people forget how much they have benefited from **someone elses** labor.

5. Children are notorious for ignoring their **elders** generosity; ingratitude is even one of the major themes of **King Lear**'s plot.

## 25c Should it be *a* or *an*?

Some writers think that they should simply use the article *a* before all words that begin with consonants and *an* before all words that begin with vowels. In fact, usage is just a bit more complicated, as a few examples show: *an* argument, *a* European, *a* house, *an* honorable person. (See also Section 33b.)

Use *a* when the word following it begins with a consonant *sound*; use *an* when the word following it begins with a vowel *sound*. In most cases, it works out that *a* actually comes before words beginning with consonants, *an* before words with vowels.

| INITIAL CONSONANTS | INITIAL VOWELS |
|---|---|
| a **b**oat | an **aa**rdvark |
| a **c**lass | an **E**gyptian monument |
| a **d**uck | an **i**gloo |
| a **f**inal opinion | an **o**dd event |
| a **h**ouse | an **O**edipus complex |
| a **X**erox product | an **u**tter disaster |

But *an* is used before words beginning with a consonant when the consonant is silent, as is sometimes the case with *h*. It is also used when a consonant itself is pronounced with an initial vowel sound ($f \rightarrow ef; n \rightarrow en; s \rightarrow es$), as often happens in acronyms.

| SILENT CONSONANT | CONSONANT WITH A VOWEL SOUND |
|---|---|
| an heir | an SAT score |
| an honest man | an HMO |
| an hors d'oeuvre | an *X*-ray star |
| an hour | an *F* in this course |

Similarly, *a* is used before words beginning with a vowel when the vowel is pronounced like a consonant. Certain vowels, for example, sound like the consonant *y*, and in a few cases, an initial *o* sounds like the consonant *w*.

**VOWEL WITH A CONSONANT SOUND**
a European vacation (**eu** sounds like **y**)
a unique painting (**u** sounds like **y**)
a one-sided argument (**o** sounds like **w**)
a U-joint (**u** sounds like **y**)

**EXERCISE 25.3** Decide whether *a* or *an* should be used before each of the following words or phrases.

1. L-shaped room

2. hyperthyroid condition

3. zygote

4. *X*-rated movie

5. Euclidean principle

6. evasive answer

7. jalapeño pepper

8. unwritten rule

9. unit of measure

10. veneer of oak

# 26 Questions About Pronoun Reference?

Pronouns usually stand in for and act like nouns, but they don't name particular persons, places, or things. As the following examples show, there are many kinds of pronouns with different functions.

**Personal:** *I, me, you, he, she, it, they, us, him, her, them*

**Possessive:** *my, your, his, her, its, our, their* (these modify nouns); *mine, yours, his, hers, ours, theirs* (these stand alone)

**Demonstrative:** *this, that, these, those*

**Indefinite:** *any, anybody, someone, no one, none, everyone, each*

**Interrogative:** *who, whose, whom, which, whoever, whomever*

**Relative:** *that, which, who, whom, whoever, whomever*

**Reflexive:** *myself, himself, herself, yourselves, themselves*

Handled well, pronouns help to make writing clear and concise. But you must pay attention to reference (Chapter 26), agreement (Chapter 27), and case (Chapter 28).

## 26a Do pronouns lack antecedents?

The person, place, or thing a pronoun refers to is called its *antecedent*, the word you'd have to repeat in a sentence if you couldn't use a pronoun.

ant.                                  pron.

*Jill* demanded that the clerk speak to **her**.

ant.                     pron.

*Workers* denied that **they** intended to strike.

A pronoun must agree with its antecedent in *number* (singular or plural), in *case* (subjective, objective, or possessive), and sometimes in *gender* (masculine or feminine). You must revise a pronoun reference if readers can't find a specific word in your sentence that could logically serve as an antecedent, the word the pronoun replaces.

When you aren't sure that the pronoun has an antecedent, ask yourself whether another word in the sentence or passage could substitute for the pronoun. If none can, replace the vague pronoun with a word or phrase that explains precisely what it is.

> **VAGUE**   The pollsters chose their participants scientifically, but **it** did not prevent a faulty prediction of the mayoral election.
>
> **REVISED**   The pollsters chose their participants scientifically, but **their random sampling** did not prevent a faulty prediction of the mayoral election.

**EXERCISE 26.1**   Revise or rewrite the following sentences to eliminate vague pronouns. Treat the sentences as a continuous passage.

1. Leah read avidly about gardening, although she had never planted one herself.

2. Her fondness for apartment living left Leah without a place for one.

3. Leah found herself buying garden tools, seeds, and catalogs, but it did not make much sense.

4. Leah's friends suggested building planters on her deck or installing a window garden, but Leah doubted that the landlord would permit it.

5. As for her parents' idea that she invest in a condominium, they overestimated her credit rating.

## 26b Are pronoun references unclear?

You have a problem with pronoun reference when a pronoun could refer to more than one antecedent.

| AMBIGUOUS | When Ms. Walker talked to Mrs. Mendoza at noon, **she** did not realize that **she** might be resigning before the end of the day. |
|---|---|
| AMBIGUOUS | As soon as the FDA approves the revolutionary antibiotic, the drug company will begin production in a new plant. **It** will make a major difference when **it** happens. |

In the first sentence, who is resigning is not clear; in the second, *it* might be the approval of the drug or the opening of a plant. You can usually eliminate such confusion by replacing the ambiguous pronouns with more specific words or by rewriting the sentence. Sometimes you have to do both.

| REVISED | When **they** talked to each other at noon, **Ms. Walker** did not realize that **Mrs. Mendoza** might be resigning before the end of the day. |
|---|---|
| REVISED | As soon as the FDA approves the revolutionary antibiotic, the drug company will begin production in a new plant. **The drug** will make a major difference **as soon as it becomes available**. |

**EXERCISE 26.2** Revise the following sentences to eliminate ambiguous pronoun references. Treat the sentences as a continuous passage. Several versions of each sentence may be possible.

1. Amanda could hardly believe that representatives from Habitat for Humanity would visit wintry Madison, Wisconsin, when it was so bad.

2. When she met them at their hotel, the winds were howling, the visitors were hungry, and it was predicted that they would get worse.

3. But the two women were ready to brave the elements, so she figured this wasn't a problem.

4. Later Amanda learned that one of the visitors, Sarah Severson, had been born in Wisconsin, and she told her she knew a great deal about northern winters.

5. The three of them took off through the blizzard in Amanda's SUV, but it didn't slow them down a bit.

## 26c Questions about *this, that, which,* and *it*?

Readers may be confused if you use the pronouns *this, that, which,* or *it* to refer to ideas you haven't named specifically in your writing. Vague pronouns of this kind are a problem not just because readers can't locate a clear antecedent, but because writers sometimes resort to vague pronouns when they aren't sure themselves what they mean in a sentence or paragraph. So unpacking a vague *this* or *that* may at times help you get a firmer grip on your ideas.

> CONFUSING  In Act III, Hamlet has a chance to avenge his dead father by stabbing his murderous uncle while the man is alone at prayer. But **it** bothers him. [What bothers him?]

> REVISED  In Act III, Hamlet has a chance to avenge his dead father by stabbing his murderous uncle while the man is alone at prayer. But **killing a man in cold blood** bothers Hamlet.

**1 Revise a sentence or passage to make it clear what *this, that, which,* or *it* means.** Constructions such as the following can be confusing or imprecise.

> CONFUSING  The minutes of the committee are usually filled with data, charts, and vivid accounts of the debate. I appreciated **this**.

Readers can't tell whether you like data, charts, or debate—or all three. You can usually clear up such confusion by putting a space after the pronoun (*this _____?* or *that _____?*) and filling it in with a word or phrase that explains what *this* or *that* is.

> CONFUSING  The minutes of the committee are usually filled with data, charts, and vivid accounts of the dialogue. I appreciated **this _____?**

Now fill in the blank.

> REVISED  I appreciated **this detailed information**.

When the unclear pronoun is *which* or *it*, you ought either to revise the sentence or supply a clear and direct antecedent. Here's an example with *it* as the vague pronoun.

> **VAGUE**    Although atomic waste products are hard to dispose of safely, **it** remains a reasonable alternative to burning fossil fuels to produce electricity.

What is the alternative to burning fossil fuels? Surely not *atomic waste products*. The *it* needs to be replaced by a more specific term.

> **REVISED**    Although atomic waste products are hard to dispose of safely, **nuclear power** remains a reasonable alternative to burning fossil fuels to produce electricity.

### ●2 Avoid using *they* or *it* without antecedents to describe people or things in general.

> **VAGUE**    In Houston, **they** drive worse than in Dallas.
>
> **REVISED**    In Houston, **people** drive worse than in Dallas.

### ●3 Avoid sentences in which a pronoun merely repeats the obvious subject. Such constructions are unacceptable in writing.

> **INCORRECT**    The **mayor**, a Democrat, **he** won the election.
>
> **REVISED**    The **mayor**, a Democrat, won the election.

### ●4 Don't let a nonpossessive pronoun refer to a word that is possessive. In the sentence below, *they* seems to refer to *pundits'*, but that word cannot be the antecedent.

> **VAGUE**    As for the television **pundits'** coverage, they either mock third-party candidates or ignore them.

*Pundits'* is a possessive form. So since *they* can't refer to *pundits'* (or to *coverage*), the sentence has to be revised.

> **REVISED**    As for the television **pundits**, **they** either mock third-party candidates or ignore them.

**EXERCISE 26.3** Decide whether a reader might find the pronouns in bold-face unclear. Revise the sentences as necessary.

1. Even tourists just visiting the building soon noticed the aging state capitol's sagging floors, unreliable plumbing, and exposed electrical conduits. **This** was embarrassing.

2. When an electrical fire in the office of the Speaker of the House was soon followed by another in the Senate chamber, it was clear **it** was a problem.

3. Old paintings and sculptures were grimy and cracked, **which** had been donated by citizens over the decades.

4. The governor's proposal for reconstructing the state capitol, the legislators endorsed **it** almost unanimously.

5. **This** was passed by a voice vote.

# 27 Questions About Pronoun Agreement?

## 27a Do antecedents and pronouns agree in number?

Pronouns and nouns are either singular or plural. Singular pronouns (such as *she, it, this, that, her, him, my, his, her, its*) refer to something singular;

plural pronouns (such as *they, these, them, their*) refer to plural nouns. This connection is called **agreement in number**.

The soccer **players** gathered **their** equipment.

The **coach** searched for **her** car.

Problems with *pronoun agreement* occur when you use a singular pronoun to stand in for a plural noun or a plural pronoun to substitute for a singular noun.

Like wax figures, pronouns stand in for the nouns they replace. This head is being prepared for the Wax Museum at Fisherman's Wharf.

**●1 Be sure that singular pronouns refer to singular antecedents and plural pronouns to plural antecedents.**

INCORRECT    An **American** always takes it for granted that government

sing.

plural

agencies will help **them** when trouble strikes.

plural
CORRECT  **Americans** always take it for granted that government

plural
agencies will help **them** when trouble strikes.

sing.
CORRECT  An **American** always takes it for granted that government

sing.
agencies will help **him or her** when trouble strikes.

Note that words such as *student, individual,* and *person* are singular, not plural. Don't use *they* to refer to them.

INCORRECT  If a **person** watches too much television, **they** may become a couch potato.

REVISED  If a **person** watches too much television, **he or she** may become a couch potato.

**2 Keep pronouns consistent in number throughout a passage.** Don't switch back and forth from singular to plural forms of pronouns and antecedents. The following paragraph—with pronouns and antecedents boldfaced—shows this common error.

One reason some **teenagers** [pl.] quit school is to work to support **their** [pl.] families. If **he or she** [sing.] is the eldest child, the **teen** [sing.] may feel an obligation to provide for the family. So **they** [pl.] look for a minimum wage job. Unfortunately, the **student** [sing.] often must work so many hours per week that **they** [pl.] cannot give much attention to schoolwork. As a result, **he or she** [sing.] grows discouraged and drops out.

To correct such a tendency, be consistent. Treat the troublesome key term—in the passage above it is *teenager*—as either singular or plural, but not both. Notice that making such a change may require adjustments throughout the passage.

One reason some **teenagers** [pl.] quit school is to work to support **their** [pl.] families. If **they** [pl.] are the eldest children, such **teens** [pl.] may feel an obligation to provide for **their** [pl.] families. So **they** [pl.] look for minimum wage jobs. Unfortunately, these **students [pl.]** often must work so many hours per week that **they [pl.]** cannot give much attention to schoolwork. As a result, **they [pl.]** grow discouraged and drop out.

**EXERCISE 27.1** Revise the following sentences wherever pronouns and antecedents do not agree in number. You may change either the pronouns or the antecedents.

1. Many a college class is conducted using the Socratic method, but they aren't always successful.

2. In the Socratic method, a teacher leads a student through a series of questions to conclusions that they believe they've reached without the instructor's prompting.

3. Yet when instructors ask leading questions, the cleverer students sometimes answer it in unexpected ways.

4. However, no instructor, except perhaps for Socrates himself, can foresee all the questions and answers clever students might have for them.

**EXERCISE 27.2** Revise the entire paragraph in Section 27a-2 to make all the boldfaced nouns or pronouns singular.

## 27b Questions about agreement with indefinite pronouns?

A troublesome and common agreement problem involves references to pronouns described as indefinite—*everyone, anybody, anyone, somebody, all, some, none, each, few,* and *most.* It is not always easy to tell whether one of these indefinite words is singular or plural.

Everyone should keep (**his? their?**) temper.

No one has a right to more than (**his or her? their?**) share.

⬤**1 Use the chart below or a dictionary to determine whether an indefinite pronoun or noun in your sentence is singular, variable, or plural.** The chart, which is not exhaustive, reflects formal and college usage.

| Chart 27.1 | **Indefinite Pronouns** | |
|---|---|---|
| | **VARIABLE** | |
| **SINGULAR** | **(SINGULAR OR PLURAL)** | **PLURAL** |
| anybody | all | few |
| anyone | any | many |
| anything | either | several |
| each | more | |
| everybody | most | |
| everyone | neither | |
| everything | none | |
| nobody | some | |
| no one | | |
| nothing | | |
| somebody | | |
| someone | | |
| something | | |

⬤**2 If the indefinite word is regarded as singular, make any pronouns that refer to it singular.**

sing.      sing.
Did **anybody** misplace **her** notes?

sing.      sing.
**Everyone** should keep **his** temper.

sing.      sing.
**No one** has a right to more than **his or her** share.

Using singular pronouns in these cases may seem odd at times because the plural forms occur so often in speech and informal writing.

| | |
|---|---|
| INFORMAL | **Each** of the candidates has **their** own ideas. |
| INFORMAL | We discovered that **everyone** had kept **their** notes. |
| REVISED—FORMAL | **Each** of the candidates has **his or her** own ideas. |
| REVISED—FORMAL | We discovered that **everyone** had kept **her** notes. |

In a few situations, however, the singular indefinite pronoun does take a plural referent, even in formal and college writing.

    sing.                     plural
Because **each** of the players arrived late, the coach gave **them** a stern lecture on punctuality.

  sing.         plural
**Nobody** was late, were **they**?

   sing.         plural
**Everybody** has plenty of money, and **they** are willing to spend it.

#### ◀▶ Point of Difference

Some grammarians and linguists now support these informal constructions. They point out that, in effect, indefinite pronouns like *everyone* or expressions like *each of the legislators* describe groups, not individuals. That's why most speakers of English intuitively consider them as plurals. Moreover, treating such indefinites as plurals avoids the need to use a clumsy *his or her* to avoid sexist language.

**Everyone** is entitled to **his or her** opinion.

Nonetheless, most editors and professional writers do not accept these forms—yet. ◆

### ● 3 If the indefinite word is usually plural, make any pronouns that refer to it plural.

  plural                    plural
**Several** of the jet fighters had to have **their** wings stiffened.

  plural               plural
**Few**, however, had given **their** pilots trouble.

**4** **If the indefinite word is variable, use your judgment to determine which pronoun suits the sentence better.** In many cases, words or phrases modifying the pronoun determine its number.

> var.                                    plural              var.
> **All** of the portraits had yellowed in **their** frames. **Some** will be restored
>       plural
> to **their** original condition.

> var.                        sing.         var.
> **All** of the wine is still in **its** casks. **Some** of the vintage is certain to have
> sing.
> **its** quality evaluated.

*None* is considered variable because it is often accepted as a plural form. However, in formal writing, you should usually treat *none* as singular. Think of *none* as meaning *not one*.

> **None** of the women is reluctant to speak **her** mind.
>
> **None** of the churches has **its** doors locked.

**EXERCISE 27.3** Select the word or phrase in parentheses that would be correct in formal and college writing.

1. Anybody can learn to drive an automobile with a manual transmission if (**they are/he or she is**) coordinated.

2. But not everyone will risk (**his or her/their**) (**life/lives**) trying.

3. Few today seem eager to take (**his or her/their**) driver's tests in a five-speed.

4. Everyone learning to drive a manual car expects (**his or her/their**) car to stall at the most inopportune moment.

5. Most of all, nobody wants to stop (**his or her/their**) manual-shift car on a steep hill.

## 27c Treat collective nouns as singular or plural?

Agreement problems are common when pronouns refer to collective nouns—that is, nouns that describe groups of things: *class, team, band, government, jury.* Collective nouns like these can be either singular or plural, depending on how they are used in a sentence.

> The **chorus** sang **its** heart out.

> The **chorus** arrived and took **their** seats.

A pronoun that refers to a collective noun should be consistently either singular or plural.

To make sure that's the case, identify any collective noun in a sentence to which a pronoun refers. Choose whether to treat that noun as a single body (the *jury*) or as a group of more than one person or object (the twelve members of the *jury*). Then be consistent. If you decide to treat the word as singular, be sure that subsequent pronouns referring to it are singular. If you decide it is plural, all pronoun references should be plural.

> The **jury** rendered **its** decision. [*jury* considered singular]

> The **jury** had **their** pictures taken. [*jury* considered plural]

In most cases, your sentences will sound more natural if you regard collective nouns as single objects. Notice how awkward the following sentence seems because the collective noun is treated as plural.

> AWKWARD    The **band** are unhappy with **their** latest recordings.

> BETTER      The **band** is unhappy with **its** latest recordings.

**EXERCISE 27.4** In the following sentences, select the appropriate words in parentheses. Be prepared to defend your answers.

1. The **class** entered the lecture hall and took (**its/their**) seats, eager to hear from the architect after (**its/their**) field trip to several of his buildings.

2. He belonged to a revitalized **school** of design that had enjoyed (**its/their**) best days four decades ago.

3. The aging architect was accompanied by several **members of his firm**, carrying (**its/their**) designs in huge portfolios.

4. Students hoped that the **board of directors** of the college might give (**its/their**) blessing to a commission by the architect.

5. Any **panel of experts** was likely to cast (**its/their**) vote in favor of such a project.

## 27d Questions about agreement involving *or, nor, either . . . or, neither . . . nor*?

When the antecedents for a pronoun are nouns joined by *or, nor, either . . . or*, or *neither . . . nor*, the choice of a pronoun can be puzzling.

**●1 When two nouns joined by *or, nor, either . . . or*, or *neither . . . nor* are singular, be sure any pronoun referring to them is singular.**

sing.
**Neither Brazil nor Mexico** will raise **its** oil prices today.

**●2 When two nouns joined by *and* or *or* are plural, be sure any pronoun referring to them is plural.**

plural
**Players or managers** may file **their** grievances with the commissioner.

**●3 When a singular noun is joined to a plural noun by *or, nor, either . . . or*, or *neither . . . nor*, be sure any pronoun agrees in number (and gender) with the noun nearer to it.**

sing.                              plural                                    plural
Either poor **diet** or long, stress-filled **hours** in the office will take **their** toll on an executive's health.

plural                        sing.        sing.
Either long, stress-filled **hours** in the office or poor **diet** will take **its** toll on an executive's health.

Pronouns also agree in gender with the nearer antecedent when two nouns are joined by *or*.

masc.      fem.                 fem.
Either a **priest** or a **nun** will escort you to **her** office.

fem.      masc.               masc.
Either a **nun** or a **priest** will escort you to **his** office.

**EXERCISE 27.5**   In the sentences below, select the appropriate words in parentheses.

1. Neither the tour guide nor any of his customers had bothered to confirm (**his/their**) flight from Chicago's O'Hare Airport back to Toledo.

2. Either the ticket agents or a flight attendant working the check-in desk had misread (**their/her**) computer terminal and accidentally canceled the group's reservations.

3. Either the tourists or their guide had to make up (**their/his**) (**minds/mind**) quickly about arranging transportation back to Toledo.

4. Neither the guide nor his wife relished the thought of spending (**his/her/their**) hard-earned money on yet another expensive ticket.

5. Wandering about the vast terminal, the guide located a commuter airline willing to fly either the group or its bags to (**its/their**) destination cheaply.

# 28 Questions About Pronoun Case?

Some personal pronouns (and *who*) change their form according to how they are used in a sentence. These different forms are called **case**. **Subjective** (or **nominative**) **case** is the form a pronoun takes when it is the subject of a sentence or a clause: *I, you, she, he, it, we, they, who*. A pronoun is also in the subjective case when it follows a linking verb as a **predicate nominative**, a word which renames the subject.

> It is **I**.
>
> It was **they** who cast the deciding votes.

**Objective case** is the form a pronoun takes when something is done to it: Elena broke *them*; Will loved *her*. This is also the form a pronoun takes after a preposition: (to) *me, her, him, us, them, whom*. The subjective and objective forms of the pronouns *you* and *it* are identical.

The **possessive case** is the form a pronoun takes when it shows ownership: *my, mine, your, yours, her, hers, his, its, our, ours, their, theirs, whose*.

## 28a Questions about pronouns in subjective and objective case?

Choose subjective forms when pronouns act as subjects, objective forms when pronouns act as objects (especially in prepositional phrases).

| Chart 28.1 Pronoun Case | |
| --- | --- |
| **SUBJECTIVE FORMS** | **OBJECTIVE FORMS** |
| I | me |
| we | us |
| you | you |

*(Continued)*

**Pronoun Case**   *(Continued)*

| SUBJECTIVE FORMS | OBJECTIVE FORMS |
|---|---|
| he | him |
| she | her |
| it | it |
| they | them |
| who | whom |

⊙ **1 Check pronoun case when pronouns are paired.** The second pronoun in a pair is often troublesome. To choose the right pronoun, figure out what the pronoun does in the sentence: Is it a subject or a predicate nominative? Is it an object?

| WHICH CASE? | You and (**I/me**) don't have the latest designs yet. |
|---|---|
| | These pronouns are subjects, so the subjective form *I* is correct. |
| CORRECT | You and **I** don't have the latest designs yet. |
| WHICH CASE? | The winners are (**he/him**) and (**I/me**). |
| | The pronouns are predicate nominatives and should be in the subjective case. |
| CORRECT | The winners are **he** and **I**. |
| WHICH CASE? | Forward the email to (**he/him**) and (**I/me**). |
| | Pronouns are objects of the preposition *to*; they take the objective case. |
| CORRECT | Forward the email to **him** and **me**. |

Alternatively, conduct a simple test by taking out the first pronoun and recasting the sentence with only the troublesome pronoun. You can often tell immediately which choice to make.

| WHICH CASE? | **You and me** don't have the latest designs yet. |
|---|---|
| WRONG | **Me** don't have the latest designs yet. |
| CORRECT | **You and I** don't have the latest designs yet. |
| WHICH CASE? | The memo praised **you and she**. |
| WRONG | The memo praised **she**. |
| CORRECT | The memo praised **you and her**. |

**EXERCISE 28.1** Select the correct pronoun from the choices offered in parentheses.

1. In the reporter's opinion, neither (**she/her**) nor (**he/him**) had done a good job in covering the city's financial crisis.

2. It was likely that both political parties would now accuse (**she/her**) and (**he/him**) of media bias.

3. Knowing her colleagues at the competing TV stations, the reporter was convinced that both she and (**they/them**) had rushed their stories.

4. "You and (**I/me**) will just have to accept the criticism," the reporter told a professional colleague.

🔹 **2 Check pronoun case when first person plural pronouns are followed by nouns.** The pronoun and noun must share the same case, either subjective or objective.

| | | |
|---|---|---|
| | subjects | |
| **SUBJECTIVE** | **We** *lucky sailors* missed the storm. | |
| | | objects |
| **OBJECTIVE** | The storm missed **us** *lucky sailors*. | |
| | obj. of preposition | |
| **OBJECTIVE** | For **us** *engineers*, the job market looks promising. | |

You can test for the correct form by leaving out the noun and recasting the sentence using only the pronoun.

| **WHICH CASE?** | Us *lucky sailors* missed the storm. |
|---|---|
| **WRONG** | **Us** missed the storm. |
| **CORRECT** | **We** *lucky sailors* missed the storm. |

🔹 **3 Check pronoun case with *who* and *whom*.** In informal spoken English, the distinction between the subject form *who* and the object form *whom* (or *whoever/whomever*) is routinely ignored. In written English, however, many readers still expect the convention to be honored. The rule is easier to state than follow: Select the subjective form (*who*) when pronouns act as subjects and the objective form (*whom*) when pronouns act as objects.

The correct choice is especially important in prepositional phrases (see Section 16c-1).

| SUBJECTIVE | **Who** wrote this letter? |
| OBJECTIVE | You addressed **whom**? |
| OBJECTIVE | To **whom** did you write? |

When *who* or *whom* (or *whoever/whomever*) is part of a dependent clause, *who* or *whom* takes the form it would have in the dependent clause, not in the sentence as a whole. Constructions of this kind are quite common. The words in italics in the following examples are clauses within full sentences.

noun clause

The system rewards ***whoever*** *works hard.*

*Whoever* is the subject of the noun clause in which it appears. It has its own verb, *works.*

noun clause

***Whomever*** *the party nominates* is likely to be elected.

The pronoun is the object of *nominates.*

adverbial clause

The deficit will increase *no matter* ***whom*** *we elect president.*

The main verb of the subordinate clause is *elect* and its subject is *we.* So the pronoun *whom* is the object of *we elect* and *president* modifies *whom.* The chart on pages 449–450 tells you that *whom*, not *who*, is correct.

You can also test for the case of a pronoun in a subordinate clause by recasting it as a question and then answering the question.

| SUBORDINATE CLAUSE | **whoever/whomever** works hard |
| RECAST AS QUESTION | **Whoever** works hard? |
| | **(or) Whomever** works hard? |
| ANSWER | **She** works hard. |
| | *She* is in the subjective case. Therefore, the pronoun in the original subordinate clause will also be in the subjective case. |
| SUBJECTIVE | The system rewards **whoever** works hard. |

Here's another example.

| | |
|---|---|
| SUBORDINATE CLAUSE | **whoever/whomever** the party nominates |
| RECAST AS QUESTION | **Whoever** will the party nominate?<br>(**or**) **Whomever** will the party nominate? |
| ANSWER | The party will nominate **her**.<br>*Her* is in the objective case, so the correct pronoun choice is also the objective form. |
| OBJECTIVE | **Whomever** the party nominates is likely to be elected. |

**EXERCISE 28.2** Decide which of the pronoun forms in parentheses is correct in each of the following sentences.

1. Jon Stewart looks like a man (**whom/who**) wouldn't trust a nun with a prayer.

2. (**Whom/Who**) wouldn't like to win the state lottery?

3. To (**who/whom**) would you go for sound financial advice?

4. Are these the young children (**who/whom**) you took by bus to Santa Fe?

5. Officials couldn't determine (**who/whom**) rigged the state elections.

⬤ 4 **Check pronoun case in comparisons.** To determine pronoun case after *than* or *as*, it helps to complete the comparison.

| | |
|---|---|
| WHICH CASE? | I am taller *than* (**him/he**). |
| CORRECT | I am taller *than* **he** (is). |
| WHICH CASE? | We don't invest as much *as* (**she/her**). |
| CORRECT | We don't invest as much *as* **she** (does). |

Some comparisons can be expanded two ways.

| | |
|---|---|
| WHICH CASE? | Politics does not interest me as much *as* (**she/her**). |

**POSSIBLE EXPANSIONS** Politics does not interest me as much *as* **she** (does).

Politics does not interest me as much *as* (it interests) **her**.

In such cases, the pronoun you select will determine what the sentence means. In these situations, it's probably better to write out the full comparison.

**EXERCISE 28.3** Select the correct pronoun from the choices offered in parentheses.

1. Although the Cowardly Lion needed the Wizard's help as much as Dorothy did, the King of the Jungle was less determined than (**she/her**) to hike to Oz.

2. Dorothy probably felt more confident than (**he/him**) that she could deal with the wonderful Wizard.

3. Perhaps Dorothy could relate more easily to (**he/him**) than a lion could.

4. Although more cautious in his appraisal of the Wizard than Dorothy, the Scarecrow was no less eager for guidance than (**she/her**).

5. Perhaps the Scarecrow even feared that Dorothy would like the Wizard more than (**he/him**).

⬤**5 Check pronoun case in appositives.** *Appositives* are nouns or phrases that add information to a previous noun.

appositive
The teacher gave special help to two of the *students*, **Cheryl and me**.

When an appositive contains a pronoun, the pronoun should be in the same case as the noun it modifies.

The teacher called *two students*, **Cheryl and (I/me)**, to the front of the classroom.

*Two students*, the noun phrase being modified, is the object of *called*. So the pronoun should also be in the objective case.

The teacher called *two students*, **Cheryl and me**, to the front of the classroom.

**◉6 Check pronoun case after linking verbs.** Linking verbs, such as *to be, to seem, to appear, to feel, to become,* connect a subject to a word or phrase that extends or completes its meaning—the predicate nominative. In most cases, use the subjective case of a pronoun when it is the complement of a linking verb.

subj.   l.v.        subj. comp.

The *culprits are* obviously **they**.

Such constructions are fairly common.

> *It* is **I**.
>
> *The next CEO* of the corporation will be **she**.
>
> *You* are **who**?

In informal speech, it is acceptable to use the objective case after a linking verb.

> It's **me**.      That's **her**.

Or work around the problem. Rather than write "The director was he," reverse the order and try "He was the director."

**EXERCISE 28.4** Select the correct pronoun from the choices in parentheses below.

1. That is (**he/him**) in the office there.

2. The guilty party certainly was not (**she/her**).

3. Spying three men in uniform, we assumed that the pilots were (**they/them**).

4. They are (**who/whom**)?

5. We were surprised that the person who had complained was (**she/her**).

## 28b Difficulties with possessive pronouns?

The most common way of showing ownership in English is to add an apostrophe + -*s* to a noun: *Akilah's book*, the *dog's owner*. The familiar -'*s* is not, however, used with **personal pronouns** (or *who*): do not add an apostrophe + *-s* with personal pronouns used to show ownership (possession). This is true whether the possessive pronoun comes before or after a noun.

| | |
|---|---|
| INCORRECT | The coat is **her's**. |
| CORRECT | The coat is **hers**. |
| INCORRECT | The TV station made **it's** editorial opinion known. |
| CORRECT | The TV station made **its** editorial opinion known. |

The following examples show the various forms of possessive pronouns. Notice that they don't add apostrophes.

| BEFORE THE NOUN | AFTER THE NOUN |
|---|---|
| That is **my** *book*. | The *book* is **mine**. |
| That is **your** *book*. | The *book* is **yours**. |
| That is **her** *book*. | The *book* is **hers**. |
| That is **his** *book*. | The *book* is **his**. |
| That is **our** *book*. | The *book* is **ours**. |
| That is **their** *book*. | The *book* is **theirs**. |
| **Whose** *book* is this? | This *book* is **whose**? |

Understand, too, that although indefinite pronouns such as *everybody* or *someone* form the possessive by adding *-'s*, others, such as *all, any, each, most, none, some,* and *few,* do not.

| | |
|---|---|
| INCORRECT | **Some's** opinion |
| CORRECT | The opinion of **some** |

## 28c Confused by *its/it's* and *whose/who's*?

Don't mistake the possessive pronoun *its* for the contraction *it's* (which means *it is* or *it has*). This error is both very common and easy to fix. Remember that *its* is a possessive form; *it's* is a contraction.

| | |
|---|---|
| POSSESSIVE FORM | The iron left **its** grim outline on the silk shirt. |
| CONTRACTION | **It's** a stupid proposal. |

Of course, the apostrophe makes the contracted form—*it's*—look suspiciously like a possessive. And the possessive form—*its*—sounds like a contraction. But don't be fooled. The possessive forms of personal pronouns never take an apostrophe, whereas contractions always require one.

| | |
|---|---|
| **WRONG** | The school lost **it's** charter because of low test scores. |
| **RIGHT** | The school lost **its** charter because of low test scores. |
| **WRONG** | **Its** unlikely that the aircraft will lose **it's** way in the dark. **Its** equipped with radar. |
| **RIGHT** | **It's** unlikely that the aircraft will lose **its** way in the dark. **It's** equipped with radar. |

If you consistently misuse *its/it's*, circle these words whenever they appear in your work and then check them. It may help if you always read *it's* as *it is*. Eventually you will eliminate this error.

A related error is mistaking *whose*, a possessive pronoun, for *who's*, which is the contraction for *who is* or *who has*.

| | |
|---|---|
| **POSSESSIVE FORM** | **Whose** teammate is on first base? |
| **CONTRACTION** | **Who's** on first? |

**EXERCISE 28.5** Circle all occurrences of *its/it's* in the following passage and correct any errors.

1. Its been decades since Americans have felt as comfortable traveling in Eastern Europe as they do now.

2. Its likely that tourism will remain a major industry in Hungary, Poland, and the Czech Republic.

3. Each of these countries has much to attract tourists to its cities.

4. Yet its the small towns of Eastern Europe that many Americans may find most appealing.

5. In rural areas, sensitive travelers often get a better feel for a country and it's people.

**EXERCISE 28.6**  Review Sections 28b and 28c. Identify and correct any pronoun-related errors in the sentences below.

1. There is usually not much doubt about whose responsible for enormous environmental disasters.

2. Its not hard to spot a capsized oil tanker.

3. Yet anybodys home or yard can contribute to environmental pollution.

4. The earth is our's to protect or despoil.

5. Ecology has to be everyone's responsibility.

# 29 Questions About Pronoun Choices?

How you use pronouns can shape how readers respond to your writing. Some issues—such as point of view and sexist pronouns—have a direct impact on the rhetoric and style of what you write. Other matters, such as the proper use of *that/which* and reflexive and intensive pronouns, are more technical. But they matter to many writers concerned with language.

## 29a When to use *I, we, you,* or *one*?

Pronouns change the distance between writers and readers. Choosing *I* or *you* puts you closer to readers; using *one* creates distance.

**◑1 Use *I* when you or your opinions belong in what you're writing.** In general, avoid the first person *I* in scientific reports and expository essays.

> **WITH *I***     **I learned** through a survey **I did** that students who drive a car on campus are more likely to have jobs than those who do not.

> **REVISED**     **A survey showed** that students who drive a car on campus are likely to have jobs.

However, when you find that avoiding *I* makes you resort to an awkward passive verb, use *I* instead.

> **WORDY**     **It is believed** that procedures for voting in campus elections are too complex.

> **REVISED**     **I believe** that procedures for voting in campus elections are too complex.

**459**

You can often eliminate an awkward passive without using *I*.

**REVISED WITHOUT *I***     Procedures for voting in campus elections are too complex.

◀ ▶ **Point of Difference**

You should know that some instructors and editors simply will not allow *I* in college, professional, or scientific prose. When writing for them, respect their rules. However, most writers today recognize that using *I* is both natural and sensible even in relatively formal work. Not using *I* or *we* (when more than one author is involved) can even lead to questions about who is taking responsibility for a statement. ◆

◉2 **Use *we* whenever two or more writers are involved in a project or when you are writing to express the opinion of a group.**

> When **we** compared our surveys, **we** discovered the conflicting evidence.
>
> **We** believe that the city council has an obligation to reconsider its zoning action.

Or use the first person *we* to indicate a general condition when it is appropriate to comment editorially.

> **We** need better control of our medical care systems in the United States.

Avoid *we* or *us* as a chummy way of addressing your reader. In most college writing, *we* used this way sounds pompous.

◉3 **Use *you* to address readers personally or to give orders or directions.** *You* sounds direct, cordial, and personal. So be sure you really want your readers included when using the second person in college writing. The following sentence, for example, may be too personal. It seems to implicate readers directly in scholastic dishonesty.

**INAPPROPRIATE**     A recent student government survey suggested that **you** will cheat in two courses during **your** college career.

REVISED    A recent student government survey suggested that **most students** will cheat in two courses during **their** college careers.

Because *you* is both vague and potentially personal, it is a pronoun to avoid in most academic writing, especially reports and research projects. *You* may be more appropriate in persuasive writing, however, where your goal is to move people to act.

## 4 Use *one* to express a general thought.    *One* may sometimes be useful for conveying moral sentiments or sweeping claims.

Consider the anxiety of not knowing where **one's** next meal is coming from.

**One** learns a great deal about pre-revolutionary Russia from reading Dostoevsky.

But notice that *one* makes the sentence more formal than it would be if *one* were replaced by *I* or *you.*

**EXERCISE 29.1**  Revise the sentences below to create a passage appropriate for a college report. Pay particular attention to the words and phrases in boldface.

1.  **I was amazed to learn that** the Chinese speak a variety of dialects of a language they describe as Han.

2.  Although there are only eight major varieties of Han, **you would find them** as different from each other as one Romance language is from another.

3.  **One finds,** moreover, that each of the eight versions of Han occurs in a great many dialects, adding to **one's** linguistic confusion.

4.  **I was surprised,** however, that the Chinese use only one system of writing—a set of common ideographs.

5.  As **you** might expect, there have been efforts to reform the Chinese language to make it easier **for you** to communicate between one region and another in the vast and populous country.

# 29b Do your pronouns treat both sexes fairly?

Today members of either sex may belong to almost every profession or group—students, athletes, coal miners, truckers, secretaries, nurses. Let your pronoun usage reflect that diversity. In situations where you cannot assume that members of a group will all be male or female, be sure your language accommodates both sexes. You can do that in a variety of ways.

### ● 1 Use the expressions *he or she, him or her,* or *his or her* instead of the pronoun of either sex alone.

| | |
|---|---|
| SEXIST | Every secretary may invite **her husband**. |
| REVISED | Every secretary may invite **his or her partner**. |

Unfortunately, variations of *he or she* grow tiresome when they occur more than once in a sentence. Other expressions have been created to express gender diversity, including *he/she, s/he,* and *(s)he.* But many readers and editors don't like these inventions. So when the widely accepted *he or she* seems clumsy, try another strategy to avoid sexist usage.

### ● 2 Make singular pronoun references plural.
Because plural pronouns do not have a specific gender in English, you can often avoid the choice between *he* and *she* simply by turning singular references into plural ones.

| | |
|---|---|
| SEXIST | **Every** secretary may invite **her husband**. |
| REVISED | **All** secretar**ies** may invite **their partners**. |
| TIRESOME | Before **he or she** leaves, **each** band member should be sure **he or she** has **his or her** music. |
| REVISED | Before leaving, **all** band members should be sure **they** have **their** music. |

Notice that these revisions eliminate *he or she* entirely.

● **3 Cut any troublesome pronouns.** Here are more examples.

**ORIGINAL**   *Anybody* may bring **his or her** favorite CD.

**REVISED**   *Anybody* may bring **a** favorite CD.

**ORIGINAL**   *Nobody* should leave until **he or she** has signed the guest book.

**REVISED**   *Nobody* should leave without **signing** the guest book.

These options are useful, but they are not always available.

● **4 Switch between *he* and *she*.** In most cases, you can vary the pronouns sensibly and naturally within chunks of prose—between paragraphs, for example, or between the examples in a series. Handled skillfully, the shift between masculine and feminine references need not attract a reader's attention.

> The dean of students knew that any student could purchase term papers through mail-order term paper services. If **he** could afford the scam, a student might construct **his** entire college career around papers **he** had purchased.
>
> Yet the dean also acknowledged that the typical plagiarist was rarely so grossly dishonest and calculating. **She** tended to resort to such highly unethical behavior only when **she** believed an assignment was beyond **her** capabilities or **her** workload was excessive.

Avoid varying pronoun gender within individual sentences.

**EXERCISE 29.2** Revise the following sentences to make them read better and to eliminate exclusionary pronouns. Treat the sentences as part of one paragraph.

1. Earlier this century, a laborer might have feared that heavy equipment would mangle his limbs or that pollutants might damage his lungs.

2. Today a worker has to be concerned with new threats to her health.

3. Anybody who faces a computer terminal eight hours a day must worry about his exposure to radiation and wonder whether his muscles and

joints are being damaged by the repetitive limb motions required by his job.

4. Frankly, the typical worker is often so concerned with her job performance that she may not consider that her workplace poses risks.

5. Of course, every worker wants their job to be safe.

## 29c Questions about *that, which,* and *who*?

In some situations, you must decide when to use the pronouns *that* and *which*. You may have learned a rule that requires *that* as the lead-in for essential or restrictive modifiers (that is, for clauses that strictly limit the meaning of the word modified).

| | |
|---|---|
| ESSENTIAL CLAUSE | The car **that hit me** rolled into the shallow ditch. |

The same rule insists that *which* be used with nonessential or nonrestrictive clauses (that is, with modifiers that add information not crucial to the meaning of a sentence).

| | |
|---|---|
| NONESSENTIAL CLAUSE | My vehicle, **which is a sport utility**, sustained little damage. |

Yet in reading you may have noticed that some writers use *which* interchangeably.

| | |
|---|---|
| ESSENTIAL CLAUSE | The car **which hit me** rolled into the shallow ditch. |

What form is correct? And when is *who* a better alternative to *which* and *that*?

**1 Use *that* to introduce essential (restrictive) clauses.** A clause introduced by *that* will almost always be essential. No commas are used around such clauses.

The concept **that intrigued the shareholders most** involved profit sharing.

Only the report **that I wrote** recommended that concept.

**2 Use *which* to introduce nonessential (nonrestrictive) clauses.** Such clauses are ordinarily surrounded by commas.

| | |
|---|---|
| **NONESSENTIAL CLAUSE** | The Web site, **which** is not on the university's server, contains controversial advice about plagiarism. |
| **NONESSENTIAL CLAUSE** | The agency, **which** was created in 1978, helps businesses use energy more efficiently. |

But understand that many writers use *which* to introduce essential clauses as well. In these clauses, context and punctuation may determine whether a *which* clause is essential or not. If the clause is essential, no commas separate it from the rest of the sentence; if nonessential, commas enclose the clause.

| | |
|---|---|
| **ESSENTIAL CLAUSE** | The business plan **which** intrigued the shareholders was the simplest one. |
| **NONESSENTIAL CLAUSE** | The business plan, **which** intrigued the shareholders, was quite simple. |

Some readers still prefer to distinguish between *that* and *which* even though the distinction is disappearing in general usage. For more about this issue, see Section 30i.

**3 Use *who* rather than *that* or *which* when modifying a person.**

| | |
|---|---|
| **INAPPROPRIATE** | The woman **that** was promoted is my boss. |
| **BETTER** | The woman **who** was promoted is my boss. |
| **INAPPROPRIATE** | The delegates, **which** represented all regions of the country, met in Philadelphia for their convention. |
| **BETTER** | The delegates, **who** represented all regions of the country, met in Philadelphia for their convention. |

**EXERCISE 29.3** Decide among *that/which/who* in the following sentences. Add commas where needed.

1. Charlie Chaplin's tramp (**that/which/who**) wore a derby, baggy trousers, and a mustache may still be the most recognized character on film.

2. The popularity (**that/which/who**) Chaplin had in the early days of film may never be equaled either.

3. His graceful gestures and matchless acrobatics (**that/which/who**) some critics likened to ballet were perfectly suited to the silent screen.

4. A flaw (**that/which/who**) weakens many of Chaplin's films is sentimentality.

5. Chaplin's tramp made a last appearance in *The Great Dictator* (1940) (**that/which/who**) satirized Hitler's regime.

## 29d Questions about reflexive and intensive pronouns?

**Reflexive** and **intensive pronouns** are created when *-self* is added to singular personal pronouns and *-selves* to plural personal pronouns: *myself, yourself, herself, himself, itself, oneself, ourselves, yourselves, themselves*. These words are *reflexive* in sentences like the following, where both the subject and the object of an action are the same person or thing.

> subj.       obj.
> *They* took **themselves** too seriously.

They are *intensive* when they modify a noun or another pronoun to add emphasis.

> *Warren* **himself** admitted he was responsible.

> noun       pron.
> *I* never vote **myself**.

**1 Don't use reflexive pronouns to make sentences sound more formal.** The basic pronoun form is adequate.

NONSTANDARD   The memo is for Ms. Matthews and **yourself**.

REVISED   The memo is for Ms. Matthews and **you**.

Use the pronoun reflexively only when the subject and object in a sentence refer to the same person or thing.

subj.   obj.
*Maggie* rediscovered **herself** in her paintings.

subj.   obj.
*Jones* had only **himself** to blame.

Similarly, don't use *myself* in place of a more suitable *I* or *me*.

NONSTANDARD   *Jose and myself* wrote the **lab report**.

REVISED   *Jose and I* wrote the **lab report**.

Compare the sentence above to a similar one using *myself* correctly as an intensive pronoun.

*I* wrote the lab report **myself**.

**2 Use intensive pronouns for emphasis.**

The gift is for *you* **yourself**.

The *residents* did all the plumbing and wiring **themselves**.

**3 Never use *hisself* or *theirselves*.** Although you may hear these expressions—especially *theirselves*—in speech, the correct forms in writing are always *himself* and *themselves*.

WRONG   They saw **theirselves** on television.

CORRECT   They saw **themselves** on television.

**EXERCISE 29.4**  Correct any problems with reflexive or intensive pronouns in the sentences below.

1. "God helps them who help themselves" is an adage credited to Benjamin Franklin.

2. The delegates to the Constitutional Convention in 1787 were not sure they could agree among theirselves on a new form of government.

3. George Washington hisself presided over the convention.

4. Aaron and myself wrote a paper on Madison's contribution to the Constitution.

5. You might want to read about the topic yourself.

# 30 Questions About Modifiers?

Much of the work in sentences is handled by modifiers—especially adjectives and adverbs (see Section 16b). These modifying words and phrases expand what we know about subjects, verbs, and other sentence elements. In this chapter, we examine some issues writers face when dealing with modifiers, including familiar problems such as misplaced modifiers and double negatives.

We also help you to distinguish between modifying clauses that are essential (restrictive) or nonessential (nonrestrictive), a tricky issue in some circumstances.

## 30a What's the problem with misplaced or dangling modifiers?

Adjectives and adverbs can cause confusion if they become detached from the words they are supposed to modify in a sentence. Two forms of this common problem are **misplaced modifying phrases** and **dangling modifiers**.

A modifier is considered *misplaced* when it hooks up with the wrong word or phrase, sometimes with comic effect.

| | |
|---|---|
| MISPLACED MODIFIER | **Carved from solid oak**, the angry mother could not break down the door. |
| CORRECTED | The angry mother could not break down the door **carved from solid oak**. |

A modifier is termed *dangling* when it doesn't have a plausible word or phrase to attach itself to in a sentence. As a result, it doesn't make a logical connection.

**469**

| DANGLING MODIFIER | **Infuriated by the groom's boorishness**, the wedding was postponed.<br><br>The boldfaced phrase doesn't describe anything in the main clause of the sentence. The sentence needs a person who might be infuriated. |
|---|---|
| CORRECTED | **Infuriated by the groom's boorishness**, the bride postponed the wedding. |

Following are strategies for avoiding problems with misplaced or dangling modifiers.

## ◉1 Be sure that an introductory modifying phrase is followed by the word it modifies.

Sometimes you will have to supply a word that the introductory phrase can modify. In other cases, the whole sentence may have to be rearranged.

| MISPLACED MODIFIER | **Insulting and predictable**, fewer and fewer television viewers are attracted to the comedian's monologues.<br><br>The boldfaced phrase doesn't describe *viewers*; it describes *monologues*. |
|---|---|
| REVISION | **Insulting and predictable**, the comedian's monologues attracted fewer and fewer television viewers. |

## ◉2 Supply a word for a dangling modifier to modify.

This often means rewriting the entire sentence, since you must usually add a word or phrase that the sentence alludes to but doesn't actually include. For example:

| DANGLING MODIFIER | **On returning to the office**, the furniture had been rearranged. |
|---|---|
| ONE POSSIBLE REVISION | **On returning to the office**, the staff found that the furniture had been rearranged. |

## ◉3 Distinguish between absolute phrases and dangling modifiers.

Some modifying phrases may look like dangling modifiers but are actually **absolute phrases**; that is, they are complete in themselves, serving only to give additional information about the sentence of which they are a part.

absolute

**Given the fiasco at dinner**, the guests weren't surprised when Martha pushed her husband into the pool.

absolute

**To be blunt**, Axel is a whiny nerd who deserves to be fired.

For more on absolute phrases, see Section 16c-3.

**EXERCISE 30.1** Rewrite or rearrange these sentences, placing modifiers in appropriate positions. You may need to add a noun for the modifier to modify. Not all of the sentences need to be revised.

1. Although they are among the most famous of reptiles, biologists have only recently begun to study rattlesnakes.

2. Rattlers belong to the family of pit vipers according to scientists, taking their name from the two characteristic pits on their snouts.

3. Given their lethal capabilities, it is not surprising that pit vipers are universally loathed.

4. Despite their fearful reputation, however, people are seldom bitten by the snakes unless they are provoked.

## 30b Where should adjectives go?

Adjectives are words that modify nouns or pronouns. They explain how many, which color, which one, and so on. All the words in boldface here function as adjectives.

A **simple** tax return is **rare** these days.

The **darkest** nights are **moonless**.

**German** beers pour slowly.

The truck, **tall** and **ungainly**, rolled down the hill.

In English, single-word adjectives usually come before the word or phrase they modify: **red** apple, **outstanding** athlete. Phrases and clauses may come before or after the words they refer to.

> the woman **in the red dress**
>
> the guy **whom I dated in high school**
>
> **Resplendent in his fur hat**, the soldier crossed the square.

Whatever kind of modifier you're using, you must position it carefully to avoid ambiguity and awkward pileups. An adjective becomes ambiguous when readers can't tell which word it modifies.

| | |
|---|---|
| AMBIGUOUS | Adam had his **enthusiastic parents' support**. |
| | *Enthusiastic* attaches itself to *parents* instead of to *support*. |
| CLARIFIED | Adam had his **parents' enthusiastic support**. |

Adjectives pile up when writers place one modifier after another until readers get confused or bored.

| | |
|---|---|
| TEDIOUS | **Recent, controversial, divisive** gambling legislation met defeat in the state legislature. |
| REVISED | **Recent** gambling legislation, **controversial and divisive**, met defeat in the state legislature. |

**●1 Relocate adjectives that are potentially confusing or ambiguous.** You may have to read your sentences carefully to appreciate how they might be misread. Better still, ask a friend to read your work and point out where readers might get confused.

| | |
|---|---|
| AMBIGUOUS | The **long-lost diplomat's memoirs** were revealing. |
| | Does *long-lost* go with *diplomat* or *memoirs*? |
| CLARIFIED | The **diplomat's long-lost memoirs** were revealing. |
| AMBIGUOUS | The **ingenious Web site's designer** resigned. |
| | Does *ingenious* go with *Web site* or *designer*? |
| CLARIFIED | The **ingenious designer of the Web site** resigned. |

**●2 Consider placing adjectives after the words or phrases they modify.** You can avoid tedious strings of adjectives this way and make sentences more graceful.

| TEDIOUS | A **new, powerful, quick**, and **easy-to-use** database program was installed today. |
|---|---|
| REVISED | A new database program, **powerful, quick**, and **easy to use**, was installed today. |

**EXERCISE 30.2** Rearrange the adjectives to make each of these sentences clearer or more effective. Several options are possible.

1. Lisa wanted to find a knowledgeable and squeaky clean neighborhood attorney to help her prepare her rezoning proposal.

2. She viewed the negative council members' attitudes as a challenge to her persuasive abilities.

3. Before explaining her plan, Lisa asked for the undivided city council's attention.

4. Obtaining a hearing was essential if she were to overcome the stubborn city planner's resistance.

## 30c How do you manage predicate adjectives?

Many people have problems selecting the right term to follow linking verbs such as *seem, become, look, appear, feel, smell*. An adjective that follows a linking verb is called a **predicate adjective**.

> I *feel* **bad**.
>
> He *seems* **uneasy**.
>
> Iris *appears* **calm**.

**1 Remember that only adjectives, not adverbs, can modify a noun.** So after a linking verb you need an adjective—not an adverb—to modify a noun. In the following example, the first version of the sentence shows the incorrect *adverb* modifier; the second version shows the correct *adjective* form.

INCORRECT   The accountant feels **awfully** about underestimating your quarterly taxes.

CORRECT   The accountant feels **awful** about underestimating your quarterly taxes.

The same principle applies when you modify a noun that acts as the object in a sentence, as in the following example.

INCORRECT   The accountant kept the leather in his Lexus **flawlessly**.
To describe *leather* (a noun), the writer should use the adjective form (*flawless*) rather than the adverb (*flawlessly*).

CORRECT   The accountant kept the leather in his Lexus **flawless**.

● **2 Pay special attention to *good/well* and *bad/badly*.** *Good* and *bad* are always adjectives. Use *good* (or *bad*) after a linking verb when you are modifying the subject of the sentence.

Tom Tewa looks **good** on paper.

His academic record is especially **good**.

Tom feels **bad** since his divorce.

In academic or formal writing, *good* and *bad* are *not* used as adverbs to describe the action of verbs.

INCORRECT   Tom's children play **good** with other children.

INCORRECT   But they usually eat **bad**, like most five-year olds.

That's the job of *well*, which usually is an adverb, or *badly*, which always is an adverb. In the following sentences, for example, *well* and *badly* clearly modify the verbs in the sentences (*play, speak*) by explaining how the actions are performed.

CORRECT   Tom's children play **well** with other children.

CORRECT   But they usually eat **badly**, like most five-year olds.

What makes matters tricky is that *well* can also function as an adjective when referring to someone's health.

Madeline hasn't felt **well** since she returned from New York.

Tommy doesn't look **well** either since the trip.

Remember, however, that *badly* is never an adjective. Although you may hear people say, "I feel badly about that," the construction is incorrect.

| | |
|---|---|
| **INCORRECT** | I feel **badly** because I have a cold. |
| **CORRECT** | I feel **bad** because I have a cold. |
| **INCORRECT** | Jackson feels **badly** about hitting my Mustang. |
| **CORRECT** | Jackson feels **bad** about hitting my Mustang. |

**EXERCISE 30.3** In these sentences, replace the boldfaced modifier with a better one.

1. In developed countries, most people feel **confidently** that their drinking water is safe.

2. In many parts of the world, however, even water that looks **well** can be full of bacteria and pollution.

3. Some major relief organizations feel **optimistically** that they can bring clean water to the rural areas of underdeveloped nations.

4. They teach villagers how to keep a sanitation system running **good**.

5. But parents who know that their children's drinking water should be boiled feel **badly** because often they cannot afford the fuel to boil it.

## 30d Questions about absolute adjectives?

Some words called *absolute adjectives* cannot be compared or qualified—at least not logically. For example, since *equal* means "exactly the same," you shouldn't write that something is *more equal* any more than you'd say it is *more empty*. Similarly, either a thing is *perfect* or it's flawed. An object is either *unique* or there are others like it.

In practice, writers and speakers do qualify absolute expressions all the time, often quite meaningfully. We know what it means to say something is *almost perfect* or *quite pregnant*. Even the preamble of the Constitution describes "a more perfect union," and the pigs in George Orwell's satire *Animal Farm* are famously *more equal* than other animals. But in most cases you should avoid using qualifiers (such as *less, more, most, least, very*) with the following absolute words: *unique, perfect, singular, empty, equal, full, definite, complete, absolute*, and, of course, *pregnant*.

Consider these examples.

| | |
|---|---|
| ILLOGICAL | We doubted that the new operating system was **absolutely perfect**. |
| REVISED | We doubted that the new operating system was **perfected yet**. |
| ILLOGICAL | Jamie's story is **more unique** than Jordan's. |
| REVISED | Jamie's story is **unique**; Jordan's is not. |

**EXERCISE 30.4** Working with other students in a group, read over these sentences and decide which ones have faulty modifiers and which might be acceptable. Confer to decide how any problems with modifiers might be solved.

1. The technician assured me that the service work on my computer was almost complete.

2. The machine had frozen because my hard drive was totally full of illegal downloads.

3. The repair had required a very complete erasure of my files.

4. Now my drive was mostly empty of music and video files.

## 30e Questions about adverb form?

Adverbs are words that modify verbs, adjectives, or other adverbs, explaining where, when, and how. Many, but not all, adverbs end in *-ly*.

The Secretary of State spoke **angrily** to the press. modifies verb *spoke*

The water was **extremely** cold. modifies adjective *cold*

The candidate spoke **quite** evasively. modifies adverb *evasively*

Some adverbs have both short and long forms.

| slow/slowly | fair/fairly | rough/roughly |
|---|---|---|
| quick/quickly | tight/tightly | deep/deeply |

The problem for many writers is that the short adverb forms look suspiciously like adjectives. Is it correct then to say "drive slow" or "tie it tight" instead of "drive slowly" and "tie it tightly"? The answer is "Yes"—but you have to consider your audience.

In most cases, the short form of the adverb sounds more casual than the long form. Consequently, in most academic and business situations, you'll do better to use the *-ly* form.

> **COLLOQUIAL** The employees expected to be treated **fair**.
>
> **STANDARD** The employees expected to be treated **fairly**.

**EXERCISE 30.5** If necessary, modify the boldfaced verbs for an academic audience.

1. Max was **real** surprised when he got a response from the IRS to his suggestion.

2. The local IRS director seemed to take his ideas for clearer tax forms very **serious**.

3. She had written back to Max **quick**.

4. But Max reacted **bad** when the IRS rejected his proposals.

## 30f Where should adverbs go?

Adverbs can take any of several positions in a sentence. For example:

> George daydreamed **endlessly** about his vacation, **thoroughly** reviewing each travel brochure.
>
> **Endlessly** George daydreamed about his vacation, reviewing each travel brochure **thoroughly**.

But because adverbs are so mobile, it's also easy to drop them in inappropriate spots, creating confusing or ambiguous sentences.

| ADVERB MISPLACED | Analyzing an argument **effectively** improves it. |
| | Does *effectively* go with *analyzing* or *improves*? |

### ◉1 Place adverbs so it is clear which words they modify.

| ADVERB MISPLACED | Before the Battle of Agincourt, King Henry V urged his troops to fight **eloquently**. |
| ADVERB REPOSITIONED | Before the Battle of Agincourt, King Henry V **eloquently** urged his troops to fight. |
| ADVERB MISPLACED | Hearing the guard's footsteps approach **quickly** Mark emptied the safe. |
| | The reader doesn't know whether *quickly* goes with *approach* or *emptied*. |
| ADVERB REPOSITIONED | Hearing the guard's footsteps approach Mark **quickly** emptied the safe. |

A comma after *approach* in either sentence would also clarify the meaning.

### ◉2 Place the adverbs *almost, even*, and *only* logically near the words they modify to ensure accurate interpretations. In everyday speech, people usually ignore this convention. But you'll want to be more precise in writing. Notice the ambiguities these words cause in the following sentences because they are misplaced.

| ADVERB MISPLACED | Much to his dismay, Connor realized he had **almost** dated every woman at the party. |
| | Putting *almost* next to *dated* implies that Connor had dated none of the women—a possibility, but probably not what the writer means. |
| ADVERB BETTER PLACED | Much to his dismay, Connor realized he had dated **almost** every woman at the party. |
| CONFUSING | Zoe **even** thought time spent driving to the office could be used productively. |
| CLEARER | Zoe thought **even** time spent driving to the office could be used productively. |

**Even** Zoe thought time spent driving to the office could be used productively.

CONFUSING          Javier **only** plays the piano.

CLEARER           Javier plays **only** the piano.
                        **Only** Javier plays the piano.

**EXERCISE 30.6** Rewrite the sentences to clarify them.

1. People who attend the theater often complain that the manners of many audience members are boorish.

2. Sitting next to a woman who spends most of the evening unwrapping Tootsie Rolls slowly can provoke even the most saintly theatergoer to violence.

3. Cellular phones, beepers, and wristwatch alarms even go off routinely.

4. For their part, actors marvel at how audiences today only manage to cough during the quietest moments of a play.

# 30g What's wrong with double negatives?

Sentences that say *no* in two different ways are emphatic and usually very colloquial.

**Can't never** remember whatshername's name!

They make their point, but you need to avoid them in academic and professional writing.

● **1 Check that you don't have two *no* words (a *double negative*) in the same sentence or independent clause.** In addition to *no*, look for such words as *not, nothing, nobody,* and *never.* If you've doubled them, you can usually just drop or alter a single word.

DOUBLE NEGATIVE    That cell phone will **not** work **no way.**
CORRECTED            That cell phone will **never** work.

| | |
|---|---|
| **DOUBLE NEGATIVE** | The child does **not** want **nobody** tying his shoes. |
| **CORRECTED** | The child does **not** want **anybody** tying his shoes. |

**2 Don't mix the adverbs *hardly, scarcely,* or *barely* with another negative word or phrase.** Such pairings create double negatives, which should be edited.

| | |
|---|---|
| **DOUBLE NEGATIVE** | The morning was so cool and clear that the hikers **couldn't hardly** wait to get started. |
| **CORRECTED** | The morning was so cool and clear that the hikers **could hardly** wait to get started. |

Double negatives shouldn't be confused with negative statements that express ideas indirectly—and perhaps with ironic twists. Consider the difference in tone between these simple sentences, framed negatively and positively.

| | |
|---|---|
| **NEGATIVE** | The proposal was not unintelligent. |
| **POSITIVE** | The proposal was intelligent. |
| **NEGATIVE** | Chris was hardly unattractive. |
| **POSITIVE** | Chris was attractive. |

**EXERCISE 30.7** Rewrite sentences that contain double negatives to eliminate the problem.

1. Some critics claim that in this media age, young people barely don't read anymore.

2. Yet many cities haven't never had so many bookstores.

3. Many bookstores aren't no longer just places to buy books.

4. They serve as community centers where people can be entertained without ever buying no books.

# 30h How do comparatives and superlatives differ?

The comparative and superlative forms of most adjectives and a few adverbs can be expressed two ways.

*ugly* (an adjective)
**Comparative**      uglier          more ugly
**Superlative**      ugliest         most ugly

*slowly* (an adverb)
**Comparative**      slower          more slowly
**Superlative**      slowest         most slowly

As a general rule, use *-er* and *-est* endings with words of one syllable and *more* and *most* (or *less* and *least*) with words of two or more syllables.

Their group is **richer** than ours.

This group is the **most conservative**.

The candidate talked **faster** than the moderator.

The incumbent speaks **more decisively** than the challenger.

Some modifiers have irregular comparatives and superlatives.

| MODIFIER | COMPARATIVE | SUPERLATIVE |
|---|---|---|
| good | better | best |
| well | better | best |
| bad | worse | worst |
| badly | worse | worst |
| little | less | least |
| many, much | more | most |
| some | more | most |

**1 Use the comparative, not the superlative, when you are comparing two items.** That means using an adverb or adjective with an *-er* ending or modified by *more* or *less*.

| | |
|---|---|
| INCORRECT | That twin is the **smartest** of the pair. |
| CORRECT | That twin is the **smarter** of the pair. |
| INCORRECT | Of the two speakers, Casey speaks **most persuasively**. |
| CORRECT | Of the two speakers, Casey speaks **more persuasively**. |

### ● 2 Use the superlative when comparing more than two items.

In most cases when you compare three or more things or qualities, you need to use *-est* adjectives or adverbs or preface the modifiers with *most* or *least*.

| | |
|---|---|
| INCORRECT | Of all New York skyscrapers, the Empire State Building is **taller**. |
| CORRECT | Of all New York skyscrapers, the Empire State Building is **tallest**. |

### ● 3 Avoid using two comparative or two superlative forms in the same phrase.

| | |
|---|---|
| INCORRECT | McDougal is a **more tougher** boss than Gonzalcz is. |
| CORRECT | McDougal is a **tougher** boss than Gonzalez is. |
| INCORRECT | Paula Sung is the **most smartest** lawyer in her firm. |
| CORRECT | Paula Sung is the **smartest** lawyer in her firm. |

### ● 4 Make sure comparisons are complete enough to be clear.

*Incomplete comparisons* come in two common forms. The first kind doesn't provide the second term of the comparison. "My paper is better" is an incomplete comparison. A complete comparison will answer the question "Better than *what*?"

Often the context makes stating the second term unnecessary. When you and a friend have been comparing your writing class papers, you won't need to say "Your paper is better than mine" for the point to be clear. In other cases, leaving off the second term invites confusion.

| | |
|---|---|
| CONFUSING | People who live in rural areas are **healthier**. |

Are these people healthier than people everywhere else? Or are they healthier than some specific group of people to whom they are being compared?

CLEARER    People who live in rural areas are **healthier than** people who live in heavily industrialized cities, but not **as healthy as** people who live in newer suburban areas near major cities.

The second kind of incomplete comparison leaves out important words needed to make the comparison clear.

CONFUSING    Sally is **more afraid** of dogs **than** Jerry.

This sentence might be read two ways.

Sally is more afraid of dogs than Jerry is.
Sally is more afraid of dogs than she is of Jerry.

To complete the comparison, supply the words that make your point clear.

**EXERCISE 30.8** Choose the appropriate forms of comparison in the following sentences.

1. Today community librarians are constantly trying to decide what is (**more/most**) important: expanding computer facilities or buying more books.

2. These librarians consider who among their clients has the (**greater/greatest**) need—schoolchildren, working adults, or retired people.

3. In general, librarians enjoy the reputation of being among the (**most helpful/helpfullest**) of city employees.

4. In good libraries, librarians are also likely to be among the (**most bright/brightest**) city employees.

5. Well-trained librarians, or information specialists as they are often called today, will find their (**better/best**) job prospects in medium-sized cities with growing populations.

## 30i Questions about nonessential and essential modifiers?

Writers sometimes puzzle over how to introduce (Section 29c) or how to punctuate (Section 36b) nonessential (or *nonrestrictive*) and essential (or *restrictive*) modifiers. In either case, you first have to understand and reliably identify these structures.

● **1 Understand nonessential modifiers.** A modifier is **nonessential** when it adds information to a sentence but can be cut without a loss of sense. It is typically surrounded by commas.

| | |
|---|---|
| WITH NONESSENTIAL MODIFIER | The police officers, **who were wearing their dress uniforms**, marched in front of the mayor's car. |
| MODIFIER REMOVED | The police officers marched in front of the mayor's car. |

Useful descriptive information is lost when the nonessential modifier is cut, but the sentence still works.

● **2 Understand essential modifiers.** When you can't remove a modifying expression from a sentence without significantly affecting its meaning, you have an *essential modifier*—which is not surrounded by commas. The sentence may make little sense with the modifier cut.

| | |
|---|---|
| ESSENTIAL MODIFIER | Diamonds **that are synthetically produced** are less expensive than natural diamonds. |
| ESSENTIAL MODIFIER REMOVED | Diamonds are less expensive than natural diamonds. |
| ESSENTIAL MODIFIER | We missed the only speaker **whose work dealt with business ethics**. |
| ESSENTIAL MODIFIER REMOVED | We missed the only speaker. |

Understand, however, that context may sometimes determine whether a modifier is essential. Remember this sentence with a nonessential modifier?

> NONESSENTIAL The police officers, **who were wearing their dress uniforms**, marched in front of the mayor's car.

We can make its modifier essential just by pairing the sentence with another that changes its overall meaning by setting up a significant contrast.

> ESSENTIAL The police officers **who were wearing their dress uniforms** marched in front of the mayor's car. The officers **who were in plain clothes** mingled with the crowd as part of a security detail.

Notice that the punctuation changes, too, with the modifiers no longer surrounded by commas.

Any clause introduced by *that* will be essential (restrictive) and should not be surrounded by commas. (See Section 29c.)

> WRONG The committee, that approved the boycott, was abolished.
>
> RIGHT The committee that approved the boycott was abolished.

**EXERCISE 30.9** Following the model provided, first write a sentence with a nonessential modifier. Then add a second sentence that would make the modifier in the first sentence essential. Be sure your version shows the same changes in punctuation that occur in the model.

> NONESSENTIAL The students, who had stood for hours in line, applauded when the ticket window opened.
>
> ESSENTIAL The students **who had stood for hours in line** applauded when the ticket window opened. Those **who had only just arrived** despaired at ever getting seats for the game.

# 31 Is English a Second Language for You (ESL)?

## by Jocelyn Steer and Carol Rhoades

ESL (English as a Second Language) is still the most familiar term to designate language instruction for people whose native tongue may not be English. But the expression probably fails to capture the circumstances of many people in college writing classes today. English may indeed be a second language for some writers—or a third or fourth. For others, English and another language may play equal, if different, roles, one the language of home and community, the other of school and workplace. For people living in border regions, two national languages may merge, so much so that so-called ESL problems may reflect attempts to negotiate hybrid grammars and vocabularies. We continue to use ESL as a familiar term, but appreciate the diversity of writers for whom more technical instruction in edited American English may be helpful. There is no single type of ESL writer.

That said, it is obvious that you will face challenges while working to express ideas in a new language. Writing in a familiar language is not always simple, and writing in a second can be even harder. But because you have experienced the grammatical systems and vocabularies of at least two languages, you have already acquired a lot of linguistic knowledge and skill that should help you become a proficient writer in English.

The next three chapters of this book are designed to help you to build on your language skills and further develop your abilities to manage English.

- This chapter, **Chapter 31**, reviews common problem areas for ESL writers. We list common errors you need to be aware of as you proofread your own writing and identify resources to which you can turn for more help. Also look for the boxed **ESL Tips**, which feature specific advice from successful ESL writers and instructors.
- **Chapter 32** gives detailed guidelines for choosing the proper verb forms in your writing.

- **Chapter 33** offers detailed advice for using gerunds, articles, count and noncount nouns, and other grammatical elements that ESL writers often ask questions about.

Of course, even though these three chapters focus specifically on the needs of ESL writers, you will also find useful material in other chapters. See Chapters 22 to 30 for general discussions of grammar and mechanics. (Chart 31.2 on pages 493–494 lists the most relevant sections of these chapters.)

## 31a Common problem areas for ESL writers

It's always a good idea to proofread papers for grammar and punctuation errors before handing in the final copy. (See Section 5c.) Reading your work aloud can help you find errors that you may not otherwise spot. You'll find that the mistakes you notice when you are proofreading are usually mistakes you know how to correct. Many errors that instructors mark on final drafts could probably have been corrected by more thorough proofreading.

If you know what your most common errors are, check for them first and then look for other problems. Also, make sure that you haven't unconsciously typed some words or word endings in your own language rather than English. This can happen even if you are thinking in English as you write.

In this section, you'll find a list of the most common problems for ESL writers—and their solutions.

---

**ESL Tip**

**State Your Thesis Early**  Monika Shehi, Albania

 When I came to America, I found writing papers to be an intimidating task. When I wrote papers in Albania, I would start with an idea and follow wherever my thoughts led, often progressing to several new ideas. My American professors found my papers very chaotic, because in U.S. universities, most papers are about establishing and developing one main point. Once I became aware of that basic structure, writing became much easier. Now I begin a draft by determining my main idea, then supplying evidence to support that idea.

**●1 Be sure each clause has a subject.** Every clause in English must have a subject, except for imperative sentences ("Sit down").

**The subject is missing.**

| INCORRECT | ∧Is difficult to write in English. |
| CORRECT | **It** is difficult to write in English. |
| | You must have *it* before the verb *is*. |

**●2 Be sure a main or an auxiliary verb isn't missing.**

**The main verb is missing.**

| INCORRECT | The teacher∧extremely helpful. *verb missing* |
| CORRECT | The teacher **is** extremely helpful. |

**The auxiliary verb is missing.**

| INCORRECT | Hurry! The plane∧leaving right now. *verb missing* |
| CORRECT | Hurry! The plane **is** leaving right now. |

**●3 Don't forget the *-s* on verbs used with third person singular nouns and pronouns (*he, she, it*).** If this is a problem for you, check all present tense verbs to make sure you haven't forgotten an *-s*.

| INCORRECT | The library close at 5:00 today. *3rd person sing. -s* |
| CORRECT | The library close**s** at 5:00 today. |

When you have the auxiliary *do* or *does* in a sentence, add *-s* to the auxiliary, not to the main verb.

| INCORRECT | He don't knows the answer to the question. |
| | *3rd person sing. -s* |
| CORRECT | He **doesn't** know the answer to the question. |

**●4 Don't forget *-ed* endings on past participles.** Check your papers to be sure that you use the past participle (*-ed* ending) for verbs in the following cases. (See Section 23b for a list of the three parts of a verb.)

**In passive voice (see Section 23e).**

| INCORRECT | The amenities were **provide** by the hotel. |
|-----------|--------------------------------------------------|
| CORRECT   | The amenities were **provided** by the hotel. |
| INCORRECT | The documents were **alter** by the thief. |
| CORRECT   | The documents were **altered** by the thief. |

**In the past perfect tense (see Section 32a).**

| INCORRECT | Juan had **finish** the race before Fred came. |
|-----------|--------------------------------------------------|
| CORRECT   | Juan had **finished** the race before Fred came. |

**In participle adjectives (see Section 16c-2).**

| INCORRECT | She was **frighten** by the dark. |
|-----------|--------------------------------------------------|
| CORRECT   | She was **frightened** by the dark. |

Be sure that you *don't* add endings to infinitives.

| INCORRECT | George started to **prepared** dinner. |
|-----------|--------------------------------------------------|
| CORRECT   | George started to **prepare** dinner. |

● **5 Don't confuse adjective pairs like *bored* and *boring*.** The following sentences are very different in meaning, although they look similar.

John is bored.
This means that John is bored by *something*—maybe his class or his homework; it is a feeling he has as a result of something.

John is boring.
This means that John has a personality that is not interesting; he is a boring person.

The ending of the adjective, *-ed* or *-ing*, is what creates a difference in meaning. Adjectives ending in *-ed* have a passive meaning. Adjectives ending in *-ing* have an active meaning. (See Section 23e for an explanation of passive voice.)

The English spelling system often confuses Jorge.

| *-ED* ENDING | Jorge is **confused** by the English spelling system. passive |
|--------------|--------------------------------------------------|
|              | The **confused** student looked up words in his spelling dictionary. passive |
| *-ING* ENDING | English spelling is **confusing**. active |
|              | It is a **confusing** system. active |

Joan's work satisfies her.

|                  |                                              |
|------------------|----------------------------------------------|
| *-ED* ENDING     | She is **satisfied** by her work. passive    |
|                  | She is a **satisfied** employee. passive     |
| *-ING* ENDING    | Her work is **satisfying**. active           |
|                  | Joan does **satisfying** work. active        |

Chart 31.1 shows some common pairs of adjectives that confuse students, along with the preposition that is used after the *-ed* adjectives.

---

**Chart 31.1    Adjective Pairs**

| | | | |
|---|---|---|---|
| amusing | amused by | exciting | excited by/about |
| annoying | annoyed by | frightening | frightened by |
| boring | bored by | interesting | interested in |
| confusing | confused by | irritating | irritated by |
| embarrassing | embarrassed by | satisfying | satisfied with |

---

**6 Avoid repeating sentence elements.** You may find that you repeat unnecessary words in your sentences. Be on your guard for the three types of repetition shown in these examples.

**In adjective clauses.**

The store that I told you about ~~it~~ closed down.
*It is not necessary because that replaces it.*

The man whom I met ~~him~~ yesterday was kind.
*Whom replaces him.*

The school where I go ~~there~~ is very expensive.
*Where replaces there.*

**In the subject of the sentence.**

My brother ~~he~~ is the director of the hospital.
*Because my brother and he refer to the same person, the he is unnecessary repetition.*

**Multiple connectors.**

Although the employee was diligent, b̶u̶t̶ she was fired.

*Although* and *but* both express contrast. You don't need two connectors in one sentence with the same meaning. You must remove one of them.

Because she fell asleep after eating a big lunch, s̶o̶ she missed her class.

*So* and *because* both express cause. Cut one of them.

---

**ESL Tip**

### Don't Repeat Points; Develop Them   Mila Tasseva, Bulgaria

The academic essay model I was accustomed to before I began college in the United States is the one typically taught to students in the countries of the former Soviet bloc. Students are taught to structure their essays so that they spiral around the thesis, repeating the same statement in different words again, and again, and again without actually developing the argument. In contrast, professors in the United States will expect students to support the thesis with details and examples.

If your instructor asks you to work on developing your paper, try the following strategy. When you review a draft, look closely into the argument's development and identify the points that give you evidence in support of the claim. Now review what you just identified and see if you can find the same point repeated in the same or different words. Do you find the spiral? I bet so. It always comes as a surprise; at least it did to me when I received back my first paper written in an American university with the note in the margin, "Why did you repeat this idea so many times?"

---

🔵 **7 Place adverbs correctly in the sentence.** Adverbs can appear in many different places in a sentence—at the beginning, in the middle, at the end. However, there are a few positions where adverbs *can't* be placed. Here are some guidelines. (For more help with adverb placement, see Section 30f.)

**Don't put an adverb between the verb and its object.**

|  | verb | adverb | obj. |
|---|---|---|---|
| **INCORRECT** | She answered | (slowly) | the question. |

|  | verb | obj. | adverb |
|---|---|---|---|
| **CORRECT** | She answered | the question | **slowly**. |

**Don't place adverbs of frequency before the verb *be*.**

> INCORRECT   Louise **regularly** is late for class.
>
> CORRECT   Louise is **regularly** late for class.

**Don't place adverbs of frequency after other verbs.**

> INCORRECT   Juan arrives **often** late to class.
>
> CORRECT   Juan **often** arrives late to class.

**EXERCISE 31.1**  Review Section 31a. Then read the following paragraph and proofread it for the mistakes described in that section. In some cases you will need to add something and in others you will delete an element. (There are seven errors. For answers, see page 495.)

There are long lines at the cashier's office because students signing up for financial aid. Is extremely frustrating to spend the entire day in line. Because some students they have other jobs and classes, so they can't wait very long. Then you very tired when you finally arrive at the desk where you can talk to the clerk there. The clerk usually give you a form to fill out, and then you have to wait in another line!

---

**ESL Tip**

### Cite Sources Carefully  Carl Jenkinson, England

For me, one of the most significant differences in America is the emphasis placed on full and accurate citation using MLA style. Although citation is required in the UK, and to a lesser extent in France, where it seems more of a courtesy than a necessity, full and accurate citation in the United States is imperative. The solution is straightforward: become as familiar as possible with the MLA handbook, and if in doubt, cite your source.

## 31b Finding other ESL resources

You may have questions about grammar or punctuation that aren't covered in Chapters 31 through 33, which deal specifically with the concerns of ESL writers. This section points you to additional resources in this book and in other publications that you can consult.

### ● 1 Consult relevant material in other chapters of this book.

Many questions you have about grammar and mechanics are not specific to ESL writers. Native speakers of English have many of these questions too. Chart 31.2 lists possible questions, each with the chapter or section in this handbook that covers that problem. If you have several areas of difficulty with grammar, focus on one at a time. Study the examples in this chapter and those in the other grammar chapters in this handbook, and work through the practice exercises on rules that you find especially tricky.

| Chart 31.2 Where to Find More Help with ESL Grammar Questions | | |
|---|---|---|
| IF YOU HAVE A QUESTION ABOUT | EXAMPLES | GO TO THIS CHAPTER/ SECTION |
| Abbreviations | Dr., APA, Ms. | 42a |
| Adjective clauses | clauses beginning with *who, which, that* | 16d, 29c |
| Capitalization | English, Japanese | 41b |
| Comparatives/ superlatives | more interesting/the most interesting | 30h |
| Dangling modifiers | Reading the paper, the phone rang. | 30a |
| Irregular verbs | *sit, sat, sat* | 23b |
| Parallelism | I like swimming and fishing | 16h, 23c |
| Passive voice | I was hit by a car. | 23e |

*(Continued)*

**Where to Find More Help with ESL Grammar Questions** *(Continued)*

| IF YOU HAVE A QUESTION ABOUT | EXAMPLES | GO TO THIS CHAPTER/ SECTION |
|---|---|---|
| Plural nouns | child: children | 25a |
| Possessives | the teacher's book | 25b |
| Pronouns | his gain; their loss | 26–29 |
| Punctuation | commas, periods | 34–40 |
| **SENTENCE PROBLEMS** | | |
| Run-ons | I am a student I come from Mexico. | 35d |
| Fragments | Because it is my house. | 35a–35b |
| Subject-verb agreement | I comes from Italy. | 22 |

**2 Consult reference books especially designed for ESL writers.** A general writer's handbook like this one cannot cover all the ESL information you need. We suggest, therefore, that you refer regularly to ESL reference books for help with grammar and usage. ESL grammar textbooks can give you more detailed grammatical explanations. Some ESL dictionaries provide useful spelling and usage information. See the following list of ESL reference books.

**Highlight    References for ESL Students**

We suggest the following reference books and Web sites for ESL students who have questions about grammar and usage.

- Betty S. Azar. *Basic English Grammar: English as a Second Language.* 3rd ed. New York: Pearson ESL, 1996.

- Betty S. Azar. *Understanding and Using English Grammar.* 3rd ed. New York: Pearson ESL, 1998.

- *Dave's ESL Café* <http://www.eslcafe.com/>.

*(Continued)*

**References for ESL Students** *(Continued)*

- ESL Resources at OWL—the Online Writing Lab at Purdue University <http://owl.english.purdue.edu/handouts/esl/eslstudent.html>.
- The *Applied English Center (AEC)* at the University of Kansas <http://www.aec.ku.edu/leo/index.html>.

We also recommend the following dictionary written for the ESL student.

- *Longman Dictionary of American English.* 3rd ed. New York: Longman, 2000.

**3 Look for opportunities to listen to, speak, read, and write English in your everyday activities.** Although books can give you thorough explanations of grammatical rules, experts agree that the best way to increase your proficiency in English is to practice, practice, practice. Look for opportunities to use English in everyday contexts: email friends and classmates in English; write letters; join a chat session on a Web site that interests you; read English novels and newspapers; and watch the news in English. Don't hesitate to ask native speakers to explain idioms, terms, or conventions of usage that are unfamiliar to you. Consider, too, using the services of your college writing center, if one is available.

## ANSWER KEY

### EXERCISE 31.1

There are long lines at the cashier's office because students **are** signing up for financial aid. **It** is extremely frustrating to spend the entire day in line. Because some students ~~they~~ have other jobs and classes, ~~so~~ they can't wait very long. Then you **are** very tired when you finally arrive at the desk where you can talk to the clerk ~~there~~. The clerk usually **gives** you a form to fill out, and then you have to wait in another line!

# 32  Questions About Verbs (ESL)?

**by Jocelyn Steer and Carol Rhoades**

English verbs are complicated. If you are a speaker for whom English is not a native or first language, you will probably still have questions about them, even after many years of studying English. For example, should you write "She is liking the class very much" or "She likes the class very much"? Are you still confused about transitive and intransitive verbs? This section addresses some common questions ESL writers have about verbs. For additional help with verbs, see Chapters 22 and 23.

## 32a Which verb tense should you use?

A verb's tense expresses time. Chart 32.1 shows the twelve most commonly used verb tenses, along with a list of common adverbs and expressions that accompany them. These words and phrases are the signposts that help you choose the best verb tense. A diagram illustrates the timeline for each tense; in the diagram, an *X* indicates an action, and a curved line indicates an action in progress.

The remainder of this section explains how to use these tenses appropriately. For more information on verb tenses, see Chapter 23.

| Chart 32.1 | Verb Tenses | | |
| --- | --- | --- | --- |
| **WHAT IT IS CALLED** | **WHAT IT LOOKS LIKE** | **WHAT IT DESCRIBES** | **TIME WORDS USED WITH IT** |
| **Simple present** | • I *sleep* eight hours every day. | Habits, regular activities | • every day<br>• often<br>• regularly<br>• always |
| | • Water *freezes* at 0°C. | Facts, general truths | • usually<br>• habitually |

*(Continued)*

## Verb Tenses *(Continued)*

| WHAT IT IS CALLED | WHAT IT LOOKS LIKE | WHAT IT DESCRIBES | TIME WORDS USED WITH IT |
|---|---|---|---|
| **Simple past** <br><br> ⊢×————┼——— | • I *slept* only four hours yesterday. <br> • He *went* to sleep three hours ago. | A finished action in the past | • yesterday <br> • last year <br> • ago |
| **Simple future** <br><br> ———┼——×——— | • I *will* try to sleep more. <br> • I *am going to sleep* early tonight. <br> • I *will* improve. | A single action in the future <br> A planned action in the future (use *be going to*) <br> Promises, offers | • tomorrow <br> • in *x* days <br> • next year |
| **Present perfect** <br><br> ⊢×————┼——— <br><br> ⊢×——→——┼——— | • I *have* already *written* my paper. <br><br> • I *have lived* here for three months. | A past action that occurred at an unspecified time in the past <br> An action that started in the past and continues to the present | • already <br> • yet <br> • before <br> • recently <br> • so far <br> • for + time period <br> • since + date |
| **Past perfect** <br><br> ⊢×·×————┼——— <br> **1 2** | • She *had* already *slept* three hours when the burglar broke into the house. | One action in the past that occurs before another action/time in the past | • when <br> • after <br> • before <br> • by the time |

*(Continued)*

**Verb Tenses** *(Continued)*

| WHAT IT IS CALLED | WHAT IT LOOKS LIKE | WHAT IT DESCRIBES | TIME WORDS USED WITH IT |
|---|---|---|---|
| **Future perfect** | • I *will have finished* the paper when you stop by tonight. | One action in the future that will be completed before another action/time in the future | • by the time<br>• when |
| **Present progressive** | • He *is sleeping* now. | A continuous activity in progress now | • right now<br>• at this time<br>• this week/year |
| **Past progressive** | • While he *was sleeping*, the telephone rang.<br><br>• He *was sleeping* at 10 A.M. | A continuous activity in progress in the past; often interrupted by another time or action | • while<br>• during that time<br>• between *x* and *y* |
| **Future progressive** | • I *will be sleeping* all day. | A continuous activity happening in the future | • all the while<br>• during that time<br>• between *x* and *y* |
| **Present perfect progressive** | • The woman *has been waiting* for many hours.<br><br>• He *has been sleeping* since eight o'clock. | A continuous activity that began in the past and continues to the present; emphasis is on the duration | • for +time period<br>• since + exact date |

*(Continued)*

**Verb Tenses** *(Continued)*

| WHAT IT IS CALLED | WHAT IT LOOKS LIKE | WHAT IT DESCRIBES | TIME WORDS USED WITH IT |
|---|---|---|---|
| **Past perfect progressive** | • She *had been waiting* for three hours when he arrived.<br><br>• He *had been sleeping* for an hour when the train crashed. | A continuous activity in the past that is finished before another action/ time in the past | • for<br>• since |
| **Future perfect progressive** | • I *will have been sleeping* for twelve hours by the time you arrive. | A continuing future activity which started before another future event | • by<br>• when |

🔵 **1 Review the difference between the simple present tense and the present progressive tense.** You may be confused because the simple present tense doesn't really refer to an action going on in the present; rather, it is used to talk about repeated and habitual actions. You should use the simple present tense when you want to talk about *regular, repeated* activity.

> **SIMPLE PRESENT**
> The mail carrier usually **arrives** at 10 A.M.
> This is an activity that is repeated daily.
>
> **PRESENT PROGRESSIVE**
> Look! She **is putting** the mail in the box now.
> This is an activity occurring at the moment of speaking— now.
>
> **PRESENT PROGRESSIVE**
> She **is delivering** mail for John this month.
> This is an activity that is in progress over a period of time. Use the progressive tense with the expression *this + time period*.

⊜**2 Review nonaction verbs and the present tense.** Some verbs in English can't be used in a progressive form because they express a state and not an activity. Nonaction verbs include verbs of existence, of thought, of emotions, and of sense perceptions. Chart 32.2 lists some of these verbs. To use one of these nonaction verbs, you must use a simple form of the verb even though the time intended is *now*.

| | |
|---|---|
| INCORRECT | I can't study because I **am hearing** my roommate's singing. |
| CORRECT | I can't study because I **hear** my roommate's singing. |
| INCORRECT | Maria **is preferring** Carlos's apartment to her own. |
| CORRECT | Maria **prefers** Carlos's apartment to her own. |

---

**Chart 32.2   Nonaction Verbs***

| | | | |
|---|---|---|---|
| appear | forget | owe | seem |
| be | hate | own | smell |
| belong | have | possess | sound |
| consist | hear | prefer | surprise |
| contain | know | recognize | taste |
| deserve | like | remember | think |
| desire | love | require | understand |
| dislike | mean | resemble | want |
| feel | need | see | wish |

*There are exceptions to the nonaction rule ("I **am thinking** about getting a job"; "He **is see-ing** a doctor about his insomnia"). These exceptions can usually be paraphrased using other verbs ("He **is seeing** a doctor about his insomnia" means "He **is consulting** a doctor about his insomnia"). You will need to keep a list of these exceptions as you come across them.

---

⊜**3 Review the difference between the simple past tense and the present perfect tense.** If an action happened in the past and is fin-ished, you can always use the simple past tense to describe it. (See Chapter 23 on how to form the past tense and for a list of irregular verbs.) Often you will also use a time word such as *ago* or *yesterday* to show the specific time of the past action.

| SIMPLE PAST | My brother **saw** that movie three days ago. |
| | We know exactly when the brother saw the movie—three days ago. You *must* use the simple past in this sentence. |

Use the **past tense** to show that something is completed, and use the **present perfect tense** to indicate that the action may continue or that it still has the possibility of occurring in the future. Compare these sentences to see how the two tenses express different ideas.

| SIMPLE PAST | My grandmother never **used** a computer. |
| | This implies that the grandmother may no longer be alive. |
| PRESENT PERFECT | My grandmother **has** never **used** a computer. |
| | This sentence indicates that the grandmother is still alive and may use a computer in the future. |

When you don't know or you don't want to state the exact time or date of a past action, use the present perfect tense.

| PRESENT PERFECT | Sarah **has seen** that movie before. |
| | We don't know when Sarah saw the movie; she saw it at an unspecified time in the past. |

You must use the present perfect for an action that began in the past and continues up to the present moment, especially when you use the time words *for* and *since*.

| PRESENT PERFECT | This theater **has shown** the same film for three months! I hope they change it soon. |
| | The action started in the past—three months ago—and continues to the present. The film is still playing. |

**◉ 4 Review the difference between the present perfect tense and the present perfect progressive tense.** You can use the **present perfect progressive** tense to show that an action is still in progress.

| PRESENT PERFECT PROGRESSIVE | Catherine **has been writing** that letter since this morning. |
| | She hasn't finished; she's still writing. |

In general, when the statement emphasizes *duration* (length of time), you need to use the present perfect progressive tense.

**PRESENT PERFECT**    My best friend **has been writing** her novel
**PROGRESSIVE**           for five years.

This tells us how long the friend has been writing; the emphasis is on duration, or length of time.

However, when the statement emphasizes *quantity* (how much), you will use the **present perfect tense**.

**PRESENT PERFECT**    Toni Morrison **has written** several well-received novels.

This tells us how many books; it talks about quantity.

**EXERCISE 32.1**  Review Sections 32a-1 and 32a-2. Choose the correct tense—simple present or present progressive. (For answers, see page 514.)

1. Many people have bizarre dreams, but I usually (**dream/am dreaming**) about something that (**happens/is happening**) during the day.

2. I often (**remember/am remembering**) my dreams right after I (**wake/am waking**) up.

3. Sometimes when I (**hear/am hearing**) a noise while I (**dream/am dreaming**), I will incorporate that into my dream.

4. I (**know/am knowing**) a lot about dreams because I (**write/am writing**) a paper about them this semester.

5. To prepare for the paper, I (**research/am researching**) many psychological explanations for various dream symbols, such as snakes, bodies of water, and people.

6. I'm not sure that I (**believe/am believing**) those explanations, but they are very interesting.

**EXERCISE 32.2**  Review Section 32a-3. Choose the best verb tense—simple past or present perfect. Use the present perfect whenever possible. (For answers, see page 514.)

1. This month the newspapers (**had/have had**) many articles about a phenomenon called the glass ceiling.

2. This refers to an unofficial limitation on promotion for women who (**worked/have worked**) in a corporation for several years and who cannot advance beyond middle management.

3. Last year my mother (**applied/has applied**) for the position of vice president of the company she works for, but they (**did not promote/ have not promoted**) her.

4. She (**had/has had**) the most experience of all the candidates for the job, but a man was chosen instead.

5. She (**was/has been**) with that company for ten years. Now she doesn't know how much longer she will stay there.

**EXERCISE 32.3** Review Section 32a. Fill in the blanks with the most precise and appropriate tense of the verb *talk*. Pay special attention to time words. Incorporate the adverbs in parentheses into your answers. (For answers, see page 515.)

1. They _____ about the issue since yesterday.

2. Some employees _____ about the issue when we arrived at work.

3. They _____ (**probably**) about the issue when they leave work.

4. We _____ about it many times in the past.

5. I never _____ about this topic last week.

6. We _____ about this problem for two hours by the time the president visited our office.

7. Workers _____ about this issue quite often these days.

8. They _____ about the subject right now.

9. After they _____ about it for many weeks, they reached a consensus.

10. They _____ (**never**) about this issue again.

## 32b How do you use transitive and intransitive verbs?

A **transitive verb** is a verb that has a direct object. This means that the verb has an effect on, or does something to, that object. The verb *raise* in the sentence "She raised her children" is transitive because the subject of the sentence (*she*) is acting on someone else (*her children*). Without the direct object (*her children*), this sentence would be incomplete; it would not make sense.

INCORRECT     She raised. This thought is incomplete; we need to know *what* she raised.

CORRECT     She raised **her children** on a farm.

There are two types of transitive verbs. (See Chart 32.3 on page 506 for a list of them.) One type—verb + direct object—*must* be followed directly by a noun or pronoun.

**VERB + DIRECT OBJECT** (trans. v. = transitive verb)

      subj.    trans. v.        noun
This university **needs** more parking lots.

      subj.    trans. v.  pronoun
The trustees **discussed** it at the last meeting.

The second type—verb + (indirect object) + direct object—*can* be followed by an indirect object (a person receiving the action) before the direct object.

When you use *to* or *for* in front of the indirect object, the position changes, as you can see in these examples.

**VERB + (INDIRECT OBJECT) + DIRECT OBJECT**

> dir. obj.
> Ron bought **a rose**.

> indir. obj.　dir. obj.
> Ron bought *his wife* **a rose**.
> *or*

> dir. obj. + *for/to* + indir. obj.
> Ron bought **a rose** *for his wife*.

An **intransitive verb** is complete without a direct object. In fact, you cannot put a direct object after an intransitive verb.

| INCORRECT | She grew up **her children**. *Her children* cannot come after the verb *grew up* because *her children* is an object; objects cannot come after intransitive verbs. |

However, other words can come after intransitive verbs.

| CORRECT | She grew up **quickly**. *Quickly* is an adverb. You can put an adverb after this verb. This sentence means that she matured at a very fast rate. |
| CORRECT | She grew up **on a farm**. *On a farm* is a prepositional phrase, not a direct object. |

There are two kinds of intransitive verbs—linking verbs and action verbs. (See Chart 32.3 on page 506 for a list of these verbs.)

| LINKING VERBS | subj.　l. v.　comp.<br>This book **seems** very old. l. v. = linking verb |
| | subj.　l. v.　comp.<br>Your professor **is** an expert in law. |
| ACTION VERBS | subj.　a. v.<br>Jacqueline **complained**. a. v. = action verb |
| | subj.　a. v.　prep. phrase<br>Jacqueline **complained** to me before breakfast. |

For more information on transitive and intransitive verbs, see Section 23e.

---

**Chart 32.3** **Transitive and Intransitive Verbs**

**TRANSITIVE VERBS***

- **Verb + direct object:** attend, bring up, choose, do, have, hit, hold, keep, lay, need, raise, say, spend, use, want, watch, wear
- **Verb + (indirect object) + direct object:** bring, buy, get, give, make, pay, send, take, tell

**INTRANSITIVE VERBS***

- **Linking verbs:** appear, be, become, seem, look
- **Action verbs:** arrive, come, get dressed, go, grow up, laugh, lie, listen, live, rise, run, sit, sleep, walk, work

---

*These lists are not complete. You can always consult your dictionary to find out whether a verb is transitive or intransitive.

---

## 32c How do you use two-word and three-word verbs?

Some verbs in English consist of two or three words, usually a main verb and a preposition. These verbs are idioms because you can't understand the meaning of the verb simply by knowing the separate meaning of each of the two or three words. For example, the verb *put* has a completely different meaning from the verb *put off* ("to postpone"), and the verb *put up with* ("to tolerate") has yet another distinct meaning. There are many two- and three-word verbs in English. Since it would be difficult to memorize all of them, it's best for you to learn them as you hear them and to keep a list of them for reference. Chart 32.4 on pages 507–508 lists common two- and three-word verbs. Two-word verbs that are transitive—which means they can have a direct object—are divided into two groups: **separable** and **inseparable**. (See Section 32b for an explanation of transitive verbs.)

## Chart 32.4   Common Two-Word and Three-Word Verbs

Here are some common two- and three-word verbs. Such verbs have two parts: the main verb and one (or more) prepositions. This list is not complete; there are many more such verbs. An asterisk (*) indicates an *inseparable* verb: the verb and the preposition cannot be separated by an object. A cross (+) indicates verbs that have additional meanings not given here.

| VERB | DEFINITION |
|---|---|
| break down* | stop functioning |
| bring on | cause something to happen |
| call off | cancel |
| catch up with*+ | attain the same position, place |
| check into* | explore, investigate |
| come across* | encounter unintentionally |
| cut down on* | reduce the amount of |
| do over | repeat |
| figure out | solve a problem, dilemma |
| find out | discover |
| get along with* | have harmonious relations |
| get in*+ | enter a car |
| get off*+ | exit from (a bus, a train, a plane) |
| get on* | enter (a bus, a train, a plane) |
| get over* | recover from (a sickness, a relationship) |
| give up | stop trying |
| go over* | review |
| grow up* | mature, become an adult |
| keep up with* | maintain the same level |
| look after* | take care of |
| look into* | explore, investigate |
| make up+ | invent |
| pass away* | die |
| pick out | make a selection |
| put off | postpone |
| put up with* | tolerate |

*(Continued)*

**Common Two-Word and Three-Word Verbs** *(Continued)*

| | |
|---|---|
| run into*+ | meet by chance |
| show up* | appear, arrive |
| stand up for* | defend, support |
| sum up | summarize, conclude |
| take after* | resemble, look alike |
| touch on* | discuss briefly |

**1 Separable verbs.** You can place the object *before* or *after* the preposition.

CORRECT     Lee checked **the book** *out* from the library.
            The object (*the book*) is placed *before* the preposition (*out*).

CORRECT     Lee checked *out* **the book** from the library.
            The object comes *after* the preposition.

However, whenever the object is a *pronoun* (such as *it* in the following example), the pronoun *must* come *before* the preposition.

INCORRECT   Gary checked out **it** from the library.
CORRECT     Gary checked **it** out from the library.

**2 Inseparable verbs.** You cannot separate the verb and the preposition.

INCORRECT   My sister **majored** history **in**.
CORRECT     My sister **majored in** history.

INCORRECT   Please **after** your brother **look**.
CORRECT     Please **look after** your brother.

**EXERCISE 32.4** Review Sections 32a through 32c. Each of the following sentences contains errors related to verb tense, transitive/intransitive verbs, or two-word verbs. Identify the errors and correct them. (For answers, see page 515.)

1. Before I study psychology, I thought it was an easy subject.

2. Now I am knowing that it isn't easy.

3. It has had a lot of statistics.

4. I am studying psychology since April, and I only begin to learn some of the concepts.

5. I have been tried to learn more of the concepts every day.

6. Last night I have studied from 9:00 to midnight.

7. I went my adviser last Monday.

8. She told to me to see her after class.

9. But when I went to see her after class, she already left.

10. It's January. By the middle of June, I have studied psychology for six months.

# 32d **Which modal should you use?**

You already know that a verb's tense expresses time. A *modal*, which is an auxiliary or helping verb, expresses an attitude about a situation. For example, if you want to be polite, you can say, "Open the door, please." To be even more polite, you can add a modal auxiliary verb: "*Would* you open the door, please?" Modals are used to express necessity, obligation, regret, and formality. Modals can be used to express ideas about the past, present, or future.

| | |
|---|---|
| **PAST** | I **could** speak Japanese as a child. |
| **PRESENT** | My brother **can** speak Japanese now. |
| **FUTURE** | I **might** learn another language next semester. |

You probably already know the common modals, such as *should, must*, and *have to*. However, you may have questions about others, such as *had better*, or perhaps you are uncertain about the difference between, for example, *have to* and *ought to*. In this section, we list the modals by their uses or functions and provide a list of common modal errors to avoid.

● 1 **Choose the modal that best expresses your idea.** Chart 32.5 on page 510 below summarizes the functions of modals. It also lists the past form of the modals. Modals in the present are followed by the base form of the verb—for example, "Kim **may** win the prize" (subject + modal + base form of the verb). The form of modals in the past varies. (See Section 32d-3 for more details.)

## Chart 32.5   Modals

| WHAT IT MEANS | PRESENT OR FUTURE FORM | PAST FORM |
|---|---|---|
| *Permission* (*Informal → Formal*) | | |
| **can** | **Can** I be excused? | He **could have** |
| **could** | **Could** I be excused? | **been** excused, but |
| **may** | **May** I be excused? | he didn't ask. |
| **would you mind**\* | **Would you mind if** I *brought* my dog? | **Would you have minded if** I *had brought* my dog? |
| *Ability* | | |
| **can** | Joe **can** drive a car. | He **couldn't** drive a car last year. |
| **be able to** | Carl **is able to** study and listen to music at the same time. | Celia **was never able to** play the Mozart concertos. |
| *Advice* | | |
| **should** | You **should** quit. | He **should have** |
| **ought to** | You **ought to** quit. | quit last year. |
| **had better** | You **had better** quit. | He didn't quit; this sentence shows regret. |
| *Necessity* | | |
| **have to** | He **has to** pay a fine. | He **had to** pay a fine last week. |
| **must** | She **must** pay her taxes. | No past form; use *had to*. |

\* *Would you mind* is followed by *if* + the past tense of the verb.

*(Continued)*

**Modals**  *(Continued)*

| WHAT IT MEANS | PRESENT OR FUTURE FORM | PAST FORM |
|---|---|---|
| *Lack of necessity* | | |
| **not have to** | You **don't have to** attend school in summer. | He **didn't have to** take the final exam last year. |
| **not need to** | You **don't need to** pay in advance. | You **didn't need to** pay in advance. |
| *Possibility* (*More sure* → *Less sure*) | | |
| **can** | It **can** get cold in May. | No past form. |
| **may** | It **may** get cold in June this year. | I'm not sure, but it **may have** just happened. |
| **could** | It **could** get cold in July this year. | It **could have** just happened. |
| **might** | It **might** get cold in July this year. | It **might have** just happened. |
| *Conclusion* | | |
| **must** | Your eyes are all red; you **must have** allergies. I'm almost certain that this is true. | You got an *A* on your test. You **must have studied** hard! I'm certain that you did this in the past. |
| *Expectation* | | |
| **should/ ought to** | Your keys **should be** on the desk where I left them. I expect them to be there. | John **should have been** elected. He didn't get elected, but I expected him to. |

*(Continued)*

**Modals**    *(Continued)*

| WHAT IT MEANS | PRESENT OR FUTURE FORM | PAST FORM |
|---|---|---|
| *Polite requests* *(Informal → Formal)* | | |
| **can** | **Can** you give me a hand? | No past forms. |
| **will** | **Will** you give me a hand? | |
| **could** | **Could** you give me a hand? | |
| **would you mind** + present participle | **Would you mind giving** me a hand? | |

**● 2 Use the correct form of the modal auxiliary and the main verb that follows it.** Modals that express present and future time have this form.

> SUBJECT + MODAL + BASE FORM OF VERB

Clarissa **had better** register for classes soon.

Here are specific tips to help you with modal formation.

- Don't use *to* or a present participle (*-ing* form of a verb) after the modal.

| INCORRECT | Jacquie **can to** play the guitar very well. |
|---|---|
| CORRECT | Jacquie **can** play the guitar very well. |
| INCORRECT | **Must** I **to** hand in this paper tomorrow? |
| CORRECT | **Must** I hand in this paper tomorrow? |
| EXCEPT | We **have to** write a ten-page paper. |
| INCORRECT | They **should reading** before class. |
| CORRECT | They **should read** before class. |

- There is no *-s* on the third person singular of a modal.

| INCORRECT | Kwang **mights** go to graduate school. |
|---|---|
| CORRECT | Kwang **might** go to graduate school. |

- Don't use two modals together.

  | INCORRECT | They **might could** drive all night. |
  |---|---|
  | CORRECT | They **might** drive all night. |

  An exception is **be able to**:

  | CORRECT | They **might be able to** drive all night. |
  |---|---|

- *Do, does,* and *did* are not used in questions with modals, except for the modal *have to.*

  | INCORRECT | **Do** I **must** answer all the questions? |
  |---|---|
  | CORRECT | **Must** I answer all the questions? |
  | EXCEPT | **Do** I **have to** answer all the questions? |

- *Do, does,* and *did* are not used in negative statements with modals; use *not* instead, placed after the modal.

  | INCORRECT | They **do not can** enter the test room. |
  |---|---|
  | CORRECT | They **cannot** enter the test room. |
  | INCORRECT | Jorge **did not could** have worked any harder. |
  | CORRECT | Jorge **could not have** worked any harder. |

**◎3 Use the perfect form to express past time.** As you can see from the chart of modals on pages 510–512, many modals have a past form. The past of modals that give advice or express possibility, expectation, and conclusion have a *perfect* verb form (modal + *have* + past participle), as you can see in the following examples.

| ADVICE | Gail **should have taken** that marketing job last year. Gail didn't take the job. |
|---|---|
| POSSIBILITY | Although he chose not to, Bob **could have gone** to Mexico over spring break. Bob didn't go to Mexico. |
| EXPECTATION | Where is Sue? She **should have been** here by now. Sue hasn't arrived yet. |
| CONCLUSION | Ted finished the paper; he **must have worked** all night. |

**EXERCISE 32.5** Review Section 32d-1. Fill in the blanks with a modal from the following list. More than one answer is possible for each blank. Try to use each modal only once. (For answers, see page 515.)

| would | must | have to | ought to | should have |
|-------|------|---------|----------|-------------|
| should | can | might | had better | must have |

1. Can you believe the line waiting to see the movie *Spider-Man*? That _____ be a good movie!

2. Where is my purse, Mom? It _____ be on the table where you put it last night.

3. I'm sorry, Professor Lopez, but I _____ take the test tomorrow because I _____ go to Immigration about my visa.

4. Jason, you _____ eat your vegetables or you won't get any dessert.

**EXERCISE 32.6** Review Section 32d. Each of the following sentences contains errors related to modal auxiliaries. Identify the errors and correct them. (For answers, see page 515.)

1. Megan's boss told her, "You had better to improve your attitude, or we will have to take disciplinary action."

2. Megan was very distressed by this news; she did not could understand the basis for her boss's complaints.

3. She tried to think of things that she had done wrong. She knew that she should had been more enthusiastic at the last meeting, but she felt she couldn't be hypocritical. She simply didn't agree with her boss.

4. Megan was really worried. Her boss mights send her a "pink slip," which would mean that she had been fired.

## ANSWER KEY

**EXERCISE 32.1**
1. dream; happens
2. remember; wake
3. hear; am dreaming
4. know; am writing
5. am researching
6. believe

**EXERCISE 32.2**
1. have had
2. have worked
3. applied; did not promote
4. had
5. has been

## EXERCISE 32.3

1. have been talking
2. were talking
3. will probably be talking
4. have talked
5. talked
6. had been talking
7. are talking (*or* talk)
8. are talking
9. had talked
10. will never talk

## EXERCISE 32.4

1. Before I **studied** psychology, I (**had**) **thought** it was an easy subject.
2. Now I **know** that it isn't easy.
3. It **has** a lot of statistics.
4. I **have been studying** psychology since April, and I **have only begun** to learn some of the concepts.
5. I **have been trying** to learn more of the concepts every day.
6. Last night I **was studying** from 9:00 to midnight.
   *or*
   Last night I **studied** from 9:00 to midnight.
7. I went **to** my adviser last Monday.
8. She told t̸o̸ me to see her after class.
9. But when I went to see her after class, she **had** already **left**.

10. It's January. By the middle of June, I **will have studied** psychology for six months.

## EXERCISE 32.5

1. must; has to; should; had better
2. should; ought to; must; had better
3. cannot/might have to; might/should
4. had better; must

## EXERCISE 32.6

1. Megan's boss told her, "You had better t̸o̸ improve your attitude, or we will have to take disciplinary action."
2. Megan was very distressed by this news; she **could not** (*or* **did not**) understand the basis for her boss's complaints.
3. She tried to think of things that she had done wrong. She knew that she **should have been** more enthusiastic at the last meeting, but she felt she couldn't be hypocritical. She simply didn't agree with her boss.
4. Megan was really worried. Her boss **might̸s̸** send her a "pink slip," which would mean that she had been fired.

# 33

# Questions About Gerunds, Infinitives, Articles, or Number (ESL)?

**by Jocelyn Steer and Carol Rhoades**

This chapter offers guidelines for handling grammatical concepts that many ESL writers find confusing: gerunds, infinitives, articles, and number agreement. If you have learned British English but will now be writing American English, pay special attention to Section 33b on articles and count/noncount nouns.

## 33a How do you use gerunds and infinitives?

In English, gerunds and infinitives have several functions. (See Section 24a for definitions of *gerund* and *infinitive*.)

A **gerund** can function as a subject, object, complement, and object of a preposition. (See the glossary for a definition of *complement*; see Section 16c-1 for more on the *object of a preposition*.)

subj.
**Finding** a parking space is impossible here!

obj.
George enjoys **reading** for half an hour before bed.

comp.
His favorite hobby is **cooking**.

obj. prep.
She is afraid of **flying**.

An **infinitive** can be the subject of a sentence, and it can be the object of a verb.

subj.
**To find** a parking space here is impossible!

obj.
My sister hopes **to be** a marine biologist.

ESL writers often have difficulty with gerunds and infinitives that act as objects in a sentence. This section will focus on this problem.

**◉1 Review which form—gerund or infinitive—to use.** You already know that some verbs in English are followed by gerunds and other verbs are followed by infinitives.

> **INFINITIVE (*TO* + BASE FORM OF VERB)**
>
> I want **to go** with you.
>
> **GERUND (BASE FORM OF VERB + *-ING*)**
>
> He enjoys **jogging** in the park.

Other verbs, however, can have *either* a gerund or an infinitive after them without a difference in meaning.

> **GERUND OR INFINITIVE (NO CHANGE IN MEANING)**
>
> gerund
> The dog began **barking** at midnight.
> infinitive
> The dog began **to bark** at midnight.
> These two sentences have exactly the same meaning.

Finally, some verbs in English (including *forget, regret, remember, stop, try*) can be followed by *either* a gerund or an infinitive, but with a change in meaning.

> **GERUND OR INFINITIVE (CHANGE IN MEANING)**
>
> Paul stopped **working** in the cafeteria.
> Paul *no longer* works in the cafeteria.
>
> Paul stopped his tennis game early **to work** on his homework.
> Paul stopped his game *in order to* work on his homework.
>
> Paul forgot **to visit** his cousin while he was in Mexico.
> He did *not* visit his cousin.
>
> Paul will never forget **visiting** Mexico.
> Paul visited Mexico and he will always remember the trip.

Native speakers know intuitively whether to use a gerund or an infinitive after a verb, but this is not usually true for ESL students.

Chart 33.1 on page 518 and Chart 33.2 on page 519 can help you; be sure to keep these charts handy when you write.

**518** **ESL** Questions About Gerunds, Infinitives, Articles, or Number (ESL)?

**33a**

**2 Review when a verb must be followed by a noun or a pronoun.** As we've seen, some verbs in English (called *transitive verbs*) need to have a noun or pronoun after them. For example, when you use *tell*, you need a direct object (*What did you tell?*) or an indirect object (*Whom did you tell?*) to complete the sentence.

---

**Chart 33.1   Verbs Followed by Gerunds or Infinitives**

**VERB + INFINITIVE**

These verbs are followed by **infinitives**.

| | | | |
|---|---|---|---|
| afford | consent | intend | pretend |
| agree | decide | learn | promise |
| appear | deserve | manage | refuse |
| arrange | expect | mean | seem |
| ask | fail | need | threaten |
| beg | hesitate | offer | wait |
| claim | hope | plan | wish |

**VERB + GERUND**

These verbs are followed by **gerunds**.

| | | | |
|---|---|---|---|
| admit | deny | mention | recommend |
| anticipate | discuss | miss | resent |
| appreciate | dislike | postpone | resist |
| avoid | enjoy | practice | risk |
| complete | finish | quit | suggest |
| consider | can't help | recall | tolerate |
| delay | keep | recollect | understand |

**VERB + GERUND OR INFINITIVE**

These verbs can be followed by either a **gerund** or an **infinitive**, with no change in meaning.

| | | | |
|---|---|---|---|
| begin | can't stand | hate | prefer |
| can't bear | continue | like | start |

**Chart 33.2 Verbs Followed by Gerunds or Infinitives with a Change in Meaning**

**VERB + GERUND OR INFINITIVE**

These verbs can be followed by either a **gerund** or an **infinitive**, but the meaning of the sentence will change depending on which one you use.

| VERB | MEANING |
|------|---------|
| try (to be) | make an attempt to be |
| try (being) | do an experiment |
| regret (to be) | feel sorry about |
| regret (being) | feel sorry about *past* action |
| remember (to be) | not forget |
| remember (being) | recall, bring to mind |
| forget (to be) | not remember |
| (never) forget (being) | always remember |
| stop (to be) | stop in order to be |
| stop (being) | interrupt an action |

| | |
|---|---|
| **INCORRECT** | I told∧to write me a letter. |
| | The object is missing; the sentence is incomplete. |
| **CORRECT** | I told **my son** to write me a letter. |
| | *My son* is the indirect object; this sentence is complete. |

Remember that an *infinitive verb* comes after transitive verb + noun or pronoun constructions. Chart 33.3 lists the verbs that follow this pattern.

**Chart 33.3 Verbs Followed by Nouns, Pronouns, or Infinitives**

**VERB + (NOUN OR PRONOUN) + INFINITIVE**

These verbs must be followed by a **noun** or a **pronoun** + an **infinitive**.

| | | | |
|---|---|---|---|
| advise | encourage | invite | tell |
| allow | forbid | order | urge |
| cause | force | persuade | warn |
| challenge | hire | remind | |
| convince | instruct | require | |

**●3 Instead of being followed by an infinitive, the verbs *have, make*, and *let* are followed by a noun or pronoun and the base form of the verb.** This means that you omit *to* before the verb.

**HAVE**   I **had** my mother *cut* my hair.

Here *had* means to cause someone to do something.

**MAKE**   The teacher **made** him *leave* the class.

Here *made* means to force someone to do something; it is stronger than *had*.

**LET**   Professor Betts **let** the class *leave* early.

Here *let* means to allow someone to do something.

**●4 Use a gerund after a preposition.** Many verbs are followed by prepositions. Sometimes adjectives are followed by prepositions. Always remember to use a gerund, not an infinitive, after prepositions. Here are two common sentence patterns with prepositions followed by gerunds.

                  verb            adj.    prep.    gerund
Carla has been very worried **about passing** her statistics class.

                  verb     prep.    gerund
Mrs. Short apologized **for interrupting** our conversation.

Chart 33.4 lists common preposition combinations with verbs and adjectives.

**Chart 33.4   Common Verb (+ Adjective) + Preposition Constructions**

| | | |
|---|---|---|
| be accustomed to | be faithful to | pray for |
| be afraid of | be familiar with | prevent from |
| approve of | be fond of | prohibit from |
| be aware of | be good at | protect from |
| believe in | be grateful to | be proud of |
| be capable of | be guilty of | rely on |
| be committed to | hope for | be responsible for |
| complain about | insist on | be satisfied with |
| be composed of | be interested in | be scared of |
| consist of | be jealous of | stop from |

*(Continued)*

**Common Verb (+ Adjective) + Preposition Constructions**  *(Continued)*

| | | |
|---|---|---|
| depend on | look forward to | succeed in |
| be disappointed in | be made of | take advantage of |
| be divorced from | be married to | take care of |
| dream of/about | object to | be tired of |
| be envious of | be opposed to | be worried about |
| be excited about | be patient with | |

**EXERCISE 33.1**  Fill in the blanks with the infinitive, gerund, or base form of the verbs in parentheses. (For answers, see page 528.)

1. Women who have not wanted (**work**) _____ because of health threats can now relax.

2. A recent study completed in California shows that women who work outside the home seem (**have**) _____ fewer health problems than those who work inside the home.

3. Another federal study reports that women employed outside the home do not risk (**have**) _____ more "stress-induced" heart attacks than women working inside the home.

4. In fact, this study appears (**support**) _____ the benefits of working outside the home for women.

5. In general, working women are found (**be**) _____ physically and mentally healthier than women who stay at home.

6. Many working women will appreciate (**hear**) _____ that their chances for depression actually increase if they decide (**drop**) _____ out of the work force.

7. These studies do not pretend (**decide**) _____ for women what is best for them.

8. However, the studies might help some women (**make**) _____ a decision about (**go**) _____ back to work outside the home or about (**quit**) _____ their jobs because they have children.

## 33b Questions about articles and number agreement?

This section gives you general guidelines about articles (*a, an,* or *the*) and expressions of quantity (such as *a few* or *a little*). For the finer points about articles not covered here, we suggest that you consult one of the ESL grammar references listed on pages 494–495.

**◉1 Decide whether the noun is count or noncount.** Before you can know which article to use, you will need to determine whether the noun in question is *count* or *noncount*. A **count noun** refers to something that you can count or that you can divide easily.

| | |
|---|---|
| **COUNT NOUNS** | There are sixty **seconds** in one **minute**.<br>Joan bought six **books** for her class. |

When there is more than one of the noun (*seconds*), the count noun must be plural. (See Section 25a for a discussion of plural nouns.) If there is only one (*one minute*), the count noun is singular.

A **noncount noun** generally refers to something that cannot usually be counted or divided. Noncount nouns include **mass nouns**, such as materials (*wood, plastic, wool*), food items (*cheese, rice, meat*), and liquids (*water, milk*), and **abstract nouns** (*beauty, knowledge, glory*).

| | |
|---|---|
| **NONCOUNT NOUNS** | Joe drank a lot of **milk** as a teenager.<br>"Give me **liberty** or give me **death**!" |

Some nouns that are noncount in English may seem like things that you can count, such as *money*. Many other noncount nouns in English can confuse ESL students: *furniture, hair, traffic, information, advice*. Consult an ESL dictionary or grammar book when you are unsure whether a noun is count or noncount.

Unlike count nouns, which can be singular or plural, noncount nouns have only the singular form. In addition, since you can't count these nouns, you can't use numbers or words that express number (*several, many*) to describe them. You will use other types of expressions to indicate quantity for noncount nouns; these expressions, called *quantifiers*, are discussed in Section 33b-5.

Most nouns are either count or noncount. However, some noncount nouns can change to have a count meaning. Using a noncount noun as a count noun usually limits the noncount noun in some way. For instance, a noncount noun changes to a count noun when you mean *an instance of, a serving of,* or *a type of* the noncount noun.

count noun
His grandmother started a **business**. one instance of business

count noun
I'd like two **coffees** to go, please. two servings of coffee

count noun
There are three new **wines** on the menu. three kinds of wine

● **2 Decide whether the count noun requires a definite article (*the*) or an indefinite article (*a/an*).** When the count noun is singular, you'll need an article, either *a/an* or *the*, in front of it. How do you know which article to use? Generally, when you introduce the noun, without having referred to it before, then you will use the *indefinite* article, *a* or *an*. (See Section 25c for the difference between *a* and *an*.)

**INDEFINITE MEANING**

*Bob:* I just signed up for **a** literature class.

*Ted:* Oh, really? I didn't know you were interested in that.

This is the first time Bob has mentioned the class to Ted.

After that, when both of them know what is being discussed, Bob will use the *definite* article, *the*.

**DEFINITE MEANING**

*Bob:* Can you believe **the** class meets on Friday evenings?

Both Bob and Ted now share the same information.

Note how the same guidelines apply to written English in the following sentences on homelessness.

There are several reasons why **a** person may end up homeless. Perhaps **the** person lost his or her job and could not pay for **an** apartment. Or perhaps **the** apartment was sold to **a** new owner who raised the rent. **The** new owner may not realize how expensive the rent is for that person.

Certain other situations also require the definite article, *the*.

- When there is only one of the noun.

  **The** earth is round. There is only one earth.

- When the noun is superlative.

  This is **the best** brand you can buy.
  There can only be one brand that is the best.

- When the noun is limited. You will usually use *the* before a noun that has been limited in some way to show that you are referring to a *specific* example of the noun.

  **The** book **that I read** is informative.
  *That I read* limits the book to a specific one.

  **The** book **on George W. Bush** is out.
  *On George W. Bush* limits the book.

If you are making a *generalization*, however, *the* is not always used.

  **A** book **on plants** can make a nice gift.
  *On plants* limits the noun, but the sentence does not refer to a specific book on plants—it refers to *any or all books on plants*. The definite article, *the*, would not be correct here.

**3 Choose articles before general nouns carefully.** When you want to make generalizations, choosing the correct article can be tricky. As a rule, use *a/an* or *the* with most *singular count nouns* to make generalizations.

  **A** dog can be good company for **a** lonely person.
  Use *a/an* to mean any dog, one of many dogs.

  **The** computer has changed the banking industry dramatically.
  Use *the* to mean *the computer in general*.

  **The** spotted owl is an endangered species.

  **The** capitalist believes in free enterprise.
  Use *the* to make general statements about specific species of animals (*spotted owl*) or groups of people (*capitalists*).

He was ill and went to **the** hospital.

American English uses the definite article with *hospital* even when we do not refer to a specific hospital; British English does not use the article with *hospital*.

Use a *plural count noun* to make general statements, without *the*.

**Capitalists** believe in free enterprise.

**Computers** have changed the banking industry dramatically.

Finally, *noncount nouns* in general statements do not have an article in front of them.

**Sugar** is a major cause of tooth decay.

Many educators question whether **intelligence** can be measured.

Consumed in moderate amounts, **red wine** is thought by some researchers to reduce chances of heart disease.

**4 Be aware of two possible article problems with noncount nouns.** First, make sure that you don't use *a/an* with noncount nouns.

| | |
|---|---|
| INCORRECT | I need a̶ **work.** |
| CORRECT | I need work. |

Second, keep in mind that a noncount noun can never be plural.

| | |
|---|---|
| INCORRECT | Joe needs some information̶s̶ about the class. |
| CORRECT | Joe needs some information about the class. |

And remember that sometimes noncount nouns can change to have a count meaning (see Section 33b-1).

**5 Pay careful attention to quantifiers.** The words that come before nouns and tell you *how much* or *how many* are called **quantifiers**. Quantifiers are not always the same for both count and noncount nouns. See Chart 33.5 on page 526 for a list of quantifiers.

---

**Chart 33.5  Quantifiers**

| USE THESE WITH COUNT AND NONCOUNT NOUNS | USE THESE WITH COUNT NOUNS ONLY | USE THESE WITH NONCOUNT NOUNS ONLY |
|---|---|---|
| **some** books/money | **several** books | **a good deal of** money |
| **a lot of** books/money | **many** books | **a great deal of** money |
| **plenty of** books/money | **a couple of** books | **(not) much** money* |
| **a lack of** books/money | **a few** books | **a little** money |
| **most of the** books/money | **few** books | **little** money |

*Much* is ordinarily used only in questions and in negative statements: "Do you have *much* milk left?" "No, there isn't *much* milk."

---

*A few/a little* **and** *few/little*   It may not seem like a big difference, but the article *a* in front of the quantifiers *few* and *little* changes the meaning. *A few* or *a little* means "not a lot, but some of the item."

> There are **a few books** in the library on capital punishment.
> Use *a few* with count nouns.

> There is **a little information** in the library on capital punishment.
> Use *a little* with noncount nouns.

*Few* or *little* (without *a*) means that there is *not enough* of something. These quantifiers have a negative meaning.

> There are **few** female leaders in the world.
> not enough of them

> My mother has **little** hope that this will change.
> not much hope

*Most* **and** *most of*   Using *most of* can be tricky. You can use *most of* before either a count or a noncount noun, but if you do, don't forget to put *the* before the noun.

*MOST OF + THE + SPECIFIC PLURAL NOUN*

**Most of the** *women* in the class were married. Not: *most of women*

*MOST OF + THE + SPECIFIC NONCOUNT NOUN*

**Most of the** *jewelry* in the house was stolen. Not: *most of jewelry*

*MOST + GENERAL PLURAL NOUN*

**Most** *cars* have seat belts. Not: *most of cars*

**EXERCISE 33.2** In the list of nouns below, write *C* after the count nouns and *NC* after the noncount nouns. If you are not sure, consult an ESL dictionary. Then make a note of the nouns you had to check. (For answers, see page 528.)

**1.** furniture

**2.** work

**3.** dollar

**4.** job

**5.** advice

**6.** people

**7.** equipment

**8.** money

**9.** newspaper

**10.** traffic

**EXERCISE 33.3** Review Section 33b. Each of the following sentences has at least one error in the use of articles or quantifiers. Circle the error and correct it. (For answers, see pages 528–529.)

**1.** Much people have visited the new restaurant downtown called Rock-and-Roll Hamburger Haven.

**2.** Most of customers are young people because music in restaurant is very loud.

**3.** The restaurant serves the usual food—hamburgers, pizza, and pasta. It is not expensive; in fact, most expensive item on the menu is only $8.

**4.** Food is not very good, but the atmosphere is very appealing to these young men and women.

**5.** There are much posters on the walls of famous rock star. There is even authentic motorcycle of one star on a platform.

**6.** Some of regular customers say they have seen some stars eating there.

**7.** These "regulars" give these advices to anyone who wants to spot a star there: look for dark glasses and a leather coat.

**EXERCISE 33.4** Write a descriptive paragraph about ordering and eating a meal at your favorite restaurant. Refer to Chart 33.5 on page 526, which lists quantifiers used with count and noncount nouns, and use at least four words from this list in your paragraph. Underline all the nouns in your paragraph and write *C* (for count nouns) and *NC* (for noncount nouns) above them. Then check your use of articles. (For help, refer to Sections 33b-2 through 33b-4.) Make sure your subject-verb agreement is correct.

## ANSWER KEY

### EXERCISE 33.1

**1.** to work
**2.** to have
**3.** having
**4.** to support
**5.** to be
**6.** hearing; to drop
**7.** to decide
**8.** to make; going; quitting

### EXERCISE 33.2

**1.** NC
**2.** NC
**3.** C
**4.** C
**5.** NC
**6.** C
**7.** NC
**8.** NC
**9.** C
**10.** NC

### EXERCISE 33.3

**1. Many** people have visited the new restaurant downtown called Rock-and-Roll Hamburger Haven.

**2.** Most of **the** customers are young people because **the** music in **the** restaurant is very loud.

**3.** The restaurant serves the usual food—hamburgers, pizza, and pasta. It is not expensive; in fact, **the** most expensive item on the menu is only $8.

**4. The** food is not very good, but the atmosphere is very appealing to these young men and women.

**5.** There are **many** posters on the walls of famous rock stars. There is even **an** authentic motorcycle of one star on a platform.

6. Some of **the** regular customers say they have seen some stars eating there.

7. These "regulars" give **this advice** to anyone who wants to spot a star there: look for dark glasses and a leather coat.

**EXERCISE 33.4**
Answers will vary.

# PART VI | Punctuation and Mechanics

# 34 How Do You Punctuate Sentence Endings?

## 34a When do you use periods?

Sentences and some abbreviations end with periods. Periods say, "That's all there is." Although periods cause few problems, writers occasionally put them in the wrong place or forget them entirely.

### ●1 Use periods at the end of statements.

*Hannibal*, a Carthaginian general, was a brilliant strategist who opposed the Romans.

### ●2 Use periods at the end of indirect questions and mild commands.

Military theorists wonder whether any battle plan has been more tactically shrewd than Hannibal's at Cannae (216 BC).

On the map, locate the Roman and Carthaginian camps.

Strong commands may also be punctuated with exclamation points.

### ●3 Use periods to punctuate some abbreviations.

Cong.                       natl.
sing., pl.                   pp.

When a statement ends with an abbreviation, the period at the end of the sentence is not doubled.

We visited the Folger Library in Washington, D.C.

The period at the end of the abbreviation is retained when the sentence is a question or an exclamation.

Have you ever been to Washington, D.C.?

Our flight departs at 6 a.m.!

When an abbreviation occurs in the middle of a sentence, it retains its period. The period may even be followed by another punctuation mark.

> Though he signed his name Quentin P. Randolph, Esq., we called him Bubba.

Abbreviations for institutions, corporations, networks, or government agencies usually don't require periods; neither do words shortened by common use.

| | | | |
|---|---|---|---|
| NFL | GM | HBO | FEMA |
| lab | auto | dorm | co-op |

Similarly, acronyms—first-letter abbreviations pronounced as words—don't take periods.

| | | |
|---|---|---|
| CARE | NATO | NOW |

When in doubt about punctuating abbreviations, check a dictionary.

**4 Use periods in conventional ways.** Not all periods mark the ends of sentences. They are also used, for example, to indicate decimals, to mark chapter and verse in biblical citations in MLA style, and to separate parts of email addresses and URLs.

| | | |
|---|---|---|
| 0.01 | $189.00 | 75.47 |

Matthew 3.1
toogie@mail.utexas.edu
<http://www.google.com>

## 34b When do you use question marks?

Question marks terminate questions; they can also be used to suggest doubt or uncertainty. Writers sometimes have problems figuring out where to place question marks when they are used with other punctuation, especially with quotation marks.

### ●1 Use question marks to end direct questions.

Have you ever studied military history?
Who fought in the Battle of Cannae?
Do you know that Hannibal smashed the Roman legions?
How?

### ●2 Use question marks to indicate that a name, date, or fact cannot be established with certainty. But don't use a question mark this way when you are unsure of facts that might be available with more research.

Hannibal (247?–183 BCE) was the Roman Republic's greatest foe.

### ●3 Do not use question marks to terminate indirect questions. **Indirect questions** are statements that seem to have questions within them. Compare these examples to see the difference.

| | |
|---|---|
| **INDIRECT QUESTION** | Varro wondered whether Hannibal's strategy would succeed. |
| **DIRECT QUESTION** | Will Hannibal's strategy succeed? |
| **QUESTION WITHIN A STATEMENT** | Varro wondered, "Will Hannibal's strategy succeed?" |
| **INDIRECT QUESTION** | The reporter asked how the new agency would be funded. |
| **DIRECT QUESTION** | How will the new agency be funded? |
| **QUESTION WITHIN A STATEMENT** | "How will the new agency be funded?" the reporter asked. |

### ●4 Punctuate as questions any compound sentences that begin with statements but end with questions.

The strategy seemed reasonable, but would it work on the battlefield?

Don't confuse these constructions with indirect questions.

**5 Place question marks after direct questions that appear in the middle of sentences.** Such questions will usually be surrounded by parentheses, quotation marks, or dashes.

> Skeptical of their tour guide's claim—"Would Hannibal really position his cavalry here?"—the scholars in the group consulted a map.

**6 Place question marks outside quotation marks except when they are part of the quoted material itself.**

> Was it Terence who wrote "Fortune helps the brave"?
> The teacher asked, "Have you read any Cicero?"

For a more detailed explanation of quotation marks, see Section 38a.

**7 Do not allow question marks to bump against other punctuation marks.** For instance, you wouldn't place a comma, colon, or semicolon after a question mark.

> WRONG     "Where did the battle begin?," the tourist asked.
> RIGHT      "Where did the battle begin?" the tourist asked.

Don't multiply question marks to add emphasis. One mark is sufficient.

> WRONG     Are you serious???
> RIGHT      Are you serious?

## 34c When should you use exclamation marks?

Exclamations give emphasis to statements. They are vigorous punctuation marks with the subtlety of a Lamborghini Murcielago. In academic writing, they should be about as rare too.

**1 Use exclamation marks to express strong reactions or commands.**

> They are infuriating!
> Our time has come at last!

Save exclamations for those occasions—rare in college and business writing—when your words really deserve emphasis. Too many exclamations can make a passage seem juvenile.

> **OVERDONE**    The Roman forces at the Battle of Cannae outnumbered Hannibal's forces roughly two to one**!** Yet Roman casualties would be ten times higher than those suffered by Hannibal's army**!**

> **TEMPERED**    The Roman forces at the Battle of Cannae outnumbered Hannibal's forces roughly two to one**.** Yet Roman casualties would be ten times higher than those suffered by Hannibal's army**.**

**2 Do not allow exclamation marks to bump against other punctuation marks.** For instance, you wouldn't place a comma, colon, or semicolon after an exclamation mark.

> **WRONG**    "Please check your records again!," the caller demanded.
> **RIGHT**    "Please check your records again**!**" the caller demanded.

Don't multiply exclamation marks to add emphasis. One mark is sufficient.

> **WRONG**    Don't shout!!
> **RIGHT**    Don't shout**!**

**EXERCISE 34.1** Edit the following passage, adding, replacing, and deleting periods, question marks, exclamation points, and any other marks of punctuation that need to be changed.

1. Hannibal simply outfoxed the Roman general Varro at Cannae!!!

2. Hannibal placed his numerically smaller army where the Aufidius River would protect his flank—could the hotheaded Varro appreciate such a move—and deployed his forces to make the Roman numbers work against themselves!

3. It must have seemed obvious to Hannibal where Varro would concentrate his forces?

4. "Advance!," Hannibal ordered!

5. Is it likely that the Roman general noticed how thin the Carthaginian forces were at the center of the battle line?

6. Predictably, the Romans pressed their attack on the weakened Carthaginian center. But in the meantime, Hannibal's cavalry had destroyed its Roman counterpart!

7. You might be wondering, "Why didn't Hannibal use his cavalry to strengthen his weak center"?

8. It was because he wanted it behind the Roman lines to attack from the rear!

9. Hannibal expected the troops at the ends of his battle line to outflank the Romans, but would such a strategy work.

10. It did! The Romans found themselves surrounded and defeated!

# 35 Problems with Sentence Boundaries: Fragments, Comma Splices, and Run-ons?

Three of the most troublesome and common punctuation problems are the fragment, the comma splice, and the run-on. All three problems arise from confusion about sentence boundaries—that is, where sentences begin and end.

## 35a How do you identify and fix sentence fragments?

**Sentence fragments** are phrases or clauses that look like complete sentences, but either they lack subjects or verbs (see Section 16a-1) or they are subordinate constructions (see Section 16g).

| | |
|---|---|
| **NO SUBJECT** | Fits perfectly! |
| **NO VERB** | The gold ring. |
| **SUBORDINATE** | That I found on the subway. |
| **COMPLETE SENTENCE** | The gold ring that I found on the subway fits perfectly. |

### ●1 Check that all sentences have complete subjects and verbs, either stated or implied.
Sometimes subjects may be understood rather than stated—for example, in commands. But complete sentences always need subjects and verbs.

The sun rose. subject is *sun*; verb is *rose*

It was a beautiful morning. subject is *it*; verb is *was*

Keep quiet. subject *you* is understood; verb is *keep*

**⊕2 Check that you have not allowed a dependent or subordinate clause to stand alone as a sentence.** Subordinate clauses—that is, clauses that begin with words such as *although, because, if, since, unless, when, while*—won't work as sentences by themselves even though they have a subject and a verb (see Section 16d-2). Such fragments can usually be repaired by attaching them to surrounding sentences.

| | |
|---|---|
| **FRAGMENT** | Rainbows can be observed only in the morning or late afternoon. **When the sun is less than forty degrees above the horizon.** |
| **COMPLETE SENTENCE** | Rainbows can be observed only in the morning or late afternoon when the sun is less than forty degrees above the horizon. |

**⊕3 Check that you have not allowed a relative clause or appositive to stand alone as a sentence.** Words such as *who, which, that*, and *where* typically signal the beginning of a relative clause—one that must be connected to a sentence to make a complete thought (see Section 19d-2). If the clause is left unattached, a fragment results.

| | |
|---|---|
| **FRAGMENT** | The Capitol is on Congress Avenue. **Which is the widest street in the city.** |
| **CORRECTED** | The Capitol is on Congress Avenue, which is the widest street in the city. |

The appositive, a group of words that gives more information about a noun, is another construction that produces fragments when left to stand alone (see Section 16c-4).

| | |
|---|---|
| **FRAGMENT** | Dr. Anderson resigned her professorship. **The Herstein Chair of Psychology.** |
| **CORRECTED** | Dr. Anderson resigned her professorship, the Herstein Chair of Psychology. |

**⊕4 Check that you have not substituted a verbal for the verb in a sentence.** If you have, the result will be a fragment. Verbals (see Sections 24a and 24b) look like verbs, but they act as nouns, adjectives, or adverbs.

Here are examples of verbals causing sentence fragments. The fragments are boldfaced.

| FRAGMENT | The reporter from Reuters asked the senator probing questions. **Frowning all the while.** |
|---|---|
| ELIMINATED | Frowning all the while, the reporter from Reuters asked the senator probing questions |
| FRAGMENT | **To break a story.** That was the reporter's goal. |
| ELIMINATED | To break a story was the reporter's goal. |

**◉5 Check that you have not treated a disconnected phrase as a sentence.** Turning a disconnected phrase into a full sentence usually requires adding a subject or a verb (sometimes both).

| FRAGMENTS | David cleaned his glasses. **Absentmindedly. With the hem of his lamb's-wool sweater.** |
|---|---|
| ELIMINATED | Absentmindedly, David cleaned his glasses with the hem of his lamb's-wool sweater. |

**◉6 Check that you have not treated a list as a complete sentence.** Sometimes a list gets detached from the sentence that introduces or explains it.

| FRAGMENT | Bucking a Washington tradition, some politicians have willingly left office to pursue new interests. **Pat Schroeder and J. C. Watts among them.** |
|---|---|
| ELIMINATED | Bucking a Washington tradition, some politicians have willingly left office to pursue new interests, among them Pat Schroeder and J. C. Watts. |

Lists are sometimes introduced by words or phrases such as *especially, for example, for instance, such as*, and *namely*.

| FRAGMENT | People suffer from many peculiar phobias. **For example, ailurophobia (fear of cats), aviophobia (fear of fly-ing), ombrophobia (fear of rain), and vestiphobia (fear of clothes).** |
|---|---|

ELIMINATED   People suffer from many peculiar phobias—for example, ailurophobia (fear of cats), aviophobia (fear of flying), ombrophobia (fear of rain), and vestiphobia (fear of clothes).

**EXERCISE 35.1**   Rewrite the following passage to eliminate any sentence fragments.

The news agenda in the United States used to be set by just a few institutions. Chiefly the news arms of the three television networks (CBS, NBC, and ABC). Along with three or four major papers. These news outlets were located mainly on the East and West Coasts. Giving these regions extra clout in political affairs. Especially influential was the *New York Times*. Considered the paper of record in the United States. However, in recent years, 24-hour news channels, radio talk shows, and Internet news outlets have challenged the power of the traditional media. Widening the range of news topics. Creating outlets for regional opinions. Providing places to examine and question mainstream news sources. The *New York Times* has become a favorite target of many critics in the new media outlets. Especially bloggers, who have had a field day finding errors and omissions in its coverage.

## 35b When are fragments okay?

Are sentence fragments considered wrong at some times but not at others? The answer is yes, depending on your purpose and audience. In advertising copy, email communications, and much fiction—phrases without subjects or verbs are routinely punctuated as sentences.

The classic sports chronometer. Rugged but elegant. Engineered to aviation standards. A cut above.

A Starbucks in Muleshoe? Bad idea. Won't get financing. Not from any local bank.

Such fragments are not actually puzzling or confusing when audiences expect them—as they might in informal, popular, or creative writing. But for that reason, fragments would be considered out of place in academic, professional, or technical writing. As a rule, avoid intentional fragments in school assignments and professional writing.

However, don't be confused by commands—words or phrases in the imperative mood. They may look like sentence fragments because they do not state a subject, but the subject is assumed—the silent or "understood" *you.* "Don't give an inch in the negotiations!" is a sentence. So is "Vote for Pedro."

**EXERCISE 35.2**  Bring to class some advertisements that use intentional fragments or locate a Web site or electronic mailing list that routinely includes fragments. Working with other students in a small group, identify these fragments; then join forces to rewrite them and eliminate all incomplete sentences. Assess the difference between the original material and the revised versions.

## 35c How can you avoid comma splices?

A comma splice occurs when you try to join two independent clauses with a comma only.

**COMMA SPLICE**
Local shopkeepers were concerned about a recent outbreak of graffiti, they feared that it indicated the arrival of troublesome gangs in the neighborhood.

The error is common and considered serious in academic and professional writing—but it is easy to identify and fix.

● 1 **Remember that commas can't link complete sentences.**  They require a linkage stronger than a comma alone to show their relationship.

| COMMA SPLICE | The report is highly critical of the news media, it has received little press coverage. |
|---|---|
| CORRECTED | The report is highly critical of the news media, so it has received little press coverage. |

| | |
|---|---|
| **COMMA SPLICE** | Shawna is an outstanding reporter, she has no formal training in journalism. |
| **CORRECTED** | Shawna is an outstanding reporter, but she has no formal training in journalism. |

Very short sentences, usually in threes, may be joined by commas. These constructions are rare.

I came, I saw, I conquered.

He ate, I paid, we left.

### ◉2 Eliminate a comma splice by replacing the faulty comma with a semicolon. Use this option when the relationship between the sentences is so close that you don't need any connecting word.

| | |
|---|---|
| **COMMA SPLICE** | When David detailed his Mustang, every brush, sponge, and swab was arranged in one neat row, he laid out each towel, chamois, and duster in another. |
| **CORRECTED** | When David detailed his Mustang, every brush, sponge, and swab was arranged in one neat row; he laid out each towel, chamois, and duster in another. |

### ◉3 Eliminate a comma splice by replacing the faulty comma with a period. Use a period when you want a clear separation between two ideas or maybe a dramatic pause.

| | |
|---|---|
| **COMMA SPLICE** | David polished a square inch of his car at a time, by the end of the day he had finished the hood and one fender. |
| **CORRECTED** | David polished a square inch of his car at a time. By the end of the day, he had finished the hood and one fender. |

### ◉4 Eliminate a comma splice by inserting a coordinating conjunction after the comma. Add a conjunction when you need a word that clarifies or explains the relationship between the two ideas. The coordinating conjunctions are *and, or, nor, for, but, yet,* and *so.*

| COMMA SPLICE | His progress was slow because he did every step by hand, it was satisfying work. |
|---|---|
| CORRECTED | His progress was slow because he did every step by hand, but it was satisfying work. |

**5 Eliminate a comma splice by subordinating one of the independent clauses.** You can do that by introducing one of the independent clauses with a subordinating word such as *although, because, since,* or *when.* The subordinating conjunction helps to put the separate ideas in a clear relationship. For more on subordination, see Section 16g.

| COMMA SPLICE | Detailing a vehicle requires skill, learning to do it can pay off in a profitable career. |
|---|---|
| CORRECTED | Although detailing a vehicle requires skill, learning to do it can pay off in a profitable career. |

**EXERCISE 35.3** Identify the sentences with comma splices and correct them.

1. At one time the walls in many Philadelphia neighborhoods were covered with graffiti, however they are covered with murals today.

2. Since 1984 a city-sponsored program has been teaming young graffiti writers with professional artists, the result is the creation of over a thousand works of public art.

3. The murals are large, they are colorful, they are 99 percent graffiti-free.

4. A forty-foot-tall mural of Julius ("Dr. J") Erving has become a local landmark, even Dr. J himself brings friends by to see it.

5. The theory behind the program is that graffiti writers, being inherently artistic themselves, will not deface a work of art they respect, so far the theory holds.

## 35d How can you fix run-on sentences?

A *run-on* occurs when no punctuation at all separates two independent clauses (see Section 16d-1). The reader is left to figure out where one sentence ends and a second begins. Note that run-ons are caused by incorrect punctuation, not by the length of the sentence.

| | |
|---|---|
| **RUN-ON** | We hoped for compromise we got nothing. |
| **CORRECTED** | We hoped for compromise. We got nothing. |

### ●1 Correct a run-on by separating independent clauses with a period.

| | |
|---|---|
| **RUN-ON** | Politicians fear reforming social security someday they will scramble to prevent its bankruptcy. |
| **CORRECTED** | Politicians fear reforming social security. Someday they will scramble to prevent its bankruptcy. |

### ●2 Correct a run-on by inserting a semicolon between independent clauses. A semicolon suggests that the ideas in the two sentences are closely related.

| | |
|---|---|
| **RUN-ON** | Emily's entire life revolves around ecological problems she can speak of little else. |
| **CORRECTED** | Emily's entire life revolves around ecological problems**;** she can speak of little else. |

For more on semicolons, see Section 37a.

### ●3 Correct a run-on by joining independent clauses with a comma and a coordinating conjunction. The coordinating conjunctions are *and, or, nor, for, but, yet,* and *so.*

| | |
|---|---|
| **RUN-ON** | Poisonous giant toads were introduced to Australia in the 1930s to control beetles they have since become an ecological menace. |

CORRECTED    Poisonous giant toads were introduced to Australia in the 1930s to control beetles, but they have since become an ecological menace.

**●4 Correct a run-on by subordinating one of the independent clauses to the other.**

RUN-ON    Albert had to finish the financial report by himself his irresponsible co-author had lost interest in the cause.

RUN-ON ELIMINATED    Albert had to finish the financial report by himself because his irresponsible co-author had lost interest in the cause.

**EXERCISE 35.4** Rewrite these sentences to eliminate punctuation problems that create run-on sentences.

1. Centuries of superstition and ignorance have given bats a bad reputation millions of the flying mammals are killed each year in a misguided effort to protect livestock, crops, and people.

2. Entire species of bats are being wiped out at an alarming rate for example, in the 1960s a new species of fruit-eating bat was discovered in the Philippines by the 1980s it was extinct.

3. In truth, bats are industrious and invaluable members of the natural order they spread the seeds of hundreds of species of plants.

4. Strange as it may sound, bats are essential to the economies of many countries the plants they pollinate or seed include such cash crops as bananas, figs, dates, vanilla beans, and avocados.

5. Many plants essential to such delicate ecosystems as the African savanna and the South American rain forest rely solely on bats for propagating should the bats disappear, the entire system could collapse.

**2 Use a comma after an introductory dependent clause.**
Dependent clauses are signaled by words such as *after, although, as, because, before, if, since, unless, when, while.*

> **While** the military band played taps **,** the flag was lowered.

> **If the CEO can't avert this crisis,** she'll be history.

When there is no comma after such an introductory clause, the reader may not understand where the main clause of the sentence begins.

> **COMMA MISSING**   Although the crack in the roadway had opened months before the bridge inspector who found it seemed surprised.
>
> *Does* before *go with the dependent clause or the main clause?*

> **COMMA ADDED**   Although the crack in the roadway had opened months before **,** the bridge inspector who found it seemed surprised.

**3 Use a comma to set off contrasts.**  Often the contrast will occur in a phrase following the main clause.

> Marietta makes mediocre pottery **, though her prices are steep.**

> In most cities, owning a car is a necessity **, not a luxury.**

Do not use a comma, however, when the additional clause or phrase is closely related to the main idea of the sentence.

> The NASDAQ market plunged **despite new rules to control computer trading.**

**4 Use commas after conjunctive adverbs at the beginning of sentences or clauses.**  Commas are needed because words of this kind—*consequently, nevertheless, however, therefore*—are interrupters that mark a shift or contrast in a sentence.

> **INCORRECT**   The poll was poorly designed. Nevertheless those who commissioned it had faith in the answers.

> **CORRECT**   The poll was poorly designed. Nevertheless **,** those who commissioned it had faith in the answers.

# 36 How Do You Use Commas?

Commas are interrupters or signals to pause. As signals, they aren't as strong as semicolons, which typically appear at major intersections between clauses. And they are certainly not as forceful as periods, which mark the ends of sentences. Instead, commas make a reader slow down and pay attention to the words and ideas they set off.

## 36a When are commas needed to separate items in a sentence?

Some commas keep words, phrases, and clauses apart. But you may have to rely on both some rules and your instincts to place them appropriately. Use too many commas, and your writing will seem plodding and fussy; use too few, and your readers may be confused.

**◉ 1 Use commas after introductory phrases of more than three or four words.** Phrases—which come in several varieties (see Section 16c)—are groups of words without subjects or verbs.

> Well before the end of the day, we were in Amarillo.
>
> Having driven nonstop most of the afternoon, we decided to spend the night in Raton.

A comma isn't needed when an introductory phrase is only a few words long and the sentence is clear without it. You may use a comma in these situations, however, when you believe it makes a sentence easier to read. Commas would be optional, though acceptable, in the following sentences.

> On Tuesday, we were in Mesa Verde National Park.
>
> Carefully, we climbed the ladder at Balcony House.

In a compound sentence (one made up of two or more independent clauses), those clauses may be joined by a semicolon. In that case, put the comma after the conjunctive adverb in the second clause.

> The budget cuts are final; **therefore**, you'll have to reduce staff.

But when a conjunctive adverb occurs in the middle of the clause modified, put a comma before and after it.

> It seemed to us, **however**, that the flames were spreading.

See Section 37a-3 for more on using and punctuating conjunctive adverbs.

**⬤5 Use commas to set off absolute phrases.** Absolutes are phrases made up of nouns and participles. You are most likely to recognize them through examples.

> **The question settled**, the strikers returned to their jobs.
> **All things considered**, the fund drive was a success.

**⬤6 Use commas to introduce quotations or to follow them.** Commas set off quotations introduced or followed by phrases such as *he said, she repeated, he argued, she insisted.*

> The lawyer kept repeating, "My client can't be held responsible for that."
> "Don't tell me he can't be held responsible," retorted the judge.

A phrase that interrupts a single independent clause is set off by commas.

> "I am sure," she said, "you will remember our earlier conversation."

No commas are needed when a quotation fits neatly into a sentence without a separate introductory phrase.

> Oscar Wilde defines experience as "the name we give to our mistakes."
> Dorothy Parker observes that "wit has truth in it; wisecracking is simply calisthenics with words."

See Section 38a for more on punctuating quotations.

## 7 Learn other uses of commas that separate.

- Commas separate words where repetitive phrases have been left out.

  Brad Pitt once worked as a giant chicken; Rod Stewart **,** as a grave-digger; Whoopi Goldberg **,** as a makeup artist for corpses.

- Commas separate parts of sentences that might cause confusion.

  The motto of some critics seems to be **,** whatever is **,** is wrong.

- Commas separate conversational expressions from the main body of the sentence.

  **No ,** I'm sure the inspector wasn't there.

- Commas set off direct address.

  "**Jane ,** bring in the newspaper when you come," I said.

- Commas separate mild interjections—short exclamations or expressions of emotion—from the main body of the sentence.

  **Oh ,** I'm sure it will be all right.

- Commas set off tag questions.

  You did remember the salsa **, didn't you?**

**EXERCISE 36.1** Insert commas in these sentences where needed.

1. When Mount St. Helens erupted in 1980 the north slope collapsed sending torrents of mud and rock down into the Toutle River valley.

2. Stripped of all vegetation for fifteen miles the valley was left virtually lifeless; whatever trees there were were dead.

3. In an effort to prevent erosion and speed the valley's recovery ecologists planted grasses and ground covers.

4. However the species they planted were not native but alien or exotic.

**5.** All things considered the scientists probably should have left nature to take its course since the alien plants are now inhibiting the regrowth of native species.

## 36b When should commas enclose words and phrases?

Enclosing some words and phrases with commas makes sentences more readable; the commas chunk information into manageable units.

**1 Use commas to set off nonessential (nonrestrictive) modifiers.** When you can remove a modifier from a sentence without affecting the primary meaning of the sentence, the modifier is *nonessential.* Such modifiers are surrounded by commas.

| | |
|---|---|
| NONESSENTIAL MODIFIER | The police officers **,** **who had been carefully screened ,** marched in front. |
| MODIFIER REMOVED | The police officers marched in front. |

When you can't remove the modifier without affecting meaning, the modifier is *essential* (restrictive). Essential modifiers do not take commas.

The car **that we had received** was not the car **that we had custom-ordered**.

A good rule of thumb: Do not use commas to set off clauses beginning with *that*.

| | |
|---|---|
| INCORRECT | The bill **,** that was passed by the city council **,** will raise property taxes again. |
| CORRECT | The bill that was passed by the city council will raise property taxes again. |

For more on essential and nonessential clauses, see Section 30i.

**●2 Use commas to enclose appositives that are nonessential.**
An *appositive* is a noun or noun phrase that describes another noun or pronoun more fully. Usually it is nonessential.

> Franklin Delano Roosevelt **, the only President to serve more than two terms ,** died in office.

There are, however, essential appositives that follow a noun and give information necessary to the sentence. The following sentence needs the essential appositive to clarify *which* of Hemingway's many novels is being discussed.

> The Hemingway novel ***The Sun Also Rises*** is set in Pamplona, Spain.

But when it's clear from the rest of the sentence which novel is meant, the appositive becomes nonessential.

> Hemingway's first successful novel **, *The Sun Also Rises* ,** is set in Pamplona, Spain.

**●3 Use commas to enclose various interrupting words, phrases, and clauses.** It is important to use commas in pairs when the interruptions come in the middle of sentences.

> The president intends **, predictably ,** to veto the bill in its current form.
>
> The first landmark we recognized **, well before the plane landed ,** was the Washington Monument.
>
> The senators **, it seemed ,** were eager for a filibuster.
>
> Tell me **, Mr. Reuter ,** what is your opinion?

**EXERCISE 36.2** Discuss the following sentences to decide which modifiers are essential and which are not; then fix the sentences that need to be changed.

1. Carter a salesclerk with a passion for Native American art urged Iona his manager at a gallery in Alpine to increase her stock of Navajo rugs.

2. On a sales trip, Carter had met with several art dealers who specialized in Native American crafts; the dealer Carter met in Gallup had offered rugs produced by several well-known artists.

3. The rugs that he showed Carter included examples of all the classic Navajo designs produced from wool which the weavers had shorn, carded, and dyed themselves.

4. Iona who had managed the store for ten years was uncertain that her regular customers would buy the premium rugs which cost as much as $6,000.

5. But because Iona the lover of art was more speculative than Iona the businesswoman, the gallery soon featured a selection of Navajo rugs which fortunately increased sales traffic.

## 36c When are commas needed to connect parts of a sentence?

Although commas often mark separations, they can also tell readers that certain ideas belong together.

**1 Use commas before the coordinating conjunctions *and, or, nor, for, but, yet*, and *so* when those words link independent clauses to form compound sentences.**

Texas is larger in land area than California **, and** its history is different too.

West Texas can seem empty at times **, yet** the vastness of its deserts and high plains is part of its appeal.

A comma is especially important when the two clauses separated by the conjunction are long.

Experts have tried to explain why dogs wag their tails **, but** they have not come up with a satisfactory reason for this attention-grabbing behavior.

Be careful—commas don't *follow* coordinating conjunctions between two independent clauses.

WRONG    My friends shared my opinion but **,** they were afraid to say so.

RIGHT    My friends shared my opinion **,** but they were afraid to say so.

Remember not to join two independent clauses by a comma. If you do, you'll create a comma splice (see Section 35c).

## ● 2 Use commas to link items in a series of three or more.

> The mapmaker had omitted the capital cities of Idaho **,** New York **,** and Delaware!

Newspaper and magazine articles follow the conventions of journalism and typically omit the final comma.

> The mapmaker had omitted the capital cities of Idaho **,** New York and Delaware!

No comma is needed between just two items in a series.

> The mapmaker had omitted the capital cities of Idaho and Delaware!

## ● 3 Use commas to link coordinate adjectives in series.

**Coordinate adjectives** modify the noun they precede, not each other (see Section 16b-1).

> The job calls for a **creative **,** experienced **,** intelligent** manager.

When adjectives are coordinate, they can be switched around without affecting the sense of a phrase.

> The job calls for an **intelligent **,** experienced **,** creative** manager.

A rule of thumb: If you can insert *and* between adjectives, they are *coordinate*.

> The job calls for an **intelligent **,** and **experienced **,** and **creative** manager.

Do not use commas to mark off noncoordinate adjectives in a series. *Non-coordinate adjectives* work together to modify a term. They cannot be switched around or have *and* inserted between them.

> He drives a **sharp blue Mustang** convertible.

> Tom Cruise has already been nominated for the **best supporting actor** Oscar.

**EXERCISE 36.3** Rewrite the following sentences, adding commas where they are needed to link ideas, moving commas that are misplaced, and correcting comma splices. Some sentences may be correct.

1. Many people freeze when they enter an electronics store cluttered with merchandise shoppers and grinning hyperactive sales staff.

2. Shrewd, and careful shoppers know exactly what they intend to buy when they walk in but, they routinely discover that those gizmos have been discontinued modified or reordered.

3. Fifteen-year-old, sales clerks direct them to ten, megapixel digital, cameras that cost an arm, and a leg.

4. When a customer explains that she just wants a clock radio, the pimply, faced sales representative will steer her toward a 52-inch plasma-screen TV that has a clock function.

5. Dazed confused and soon-to-be penniless, customers trudge toward gleaming, check-out counters lugging more electronics gear than 007.

## 36d Where are commas not necessary or wrong?

Every comma in a sentence should be placed for a reason: to mark a pause, to set off a unit, to keep words from running together. Cut those that don't serve any such purpose.

### ◑ 1 Eliminate commas that interrupt the flow of a sentence.
Sometimes a comma disrupts what would otherwise be a clear statement.

| | |
|---|---|
| **UNNECESSARY COMMA** | Five years into graduate school, Frida found herself**,** without a degree or prospects for a job. |
| **COMMA CUT** | Five years into graduate school, Frida found herself without a degree or prospects for a job. |

At other times, unneeded commas seem to follow a guideline, but they really don't. In the following example, the writer may recall that commas often follow introductory words, phrases, and clauses.

| | |
|---|---|
| UNNECESSARY COMMA | However **,** cold it gets, the train arrives on time. |
| COMMA CUT | However cold it gets, the train arrives on time. |

**● 2 Don't let a comma separate a subject from a verb.** Such problems usually occur when the subject of a sentence is more complex than usual—perhaps a noun clause or a verb phrase.

| | |
|---|---|
| UNNECESSARY COMMA | What happened to the team since last season **,** isn't clear. |
| COMMA CUT | What happened to the team since last season isn't clear. |
| WRONG | To keep the team's spirit up **,** won't be easy. |
| RIGHT | To keep the team's spirit up won't be easy. |

Only in rare cases may a comma be required between subject and verb to ensure clarity.

Those who hope **,** thrive; those who despair **,** fail.

Note that when nonessential modifiers or interrupters separate subjects from their verbs, the modifying phrases are set off by *pairs* of commas.

**MODIFIER SET OFF BY COMMAS**

Frida **,** who just turned 51 **,** is determined to improve her job qualifications.

See Section 30i for more on nonessential modifiers.

**● 3 Don't let a comma separate a verb from its object.**

| | |
|---|---|
| UNNECESSARY COMMA | During the Cold War, the Pentagon developed and deployed **,** nuclear submarines, cruise missiles, and MIRV warheads. |

| COMMA CUT | During the Cold War, the Pentagon developed and deployed nuclear submarines, cruise missiles, and MIRV warheads. |
|---|---|

## ⊙4 Don't use commas to separate compound subjects, predicates, or objects.

| WRONG | The Mississippi**,** and the Missouri are two of the United States' great rivers. |
|---|---|
| RIGHT | The Mississippi and the Missouri are two of the United States' great rivers. |
| WRONG | We toured the museum**,** and then explored the monument. |
| RIGHT | We toured the museum and then explored the monument. |
| WRONG | Alexander broke his promise to his agent**,** and his contract with his publisher. |
| RIGHT | Alexander broke his promise to his agent and his contract with his publisher. |

Of course, commas are used to separate full independent clauses joined by conjunctions. Compare the following sentences, both punctuated correctly.

| RIGHT | We toured the museum and then explored the monument. |
|---|---|
| RIGHT | We toured the museum, and then we explored the monument. |

## ⊙5 Don't use commas to introduce lists.

| WRONG | States with impressive national parks include**,** California, Utah, Arizona, and New Mexico. |
|---|---|
| RIGHT | States with impressive national parks include California, Utah, Arizona, and New Mexico. |

Note, though, how commas works in the following sentences to set off lists introduced by "including" and "such as."

| RIGHT | Many states have impressive national parks, including California, Utah, Arizona, and New Mexico. |
|---|---|

RIGHT    Many states, such as California, Utah, Arizona, and New Mexico, have impressive national parks.

Commas may be used to enclose lists that function as nonessential modifiers.

RIGHT    Universities with major football programs, Notre Dame, Michigan, and LSU among them, benefit from generous alumni contributions.

In such cases, however, all the commas can be confusing. The modifier might be better enclosed by dashes (see Section 40a).

RIGHT    Universities with major football programs—Notre Dame, Michigan, and LSU among them—benefit from generous alumni contributions.

**EXERCISE 36.4** Working in a group, analyze these sentences to see if all the commas are needed. Then work together to rewrite sentences to get rid of commas that cause awkward interruptions. Notice that some of the commas are necessary.

1. Psychologists, who have studied moods, say that such emotional states are contagious, and compare them to social viruses.

2. Moreover, some people are emotionally expressive, and likely to transmit moods; others, seem to be more inclined to "catch" moods.

3. Trying to pinpoint the exact means by which moods are transmitted, is difficult, since the process happens almost instantaneously.

4. One transmission mechanism is imitation: by unconsciously imitating facial expressions, people produce, in themselves a mood that goes with the expression.

5. People who get along well with others, generally, synchronize their moods, by making a series of changes in their body language.

## 36e **What special uses do commas have?**

Aside from the important role commas play within sentences both in linking and separating ideas, commas have many conventional uses you simply have to know to get right.

● 1 **Use commas correctly to separate units of three within numbers.** Commas are optional in four-digit numbers.

> 4,110 or 4110
>
> 99,890
>
> 1,235,470

Do not use commas in decimals, social security numbers, street addresses, or zip codes.

> 3.141592653
>
> 286-50-0012
>
> 14145 Lisa Dr.
>
> 78750-8124

● 2 **Use commas correctly in dates.** In American usage, commas separate the day from the year. Note that a year is enclosed by commas when it appears in the middle of a sentence.

> World War II began on September 1, 1939.
>
> Germany expanded the war on June 22, 1941, when its armies invaded Russia.

Commas aren't required when only the month and year are given.

> World War II began in September 1939.

Commas are not used when dates are given in British form, with the day preceding the month.

> World War II began on 1 September 1939.

**3 Use commas correctly in addresses.** Commas ordinarily separate street addresses, cities, states, and countries. When these items occur in the middle of a sentence, they are enclosed by commas.

Miami University is in Oxford, Ohio.

Though born in London, England, Denise Levertov is considered an American writer.

The prime minister lives at No. 10 Downing Street, Westminster, London, England.

Commas aren't used between states and zip codes.

Austin, Texas  78712

**4 Use commas correctly to separate proper names from titles and degrees that follow.**

Tonya Galvin, Ph.D., has been chosen to replace Howard Brill, M.D.

**5 Use commas to follow the salutation and closing in personal letters.**

Dear Aunt Sue,

Dear Friends,

Sincerely yours,

With regards,

**EXERCISE 36.5** Review the following sentences and add commas where necessary.

1. In the autumn of 1863, Abraham Lincoln President of the United States traveled to Gettysburg Pennsylvania to speak at the dedication of a cemetery there.

2. The cemetery was for the soldiers who had fallen at the Battle of Gettysburg, and Lincoln's speech—now known as the Gettysburg Address—opened with the famous words "Fourscore and seven years ago."

3. The Battle of Gettysburg had started on July 1 1863 and had raged for three days.

4. The Civil War would not end until April 1865.

5. The bloodiest battle of the war took place near Sharpsburg Maryland along the banks of Antietam Creek, where a single day of fighting produced over 23000 casualties.

# 37 Questions About Semicolons and Colons?

## 37a When do you use semicolons?

In a sentence, a semicolon ( ; ) marks a stronger pause than a comma, but a weaker pause than a period. Many writers find semicolons confusing. So they avoid them and place commas where semicolons are needed. Or they misuse them, using semicolons where commas work better.

**● 1 Use semicolons to separate items of equal grammatical weight.** Semicolons can be used to separate one independent clause from another, one phrase from another, or one item in a list from another.

independent clause ; independent clause

Director John Ford released *Stagecoach* in 1939 ; a year later, he made *The Grapes of Wrath.*

phrase ; phrase

My film course taught the basics, including how to write treatments, outlines, and scripts ; how to direct actors ; and how to edit.

item in a list ; item in a list ; item in a list

We rented DVDs of *Resident Evil: Apocalypse* ; *Napoleon Dynamite* ; and *Blade Runner—The Director's Cut.*

Because semicolons work only between comparable items, it would be wrong to place a semicolon, for example, between an independent clause and a prepositional phrase or a dependent clause and an independent clause. Commas are usually the correct punctuation in such cases.

independent clause , prepositional phrase

**WRONG** Many young filmmakers regularly exceed their budgets ; in the tradition of the finest Hollywood directors.

**RIGHT** Many young filmmakers regularly exceed their budgets , in the tradition of the finest Hollywood directors.

dependent clause **,** independent clause

**WRONG**     Although director Alfred Hitchcock once said that
actors should be treated like cattle **;** he got fine performances from many of them.

**RIGHT**      Although director Alfred Hitchcock once said that
actors should be treated like cattle **,** he got fine performances from many of them.

**2 Use semicolons to join independent clauses closely related
in thought.** Coordinating conjunctions (such as *and, or, nor, for, but, yet,
so*) aren't needed when clauses are linked by semicolons.

> Italian cinema blossomed after World War II **;** directors like Fellini and
> Antonioni won critical acclaim.

Omitting the semicolon in the example above would create a run-on sentence
(see Section 35d). Using a comma would produce a comma splice (see Section
35c). Sometimes, however, it can seem like punctuation overkill to place semicolons between independent clauses that are both parallel in structure (see
Section 16h) and very short. In these rare cases, commas might be acceptable:

**WITH COMMAS**    For best director **,** Todd picked Alfred Hitchcock **,**
Ryan nominated François Truffaut **,** and Jodi chose
Agnès Varda.

**3 Use semicolons between independent clauses joined by
conjunctive adverbs such as *however, therefore, nevertheless,
nonetheless, moreover*, and *consequently*.** These words by themselves cannot link sentences.

> The original *Rocky* was an Oscar-winning movie **; however,** its many
> sequels exhausted the original idea.

> Films about British spy 007 have been in decline for years **; neverthe-
> less,** new James Bond films continue to appear.

In sentences such as those above, using a comma instead of a semicolon
before the conjunctive adverb would produce a comma splice, an error (see
Section 35c-2).

But when a word like *however* or *therefore* occurs in the middle of an independent clause, it *is* preceded and followed by commas. In the following pair of sentences, note where the boldfaced words appear and how the shifts in location change the punctuation required.

*Casablanca* is now a film classic **; however ,** its stars regarded it as an average spy thriller.

*Casablanca* is now a film classic; its stars **, however ,** regarded it as an average spy thriller.

| Chart 37.1 **Frequently Used Conjunctive Adverbs** | | |
|---|---|---|
| consequently | meanwhile | rather |
| furthermore | moreover | then |
| hence | nonetheless | therefore |
| however | otherwise | thus |

**4 Use semicolons to join independent clauses connected by words or phrases such as *indeed, in fact, at any rate, for example,* and *on the other hand.*** These expressions, like conjunctive adverbs, ordinarily require a semicolon before them and a comma after.

Box office receipts for *Spider-Man's* opening week were spectacular **; indeed,** the film unexpectedly broke records for a summer release.

Tobey Maguire had never opened a major film before **; on the other hand,** he was perfectly cast as the boy-next-door superhero.

A period could be used instead of the semicolon in these situations.

Naturally, *Spider-Man* will spawn many sequels. **In fact,** *Spider-Man 2* was a better film than the original.

**5 Use semicolons to separate clauses, phrases, or items in a series that might be confusing if commas alone were used to mark boundaries.** Semicolons are especially helpful when complicated phrases or items in a list already contain commas or other punctuation.

The sound track for the film included the Supremes' "Stop in the Name of Love!" ; Bob Dylan's "Rainy Day Women #12 & 35" ; and Rodgers and Hart's "Glad to Be Unhappy."

Matt Damon's filmography includes *School Ties*, which is set in an upper-class prep school ; *Saving Private Ryan*, a Steven Spielberg movie in which Damon plays the title character ; and *Good Will Hunting*, a drama that earned him an Oscar for best screenplay.

**6 Do not use semicolons to introduce quotations.** Direct quotations can be introduced by commas or colons.

> WRONG    Wasn't it Mae West who said **;** "When I'm good I'm very good, but when I'm bad, I'm better"?
>
> RIGHT    Wasn't it Mae West who said **,** "When I'm good I'm very good, but when I'm bad, I'm better"?

**7 Never use semicolons to introduce lists.**

> WRONG    Paul Robeson performed in several classic films **;** *Show Boat, Song of Freedom, King Solomon's Mines.*
>
> RIGHT    Paul Robeson performed in several classic films **:** *Show Boat, Song of Freedom, King Solomon's Mines.*

In some cases, semicolons may separate items *within* a list (see Section 37a-1).

**8 Use semicolons correctly with quotation marks.** Semicolons ordinarily fall outside quotation marks (see Section 38a-6).

> The first Edgar Allan Poe work filmed was "The Raven"**;** movies based on the poem appeared in 1912, 1915, and 1935.

**EXERCISE 37.1** Revise the following sentences, adding or deleting semicolons as needed. Not all semicolons below are incorrect. You may have to substitute other punctuation marks for some semicolons.

1. For many years, biblical spectacles were a staple of the Hollywood film industry, however, in recent years, few such films have been produced.

2. Cecil B. DeMille made the grandest epics; he is quoted as saying;"Give me any couple of pages of the Bible and I'll give you a picture."

3. He made *The Ten Commandments* twice, the 1956 version starred Charlton Heston as Moses.

4. The most famous scene in *The Ten Commandments* is the parting of the Red Sea; the waters opening to enable the Israelites to escape the pursuing army of Pharaoh.

5. DeMille made many nonbiblical movies, some of them, however, were also epic productions with casts of thousands and spectacular settings.

# 37b When do you use colons?

Colons (:) are strong directional signals. They show movement in a sentence, pointing your reader's attention to precisely what you wish to highlight, whether it is an idea, a list, a quotation, or even another independent clause. It may help to think of a colon as an equal sign: what is on one side of the colon is roughly equivalent to what's on the other. Colons require your attention because their functions are limited and quite specific.

### 1 Use colons to direct readers to examples, explanations, or significant words and phrases.

Orson Welles's greatest problem may also have been his greatest achievement : the brilliance of his first film, *Citizen Kane*.

*Citizen Kane* turns on the meaning of one word uttered by a dying man : "Rosebud."

A colon that highlights an item in this way ordinarily follows a complete sentence. In fact, many readers object strongly to colons placed after linking verbs.

| WRONG | America's most bankable film star is ; Julia Roberts. |
| RIGHT | America's most bankable film star is Julia Roberts. |

## 2 Use colons to direct readers to lists.

Besides *Citizen Kane*, Welles directed, produced, or acted in many movies : *The Magnificent Ambersons, Journey into Fear, The Lady from Shanghai*, and *Macbeth*, to name a few.

Colons that introduce lists ordinarily follow complete sentences.

The filmmakers the professor admired most were a diverse group : Alain Robbe-Grillet, François Truffaut, Spike Lee, and Penny Marshall.

Colons are omitted after expressions such as *like, for example, such as*, and *that is*. In fact, colons replace these terms.

| | |
|---|---|
| **WRONG** | Shoestring budgets have produced many artistically successful films, such as ; *Plutonium Circus, Breaking Away*, and *Slackers*. |
| **RIGHT** | Shoestring budgets have produced many artistically successful films, such as *Plutonium Circus, Breaking Away*, and *Slackers*. |

Colons are used, however, after phrases that specifically announce a list, expressions such as *including these, as follows*, and *such as the following*. Review the following sentence to understand the difference.

| | |
|---|---|
| **WITH A COLON** | The producer trimmed her budget by cutting out frills **such as the following:** special lighting, rental costumes for the cast, and crew lunches. |

Never introduce a list with a colon that separates a preposition from its object(s).

| | |
|---|---|
| **WRONG** | Katharine Hepburn starred in ; *Little Women, The Philadelphia Story*, and *The African Queen*. |
| **RIGHT** | Katharine Hepburn starred in *Little Women, The Philadelphia Story*, and *The African Queen*. |

## 3 Use colons to direct readers to quotations or dialogue.

Orson Welles commented poignantly on his own career : "I started at the top and worked down."

Don't introduce short quotations with colons. A comma or no punctuation mark at all will suffice. Compare the following sentences.

Dirty Harry said   "Make my day!"

As Dirty Harry said , "Make my day!"

We recalled Dirty Harry's memorable phrase : "Make my day!"

In the last example, the colon *is* appropriate because it directs attention to a particular comment.

**◉4 Use colons to join two complete sentences when the second sentence illustrates or explains the first.**

Making a film is like writing a paper : it absorbs all the time you'll give it.

Don't use more than one colon in a sentence. A dash can usually replace one of the colons.

PROBLEM   Most critics agree on this point : Orson Welles made one of the greatest of films : *Citizen Kane.*

SOLUTION   Most critics agree on this point : Orson Welles made one of the greatest of films—*Citizen Kane.*

Colons and semicolons are not interchangeable, but you can use both marks in the same sentence. A colon, for example, might introduce a list of items separated by semicolons.

The 1950s produced an odd array of science fiction films : *It! The Terror from Beyond Space*; *Earth vs. the Flying Saucers*; *Forbidden Planet.*

**◉5 Use colons to separate titles from subtitles.**

*Nightmare on Elm Street 3* : *Dream Warriors*
"Darkest Night : Conscience in *Macbeth*"

**◉6 Use colons in conventional situations.** Colons separate numbers when indicating time or citing Bible passages—though MLA style uses a period in biblical citations.

12 : 35 p.m.            Matthew 3 : 1 (or Matthew 3.1 in MLA style)

Colons traditionally follow salutations in business letters.

> Dear Ms. Dowd :     Dear Mr. Ebert :

Colons separate place of publication from publisher and separate date from page numbers in various MLA bibliography entries.

> Glenview : Scott, 1961     14 Aug. 1991 : 154–63

Colons appear in Web addresses, with no space left after the mark.

> <http : //google.com>

**EXERCISE 37.2** Revise the following sentences by adding colons or making sure colons are used correctly. Don't assume that every sentence contains an error.

1. No one ever forgets the conclusion of Hitchcock's *Psycho*; the discovery of Norman's mother in the rocking chair.

2. Hitchcock liked to use memorable settings in his films, including: Mt. Rushmore in *North by Northwest*, Radio City Music Hall in *Saboteur*, and the British Museum in *Blackmail*.

3. One actor appears in every Hitchcock film Hitchcock himself.

4. *Rear Window* is a cinematic tour de force: all the action focuses on what Jimmy Stewart sees from his window.

5. Hitchcock probably summed up his own technique best; "There is no terror in a bang, only in the anticipation of it."

# 38   How Do You Use Quotation Marks and Ellipses?

## 38a When do you use quotation marks?

Quotation marks, which always occur in pairs, highlight what appears between them. Use double marks (" ") around most quoted material and around titles. Use single quotation marks (' ') when quoted material (or titles) fall within double quotations.

### ●1 Use quotation marks around material you are borrowing word for word from sources.

> Emerson reminds us that "nothing great was ever achieved without enthusiasm."

> "Next to the originator of a good sentence is the first quoter of it," writes Emerson.

### ●2 Use quotation marks to set off dialogue. When writing a passage with several speakers, start a new paragraph each time the speaker changes.

> Mrs. Bennet deigned not to make any reply; but unable to contain herself, she began scolding one of her daughters.
> "Don't keep coughing so, Kitty, for heaven's sake! Have a little compassion on my nerves. You tear them to pieces."
> "Kitty has no discretion in her coughs," said her father; "she times them ill."
> "I do not cough for my own amusement," replied Kitty fretfully.
> —Jane Austen, *Pride and Prejudice*

When dialogue is provided not for its own sake but to make some other point, the words of several speakers may appear within a single paragraph.

> Professor Norman was confident that his colleagues would eventually see his point. "They'll come around," he predicted. "They

always do. " And Professor Brown, for one, was beginning to soften. " I've supported many proposals not half so bone-headed. "

**3 Use quotation marks to cite the titles of short works.** These include titles of songs, essays, magazine and newspaper articles, TV episodes, unpublished speeches, chapters of books, and short poems. Titles of longer works appear in *italics* (see Section 41a-1).

> " Love Is Just a Four-Letter Word " song
>
> " Love Is a Fallacy " title of an essay

**4 Use quotation marks to draw attention to specific words.** Italics can also be used in these situations (see Section 41a-3).

> Politicians clearly mean different things when they write about " democracy. "

You might also use quotation marks to signal that you are using a word ironically, sarcastically, or derisively.

> The clerk at the desk directed the tourists to their " suites "—bare rooms crowded with cots. A bathroom down the hall would serve as the " spa. "

But don't overdo it. Highlighting a tired phrase or cliché just makes it seem more fatigued.

> Working around electrical fixtures makes me more nervous than ✗a cat on a hot tin roof.✗

**5 Surround quotation marks with appropriate punctuation.** A quotation introduced or followed by *said, remarked, observed*, or a similar expression takes a comma.

> Benjamin Disraeli *observed* , " It is much easier to be critical than to be correct. "

Commas are used, too, when a single-sentence quotation is broken up by an interrupting expression such as *he asked* or *she noted*.

> "If the world were a logical place ," Rita Mae Brown *notes* , "men would ride sidesaddle. "

When such an expression comes between two successive sentences quoted from a single source, a comma and a period are required.

> "There is no such thing as a moral or an immoral book ," *says* Oscar Wilde . "Books are well written, or badly written. That is all. "

No additional punctuation is required when a quotation runs smoothly into a sentence you have written.

> Abraham Lincoln observed that "in giving freedom to the slave we assure freedom to the free . "

See Section 47a for guidelines on introducing and framing quotations.

**● 6 Use quotation marks correctly with other pieces of punctuation.** Commas and periods ordinarily go *inside* closing quotation marks.

> "This must be what the sixties were like ," I thought.

> Down a dormitory corridor lined with antiwar posters, I heard someone humming "Blowin' in the Wind . "

However, when a sentence ends with a citation in parentheses, the period follows the parenthesis.

> Mike Rose argues that we hurt education if we think of it "in limited or limiting ways" (3) .

In American usage, colons and semicolons go *outside* closing quotation marks.

> Riley claimed to be "a human calculator ": he did quadratic equations in his head.

> The young Cassius Clay bragged about being "the greatest "; his opponents in the ring soon learned he wasn't kidding.

Question marks, exclamation points, and dashes can fall either inside or outside quotation marks. They fall *inside* when they apply only to the quotation.

When Mrs. Rattle saw her hotel room, she muttered, "Good grief !"

She turned to her husband and said, "Do you really expect me to stay here ?"

They fall *outside* the closing quotation mark when they apply to the complete sentence.

Who was it who said, "Truth is always the strongest argument "?

**EXERCISE 38.1** Rework the following passage by adding or deleting quotation marks, moving punctuation as necessary, and indenting paragraphs where you think appropriate.

Much to the tourists' surprise, their "uproar" over conditions at their so-called "luxury resort" attracted the attention of a local television station. (In fact, Mrs. Rattle had read "the riot act" to a consumer advocate who worked for the station.) A reporter interviewed Mrs. Rattle, who claimed that she had been promised luxury accommodations. This place smells like old fish she fumed. Even the roaches look disappointed. Didn't you check out the accommodations before paying? the reporter asked, turning to Mr. Rattle. He replied that unfortunately they had prepaid the entire vacation. But Mrs. Rattle interrupted. I knew we should have gone to Paris. You never said that! Mr. Rattle objected. As I was trying to say, Mrs. Rattle continued, I'd even rather be in Philadelphia.

**EXERCISE 38.2** Write a passage extending the reporter's interview in Exercise 38.1. Or create a dialogue on a subject of your own.

◀▶ **Point of Difference**

The guidelines in this section on quotation marks apply in the United States. Conventions for marking quotations differ significantly from language to language and country to country. French quotation marks, called *guillemets,* look like this: « ». Guillemets are also employed as quotation marks in Spanish, which uses dashes to indicate dialogue. In books published in Britain, you'll find single quotation marks (' ') where American publishers use double marks (" "), and vice versa.

| | |
|---|---|
| **AMERICAN** | Carla said, "I haven't read 'The Raven.'" |
| **BRITISH** | Carla said, 'I haven't read "The Raven".' |

American and British practices differ, too, on the placement of punctuation marks within quotation marks. In general, British usage tends to locate more punctuation marks (commas especially) outside quotation marks than does American usage.

| | |
|---|---|
| **AMERICAN** | To be proper, say "I *shall* go," not "*will.*" |
| **BRITISH** | To be proper, say 'I *shall* go', not '*will*'. |

In the United States, follow American practice. ◆

## 38b When do you use ellipses?

The three spaced periods that form an ellipsis mark (**. . .**) signal that words, phrases, or whole sentences have been cut from a passage you are quoting.

**◉1 Place ellipses where material has been omitted from a direct quotation.** This material may be a word, a phrase, a complete sentence, or more.

**COMPLETE PASSAGE**

Abraham Lincoln closed his First Inaugural Address (March 4, 1861) with these words: "We are not enemies, but friends. We must not be enemies. Though passion may have strained it must not break our bonds of affection. The mystic chords of memory, stretching from every battlefield and patriot grave to every living heart and hearthstone all over this broad land, will yet swell the chorus of the Union, when again touched, as surely they will be, by the better angels of our nature."

**PASSAGE WITH ELLIPSES**

Abraham Lincoln closed his First Inaugural Address (March 4, 1861) with these words: "We are not enemies, but friends. **. . .** The mystic chords of memory **. . .** will yet swell the chorus of the Union, when again touched, as surely they will be, by the better angels of our nature."

If you are quoting an author who uses ellipses, put any ellipses you create in brackets [. . .] to distinguish them from the author's original punctuation. See the sample MLA paper, page 732, for an example.

### ⊘ 2 Use ellipses to indicate pauses of any kind or to suggest that an action is incomplete or continuing.

We were certain we would finish the report on time . . . until the computer crashed and wouldn't reboot.

The rocket rumbled on its launch pad as the countdown wound down, "six, five, four . . ."

### ⊘ 3 Use the correct spacing and punctuation before and after ellipsis marks. An ellipsis is typed as three spaced periods (. . . not ...).
When an ellipsis mark appears in the middle of a quoted sentence, leave a space before the first and after the last period.

mystic chords of memory . . . will yet swell

If punctuation occurs before the ellipsis, include the mark when it makes your sentence easier to read. The punctuation mark is followed by a space, then the ellipsis mark.

The mystic chords of memory, . . . all over this broad land, will yet swell the chorus of the Union.

When an ellipsis occurs at the end of a complete sentence from a quoted passage or when you cut a full sentence or more, place a period at the end of the sentence, followed by a space and then the ellipsis.

We must not be enemies. . . . The mystic chords

When a parenthetical citation follows a sentence that ends with an ellipsis, leave a space between the last word in the sentence and the ellipsis. Then provide the parenthetical reference, followed by the closing punctuation mark.

passion may have strained it . . ." (2001).

**⊕4 Keep ellipses to a minimum at the beginning and end of sentences.** You don't need ellipses every time you break into a sentence. If your quoted material begins with a capital letter, readers will know you are quoting a complete sentence.

> According to Richard Bernstein, "The plain and inescapable fact is that
>
> the derived Western European culture of American life [has] produced
>
> the highest degree of prosperity in the conditions of the greatest
>
> freedom ever known on planet Earth" (11).

You need ellipses at the beginning of a quotation only when a capital letter in a proper noun (or the pronoun *I*) might lead readers to believe that you're quoting a complete sentence when, in fact, you are not.

> According to Richard Bernstein, " **. . .** American life [has] produced the
>
> highest degree of prosperity in the conditions of the greatest freedom
>
> ever known on planet Earth" (11).

Whenever you use an ellipsis, be sure your shortened quotation accurately reflects the meaning of the uncut passage.

**⊕5 Use a full line of spaced dots when you delete more than a line of verse.**

> For Mercy has a human heart,
>
> Pity a human face,
>
> . . . . . . . . . . . . . . . . .
>
> And Peace, the human dress.
>
> —William Blake, "The Divine Image" (1789)

**EXERCISE 38.3** Abridge the following passage, using at least three ellipses. Be sure the passage is still readable after you have made your cuts.

> Within a week, the neglected Victorian-style house being repaired by volunteers began to look livable again, its gables repaired, its gutters rehung, its roof reshingled. Even the grand staircase, rickety and worm-

eaten, had been rebuilt. The amateur artisans made numerous mistakes during the project, including painting several windows shut, papering over a heating register, and hanging a door upside down, but no one doubted their commitment to restoring the historic structure. Some spent hours sanding away layers of varnish accumulated over almost six decades to reveal beautiful hardwood floors. Others contributed their organizational talents—many were managers or paper-pushers in their day jobs—to keep other workers supplied with raw materials, equipment, and inspiration. The volunteers worked from seven in the morning to seven at night, occasionally pausing to talk with neighbors from the area who stopped by with snacks and lunches, but laboring like mules until there was too little light to continue. They all felt the effort was worth it every time they saw the great house standing on the corner in all its former glory.

# 39 How Do Parentheses and Brackets Differ?

## 39a When do you use parentheses?

Parentheses ( ) are common marks of punctuation that allow a writer to add an extra bit of information, a comment, or an aside to a sentence. Precisely because parentheses are so useful, you may find yourself relying on them so often that readers find them intrusive. Keep them to a minimum. Parentheses also enclose in-text notes for MLA and APA documentation (see Chapters 50 and 51).

Don't use parentheses to explain what will be obvious to most readers.

**●1** Use parentheses to separate material from the main body of a sentence or paragraph. This material may be a word, a phrase, a list, even a complete sentence.

The helicopter flight to Ouray **(in southwestern Colorado)** was quick and scenic.

The emergency kit contains essential road trip gear **(jumper cables, tire inflator, flares)**.

The buses arrived early, and by noon the stagehands were working at the stadium. **(One of the vans carried a portable stage.)** Preparations for the concert were on schedule.

**●2** Use parentheses to insert examples, directions, or other details into a sentence.

The call to the police included an address **(107 West St.)**.

If the children get lost, have them call the school **(346-1317)** or the church office **(471-6109)**.

**●3 Use parentheses to highlight numbers or letters used in listing items.**

The labor negotiators realized they faced three alternatives: **(1)** concede on all issues immediately, **(2)** stonewall until the public demanded a settlement, or **(3)** hammer out a compromise.

**●4 Use the correct punctuation with or around parentheses.** When a complete sentence standing alone is surrounded by parentheses, place its end punctuation inside the parentheses.

The neighborhood was run-down. (Some houses looked as if they hadn't been painted in decades **.)**

However, when a sentence concludes with a parenthesis, the end punctuation for the complete sentence falls outside the final parenthesis mark.

On the corner was a small church (actually a converted store **).**

When parentheses enclose a very short sentence within another sentence, the enclosed sentence ordinarily begins without capitalization and ends without punctuation.

The editor pointed out a misplaced modifier **(the writer glared at her)**, crossed out three paragraphs **(the writer grumbled)**, and then demanded a complete rewrite.

Punctuation may be used, however, when an enclosed sentence is a question or exclamation.

The revolution ended **(who would have guessed it?)** almost as quickly as it began.

**●5 Don't use punctuation before a parenthesis in the middle of sentences.** A comma before a parenthesis is incorrect; if necessary, a parenthesis may be followed by a comma.

**WRONG**    Although the Crusades failed in their announced objective✗ **(Jerusalem still remained in Muslim hands afterward)** the expeditions changed the West dramatically.

RIGHT    Although the Crusades failed in their announced objective **(Jerusalem still remained in Muslim hands afterward)**, the expeditions changed the West dramatically.

**EXERCISE 39.1**   Add parentheses as needed to the following sentences.

1. Native Americans inhabited almost every region of North America, from the peoples farthest north the Inuit to those in the Southwest the Hopi, the Zuni.

2. In parts of what are now New Mexico and Colorado, during the thirteenth century, some ancient tribes moved off the mesas no one knows exactly why to live in cliff dwellings.

3. One cliff dwelling at Mesa Verde covers an area of 66 meters 217 feet by 27 meters 89 feet.

4. Spectacular as they are, the cliff dwellings served the tribes known as the Anasazi for only a short time.

5. The Anasazi left their cliff dwellings, possibly because of a prolonged drought A.D. 1276–1299 in the entire region.

## 39b When do you use brackets?

Like parentheses, brackets [ ] are enclosures. But brackets have fewer and more specialized uses. Brackets and parentheses are usually *not* interchangeable.

● 1 **Use brackets to insert comments or explanations into direct quotations.** Although you cannot change the words of a direct quotation, you can add information between brackets.

"He **[George Lucas]** reminded me a little of Walt Disney's version of a mad scientist."

—Steven Spielberg

In other cases, you can insert bracketed material to make the grammar of a quotation fit smoothly into your own syntax. But use this strategy sparingly, taking care not to change the meaning of the original.

Any change you make in an original text, even if only from an uppercase to a lowercase letter or vice versa, should be signaled with brackets.

> In *The Dinosaur Heresies*, Robert T. Bakker rejects "[o]rthodox theory" that treats the giant reptiles as early creatures of evolution. "By the time they [dinosaurs] appear in the land ecosystem," Bakker notes, "the woodlands and waterways were already full of creatures" (16).

Brackets around the letter *o* indicate that you have changed Bakker's original capital letter to lowercase.

**2 Use brackets to avoid one set of parentheses falling within another.** Turn the inner pair of parentheses into brackets.

> The Web site included a full text of the resolution (expressing the sense of Congress on the calculation of the consumer price index **[H.RES.99]**).

**3 Use brackets to acknowledge or highlight errors that originate in quoted materials.** In such cases, the Latin word *sic* ("thus") is enclosed in brackets immediately after the error. See Section 47c-1 for details.

> The sign over the cash register read "We don't except **[sic]** personal checks for payment."

# 40 Questions About Dashes, Hyphens, and Slashes?

Dashes, hyphens, and slashes have specific and different uses in English, some highly rhetorical like the dash, others more mechanical like the hyphen and slash. We also make a distinction you may have never noticed between dashes of different lengths, the em dash and the en dash.

## 40a When do you use an em dash?

The em dash is the mark you are most familiar with, the longish dash roughly equal in width to the printed letter *m* (where the name comes from). Em dashes can be typed as two connected hyphens (--) with no space left before or after the mark. Or, more elegantly, you can create a dash that appears as a single line (—) by using the appropriate computer keystrokes. On a PC, try "Alt" + "Ctrl" + minus (on the keypad); for a Mac, depress "shift" + "option" and the hyphen key.

**●1 Use em dashes to add illustrations, examples, or summaries to the ends of sentences or to emphasize a shift in tone or thought.** A dash gives emphasis to any addition.

> Dvorak's *New World* Symphony reflects musical themes the composer heard in the United States — including Native American melodies and black spirituals.

> At the podium, Coach Bull claimed that he was at a loss for words — and then he proved it for more than an hour.

**●2 Use a pair of em dashes to insert information into a sentence.** Information between dashes gets noticed.

> Many regard Verdi's *Otello* — based on Shakespeare's story of a marriage ruined by jealousy — as the greatest of Italian tragic operas.

Dashes are especially useful for setting off material that already contains its own internal punctuation.

> Marie's writing style — complex, subtle, yet also incisive — earned the admiration of her colleagues.

### ◉ 3 Use an em dash in dialogue to indicate that a speaker has broken off abruptly or has been interrupted.

> "I want some poison," she said.
> "Yes, Miss Emily. What kind? For rats and such? I'd recom —"
> "I want the best you have. I don't care what kind."
> —William Faulkner, "A Rose for Emily"

### ◉ 4 Don't use a hyphen when a dash is required. Use hyphens to connect items rather than to separate them (see Section 40c).

| NOT | Beethoven's music -unlike that of Mozart -uses emphatic rhythms. |
|---|---|
| BUT | Beethoven's music — unlike that of Mozart — uses emphatic rhythms. |

### ◉ 5 Don't use too many dashes. Dashes can clutter a passage; one pair per sentence is the limit.

| TOO MANY DASHES | Mozart — recognized as a genius while still a child — produced more than 600 compositions during his life — including symphonies, operas, and concertos. |
|---|---|
| REVISED | Mozart — recognized as a genius while still a child — produced more than 600 compositions during his life, including symphonies, operas, and concertos. |

**EXERCISE 40.1** Add and delete em dashes as necessary to improve the sentences below.

1. Legend has it that Beethoven's Third Symphony was dedicated to Napoleon Bonaparte the champion of French revolutionary ideals until he declared himself emperor.

2. Scholars believe—though they can't be sure—that the symphony was initially called *Bonaparte*—testimony to just how much the idealistic Beethoven admired the French leader.

3. The Third Symphony a revolutionary work itself is now known by the title *Eroica*.

4. The Third, the Fifth, the Sixth, the Seventh, the Ninth Symphonies, they all contain musical passages that most people recognize immediately.

5. The opening four notes of Beethoven's Fifth, da, da, da, dum, may be the most famous in all of music.

## 40b When do you use an en dash?

The en dash is slightly shorter than the em dash, roughly equal in width to the printed letter *n*. Reserve it for the special circumstances listed below. To produce an en dash with word-processing software, hit "Ctrl" + minus (on the keypad) when using a PC; with a Mac, depress "option" and the hyphen key.

● **1 Use en dashes to connect words and numbers.** Think of it as a substitute for the word *to*.

> Richard Nixon (1913–1994) was the thirty-seventh President of the United States.
>
> The meeting is on Thursday, 2:00–4:30 p.m., in the Dobie Room.
>
> We caught the only direct Austin–Santa Fe flight of the day.

You should not use an en dash, however, when the items you are connecting are preceded by *from* or *between*. Use "to" or "and" instead.

> The meeting is on Thursday, **from** 2:00 **to** 4:30 p.m., in the Dobie Room.
>
> We caught the only direct flight that day **between** Austin **and** Santa Fe.

● **2 Use en dashes to indicate that a period of time is continuing.** You'll see this usage most often when the birth date is given for a person still living.

> Scott Blackwood (1965–) has already published two novels.

**3 Use en dashes to connect complicated compound expressions.** When you have to connect compound or hyphenated words or expressions, you may want to use an en dash.

> Our senator presented herself as an odd pro-choice – pro-gun candidate.
>
> We were organizing a college – high school debate team colloquium.

## 40c When do you use hyphens?

Hyphens either join words or divide them between syllables. Don't confuse them with dashes, which have different functions (see Sections 40a and 40b).

**1 Learn common hyphenation patterns.** Hyphenate words beginning with the prefixes *all-, self-,* and *ex-* or ending with the suffix *-elect.*

| | |
|---|---|
| **all** - encompassing | **ex** - hockey player |
| **self** - contained | mayor - **elect** |

Hyphenate most words beginning with *well-, ill-,* and *heavy-* when these expressions precede a noun.

| | | |
|---|---|---|
| **well** - dressed man | **ill** -conceived notion | **heavy** -handed tactics |

Most, though not all, words beginning with *un-, non-, anti-, pro-,* and *pre-* are not hyphenated.

| | | |
|---|---|---|
| **un**certain | **anti**slavery | **pre**nuptial |
| **non**smoker | **pro**democracy | |

When in doubt about whether to use a hyphen with a prefix, check a dictionary. Most larger dictionaries provide extensive lists of words formed from prefixes.

**2 Follow the conventional uses of hyphens.** Use hyphens to write out numbers from twenty-one to ninety-nine. Fractions also take hyphens, but use only one hyphen per fraction.

twenty-nine                    one forty-seventh of a mile

one-quarter inch               two hundred forty-six

Use hyphens to indicate double titles, elements, functions, or attributes.

the secretary-treasurer of our club

members of the AFL-CIO

a city-state such as Sparta

in the space-time continuum

Use hyphens in some technical expressions:

uranium-235                    A-bomb

Use hyphens to link prefixes to proper nouns and their corresponding adjectives.

**pre**-Columbian               **anti**-American

**mid**-Victorian               **neo**-Darwinism

Use hyphens to prevent words from being misread.

a recreation area              the re-creation of an event

a chicken coop                 a student co-op

## ●3 Use hyphens to link some compound nouns and verbs.

The conventions for hyphenating words are complicated and inconsistent. Here are some expressions that do take hyphens.

brother-in-law       great-grandmother       cold-shoulder

hocus-pocus          president-elect          double-talk

Here are compounds that aren't hyphenated. Some can be written as either single words or separate words.

cabdriver            best man                sea dog

cab owner            blockhouse              hole in one

When in doubt, check a dictionary or a style manual.

**4 Use hyphens to create compound phrases and expressions.**

Some classmates resented her **holier-than-thou** attitude.

Product innovation suffered because of a **not-invented-here** bias.

**5 Use hyphens to link unit modifiers before a noun.** A *unit modifier* is a two-word modifier in which the first word modifies the second. The combination formed by these two words modifies a following noun.

a **bare-chested** warrior

an **English-speaking** city

a **no-growth** policy

a **fifty-dollar** book

When putting a comma between modifying words produces nonsense, you probably have a unit modifier that requires a hyphen.

bare, chested warrior (?)

an English, speaking city (?)

But don't use hyphens to link compound modifiers following a noun.

The warrior was **bare chested**.

The book cost **fifty dollars**.

Nor should you use hyphens with *very* or with adverbs that end in *-ly*.

a **very hot** day          a **sharply honed** knife

**6 Handle suspended modifiers correctly.** Sometimes a word or phrase may have more than a single hyphenated modifier. These **suspended modifiers** should look like the following.

Anne planned her vacation wardrobe to accommodate **cold-, cool-,** and **wet-weather** days.

We couldn't determine whether the class should be a **first-** or **second-semester** course.

**7 Don't hyphenate words or numbers at the ends of lines.**
Most style manuals advise against such divisions when you are typing. If you

are using a computer, turning on the "word wrap" function will automatically eliminate end-of-line divisions. When you must divide a word, break it only at a syllable and then check a dictionary for the syllable break. Don't guess; your ear and eye will often fool you. Never hyphenate one-syllable words.

**EXERCISE 40.2** In the following sentences, indicate which form of the words in parentheses is preferable. Use a dictionary if you are not familiar with the terms.

1. Local citizens have a (**once in a lifetime/once-in-a-lifetime**) opportunity to preserve an (**old-growth/oldgrowth**) forest.

2. A large, wooded parcel of land is about to be turned into a shopping mall by (**real-estate/realestate**) speculators and (**pinstripe suited/pinstripe-suited**) investors.

3. The forest provides a haven for (**wild-life/wildlife**) of all varieties, from (**great horned** owls/**great-horned** owls) to (**ruby throated/ ruby-throated**) hummingbirds.

4. Does any community need (**video stores/video-stores**), (**T shirt/ T-shirt**) shops, and (**over priced/overpriced**) boutiques more than acres of natural habitat?

5. This (**recently-proposed/recently proposed**) development can be stopped by petitioning the (**city-council/city council**).

# 40d When do you use slashes?

Slashes are used to indicate divisions. They are rare pieces of punctuation with a few specific functions.

### ●1 Use slashes to separate expressions that indicate a choice.
In these cases, no space is left before or after the slash.

either/or      he/she      yes/no      pass/fail

Some readers object to these expressions, preferring *he or she*, for example, to *he/she* (sometimes even written as *s/he* ).

### ● 2 Use slashes to indicate fractions.

> 2/3      2 2/3      5 3/8

### ● 3 Use slashes in typing World Wide Web addresses.

> <http: // www.nps.gov / parks.html>

Note that no spaces precede or follow slashes in Web addresses.

### ● 4 Use slashes to divide lines of poetry quoted within sentences. When used in this way, a space is left on either side of the slash.

> Only then does Lear understand that he has been a failure as a king:
>
> "O, I have taken / Too little care of this!"

# 41 Questions About Italics and Capitalization?

## 41a When do you use italics?

Italics, like quotation marks, draw attention to a title, word, or phrase. In a printed text, italics are *slanted letters*. In typed or handwritten papers, italics are often signaled by <u>underlining the appropriate words</u>. If you are using a computer that can print italicized words, ask your instructors or editors whether you should print actual italics in a paper. (They may still prefer that you use an underscore.)

**1 Use italics to set off some titles.** Some titles and names are italicized; others appear between quotation marks. Chart 41.1 on the facing page provides guidance.

Neither italics nor quotation marks are used for the names of *types* of trains, ships, aircraft, or spacecraft.

DC-10        Trident submarine

Neither italics nor quotation marks are used with titles of major religious texts, books of the Bible, or classic legal documents.

the Bible                    the Magna Carta
the Qur'an                   the Constitution
1 Corinthians                the Declaration of Independence

**2 Use italics to set off foreign words or phrases.** Italics emphasize scientific names and foreign terms that haven't become accepted into the English vocabulary.

Pierre often described his co-workers as *les bêtes humaines*.

---

**Chart 41.1 Titles *Italicized* or "In Quotes"**

**TITLES *ITALICIZED***

| | |
|---|---|
| books | *Blink* or <u>Blink</u> |
| magazines | *Time* or <u>Time</u> |
| journals | *JAMA* or <u>JAMA</u>, *Commentary* or <u>Commentary</u> |
| newspapers | *USA Today* or <u>USA Today</u> |
| films | *Casablanca* or <u>Casablanca</u> |
| TV shows | *Punked* or <u>Punked</u> |
| radio programs | *All Things Considered* or <u>All Things Considered</u> |
| plays | *Macbeth* or <u>Macbeth</u> |
| long poems | *Beowulf* or <u>Beowulf</u> |
| long musical pieces | *The Mikado* or <u>The Mikado</u> |
| albums | Green Day's *American Idiot* or <u>American Idiot</u> |
| works of art | Schnabel's *Adieu* or <u>Adieu</u> |
| spacecraft | *Apollo 11* or <u>Apollo 11</u> |
| software programs | *Microsoft Word* or <u>Microsoft Word</u> |

**TITLES "IN QUOTES"**

| | |
|---|---|
| chapters of books | "Lessons from the Pros" |
| articles in journals/magazines | "Is the Stock Market Too High?" |
| articles in newspapers | "Inflation Heats Up" |
| TV episodes | "The Soup Nazi" |
| short stories | "Araby" |
| short poems | "The Red Wheelbarrow" |
| songs | "God Bless America" |

Foreign words absorbed by English over the centuries should not be italicized. To be certain, look them up in a recent dictionary.

crèche     gumbo     gestalt     arroyo

Common abbreviations from Latin appear without italics or underscoring.

etc.        et al.        i.e.        viz.

**● 3 Use italics (or quotation marks) to emphasize or clarify a letter, a word, or a phrase.**

Does that word begin with an *f* or a *ph*?

"That may be how you define *fascist*," she replied.

When some people talk about *school spirit*, they really mean "Let's party."

**EXERCISE 41.1**   Indicate whether the following titles or names in boldface should be italicized, in quotation marks, or unmarked. If you don't recognize a name below, consult an encyclopedia or another reference work.

1. watching **I Love Lucy**

2. returning **A Farewell to Arms** to the public library

3. discussing the colors of Picasso's **The Old Guitarist**

4. reading Jackson's **The Lottery** one more time

5. whistling **Here Comes the Sun** from the Beatles' **Abbey Road**

## 41b When do you capitalize?

Capital letters can cause problems simply because you have to remember that conventions guide their use—which may vary, depending on what style sheet or institution (newspaper, magazine, federal government) defines the principles. Here, for instance, we follow MLA recommendations for titles.

**● 1 Capitalize the first word in a sentence.**   You can set most word processors to capitalize sentence beginnings automatically.

**N**aomi picked up the tourists at their hotel.

**W**hat a remarkable city Washington is!

**2 Capitalize the first word in a direct quotation that is a full sentence.**

> Ira asked, "**W**here's the National Air and Space Museum?"
>
> "**G**ood idea!" Naomi agreed. "**L**et's go there."

Use lowercase for quotations that continue after an interruption.

> "It's on the Mall," Naomi explained, "**n**ear the Hirshhorn gallery."

**3 Don't capitalize the first word of a phrase or clause that follows a colon unless you want to emphasize the word.** You may also capitalize the first word after a colon if it is part of a student paper title.

| | |
|---|---|
| NO CAPS AFTER COLON | They ignored one item while parking the car: **a** no-parking sign. |
| CAPS FOR EMPHASIS | The phrase haunted her: **Y**our car has been towed! |
| CAPS FOR TITLE | *Rebuilt: How Becoming Part Computer Made Me More Human* |

**4 Don't capitalize the first word of a phrase or sentence enclosed by dashes.**

> Audrey's first screenplay—**a** thriller about nanotechnology—had been picked up by an agent.
>
> Her work—**s**he couldn't believe it—was now in the hands of a studio executive.

**5 Capitalize the major words in the titles of papers, books, articles, poems.**

> *All the Trouble in the World*
> The Genome Initiative: How to Spell "Human"
> "Stopping by Woods on a Snowy Evening"

Follow these general guidelines for capitalizing titles.

- Capitalize the first word.
- Capitalize the last word.

- Capitalize the first word of any subtitle.
- Capitalize all other words *except*
  —articles (*a, an, the*)
  —prepositions
  —coordinating conjunctions
  —the *to* in infinitives

Note, however, that the American Psychological Association (APA) does not follow these guidelines for capitalizing titles (see Chapter 51).

**6 Capitalize the first word in each line of quoted poetry unless the poet has used lowercase letters.**

> **S**umer is ycomen in,
> **L**oude sing cuckoo!
>
> —"The Cuckoo Song"

> **a**nyone lived in a pretty how town
> (**w**ith up so floating many bells down)
>
> —e. e. Cummings, "anyone lived in a pretty how town"

**7 Capitalize the names of people.** People's names are *proper nouns*, which refer to specific people, places, and things, whereas nouns that refer to people, places, and things in general are called *common nouns*.

| PROPER NOUNS | COMMON NOUNS |
|---|---|
| Emily Dickinson | poet |
| John | brother |
| Ted Kennedy | senator |

Capitalize the initials in people's names and titles identified with specific people.

| | |
|---|---|
| Justice Clarence Thomas | I. M. Pei |
| J. Hector St. Jean Crèvecoeur | Aunt Josephine |
| Robert King, Dean of Liberal Arts | Rosa Eberly, PhD |

But don't capitalize titles used less specifically or minor titles that stand alone—that is, unattached to a particular proper noun. As a general rule, capitalize titles that precede the noun but do not capitalize titles that follow the noun.

> Josephine, my favorite **a**unt
> Robert King, a **d**ean at the university
> a **c**ommissioner in Cuyahoga County

More prestigious titles may be capitalized even when they stand alone, though style manuals disagree on this point. It is generally acceptable to capitalize a title that is being used in place of a proper name.

> the **P**resident *or* the **p**resident
> the **S**ecretary of **S**tate *or* the **s**ecretary of **s**tate
> the **C**hair of the Classics Department
> The **S**enator will be arriving at six o'clock.

Capitalize *God* when you are referring specifically to the god of the Judeo-Christian tradition, but not when you are referring to *gods* in general.

> In the Old Testament, **G**od punished those who chose to worship the pagan **g**ods.

⊜**8 Capitalize the names of national, political, and ethnic groups.** These are proper nouns, since they refer to specific groups.

> **K**enyans            **C**hicanos            **A**frican **A**mericans
> **L**ibertarians       **D**emocrats          **R**epublicans

The names of racial groups, economic groups, and social classes are usually not capitalized—though you will often encounter exceptions.

> blacks                 whites
> the proletariat        the knowledge class

⊜**9 Capitalize the names of institutions and specific objects.** These include the following.

> businesses             **D**aimler**C**hrysler
> organizations          **N**ational **R**ifle **A**ssociation

| schools | University of **M**emphis |
| religions | **B**uddhism |
| sacred books | the **B**ible, the **T**orah |
| place names | **A**sia, **F**rance |
| geographic features | the **G**ulf of **M**exico |
| buildings | the **E**mpire **S**tate **B**uilding |
| ships and planes | **S.S.** *Titanic*, **B**oeing 767 |
| documents | the **D**eclaration of **I**ndependence |
| cultural movements | **R**omanticism, **V**orticism |
| historical periods | **P**ax **R**omana, **V**ictorian **A**ge |
| days and months | **M**onday, **J**uly |
| holidays | **H**alloween, **F**ourth of **J**uly |
| course titles | **H**istory 101 |

Capitalize words such as *river, park, street,* and *road* only when they refer to a specific road, river, or street.

| Georgetown **R**oad | a dusty **r**oad |
| the Mississippi **R**iver | an American **r**iver |

Capitalize the days of the week (***Monday, Friday***)—word processors can be set to do it for you. Do not capitalize seasons (*winter, spring*) or compass directions (*north, west*) unless they are part of a place name (***North America***) or unless they are being used as a place name (*the **West***). Do not capitalize school subjects unless they are themselves proper nouns (*mathematics, **Russian** history, **English***).

◉ **10 Capitalize brand names.** Many familiar words are really trade-marked brand names—proper names that legally refer only to the product of a particular company. Dictionaries will help you decide when to capitalize such names.

**X**erox                    **P**ost-**I**t

◉ **11 Capitalize adjectives formed from proper nouns.**

**E**lizabethan literature          **C**hurchillian steadfastness

**⊘12 Capitalize abstractions when you want to give them special emphasis.** Compare the following examples.

What is this thing called **Love**?
Adil had fallen in **l**ove again.

**⊘13 Capitalize all the letters in most acronyms.**

**NATO**       **OPEC**       **SALT** Treaty

Don't capitalize familiar acronyms that seem like ordinary words. When in doubt, check a dictionary.

radar       sonar       laser

**EXERCISE 41.2** Correct the problems in capitalization in the following sentences.

1. The passenger next to me asked, "do you remember when air travel used to be a pleasure?"

2. I couldn't reply immediately: My tray table had just flopped open and hit me on the knees.

3. The plane we were on—A jumbo jet that seated nine or ten across—had been circling Dulles International for hours.

4. "We'll be landing momentarily," the flight attendant mumbled, "If we are lucky."

5. I had seen the film version of this flight: *airplane!*

**EXERCISE 41.3** Capitalize in the following sentences as necessary.

1. The constitution and the declaration of independence are on view at the national archives.

2. I heard the doorkeeper at the hilton speaking spanish to the general secretary of the united nations.

**3.** Visitors to washington, d.c., include people from around the world: russians from moscow, egyptians from cairo, aggies from texas, buckeyes from ohio.

**4.** At the white house, the president will host a conference on democracy and free enterprise in the spring, probably in april.

# 42 Questions About Abbreviations and Numbers?

## 42a How do you handle abbreviations?

Using abbreviations, acronyms (*NATO, radar*), and initialisms (*HBO, IRS*) can make some writing simpler. Many conventional abbreviations are acceptable in all kinds of papers.

| | | | |
|---|---|---|---|
| a.m. | p.m. | B.C. | A.D. |
| Ph.D. | M.D. | Mrs. | Mr. |

Other abbreviations are appropriate on forms, reports, and statistics sheets, but not in more formal writing.

Jan.—January          no.—number
ft.—foot              mo.—month

### ● 1 Be consistent in punctuating abbreviations and acronyms.

Abbreviations of single words usually take periods.

vols.          Jan.          Mr.

Acronyms and initialisms are usually written without periods.

| | | |
|---|---|---|
| IRS | NATO | NOW |
| HBO | AFL-CIO | URL |

Acronyms that have become accepted words never need periods.

sonar          radar          laser          scuba

Periods are usually omitted after abbreviations in technical writing unless a measurement or other item might be misread without a period—for example, *in.*

Consistently use three periods or none at all in terms such as the following. Current usage generally omits the periods.

m.p.g. *or* mpg          r.p.m. *or* rpm          m.p.h. *or* mph

**2 Be consistent in capitalizing abbreviations, acronyms, and initialisms.** Capitalize the abbreviations of words that are capitalized when written out in full.

General Motors—GM  University of Toledo—UT
U.S. Navy—USN  98° Fahrenheit—98° F

Don't capitalize the abbreviations of words not capitalized when written out in full.

pound—lb.  minutes—min.

Always capitalize *B.C.E.* and *C.E.* or *B.C.* and *A.D.* Printers may set these items in small caps: *B.C.E.* and *A.D.*

You may capitalize *A.M.* and *P.M.*, but they often appear in small letters: *a.m.* and *p.m.* Printers may set them as small caps: *A.M.* and *P.M.*

Don't capitalize acronyms that have become accepted words: *sonar, radar, laser, scuba.*

**3 Use the appropriate abbreviations for titles, degrees, and names.** Some titles are almost always abbreviated (*Mr., Ms., Mrs., Jr.*). Other titles are normally written out in full, though they may be abbreviated when they precede a first name or initial.

President  President Bush  Pres. George W. Bush
Professor  Professor Davis  Prof. Diane Davis
Reverend  Reverend Call  Rev. Ann Call
 the Reverend Dr. Call  Rev. Dr. Call

Never let abbreviated titles of this kind appear alone in a sentence.

WRONG  The **gov.** urged the **sen.** to support the bill.

RIGHT  The **governor** urged the **senator** to support the bill.

Give credit for academic degrees either before a name or after—not both. Don't, for example, use both *Dr.* and *Ph.D.* in the same name.

WRONG  **Dr.** Katherine Martinich, **PhD.**

RIGHT  **Dr.** Katherine Martinich
 Katherine Martinich, **PhD.**

Abbreviations for academic titles often stand by themselves, without names attached.

> Professor Kim received her **PhD** from Penn State and her **BS** from St. Vincent College.

**⊚4 Use the appropriate technical abbreviations.** Abbreviations are often used in professional, governmental, scientific, military, and technical writing.

| | | | |
|---|---|---|---|
| DNA | UHF | EKG | START |
| SALT | GNP | LEM | kW |

When writing for nontechnical audiences, spell out technical terms in full the first time you use them. Then in parentheses give the specialized abbreviation you will use in the rest of the paper.

> The two congressional candidates debated the effects a tax increase might have on the gross national product (GNP).

**⊚5 Use the appropriate abbreviations for agencies and organizations.** In some cases, the abbreviation or acronym regularly replaces the full name of a company, agency, or organization.

| | | | |
|---|---|---|---|
| FBI | IBM | MCI | AT&T |

**⊚6 Use the appropriate abbreviations for dates.** Dates are not abbreviated in most writing. Write out in full the days of the week and months of the year.

> **WRONG**   They arrived in Washington on a **Wed.** in **Apr.**
>
> **RIGHT**   They arrived in Washington on a **Wednesday** in **April**.

Abbreviations of months and days are used primarily in notes, lists, forms, and reference works.

**⊚7 Use the appropriate abbreviations for time and temperatures.** Abbreviations that accompany time and temperatures are acceptable in all kinds of writing.

| | | | |
|---|---|---|---|
| 43 B.C. | A.D. 144 | 1:00 a.m. | 98° F |
| 143 B.C.E. | 1066 C.E. | 4:36 p.m. | 13° C |

Notice that the abbreviation *B.C.* appears after a date, *A.D.* usually before one. You may also see *B.C.E.* (*Before the Common Era*) used in place of *B.C.* and *C.E.* (*Common Era*) substituted for *A.D.* Both follow the date. MLA style deletes the periods in these items: BC, BCE, AD, CE.

**8 Use the appropriate abbreviations for weights, measures, and times.** Technical terms or measurements are commonly abbreviated when used with numbers, but they are written out in full when they stand alone in sentences. Even when accompanied by numbers, the terms usually look better in sentences when spelled out completely.

| | | | |
|---|---|---|---|
| 28 mpg | 1 tsp. | 40 km. | 420 lbs. |
| 50 min. | 30 kg. | 2 hrs. | 40 mph |

Ella didn't really care how many **miles per gallon** her Escalade got in the city.

The abbreviation for number—*No.* or *no.*—is appropriate in technical writing, but only when immediately followed by a number.

**NOT**  The **no.** on the contaminated dish was **073**.

**BUT**  The contaminated dish was **no. 073**.

*No.* also appears in footnotes, endnotes, and citations.

**9 Use the appropriate abbreviations for places.** In most writing, place names are not abbreviated except in addresses and in reference tools and lists. However, certain abbreviations are accepted in academic and business writing.

| | | | |
|---|---|---|---|
| USA | USSR | UK | Washington, D.C. |

In addresses (but not in written text), use the standard postal abbreviations, without periods, for the states.

| | | | |
|---|---|---|---|
| Alabama | AL | Arizona | AZ |
| Alaska | AK | Arkansas | AR |

| California | CA | Nevada | NV |
| Colorado | CO | New Hampshire | NH |
| Connecticut | CT | New Jersey | NJ |
| Delaware | DE | New Mexico | NM |
| Florida | FL | New York | NY |
| Georgia | GA | North Carolina | NC |
| Hawaii | HI | North Dakota | ND |
| Idaho | ID | Ohio | OH |
| Illinois | IL | Oklahoma | OK |
| Indiana | IN | Oregon | OR |
| Iowa | IA | Pennsylvania | PA |
| Kansas | KS | Rhode Island | RI |
| Kentucky | KY | South Carolina | SC |
| Louisiana | LA | South Dakota | SD |
| Maine | ME | Tennessee | TN |
| Maryland | MD | Texas | TX |
| Massachusetts | MA | Utah | UT |
| Michigan | MI | Vermont | VT |
| Minnesota | MN | Virginia | VA |
| Mississippi | MS | Washington | WA |
| Missouri | MO | West Virginia | WV |
| Montana | MT | Wisconsin | WI |
| Nebraska | NE | Wyoming | WY |

All the various terms for *street* are written out in full, except in addresses.

| boulevard | road | avenue | parkway |
| highway | alley | place | circle |

But *Mt.* (for *mount*) and *St.* (for *saint*) are acceptable abbreviations in place names when they precede a proper name.

**Mt.** Vesuvius        **St.** Charles Street

● **10** Use the correct abbreviations for certain expressions preserved from Latin.

i.e. (*id est*—that is)
e.g. (*exempli gratia*—for example)

et al. (*et alii*—and others)
etc. (*et cetera*—and so on)

In most writing, it is better to use English versions of these and other Latin abbreviations. Avoid using the abbreviation *etc.* in formal or academic writing. Never write *and etc.*

**11 Use the appropriate abbreviations for divisions of books.**
The many abbreviations for books and manuscripts (*p., pp., vols., ch., chpts., bk., sect.*) are fine in footnotes or parenthetical citations, but don't use them alone in sentences.

| | |
|---|---|
| WRONG | Richard stuck the **bk.** in his pocket after reading **ch.** 5. |
| RIGHT | Richard stuck the **book** in his pocket after reading **chapter** 5. |

**12 Use symbols as abbreviations carefully.** Symbols such as %, +, =, ≠, <, > make sense in technical and scientific writing, but in other academic papers, spell out the full words. Most likely to cause a problem is *%* for *percent*.

| | |
|---|---|
| ACCEPTABLE | Mariah was shocked to learn that **80%** of the cars towed belong to tourists. |
| PREFERRED | Mariah was shocked to learn that **80 percent** of the cars towed belong to tourists. |

You can use a dollar sign—$—in any writing as long as it is followed by an amount. Don't use both the dollar sign and the word *dollar*.

| | |
|---|---|
| WRONG | The fine for parking in a towing zone is $125 dollars. |
| RIGHT | The fine for parking in a towing zone is **$125**. |
| RIGHT | The fine for parking in a towing zone is **one hundred twenty-five dollars**. |

The ampersand (&) is an abbreviation for *and*. Do not use it in formal writing except when it appears in a title or name: *Road & Track*.

**EXERCISE 42.1** Correct the sentences below, abbreviating where appropriate or expanding abbreviations that would be incorrect in college or professional writing. Check the punctuation for accuracy and consistency. If you insist on periods with acronyms and initialisms, use them throughout the passage.

1. There's a better than 70% chance of rain today.

2. Irene sent angry ltrs. to a dozen networks, including NBC, A.B.C., ESPN, and CNN.

3. The Emperor Claudius was born in 10 b.c. and died in 54 A.D.

4. Dr. Kovatch, M.D., works for the Federal Department of Agriculture (FDA).

5. I owe the company only $175 dollars, & expect to pay the full amount before the end of the mo.

## 42b How do you handle numbers?

You can express numbers in writing either through numerals or through words.

| | |
|---|---|
| 1 | one |
| 25 | twenty-five |
| 100 | one hundred |
| 1/4 | one-fourth |
| 0.05% | five hundredths of a percent *or* |
| | five one-hundredths of a percent |

You'll likely use numerals in technical, scientific, and business writing. In other kinds of documents, you may combine words and numerals. (For guidelines on using hyphens with numbers that are spelled out, see Section 40c-2.)

**◉1 Write out numbers from one to nine; use numerals for numbers larger than nine.**

| | | |
|---|---|---|
| 10 | 15 | 39 |
| 101 | 115 | 220 |
| 1001 | 1021 | 59,000 |
| 101,000 | 10,000,101 | 50,306,673,432 |

In most cases, spell out ordinal numbers (that is, numbers that express a sequence): *first, second, third, fourth,* and so on. Spell out numbers that identify centuries.

in the fifteenth century
twentieth-century philosophers

These guidelines have variations and exceptions. The MLA style manual, for example, recommends spelling out any number that can be expressed in one or two words.

| | |
|---|---|
| thirteen | twenty-one |
| three hundred | fifteen thousand |

The APA style manual suggests using figures for most numbers above ten unless they appear at the beginning of a sentence.

Thirty-three workers were rescued from an oil platform.

Check the style manual in your field to confirm how numbers ought to be presented in your writing.

**◉2 Combine words and figures when you need to express large round numbers.**

| | | |
|---|---|---|
| 100 billion | $32 million | 103 trillion |

Avoid shifting between words and figures. When you need numerals to express some numbers in a sentence, use numbers throughout.

There were over **125,000** people at the protest and **950** police officers, but only **9** arrests.

When one number follows another, alternate words and figures for clarity.

33 fifth graders                    12 first-term representatives
2 four-wheel-drive vehicles         five 5-gallon buckets

**3 Use numerals when comparing numbers or suggesting a range.** Numerals are easier to spot and compare than words.

A blackboard at the traffic office listed a **$50** fine for jaywalking, **$100** for speeding, and **$125** for parking in a towing zone.

**4 Don't begin sentences with numerals.** Either spell out the number or rephrase the sentence so that the numeral is not the first word.

WRONG     32 people were standing in line at the parking violation center.

RIGHT     Thirty-two people were standing in line at the parking violation center.

**5 Use numerals for dates, street numbers, page numbers, sums of money, and various ID and call numbers.**

July 4, 1776                    1860–1864
6708 Beauford Dr.               1900 East Blvd.
p. 352                          pp. 23–24
$2,749.00                       43£
Channel 8                       103.5 FM
PR 105.5 R8                     SSN 111-00-1111

Don't use an ordinal form in dates.

WRONG     May 2nd, 1991

RIGHT     May 2, 1991 *or* 2 May 1991

**6 Use numerals for measurements, percentages, statistics, and scores.**

35 mph          13° C          Austin, TX 78750
75 percent      0.2 liters     5.5 pupils per teacher
2½ miles        15%            Browns 42—Steelers 7

Use numerals for time with *a.m.* and *p.m.*; use words with *o'clock*.

**2:15** p.m.         **6:00** a.m.         **six** o'clock

**⊚7 Form the plural of numbers by adding -s or -'s.**

five 6 s in a row         five 98's

See Section 25a for more on plurals.

**EXERCISE 42.2** Decide whether numbers used in the following sentences are handled appropriately. Where necessary, change numerals to words and words to numerals. Some expressions may not need revision.

1. 4 people will be honored at the ceremony beginning at nine p.m.

2. The culture contained more than 500,000,000,000 cells.

3. We forgot who won the Nobel Peace Prize in nineteen ninety-one.

4. The examination will include a question about the 1st, the 4th, or the Tenth Amendment.

5. We paid $79.80 for the hotel room and twenty dollars for admission to the park.

# PART VII | Research and Writing

# 43 How Do You Design a Research Project?

You may not think of yourself as someone interested in doing research. But people in almost every career and walk of life today increasingly find themselves expected to locate and present information to their colleagues, clients, or the general public. Scientists prepare grant proposals and research articles; people in business manage endless streams of information; lawyers and medical professionals write constantly. The research papers and projects you do in college will introduce you to the way people think, write, and share information in a variety of fields.

We can't anticipate the kinds of work you'll do in college and beyond, but we can offer some reliable methods for finding and developing a topic, using research resources, and evaluating, organizing, and documenting the sources you locate. Don't let any of our advice restrict your creativity: the point of research, after all, is not to limit horizons, but to expand them.

> **e-Tips**
>
> For more about undergraduate research opportunities, see the Council on Undergraduate Research at <http://www.cur.org>.

## 43a How do you claim a topic?

Think of research as an active process of creating knowledge rather than a passive one of reporting information. College projects can, in fact, start intellectual voyages that last a lifetime; many students change their majors and redirect their careers as a result of work they began in a paper.

● **1 Size up an assignment carefully.** In most cases, you'll receive a sheet of instructions when you are assigned a major college research project. Go over the sheet carefully, highlighting its key features. Consider issues such as the following.

- **Scope and media.** Understand what you must do (paper? Web site? flipchart? PowerPoint presentation?) and at what length. Look for word, page, or time limits at both ends (*no less than, no more than*).
- **Due dates.** There may be separate due dates for different stages of the project: topic proposal, annotated bibliography, outline, first draft or prototype, final version.
- **Format and documentation.** A project may have to include specific features: cover sheet, abstract, appendixes, bibliographies, illustrations, charts and so on. Note also any specific requirements for margins, page numbers, line spacing, titles, headings, illustrations, and so on. If an instructor doesn't specify a format, use one of the documentation styles explained in this book: MLA—for papers in English; APA—for psychology and the social sciences; CMS—for humanities. In the sciences, consult guides to CSE style.
- **Collaboration.** Instructors may encourage collaboration on research papers. If that's the case with your project, read the ground rules carefully. Pay attention, especially, to how the project will be evaluated and graded.
- **Key words.** Underscore any key words in the assignment: *analyze, classify, define, discuss, evaluate, review, explain, compare, contrast, prove, disprove, persuade, survey.* Each of these words means something different. (For a discussion of such terms, see Chart 6.1.)

● **2 Browse your topic area.** When you can pick your topic for a project, look for a subject, cause, or concern about which you can honestly say, "I'd really like to learn much more about it." Avoid stale controversies students have been writing about for decades: gun control, capital punishment, abortion, or legalization of marijuana.

---

**Checklist 43.1    Your Browsing and Background Reading Should . . .**

- Confirm whether you are, in fact, interested in your topic.

- Survey your subject so you can identify key issues and begin narrowing the scope of your project, as appropriate.

- Determine whether enough resources exist to support your project in the time available.

---

Get closer to your subject by spending a few hours browsing, first in your library and then on the Web. One shrewd way to begin exploring an academic topic is to read a specialized encyclopedia, one that deals specifically with your subject. You'll learn enough about your topic to decide whether you really want to stay with it. See the checklist below and ask reference librarians for their help.

---

**Checklist 43.2    Specialized Encyclopedias**

| DOING A PAPER ON . . . ? | BEGIN BY CHECKING . . . |
| --- | --- |
| Art | *Encyclopedia of World Art* |
| Economics | *Encyclopedia of American Economic History* |
| Environment | *Encyclopedia of the Environment* |
| Film | *International Encyclopedia of Film* |
| Health/medicine | *Health and Medicine Horizons* |
| History | *Dictionary of American History; Guide to Historical Literature* |
| Music | *The New Grove Dictionary of American Music* |
| Political science | *Encyclopedia of American Political History; Oxford Companion to Politics of the World* |
| Psychology, psychiatry | *International Encyclopedia of Psychiatry, Psychology, Psychoanalysis and Neurology* |
| Rhetoric | *Encyclopedia of Rhetoric* |
| Science | *McGraw-Hill Encyclopedia of Science and Technology* |
| Social sciences | *International Encyclopedia of the Social Sciences* |

To get a feel for your topic area, examine books or journals in the field. What are the major issues? Who is affected by them? Who is writing on the topic? Find two or three books on the subject you are researching and compare their bibliographies. Books that appear in more than one bibliography are likely to be key sources on the subject. Use a search engine to explore any major Web sites on your topic—preferably one sponsored by a reputable group or organization.

## 43b How do you plan a project?

You shouldn't wait to organize your project. From the start, you'll need a plan to deal with the complexities of a research project that may draw on many different kinds of sources and technologies.

● 1 **Write a research proposal.** For some research assignments, you may be asked to prepare a proposal that outlines your project. The prospectus for a short project might fit on a single page; that for a senior thesis might run many pages. Any proposal, however, will likely include some of the following elements.

- **Identification of a topic or topic area.** Explain your topic area and, if required, provide a reason for selecting this subject. See Chapter 2 for detailed advice.
- **A hypothesis, research question, or thesis.** State your hypothesis or question clearly. If required, discuss the hypothesis in some detail and defend its significance, relevance, or appropriateness. See Chapter 3 for help in formulating a thesis.
- **Background information or review of literature.** Identify the books, articles, and other materials you expect to read to gain background information on your subject. For major projects, you may need to do a thorough literature review, surveying all major work done in your research area.
- **A review of research resources.** Identify the types of materials you'll need for your project and determine their availability: books, articles, newspapers, documents, manuscripts, recordings, videos, artworks,

databases, online sources, and so on. You might list these items in a preliminary bibliography. See Chapter 44 for much more about research resources.

- **A description of your research methodology.** Outline the procedures you will follow in your research, and justify your choice of methodology.
- **An assessment of the ethics of your project if it involves experiments on people or animals.** Most universities have institutional review boards that govern research with human or animal subjects. Your instructor will likely tell you about these rules, especially in fields where such research is common, such as psychology and the social sciences.
- **A schedule or timeline.** For more information about scheduling a project, see Section 43c.

**● 2 Decide how you will handle your research materials.** Most writers now routinely use both printed and electronic sources and rely on their computers or database research programs (such as *ProCite*) to organize their work. Many projects today also require charts, graphs, and illustrations, some of them created on software, some downloaded from electronic sources. To store all this data, you'll want to rely both on the hard disk in your computer and a backup, either some portable media such as a USB Drive or Web space on a server.

**● 3 Keep track of your sources.** Whether you are using print or electronic sources, you need to know where your information came from. Develop a list of all the sources you use as you use them. Eventually you will need the bibliographical data to generate the Works Cited or References pages required of every standard academic paper. Each bibliographical record should contain all the information necessary to find a source again later.

The exact information you need will vary considerably for books, articles, newspapers, and electronic sources: check the MLA, APA, and CMS models in Chapters 50 through 52. When using a Web page, always record the URL and the date you viewed the site.

**● 4 Make copies of printed sources.** Photocopy or print out passages from printed sources that you expect to quote from directly and extensively. In such cases, be sure your copies are complete and legible (especially any page numbers). When you are copying from a book or magazine, duplicate both the title page and the publication information page that follows. You'll need that data later.

Also write basic bibliographical information directly on photocopies and printouts so that you remember where they came from, making sure each document is keyed somehow to a fuller bibliography record. Double-check bibliographical information, especially the spelling of names. Use highlighter pens to mark key passages in photocopies and printouts, and keep these materials in a folder. (Never highlight material in library books.)

**⬤5 Print or download electronic sources.** How you record data from an electronic source will depend on how you expect to use it. If you're simply looking for facts, record key data on note cards or print out the source itself. Printouts may be the easiest way to preserve information on Web resources whose content changes from day to day. Some of this material may be archived electronically, but it is always safer to print out material you will later cite. Record when you made the printout, since most documentation for electronic material requires a date of access.

It is possible to copy most electronic sources directly to disk. The finder on your computer may already have folders where you can store text files, movies, pictures, music files, and Web sites. Carefully, label any folders you create so that you or a colleague on the project can find information easily. Do back up all such materials. Know where *all* downloaded images come from and who owns their copyrights; you will have to document and credit all copyrighted pictures, photographs, and images borrowed from the Web. To use copyrighted material in your own electronic publications, you must get permission from the holder of the copyright.

For serious or long-term research projects, you might investigate a resource such as CiteULike at <http://www.citeulike.org/>, which will keep track of scholarly articles you are reading and even record the bibliographical information you will later need for your citations.

**⬤6 Consider collaborative research.** You may be expected or invited to work as part of a team for some college projects. You'll quickly discover that careful management is an important part of any collaborative effort. Settle questions such as the following with your team. (See Section 4e for more on collaborative writing.)

- What research and writing skills will your project require?
- How will you organize your team?
- How will decisions be made?
- Who—if anyone—will be in charge?
- How will you communicate and coordinate your efforts? Should you set up a wiki?
- How will you schedule the work, and how will you deal with deviations from the schedule?
- How will you assess your work and share the credit?

## 43c How do you schedule a project?

Many college assignments will have only one due date: the day the project must be turned in. Take it seriously; instructors rarely tolerate late work. However, some instructors may give you a series of due dates for a major project, asking that you submit items such as the following at specific times.

- Project proposal, prospectus, or thesis
- Annotated working bibliography
- Storyboards (for projects with graphics)
- First draft
- Responses to peer editing

When you are given several due dates, sketch out a calendar. Mark down the due dates of a project, leaving enough space between them to list the work necessary to meet those deadlines. Then estimate the time available for each step in the project. Here's a calendar for a paper with three major due dates and a variety of support activities. You would have to determine an appropriate completion date for each activity.

**CALENDAR: RESEARCH PAPER**

_____ Choosing a topic and defining the project

_____ Determining campus resources

_____ Drafting the proposal

Topic proposal: Due October 2

_____ Gathering and evaluating materials

_____ Summarizing and paraphrasing sources

_____ Organizing/designing the paper

_____ Drafting the project

First draft: Due October 23

_____ Getting/responding to feedback on the draft

_____ Refining/rewriting the project

_____ Documenting the project

_____ Preparing the final materials

Final draft: Due November 6

Keep the calendar simple; you can't schedule every moment in a complicated process.

You can also schedule your project on an appointment calendar or PDA. Always allow some slack in your schedule to account for activities that take more time than you allotted.

# 44 How Do You Find Information?

As you begin a research paper or project, your goal is to find potential sources and, in some cases, to prepare a *working* or *annotated bibliography*—that is, a preliminary list of materials related to your topic (see pages 80–81 for an example). Today, you can tap in to more information than ever before. By the same token, the enormous range of possibilities can be intimidating. In this section, we outline strategies to use in finding information.

## 44a How do you use a library?

A first priority for any college student is to become comfortable with basic tools for research. Three of these are your campus library, the library catalog, and the World Wide Web.

**1 Explore your campus library or research collections.** Don't be intimidated. Take a tour of these buildings, study their materials, and, above all, get to know the research librarians. Be sure you can locate the following places, features, and services important to your research.

- **Online catalog.** Learn how to use these terminals, which are the pathway into your library's books, journals, and other materials. Many libraries also have comprehensive online catalogs and Web sites with links to available indexes, databases, and online reference tools.
- **Card catalog.** Most libraries now have extensive electronic catalogs. But online terminals sometimes may not cover older library materials or special collections.
- **Reference room.** Study this useful collection carefully. Notice how its materials are arranged and where heavily used items (encyclopedias, almanacs, phone books, databases) are located.
- **Databases and bibliographies.** Research databases will usually be arrayed around computer terminals, with information either online or

accessed via CD-ROM disks. Older print bibliographies in various fields will often be large multi-volume collections. Ask librarians for help.

- **Microforms collections.** Some older documents, newspapers, and periodicals have been preserved on rolls of film called *microfilm* or rectangular sheets of film called *microfiche*. Know where these collections are and learn how to use them.

- **Periodical collections.** Know where to find both current journals and periodicals and older bound or microfilmed copies.

- **Newspapers.** Current newspapers are usually available in a reading room. A limited selection of older newspapers will often be available on microfilm or in online archives.

- **Special collections.** Note the location of any important collections in your library: pictures and photographs, maps, government documents, and so on.

- **Audio/video collections.** Know where to locate audio/video materials as well as facilities for listening to or viewing CDs, DVDs, tapes, and video disks.

- **Circulation desk/library services.** Learn about circulation desk services. You can usually recall materials already on loan. Most libraries also offer interlibrary loan programs that enable you to borrow materials your library may not own. (These orders take time; don't wait until the last minute.)

- **Photocopiers/computers/study areas.** Look for quiet places to study, photocopiers, and computer terminals, ports and plugs for laptops, and wireless areas.

- **Study carrels.** Many colleges and university libraries provide library carrels for people doing serious research. Find out whether you are eligible for such a carrel.

**●2 Use traditional and online library catalogs efficiently.** Almost all libraries now provide access to their resources via computer terminals or the World Wide Web. Many libraries also participate in the database called *OCLC WorldCat*, which links the catalogs of libraries around the world, giving you almost unlimited access to materials. In traditional card catalogs, books and other sources could be located by author, title, and key term. Electronic catalogs can be searched by similar categories, but more quickly and with more options. Learn the basic search techniques and commands used by your library catalog. Most opening screens support a variety of author-title-subject keyword search combinations, and more advanced searches enable you to pick the date, location, format, and language of the research material. Librarians find that most people enter online catalogs by using keyword searches. For much more about keyword searches, see Section 44c.

**e-Tips**

For a list of online library catalogs, examine the LIBCAT Web site at <http://www.metronet.lib.mn.us/lc/lca.cfm>.

An online catalog offers detailed information about most library holdings. On screen, you'll often be given a list of brief entries on your subject—typically the author, title, publishing information, date, and call number—with

WHAT STARTS HERE CHANGES THE WORLD
THE UNIVERSITY OF TEXAS AT AUSTIN

**The Library Catalog** : UTNetCAT    The catalog of the University of Texas Libraries

## Search Results

Ask a Librarian

New Search  [ Title (omit initial article) ▾ ]  [                    ]  ( Search )

### FULL DISPLAY

TITLE:
  Henry James.
PUBLISHED:
  Sydney : Wentworth Press, 1960.
DESCRIPTION:
  37, (2) p. ; 21 cm.
NOTES:
  "Read before the English Association (Sydney Branch) on 6th August, 1958"--P. (2) at end.
  Contents: Some impressions to introduce Henry James / Eleanor Green -- Ambiguity and eloquence in T
SUBJECTS:
  James, Henry, 1843-1916--Criticism and interpretation.
  James, Henry, 1843-1916 Golden bowl--Criticism and interpretation.
OTHER AUTHORS:
  Green, Eleanor, 1929- / Some impressions to introduce Henry James.
  Wilson, Richard Bartley Joseph / Ambiguity and eloquence in The golden bowl.
  English Association. Sydney Branch.
OTHER TITLES:
  Some impressions to introduce Henry James.
  Ambiguity and eloquence in The golden bowl.
OCLC NUMBER:
  10999719

**Call Number and Library for item location:**
PS 2124 G715 PCL Stacks

GO TO: User's Guide | Help | Browse Search | Keyword Search | Search Commands | Reserves Lists | Services

an option to select a fuller listing. The full listing describes additional features of the item—whether it is illustrated or has an index or a bibliography.

Most card and online catalogs use subject headings determined by the Library of Congress and compiled in the multi-volume *Library of Congress Subject Headings,* commonly known by its abbreviation *LCSH.* Be sure to consult this volume (or its electronic equivalent) in the reference room of your library at the start of your research: it will tell you how your topic is described and treated in the library catalog. On any given subject card or screen, pay attention, too, to any additional subject headings offered because these may be keywords to use for additional searches. For instance, if you were exploring "hieroglyphics," a listing on that topic might offer the keywords "Egyptian language—grammar" and "Egyptian language—writing." You might not have considered using those terms in a keyword search of your own.

**● 3 Check the World Wide Web.** The Web is not, like a library, designed, catalogued, and selected to support research. So while finding information is easy, finding reliable source material can be more of a challenge. You probably do most of your Web searching using *Google* or *Yahoo!* But you should be careful not to let these resources become your only tools for research. Good as they are, they follow logical pathways that may miss material that you need. At a minimum, try several search engines for any major project. Here are alternatives:

| SEARCH TOOLS | ADDRESS |
|---|---|
| *AltaVista* | <http://altavista.com> |
| *Ask* | <http://ask.com> |
| *Dogpile* | <http://www.dogpile.com> |
| *Excite* | <http://excite.com> |

Libraries, universities, and government agencies have also created hundreds of reference tools with more scholarly goals. Here are some places to look. (Be warned that Web addresses change frequently.)

| REFERENCE SITE | ADDRESS |
|---|---|
| *Infomine* | <http://infomine.ucr.edu> |
| *The Internet Public Library* | <http://www.ipl.org> |
| *Librarians' Index to the Internet* | <http://lii.org> |

The basic tool of many search engines and databases is the keyword search. For keyword search strategies, see Section 44c. Don't be satisfied with your initial searches, even when they supply lots of information. Another combination of keywords or a different search path might provide still better material. If you get a disappointing or unexpected response from a search, ask why. Look for clues in the results you receive (or don't receive). Check spellings and try synonyms. Don't give up.

Finally, pay attention to fast-evolving online sources for scholarly books and documents: *Google Scholar* at <http://scholar.google.com> and *Google Book Search* at <http://books.google.com>.

## 44b How do you find research materials?

In this section, we survey some basic search tools and strategies you might use on a project. We look at both printed and electronic sources since they have largely merged—especially when you are consulting newspapers, magazines, and journals.

● **1 Locate suitable bibliographies.** Bibliographies are lists of books, articles, and other documentary materials that deal with particular subjects or subject areas. Ask a reference room librarian whether a bibliography on your specific subject has been compiled. If not, consult one of the more general bibliographies available in almost every field.

---

**Chart 44.1　Types of Printed Bibliographies**

- **Selective bibliographies** usually list the best-known or most respected books and articles in a subject area.
- **Annotated bibliographies** briefly describe the works they list and may evaluate them.
- **Annual bibliographies** catalog the works produced within a field or discipline in a given year.

Printed bibliographies, however, are quickly losing ground to electronic indexes and databases, but they are still available on many subjects. Don't ignore bibliographies at the back of scholarly books, articles, and dissertations. Such bibliographies offer a focused look at a specific topic. Only a few of the thousands of bibliographic resources in specific disciplines are listed in Checklist 44.1.

---

**Checklist 44.1    Bibliographies**

| DOING A PAPER ON . . . ? | CHECK THIS BIBLIOGRAPHY . . . |
| --- | --- |
| American history | *Bibliographies in American History* |
| Art | *Guide to the Literature of Art History* |
| Classics | *Greek and Roman Authors: A Checklist of Criticism* |
| Communications | *Communication: A Guide to Information Sources* |
| Engineering | *Science and Engineering Literature* |
| Literature | *MLA International Bibliography* |
| Mathematics | *Using the Mathematical Literature* |
| Philosophy | *A Bibliography of Philosophical Bibliographies* |
| Psychology | *Harvard List of Books in Psychology* |
| Social work | *Social Work Education: A Bibliography* |

---

**● 2 Locate suitable databases to search the periodical literature.** Database indexes list items such as journal articles, magazine pieces, and newspapers stories that are not included in library catalogs. Such material is called the *periodical literature* on a subject. You shouldn't undertake any college-level research paper without checking out this important body of information. For example, to write about school vouchers, you'd likely want information from magazines such as *Newsweek* and *Time* and newspapers such as the *New York Times*. To find such materials, you would go to indexes, not library catalogs.

In the past, all periodical indexes were printed works, and you may still have to use these helpful volumes to find older sources. More recent materials, however, are indexed electronically. Such databases now typically offer not only basic bibliographical information on an article—who published it, where, and when—but also an abstract of the piece or even the full text. Depending on copyright rules, you can print out the text, download it to your computer, or have it sent to you via email.

You may want to begin periodical searches with general and multidisciplinary indexes to which your school or public library may subscribe, such as the following:

> *Expand Academic ASAP* (electronic)
>
> *EBSCOhost* (electronic)
>
> *LexisNexis Academic* (electronic)

A new and developing resource is *Google Scholar* at <http://scholar.google.com>. You can search for authors, articles, and more—but begin by reading Scholar Help.

All major academic fields and majors now have several indexes for their periodical literatures, most of them computerized and requiring that your library subscribe to them. And because new indexes may be added at any time, check with your reference librarian or your library's Web site to find the index best suited to your work. Or consult one of the frequently updated electronic subject guides offered free by major public libraries. Locate a study guide for your subject or field, and you'll find links to much important research material:

- New York Public Library (search for research guides and subject guides)
  <http://www.nypl.org/>
- Columbia University Library Web "Selected Subject Guides and Resources"
  <http://www.columbia.edu/cu/lweb/eguides>
- The University of California at Berkeley Libraries (search for subject guides)
  <http://www.lib.berkeley.edu>
- The University of Chicago "Libraries, Collections, and Subjects"
  <http://www.lib.uchicago.edu/e/lcs.html>

---

### Checklist 44.2    Searching an Electronic Index or Database

- Be sure you are logged on to the right index. A library terminal may provide access to several different databases or indexes. Find the one appropriate for your subject.

- Read the description of the index to find out how to use its information. Not all databases and indexes work the same way.

- Try synonyms if an initial keyword search turns up too few items.

- Check your spelling of titles, author's names, and keywords.

---

● **3 Consult biographical resources.** In a research project, you may need information about notable people, living and dead. Resources in the library reference room will help you. Good places to start include *The McGraw-Hill Encyclopedia of World Biography, Biography Index, Bio-Base, LexisNexis,* and *Current Biography.*

Probably the two most famous dictionaries of biography are the *Dictionary of National Biography* (British) and the *Dictionary of American Biography.* There are also *Who's Who* volumes for living British, American, and world notables, as well as volumes for African Americans and women. Deceased figures may appear in *Who Was Who.* The Arts and Entertainment Network program *Biography* at <http://www.biography.com> provides information on 25,000 people. To search for private individuals, you can use *Yahoo!'s* "people search" on the Web. It provides addresses and phone numbers with almost frightening ease.

---

### Checklist 44.3    Biographical Information

| YOUR SUBJECT IS IN . . . ? | CHECK THIS SOURCE . . . |
| --- | --- |
| Music | *The New Grove Dictionary of Music and Musicians* |
| Politics | *Politics in America; Almanac of American Politics* |
| Science | *Dictionary of Scientific Biography* |

*(Continued)*

**Biographical Information**   *(Continued)*

| YOUR SUBJECT IS . . . ? | CHECK THIS SOURCE . . . |
|---|---|
| African American | *Dictionary of American Negro Biography* |
| Asian | *Encyclopedia of Asian History* |
| Female | *Index to Women; Notable American Women* |
| Mexican American | *Mexican American Biographies* |

● **4 Locate statistics.** Statistics about every imaginable topic are available in library reference rooms and online. Be sure to find up-to-date and reliable figures.

**Checklist 44.4   Statistics**

| TO FIND . . . | CHECK THIS SOURCE . . . |
|---|---|
| General statistics | *World Almanac; Current Index to Statistics* (electronic) |
| Statistics about the United States | *Historical Statistics of the United States; Statistical Abstract of the United States; STAT-USA* (electronic); *GPO Access* (electronic) |
| World information | *The Statesman's Yearbook; National Intelligence Factbook; UN Demographic Yearbook; UNESCO Statistical Yearbook* |
| Business facts | *Handbook of Basic Economic Statistics; Survey of Current Business; Dow Jones–Irwin Business Almanac* |
| Public opinion polls | *Gallup Poll* |
| Population data | *Population Index* (electronic) |

**e-Tips**

For statistics from more than 70 agencies of the federal government, explore FedStats at <http://www.fedstats.gov>. Also consult resources such as *The Internet Public Library* at <http://www.ipl.org>, <iTools.com>, and *Wikipedia: The Free Encyclopedia* at <http://en.wikipedia.org/wiki/Main_Page>. Note, however, that *Wikipedia* is an open-source work, created and revised by the people who use it. The quality of its entries will vary and you might want to double-check its factual claims.

**◉5 Check news sources.** To find information from newspapers published earlier than the mid-1990s, you'll usually have to rely on printed or microfilm copies. When you know the date of an event, however, you can usually locate the information you want. If your subject isn't an event, you may have to trace it through an index or online archive. Only a few printed papers are fully indexed, notably the *New York Times*. A reference librarian can guide you to other news indexes available in your library—products such as *Newsbank* or *InfoTrac*.

For very current events, you can search hundreds of online newspapers and news services. But some may require you to register and, more and more, some are charging fees for their materials. As with any source, exercise caution when using information you find on the Web, making sure that its source is reputable (see Chapter 45). The speed of online journalism seems to have put pressure on fact checkers and editors: don't assume that the facts, quotations, and dates you find even in reputable sources will always be correct.

| NEWS RESOURCE | ADDRESS |
|---|---|
| *CNN Interactive* | \<http://www.cnn.com\> |
| *C-SPAN Online* | \<http://c-span.org\> |
| *Fox News* | \<http://foxnews.com\> |
| *Google News* | \<http://news.google.com\> |
| *London Times* | \<http://www.thetimes.co.uk\> |
| *National Public Radio* | \<http://www.npr.org/\> |
| *New York Times* | \<http://www.nytimes.com\> |

A directory such as *Yahoo!* at \<http://www.yahoo.com\> can point you to hundreds of online newspapers of every sort. Check under its "News & Media" category. You may have to register to use some online newspapers and pay to download archived materials.

**◉6 Check book and film reviews.** Sometimes you may want to know how a given book or film was received when it first appeared. To locate reviews of older books, see *Book Review Digest* (1905), *Book Review Index* (1965), or *Current Book Review Citations* (1976). *Book Review Digest* lists fewer reviews than the other two collections, but it summarizes those it does include—a useful feature. Many electronic periodical indexes also catalog book reviews. Enter "book reviews" on a search engine or directory, and you will turn up many sites, such as the *New York Times Sunday Book Review* at <http://www.nytimes.com/pages/books/review/index.html> and *The New York Review of Books* at <http://www.nybooks.com>.

For film reviews and criticism, see the printed volumes *Film Review Index* (1986) and *Film Criticism: An Index to Critics' Anthologies* (1975) as well as the electronic index *Film Index International*. Numerous Web sites—of wildly varying quality—are devoted to films and film reviews.

**● 7 Write or email professional organizations.** Almost every subject, cause, concept, or idea is represented by a professional organization, society, bureau, office, or lobby. Write or email an appropriate organization for information on your topic. For mailing addresses of organizations, consult the *Encyclopedia of Associations*, published by Gale Research. Use a search engine to find Web sites.

**● 8 Consult collections of images.** Online resources make it possible to locate images you may need for your research projects. Some search engines—such as *AltaVista* and *Google*—look for images (as well as audio and video clips). Among the numerous collections of images and clip art on the Web are the following.

| IMAGE SITE | ADDRESS |
|---|---|
| *About.com* | <http://webclipart.about.com> |
| Surveys clip art and graphic sites on the Web. | |
| *Google Maps* | <http://maps.google.com> |
| Provides both maps and satellite images of all locations. | |
| *GraphicMaps.com* | <http://www.graphicmaps.com> |
| Provides information about maps on the Web. | |
| *Time & Life Pictures* | <http://www.timelifepictures.com> |
| Presents images from the Time, Inc., collection. | |

Note that you may have to pay to acquire or use some images. You'll also need to document any borrowed images you include in your finished project, just as you cite and document other research sources.

**⊕9 Consult Usenet groups and blogs in research.** Usenet groups make it possible for you to read or participate in discussions on a huge variety of topics—arts, sciences, religion, popular culture, and so on. You can access these groups easily by selecting "Groups" at either <http://www.yahoo.com> or <http://www.google.com>. But be cautious with any information you take from such an open environment: confirm any statistic, fact, or claim from such a source with information from a second and different type of authority—a published book, an article, a reference work.

Similarly, many blogs offer commentary on the news and critiques of mainstream media sources. The best of these often highly personal and frequently updated sites can be useful when you want to gauge opinion on almost any subject. But remember that you are usually reading the unfiltered opinions of one person or group.

## 44c How do you search by keywords?

Writers now routinely find information online by typing names, phrases, or other key terms into *Google* to see what pops up. That habit has largely replaced more refined keyword searches. Yet you still will need keyword search techniques to explore many electronic resources. A *keyword search* is simply a scan of an electronic text or database to find each occurrence of a given word or phrase.

> **e-Tips**
>
> Be sure to type keywords carefully, especially proper nouns. A misspelled search term can prevent you from finding available information.

**⊕1 Understand how a simple keyword search works.** A keyword search finds the items in a catalog or database that contain the keyword(s) you have typed into a box or line on the screen. You might get keyword ideas from the *Library of Congress Subject Headings* (*LCSH*) in the reference room of your library. Or ask a reference librarian for help.

When searching a library catalog, always look for cross-listings for your particular subject—that is, other terms under which your subject is entered. For example, if your project on Civil War ironclad ships leads you to search with the term *Monitor* (the name of a famous Union ship), a particular catalog entry might include the cross-listings *Civil War; Merrimac; U.S. Navy, history; Ericsson, John.* You could then probe the catalog using each of these new terms.

You will have to be ingenious at times in choosing keywords for Web searches. Use your preliminary reading on a subject to come up with more specific keywords. If you need to know whether alcohol is legally considered a drug, for example, you could begin with general keywords such as "alcohol" or "drugs." But if you have read that drugs are regulated by the Federal Drug Administration, FDA might be a better search term.

So the keywords you choose—whether names, places, titles, concepts, or people—will shape your search. A comparatively small database, such as an online library catalog, may ask you to indicate whether a word you are searching is a title (t), author (a), subject (s), or some other term the system recognizes. But more sophisticated search techniques may be required when you get more hits from a keyword search than you can reasonably research. One such technique is called Boolean searching.

**● 2 Understand the principles of Boolean searching.** A Boolean search uses specific terms (or symbols) to give you more control over what you are seeking. Most search engines in online catalogs, databases, or Web sites use some form of Boolean search.

In a Boolean search, by linking keywords with the term AND, you will pull up only those database items in which the linked terms intersect. It may help to visualize these items in terms of sets.

schnauzer AND training

Washington AND Jefferson AND Constitution

Another way to initiate a Boolean search is to select an appropriate command from a search engine menu, such as an "all the words" option. Narrowing your search to look for only those items in which occur *all* the words you specify usually reduces the information glut.

Other Boolean operators allow you to direct database searches in different ways.

**OR** Using OR between keywords directs the search engine to find any examples of either keyword. Using OR might widen a search, but it would also allow you to locate all documents that cover related concepts.

> **dog OR puppy**
>
> **Congress OR Senate**

**NOT**   Using NOT between terms permits you to search for sites that include one term but not another. This may be useful when you want to exclude certain meanings of a term irrelevant to your search.

> **Indians NOT Cleveland**
>
> **republican NOT party**

**( )**   Putting items in parentheses allows for additional fine tuning of a search. In the first example below, you could locate documents that mention either Senator Clinton or Senator Hutchison.

> **Senator AND (Clinton OR Hutchison)**
>
> **pickup NOT (Ford OR Dodge)**

● **3 Search by exact phrase.** To narrow a search even more, you can search for a specific and distinctive phrase either by placing it between quotation marks or selecting the "exact phrase" option on a search screen. You can use exact-phrase searches creatively in many ways. When you can't recall who is responsible for a particular expression or quotation—for example, "defining deviancy down"—you can make it the subject of an exact-phrase search. Do so on a Web search engine and you may find the expression attributed to former Senator Daniel Patrick Moynihan.

You can also combine exact-phrase searches with various Boolean commands to find precisely what you need if you identify appropriate keywords.

> "Ten Commandments" AND ("Charlton Heston" OR "Yul Brynner")
>
> "pickup truck" NOT (Ford OR Dodge)

**e-Tips**

To learn more about using Web search engines, see Ellen Chamberlain's "Bare Bones 101," a site at the University of South Carolina Beaufort that includes detailed descriptions of important search engines, at<http://www.sc.edu/beaufort/library/pages/bones/bones.shtml>.

## 44d How do you do field research?

Some of your research—especially in service-learning projects—may require interviews, surveys, and close observation. Such *fieldwork* is common in disciplines such as psychology, anthropology, and education; if you are pursuing degrees in these areas, you'll learn formal techniques for field research. But informal fieldwork can be useful in other research situations provided that you describe your procedures accurately and properly qualify your conclusions. Here we'll look briefly at conducting interviews and using questionnaires. One caution: before you begin, be sure to check your school's policies on what is often called *institutional research*. You may be required to get approval from a committee before you may survey, experiment with, or do systematic observation of fellow students.

● **1 Conduct interviews.** People are often the best sources of authoritative or firsthand information. When you can discuss your subject with experts or learn from people in a community, you add credibility, authenticity, and immediacy to a research report or service project. For example, if you're writing about problems in the building industry, find a builder or banker with thirty minutes to spare.

Consider, too, how technology might enhance the information gained from an interview. For instance, you might photograph or videotape the people you interview and make those images part of a *PowerPoint* or Web presentation. Current digital imaging tools make such enhancements not only possible but also relatively easy.

---

**Checklist 44.5 Conducting a One-on-One Interview**

- Write or telephone your subject for an appointment, and make it clear why you want the interview.

- Confirm your meeting the day before, and be on time for your appointment.

- Be prepared for the meeting. If possible, learn all you can about your subject's professional background, education, work history, and publications.

- Have a list of questions and possible follow-ups ready in your notebook. Establish the basic facts: Who? What? Where? When? How? Why? Then, when appropriate, pose questions that require more than one-word answers.

- Focus your queries on your research question: don't wander from the subject.

- Take careful notes, especially if you intend to quote your source.

- Double-check direct quotations, and be sure your source is willing to be cited "on the record."

- Get your subject's approval before turning on an audio or video recorder.

- Promise to send your subject a copy of your completed project.

- Send a thank-you note to an authority who has been especially helpful.

---

**2 Conduct surveys.** Research projects that focus on your local community may require surveys of public opinion and attitudes not available from other sources. So you may have to supply the information yourself by preparing questionnaires and conducting studies. To begin with, have a clear idea about the information you are seeking. Look for answers to specific research questions: *Do people on my dormitory floor feel personally secure in their rooms? Would people in my neighborhood support the presence of a halfway house for juvenile offenders? Are people willing to pay additional taxes for improved public transportation?*

Asking the right questions isn't easy. You don't want to skew the answers you get by posing vague, biased, or leading questions. (Leading questions have the effect of pushing respondents toward a particular answer.)

| | |
|---|---|
| **VAGUE** | What do you think about dorm security? |
| **REVISED** | Do you have any concerns about personal security in Aurelius Hall? |
| **BIASED** | Would you support yet another tax increase to fund a scheme for light rail in the city? |
| **REVISED** | Would you support a one-cent increase in the current sales tax to fund a light rail system for the city? |
| **LEADING** | Are you in favor of the city's building a halfway house for juvenile criminals right in the middle of our peaceful Enfield neighborhood? |
| **REVISED** | Do you favor the city's plan to build a halfway house for juvenile offenders in the Enfield neighborhood? |

To make responses easy to tabulate, provide readers with a range of options for answering your questions, such as the five possible responses in the following example.

How do you feel about the following statements? Respond using the appropriate number:

1. I disagree totally.
2. I disagree somewhat.
3. I neither agree nor disagree.
4. I agree somewhat.
5. I agree totally.

| | |
|---|---|
| Our bus system serves the whole community. | _____ |
| Our bus system operates efficiently. | _____ |
| Our bus system runs on time. | _____ |
| Bus fares are too high. | _____ |
| A sales tax increase for buses makes sense. | _____ |

In addition to exploring your specific issues, you may need to gather *relevant* demographic data on the people you are surveying (e.g., gender, marital status, age, race, ethnicity, level of education or income); this information may be useful later in interpreting your findings. You must also be able to protect the privacy of the people you survey and offer reasonable assurances that any information they volunteer will not be used against them in any way.

Be sure you survey enough people from your target group so that readers will find your sample adequate. You ordinarily need to choose people at random for your study, yet those polled should represent a cross-section of the whole population. Surveying just your friends, just people who agree with you, or only people like yourself will almost certainly produce inaccurate research.

Finally, you'll have to tabulate your findings accurately, present the results in a fashion that makes sense to readers, let readers know the techniques you used to gather your information, and, most important, report the limits of your study. Those limits provide the qualifications for any conclusions you draw. Don't overstate the results.

---

**Checklist 44.6  Conducting a Survey**

- Understand the purpose of your survey or questionnaire before you create it. What information do you want to gather?

- Prepare clear, fair, and unbiased questions. Test your questions on others to be sure participants in your actual survey will understand them.

- Consider the type of responses you need from respondents. Should they respond to a scale? To a list of options you provide? Should they fill in blanks?

- Consider how much space might be adequate for responses and how much space might be too much.

- Create questionnaires that are easy to read, easy to fill out, and easy to tabulate.

- Create questionnaires that are convenient to return. If necessary, provide properly addressed envelopes and return postage.

- Give respondents appropriate assurances about the confidentiality of their responses, and then abide by your commitment.

- Keep track of all your sampling procedures so you can report them accurately in your research paper.

# 45 How Do You Evaluate Sources?

Finding research materials, as described in Chapter 44, doesn't grind to a halt when you begin developing a project. Instead, you may find yourself seeking more information to address new questions or plug gaps in what you've learned. At the same time, you'll be assessing sources you've already gathered—first *evaluating* them to see whether they will be useful to you and then *positioning* them to understand their purpose and genre.

## 45a How do you evaluate research materials?

Writers have always had to be careful about the sources they cited in research projects, but at least they could be confident that the library materials they used had been reviewed by publishers, editors, and librarians. Today, however, some materials—for example, pages from the Web and messages from electronic mailing lists—may come to you almost directly from their authors, unreviewed and unrefereed. It falls to you, then, to judge their authority, quality, and credibility.

● **1 Consider the purpose of a source.** Sources aren't simply *good* or *bad*. Their value will depend, in part, on how you intend to use them. Writing a report on Abraham Lincoln's positions during the 1860 presidential campaign, you'd depend on scholarly works or, perhaps, newspaper accounts of his speeches on microfilm. Writing about current political campaigns, you'd likely have to use less scholarly materials—campaign literature, articles in recent magazines, maybe even some blogs. These sources would lack the authority of scholarly books (which wouldn't be available yet), but they could still provide a valid snapshot of current political attitudes.

Even if sources can't be described as simply good or bad without considering their purposes, they do have strengths and weaknesses to weigh. We've summarized some of those qualities in the table on pages 640–641. Of course, any single source might differ from our characterizations. In researching any subject, the best sources for you are likely those just a step or two above your current level of knowledge. Push yourself to learn more without exceeding your depth.

**⊙2 Consider the authority and reputation of a source.** As you accumulate materials for a project, you may find that certain sources are cited more often than others. These are likely to be essential materials that people in the field assume most other researchers know. If you haven't already consulted these materials, go to the library and review them. Ask librarians or instructors, too, about the quality of sources that you expect to use. Take their advice about reputable publishers, journals, and bibliographies.

Do the same with electronic sources: track down the best items so far as you can determine. Inevitably, the most valuable sites will appear on many "favorites" lists. Sometimes the Web address (URL) can also help you identify the nature of a source. Checking the domain in the address will give you some sense of who is sponsoring the site—though the designation can be misleading since anyone can claim some of these domains.

.edu—a U.S. educational institution
.org—an organization
.gov—restricted to U.S. government
.com—a commercial/business site
.biz—an alternative to .com
.net—may be an Internet service provider
.info—an informative site
.museum—restricted to museums
.travel—restricted to travel
.fr—country code for France

**⊙3 Consider the credentials of authors and sponsoring agencies.** This advice might not seem practical when you are exploring a subject new to you. But you'll quickly pick up the names of people mentioned frequently as experts or authorities. When scanning a lengthy printout of potential sources, look for these familiar authors. But don't be drawn in by celebrity alone, particularly when the names of celebrities are attached to subjects about which they may have no expertise.

You can be more confident about electronic information when the sponsoring agency of the source is one you would trust in a print environment. Acquiring information online from *Reuters News Service* or the *New York Times* is equivalent to seeing the same information in print. But don't hesitate even in these cases to raise questions about fairness, bias, and completeness.

**●4 Consider the timeliness and stability of a source.** Timeliness is relative. For some projects, you might need sources that are both immediate and interactive like the conversations in news groups and blogs. For other projects, you may turn to the more studied discussion of current issues you'll find in some newspapers, magazines, and popular journals. For still other academic work, you'll want sources that offer the kind of thoughtful commentary or observation that requires time, research, and study.

With books and articles, then, the date of publication is crucial. In general, you want to support your projects with the most current and reputable information in a field. But your instructors and librarians may refer you to classic pieces, too, writings that have shaped thinking in your topic area. For many college papers, you should have a mix of sources, some from the past, some quite recent.

Timeliness is a different matter in newer electronic environments. In general, electronic sources are not yet as stable, comprehensive, and dependable over the long run as printed books and articles—though the situation is improving rapidly and some materials (such as scholarly e-journals) may be available only online. In general, avoid sites that do not date either their original postings or updates. And be sure a site is current when you use it: some pages remain on servers years after they were originally posted. Check too whether a site archives its materials. If it doesn't, it may not be useful for research.

**● 5 Consider who supports or sponsors a source.** Sponsored materials will often reflect the commercial connections of their owners, especially when news or information outlets (TV, radio, publishers) are in fact owned by larger companies with specific mercantile interests or political agendas. Who supports the message may determine what appears—or doesn't appear—in the media (see Section 45b). This may also be true of the work of think tanks and trusts, such as Brookings, Cato, or PEW, whose research may reflect the views of those who sponsor such groups. That's not to say that the research produced is not credible or honest, just that it may be produced in support of specific causes or positions.

---

**Checklist 45.1    Evaluating a World Wide Web Site**

- Is the site sponsored by a reputable group you can identify?

- Do the authors of the site give evidence of their credentials?

- Is this the site of an advocacy group? Are they forthright about their advocacy?

- Is the site conveniently searchable?

- Is information in the site logically arranged?

- Is the site easy to navigate?

- Does the site provide an email address where you might send questions?

- Is the site updated regularly or properly maintained?

- Does the site archive older information?

- Is the content of the site affected by commercial sponsorship?

**Assessing Sources**

| Source | Purpose | Authors | Audience/ Language |
|---|---|---|---|
| *Scholarly books* | Advance or report new knowledge | Experts | Academic/ Technical |
| *Scholarly articles* | Advance or report new knowledge | Experts | Academic/ Technical |
| *Serious books & articles* | Report or summarize information | Experts or professional writers | Educated public/ Formal |
| *Popular magazines* | Report or summarize information | Professional writers or journalists | General public/ Informal |
| *Newspapers, news services* | Report current information | Journalists | Popular/ Informal |
| *Sponsored Web sites* | Varies from report information to advertise | Varies, usually Web expert | Varies/Usually informal |
| *Individual Web sites/Blogs* | Varies | Expert to novice | Varies/Casual to slang |
| *Interviews* | Consult with experts | Experts | Varies/Technical to colloquial |
| *Electronic mailing lists* | Discuss specific subjects | Experts to interested amateurs | Varies/Technical to colloquial |
| *Usenet newsgroups* | Discuss specific subjects | Open to everyone | Varies/Technical to colloquial |

| Publisher or Medium | Reviewed/ Documented? | Current/ Stable? | Dialogic/ Interactive? |
|---|---|---|---|
| University Press | Yes/Yes | No/Yes | No/No |
| Scholarly or professional journal | Yes/Yes | Usually no/ Yes | No/No (unless online) |
| Commercial publishers | Yes/No | Depends on subject/Yes | No/No (unless online) |
| Commercial publishers | Yes/No | Yes/Yes | No/No (unless online) |
| Commercial press or online | Yes/No | Yes/Yes | No/No (unless online) |
| Online WWW | Sometimes/ Links to other sites | Regularly updated/ Sometimes | Sometimes/ Often |
| Online WWW | Usually no/ Links to other sites | Varies/Varies | Sometimes/ Sometimes |
| Notes, recordings, email | No/No | Yes/No | Yes/Yes |
| Online email | No/No | Yes/ Sometimes | Yes/Yes |
| Online email | No/No | Yes/No | Yes/Yes |

## 45b How do you position research sources?

Before you annotate (see Section 46a), summarize, or paraphrase a source (see Section 46b), be sure you understand its context—what we call *positioning a source.* You position a source by trying to identify its point of view, biases, strengths, and limitations. Of course, you will use different sources in different ways. Sometimes you'll want sources that offer the most balanced or authoritative treatment of a subject. At other times you'll choose sources that exemplify specific points of view—a libertarian view, a feminist perspective, a Catholic outlook. Positioning a source ensures that you'll make such decisions with your eyes open and not misconstrue information when you report it.

*Utne Reader* at <http://utne.com> appeals to a predominantly left-of-center readership concerned with issues of culture, earth, body, spirit, and politics.

The titles of articles in *The Weekly Standard* at <http://www.weeklystandard.com> might suggest its right-of-center politics. Or you might recognize the names of some of its authors.

The perspectives of a magazine like *Rolling Stone*, which focuses on popular culture, may not be as self-evident or consistent as those of a political journal. But the magazine will still reflect the interests and biases of its writers and publishers. To position such a source, you might examine the titles of its articles, the tone of its editorials (if any), the character of its illustrations and graphics, and even the types of ads it attracts. View its Web site at <http://www.rollingstone.com>.

## Checklist 45.2   Positioning a Source

- What are the background and interests of the author(s)?

- What are the interests and biases of the publisher?

- How much authority does the source claim? (Look for such words as "official," "leading," "authorized," and so on.)

- Are its assertions of authority justified?

- Does the source claim to be objective and/or scientific?

- Does the source present itself as subjective and/or personal?

- Whose interests or outlook does the source represent?

- Whose interests does the source seem to ignore?

- To what audience(s) is the source directed?

- What do readers need to know about the source?

- Where do links in the source lead? Who advertises in the source?

- What role should the source play in my project: Authority? Opinion? Illustration?

# 46 How Do You Use Sources Responsibly?

Once you have found solid sources for your project, you may need to annotate, summarize, and paraphrase the material to make good use of it and to avoid problems with plagiarism and collusion. Plagiarism is submitting someone else's work as your own; collusion is unauthorized collaboration—that is, having someone else work on your project without an instructor's knowledge and approval.

## 46a How do you annotate research materials?

Once you have evaluated and positioned a source (see Chapter 45), read it carefully, attaching comments, questions, and reactions directly to the text to mark information worth noting and recalling. Such annotation is difficult when you are reading library books and materials; in these cases, record your reactions in notes, summaries, and paraphrases (see Section 46b). But much research material today is photocopied, downloaded, or read online—and these media support more direct forms of annotation.

Many researchers use highlighter pens to tag important passages in photocopied materials. But be sure to attach a marginal comment to any section you highlight this way to explain its importance or record your reaction. For electronic files, you can record your reactions by using both the highlighting and commenting features of word-processing programs. If such annotations are thoughtful and entirely in your own words, they

---

**e-Tips**

For a detailed online guide to *Microsoft Word*'s commenting features, search "word commenting" at <http://www.cwrl.utexas.edu> or try <http://www.cwrl.utexas.edu/?q=node/56>. The tutorial explains how to either edit or comment on any document you can download in *Word*.

## An Annotated Essay

### "Educational Insensitivity"

#### Diane Ravitch

An enterprising parent of a high school senior recently discovered that the literary texts on the New York Regents examinations had been expurgated. Excerpts from the writings of many prominent authors were doctored, without their knowledge or permission, to delete references to religion, profanity, sex, alcohol or other potentially troublesome topics.

The story was a huge embarrassment to the New York State Education Department, which prepares the examinations, and yesterday Richard P. Mills, the state education commissioner, ordered the practice stopped. From now on, all literary passages used on state tests will be unchanged except for length.

Mr. Mills is to be commended for this new policy. But the dimensions of this absurd practice reach far beyond the borders of New York, and there are many culprits. Censorship of tests and textbooks is not merely widespread: across the nation, it has become institutionalized.

For decades, American publishers have quietly trimmed sexual and religious allusions from their textbooks and tests. When publishers assemble reading books, they keep a wary eye on states like California, Texas and Florida, where textbooks are adopted for the entire state and any hint of controversy can prevent a book's placement on the state's list. In Texas, Florida and other southern states, the religious right objects to any stories that introduce fantasy, witchcraft, the occult, sex or religious practices different from its own. In California, no textbook can win adoption unless it meets the state's strict demands for gender balance and multicultural representation and avoids mention of unhealthy foods, drugs or alcohol.

Over the past several decades, the nation's testing industry has embraced censorship. In almost every state, tests are closely scrutinized in an official process known as a bias and sensitivity review. This procedure was created in the late 1960's and early 1970's to scrutinize questions for any hint of racial or gender bias. Over the years, every test development company in the nation has established a bias and sensitivity review process to ensure that test questions do not contain anything that might upset students and prevent them from showing their true abilities on a test. Now these reviews routinely expurgate references to social problems, politics, disobedient children or any other potentially controversial topic.

*Original audience was readers of the New York Times, America's paper of record.*

*Find out more about NY Regents exams.*

*What's the issue now if the policy has been changed?*

*Ravitch's claim.*

*Can both right and left be responsible for censorship?*

*Looks like good intentions gone haywire. Shouldn't good literature challenge students?*

This is the rationale now used within the testing industry to delete references to any topic that someone might find objectionable. As a top official in one of the major testing companies told me: "If anyone objects to a test question, we delete it. Period."

This self-censorship is hardly a secret. Every major publisher of educational materials uses "bias guidelines," which list hundreds of words and images that are banned or avoided. Words like "brotherhood" and "mankind" have been banished. A story about mountain climbing may be excluded because it favors test-takers who live near mountains over those who don't. Older people may not be portrayed walking with canes or sitting in rocking chairs.

> Is Ravitch being sarcastic in this ¶ or are her examples real?

I serve on the board of a federal testing agency, the National Assessment Governing Board, which is directly responsible for reviewing all test questions on the National Assessment of Educational Progress. We have learned that bias and sensitivity rules are subject to expansive interpretations. Once reviewers proposed to eliminate a reading passage about Mount Rushmore because the monument offends Lakota Indians, who consider the Black Hills of South Dakota a sacred site.

This censorship is now standard practice in the testing industry and in educational publishing. One way to end it is to expose the practice to public scrutiny, forcing officials like Mr. Mills to abandon it. Another way, adopted by the National Assessment Governing Board, is to review every deletion proposed by those applying bias and sensitivity standards to determine whether it passes the test of common sense. I would also recommend that whenever material is deleted from a literary passage in a test, the omission should be indicated with ellipses.

> Proposals to solve censorship in schools and textbooks.

The bias and sensitivity review process, as it has recently evolved, is an embarrassment to the educational publishing industry. It may satisfy the demands of the religious right (in censoring topics) and of the politically correct left (in censoring language). But it robs our children of their cultural heritage and their right to read—free of censorship.

> Ravitch's actual claim—and a possible quotation.

Diane Ravitch, a historian of education at New York University, is writing a book about censorship in the educational publishing industry.

> What else has she written? What are her politics?

might later be incorporated directly into your paper or project. Following is an example of a source that has been annotated in its margins. This same article is both summarized and paraphrased in Section 46b.

## 46b Should you summarize or paraphrase research materials?

Summarizing and paraphrasing represent different ways of responding to materials you read.

A *summary* captures the gist of a source or some portion of it, boiling it down to a few words or sentences. Summaries tend to be short, describing only what is immediately relevant from a source. Summarize those materials that support your thesis, but do not provide an extended argument or idea that you need to share in detail with readers.

When summarizing a source, identify its key facts or ideas and put them in your own words. When an article is quite long, look for topic ideas in each major section. If you have a photocopy of the source, highlight any sentences that state or emphasize its key themes. Then assemble these ideas into a short, coherent statement about the whole piece, one detailed enough to stand on its own and make sense several weeks after you examine the material. The summary should be entirely in your own words.

A *paraphrase* usually reviews a complete source in much greater detail than does a summary. When paraphrasing a work, you report its key information or restate its core arguments point by point *in your own words*.

An effective paraphrase will meet the following conditions.

- The paraphrase follows the structure of the original piece.
- The paraphrase reflects the ideas of the original author, not your thoughts on them.
- Each important fact or direct quotation is accompanied by a specific page number from the source when possible.
- The material you record is relevant to your theme. (Don't waste time paraphrasing parts of the source that are of no use to your project.)
- The material is entirely in your own words—except for clearly marked quotations.

In gathering information, you'll often find yourself switching between summary and paraphrase, depending on what you are reading.

Let's look at a source first summarized and then paraphrased—the article "Educational Insensitivity" by Diane Ravitch annotated in Section 46a (see pages 646–647). This op-ed piece originally appeared in the *New York Times* on June 5, 2002, shortly after the New York State Department of Education admitted that, to avoid offending students, it had been censoring works of literature included in a standard examination.

To prepare a summary, assemble the key claim and supporting elements into a concise restatement of the overall argument that makes sense on its own. Don't be surprised if you go through several versions of that sentence before you come up with one that satisfies you.

**EFFECTIVE SUMMARY**   Diane Ravitch, a professor at New York University, argues in the *New York Times* (5 June 2002) that educators and textbook authors should not cave in to the demands of the political right or left to censor the topics and the language of literary works because such editing robs students of their cultural heritage.

How can something as simple as a summary go wrong? You might, for example, leave out crucial details. Such a summary scribbled on a note card might be useless when, days later, you try to make sense of it.

**INEFFECTIVE SUMMARY**   She argues that it's wrong to censor literature. Both the left and right want it.

Or your summary might fail because it misses the central point of a piece by focusing on details that are not relevant to the argument.

**INACCURATE SUMMARY**   Diane Ravitch, a professor at New York University, knows about censorship in education because she serves on the National Assessment Governing Board, which reviews questions on tests.

Yet another danger lies in using the actual words of the original author in your summary. If these borrowings make their way into your project itself without *both* quotation marks and documentation, you are guilty of plagiarism (see Section 46c). In the following example, language taken directly and inappropriately from Ravitch's op-ed piece is underlined.

| | |
|---|---|
| **PLAGIARIZED** | Diane Ravitch, a professor at New York University, |
| **SUMMARY** | argues in the *New York Times* (5 June 2002) that the |
| | expurgation of literary works by educators and textbook |
| | publishers <u>robs our children of their cultural heritage</u> |
| | <u>and their right to read--free of censorship</u>. |

To avoid plagiarism, the safest practice is *always* to use your own words in summaries.

A paraphrase of "Educational Insensitivity" would be appreciably longer than a summary because a researcher would expect to use the information differently, probably referring to the source in much greater detail. Here's one possible paraphrase of Ravitch's op-ed article.

| | |
|---|---|
| **EFFECTIVE** | Responding to criticism that it had edited sensitive and |
| **PARAPHRASE** | controversial passages from literary works on its Regents |
| | examinations, the New York State Education Department |
| | announced that it would abandon the practice. But Diane |
| | Ravitch argues in a *New York Times* op-ed piece (5 June |
| | 2002) that the practice of trimming controversial materials |
| | from educational materials is so common that it is |
| | institutionalized. Those on the political right demand that |
| | morally offensive topics and ideas be cut from exams and |
| | textbooks; those on the political left demand gender and |
| | ethnic balance. Standardized tests are now routinely |
| | subject to reviews for bias and insensitivity, as are other |
| | educational materials. Ravitch argues that this |

embarrassing practice should be ended by letting the public know what is happening and by carefully reviewing any standards applied to educational materials. Censorship robs students of their cultural right to read literature as it was written.

This paraphrase covers all the major points in the editorial in the same order as the original. It also borrows none of the author's language. With proper documentation, any part of the paraphrase could become part of a final research project without a need for quotation marks.

How can paraphrases go wrong? A paraphrase shouldn't include your comments and asides because you might later confuse your ideas with those of your source. Consider how the underlined passages in the following paraphrase misreport the views of Diane Ravitch.

**INACCURATE PARAPHRASE** Responding to criticism that it had edited sensitive and controversial passages from literary works on its Regents examinations, the New York State Education Department announced that it would abandon the practice <u>even though one could argue that many students benefited from the censorship</u>. But Diane Ravitch argues in a *New York Times* op-ed piece (5 June 2002) that trimming controversial materials from educational materials is so common that it is institutionalized. Those on the political right, <u>who probably don't want their children exposed to any challenging ideas</u>, demand that morally offensive topics be cut from exams and textbooks; those on the political left demand gender and ethnic balance, <u>which Ravitch should admit is often lacking in so-called classical works of literature</u>. Standardized tests are now routinely subject to reviews for bias and insensitivity, as are other educational materials. Ravitch argues that this

embarrassing practice should be ended by letting the
public know what is happening and by carefully
reviewing any standards applied to educational
materials. Censorship robs students of their cultural right
to read literature as it was written.

A paraphrase also should not reorganize the structure or argument of the
original piece. For example, the following paraphrase of Ravitch's editorial
rearranges its information radically.

| | |
|---|---|
| **INACCURATE** | Children in school should not be robbed of their cultural |
| **PARAPHRASE** | heritage by educators and publishers worried that |
| | reading what literary authors actually wrote might harm |
| | their tender sensitivities. But that's what is happening all |
| | across the country according to Diane Ravitch, a member |
| | of the National Assessment Governing Board, a group |
| | that reviews questions posed on the National |
| | Assessment of Educational Progress. Maybe if Ms. |
| | Ravitch served in the New York State Education |
| | Department, it would not have gotten into the business |
| | of censoring the literary works that appeared on its |
| | Regents examinations--sparking a controversy about |
| | how much censorship is occurring in education today |
| | as a result of pressure from both the right and the left |
| | to advance their political agendas in our nation's |
| | schools. |

The most dangerous and academically dishonest paraphrase is one in
which a researcher borrows the ideas, structure, and details of a source
wholesale, changing a few words here and there in order to claim originality.
This sort of paraphrase is plagiarism even if the material is documented in
the research project.

| PLAGIARIZED | An inquisitive parent of a high school student figured |
| PARAPHRASE | out recently that the works of literature used on the New |
| | York Regents examinations had been cut and edited. |

Passages from the novels and poems of many famous writers were changed, without their permission or knowledge, to remove all mention of religion, drugs, sexuality, and other such offensive subjects.

The story embarrassed the New York State Education Department, which creates the tests, and so the state education commissioner ordered a stop to the practice. Henceforth, all literary passages used on New York tests will be unchanged except for length. . . .

You'll see the fault very readily if you compare these plagiarized paragraphs with the opening paragraphs in Ravitch's original editorial.

# 46c Do you understand academic responsibility?

Most students understand that it is wrong to buy or download a paper, to let someone heavily edit a paper for them, or to submit someone else's work as their own. This kind of activity is dishonest, and most institutions have procedures for handling scholastic dishonesty when it occurs (see Section 3b).

But many students do not realize that taking notes carelessly or documenting sources inadequately may also raise doubts about the integrity of a paper. Plagiarism is easily avoided if you take good notes (see Section 46b) and follow the guidelines in this section.

● **1 For conventional sources, acknowledge all direct uses of anyone else's work.** Suppose, for example, that in preparing a research paper on mountain biking, you come across the following passage from *The Mountain Bike Book* by Rob van der Plas.

106

In fact, access and right-of-way are the two intangibles in trail cycling these days. The sport is getting too popular too fast, and in defense, or out of fear, authorities have banned cyclists from many potentially suitable areas.

You will probably use forest service or fire roads and trails intended for hikers most of the time. Don't stray off these trails, since this may cause damage, both to the environment and to our reputation. As long as you stay on the trails and do it with a modicum of consideration for others, you have nothing to fear and should not risk being banned from them by public agencies.

In many areas a distinction is made between single-track trails and wider ones. Single tracks are often considered off-limits to mountain bikers, although in most cases they are perfectly suitable and there are not enough hikers and other trail users to worry about potential conflicts. In fact, single trails naturally limit the biker's speed to an acceptable level.

If you decide to quote all or part of the selection above in your essay, you must use quotation marks (or indention) to indicate that you are borrowing the writer's exact words. You must also identify the author, work, publisher, date, and location of the passage through documentation. If you are using MLA documentation (see Chapter 50), the in-text acknowledgment and corresponding Works Cited entry might look like this.

As Rob van der Plas reminds bikers, they need only use common sense in riding public trails: "As long as you stay on the trails and do it with a modicum of consideration for others, you have nothing to fear and should not risk being banned from them by public agencies" (106).

Works Cited

van der Plas, Rob. *The Mountain Bike Book: Choosing, Riding and Maintaining the Off-Road Bicycle.* 3rd ed. San Francisco: Bicycle, 1993. Print.

You must use *both* quotation marks and an in-text note when you quote directly. Quotation marks alone would not tell your readers what your source was. A note alone would acknowledge that you are using a source, but it would not explain that the words in a specific portion of your paper are not entirely your own.

⦿**2 Summarize and paraphrase carefully.** When you summarize or paraphrase a source (see Section 46b), be certain that your notes are entirely in your own words. Some writers mistakenly believe that they can avoid a charge of plagiarism just by rearranging the elements or changing a few words in a source they are using. They are flat wrong.

For example, you may want to discuss the ideas raised in the selection from *The Mountain Bike Book* on the facing page, borrowing the information in van der Plas's paragraphs but not his words. Here are two acceptable summaries of the passage on mountain biking that report its facts appropriately and honestly. Notice that both versions include a parenthetical note acknowledging van der Plas's *The Mountain Bike Book* as the source of information.

> Rob van der Plas asserts that mountain bikers need not fear limitation of their right-of-ways if they ride trails responsibly (106).

> Though using so-called single-track trails might put mountain bikers in conflict with the hikers, such tracks are often empty and underutilized (van der Plas 106).

Without those parenthetical notes, both versions above might be considered plagiarized even though only van der Plas's ideas—not his actual words—are borrowed. That's because you *must give credit even for ideas* you take from your sources unless you are dealing with common knowledge. Review Section 46b for detailed advice on how to write effective summaries and paraphrases and how to avoid plagiarizing in the process.

⦿**3 Be careful with information you find on the Web.** The basic rules of scholastic honesty still apply in electronic environments. You may not copy and paste information from a Web site, electronic mailing list, newsgroup, or other electronic source to your own project without fully documenting that material.

# 47 How Do You Introduce and Quote from Sources?

Every quotation in an article should contribute something your own words cannot. So choose these quotations strategically and then introduce them seamlessly into the paper or project. Use quotations for reasons such as the following.

- To focus on a particularly well-phrased idea in a source.
- To show what others think about a subject.
- To give impact to important facts or color and character to an argument.
- To show a range of opinion.
- To clarify a difficult or contested point.
- To demonstrate the complexity of an issue.

Never use quotations to pad your work or just to avoid writing yourself. And don't use so many quoted passages in a paper (even good ones) that a reader loses sense of what your contributions to the project are.

However, most of the source material you present in a paper will be either summarized or paraphrased (see Section 46b). This material, too, will need to be appropriately introduced so that readers appreciate its authority and significance.

## 47a How do you introduce material borrowed from sources?

Introduce readers to any borrowed words and ideas by supplying a context or *frame*. Such frames can be relatively simple, and they can *precede, follow,* or *interrupt* the quoted material. The frame need not even be in the same sentence as the quotation; it may be part of the surrounding paragraph. Here are examples of ways that quoted material can be introduced.

- *Frame precedes borrowed material:*

  **In 1896, Woodrow Wilson, who would become Princeton's president in 1902, declared,** "It is not learning but the spirit of service that will give a college a place in the public annals of the nation."

  —Ernest L. Boyer

- *Frame follows borrowed material:*

  "One reason you may have more colds if you hold back tears is that, when you're under stress, your body puts out steroids which affect your immune system and reduce your resistance to disease," **Dr. Broomfield comments.**

  —Barbara Lang Stern

- *Frame interrupts borrowed material:*

  "Whatever happens," **he [Karl Marx] wrote grimly to Engels,** "I hope the bourgeoisie as long as they exist will have cause to remember my carbuncles."

  —Paul Johnson

- *Surrounding sentences frame borrowed material:*

  **In the meantime, [Luis] Jimenez was experimenting with three-dimensional form.** "Perhaps because of the experience of working in the sign shop, I realized early on that I wanted to do it all—paint, draw, work with wood, metal, clay." **His images were those of 1960s pop culture, chosen for their familiarity and shock value.**

  —Chiori Santiago

- *Borrowed material integrated with passage:*

  **The study concludes that a faulty work ethic is not responsible for the decline in our productivity; quite the contrary, the study identifies** "a widespread commitment among U.S. workers to improve productivity" **and suggests that** "there are large reservoirs of potential upon which management can draw to improve performance and increase productivity."

—Daniel Yankelovich

You should also introduce ideas that you borrow when you summarize or paraphrase a source rather than quote from it. The frames you provide may vary according to the style of documentation you are using; we show examples in MLA and APA style here.

- *Frame precedes borrowed material* (MLA):

  **In *Freakonomics*, Steven D. Levitt and Stephen J. Dubner observe that** there seems to be little correlation between children's success on standardized tests and whether they watch television (168).

- *Frame follows borrowed material* (APA):

  Contrary to experts who predicted a sterile future, ours is an age of expressive and inventive design, **Postrel (2003) argues**.

- *Frame interrupts borrowed material* (MLA):

  Federal standards for meat processing are so lax, ***Fast Food Nation* author Eric Schlosser claims**, that consumers should regard ground beef as a hazardous material (221).

The basic principle for introducing borrowed material is simple: either name (directly or indirectly) the author, the speaker, or the work the passage is from, or explain why the words you are quoting are significant. Many phrases of introduction or *attribution* are available. Note that the verb of attribution you choose can shape the way readers perceive the quotation that follows. Compare your reactions to the following statements that differ only in their verb of attribution.

Benson **reports** that high school test scores have dropped again.

Benson **laments** that high school test scores have dropped again.

Benson **complains** that high school test scores have dropped again.

| Chart 47.1 | **Verbs of Attribution** (there are many more) | | | |
|---|---|---|---|---|
| accept | allege | demonstrate | insist | say |
| add | argue | deny | mention | show |
| admit | believe | disagree | posit | state |
| affirm | confirm | emphasize | propose | verify |

# 47b How may you modify direct quotations?

You must always quote accurately and never omit words or phrases just to make sources seem to support your thesis. Such modifications would undermine the credibility of your entire research project. But there are ways to make quotations flow naturally with the style of your paper. These techniques preserve the integrity of quotations while giving you some flexibility in their use.

**● 1 Tailor your language so that direct quotations fit into the grammar of your sentences.** To create a seamless merger, you may have to modify the words you use to frame a quotation or modify the quotation itself by careful selections, ellipses (see Section 38b-1), or additions made within brackets (see Section 39b-1).

CLUMSY    The chemical capsaicin that makes chili hot: "it is so hot it is used to make antidog and antimugger sprays" (Bork 184).

REVISED    Capsaicin, the chemical that makes chili hot, is so strong "it is used to make antidog and antimugger sprays" (Bork 184).

CLUMSY    Computers have not succeeded as translators of language because, says Douglas Hofstadter, "nor is the difficulty caused by a lack of knowledge of idiomatic phrases. The fact is that translation involves having a mental model of the world being discussed, and manipulating symbols in the model" (603).

**REVISED** "A lack of knowledge of idiomatic phrases" is not the reason computers have failed as translators of languages. "The fact is," says Douglas Hofstadter, "that translation involves having a mental model of the world being discussed, and manipulating symbols in the model" (603).

● **2 Use ellipses (three *spaced* periods . . . ) to indicate where you have cut material from direct quotations.** For example, ellipses might be used to trim the lengthy passage following to focus on the oldest portions of the biblical text. The ellipses will tell readers where words, phrases, and even whole sentences have been cut.

**ORIGINAL PASSAGE**

The text of the Old Testament is in places the stuff of scholarly nightmares. Whereas the entire New Testament was written within fifty to a hundred years, the books of the Old Testament were composed and edited over a period of about a thousand. The youngest book is Daniel, from the second century B.C. The oldest portions of the Old Testament (if we limit ourselves to the present form of the literature and exclude from consideration the streams of oral tradition that fed it) are probably a group of poems that appear, on the basis of linguistic features and historical allusions contained in them, to date from roughly the twelfth and eleventh centuries B.C. . . .

—Barry Hoberman, "Translating the Bible"

**PASSAGE AS CUT FOR USE IN AN ESSAY**

Although working with any part of an original scripture text is difficult, Hoberman describes the text of the Old Testament as "the stuff of scholarly nightmares." He explains in "Translating the Bible" that although "the entire New Testament was written within fifty to a hundred years, the books of the Old Testament were composed and edited over a period of about a thousand. . . . The oldest portions of the Old Testament . . . are probably a group of poems that appear . . . to date from roughly the twelfth and eleventh centuries B.C."

**● 3 Use square brackets [ ] to add necessary information to a quotation.** You may want to explain who or what a pronoun refers to, or you may have to provide a short explanation, furnish a date, and explain or translate a puzzling word.

> Some critics clearly prefer Wagner's *Tannhäuser* to *Lohengrin*: "The well-written choruses [of *Tannhäuser*] are combined with solo singing and orchestral background into long, unified musical scenes" (Grout 629).

But don't overdo it. Readers will resent the explanation of obvious details.

# 47c What conventions govern direct quotations?

Following are some specific conventions that apply to direct quotations. Quotation marks themselves (" ") do more than set off direct quotations, so you may want to review Section 38a to appreciate all their uses. In that section, you'll also find guidelines that explain where to place quotation marks when they meet up with other punctuation marks in sentences.

**● 1 Use [sic] to indicate an obvious error copied faithfully from a source.** Quotations must be copied, word by word, from your source— errors and all. To show that you have copied a passage faithfully, place the expression *sic* (the Latin word for "thus" or "so") in brackets one space after any mistake.

> Mr. Vincent's letter went on: "I would have preferred a younger bride, but I decided to marry the old window [sic] anyway."

If *sic* can be placed outside the quotation itself, it appears between parentheses, not brackets.

> Molly's paper was titled "King Leer" (sic).

**●2 Place prose quotations shorter than four typed lines (MLA) or forty words (APA) between quotation marks.**

> In *Utilitarianism* (1863), John Stuart Mill declares, "It is better to be Socrates dissatisfied than a pig satisfied."

**●3 Indent more than three lines of poetry (MLA).** Up to three lines of poetry may be handled just like a prose passage, with slashes marking the separate lines. Quotation marks are used.

> As death approaches, Cleopatra grows in both grandeur and dignity: "Husband, I come! / Now to that name my courage prove my title! / I am fire and air" (5.2.287-89).

More than three lines of poetry are indented 10 spaces and quotation marks are not used. (If the lines of poetry are unusually long, you may indent fewer than 10 spaces.) Be sure to copy the poetry accurately, right down to the punctuation.

> Among the most famous lines in English literature are those that open William Blake's "The Tyger":
>
> > Tyger tyger, burning bright,
> >
> > In the forests of the night;
> >
> > What immortal hand or eye,
> >
> > Could frame thy fearful symmetry? (1-4)

**●4 Indent any prose quotation longer than four typed lines (MLA) or forty words (APA).** MLA form recommends an indention of one inch, or 10 spaces if you are using a typewriter; APA form requires 5 spaces. Quotation marks are *not* used around the indented material. If the quotation extends beyond a single paragraph, the first lines of subsequent paragraphs are indented an additional quarter inch, or 3 typed spaces (MLA) or 5 spaces (APA). In typed papers, the indented material—like the rest of the essay—is double spaced.

You may indent passages of fewer than four lines when you want them to have special emphasis. But don't do this with every short quotation or your paper will look choppy.

# 48 How Do You Produce a Final Draft?

Since academic research projects represent a first level of serious professional work, they must meet exacting standards as you bring them to completion. These requirements vary from discipline to discipline, but the principles and concerns examined in this section apply to most papers and projects. (See also Chapter 5.)

## 48a Is the organization solid?

Organizing a sizable paper or project is rarely an easy job. For the draft of a long paper, you may want to check the overall structure using a method such as the following.

- **Underline the topic idea, or thesis, in your draft.**
- **Underline just the first sentence in each subsequent paragraph.**
- **Read the underlined sentences straight through as if they formed an essay in themselves.** Ask whether each sentence advances or explains the main point or thesis. If the sentences—taken together— read coherently, chances are good that the paper is well organized.
- **If the underlined sentences don't make sense, reexamine those paragraphs not clearly related to the topic idea.** If the ideas really are not connected, delete the whole paragraph. If the ideas are related, revise the paragraph to make the ties clearer. (See Section 14b.)
- **Test your conclusion against your introduction.** Sometimes the conclusions of essays contradict their openings because of changes that occurred as the paper developed. Revise as necessary.

Of course, there are exceptions to this structure: some papers lead toward a conclusion—where the thesis may be finally stated. Still, each major section of the paper should lead clearly toward that main idea.

Test the structure of other projects similarly. For a Web site, try to imagine how a reader encountering it for the first time might search for information: Will users find what they are seeking by following only a short sequence of links?

# 48b Is the format correct?

Whether you are reporting your research in a conventional paper or on a Web site, you want the presentation to be effective. Here we focus chiefly on research papers, but you can find advice about crafting other types of projects in Part IV, Design and Shape of Writing.

● **1 Pay attention to the format of work you submit.** Be sure a paper is submitted on good-quality white paper. Print on only one side of the pages, double-spacing the body of your essay and the notes. Keep fonts simple and use boldface rarely, perhaps to highlight important headings.

Specifications for MLA and APA papers are given in Sections 50c and 51c, respectively. These guidelines can be applied even to papers that don't need to follow a specific professional style.

● **2 Insert tables and figures as needed.** Use graphics whenever they help readers understand your ideas better than words alone can. Pie charts, graphs, and tables (see Section 18d) can make information easier to interpret.

But be careful, too, not to clutter your work with what one design expert calls "chartjunk." Just because you have easy access to graphics doesn't mean you must illustrate every page. (See Chapter 18 on visual design.)

MLA form requires that you label tables (columns of data) and figures (pictures or illustrations), number them, and briefly identify what they illustrate. Spell out the word *Table*, and position the heading above the table, aligned with the left margin.

Table 1

First-Year Student Applications by Region

| Fall 1995 | Fall 1994 | Difference | Percent | Change |
|-----------|-----------|------------|---------|--------|
| Texas | 12,022 | 11,590 | 432 | +4 |
| Out of state | 2,121 | 2,058 | 63 | +3 |
| Foreign | 756 | 673 | 83 | +11 |

*Figure*, which is usually abbreviated in the caption as *Fig.*, appears below the illustration, flush left. To point to an image in the text of an essay, use the form we show at the end of this sentence (see Fig. 7).

Fig. 7. Mountain bike.

When preparing an APA paper, you may want to check the detailed coverage of figures and tables in the *Publication Manual of the American Psychological Association*. For APA-style student papers, figures (including graphs, illustrations, and photos) and tables should appear in the body of the essay itself, but placed on separate pages, immediately following their mention in the text.

Chromosomes consist of four different nucleotides or bases—adenine, guanine, thymine, and cytosine—which, working together, provide the code for different genes (see Figure 1).

Short tables may even appear on the same page as text material.

Figures and tables are numbered consecutively. Captions for figures appear below the item. If the illustration is borrowed from a source, you must get permission to reproduce it and acknowledge the borrowing as shown.

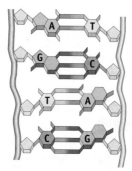

**Figure 1.** The four bases of the genetic code: adenine (A), guanine (G), thymine (T), and cytosine (C). From *Your Genes, Your Choice*, by C. Baker, 1997. Copyright 1997 by the American Association for the Advancement of Science. Reprinted with permission.

Titles for tables appear above the item.

Table 2

*Errors by Levels of Difficulty*

● **3 Be consistent with headings.** You can use headings to give shape to any project. A short research paper (five to six pages) ordinarily needs only a title. In longer papers, however, readers may appreciate headings that explain the content of major sections. (You may want to check with instructors about their preferences.) All such heads should be brief, parallel in phrasing, and consistent in format like the items in a formal outline (see

Section 3d-3). For most academic papers, you probably won't use more than one level of heading after the title.

MLA style (described in Chapter 50) provides fairly loose standards for headings. Titles of MLA papers are ordinarily centered on the first page of an essay and headings appear in the text, flush with the left-hand margin. If you descend to a second level, you'll have to distinguish second-level heads by numbering or lettering them or by setting them off typographically (usually by variations in capitalization or underlining). MLA style leaves you to decide how you will handle such choices, but in all cases, you must keep the headings clean and unobtrusive.

APA style (described in Chapter 51) provides five levels of headings for professional articles—more than you'll probably use in a college paper. But APA rules are complex and precise. Here's how to handle a paper that requires just two levels of headings.

- First-level heads are centered, using both uppercase and lowercase letters as shown below.
- Second-level heads are capitalized like titles, but also italicized and placed flush with the left-hand margin.

Here's how those APA guidelines look in operation. For more complex papers or articles you submit for publication, consult the *Publication Manual of the American Psychological Association.*

Differences in Reading Habits of

College Sophomores      Title

Abstract      1st level

Method      1st level

*Participants*      2nd level

*Materials*      2nd level

*Design and Procedure*      2nd level

Results      1st level

Discussion      1st level

## 48c Are the details correct?

Give the final version of your project a careful review. Don't skip this step.

● 1 **Include all the components your project requires.** Before you submit a project, reread the specifications of either the instructor or the professional society whose guidelines you are following. A research paper typically follows a specific order.

- Title page (not recommended in MLA; required in APA)
- Outline (optional; begins on its own page; requires separate title page)
- Abstract (optional, but common in APA; usually on its own page)
- Body of the essay (in MLA, Arabic pagination begins with the body of the essay in MLA; in APA, with the title page)
- Content or bibliographic notes
- Works Cited/References (begins on its own page separate from the body of the essay and any content or bibliographic notes)

The sample research essay on pages 733–746 illustrates MLA style, and the essay on pages 779–796 illustrates APA style. For a more complex paper such as a master's thesis or a doctoral dissertation, follow the order recommended in a volume such as *The MLA Style Manual* (MLA) or the *Publication Manual of the American Psychological Association* (APA). Many schools publish their own guidelines for submitting graduate-level theses.

● 2 **Follow the rules for documentation right down to the punctuation and spacing.** Accurate documentation is a part of professional research. Instructors and editors notice even minor variations in documentation form. Perhaps the two most common errors in handling the MLA format, for example, are forgetting to put a period at the end of entries in the Works Cited list and placing a comma where none is needed in parenthetical documentation.

> **WRONG**  Pluto, Terry. *The Curse of Rocky Colavito.* New York: Simon, 1994. Print
>
> **RIGHT**  Pluto, Terry. *The Curse of Rocky Colavito.* New York: Simon, 1994. Print.

**WRONG**   (Pluto, 132-36)

**RIGHT**   (Pluto 132-36)

You will survive both errors, but they are easy to avoid.

---

### Checklist 48.1   Research Project Requirements

- Have you placed your name, your instructor's name, the date, and the course name on the first or title page?

- Is the title centered? Are only the major words capitalized? (Your title should not be underlined or appear between quotation marks.)

- Did you number the pages? Are they in the right order?

- Have you used quotation marks and parentheses correctly and in pairs? (The closing quotation mark and parenthesis are often forgotten.)

- Have you placed quotation marks around all direct quotations that are shorter than four lines?

- Have you indented all direct quotations of more than four typed lines (MLA) or of forty words or more (APA)?

- Have you remembered that indented quotations are not placed between quotation marks?

- Did you introduce all direct quotations with some identification of their author, source, or significance?

- Did you use the correct form for parenthetical notes?

- Have you handled titles correctly, italicizing or underscoring (depending on style) book titles and putting the titles of articles between quotation marks?

- Did you include a Works Cited or References list? Is your list of works cited alphabetized? Did you indent the entries correctly?

**PART VIII** | **Documentation**

# 49 How Do You Document a Research Paper?

In your research project you will create a dialogue among the sources you have assembled. But readers will want to know which ideas and claims are your own and which should be credited to your sources. They may also want to assess your work and pursue it further. For these reasons, you need to acknowledge your sources in academic or professional projects conscientiously, honestly, and gracefully, using an appropriate system of documentation. Presented in subsequent chapters are documentation systems of the Modern Language Association (MLA), the American Psychological Association (APA), and the *Chicago Manual of Style* (CMS). This chapter examines the general principles for acknowledging and using sources.

## 49a What are documentation styles?

*Documentation* refers to the forms devised to keep track of sources used in a project—typically some type of notes (endnotes, footnotes, parenthetical notes) and a full bibliography. Systems of documentation typically offer detailed models for handling a wide variety of sources, from traditional books and articles to less familiar electronic media. In high school and college, most student writers learn the documentation procedures established by the Modern Language Association (MLA). But different rules about documentation and style have evolved in other fields. Use the documentation style appropriate to your field or recommended by your instructor.

| Chart 49.1 Style Guides in Various Fields |
| --- |
| • **Biology:** *Scientific Style and Format: The CBE Manual for Authors, Editors, and Publishers* (6th ed., 1994) by the Council of Science Editors |
| • **Chemistry:** *The ACS Style Guide: A Manual for Authors and Editors* (2nd ed., 1997) by the American Chemical Society and Janet S. Dodd |
| *(Continued)* |

---

**Style Guides in Various Fields**  *(Continued)*

- **Earth science:** *Geowriting: A Guide to Writing, Editing, and Printing in Earth Science* (5th ed., 1995) by Robert Bates

- **English language and literature/humanities:** *MLA Handbook for Writers of Research Papers* (6th ed., 2003) by Joseph Gibaldi (the student version of *MLA Style Manual*)

- **Federal government:** *United States Government Printing Office Manual* (2000) by the United States Government Printing Office (GPO)

- **Journalism:** *The Associated Press Stylebook and Briefing on Media Law* (2002)

- **Law:** *Uniform System of Citation: The Bluebook* (18th ed., 2005) by the Harvard Law Review Association

- **Mathematics:** *A Manual for Writers of Mathematical Papers* (8th ed., 1990) by the American Mathematical Society

- **Music:** *Writing About Music: An Introductory Guide* (3rd ed., 2001) by Richard J. Wingell

- **Nursing:** *Writing for Nursing Publications* (1981) by Andrea B. O'Connor

- **Political science:** *Style Manual for Political Science* (rev. ed., 2002) by the American Political Science Association and Michael K. Lane

- **Psychology and social sciences:** *Publication Manual of the American Psychological Association* (5th ed., 2001)

- **Physics:** *AIP Style Manual* (4th ed., 1990) by the American Institute of Physics

---

## 49b How do you document a research project?

Knowing what to document in a research paper can be as complicated as the documentation styles themselves. Here are some guidelines. (See Figure 49.1 on page 675 for specific examples.)

**● 1 Provide a source for every direct quotation.** A *direct quotation* is any material repeated word for word from a source. Direct quotations in college papers typically require some form of parenthetical documentation—

that is, a citation of author and page number (MLA) or author, date, and page number (APA).

MLA    It is possible to define literature as simply "that text which the community insists on having repeated from time to time intact" (Joos 51–52).

APA    Hashimoto (1986) questions the value of attention-getting essay openings that "presuppose passive, uninterested (probably uninteresting) readers" (p. 126).

You are similarly expected to identify the sources for any diagrams, statistics, charts, or pictures in your paper. You need not document famous sayings, proverbs, or biblical citations.

In less formal writing, you should still identify the author, speaker, or work from which you borrow any passage and indicate why the words you are quoting are significant. Many phrases of introduction or attribution are available (see Section 47a). Here are just a few.

One noted astronomer **reported** that . . .

**According to** the GAO, the figures  . . .

● **2 Document all ideas, opinions, facts, and information that cannot be considered common knowledge.** *Common knowledge* includes the facts, dates, events, information, and concepts that a person in your *intended* audience can be assumed to know or which would be uncontroversial if they had to look them up. Writing a history paper, you might need an encyclopedia to find out that the Battle of Waterloo was fought on June 18, 1815, but such an important date would be considered common knowledge because it is well established and undisputed. You would not have to give credit to a particular source to use such a fact in a paper.

Similarly when you find that a given piece of information or an idea is shared among several of the sources you are using within an academic field or discipline, you usually need not document it. For example, if in writing a paper on anorexia nervosa you discover that most authorities define it in the same way, you probably don't have to provide a citation for that definition. What experts know collectively constitutes the common knowledge within a

> 2        WALTER ISAACSON
>
> Benjamin Franklin is the founding father who winks at us. George Washington's colleagues found it hard to imagine touching the austere general on the shoulder, and we would find it even more so today. Jefferson and Adams are just as intimidating. But Ben Franklin, that ambitious urban entrepreneur, seems made of flesh rather than marble, addressable by nickname, and he turns to us from history's stage with eyes that twinkle from behind those newfangled spectacles. He speaks to us, through his letters and hoaxes and autobiography, not with orotund rhetoric but with a chattiness and clever irony that is very contemporary, sometimes unnervingly so. We see his reflection in our own time.
>
> He was, during his eighty-four-year-long life, America's best scientist, inventor, diplomat, writer, and business strategist, and he was also one of its most practical, though not most profound, political thinkers. He proved by flying a kite that lightning was electricity, and he invented a rod to tame it. He devised bifocal glasses and clean-burning stoves, charts of the Gulf Stream and theories about the contagious nature of the common cold. He launched various civic improvement schemes, such as a lending library, college, volunteer fire corps, insurance association, and matching grant fund-raiser. He helped invent America's unique style of homespun humor and philosophical pragmatism. In foreign policy, he created an approach that wove together idealism with balance-of-power realism. And in politics, he proposed seminal plans for uniting the colonies and creating a federal model for a national government.
>
> But the most interesting thing that Franklin invented, and contin-

Isaacson's memorable description of Franklin would be a good passage to quote directly (and document properly).

Franklin's kite flying is common knowledge even to the general public. You could mention it without citing this source—but not use Isaacson's words in your work.

The information here is not common knowledge. In a paper, the idea should be paraphrased and credited to Isaacson so readers could check your sources and his.

**Figure 49.1** In this selection from Walter Isaacson's *Ben Franklin: An American Life* (2003) you can see how a single source might offer different kinds of information for a paper.

field; what they claim individually—their opinions, studies, theories, research projects, hypotheses—is the material you *must* document in a paper.

### ● 3 Document materials that readers might question or wish to explore further.

If your subject is controversial, you may want to document even those facts or ideas considered common knowledge in the field. Suppose that in writing about witchcraft you make a historical assertion well known by scholars within a field but liable to surprise nonspecialists. Writing for nonspecialists, you should certainly document the assertion. Writing for experts, you might skip the note. But when in doubt, document.

### ● 4 Furnish dates, credentials, and other information to assist readers.

Provide dates for important events, major figures, and works of literature and art. Identify any person readers might not recognize.

After the great fire of London (1666), the city was . . .

Henry Highland Garnet (1815–82), American abolitionist and radical, . . .

*Pearl* (c. 1400), an elegy about . . .

In the last example, the *c.* before the date stands for *circa*, which means "about."

When quoting from literary works, help readers locate the passages you are citing. For novels, identify page numbers; for plays, give act/scene/line information; for long poems, provide line numbers and, when appropriate, division numbers (book, canto, or other divisions).

● **5 Use links to document electronic sources.** Links in Web pages can function as a type of documentation: they can take readers directly to supporting material or sources. But it's important that readers of hypertexts understand where a highlighted passage is leading them. Hyperlinks should be used judiciously to provide real information. Don't overwhelm a Web page with links; they can seem as fussy as a page with too many footnotes. And make sure the links work because Web addresses change with distressing frequency.

● **6 Use computer programs to document your project.** Some software programs are available to help you document a paper or create a bibliography. Even most word processors have automatic footnote or endnote features. If you choose to use such a feature, be sure it supports the documentation style—for example, MLA, APA, CMS—required for your project. Also be certain that the program is up to date.

# 49c Where do you find information to document a source?

When working with research materials, you'll encounter many unfamiliar terms and concepts. An instructor may assume, for example, that you know what an *edition* is, where the publication information for a book can be found, or why some magazines have volume numbers and others do not. We'll cover some basics of documenting books, articles, and electronic sources here, but don't hesitate to ask an instructor or librarian questions. The documentation "maps" at the end of this section give clear, visual hints for finding source information.

### ● 1 Check the title and copyright pages on books for documentation information.

For books published in English, you'll find the title page just a page or two inside the front cover. Most title pages will include a full title (including any subtitle); the names of the author(s), editors, or translators; the number of the edition; and the publisher. For the year and place of publication, check the copyright page, which follows immediately. The copyright page may also offer details about previous editions of the book, as well as its Library of Congress call number and its International Standard Book Number (ISBN). If information you need is not in the book—a place of publication, a date, or even an author's name—just omit that information from your citation. Don't guess or make it up.

Large books may appear in several *volumes* because a single volume would be too large or because the book was produced over a long time, with different volumes appearing in different years. A book in a *series* is a separate work that is part of a collection of books by different authors on a common theme. If a book is published in several volumes or is part of a series, you'll need to mention the fact in your citation.

### ● 2 Check the cover or contents page of scholarly journals for documentation information.

Any additional information you need may be in a table of contents—though you'll need to check the article itself to get its closing page number. Most scholarly journals use *volume* numbers to identify the work produced in a particular year because they rarely come out monthly or on a particular date. For easy reference, all the issues of a journal produced during a single year constitute one *continuously paginated* volume. (For example, the "winter" issue of a journal may begin on page 389.) When citing a journal article, you will always need the volume number, the year of publication, and the page numbers of the article you are using.

### ● 3 Check magazines articles for documentation information.

Most of the information you need to cite an article in a popular magazine (name of periodical, date, author, title of article) will appear in the table of contents. But to get an exact title, rely on the article itself. Page numbers can be tricky too. Although articles in scholarly journals run uninterrupted from beginning to end, those in magazines are often broken up by ads and other stories. In MLA style, you give the first page of an interrupted story followed by a plus sign: *60+.* In APA style, you list all the pages on which the interrupted story appears: *60–65, 96, 98–99.*

Quite often, you'll be citing a magazine article not from an original copy, but from a printed version provided by a library subscription service, perhaps emailed to you. The piece will ordinarily provide all the bibliographical information you need for a citation, including page numbers. But it may not include images or other textual features of the original article.

● **4 Check the masthead and credits column of newspapers for documentation information.** A masthead is the distinctive banner that runs across the front page identifying the paper. If the masthead indicates that you are using a particular edition of the paper—*morning, evening, suburban*—be sure to note it. Copy the headline of any article you cite from the first page of the story; a continuation of the story on a later page might have an altered title. When stories appear across a series of pages, follow the same procedure for newspapers as for magazines. But note that newspapers are paginated by sections as well as numbers. In MLA style, you simply give the first section and page of the story, followed by a plus sign: *B60+.* In APA style, list all the pages on which the story appears: *B60–B65, B96, B98–B99.*

A copy of the article provided by a library news service such as Lexis-Nexis will provide full bibliographical information, usually before the body of the article.

● **5 Expect full documentation from the Web sites you use.** The Web page for a site you use for a research paper should give you enough information to provide adequate documentation—at a minimum the name of the site, an institutional sponsor, and a date for the most recent material. (Sometimes you may have to go back to the home page of the site for information.) For online books, articles, and newspapers, look for the same bibliographical date that you would gather for printed versions of these materials, with the possible exception of page numbers. When a Web site provides virtually no documentation information, aside from the title of the page and the URL, you might question its value as a source for your project.

Refer to the following documentation "maps" for hints on finding information needed to document sources.

## How Do You Cite a Book?

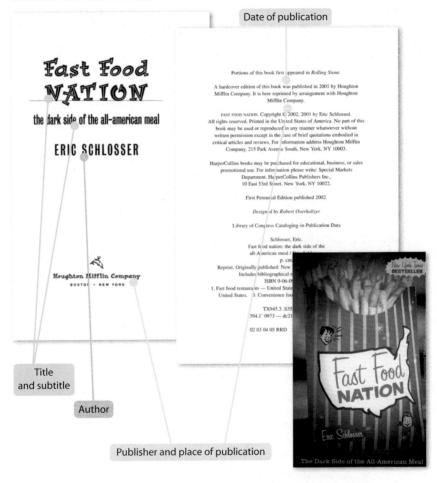

Date of publication

Portions of this book first appeared in *Rolling Stone*.

A hardcover edition of this book was published in 2001 by Houghton Mifflin Company. It is here reprinted by arrangement with Houghton Mifflin Company.

FAST FOOD NATION. Copyright © 2002, 2001 by Eric Schlosser. All rights reserved. Printed in the United States of America. No part of this book may be used or reproduced in any manner whatsoever without written permission except in the case of brief quotations embodied in critical articles and reviews. For information address Houghton Mifflin Company, 215 Park Avenue South, New York, NY 10003.

HarperCollins books may be purchased for educational, business, or sales promotional use. For information please write: Special Markets Department, HarperCollins Publishers Inc., 10 East 53rd Street, New York, NY 10022.

First Perennial Edition published 2002.

*Designed by Robert Overholtzer*

Library of Congress Cataloging-in-Publication Data

Schlosser, Eric.
Fast food nation: the dark side of the
all-American meal /
p. cm.
Reprint. Originally published: New
Includes bibliographical r
ISBN 0-06-0
1. Fast food restaurants — United State
United States. 3. Convenience foo

TX945.3 .S35
394.1' 0973 — dc21

02 03 04 05 RRD

*Fast Food*
**NATION**
the dark side of the all-american meal

**ERIC SCHLOSSER**

**Houghton Mifflin Company**
BOSTON · NEW YORK

Title and subtitle

Author

Publisher and place of publication

**MLA:** Schlosser, Eric. *Fast Food Nation: The Dark Side of the All-American Meal*. New York : Houghton, 2005. Print.

**APA:** Schlosser, E. (2005) *Fast food nation: The dark side of the all-American meal*. New York : Houghton, Mifflin.

## How Do You Cite Scholarly Articles?

A scholarly article in printed form ordinarily provides all necessary bibliographic information on its first page.

For scholarly articles found via database services, look for bibliographical information on a preview page or on the article itself (often reproduced in .pdf format). Such databases may even offer model citations.

**MLA:** Anderson, Virginia. "'The Perfect Enemy': Clinton, the Contradictions of Capitalism, and Slaying the Sin Within." *Rhetoric Review* 21 (2002): 384-400. Print.

**APA:** Gosling, S.D. & John, O.P. (1999) Personality dimensions in nonhuman animals: A cross-species review. *Current Dimensions in Psychological Science, 8*(3), 69-75. Retrieved May 1, 2005, from Blackwell Synergy database.

## How Do You Cite a Magazine Article?

Title

Publication,
date, page number

Author

Full bibliographical information
attached to library service printout
of the *Texas Monthly* article
entitled "Tyler Hollandsworth"

**MLA:** Hollandsworth, Skip. "Tyler Hollandsworth." *Texas Monthly*
Sept. 2003: 64. Print.

**APA:** Hollandsworth, S. (2003, September). Tyler Hollandsworth.
*Texas Monthly*, 64.

## How Do You Cite a Newspaper?

The same article provided by LexisNexis search includes full bibliographical information.

No page number appears on this front page. But a box makes it clear that this edition has sections. So this page is A1 and the article continues on B4.

Author

Title

Name of newspaper

Edition

Date of publication

MLA: Apple, R.W., Jr. "A High Point in 2 Decades of U.S. Might." *New York Times* 10 Apr. 2003, late ed.: A1+. Print.

APA: Apple, R.W., Jr. (2003, April 10). A high point in 2 decades of U.S. might. *New York Times*, pp. A1, B4.

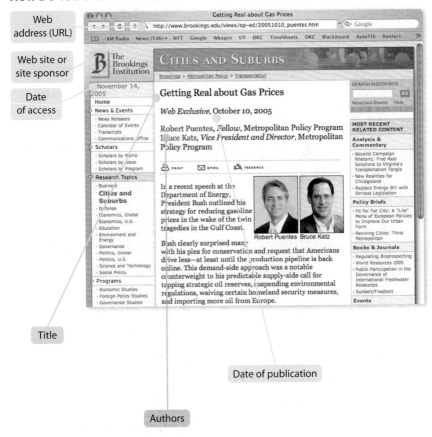

## How Do You Cite a Website?

Web address (URL)

Web site or site sponsor

Date of access

Title

Date of publication

Authors

**MLA:** Puentes, Robert, and Bruce Katz. "Getting Real About Gas Prices." *The Brookings Institution* 10 Oct. 2005. Web. 14 Nov. 2005.

**APA:** Puentes, R. & Katz B. (2005, October 10) Getting real about gas prices. Retrieved November 14, 2005, from http://www.brookings.edu/views/op-ed/20051010_puentes

# Directory to MLA Notes—by Type

(See inside back cover for alphabetical directory.)

# 50 How Do You Use MLA Documentation?

In the humanities and liberal arts, many writers and publishers follow the guidelines for documentation and formatting recommended by the Modern Language Association (MLA). The basic procedures for documenting an MLA-style paper involve just two steps: placing a note at the point where you

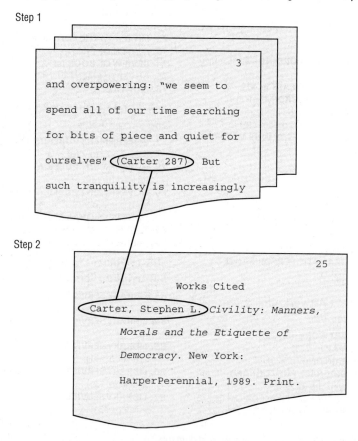

Step 1

3

and overpowering: "we seem to
spend all of our time searching
for bits of piece and quiet for
ourselves" (Carter 287) But
such tranquility is increasingly

Step 2

25

Works Cited

Carter, Stephen L. *Civility: Manners,
Morals and the Etiquette of
Democracy.* New York:
HarperPerennial, 1989. Print.

use a source in a paper or project (Section 50a) and then creating an entry on a Works Cited page for that source (Section 50b). If you run into problems not discussed here, refer to the *MLA Handbook for Writers of Research Papers* (7th ed., 2009) by the Modern Language Association. Updates are also available at the MLA Web site: <http://www.mla.org/style>. If you want more information about citation styles in general or are uncertain about what exactly you should document in a paper, see Chapter 49, "How Do You Document a Research Paper?"

## 50a Step 1: In the body of your paper, place a note for each source you use.

Each time you quote, paraphrase, or in some way use ideas from outside sources, you must acknowledge that you've done so with some form of note. You can create in-text notes several ways. One is to use *parenthetical citations*, which put information about a source between parentheses, usually at the end of a sentence: **(Prosek 246-47)**. Or you may use *signal phrases*, which identify sources within the normal flow of the sentence: **According to Eric Foner** in *The Story of American Freedom*. . . . Often you will combine these basic forms, using both a signal phrase and a page number in parentheses: **Anderson claims** that the TV show *South Park* "spares no sensitivity" **(76)**.

Parenthetical notes tend to be the easiest form of citation to create, but they can interrupt the flow of your writing. Consequently, MLA guidelines suggest that you use them sparingly and make them as concise as possible. Signal phrases, on the other hand, allow you to mention details about your source that establish its credibility, explain its relevance, or clarify its positions. (Review Section 47a for more on how to introduce borrowed material effectively.)

### ● 1 Identify outside sources clearly each time you use them.

Whether you introduce sources with parenthetical notes or signal phrases, your readers will always need to know precisely which the source on the works-cited list you're using. You establish that connection by making certain that the note itself clearly refers to the word by which source is alphabetized in the works-cited list, whether that is a person's last name (an author or editor, for example), a set of names (groups of authors or editors, for example), or a title.

**IN-TEXT NOTE:** . . . while fishing in England (**Prosek** 246-47)

Works Cited

**Prosek**, James. *The Complete Angler: A Connecticut Yankee Follows in the Footsteps of Walton.* New York: Harper, 1999.

**IN-TEXT NOTE:** More information on National Parks in the United States can be found at the Web site *Parknet*

Works Cited

*"Parknet." National Park* Service. 12 Dec. 1999. Web. 6 Dec. 2008.

As you can see, you will need to know how a source will appear on your works-cited list in order to create a note. But in most cases, that will be easy once you have identified the author(s) or title of a source. Simply apply the guidelines below that fit the particular sources you are citing. (The works-cited entries for the examples in these guidelines appear on pp. 691–692.)

**1.1  Citing a source listed under a single person's name.** This is a common type of note.

As one historian says, "The scientist, like the artist, is one of us" (**Jardine** 5).

In signal phrases, you may use full first names to make your passage more readable.

"Today's secular disruption between the creative aspect of art and that of science," anthropologist **Loren Eiseley** contends, "is a barbarism that would have brought lifted eyebrows in a Cro-Magnon cave" (271).

When your works-cited listing contains sources by different people having the same last name, use initials or full first names to refer to their works without confusion.

**1.2 Citing a source listed under a group of people's names.** Provide the *last names of all individuals* in the same order they will appear at the beginning of the works-cited entry. When a source is listed under four or more persons' names, you have the option of using the Latin abbreviation *et al.* (*et alia,* "and others") after the first person's name. If you choose the shortened form *et al.* for your works-cited entries, use it also for all in-text notes.

> **Varela, Thompson, and Rosch** ask, "What challenges does human experience face as a result of the scientific study of the mind?" (xvii).

> The Royal Society was chartered in 1662 to further scientific enquiry and advance the study of natural philosophy (**Abrams et al.** 1: 1571).

**1.3 Citing a source listed under a corporate or group author.** In this case, a signal phrase is often more readable than a parenthetical note. When you do use a parenthetical note to identify the source, abbreviate the name of the author.

> "The Shuttle will return to flight only after we have met all the safety requirements and milestone goals—and not before" (**NASA**).

**1.4 Citing a source listed by title.** Put the *title* in your in-text citation when a work doesn't have an author or creator. Shorten that title as much as possible: the shortened title, however, should always include its first word (excluding *A, An,* and *The*), so readers can easily find the entry on the alphabetized Works Cited page.

> Scientific creativity tends to be limited more by money than ideas (**"Art"**).

**1.5 Citing a source that is one of many listed under the same person's name.** Mention *both* the *last name* of the author and the *title* of the particular source. When using parenthetical citation, follow the person's last name with a comma and a shortened version of the title (see the preceding section).

> Even the most cultivated "habit of thought" can be questioned when we acknowledge that "conviction of the 'truth' . . . is founded exclusively on rather incomplete experience" (**Einstein**, *Relativity* 3-4).

A readable way of handling such a citation is to mention the person's name in a signal phrase and then use a parenthetical citation to clarify which work you are referring to in the particular passage.

> **Spielberg**'s recent films have explored how science and technology shape our views of morality (*Minority Report*), as well as how they challenge our ideas of humanity (*A.I.*)—traditional concerns of humanist scholars.

**1.6 Citing material from sacred texts, classical literary works, and legal documents.** These works are often identified by standard abbreviations, especially when parenthetical notes are used. For classical literary works, look for a standard abbreviation in the textual notes of the edition you're using, or find a list compiled by scholars; if none is available, follow the guidelines presented in "Citing a source listed by title" on page 689.

> **Shakespeare**'s Caliban values his education in the language arts only because it helped him "know how to curse" (*Tmp.* 1.2.364).

For sacred texts, standard abbreviations are often used to identify the work in both signal phrases and parenthetical notes. When you use the generic name of a sacred work—including terms such as the Bible, Torah, Qur'an, as well as sections and chapters within them—do *not* underline the title in your in-text notes.

> The spiritual and emotional value of pursuing the truth is articulated well in the **King James Version** of the **Bible**: "He that hath knowledge spareth his words: and a man of understanding is of an excellent spirit" (**Prov.** 17.27).

Do, however, underscore the title of any particular published editions of such works.

> It is not clear how the works that comprise the Torah came to be seen as one book (*New Oxford Annotated Bible*, HB 6).

Similar rules apply to historic legal documents (for example, the Declaration of Independence and the Treaty of Versailles), and also to specific government acts and laws (for example, the Selective Service Act). You would, ordinarily, not underline such titles.

**1.7 Citing multiple sources in a single parenthetical note.** Separate each citation by a semicolon, following the other guidelines listed above. Do this sparingly, however, since such notes can become long and distracting.

> Newer editions of literary anthologies include scientific texts of historical significance (**Abrams et al.** xxiii; **Henderson and Sharpe** vii, xii).

**1.8 Citing material repeatedly from the same source.** Readers can assume that any parenthetical notes that don't identify a source refer to the last works-cited entry mentioned in the body of the paper. Omit the source identifier in notes referring repeatedly to the same work when no other is mentioned.

> Dr. Frankenstein, whose "sole occupation" is "natural philosophy" (**M. Shelley** 49; vol. 1, ch. 4), studies the human animal through biological experiments. His creation, a so-called "monster" (60; vol. 1, ch. 5), *learns to be human* by reading poetry and history (124-27; vol. 2, ch. 7).

Works Cited

Abrams, M. H., et al., eds. *The Norton Anthology of English Literature.*
    6th ed. 2 vols. New York: Norton, 1993. Print.

"The Art of Science—Big or Small." Editorial. *Los Angeles Times*
    13 Dec. 1993: B6. Print.

Einstein, Albert. *Letters to Solovine.* New York: Philosophical Lib.,
    1987. Print.

---. *Relativity: The Special and General Theory.* Trans. Robert W.
    Lawson. New York: Bonanza, 1961. Print.

Eiseley, Loren. *The Star Thrower.* Intro. W. H. Auden. San Diego:
    Harcourt, 1978. Print.

Henderson, Heather, and William Sharpe, eds. *The Longman Anthology
    of British Literature.* 2nd ed. Vol. 2B. New York: Longman, 2003.
    Print.

*The Interpreter's Bible.* Ed. John W. Bailey et al. 12 vols. New York: Abingdon, 1952. Print.

Jardine, Lisa. *Ingenious Pursuits: Building the Scientific Revolution.* New York: Anchor-Random, 2000. Print.

National Aeronautics and Space Administration. "Frequently Asked Questions." *NASA.* 2004. Web. 14 Sept. 2008.

Shakespeare, William. *The Riverside Shakespeare.* Ed. G. Blakemore Evans. Boston: Houghton, 1974. Print.

Shelley, Mary. *Frankenstein: The Modern Prometheus.* 1818. Ed. and intro. Maurice Hindle. London: Penguin, 1992. Print.

Shelley, Percy Bysshe. *Prometheus Unbound.* 1820. *LiteratureClassics.com.* 2005. Web. 2 Dec. 2008.

Spielberg, Stephen, dir. *A.I.: Artificial Intelligence.* Warner, 2001. DVD.

---. *Minority Report.* Fox, 2002. DVD.

Varela, Francisco J., Evan Thompson, and Eleanor Rosch. *The Embodied Mind: Cognitive Science and Human Experience.* Cambridge: MIT P, 1991. Print.

**● 2 Locate referenced material as precisely as possible.** Besides identifying a source, in-text notes also tell readers exactly where to find that material you are borrowing or citing. Typically, you would simply provide page numbers, but many electronic sources don't give you that option. The guidelines below present your options.

**2.1 Locating passages in sources with standard pagination.** In a parenthetical note, give the page number(s) after naming the source, separating the two with a space only. If the author or source is not named, you can just enclose the page numbers. Use whatever page-numbering scheme the source itself uses—roman numerals, letter-number combination, etc.

| | |
|---|---|
| **SINGLE PAGE** (You can omit the page reference when the source is only one page long) | (Jones **142**) According to Jones . . . (**142**) ("Blame" **21**) |
| **RANGE OF PAGES** Separate the first and last pages in the range with a hyphen | (Dyson, *Disturbing* **11-13**) (Savlov **E4-E5**) |
| **NONCONSECUTIVE PAGES** Separate by a comma and space each page where idea is referenced | (**151, 156, 198**) (Gilbert and Gubar **xxix, xxxiv**) |
| **PAGES IN MULTI-VOLUME SOURCES** Insert the volume number, a colon, and a space before page references | (**2: 132**) (Churchill **4: 3461-62**) |

**2.2 Locating passages in sources using alternative numbering schemes.** Works in newer media often have numbered paragraphs or screens, rather than pages, and most classical works have traditional numbering mechanisms: chapters and sections for novels and treatises; acts and scenes for dramatic works; cantos and line numbers for poetry. Traditional numbering schemes help readers find material no matter which edition they use.

| | |
|---|---|
| **SOURCES WITH NO PAGINATION** After the source identifier (if given in the note), insert a comma, an abbreviation for the numbering scheme, and a reference number | (Neruda, **lines 2-9**) (USPTO, "Intellectual Property," **par. 4**) (**screen 3**) |
| **LITERARY WORKS WITH PAGINATION** Follow the page reference with a semicolon and reference to the chapter, section, etc. | (Eliot, *Middlemarch* **273; ch. 28**) (**75-76; ch. 4, sec. 1.5**) (Stoppard **58-59; act 2**) |

**WORKS WITH TRADITIONAL NUMBERING**
Classic works that are divided into precise hierarchical sections need no page references. Instead, list each section from largest to smallest with periods in between—even between chapter and verse in biblical citations. Use hyphens to indicate a range.

(Aristotle, *Prior* **68b.9-15**)

(*Ham.* **3.6.4-5**)

(*Interpreter's Bible*, **Mark 10.25**)

**2.3 Quoting or paraphrasing a statement that your source itself quotes.** Start a note with *qtd. in* to indicate that the author of the work did not make these statements, but rather someone named within the source:

> According to eminent scientist Albert Einstein, "Imagination is more important than knowledge" (**qtd. in** Thomas 1).

**● 3 Place and punctuate parenthetical citations correctly.** Place parenthetical citations just before the first natural pause that follows the cited material: after closing quotation marks but before ending or connecting punctuation marks.

**AFTER BORROWED IDEA OR QUOTE, BEFORE END PERIOD**

As Carter notes, "we seem to spend all of our time searching for bits of peace and quiet" (287)

**TWO PARENTHETICAL NOTES IN ONE SENTENCE**

The seclusion of the Lake District would often result in "the deepest melancholy" (D. Wordsworth 19), but the lakes themselves could be "soft . . . and beautiful" (36).

**AFTER FINAL PUNCTUATION FOR BLOCK QUOTATIONS (SEE CHECKLIST 50.3)**

Fixed ideas of permanence

And transience,

Finitude and infinity,

Have no place when all is well.

(Nagarjuna, lines 28-31)

# 50b Step 2: On a separate page at the end of your project, list alphabetically every source you have cited.

The Works Cited page, which appears after the body of the essay, provides readers with full bibliographical information on each source mentioned in your in-text notes: when it was published, by whom, in what format, and so on. List only sources you actually mention in your writing, even if you examined many others in the course of developing your project. The format of each works-cited entry will vary, depending on the type of source you are citing. To help you manage these variations, we've provided numerous model citations on pages 702–731.

As you create entries, you'll note that some sources are the work of many people: movies and plays have directors, scriptwriters; books may have editors and translators, as well as authors. So whom do you credit? You can usually name all the major contributors—but you may need to decide whose contribution will receive **primary acknowledgment** and whose **secondary**. This choice will depend on which contributor's work is most important to your project. If you discuss the films of a particular director, give him or her primary acknowledgment for each film you cite. If you intend to analyze the work of an editor, list his or her name first, rather than the author's.

**Creating Works-cited Entries.** The following pages describe each component of a works-cited entry in detail. Then, on pages 702–731, you will find model works-cited entries (with their accompanying in-text notes) for more than eighty kinds of sources. Note that the models have these rules in common:

- **Each part of an entry begins with a capitalized word and ends with a period.**
- **A space follows each comma, semicolon, and period**—*except* when the mark is followed by other punctuation, when it is part of an online address, or when it is part of a title that omits such spacing intentionally.

# BASIC PARTS OF MLA WORKS-CITED ENTRIES

Works-cited entries are composed of five basic parts, each of which is listed below, then marked and color-coded in the sample entries at the bottom of the page.

**Primary Acknowledgment (Author).**   Each entry usually begins with the name(s) of the author(s) or artist(s). In some cases you'll have the option of focusing on other contributors—for example, a book's editor, a CD's producer, or a movie's director.

**Title.**   Usually the second item of an entry, title sometimes appear first—for instance, with an unsigned source. You might also list two titles within your entry—for example, the title of a book and that of a chapter inside.

**Secondary Acknowledgments.**   Some works are created by many hands. After the title, list the names of other people (aside from the primary acknowledgment) who are given credit for creating the source.

**Publication or Production Information.**   This part can be the most complicated—especially when dealing with electronic documents—but you're offering readers three key details: *who published the source, where,* and *when.*

**Online Access Information.**   For online sources, state the date you last viewed the source.

**Medium of Publication.**   For every entry for a print source, include "Print" at the end followed by a period.  Every source from the World Wide Web must include "Web" at the end, followed by a period and the date that source was accessed.

---

Works Cited

Achebe, Chinua. *Things Fall Apart.* 1954. New York: Anchor-Doubleday, 1994. Print.

Schoolnik, Skip, dir. "Slouching towards Bethlehem." Writ. Jeffrey Bell. Perf. David Boreanaz and Charisma Carpenter. *Angel.* WB. KTLA, Los Angeles. 27 Oct. 2002. Television.

"W. B. Yeats." *Poets.org.* Academy of American Poets. 6 Nov. 2002. Web. 2 July 2008.

## Primary Acknowledgments (Author)

Identify the author of a source in last-name-first order, spelling names as they appear in the source, even if those given are known pseudonyms.

- Omit titles and degrees, such as *M.D., S.J., Ph.D., President.*
- Include, however, identifying suffixes such as *Jr.* or *III.* Suffixes should be listed immediately after an individual's name, preceded by a comma.
- Include also traditional identifying modifiers (*de Medici*, for example) for persons not having last names, placing them immediately after the first name.

| | |
|---|---|
| **One author or artist.** List the last name first, followed by a comma, and first names and initials as they appear on the title page of the source. Add essential suffixes after the first name. When no last name is given, simply list the name by which the individual is recognized in the source. | Bloom, Amy. —<br>Christine de Pisan. —<br>King, Martin Luther, Jr. —<br>O'Keefe, Georgia. —<br>Shakira. — |
| **Two or more authors or artists.** List their names in the same order they appear on the title page or byline. The first person appears last-name-first, followed by all others in normal order. Separate each with a comma (even when only two persons are listed), preceding the last person's name with the word *and.* | Armstrong, Lance, and Sally Jenkins. —<br>Black, Francis, and Kim Deal. —<br>Harrison, Maureen A., Ian F. Rae, and Ann Harris. —<br>See Models 3, 5, 15, 23, 24, 29, 42 |
| **Four or more authors or artists.** You may use a shortened form, listing only the Latin abbreviation *et al.* ("and others") after the first author's name (last-name-first). | Page, Jimmy, et al. —<br>Roberts, Henry M., III, et al. —<br>See Models 33, 84 |
| **Corporate or group authors or artists.** List them as they appear on the title page or byline of the source, omitting initial articles (*A, An,* or *The*) when the name stands for a corporation or institution. | Blue Man Group. —<br>The Who. —<br>World Health Organization. —<br>See Models 48, 77, 78, 79 |
| **Editors, translators, compilers, etc.** When they are given primary acknowledgment, these individuals are listed just like authors—*except* before the ending period insert a comma and an abbreviation that identifies the form of contribution (see Chart 50.1). When listing multiple persons, place the abbreviation (pluralized by inserting *s* before the period) after the last individual's name. | Cash, Johnny, and June Carter, perfs. —<br>Heaney, Seamus, trans. —<br>Lee, Spike, dir. —<br>Selfe, Cynthia L., and Susan Hilligoss, eds. —<br>See Models 9, 13, 31, 49, 51 |

## Titles

Capitalize the first word of each title and all other words, except articles (*a*, *an*, and *the*), prepositions (also *to* when part of an infinitive), and coordinating conjunctions. Most titles have other formatting as well.

**Italicized titles.**    Italicize the titles of major works, including books, plays, operas, musicals, TV programs, radio programs, artworks, CDs, movies, long poems, and periodicals. (See also Section 41a.) *Do not* format the end period, but *do* italicize exclamation points and question marks that are part of the title.

> *The Da Vinci Code.*
> *Friends.*
> *Bullet in a Bible.*
> *Mamma Mia!*
> *Omeros.*
> *Rolling Stone.*
> *Starry Night.*

**Titles in quotation marks.**    Enclose in quotation marks the titles of short works, such as periodical articles, essays, speeches, short poems, short stories, individual TV episodes, radio broadcasts, and songs. End punctuation goes within the closing quotation mark.

> "Island in the Sun."
> "The One with Russ."
> "Redwoods Go Wireless."
> "Self-Reliance."
> "The Tyger."

**Subtitles.**    Place subtitles after the main title, inserting a colon and a space between the two. Capitalize letters in the subtitle like any other title.

> *Seeing Voices: A Journey into the World of the Deaf.*
> See Models 1, 6, 9, 12, 15, 17, 24, 25, 28, 32, 52, 53, 69, 74, 81

**Descriptive titles.**    Some works are identified by descriptive phrases, rather than standard titles. Capitalize the first letter of the first word only and do not italicize the phrase or place it in quotation marks—but do format titles within the phrase.

> Interview with Toni Morrison.
> Online posting. 17 Aug. 2003.
> Review of *Clueless.*
> See Models 15, 16, 36, 40, 43, 45, 54, 59, 61, 62, 64, 68, 70-76

**Titles within titles.**    Many works refer to other works within their titles. Refrain from italicizing a title when it appears within another italicized title. For titles ordinarily enclosed in double quotation marks, use single quotes when they appear within another title enclosed by double quotes. Otherwise, follow the standard rules for formatting titles.

> *The Apocalypse Now Book.*
> "*Four Weddings* Director Eyes *Potter IV*."
> "New Beatles 'Let it Be' Due."
> See Models 13, 14, 16, 22, 32, 68

## Secondary Acknowledgments

List any secondary contributors after the title of the work they helped create
and before publication details. Present their names in normal order, preceding each with an abbreviation indicating the form of contribution (see
Chart 50.1 on page 701). You may list more than one secondary contributor—group into a single acknowledgment the names of those who contribute in the same way. Note that sometimes authors and artists are not
listed before the title, but instead after (following the word *By*).

> ---. By William Shakespeare. Dir. Laurence Olivier. ---
>
> ---. Ed. Andrea Lunsford and John Ruszkiewicz. ---
>
> ---. Writ. and dir. Andy Wachowski and Larry Wachowski. Perf. Keanu
>
>     Reeves, Laurence Fishburne, and Carrie-Anne Moss. ---

See Models 8, 10-13, 16-18, 30, 47-51, 56, 57, 69, 81, 82

## Publication and Production Information

These details vary greatly depending on the type of source you're documenting. The models in Sections 50b-1–14 cover most of the sources you'll encounter. As you look at the models, notice how the following details are formatted:

**Places.** When cities are well known, omit state and nation specifications. When no place of publication is available for books, use the abbreviation *n.p.* For some sources, such as performances, identify a specific venue before the city.

> Englewood Cliffs, NJ
> London
> Odyssey Theatre, Los Angeles

**Names of publishers.** You can abbreviate publishers' names by omitting articles and indistinctive words (*Inc., Co.,* etc.) and by using standard abbreviations (see Chart 50.1). When no publisher is given where expected, use the abbreviation *n.p.*

> Amer. Medical Assn.
> Norton
> U of Texas P

**Dates.** MLA works-cited entries include one or more dates depending on the type of source. All dates should be presented in day-month-year order. Abbreviate all months except *May, June,* and *July.* If no date is given where expected, put *n.d.*

> 4 July 1776
> Oct. 1929
> 2001

**Pages, etc.** For page ranges list the first and last with a hyphen between. For nonconsecutive pages, list only the first page followed by a plus sign. Use the same format (roman numerals, letters, etc.) as the source. Use the abbreviation *n. pag.* when the source is not paginated, unless a different scheme is used (paragraphing, etc.); indicate the type of numbering with an abbreviation.

> 9-16, 145-49, 501-615,
> E1+
> iii-xi
> pars. 4-10
> screen 3

## Medium of Publication

Include the medium of publication for each entry. For every entry for a print source, include "Print" at the end followed by a period. Every source from the World Wide Web must include "Web" at the end, followed by a period and the date that source was accessed. Be specific about other media of publication, such as "Radio," "Television," "CD," "Live performance," "Musical score," and so on.

---

## Online Access Information

Include the URL for an online citation *only* when the reader probably could not locate the source without it. In most cases, entries should simply the Web site's name and publisher, and the inclusion of "Web" as the medium of publication. When a URL is included, enclose the URL in angle brackets <like these>.

> ---. 5 May. 2003 <http://www.visualthesaurus.com/>.
>
> ---. 12 Dec. 2002 <http://www.moviesunlimited.com/>. Keyword: Coppola.
>
> ---. 1 July 2003 <http://www.energystar.gov/>. Path: Education; Computers.
>
> ---. 5 Sept. 2002 <http://www.cnn.com/2003/TECH/science/08/15/
>
> coolsc.redwoods/index.html>.

---

### Chart 50.1  Useful MLA Abbreviations

**SECONDARY ACKNOWLEDGMENTS**

| | | | |
|---|---|---|---|
| Adapted by | adapt. | Introduced by | introd. |
| Compiler | comp. | Narrator | narr. |
| Conductor | cond. | Performer | perf. |
| Director | dir. | Preface by | pref. |
| Editor | ed. | Producer | prod. |
| Foreword by | fore. | Translator | trans. |
| Illustrator | illus. | Written by | writ. |

**PUBLICATION INFORMATION**

| | | | |
|---|---|---|---|
| Book | bk. | Press | P |
| Chapter | ch. or chap. | Scene | sc. |
| Edition | ed. | Section | sec. or sect. |
| Line | line or l. | Series | ser. |
| Lines | lines or ll. | University | U |
| Page | p. | University Press | UP |
| Pages | pp. | Volume | vol. |
| Paragraph | par. | Volumes | vols. |

# MLA MODELS 50B-1  Books and pamphlets

## 1. BOOK—BASIC ENTRY

Author          Title

Balliett, Whitney. *New York Notes: A Journal of Jazz,*

*1972-1975.* Boston: Houghton, 1976. Print.

Publication information  Medium of
(Place: Publisher, Year.)  publication

IN-TEXT NOTE: (Balliett 5)

For most books and pamphlets, list only author(s), title, and basic publication details (place, publisher, and year). For some, however, provide additional details:

- **Is an editor, translator, or other contributor listed on the title page?** List secondary acknowledgments after the title. See Models 10, 11, 12.
- **Is the book's original publication date known?** Insert the original year of publication after the title, before the publication details for the edition used. See Models 2, 3.
- **Does the title page list a name or number for this edition?** Insert the name or number of the edition after the title and secondary contributors (if any). See Models 3, 4.
- **Is the book part of a multi-volume set?** After the name of the edition (if any), list the volume number you are using or, if using more than one volume, the total volume count, citing specific volume numbers in your in-text notes. See Models 4, 5.
- **Is the book part of a series?** List the series title (neither underlined nor in quotes) and the series number (if any) just before the place of publication. See Model 6.

**Works Cited and In-text Citations (Notes)**

**2. BOOK—**
With Original
Publication
Date

Angelou, Maya. *I Know Why the Caged Bird Sings.*
1969. New York: Bantam, 1997. Print.

IN-TEXT NOTE: (Angelou 45)

**3. BOOK—**
Subsequent
Edition

Holiday, Billie, and William Dufty. *Lady Sings the*
*Blues.* 1956. Revised discography ed. London:
Penguin, 1992. Print.

IN-TEXT NOTE: (Holiday and Dufty 113-14)

**4. BOOK—**
Multi-volume
Set, Referring
to One

Rampersad, Arnold. *The Life of Langston Hughes.*
2nd ed. Vol. 2. New York: Oxford UP, 2002. Print.

IN-TEXT NOTE: (Rampersad 14, 21)

**5. BOOK—**
Multi-volume
Set, Referring
to Many

Titon, Jeff Todd, and Bob Carlin. *American Musical*
*Traditions.* 5 vols. New York: Schirmer-Gale, 2002.
Print.

IN-TEXT NOTE: (Titon and Carlin 4: 36)

**6. BOOK—**
One That Is Part
of a Series of
Books

Tuso, Joseph F. *Singing the Vietnam Blues: Songs of the*
*Air Force in Southeast Asia.* Texas A&M U
Military History Ser. 19. College Station: Texas
A&M UP, 1990. Print.

IN-TEXT NOTE: (Tuso 78)

**7. PAMPHLET**

*Women in Music and Art.* Pittsburgh: Carnegie Lib.,
1981. Print.

IN-TEXT NOTE: (*Women* 2)

## MLA MODELS 50B-2  Books with editors, translators, etc.

### 8. BOOK—EDITED

Author            Title

Weems, Mason L. *The Life of Washington*. 1800.

Ed. Marcus Cunliffe. Cambridge: Harvard UP, 1962. Print.

Editor            Publication information            Medium of
(Place: Publisher, Year.)            publication

IN-TEXT NOTE: (Weems 202)

When editors, translators, or other contributors appear on the title page of a book, list their names and contributions after the title. Consider also the following factors when listing secondary contributors:

- **Are you citing a reader or anthology not focused on a single author?** List the editors or compilers first, unless citing a specific selection. See Model 9.

- **Are multiple secondary contributors listed on the title page?** A book might be both edited and translated, for example. List all contributors shown on the title page as either the primary acknowledgment or a secondary one. See Models 10, 11.

- **Is someone listed as contributing in two ways?** List both contributions before the person's name; after, if the person is given primary acknowledgment. See Model 12.

- **Does it make sense to focus on someone other than the author?** If you need to focus on an editor or translator, for example, present that person first in the entry, before the title. Then list the author of the book after the title (following the word *By*), where you would normally provide secondary acknowledgments. See Model 13.

**Works Cited and In-text Citations (Notes)**

**9. ANTHOLOGY OR READER** (or Other Compilation)

Crane, Diana, Nobuko Kawashima, and Ken'ichi Kawasaki, eds. *Global Culture: Media, Arts, Policy, and Globalization*. New York: Routledge, 2002. Print.

**IN-TEXT NOTE:** (Crane, Kawashima, and Kawasaki iv-v)

**10. BOOK**— Translated (with Help of Author)

Fuentes, Carlos. *A New Time for Mexico*. Trans. Marine Gutman Castaneda and Fuentes. Berkeley: U of California P, 1997. Print.

**IN-TEXT NOTE:** (Fuentes 89)

**11. BOOK**— Multiple Secondary Contributors

Gandhi, M. K. *The India of My Dreams*. Comp. R. K. Prabhu. Fore. Rajendra Prasad. Bombay: Hind Kitabs, 1947. Print.

**IN-TEXT NOTE:** (Gandhi 131)

**12. BOOK**— One Person Contributing in Two Ways

Nagarjuna. *Verses from the Center: A Buddhist Vision of the Sublime*. Ed. and trans. Stephen Batchelor. New York: Riverhead, 2000. Print.

**IN-TEXT NOTE:** (Nagarjuna 91)

**13. BOOK**— Focus on Editor

Rice, Julian, ed. *Ella Deloria's* The Buffalo People. By Ella Deloria. Albuquerque: U of New Mexico P, 1994. Print.

**IN-TEXT NOTE:** (Rice 45)

# MLA MODELS 50B-3 Book parts, excerpts, and selections

### 14. BOOK PART

| Author | Title of book part | Title of book |
|---|---|---|

Mason, Bobbie Ann. "Detroit Skyline, 1949." *"Shiloh" and Other Stories.*

New York: Colophon-Harper, 1982. 34-52. Print.

| Publication information | Medium of |
|---|---|
| (Place: Publisher, Year. Pages.) | publication |

IN-TEXT NOTE: (Mason 36)

When using only part of a book, create an entry for the book itself, inserting the title of the selection just before the title of the book. After the book's publication information, provide the pages where the selection appears. Some book parts are cited differently, especially those not written by the book's main author(s):

- **Is the selection an introduction, preface, forward, or afterward?** Describe the type of selection after the name of the selection's author(s) or title (if any). See Models 15, 16.
- **Is the selection by someone other than the book's author?** List the selection's author(s) first, then its title, the book's title, and the book's author(s) as a secondary acknowledgment, all before the publication details and pages. See Model 16.
- **Is the selection from an anthology?** List the selection's author(s) first, then the title of the selection. Name editors or compilers after the title of the book. See Model 17.
- **Is the selection an article from a reference work?** For well-known reference works, omit page numbers. secondary acknowledgments, volume information, place, and publisher. But provide this information for less familiar reference works. Always list edition and year. See Models 18, 19, 87.

**Works Cited and In-text Citations (Notes)**

| | |
|---|---|
| **15. BOOK PART**—Untitled Preface by Authors of Book | Alfrey, Judith, and Catherine Clark. Preface. *The Landscape of Industry: Patterns of Change in the Ironbridge Gorge*. London: Routledge, 1993. xi-xii. Print. <br> IN-TEXT NOTE: (Alfrey and Clark xi) |
| **16. BOOK PART**—By Secondary Contributor | Surtz, Edward. "*Utopia* Past and Present." Introduction. *Utopia*. By Thomas More. Ed. Surtz. New Haven: Yale UP, 1964. vii-xxx. Print. <br> IN-TEXT NOTE: (Surtz xii) |
| **17. BOOK PART**—From Reader, Anthology, Compilation | Tschumi, Benard. "Architecture and the City." *The Unknown City: Contesting Architecture and Social Space*. Ed. Iain Borden et al. Cambridge: MITP, 2001. 370-85. Print. <br> IN-TEXT NOTE: (Tschumi 382) |
| **18. REFERENCE ARTICLE**—Less-known Reference | "Polixenes." *The Oxford Companion to English Literature*. Ed. M. Drabble. Oxford: Oxford UP, 1998. Print. <br> IN-TEXT NOTE: ("Polixenes") |
| **19. REFERENCE ARTICLE**—Well-known Reference | "Ypsilanti." *The New Encyclopædia Britannica: Micropædia*. 15th ed. 1987. Print. <br> IN-TEXT NOTE: ("Ypsilanti") |

## MLA MODELS 50B-4 Periodical articles: newspapers, magazines

### 20. ARTICLE—NEWSPAPER

Author        Title

Reifenberg, Anne. "Nobody Said 'Boo' When Anne Rice Came

to New Orleans." *Wall Street Journal* 2 Jan. 2003: D8. Print.

Publication information  Medium of
(Periodical Issue: Pages.)   publication

IN-TEXT NOTE: (Reifenberg)

Begin with the author(s) and title of the article, as you would a book part. Then list the title of the periodical, the issue, and pages where the article can be found. Note that different types of periodicals identify their issues in different ways:

- **Are you citing an editorial, review, letter, or advertisement?** See also Section 50b-13 on pages 726–727.
- **Are you citing a newspaper article?** Identify the paper by the date that appears on its masthead. After the date, provide information about the edition or section where you found the article. *Do not* list volume or issue numbers. See Models 20, 21.
- **Are you citing a magazine article?** Identify the issue of the magazine by the date that appears on the cover—*do not* list volume or issue number. See Models 22, 23.
- **Are you citing a journal article?** Identify the issue of the journal by its volume and issue numbers (separated by a period) and year (in parentheses). You may omit the issue number when the journal is paginated by volume, rather than issue. See Models 24, 25.

## Works Cited and In-text Citations (Notes)

**21. NEWSPAPER ARTICLE**—With Edition

"Despite Recent Appeals, Blood Supplies Are Low."
*New York Times* 3 Aug. 1998, late ed.: B4. Print.

IN-TEXT NOTE: ("Despite")

**22. MAGAZINE ARTICLE**—Weekly

Klein, David. "Emmy-Worthy *Buffy* Musical Slays This
Critic." *Television Weekly* 8 July 2002: 6. Print.

IN-TEXT NOTE: (Klein)

**23. MAGAZINE ARTICLE**—Monthly

Olders, Henry G., and Anthony D. Del Genio. "What
Causes Insomnia?" *Scientific American*
Oct. 2003: 103. Print.

IN-TEXT NOTE: (Olders and Del Genio)

**24. JOURNAL ARTICLE**—Paged by Volume

Ratcliffe, John M., Brock M. Fenton, and Bennett G.
Galef. "An Exception to the Rule: Common
Vampire Bats Do Not Learn Taste Aversions."
*Animal Behavior* 65 (2003): 385-89. Print.

IN-TEXT NOTE: (Ratcliffe, Fenton, and Galef 386-87)

**25. JOURNAL ARTICLE**—Paged by Issue

Whalen, Tom. "Romancing Film: Images of Dracula."
*Literature-Film Quarterly* 23.2 (1995): 99-101. Print.

IN-TEXT NOTE: (Whalen 99)

## MLA MODELS 50B-5  ONLINE SOURCES: WEB PAGES, WEB SITES

### 26. WEB PAGE—UNSIGNED

|  | **Publication information** |
| **Title of Web page** | (Site Name. Last Update.) |

"Greater Cheyenne Greenway." *CheyenneWyoming*. City of Cheyenne.

18 July 2003. Web. 20 July 2003.

|  | **Medium of** | **Date of** |
|  | **publication** | **access** |

IN-TEXT NOTE: ("Greater Cheyenne")

Begin by listing author(s), title, and secondary contributors (if any), as with a print source. Then provide electronic publication details, including the title of the Internet site housing the source and when the site was last updated. Finally, give details about how you accessed the source, including the date you last viewed it and its online address. The models on the facing page identify other publication details to include; those on the next list address more difficult online genres.

- **Are you citing an entire Web site?** List only publication and access details. See Model 27.
- **Is it clear who sponsors the site?** If not, list sponsors after the update. See Models 27, 28.
- **Is a posting date listed for the specific page(s) you're using?** List the date after page title, before the site name and other publication details. See Model 28.
- **Is an editor or version listed for the site containing the source?** List the editor of the site after the name of the site. Insert the version or edition just before the update information for the site, after its title and editors (if any). See Model 30.

## Works Cited and In-text Citations (Notes)

**27. WEB SITE**

*Active Living By Design.* U of North Carolina School of Public Health. 2003. Web. 24 July 2003.

IN-TEXT NOTE: (*Active Living*)

**28. WEB PAGE**—With Date of Posting

"B&O Trail Benefits: Recreation and Health." *B&O Trail Netliner.* Rail Corridor Development Inc. 14 July 2003. Web. 24 July 2003.

IN-TEXT NOTE: ("B&O Trail")

**29. WEB PAGE**—Signed by Authors

Riter, Jan, and Mike Riter. "Essential Tools for Trailwork." *International Mountain Biking Association.* Web. 29 July 2003.

IN-TEXT NOTE: (Riter and Riter)

**30. WEB PAGE**—On Edited and Versioned Site

"Tsali Trail Information." *Mountain Biking in Western North Carolina.* Ed. J. Mitchell. Vers. 4.77. 10 July 2003. Web. 27 July 2003.

IN-TEXT NOTE: ("Tsali")

**31. WEB PAGE**—Signed by Compiler

Weir, Don, comp. "A Bibliography of Trail and Recreation Issues." *International Mountain Biking Association.* Web. 29 July 2003.

IN-TEXT NOTE: (Weir)

## MLA MODELS 50B-6  Online sources: articles, newspapers, books

### 32. ONLINE ARTICLE

| Author | | Title |
|---|---|---|

Heffernan, Virginia. "Dial Miami for Murder: *CSI's* Florida Sojourn." *Slate*.

Washington Post.Newsweek Interactive.  3 Oct. 2002.  Web. 10 Oct. 2003.

| Publication information | Medium of | Date of |
|---|---|---|
| (Periodical Issue.) | publication | access |

IN-TEXT NOTE: (Heffernan)

Some genres of Web sites and Web pages have special formatting:

- **Are you citing an online article?** For an article in an online magazine or journal, list as you would a printed article, using the site name for the periodical name; then identify the issue volume or date (see Section 50b-4 on pages 708–709), followed by online access information. See Models 32, 33. If you pull the article from an online database, list the name of the database after the issue information. See Model 33 (second item).

- **Are you citing an online newspaper article?** Provide all the basic publication information, including the name of the newspaper—which may or may not indicate that it is a Web version. Provide both the original date of article and a date of access: list both separately even when the dates are the same. See Model 34 (first item).

- **Are you citing an online version of a book or other print source?** List all print publication details that are given (using the guidelines for books, book parts, and articles) just before the standard electronic publication information. See Model 35.

### Works Cited and In-text Citations (Notes)

| | |
|---|---|
| **33. ONLINE ARTICLE—**<br>From Online Journal,<br>From Database Repository | Castello, Ana, et al. "Long-Lasting Lipstick and Latent Prints." *Forensic Science Communications* 4.2 (2002). n. pag. Web. 3 Jan. 2009.<br><br>IN-TEXT NOTE: (Castello et al.)<br><br>Emmerichs, Mary Beth. "Getting Away with Murder: Homicide and the Coroners in Nineteenth-Century London." *Social Science History* 25.1 (2001): 93-100. *Project Muse.* Web. 12 Mar. 2008.<br><br>IN-TEXT NOTE: (Emmerichs 95) |
| **34. ONLINE NEWSPAPER** | Olson, Elizabeth. "Peer Support Cited in Black Students' Success." *New York Times.* New York Times, 17 May 2006. Web. 2 Nov. 2008.<br><br>IN-TEXT NOTE: (Olson)<br><br>"Save Our Springs." *Daily Texan.* Daily Texan, 10 Mar. 2006. Web. 14 Nov. 2008.<br><br>IN-TEXT NOTE: ("Save") |
| **35. ONLINE BOOK—**<br>Electronic Version of Print Edition | Rinehart, Mary Roberts. *The Circular Staircase.* New York: Grosset, 1908. *Electronic Text Center.* 12 June 2003. Web. 13 July 2007.<br><br>IN-TEXT NOTE: (Rinehart, ch. 4) |

# MLA MODELS 50B-7 Online discussion postings and blogs

### 36. ONLINE POSTING

| Author | Title | Publication information (Posting Date. Forum Name.) |

Sebring95. "Re: 96 Tacoma." Online posting. 3 Jan. 2003. *Car Questions.*
Web. 10 Aug. 2003.

| Medium of publication | Date of access |

IN-TEXT NOTE: (Sebring95)

Cite a message in an online discussion—whether posted to a Web forum, an electronic mailing list, or a Usenet newsgroup—by listing the author of the posting, the subject line of the message (in quotation marks), the words *Online posting,* the date the message was posted, and typical access information, including the date you last viewed the message and its URL. Note that some forms of online discussion have different kinds of URL addresses, ones that don't begin with *http.* See Models 36, 37, 38.

- **Is the message a Web forum posting?** Insert the name of the discussion forum (neither underlined nor in quotation marks) before the date of access. See Model 36.
- **Is the message from a blog?** Blog items with obvious authors and titles for daily entries can be cited without much difficulty, but many blog entries won't have conventional titles or pagination. If you think the reader probably could not locate the source without the URL, give the site address for the blog or the URL for its archived material. See Model 39.
- **Is the message available in a discussion archive?** Many online discussions are archived and published in a fixed form. If available, refer to the archive's URL, rather than that of the original posting, keeping other details the same. See Model 40.

## Works Cited and In-text Citations (Notes)

**37. EMAIL LIST**

Cook, Janice. "Re: What New Day Is Dawning?"
    Online posting. *Alliance for Computers and
    Writing Listserv.* 19 June 1997. Web. 4 Feb. 1998.

IN-TEXT NOTE: (Cook)

**38. USENET POSTING**

Heady, Christy. "Buy or Lease? Depends on How Long
    You'll Keep the Car." Online posting. N.p. 7 July
    1997. Web. 14 July 1997.

IN-TEXT NOTE: (Heady)

**39. BLOG**

Johnson, Scott. "God and Juan at Yale." Blog posting.
    *Powerline.* 26 Mar. 2006. Web. 11 May 2008.

IN-TEXT NOTE: (Johnson)

Postrel, Virginia. "The Box That Changed the World."
    Blog posting. *Dynamist.com.* 26 Mar. 2006. Web.
    15 Aug. 2008.

IN-TEXT NOTE: (Postrel)

**40. ARCHIVED POSTING**

Knight. "Will BMW Let ME Test Drive?" Online posting.
    4 Mar. 2000. *Bimmer.* Forums: E 46. Web. 6 Mar.
    2000.

IN-TEXT NOTE: (Knight)

## MLA MODELS 50B-8 Downloaded files, CD-ROMs, software

### 41. PHOTOGRAPH—DOWNLOADED

| Artist | Title | Online publication information |
|--------|-------|-------------------------------|

Nohl, Mark. "Taos Pueblo Pottery." 2002. *NewMexico.org*. New Mexico

Dept. of Tourism. N.d. Web. 13 Aug. 2003.

Medium of   Date of
publication   access

IN-TEXT NOTE: (Nohl)

Almost any kind of work can be published as a computer file or program:

- **Are you citing an article, book, or pamphlet downloaded as a file?** Cite downloaded word-processing documents and PDF files like online documents. See Model 42.

- **Are you citing a downloaded multimedia file?** For recordings and images distributed over the Internet, use the guidelines for typical audio/video works (see Sections 50b-9–11 on pages 718–723), but replace the standard publication details with electronic publication and access information. See Models 41, 43.

- **Is the source published on a CD-ROM or other electronic reference?** Some electronic sources are found on recorded media (see Section 50b-9 on pages 718–719), not the public Internet. Instead of typical online publication details, list the version being used, the vendor, and the year of production. Entries begin with typical acknowledgments and titles for a source of similar genre (article, drawing, painting, etc.). See Models 44, 45.

- **Are you citing a computer program, rather than its contents?** List the software's title (italicized) and publication details for the installation media. See Model 46.

## Works Cited and In-text Citations (Notes)

**42. ONLINE ITEM—** Downloaded in PDF Format

Belanus, Betty, and Marjorie Hunt. "Building with Adobe." *Masters of the Building Arts.* (2001): 24-27. Smithsonian Center for Folklife and Cultural Heritage. N.d. Web. 6 Mar. 2008.

IN-TEXT NOTE: (Belanus and Hunt 25)

**43. AUDIO INTERVIEW—** Downloaded Recording (from Site with Multiple Sponsors)

Flores, Dolores. "Herbal Healer." Interview. *The Pascua Yaqui Connection.* Pascua Yaqui Tribe, Pima CC, and U of Arizona. 15 Aug. 2003. Web. 24 Sept 2007.

IN-TEXT NOTE: (Flores)

**44. ARTICLE—** On CD-ROM

"Gallup." *Microsoft Bookshelf 2000.* Redmond: Microsoft, 2000. CD-ROM.

IN-TEXT NOTE: ("Gallup")

**45. MAP—** On CD-ROM reference

"New Mexico." Map. *Britannica 2003 Ultimate Reference Suite.* Encyclopædia Britannica, 2003. CD-ROM.

IN-TEXT NOTE: ("New Mexico")

**46. COMPUTER SOFTWARE**

*iTunes.* Vers. 5. Apple, 2005. Software.

IN-TEXT NOTE: (*iTunes*)

## MLA MODELS 50B-9   Recorded media: Films, CDs, DVDs, etc.

### 47. AUDIO RECORDING

| Artist | Title of recording | Production information (Format. Vendor, Year.) | Medium of publication |
|---|---|---|---|

Mayer, John. *Heavier Things*. Prod. Jack Joseph Puig. Sony, 2003. CD.

IN-TEXT NOTE: (Mayer)

For recorded media, list the format (*CD, DVD, Cassette, VHS, MP3, Podcast*, etc.), vendor, and year. (Omit the format for audio CDs and films viewed in a theater.) What's listed before these production details depends on the type of source:

- **Is the source an audio recording?** Begin with the artist(s) or composer(s), unless it makes sense to focus on a different contributor (a producer, for example). Next list the title and other contributors. If you want to focus on a single selection, a song or other kind of track or download, list its title before the recording's. See Models 47, 48.

- **Is the source a film or video recording?** Begin with the title, unless you wish to foreground a particular contributor (the director, scriptwriters, etc.). See Models 49, 50, 51.

- **Are you referring to supplementary material (liner notes, booklets, "bonus" material on a DVD, etc.)?** List the author(s) of the supplement first; then describe the material (*Libretto, Liner notes, Documentary, Director's audio commentary*, etc.). Finally, provide basic production details for the recording. See Model 52.

- **Is the recording distributed online?** Provide online publication and access information after the title, acknowledgments, and production details. See Section 50b-8 on pages 716–717.

- **Is it a recording of a live performance, interview, or TV/radio broadcast?** List information about the performance, interview, or broadcast before the production details for the audio or video recording. See Sections 50b-10 on pages 720–721 and 50b-12 on pages 724–725.

## Works Cited and In-text Citations (Notes)

**48. SONG, PODCAST**

Funkadelic. "Biological Speculation." *America Eats Its Young*. Perf. George Clinton. Westbound, 1972. MP3 File.

IN-TEXT NOTE: (Funkadelic)

Armstrong, Billie Joe. Interview with John Pareles. *TimesTalk*. New York Times Co. 7 Jan. 2006. Web. 1 Feb. 2006.

IN-TEXT NOTE: (Armstrong)

**49. VIDEO RECORDING—** Adaptation of Book

Haas, Philip, and Belinda Haas, adapt. *Angels and Insects*. By A. S. Byatt. Dir. P. Haas. Samuel Goldwyn, 1996. DVD.

IN-TEXT NOTE: (Haas and Haas)

**50. FILM—** Viewed in Theater

*Species*. Dir. Roger Donaldson. Perf. Ben Kingsley, Forest Whitaker, and Natasha Henstridge. MGM, 1995. DVD.

IN-TEXT NOTE: (*Species*)

**51. FILM—** Focus on Director

Spielberg, Stephen, dir. *Jurassic Park*. Perf. Jeff Goldblum, Wayne Knight, and Sam Neill. Universal, 1993. DVD.

IN-TEXT NOTE: (Spielberg)

**52. LINER NOTES, BONUS MATERIAL**

Terrell, Tom. Liner notes. *Evolution (and Flashback): The Very Best of Gil Scott-Heron*. BMG, 1999. Print.

IN-TEXT NOTE: (Terrell)

Maguire, Tobey. Actor's audio commentary. *Spider-Man 2*. Columbia, 2004. DVD.

IN-TEXT NOTE: (Maguire)

# MLA MODELS 50B-10  TV and radio broadcast, live performance

### 53. SPEECH

Speaker           Title of speech

Kelly, Randy. "The Future of Saint Paul: Progress through Partnerships."

U of Minnesota Student Center Theatre, St. Paul. 10 Apr. 2003. Address.

Production information
(Venue, City. Date.)

Medium of publication

IN-TEXT NOTE: (Kelly)

Performances, speeches, and broadcast programs (TV or radio) occur at specific times and places. Their citation formats reflect this. (But list published recordings or transcripts of these sources like other printed, online, or recorded works.)

- **Are you citing a lecture, reading, or speech?** List the speaker and title of the talk (or *Reading of . . .*, *Keynote address*, etc.). Then list the name of the event and its sponsoring group (if applicable), the venue, the city, and the date. See Models 53, 54.

- **Are you citing a television or radio program?** Begin with the title of the program, unless you wish to foreground a particular contributor (a narrator or an actor, for example). After the program title, list secondary contributors, the broadcasting network, the station, the city, and the date. See Model 55.

- **Are you citing a specific episode or segment of a TV or radio program?** Insert the episode or segment title before the program title. (Note that secondary acknowledgments may apply to the episode or segment, but not the entire program—place contributors' names after the appropriate title.) See Model 56.

- **Are you citing a dramatic performance?** Begin with the title of the work being performed, unless you wish to foreground a particular contributor (a scriptwriter or the director, for example). After the title, list secondary contributors, the performance venue, the city, and the date of the show. See Model 57.

## Works Cited and In-text Citations (Notes)

**54. READING OF A BOOK—**
Given at Sponsored Group Event

Anderson, Beth. Reading of Robert D. Putnam's *Bowling Alone*. New Book Forum. Sociology Book Club. The Midnight Reader's Lounge, Atlanta. 21 Feb. 2002. Performance.

IN-TEXT NOTE: (Anderson)

**55. TV SHOW**

*Buena Vista Social Club*. PBS. KBYU, Provo. 19 July 2000. Television.

IN-TEXT NOTE: (*Buena Vista*)

**56. RADIO BROADCAST**

"L.A. Votes to Break Up Its Landmark—Hollywood." *Which Way L.A.?* Host Warren Olney. Natl Public Radio. KCRW, Santa Monica. 5 June 2002. Radio.

IN-TEXT NOTE: ("L.A. Votes")

**57. DRAMATIC PERFORMANCE**

*The Producers*. By Mel Brooks. Perf. Jason Alexander and Martin Short. Dir. and chor. Susan Stroman. Pantages Theatre, Los Angeles. 25 June 2003. Performance.

IN-TEXT NOTE: (*Producers*)

## MLA MODELS 50B-11 Artwork, charts, musical scores, etc.

### 58. ARTWORK

| Artist | Title of work (in this case with completion date) | Display information (Current Venue, City.) |
|---|---|---|

Rodia, Simon. *Watts Towers*. 1954. Watts Towers Art Center,

Los Angeles.

IN-TEXT NOTE: (Rodia)

Cite visual works by listing the artist(s), the title of the work, completion date (if known), and current display information, which will depend on how and where you viewed the source and what kind of work it is:

- **Are you citing a painting, photograph, or sculpture?** After the artist and the title (italicized), identify the owner (a person or institution) and the city where the work is housed. If using a published image or reproduction of the work, attach standard publication details for that source at the end of your entry. See Models 58, 60.
- **Are you citing maps, charts, photographs, or other graphical publications?** When the item is published separately, list the artist (if known), the title (italicized), a description (*Map, Chart*, etc.), and publication details (place, publisher, and year). When the item appears inside another source, such as a book or Web page, place the title in quotes and provide publication details for the containing source. See Models 59, 61, 62.
- **Are you citing a musical composition?** If citing a published score, format the entry like a book or online book, depending on how published. If not using a particular recording or published score, simply list the artist, title, and year. See Model 63.

**Works Cited and In-text Citations (Notes)**

**59. MAP**    *Arches National Park*. Map. U.S. Natl. Park Service, 2001. Print.

IN-TEXT NOTE: (Arches)

**60. PAINTING**    Cassatt, Mary. *In the Omnibus*. Ca. 1891. Oil on canvas. Chester Dale Collection. Natl. Gallery of Art, Washington.

IN-TEXT NOTE: (Cassatt)

**61. DIAGRAM, PHOTOGRAPH—** Published on a Web Site    "How Small Wind Turbines Work." Diagram. *American Wind Energy Association*, 2002. Web. 2 Sept. 2008.

IN-TEXT NOTE: ("How Turbines Work")

Evans, James. *Dancing Feet*. 1993. Photograph. *Alterimage Gallery*. Web. 28 Feb. 2008.

IN-TEXT NOTE: (Evans)

**62. DRAWING—** On CD-ROM Reference    Vitullo, Richard J. "Dome Unit Skylight—Flat Roof." Drawing. *Architectural Graphic Standards*. Vers. 3. New York: Wiley, 2000. CD-ROM.

IN-TEXT NOTE: (Vitullo)

**63. MUSICAL COMPOSITION**    Vivaldi, Antonio. *The Contest between Harmony and Invention*. 1725. Print.

IN-TEXT NOTE: (Vivaldi)

## MLA MODELS 50B-12 Interviews, letters, memos, emails

### 64. INTERVIEW—IN MAGAZINE

Interviewee                    Title of interview

Kingston, Maxine Hong. Interview with Karen Horton.

*Honolulu* Dec. 1979: 49-56. Print.

Publication      Medium of
information      publication

**IN-TEXT NOTE:** (Kingston 50)

Works-cited entries for letters, memos, emails, and interviews are formatted according to how they are gathered by the researcher:

- **Is the source a published, broadcast, or recorded interview?** Cite the interview as you would any other book part, article, online document, recording, or broadcast—but list the interviewee first, as primary acknowledgment. Then insert the title (if given) and a descriptive phrase, *Interview with . . . .* See Models 43, 64, 65.
- **Is the source an interview you conducted?** List the interviewee, a description (*Personal interview, Telephone interview,* etc.) and the date(s). See Model 66.
- **Is the source an unpublished letter, memo, or email?** List the author(s), the subject line in quotation marks (for emails, memos), a description of the format and audience (*Letter to . . .* , *Email to the author,* etc.), and the date sent. See Models 67, 68.
- **Is the source published correspondence?** Cite a published letter, memo, or email as you would any other book part, periodical entry, or online document, depending on the form of publication. After the title of the letter, insert the date of the correspondence and any identifying number added by the editor. See Models 69, 72.

## Works Cited and In-text Citations (Notes)

**65. INTERVIEW—** Didion, Joan. Interview with David Eggers. *Salon*. N.p.
Published in          28 Oct. 1996. Web. 4 May 2008.
Online Magazine   IN-TEXT NOTE: (Didion 2)

**66. INTERVIEW—** Halsam, Gerald. Personal interview. 23–24 Apr. 2003.
By Researcher   IN-TEXT NOTE: (Halsam)

**67. EMAIL—** Schwarz, Sigmar. "Who's Going to Sacramento?"
Unpublished         Message to the author. 8 Oct. 2003. E-mail.
IN-TEXT NOTE: (Schwarz)

**68. MEMO—** Seward, Daniel. "Proposal for Forum on Richard
Unpublished        Rodriguez's *Hunger of Memory*." Memo to English
Dept. fac., California Lutheran U. 1 May 2003.
Print.
IN-TEXT NOTE: (Seward)

**69. LETTER—** Steinbeck, John. "To Lyndon B. Johnson." 24 Nov. 1963.
Published in a   *Steinbeck: A Life in Letters*. Ed. Elaine Steinbeck
Book          and Robert Wallsten. New York: Viking, 1975.
787–88. Print.
IN-TEXT NOTE: (Steinbeck 788)

## MLA MODELS 50B-13 Editorials, reviews, ads, cartoons, etc.

#### 70. EDITORIAL—SIGNED

| Author | Title of piece | Publication information |
|---|---|---|

Goett, Pamela. "Houston, We Have a Problem." Editorial. *Journal of*

*Business Strategy* 23.1 (2002): 2. Print.

Medium of
publication

IN-TEXT NOTE: (Goett)

Many periodicals and online publications contain special genres of writing that you should identify by inserting a descriptive word or phrase into the entry:

- **Is the source an editorial?** After the title, insert *Editorial.* See Models 70, 71.
- **Is the source a letter to the editor?** After the title (if any), insert *Letter.* See Model 72.
- **Is the source a review?** After the title (if any) insert *Rev. of* followed by the title of what's being reviewed. You may list contributors for the work being reviewed after its title, separated by commas (not periods here). See Models 73, 74.
- **Is the source an advertisement?** Begin with the name of the product or the company (if no product is mentioned). Then insert *Advertisement.* See Model 75.
- **Is the source a cartoon or comic strip?** Insert *Cartoon* or *Comic strip.* See Model 76.

## Works Cited and In-text Citations (Notes)

**71. EDITORIAL—**
Unsigned

"Houston, You Have a Problem." Editorial. *Scientific American* Aug. 2003: 10. Print.

**IN-TEXT NOTE:** ("Houston")

**72. LETTER TO THE EDITOR—**
Signed

Ceniceros, Claudia. Letter. *New York Times* 20 Aug. 2002, late ed.: A18. Print.

**IN-TEXT NOTE:** (Ceniceros)

**73. REVIEW OF FILM—**
From Nonperiodical Web Site

Johanson, Mary Ann. "Sounds of Silence." Rev. of *Apollo 13*, dir. Ron Howard. *The Flick Filosopher*. 13 Mar. 2000. Web. 8 Mar. 2003.

**IN-TEXT NOTE:** (Johanson)

**74. REVIEW OF BOOK—**In Printed Journal

Bauman, Zygmunt. Rev. of *Risk and Blame: Essays in Cultural Theory*, by Mary Douglas. *British Journal of Sociology* 45.1 (1994): 143. Print.

**IN-TEXT NOTE:** (Bauman)

**75. ADVERTISEMENT—**
In Magazine

PeopleSoft's Real-Time Enterprise. Advertisement. *Business Week* 9 June 2003: 17. Print.

**IN-TEXT NOTE:** (PeopleSoft)

**76. CARTOON—**
Untitled, Published in Online Periodical

McKee, Rick. Cartoon. *Slate*. Washington Post. Newsweek Interactive, 23 July 2003. Web. 6 Mar. 2008.

**IN-TEXT NOTE:** (Mckee)

## MLA MODELS 50B-14  Government documents and sacred texts

### 77. GOVERNMENT PUBLICATION

Government entity          Title of publication

Columbus, Ohio. Recreation and Parks Dept. *Camp Fair.*

Columbus: n.p., 2003. Print.

Publication      Medium of
information      publication

IN-TEXT NOTE: (Columbus)

Although these works have traditionally appeared in print, they now are regularly accessed online. Provide standard publication information for the edition you are using, which for electronic versions might also include original print publication details before the site name or software reference where you found the source.

- **Are you citing a government document?** Begin with the government entity (nation, state, etc.) and specific agency or department (if any). Then list the title (usually italicized, but in quotes for Web pages or parts of documents), secondary contributors (if any), and available publication information. For congressional documents, list the session (abbreviated) before the publication information, noting also the type of document and assigned number. See Models 77, 78, 79.
- **Are you citing the *Congressional Record*?** Simply list the abbreviated title *Cong. Rec.*, the date, and the page numbers. No other information is needed. See Model 80.
- **Are you citing a sacred text?** Cite the source as an anonymous work, beginning with the title of the edition (underlined); then list the date the particular edition was originally published, secondary acknowledgments from the edition's title page or byline, and print or electronic publication details. See Models 81, 82.

## Works Cited and In-text Citations (Notes)

**78. GOVERNMENT PUBLICATION—** Printed Official Document of U.S. Congress

United States. Cong. Joint Committee on Printing. *1985-86 Official Congressional Directory.* 99th Cong., 1st sess. Washington: GPO, 1985. Print.

IN-TEXT NOTE: (U.S. Cong. Joint Committee on Printing)

**79. GOVERNMENT PUBLICATION—** Web Page on Government Site

Vermont Agency of Natural Resources. "Introduction and Greeting." *Vermont Agency of Natural Resources.* Vermont Agency of Natural Resources. 2008. Web. 3 Jan. 2009.

IN-TEXT NOTE: (Vermont)

**80. CONGRES-SIONAL RECORD**

*Cong. Rec.* 8 Feb. 1974: 3942-43. Print.

IN-TEXT NOTE: (*Cong. Rec.* 8 Feb. 1974)

**81. SACRED TEXT**—Printed in Book Form

*The Bible: Authorized King James Version.* 1611. Ed. Robert Carroll and Stephen Pricket. Oxford: Oxford UP, 1997. Print.

IN-TEXT NOTE: (Matt. 19.24)

**82. SACRED TEXT**—Online Version of Previously Printed Edition

*Rig Veda.* Trans. Ralph T. H. Griffith. 1896. *SacredTexts.com.* John Bruno Hare. N.d. Web. 29 Aug. 2008.

IN-TEXT NOTE: (Rig Veda 7.32)

## MLA MODELS 50B-15 Sources from library subscription services

### 83. LIBRARY SERVICE—ARTICLE

Author ▼                                    Title ▼

Lim, Beng Choo. "Performing *Furyu No*: The Theatre of Konparu

Publication information (Periodical Issue: Pages.) ▼   Database ▼

Zenpo." *Asian Theatre Journal* 22.1 (2005): 33-51. *International*

Information   Medium of   Date of
service   publication   access
▼             ▼            ▼

*Index to Performing Arts.* ProQuest. Web. 2 Feb. 2006.

IN-TEXT NOTE: (Lim)

Many writers now gain access to materials from information services to which their local or school libraries subscribe, such as *LexisNexis*, *Gale*, or *EBSCO*. Such services typically offer a full menu of databases.

- **Are you citing an online article?** To cite an article you find in a library subscription database, provide author, title of the article, complete publication information, database and/or information service where the material was found. Also provide a date of access. See Models 83, 84.

- **Are you citing a magazine article from a subscription service?** Treat the magazine as you would a print item. But also identify the database, subscription service, and library. The subscription service is generally identified on the bottom of search screens or as a logo elsewhere on the page. Titles of databases are italicized. See Model 85.

- **Are you citing a newspaper source?** Pay attention to any information used to identify the section number of the article as it appeared in print. See Model 86.

- **Are you citing an online encyclopedia?** Many libraries subscribe to online encyclopedias or reference works. Cite the entry you have consulted and provide a date of access. You need not identify the library or location. See Model 87.

**Works Cited and In-text Citations (Notes)**

| | |
|---|---|
| **84. LIBRARY SERVICE—** Journal Article | Lewis, Richard D., et al. "Prevalence and Degree of Childhood and Adolescent Overweight in Rural, Urban, and Suburban Georgia." *Journal of School Health* 76.4 (2006): 126-32. *Expanded Academic ASAP*. Web. 15 Sept. 2006. |

IN-TEXT NOTE: (Lewis et al. 129)

| | |
|---|---|
| **85. LIBRARY SERVICE—** Magazine Article | Harrison, Bobby R. "Phantom of the Bayou." *Natural History* Sept. 2005: 18-52. *Academic Search Premier*. Web. 15 Sept. 2006. |

IN-TEXT NOTE: (Harrison 18)

| | |
|---|---|
| **86. LIBRARY SERVICE—** Newspaper Article | Toner, Mike. "Back to the Moon." *Atlanta Journal-Constitution* 13 Oct. 2005: A1. *LexisNexis*. Web. 11 May 2006. |

IN-TEXT NOTE: (Toner)

| | |
|---|---|
| **87. LIBRARY SERVICE—** Encyclopedia Entry | "Schnauzer." *Encyclopædia Britannica Online*. 2006. Encyclopædia Britannica. Web. 29 May 2006. |

IN-TEXT NOTE: ("Schnauzer")

## 50c Sample Research Paper—MLA

Nelson Rivera, a first-year student at the University of South Carolina, wrote "Taking a Closer Look at the Motorcycle Boom" in March 2005 while a student in "English 101: Rhetoric and Composition." The assignment sheet for the paper asked students to write a casual argument, that is, a paper that tries to explain a phenomenon—in this case, the growing popularity of motorcycles. The paper appears here substantially as Rivera wrote it, though with some modifications to highlight specific features of MLA style. It is accompanied by annotations and checklists designed to help you set up a paper correctly.

---

### Checklist 50.1   Formatting the Paper—MLA

Use the following general settings in your word processor for an MLA paper, but adjust them to match any special preferences set by your instructor. (Note: If using a typewriter or fixed-width font, you can insert five spaces in place of each half-inch of indentation.) Subsequent checklists provide details for the title page, special items (quotations, tables, and figures), and the Works Cited page.

a. **Use white, 8½-by-11-inch paper.** For a traditional academic assignment, never use color or lined paper. Handwrite a paper only with an instructor's permission.

b. **Insert your last name and page number one-half inch from the top of *every* page, aligned with the right-hand margin.** The best way to achieve this is to insert a running page header. (See the View or Insert menus.)

c. **Use the same readable font face throughout your paper.** Avoid fonts with too much decoration, since they can be hard on the eyes. Also be sure to use a moderate text size, 10 to 12 points depending on the font face.

d. **Double-space the entire document.** This includes the Works Cited page and title page. (Use your word processor's Format or Paragraph menus to select line spacing.)

e. **Left-align the body of the paper and do not hyphenate words at the end of the line.** You may need to turn off your word processor's automatic hyphenation tool.

f. **Indent the first word of each paragraph one-half inch.** Most word processors have a way to auto set an indent for the first line of paragraphs.

---

**Checklist 50.2   Formatting the Title Page—MLA**

MLA does not require a separate cover sheet or title page—instead, at the *top of the first page* list each of the following items on a *separate* line. All these items are double spaced. In particular, do not insert extra spaces above or below the title.

**a.  List your full name on the first line of the first page, aligned to the left.**

**b.  List your instructor's name with appropriate title, aligned to the left.** When uncertain about academic rank, use *Mr., Ms.,* or *Prof.* Better, look up the title in a campus directory or simply ask your instructor.

**c.  List the course title, aligned to the left.**

**d.  List the date you submit the assignment, aligned to the left.**

**e.  Give the title of your paper, capitalized and centered.** Capitalize the first and last words of the title, and all words in between *except* articles (*a, an*, and *the*), prepositions (including *to* when part of an infinitive), and coordinating conjunctions. Do not end the title with a period, but use a question mark when appropriate. Do not bold, underline, italicize, or specially format your title *except* for specific words and phrases that generally require special formatting.

Taking a Closer Look at the Motorcycle Boom

Nelson Rivera

Ms. Melissa Jantz

English 101: Rhetoric and Composition

25 March 2005

---

**Note:** If your instructor does ask for a title page, center the title of your paper and your name in the upper third of the paper. Center the course title, your instructor's name, and the date on the lower third of the sheet, double-spacing each item. (See sample above.)

---

**Checklist 50.3  Quotations, Tables, and Figures—MLA**

a. **Format quotations correctly.** MLA requires that you present long quotations—more than four lines—in block format. *Block quotations* are *not* enclosed by quotation marks. The entire quotation is indented 1 inch from the left margin. Use the same double spacing as the rest of the document.

b. **Label and number tables, placing them as close as possible to related text.** Before the table, provide the label *Table*, an identifying number, and a caption, capitalized according to the standard rules for titles. Double-space the table (assuming you're not using an image of a table, as student writer Nelson Rivera does), citing the source (if you didn't create it yourself) in a caption at the bottom. The caption should use the same 1-inch margin as the rest of the paper.

c. **Label and number illustrations and other visual material.** Place the item as close as possible to the related text, providing underneath the label *Fig.* (or *Figure*), an identifying number, and the title (or a descriptive label or caption). For more on figures and tables, see Section 48b-2.

1/2 inch
Rivera 1

1 inch

Nelson Rivera

Center the title and use same font/ font size as in the paper: no boldface, underscore, or display fonts.

Ms. Melissa Jantz

English 101: Rhetoric and Composition

25 March 2005

Double-space all elements on the title page. No special spacing or enlarged or enhanced fonts.

1/2 inch

Taking a Closer Look at the Motorcycle Boom

In 1969 the film *Easy Rider* revolutionized the motorcycle

world by creating the bad boy biker image that is familiar to most

people today (see fig. 1). Bikers were renegades, counterculture

Use a note to connect text and images.

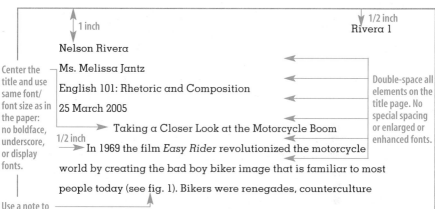

Label, number, and provide a caption for figures below the item, using "Fig." or "Figure."

Fig. 1. Peter Fonda and Dennis Hopper growling down the

highway in *Easy Rider* (1969), representing bikers as rebels.

road warriors who, according to scholars Jeremy Packer and Mary

K. Coffey, were "violent, heteronormative, and (for the most part)

masculine as they may be" (641). Though they weren't typical

heroes, Peter Fonda and Dennis Hopper portrayed life on the road

1 inch

as life on their own terms, and after the release of this movie, the

1 inch

motorcycle industry experienced a 98% increase in sales between

1970 and 1980. This increase diminished, however,

1 inch

Author's last name
appears on every page
Rivera 2

soon after it peaked. It wasn't until 1992 that the industry experienced a rebirth with increases in motorcycle sales "not seen since the 1970's" ("Annual"). Today the industry has

*This source does not use page numbers.*

reached the one million mark in motorcycle sales. Up from just 278,000 motorcycles sold in 1992, these sales numbers represent an increase of over 270%, as seen in Table 1.

*Label, number, and provide a caption for tables above the item.*

Table 1

Estimated New Motorcycle Sales: 1992-2004

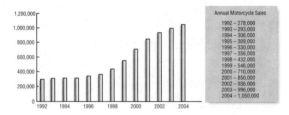

Annual Motorcycle Sales

1992 – 278,000
1993 – 293,000
1994 – 306,000
1995 – 309,000
1996 – 330,000
1997 – 356,000
1998 – 432,000
1999 – 546,000
2000 – 710,000
2001 – 850,000
2002 – 936,000
2003 – 996,000
2004 – 1,050,000

*List source information beneath the table.*

Source: *2003 Motorcycle Statistical Annual Report. Free Student Kit.* Motorcycle Industry Council. 2004. Web. 16 Mar. 2008.

This trend has continued into what is now a twelfth consecutive year of record-breaking motorcycle sales. Unlike those involved in the first motorcycle craze in the 1970s, today's motorcycle enthusiasts do not have a box office hit movie to fuel their interest, and they do not dream of giving up the social

Rivera 3

This ¶ states the thesis of the causal argument.

responsibilities of work and family in the vein of *Easy Rider*'s free-living protagonists. Instead, this sales increase is likely due to several interrelated social and economic causes, especially including the rise in expendable income now enjoyed by the Baby Boom generation. Generally speaking, the counterculture biker image appeals to this group of aging activists, and the biker lifestyle is now much more accessible to those with the social responsibilities of work and family.

Indeed, the stereotyped image of the average biker has dramatically changed over the last 20 years. Today's bikers are a new breed. No longer are they simply leather-clad, beer-drinking Hell's Angels, described in 1966 by Hunter S. Thompson as

Indent block quote 1 inch from left-hand margin and double-space it. Omit " " around quote.

1 inch

> running fast and loud on the early morning freeway, low in the saddle, nobody smiles, jamming crazy through traffic and ninety miles an hour down the center stripe,

The ellipsis mark *without* brackets actually appears in Thompson's ¶.

> missing by inches . . . like Genghis Khan on an iron horse, a monster steed [ . . . ] long hair in the wind, beards and bandanas flapping, earrings, armpits, chain whips [ . . . ] and stripped-down Harleys flashing chrome as traffic on 101 moves over, nervous, to let the formation pass like a

The in-text note comes after the punctuation at the end of a block quote.

> burst of dirty thunder. (3)

Even though much of this rebellious style remains, today's biker lifestyle does not necessarily exclude the demands of a more traditional lifestyle. In fact, many of today's bikers are law firm partners, accountants, and doctors--a lifestyle still frowned upon in the early 1980s, when for example a cycle-riding metropolitan

Rivera 4

court judge from New Mexico admitted in the *American Bar Association Journal* that "people think you're crazy riding a motorcycle, period" (Winter 527). Now, however, the biker you see growling down the highway might even be your boss. This change in image has made the biker lifestyle seem more accessible to professionals who might have otherwise felt too mainstream to take part in a counterculture.

Even cable TV networks now spotlight the biker world with programs such as *World Biker Build-off*, *American Steel*, and *American Choppers* (see Fig. 2), and so "the bikes that once invoked images of greasy leathers and snarling gangs are now just as likely to turn

> ← Italicize television series titles.

Fig. 2. Biking goes mainstream with Paul Teutul, Sr., and Paul Teutul, Jr., of *American Chopper*.

Rivera 5

"G5" is a section/page number in a newspaper.

up in executives' garages" (Hopkins G5). This attention by the media has lured names such as Jay Leno, Dennis Rodman, and Shaquille O'Neal to join the biker lifestyle. And the increase in media coverage has in turn sparked the interest of a wider range of Americans, creating a greater market field and expanding the buyer segments.

Perhaps it is not that surprising, then, that women make up a significant new addition to the motorcycle market. In fact, women are the fastest-growing segment in the market and, as Steve Pilkington succinctly notes, they "are no longer taking a back seat to men" (9). According to the Motorcycle Industry Council, female ridership increased from 2% in 1985 to 10% in 2003. An article in

Brackets indicate that the "t" was originally a capital letter.

*Working Woman* reports that "[t]oday 1 out of every 11 American motorcycle owners is a woman, compared with 1 out of 100 in 1960" (Aronson 18). The overall increase in motorcycle sales can be attributed, in part, to this increase in female riders. Because many women have experienced a growth in disposable income, they can now make motorcycle purchases on their own, without the help of their male partners. The biker image now seems more accessible and acceptable, and women can more comfortably fit into this lifestyle.

This new gentler image is in large part created by a return to the saddle by the Baby Boomers who had previously abandoned their riding days in exchange for families and careers. During the last motorcycle boom, the average rate of increase in motorcycle sales matched that of the annual increase in the number of Baby

Rivera 6

Boom males reaching their 18th birthdays. Ken Kurson, who points out these facts in "Motorcycles for Grown-ups," adds that "30 years later, much of this round of expansion comes from the fact that Baby Boomers are rediscovering their love of motorcycles" (112). In the last 12 years the motorcycling lifestyle has attracted wealthier and older owners, both male and female, and this is largely due to the fact that the Baby Boom generation is now entering into a stage of financial stability with no dependents. The results of a 2003 consumer research report show the average age of bikers to be 41 with a median household income of $55,850 annually (see table 2).

Table 2

Owner Profile by Age, Marital Status, Education, Occupation, and Income: 1985-2003

| | % OF TOTAL OWNERS | | | |
|---|---|---|---|---|
| | 2003 | 1998 | 1990 | 1985 |
| **AGE** | | | | |
| Under 18 | 3.7% | 4.1% | 8.3% | 14.9% |
| 18 – 24 | 10.8% | 10.6% | 15.5% | 20.7% |
| 25 – 29 | 7.6% | 10.9% | 17.1% | 18.7% |
| 30 – 34 | 8.9% | 11.5% | 16.4% | 13.8% |
| 35 – 39 | 10.4% | 16.0% | 14.3% | 8.7% |
| 40 – 49 | 27.9% | 24.6% | 16.3% | 13.2% |
| 50 and Over | 25.1% | 19.1% | 10.1% | 8.1% |
| Not Stated | 5.6% | 3.2% | 2.0% | 1.9% |
| Median Age | 41.0 yrs. | 38.0 yrs. | 32.0 yrs. | 27.1 yrs. |
| Mean Age | 40.2 yrs. | 38.1 yrs. | 33.1 yrs. | 28.5 yrs. |
| **HOUSEHOLD INCOME FOR PRIOR YEAR** | | | | |
| Under $20,000 | 5.9% | 9.3% | 15.6% | 31.8% |
| $20,000–$34,999 | 13.1% | 19.4% | 32.2% | 26.7% |
| $35,000–$49,999 | 18.1% | 19.1% | 19.6% | 14.4% |
| $50,000–$74,999 | 19.3% | 18.8% | 13.1% | ** 6.1% |
| $75,000–$99,999 | 13.7% | 8.3% | 4.1% | |
| $100,000–$149,999 | 8.4% | 3.8% | * 2.7% | |
| $150,000 and Over | 4.8% | 2.3% | | |
| Not Stated | 16.7% | 19.0% | 12.7% | 21.0% |
| Median | $55,850 | $44,250 | $33,100 | $25,600 |
| * $100,000 and Over | | | | |
| ** $50,000 and Over | | | | |
| **MARITAL STATUS** | | | | |
| Single | 41.1% | 40.0% | 41.1% | 47.6% |
| Married | 55.5% | 58.8% | 56.6% | 50.3% |
| Not Stated | 3.4% | 1.2% | 2.3% | 2.1% |
| **HIGHEST LEVEL OF EDUCATION** | | | | |
| Grade School | 3.1% | 3.3% | 5.9% | 7.5% |
| Some High School | 6.9% | 9.6% | 9.5% | 15.3% |
| High School Graduate | 30.2% | 36.0% | 39.4% | 36.5% |
| Some College/Technical | 25.9% | 26.5% | 25.2% | 21.6% |
| College Graduate | 18.6% | 16.0% | 12.4% | 12.2% |
| Post Graduate | 10.5% | 6.9% | 5.2% | 5.2% |
| Not Stated | 4.8% | 1.7% | 2.4% | 1.7% |
| **OCCUPATION OF OWNER** | | | | |
| Professional/Technical | 31.2% | 31.3% | 20.3% | 19.0% |
| Mechanic/Craftsman | 11.7% | 15.3% | 13.1% | 15.1% |
| Manager/Proprietor | 10.8% | 7.5% | 9.3% | 8.9% |
| Laborer/Semi-Skilled | 6.9% | 12.7% | 24.1% | 23.2% |
| Service Worker | 6.0% | 7.5% | 6.6% | 6.4% |
| Clerical/Sales | 4.4% | 3.6% | 6.8% | 7.8% |
| Farmer/Farm Laborer | 1.9% | 2.8% | 2.1% | 5.1% |
| Military | 1.3% | 2.6% | 1.5% | 1.6% |
| Other | 18.3% | 13.5% | 13.1% | 4.6% |
| Not Stated | 7.5% | 3.2% | 3.1% | 8.3% |
| Note: Percentages based on owners employed | | | | |

Source: *2004 Motorcycle Statistical Annual Report. Free Student Kit.* Motorcycle Industry Council. 2005. Web. 16 Mar. 2008.

Rivera 8

Because of the Baby Boomers' large numbers and their inclination toward free spending, it was just a matter of time before the tourist industry jumped onto the motorcycle boom bandwagon ("Baby Boomers"). This, in turn, prompted some major cities to sponsor weeklong celebrations geared toward welcoming motorcycle enthusiasts and creating a $774 million a year tourist industry in Daytona Beach alone. A 2001 study conducted by the University of Central Florida shows that "this is significantly more than the $561 million generated by the Daytona 500 [ . . . ] or the $196 million from spring break" (Schneider 14). Not only is the motorcycle industry now more accessible to individuals who might have been reluctant or unable to take part before, but it is also more lucrative for the tourist industry, which now has a financial incentive to sponsor biker events.

Though the Baby Boomers are known for their capacity for free spending, some research suggests that sales are up in part because motorcycles provide the rider with an economical and environmentally friendly method of transportation. At a time when gas prices are soaring, more people are becoming aware of the economic benefits of owning a motorcycle. According to the U.S. Department of Transportation, the average cost of self-serve gasoline has risen from $1.12 in 1992 to $2.20 per gallon in 2004 ("Table 3-8"). These figures reflect an increase of 96%. With motorcycles averaging 50 miles per gallon of gasoline versus 22 miles per gallon of gasoline for cars and small trucks (U.S. Department of Transportation, "Table 4-11"), one can either ride

"Table 3-8" is a title in the Works Cited list, not a link to a table shown in the paper.

This lengthy note sends readers to the right Works Cited entry.

Rivera 9

back and forth to work all week or go joy riding for an entire weekend on just $20 worth of fuel. Some motorcycle dealers have attributed the sharp increase in motorcycle sales to the higher cost of fuel, claiming that when faced with higher prices at the pump "traditionally [ . . . ] people put motorcycles into the mode of transportation versus the mode it is usually in and that is recreation" (Kenny 1D). Though it might seem odd that the very Baby Boomers who can now enter the biker life because of their expendable income are also attracted by the cost-saving elements of owning a bike, the two causes are not contradictory. According to the Strategic Edge, a market research company that predicts the buying patterns of various target groups, many Baby Boomers were concerned with environmental issues when they came of age ("Baby Boomers"). In addition to the promise of the open road, then, the economic and environmentally responsible elements of the biker lifestyle also appeal to the Baby Boomer.

Concluding ¶ summarizes causes for growth in motorcycle sales.

For both social and economic reasons, motorcycling is now enjoying a greater role in mainstream American culture. Of course, Peter Fonda's and Dennis Hopper's characters would never have considered the cost of fuel as they took to the road, and they certainly wouldn't have returned to the office after a weekend ride. But today's easy riders do not have to trade in their conventional lives for the chance to live and ride free. The new, more accessible and acceptable biker lifestyle has afforded them a taste of the open road, even if only for the weekend.

1 inch

1/2 inch

Rivera 10

Works Cited

"Annual Motorcycle Sales Roar through the One Million Mark: Upward Trend Continues for 12th Consecutive Year." *Business Wire* 21 Jan. 2005. Web. 17 Mar. 2005.

Aronson, Amy. "A Vroom of One's Own: Women Riders Are Fueling a Motorcycling Boom." *Working Woman* June 1999: 18. Print.

"Baby Boomers Grow Up." *The Strategic Solution*. The Strategic Edge. Fall 1996. Web. 15 Mar. 2005.

*Easy Rider*. Dir. Dennis Hopper. Perf. Peter Fonda and Dennis Hopper. Columbia/TriStar Studios, 1969. DVD.

*Easy Rider*. Image. *40 Years of Easy Rider*. N.d. Web. 14 Mar. 2005.

"Estimated New Units Retail Sales." *2003 Motorcycle Statistical Annual Report. Free Student Kit*. Motorcycle Industry Council. 2004. Web. 16 Mar. 2008.

Hopkins, Brent. "Mid-Life Executives Help Alter Bike Rider's Image." *Edmonton Journal* 24 Dec. 2004: G5. *LexisNexis*. Web. 15 Mar. 2005.

Kenny, Megan. "Husbands: Another Reason to Get a Bike. Some Say Rising Prices at the Pump Are Leading to a Spike in Motorcycle Sales." *Charleston Daily Mail* 20 Sept. 2004: 1D. Print.

Kurson, Ken. "Motorcycles for Grown-ups: Bikes Aren't Just for Teenagers and Hell's Angels Anymore." *Money* May 2001: 112-13. Print.

1 inch

1/2 inch (hanging indent)

1 inch (left margin)

1 inch (right margin)

Source comes from a library subscription service.

*The Strategic Solution* is italicized because it is the title of a newsletter. The Strategic Edge is the name of a company.

*Easy Rider* is listed by its title since that is how it is referred to in the paper. Secondary acknowledgments give credit to its director and stars.

Rivera 11

"Owner Profile by Age, Occupation, Marital Status, Occupation, and Income: 1985–2003." *2004 Motorcycle Statistical Annual Report. Free Student Kit*. Motorcycle Industry Council. 2005. Web. 16 Mar. 2008.

Packer, Jeremy, and Mary K. Coffey. "Hogging the Road: Cultural Governance and the Citizen Cyclist." *Cultural Studies* 18.1 (2004): 641-74. Print.

*Paul Teutul, Sr. and Paul Teutul, Jr*. Photograph. *The Discovery Channel: American Chopper*. N.d. Web. 10 Mar. 2005.

Pilkington, Steve. "Women Roll into House of Harley." *Alaska Business Monthly* Feb. 2005: 9. Print.

Thompson, Hunter S. *Hell's Angels: A Strange and Terrible Saga*. New York: Ballantine, 1966. Print.

United States Dept. of Transportation. "Table 3-8: Sales Price of Transportation Fuel to End-Users." *NTS Report 2004*. Bureau of Transportation Statistics. 17 Nov. 2004. Web. 15 Mar. 2005.

---"Table 4-11: Passenger Car and Motorcycle Fuel Consumption and Travel." *NTS Report 2004*. Bureau of Transportation Statistics. 17 Nov. 2004. Web. 15 Mar. 2005.

Winter, Bill. "Biker-Judges and Lawyers Rev Up Their Image." *American Bar Association Journal* 68.1 (1982): 527-28. Print.

The data cited here is not actually available at the site. It must be requested by mail.

---

**Checklist 50.4  Formatting the Works Cited Page—MLA**

Works Cited pages use the same double spacing, 1-inch margins, and running headers (including your last name and page number) as all other sections of an MLA document, so you can easily insert this page at the end of the electronic file you use to store your paper. But use these additional guidelines:

a. **Insert a page break before your Works Cited page.** The works-cited list should start at the top of the first full page following the body of the paper.

b. **Center the title "Works Cited" on the first line.** If the list of works-cited entries overflows this page, *do not* repeat this title on subsequent pages.

c. **Provide works-cited entries for every source you mention in the paper.** Do not list materials you examined but do not cite in the body of the paper. (If you do include such items, the list can be retitled *Works Consulted.*

d. **Arrange the entries alphabetically.** Use the first words of each entry (excluding *A, An*, and *The*) to alphabetize the list.

e. **Use a hanging indentation of one-half inch for each entry.** Unlike paragraphs in the body of the paper, the first line of each works-cited entry is not indented, but subsequent lines are. To adjust the indentation, use your word processor's paragraph formatting feature or, if provided, its indentation and tabbing ruler.

f. **When more than one entry begins with the same person's name,** replace the repeated information with three hyphens followed by a period. This helps readers see easily that the same person is responsible for more than one source on your list:

> van der Plas, Rob. *The Mountain Bike Book: Choosing, Riding and Maintaining the Off-Road Bicycle.* 3rd ed. San Francisco: Bicycle, 1993. Print.
>
> ---. *Mountain Bike Magic.* Mill Valley: Bicycle, 1991. Print.

g. **Use cross-references to shorten entries.** If citing multiple selections from the same book, you don't need to repeat all information about the book for each works-cited entry. Instead, create a separate, full entry for

*(Continued)*

**Formatting the Works Cited Page—MLA** *(Continued)*

the book itself, referring to this entry as you create entries for individual selections. Insert the cross-reference after the selection's title, where you would normally put the book's title and publication details, using the same guidelines for identifying sources here that you do for identifying them with in-text notes. (See Section 50a-1.)

Behrens, Laurence, and Leonard J. Rosen. *Writing and Reading across the Curriculum*. 8th ed. New York: Longman, 2003. Print.

Koplan, Jeffrey P., and William H. Dietz. "Caloric Imbalance and Public Health Policy." Behrens and Rosen 440-47.

Morrison, Toni. "Cinderella's Stepsisters." Behrens and Rosen 590-92.

# Directory to APA Notes—by Type

(See inside back cover for alphabetical directory.)

# 51 How Do You Use APA Documentation?

In many social science and related courses (anthropology, education, economics, linguistics, political science, psychology, sociology), writers are expected to document their sources using the style recommended by the American Psychological Association (APA). The basic procedures for produc-

Step 1 (in the body of the paper)

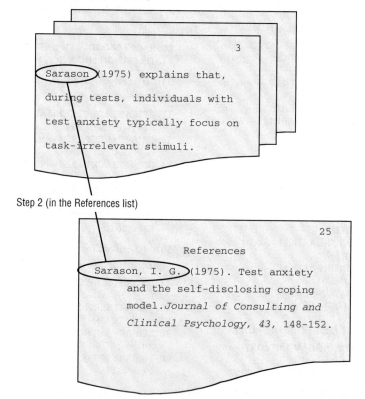

Sarason (1975) explains that, during tests, individuals with test anxiety typically focus on task-irrelevant stimuli.

Step 2 (in the References list)

References

Sarason, I. G. (1975). Test anxiety and the self-disclosing coping model. *Journal of Consulting and Clinical Psychology, 43,* 148-152.

ing a paper in APA style are spelled out in this chapter. APA documentation involves just two basic steps: inserting an in-text note at each point where a paper or project needs documentation (Section 51a) and then recording all sources used in these notes in a References list (Section 51b). A full explanation of APA procedures is provided by the *Publication Manual of the American Psychological Association*, (5th edition, 2001), available in most college libraries. See also <http://www. apa.org/students>.

# 51a Step 1: In the body of your paper, place a note for each source you use.

Each time you introduce material from an outside source into an APA paper, you insert a note to tell readers what your source is and when it was published. You create such notes by using a combination of *parenthetical citations*, which put information about a source between parentheses, and *signal phrases*, which name sources within the normal flow of the sentence. The following example shows how you can combine the two devices when quoting a source in APA documentation style:

Identifies outside source                              Locates source material

Zuboff (1988) observes, "While it is true that computer-based automation continues to displace the human body and its know-how (a process . . . known as deskilling), the information power of the technology simultaneously creates pressure for a profound reskilling" (p. 57).

In APA style, you need a page number only when you are quoting directly or citing material you have paraphrased. As you read the following guidelines, you'll see other patterns for citing sources in your paper.

**● 1 Identify sources clearly each time you use them.** Whether you introduce sources with parenthetical notes or signal phrases, your readers will always need to know which source on the reference list at the end of the paper you're using. You establish that connection by making sure that the note itself clearly refers to the word by which the source is alphabetized in that reference list, whether that is a person's last name (an author or editor, for example), a set of names (groups of authors or editors), or a title.

To help identify sources better, APA also requires that you give the year the source was published, which is always the second item in the reference-list entry.

IN-TEXT NOTE: . . . **Sarason (1975)** observes that a student's performance . . .

References

**Sarason**, I. G. **(1975)**. Test anxiety and the self-disclosing coping model. *Journal of Consulting and Clinical Psychology, 43,* 148–152.

IN-TEXT NOTE: . . . proves the need for more attention to national parks (**"Deferred Repairs," 2003**).

References

**Deferred repairs** take toll on parks. (**2003**, June 15). *The Los Angeles Times.* Retrieved November 2, 2003, from http:// pqasb.pqarchiver.com/latimes

**1.1 Citing a source listed under one person's name.** Mention the individual's *last name,* either in the signal phrase or the parenthetical note. Provide first and middle initials before the last name when another entry on your reference list begins with an individual having the same last name.

"Any institution that is going to keep its shape needs to gain legitimacy by distinctive grounding in nature and in reason" (**Douglas, 1986**, p. 112).

**Nightingale (1858)** reveals that a major cause of deaths in the Crimean War was unsanitary living conditions, not conflict on the battlefield.

**1.2 Citing a source listed under two individuals' names.** Mention the *last names of both individuals,* separated by *and* (or & for parenthetical notes).

**Tarr and Pinker (1990)** define *object constancy* as "the ability to recognize an object despite changes in its retinal image" (p. 253).

Previous research (**Hazelhurst & Hutchins, 1998**) has shown that logical propositions are not so much the product of an innate ability to reason, but rather the result of trying to communicate in a shared world.

**1.3 Citing a source listed under three to six individuals' names.** The first time you cite the source, list the *last name of every person*, separated by commas. Precede the last name in the list with *and* (or *&* for parenthetical notes). Shorten subsequent notes by naming only the first author followed by the abbreviation *et al.* (Latin for "and others").

Human experience is something of a conundrum: "Minds awaken in a world. We did not design our world. We simply found ourselves with it; we awoke both to ourselves and the world we inhabit" (**Varela, Thompson, & Rosch, 1991**, p. 3). . . . [*later in same paper*] . . . **Varela et al. (1991)** reconcile the Eastern and Western views of human experience in order to . . .

**1.4 Citing a source listed under more than six individuals' names.** Mention only the *last name of the first person*, followed by *et al.*

Youth who are unsatisfied with their outside obligations have a greater tendency towards risky behavior (**Donohue et al., 2003**).

**1.5 Citing a source listed under the name of a corporation or group.** Give the full name of the organization. If you need to mention the source again, you may use a well-known abbreviation or acronym, providing it in parentheses (or brackets if already in parentheses) after the first citation; use only this short version in subsequent notes.

In 1999 over 350,000 were home-schooled for religious reasons, 38.4% of all home-schooled students (**National Center for Education Statistics [NCES], 2001**). . . . [*later in same paper*] . . . According to the **NCES (2001)** . . .

**1.6 Citing a source listed by title.** For sources without authors, the title will appear first in the reference-list entry—so in corresponding in-text citations, give a shortened version of the title (including always the first alphabetized word). Italicize titles that are italicized on the References page; place other titles in quotation marks when citing them in in-text notes.

> A tight labor market does not necessarily result in greater job satisfac-
>
> tion for those who are already employed (**"Job Satisfaction," 2003**).

**1.7 Citing a source that is one of many listed under an author or title.** Do nothing special for most sources, because the year can be used to distinguish the entries. But when two sources are listed under the same name(s) in the same year, distinguish between them by attaching an identifying lower-case letter to the year (*1991a, 1991b,* etc.). The same letter should appear in the date of the corresponding reference-list entry.

> The charge is raised by **Rosner (2004a)**, quickly answered by **Anderson**
>
> **(2004)**, and then raised again by **Rosner (2004b)**.

**1.8 Citing multiple sources in one in-text note.** For multiple works all by one author, provide the years for each source after the name, separating each by a comma. When listing multiple sources by different authors, separate the references by a semicolon when using a parenthetical note; separate them by commas when using a signal phrase. Notice that authors who work with different co-authors are listed separately for each group of collaborators, even when their names appear first in all entries.

> Similar results have been observed in previous studies of the
>
> therapeutic effects of music on children with special developmental
>
> needs (**Goldstein, 1964; Goldstein, Lingas, & Sheafor, 1965; Murphy, 1957,**
>
> **1958**).

**1.9 Citing sacred texts, classical works, entire Web sites, and unpublished correspondence.** None of these sources needs to be listed on your References page, but they do need to be cited in the body of your paper when used. For sacred texts and classical works (those that are widely available in commonly accepted versions), simply identify the source, naming the version in parentheses after the first reference.

> **Exodus** 22:33–37 (**New American Bible**) provides a basis for assessing and compensating damages in private torts. **Deuteronomy** 25:1–4 further . . .

When referring to an entire Web site (rather than just a page or section), give the name of the site in your signal phrase followed by its Internet address in parentheses (for the first reference only).

> The **U.S. Census Bureau** regularly publishes statistics on homeownership (http://www.census.gov), along with other demographic data.

For unpublished correspondence, name the person who wrote the letter or email in the signal phrase, followed in parentheses by the words *personal communication*, a comma, and the date the piece was written.

> According to **Rice (personal communication, August 28, 2002)**, . . .

**●2 Provide page numbers to locate quotations and paraphrased passages.** When you reference a specific passage from a source, you need to provide page numbers—or another kind of specific reference—in addition to identifying the source and its publication year. Page numbers appear in parentheses just after quoted or paraphrased material. If presented in a parenthetical note with author and year, the page reference follows a comma.

| | |
|---|---|
| **SOURCES WITH STANDARD PAGINATION** | **(p. 42)** |
| Use *p.* or *pp.* (two or more pages) before the reference. Use an en dash to separate page ranges—for example, when a quote runs onto the next page. | (Tannen, 1990, **pp. 130–131**) |
| | (Man, Tam, & Li, 2003, **p. 778**) |

SOURCES WITH NO PAGINATION
Indicate the numbering scheme
used (¶ for paragraphs, *chap.*
for chapter, etc.), and provide
a reference number. If no
numbering is available, state
the heading of the nearest
subsection, and identify the
paragraph within the section.

(TEA, 1998, **chap. 110.c–d**)
(**¶ 4**)
(Green Day, 2004, **track 2**)
(Cheadle, 2001, **"Methods," ¶ 2–3**)

WORKS WITH TRADITIONAL NUMBERING
Classic works that are divided
into precise hierarchical sections
need no page references. Instead,
identify the relevant sections
using the standard numbering.

(Aristotle, *Prior Analytics*, **68b.9–15**)
(Mark **10:25**)

## 3 Place and punctuate parenthetical notes appropriately.

Insert citations immediately after the relevant quoted or paraphrased
material.

> Predictions that the future would be uniform and sterile are proving to
> be wrong **(Postrel, 2003)**.

If the citation occurs in the middle of a sentence, add no extra punctuation
after the closing parenthesis, except what may be needed to resume the normal flow of the sentence.

> Statistical analyses **(Levitt & Dubner, 2005)** suggest that what
> candidates spend on political campaigns matters much less than
> who they are and how much the public likes them.

When the citation occurs at the end of the sentence, place the parenthetical
note before the ending period and after the end quotation mark.

> Schlosser **(2001)** claims that fast food is a "revolutionary force in
> American life" **(p. 3)**.

# 51b Step 2: On a separate page at the end of your project, list alphabetically every source you have cited.

An APA References page, which appears after the body of the paper and before any appendixes, provides readers with full bibliographical information on all the sources that you mention in the body of your paper—except sacred texts, Web sites (when referring to the entire site), and unpublished correspondence. The following pages outline the basic formatting of those APA reference-list entries and show how specific kinds of sources might appear using these guidelines. If no model is given for the kind of source you're citing, use the details you know about a source to fill in the different parts of a similar kind of entry. You can also consult the official APA *Publication Manual* (2001) or look for similar entries cited on the References pages of articles published in journals using *APA* style.

## BASIC PARTS OF APA REFERENCE-LIST ENTRIES

Reference-list entries are composed of four or five (for some online sources) basic parts, each of which is listed below, marked and color-coded in the corresponding sample entries. Notice that each item ends with a period and begins with a capitalized word.

**Author.**   APA defines authors as the "primary contributors" to a particular source. For most entries, the author(s) will be the researcher(s) who wrote the study. In some cases, however, you'll list others types of contributors—for example, the editors of a book, a producer of a CD, or the director of a movie.

**Date.**   The date of publication appears in parentheses as the second item in an entry. The year will appear in any in-text notes that refer to the entry.

**Title.**    Usually the third item of a reference-list entry, a title will appear first when a source does not have an author. When a title is listed first, place the date after the title. Sometimes, you might need to list two titles within an entry—for example, both the title of an anthology and that of a selection it contains.

**Publication or Production Information.**    Tell readers where the source was published and by whom—details that depend on the type of source you're referencing. For example, list place of publication and publisher for books; periodical, issue, and page numbers for articles; and place and/or vendor for CDs or musical downloads.

**Online Retrieval Information.**    For online sources, state the date you last viewed the source, the site name (if not clear from other parts of the citation), and the online address (URL) or database containing the source. Don't place a period after this item when the final part of the entry is an online address.

---

References

Hawkes, N. (2003, October 13). Monkeys' mind games. *The Times* (London), p. H9.

O'Ehley, J. (2002). Just what do you think you're doing, Dave? [Review of the motion picture *2001: A space odyssey*]. Retrieved August 3, 2003, from http://www.sciflicks.com/2001/review.html

Suchman, L. A. (1987). *Plans and situated actions: The problem of human-machine communication*. Cambridge, England: Cambridge University Press.

## Authors

List all authors last-name-first, using initials instead of full first names. Omit titles (*M.D., S.J.*, etc.), but provide essential suffixes (*Jr., III*, etc.) after the name.

| | |
|---|---|
| **One author.** List the last name first, followed by a comma, the initials of first and middle names appearing on the title page of the source, and a period. | Ruffin, M. T., IV.<br>Sacks, O.<br>Tannen, D. |
| **Two or more authors.** List their names in the same order they appear on the title page or byline. Present all names last-name-first, separating them by commas (even when only two are listed). Precede the final name with an ampersand (&). | Crowley, B. J., Hayslip, B., Jr., & Hobdy, J.<br>Tarr, M. J., & Pinker, S.<br>See Models 7, 19, 23, 28, 34, 37 |
| **More than six authors.** List the first six, then provide the Latin abbreviation *et al.* ("and others"), preceded by a comma. | See Model 9 |
| **Corporate or group authors or artists.** Provide the complete name of the organization or corporation. | California Legislative Counsel.<br>See Models 6, 21, 27, 30, 32 |
| **Editors, directors, etc.** When the main authors of a work are listed as contributing in a special way, describe the contribution in parentheses after each name. When several people contribute in the same way, place a pluralized description after the last person's name: (Writers). | Alda, A. (Writer/Director).<br>Coyne, J. (Ed.).<br>Sherman-Palladino, A. (Writer), & Glatter, L. L. (Director).<br>See Models 2, 29, 30, 31 |
| **Consulting authors.** An author listed on the title page preceded by *with* appears in parentheses after the primary author(s) in a reference-list entry, but is *not* mentioned in in-text notes. | Armstrong, L., & Carmichael, C. (with Nye, P. J.).<br>Symonds, M. (with Ellison, L.). |

## Dates

List the publication date in parentheses.

> Jones, A. (1975).

When providing more than just a year, insert a comma before the month (unabbreviated) and date. (Note: Dates in other parts of an entry appear in month/day/year order.)

> Garza, J. (1971, May 15).
>
> Smith, C. (1975, January).

When more than one source is listed under the same author for a given year, place a small lowercase letter after the year to distinguish the sources.

> Doe, J. (1972a).
>
> Doe, J. (1972b, July 20).

## Titles

Capitalize the first word of the title of each source and all proper nouns within the title. Some titles have other formatting as well.

**Italicized titles.** Italicize titles of complete works and publications, including books, brochures, reports, TV and radio programs, CDs, and movies. *Do not italicize* titles of articles, chapters, individual TV episodes, radio segments, songs, etc.

*Civilization and its discontents.*
*A dictionary of sociology.*
*Every second counts.*
*Report on medical services.*

**Subtitles.** Place a subtitle after the main title, inserting a colon between the two. Handle subtitles like any other title—that is, only the first words and proper nouns are capitalized.

*Seeing voices: A journey into the world of the deaf.*
See Models 1, 3, 4, 24.

**Supplementary details.** For some works you'll list supplementary details in parentheses after the title, including the names of editions, volume numbers, translators, etc. You may also need to indicate the format of the source in brackets after the title. Do not italicize these details.

*Interpretation of dreams* (3rd ed., A. A. Brill, Trans.).
*The ring* (Widescreen ed.) [DVD].
*American idiot* [CD].
See Models 2, 3, 5, 14, 16, 25–31.

## Publication and Production Information

Apply the following guidelines when listing publication and production details.

| | |
|---|---|
| **Places.**   List the city of publication for books and reports. Identify also the state (or country, or province, etc.), unless the city is well known for publishing or another part of the entry clarifies the location. | Englewood Cliffs, NJ<br>London<br>Cambridge, England |
| **Publishers and organizations.**   Give the full name of the organization, but omit designations such as *Inc.*, *Co.*, and *Ltd.* | Norton<br>Oxford University Press |
| **Periodical names.**   When listing publication details for articles, capitalize all words in the periodical's name, except articles, conjunctions, and prepositions less than four letters. After the periodical name (italicized), identify the volume and issue (if any). | *Monitor on Psychology, 34*(2)<br>*USA Today*<br>*Journal of Applied<br>    Psychology, 21* |
| **Pages.**   Separate page ranges by en dashes and nonconsecutive pages by commas. | pp. 103–140<br>pp. A3, A7 |

## Online Retrieval Information

After an online source's publication information, list the date you retrieved the material and provide the URL for a Web site. You can name the site if it would not be clear from the URL. If the online source is a database, identify it, but don't provide a lengthy URL. When an entry ends with a URL, do not add a period after it.

—. Retrieved October 15, 2003, from http://archive.salon.com/
    people.com/people/feature/2002/03/28buffalo_soldiers/

—. Retrieved August 29, 2003, from Rocky Mountain College Web site,
    http://www.rocky.edu/campus/billings.html

—. Retrieved October 31, 2003, from Psychology and Behavioral
    Sciences Collection database.

—. Abstract retrieved October 20, 2002, from Social Science Abstracts
    database.

## APA MODELS 51B-1   Books, book parts, and reports

### 1. BOOK—BASIC ENTRY

|  Author  |  Date  |         |  Title  |
|----------|--------|---------|---------|

Stone, C. N. (1989). *Regime politics: Governing Atlanta 1946–1988.*

Lawrence: University Press of Kansas.

**Publication information** (Place: Publisher.)

**IN-TEXT NOTE:** (Stone, 1989, p. 78)

The basic parts of a book citation are listed above; consider also these factors:

- **Are editors listed as the primary contributors?** List them first in the entry. See Model 2.
- **Is the book or report a revised edition, part of a multi-volume set, or a numbered item in a series?** Insert edition names, volume numbers, and report IDs in parentheses after the title. Here you would list translators, as well. See Models 3, 5.
- **Are you citing only part of a book or reference work?** List the author(s) of the part first, then the book's date, and the selection's title. Next, list standard book details, inserting pages for the selection in parentheses after the title (and any edition or volume info). List names in normal order when not in the first part of the entry. See Models 4, 5, 7.
- **Are you citing a brochure or pamphlet?** Describe the work in brackets following the title. Such items may lack authors or publication information. Provide all the details you can find on the document. See Model 6.

## References

**2. BOOK—**
Edited Multi-
volume Set

Eldredge, H. W. (Ed.). (1967). *Taming megalopolis* (Vol. 2).
    New York: Doubleday.

**IN-TEXT NOTE:** Eldredge (1967) includes . . .

**3. BOOK—**
Subsequent
Edition

Philips, E. B. (1996). *City light: Urban-suburban life in
    the global society* (2nd ed.). New York: Oxford
    University Press.

**IN-TEXT NOTE:** Philips (1996) claims, " . . . " (p. 132).

**4. BOOK
CHAPTER—**
By Author

Putnam, R. D. (2000). Mobility and sprawl. In *Bowling
    alone: The collapse and revival of American
    community* (pp. 204–215). New York: Simon &
    Schuster.

**IN-TEXT NOTE:** Putnam (2000) concludes . . .

**5. REFERENCE
WORK—**Article

Rapid transit. (2002). In *Encyclopædia Britannica*
    (15th ed., Vol. 9, p. 943). Chicago: Encyclopædia
    Britannica.

**IN-TEXT NOTE:** ("Rapid Transit," 2002)

**6. BROCHURE**

Apple Computer. (2002). *Welcome to Mac OS X* [Brochure].

**IN-TEXT NOTE:** (Apple Computer, 2002)

**7. ANTHOLOGY,
COLLECTION—**
Selection in
Edited Book

Williams, O. P., Herman, H., Liebman, C. S., & Dye, T. R.
    (1988). Suburban differences and metropolitan
    policies. In R. L. Warren & L. Lyon (Eds.),
    *New perspectives on the American community*
    (pp. 214–219). Chicago: Dorsey.

**IN-TEXT NOTE:** Williams, Herman, Liebman, and Dye
(1988) find . . .

## APA MODELS 51B-2  Periodical articles

### 8. ARTICLE—BASIC ENTRY

Author    Date    Title

Matthews, J. (2003). The Philadelphia experiment.

*Education Next, 3*(1), 51–56.

**Publication information**
(Periodical Name, Volume (issue), Pages.)

**IN-TEXT NOTE:** (Matthews, 2003, p. 52)

List the author(s), date of the issue, title of the article, periodical name, volume (with issue in parentheses), and page reference (omitting the usual *p.* or *pp.*). Some details might vary, however, depending on the type of periodical being used:

- **Is the article from a journal?** List only the year for the date. Omit the issue if page numbering does not restart at 1 with each issue. See Models 8–10, 13
- **Is the article from a magazine or newsletter?** Always give the date exactly as it appears on the cover. Note that magazines often don't number volumes. See Model 8
- **Is the article from a newspaper?** For both dailies and weeklies, omit volume information and provide the abbreviation *p.* or *pp.* before page references. See Models 11, 12
- **Is the source a review, abstract, or letter to the editor?** Indicate the special form in brackets after the title, or in place of the title when none exists. See Models 13, 14

## References

**9. JOURNAL ARTICLE**—
Paged by Volume (More Than Six Authors)

Allie, S., Buffler, A., Campbell, B., Lubben, F., Evangelinos, D., Psillos, D., et al. (2003). Teaching measurement in the introductory physics laboratory. *Physics Teacher, 41*, 394–401.

**IN-TEXT NOTE:** (Allie et al., 2003)

**10. JOURNAL ARTICLE**—
Paged by Issue

Kennedy, M. (2003). Building better schools. *American School & University, 75*(5), 30–35.

**IN-TEXT NOTE:** Kennedy (2003) shows . . .

**11. NEWSPAPER ARTICLE**

Brown, L. (2002, September 28). Funding formula broken, panel told. *The Toronto Star*, p. A08.

**IN-TEXT NOTE:** Brown (2002) suggests . . .

**12. NEWSPAPER ARTICLE**—
Weekly, Unsigned

Costs mar science training plan. (2003, January 17). *Times Educational Supplement* (London), p. 4.

**IN-TEXT NOTE:** ("Costs Mar Science," 2003)

**13. BOOK REVIEW**—
Untitled

Egan, B. (2003). [Review of the book *Teaching and learning design and technology*]. *Education Review, 55*, 82–83.

**IN-TEXT NOTE:** (Egan, 2003, pp. 82–83)

**14. LETTER TO THE EDITOR**—
Untitled, Monthly Magazine

Sullivan, K. (2003, August). [Letter to the editor]. *Building Design and Construction*, 10.

**IN-TEXT NOTE:** (Sullivan, 2003)

## APA MODELS 51B-3  Web pages, online periodical articles, blogs

### 15.  WEB PAGE—UNSIGNED

Title of page    Date                    Online retrieval information

History of Billings. (2003). Retrieved August 29, 2003, from Rocky Mountain

College Web site: http://www.rocky.edu/campus/billings.html

IN-TEXT NOTE: ("History of Billings," 2003)

List the author(s), date of posting (or copyright date), the title of the page, and online retrieval information, including date viewed and address. Consider also:

- **Is the source an article from an Internet-only periodical?** Cite like a Web page, but insert the name of the periodical, volume (if any), and pages after the title. See Model 17.

- **Is the source an article from the online version of a print periodical?** If older articles are organized by issue, cite the source like a print article, inserting *[Electronic version]* after the title. See Model 18.

- **Is the source from an online database containing materials from many periodicals?** Simply provide the name of the database, rather than the online address. You can add an accession number if one is given, but you do not have to provide the URL of the online database. See Models 19, 37–39.

- **Is the source an article from a blog?** Cite like a Web page article with the current URL for the site. If the article has been archived, provide the URL for the archive. See Model 20.

## References

**16. WEB PAGE**—Untitled, Signed, Review of Movie

Cracknell, R. (2003, August 28). [Review of the movie *Northfork*]. Retrieved November 3, 2003, from http://www.theplaza.ca/moview/Films/N/ northfork.html

IN-TEXT NOTE: (Cracknell, 2003)

**17. ONLINE ARTICLE**— Internet-only Periodical

Allan, A. (2002, March 28). Buffalo soldiers. *Salon.com*, 1–4. Retrieved October 15, 2003, from http:// archive.salon.com/people/feature/2002/03/28/ buffalo_soldiers.html

IN-TEXT NOTE: (Allan, 2002)

**18. ONLINE ARTICLE**— Same as Print

Dittman, M. (2003, June). Maintaining ethics in a rural setting [Electronic version]. *Monitor on Psychology, 34*(6), 66.

IN-TEXT NOTE: (Dittman, 2003)

**19. DATABASE**— Article

Walker, G. J., Deng, J., & Dieser, R. B. (2001, October). Ethnicity, acculturation, self-construal, and motivations for outdoor recreation. *Leisure Sciences, 23*, 263–283. Retrieved October 31, 2003, from Psychology and Behavioral Sciences Collection database.

IN-TEXT NOTE: (Walker, Deng, & Dieser, 2001, p. 263)

**20. BLOG**— Entry from Archive

Postrel, V. (2006, March 26). The box that changed the world. *Dynamist.com*. Retrieved August 15, 2006, from http://www.vpostrel.com/weblog/archives/ index.html

IN-TEXT NOTE: (Postrel, 2006)

## APA MODELS 51B-4 Other online sources

### 21. ONLINE GOVERNMENT REPORT

| Author | Date | Title of report |
|---|---|---|

Texas Department of Transportation. (2003). *1–10 East corridor*

*study—El Paso, Texas.* Retrieved October 20, 2003, from http://

**Online retrieval information**

www.dot.state.tx.us/elp/mis/i10east/project.htm

**IN-TEXT NOTE:** (Texas Department of Transportation [TDOT], 2003)

Other online documents have slightly different formats:

- **Is the source an online report or book?** Italicize the title of the source, just as you would a print source, but list online retrieval details instead of place and publisher. Cite parts of the document by placing the title of the section (article, chapter, etc.) before the report's title—but don't italicize the part's title. See Models 21, 22.

- **Is the source an online abstract from an online database or library subscription service?** Cite an online abstract as you would cite the document described in the abstract, but begin the retrieval statement with the phrase *Abstract retrieved from.* . . . See Models 23, 24.

- **Is the source a posting to an online discussion?** List author, posting date, and subject line, followed by the message identifier (in brackets) and the URL of the forum (preceded by the phrase *Message posted to* . . .). See Model 25.

## References

**22. ONLINE BOOK PART**—Unsigned, from Online Reference

Commerce Clause. (2003). In *Britannica Concise Encyclopædia*. Retrieved October 18, 2003, from http://www.britannica.com/ebc/article?eu=386538

IN-TEXT NOTE: ("Commerce Clause," 2003)

**23. ONLINE ABSTRACT**—For Article, from Database

Cox, B. S., Cox, A. B., & Cox, D. J. (2000). Motivating signage prompts safety belt use. *Journal of Applied Behavior Analysis, 33*, 635–638. Abstract retrieved October 20, 2002, from Social Science Abstracts database.

IN-TEXT NOTE: (Cox, Cox, & Cox, 2000)

**24. ONLINE ABSTRACT**—For Book, from Database

Groegor, J. A. (2000). *Understanding driving: Applying cognitive psychology to a complex everyday task.* Philadelphia: Psychology Press. Abstract retrieved October 10, 2003, from PsycINFO database.

IN-TEXT NOTE: Groegor (2000) studies . . .

**25. ONLINE POSTING**—No Subject Line

Olson, F. M., III. (2003, October 16). [Msg. 4]. Message posted to http://yourturn.npr.org/cgi-bin/WebX?230@112.UaIsajPkfPR.43901@.1dd0664c

IN-TEXT NOTE: (Olson, 2003)

## APA MODELS 51B-5  Special formats: CDs, films, and broadcasts

#### 26. VIDEOTAPE OR FILM

| Author | Date | Title |
| --- | --- | --- |

Pennebaker, D. A. (Director). (1997). *Monterey pop* [Videotape].

United States: Rhino. (Original date, 1967)

**Publication information**

**IN-TEXT NOTE:** Pennebaker (1967/1997) documents . . .

Recorded media, broadcast programs, and brochures should all be cited by indicating the format of the source within brackets after the title. Note that many of these formats don't have typical kinds of authors:

- **Are you citing a film?** Give scriptwriters, directors, and producers primary credit. List the format as [*Motion picture*] if viewed in a movie theater. See Models 26, 29.
- **Are you citing a music recording?** List first the name given on the byline of the recording. If citing a specific song, list the songwriter first, the song's copyright date, the song's title, and the person recording the song (if not the songwriter) in brackets, all before giving the details for the full recording. See Models 27, 28.
- **Are you citing a broadcast program?** List producers, directors, and scriptwriters first. If applicable, name a specific episode before the program title. See Models 30, 31.

## References

**27. AUDIO RECORDING**

Big Brother and the Holding Company. (2002). *Live in San Francisco 1966* [CD]. Studio City, CA: Verèse Sarabande.

IN-TEXT NOTE: (Big Brother and the Holding Company, 1966/2002)

**28. AUDIO RECORDING**—Specific Song, Not Recorded by Author

Cropper, S., & Redding, O. (1967). (Sittin' on) the dock of the bay [Recorded by M. Bolton]. On *The hunger* [CD]. United States: Sony. (1987)

IN-TEXT NOTE: Cropper and Redding (1967) wrote . . .

**29. FILM**—Theatrical Release

Crowe, C. (Writer/Director/Producer), & Bryce, I. (Producer). (2000). *Almost famous* [Motion picture]. United States: Dreamworks.

IN-TEXT NOTE: (Crowe & Bryce, 2000)

**30. RADIO BROADCAST**

King Biscuit Entertainment (Producer). (2003, July 6). *King Biscuit flower hour* [Radio program]. Santa Rosa, CA: KMGG.

IN-TEXT NOTE: (King Biscuit Entertainment, 2003)

**31. TELEVISION SHOW**—Specific Episode

Kuhn, R. L. (Creator/Host), & Fefernan, L. (Director/Producer). (2003, May 13). What makes music so significant? [Television series episode]. In L. Fefernan *Closer to the truth*. Los Angeles: KCET.

IN-TEXT NOTE: (Kuhn & Fefernan, 2003)

## APA MODELS 51B-6  Academic reports and publications

### 32.  RESEARCH OR TECHNICAL REPORT

|        Author        |      Date      |      Title      |

National Endowment for the Arts. (2004). *Reading at risk: A survey of*

*literary reading in America* (Research Division Report #46).

Washington, DC: Author.    **Publication information**

**IN-TEXT NOTE:** (National Endowment for the Arts [NEA], 2004, p. 3)

Academic documents such as reports, conference papers, and dissertations may have special features when listed on a References page.

- **Are you citing a report prepared by a group or agency?** When no individual authors are given, list the agency or institution as the author of the report. If the report is part of a series, identify the series within parentheses as it is given on the title page. If the agency responsible for the report also published it, give "Author" as the publisher. See Model 32.
- **Are you citing a paper delivered at an academic conference?** Academic papers read at conferences but not subsequently published may be cited simply by identifying the meeting and location. See Model 33.
- **Are you citing a paper published in the proceedings of a conference?** Identify the paper and then give the title of the proceedings or publication following "In." Identify the editor if one is given. See Model 34.
- **Are you citing an unpublished dissertation or thesis?** Most dissertations are listed in *Dissertation Abstracts International* (DAI) and published by University Microfilms International (UMI). Those not yet in this service are cited by title and institution—with the title of the work in italics. See Model 35.
- **Are you citing a published dissertation or thesis?** Dissertations listed in *Dissertation Abstracts International* (DAI) and available via UMI are considered published. Provide both the DAI listing (volume/issue/page number) and the order number from UMI. The title of the dissertation is not italicized. See Model 36.

## References

**33. CONFERENCE PAPER—** Unpublished

Tebeaux, E. (2005, March). *The evolution of technical writing: From text to visual text in applied discourse.* Paper presented at the annual meeting of the Conference on College Composition and Communication, San Francisco.

**IN-TEXT NOTE:** Tebeaux (2005) explains . . .

**34. CONFERENCE PAPER—** Published in Proceedings

Matthews, T., Fong, J., & Mankoff, J. (2005). Visualizing non-speech sounds for the deaf. In *Assets 2005. The seventh international ACM SIGACCESS conference on computers and accessibility* (pp. 52–59). New York: ACM Press.

**IN-TEXT NOTE:** (Matthews, Fong, & Mankoff, 2005)

**35. DISSERTATION—** Unpublished

Kinkade, J. (2005). *Samuel Johnson's Rambler and the invention of self-help literature.* Unpublished doctoral dissertation, University of Texas, Austin.

**IN-TEXT NOTE:** (Kinkade, 2005)

**36. DISSERTATION—** Published

Anderson, V. (1997). Unpersuasive truths: Critical theory, pedagogy, and democratic education. *Dissertation Abstracts International 59* (01), 154. (UMI No. 9822533)

**IN-TEXT NOTE:** Anderson (1997) argues . . .

## APA MODELS 51B-7 Sources from library subscription services

### 37. LIBRARY SERVICE—ARTICLE

Author            Date      Title

Gosling, S., Vazire, S., Srivastava, S., & John, O. P. (2004). Should we trust Web-based studies? A comparative analysis of six preconceptions about Internet questionnaires. *American Psychologist, 59*, 93–104.

Publication information

Retrieved May 29, 2006, from PsycINFO database.

Database

**IN-TEXT NOTE:** (Gosling, Vazire, Srivastava, & John, 2004, p. 97)

Many writers now gain access to materials from information services to which their local or school libraries subscribe, such as LexisNexis, Gale, or EBSCO. Such services typically offer a full menu of databases. But APA style does not require any special information when using such services, beyond providing the date the material was accessed and the name of the database.

- **Are you citing an online article?** To cite an article you find in a library subscription database, provide author, date, title of the article, and complete publication information. Then explain when and where the information was found. You can provide additional information if helpful, including an item or accession number. But you need not supply a lengthy URL. See Model 37.
- **Are you citing a magazine article from a subscription service?** Treat the magazine as you would a print item. But also furnish the date of access and the name of the database used. See Model 38.
- **Are you citing a newspaper source?** How you identify the database may vary. You can cite a general database such as LexisNexis or provide the URL of the newspaper you searched: http://www.nytimes.com. See Model 39.
- **Are you citing an online encyclopedia?** Many libraries subscribe to online encyclopedias or reference works. Cite the entry you have consulted and provide a date of access and URL. The *Britannica Online* usually provides a preferred URL. See Model 40.

# References

**38. LIBRARY SERVICE—** Magazine Article

Harrison, B. R. (2005, September 15). Phantom of the bayou. *Natural History*, 18–52. Retrieved March 15, 2006, from Academic Search Premier database.

**IN-TEXT NOTE:** Harrison (2005) reports . . .

**39. LIBRARY SERVICE—** Newspaper Article

Toner, M. (2005, October 13). Back to the moon. *Atlanta Journal-Constitution*. Retrieved May 11, 2006, from LexisNexis database.

**IN-TEXT NOTE:** (Toner, 2005)

Leeds, J. (2005, December 14). It's star wars on satellite radio. *The New York Times*. Retrieved April 1, 2006, from http://www.nytimes.com

**IN-TEXT NOTE:** Leeds (2005) reports . . .

**40. LIBRARY SERVICE—** Encyclopedia Entry

Schnauzer. (2006). In *Encyclopaedia Britannica*. Retrieved May 29, 2006, from Encyclopædia Britannica Online at http://search.eb.com/eb/article-9066176

**IN-TEXT NOTE:** ("Schnauzer," 2006)

# 51c Sample Empirical Research Paper—APA

The following APA-style research report was written by Jessica Carfolite at the University of South Carolina. In structure and language, it represents the kind of essay routinely prepared in psychology courses: it includes a title page, an abstract, a statement of hypothesis, sections explaining method and results, a formal discussion section, references, and two tables. Carfolite's paper assumes that readers will be familiar with many technical terms and statistical procedures, as well as various research conventions in the field. Not every part of the paper will be easily accessible to every reader, but that is often the case with research in various scientific disciplines.

---

### Checklist 51.1 Parts of a Research Report—APA

When presenting the results of an empirical study, divide your paper into the following sections. Provide a header at the beginning of each section. Each header should be centered on a separate line. You can also create subsections (see, for example, the Method section in the sample paper), which should begin with an italicized header (on a separate line) aligned to the left-hand margin. Note that some sections should start on a new page.

**a. Title page.** This page presents the title of the study and identifies the researchers and their affiliations. It is always page 1. (See also Checklist 51.2.)

**b. Abstract.** The abstract is a concise summary of the paper. Start the abstract on a separate page. It is always page 2. (See also Checklist 51.3.)

**c. Introduction.** The introduction is the first section of the main text of the paper. In this section you present your hypothesis and a review of literature related to your study. Unlike the other sections, don't begin the introduction with a header—instead, repeat the title of the paper you placed on the title page. Start this section on page 3.

**d. Method.** This section provides a detailed description of the procedures used in the research. Because the validity of the research depends on how the data were gathered, this is a critical section for

*(Continued)*

**Parts of a Research Report—APA**    *(Continued)*

readers assessing the report. Don't start this section on a new page—start this section on the line immediately following the Introduction section.

**e. Results.** This section reports the data, often given through figures, charts, graphs, and so on. The reliability of the data is explained here, but little comment is made on the study's implications. Don't start this section on a new page—start this section on the line immediately following the Method section.

**f. Discussion/Conclusions.** Here you analyze and interpret the data presented in the Results section. Don't start this section on a new page—start this section on the line immediately following the Results section.

**g. References.** As covered in Section 51b, this section is an alphabetized list of research materials cited in the report. Begin this section on a new page. (See also Checklist 51.5.)

**h. Appendixes.** Provide, in consecutively lettered appendixes, materials germane to the study but too lengthy to include in the body of the paper. You might, for example, provide a copy of a questionnaire you presented to participants in Appendix A, provide a copy of your consent form in Appendix B, and so on.

**Checklist 51.2 Formatting the Title Page—APA**

APA style requires a separate title page; use the facing page as a model and apply the following guidelines:

a. **Choose an effective title.** Don't state the obvious, that you're presenting the results of a study. Instead, state the key variables you're researching.

b. **Present the title of your paper, centered, on the upper half of the page.** Capitalize all words *except* articles (*a*, *an*, and *the*), prepositions, and conjunctions that are shorter than four letters.

c. **List your first name, middle initial, and last name, centered under the title.**

d. **List your institutional affiliation under your name, centered on the page.**

e. **Make sure the title page is numbered like the rest of your paper.** The page header should include (aligned to the right) a shortened title of the paper (two or three words) and the page number *1*. Separate the page number and shortened title by five spaces.

f. **For an article that will be published,** indicate at the top of the page what the running head for the essay should be in all caps. Running heads should not exceed fifty characters.

g. **Repeat the title at the top of the first page of the body of the paper.** Center the title on the top line(s) of the first page of the body of the paper.

1/2 inch

Assessing Social Skills Measurements          1

5 spaces

Assessing Social Skills Measurements in

Middle School Students

Jessica Carfolite

University of South Carolina

---

**Checklist 51.3   Creating an Abstract—APA**

Abstracts are common in papers using APA style and are required for articles submitted for publication.

a. **Place the abstract on a separate page after the title page.** This page should have the same spacing and margins as the rest of the document.

b. **Make sure the running head and correct page number (2) appear at the top of the page.**

c. **Insert the heading "Abstract" on the first line of the body of the page.** Start the paragraph containing the abstract on the following line.

d. **Do not indent the first line of the abstract.** Present the paragraph containing the abstract in block form, unlike paragraphs in the body of the paper.

e. **Summarize the paper accurately and concisely (120 or fewer words).** To be accurate, avoid discussing material not treated in the body of the paper. Also, avoid using abbreviations or references that aren't clear within the abstract itself—which is usually intended to be read as a stand-alone description of the paper. Describe in the abstract the problem or issue treated, the type of research used, and conclusions drawn from the study.

## Abstract

This study investigates the validity of the newly developed Social Activities Questionnaire (SAQ) for measuring children's social skills relative to an established measure, the Social Skills Rating System (SSRS). Based on data from 34 middle-school students and their parents who were participating in an after-school program for children with learning or behavior problems, the SAQ was found to have small-to-moderate correlations with the widely used SSRS. However, unlike the SSRS, the SAQ showed moderate correlations with children's grade point averages in school, which research suggests is an important predictor of children's social success. This study suggests the SAQ is a promising measurement tool that should be subjected to further development and validation studies with larger and more diverse samples.

## Checklist 51.4    Document Formatting—APA

a. **Use white, 8½-by-11-inch bond paper with at least 1-inch margins.** You can easily set margins by adjusting the document's Page Setup.

b. **Use 12-point Times, American Typewriter, or Courier font faces** when available. If not available, use a readable font.

c. **Double-space the entire document.** This includes the References page and title page. In certain circumstances you may use single spacing to improve readability—for example, with tables, captions, and extended block quotations.

d. **Indent the first word of each paragraph one-half inch.** Note that the Abstract and the References pages do not follow this standard indentation.

e. **Left-align the body of the paper and do not hyphenate words at line breaks.**

f. **Insert a shortened title for your paper and consecutive page numbers one-half inch from the top of *every* page, aligned to the right.** The best way to achieve this is to insert a running page header.

1/2 inch

1 inch    Assessing Social Skills Measurements    3

Assessing Social Skills Measurements
in Middle School Students

Effective social functioning can be a protective factor for students struggling with successful middle school adjustment. Social Skills Training (SST) intervention to improve a child's functioning is often employed, but it repeatedly fails to attain generalization (Gresham, 1998). One of the limitations in prior research on SST programs is the lack of empirically valid tools to measure social functioning. To address this issue, this study investigates the validity of the newly developed Social Activities Questionnaire (SAQ). This paper begins by addressing the complex and often ambiguous definition of social skills. It then explains the importance of social competence to children in the middle school age group. It also describes problems with past measurement tools and the recently proposed development of a Social Activities Questionnaire (SAQ). Finally, the introduction states the hypotheses for this study.

*Importance of Social Functioning*

Repeatedly, researchers have found evidence that poor peer adjustment can put children at risk for later difficulties in life. Peer interactions affect the development of social competence, and, if children are not accepted by peers, they are more likely to lack key social competencies (Parker & Asher, 1987). Conversely, positive peer relations may buffer the other vulnerabilities children experience. For instance, research shows that peer acceptance, as well as the number and quality of friendships, relates to

1 inch

Assessing Social Skills Measurements     4

loneliness and depression in children (Nagle & Erdley, 2001).

Research on social competence in schools has found lower

substance abuse and a decrease in aggression and emotional

distress among socially skilled students (Hartup, 1996).

Because social skills lessen the day-to-day frustrations

adolescents face in schools, it is not surprising that they might

also enhance academic performance. Social skills create a "social

context" for learning by providing rules and role expectations for

students. As a result, social skills can facilitate academic success

by working in tandem with learning goals (Maleki & Elliott, 2002).

But it is not necessarily social competence that leads to academic

competence. It is possible that academic competence leads to

social competence. Welsh, Parke, Widaman, and O'Neil (2001)

found that academic competence in first grade influenced second

grade social competence. Thus there is probably a reciprocal

relationship between social competence and academic

performance. Success in one arena likely promotes success in the

other. Conversely, problems with teachers and peers might

obstruct learning, while difficulties in academics might create a

stigma that causes social problems.

*Defining Social Skills*

Despite the hundreds of published studies on the topic, there

is no general consensus on what constitutes "social skills" and

how they should be measured in children. Several studies have

defined social skills in terms of peer acceptance or popularity

(Asher, Oden, & Gottman, 1977). These definitions do not actually

---

When multiple authors are named outside parentheses, "and" is used instead of &.

Problems defining "social skills," a key term, are examined.

Assessing Social Skills Measurements 5

target the social skills themselves, but the outcome of using them. Other studies define social skills by actual behavior, such as the ability to start a conversation, make a joke, or resist the urge to interrupt mid-conversation (Foster & Ritchey, 1979). Still others look at a combination of social behaviors and levels of peer acceptance (Asher, 1978).

Social validity, a term coined by Gresham (1998), defines social skills as socially significant behaviors exhibited in specific situations that predict important social outcomes. These outcomes might include friendships, teacher and parent acceptance, and even school adjustment. Gresham's emphasis on establishing the social validity of interpersonal behaviors helps to focus social skills measurement and intervention on specific behaviors and outcomes important for current and future functioning.

*Development of the SAQ*

The SAQ was designed to measure outcomes of social skills training. The SAQ questions are direct, short, and easy to answer. A parent completes a report of 12 items about the social activities of his or her child. Items were selected based on a combination of practical experiences, mostly social outcome-related treatment goals, in the Challenging Horizons Program (CHP). The final version of the SAQ was refined by suggestions made by the research staff of faculty advisors, graduate students, CHP counselors, and parents at James Madison University. This study is one of the first empirical tests of the SAQ.

Another key term is defined.

Assessing Social Skills Measurements    6

*Statement of Hypotheses*

       The purpose of this study is to explore the predictive validity of the Social Activities Questionnaire (SAQ). It is expected that the SAQ and the SSRS should moderately correlate, and these scales should also predict grade point average (GPA) and disciplinary referrals among children.

Headings at this level are centered.

                              Method

Headings at this level are flush left and italicized.

*Participants*

       The participants of this study were the 34 middle school students and 34 parents who completed and returned the survey packet. The sample was taken from the Challenging Horizons Program, an after-school program for students with AD/HD at Hand Middle School and Crayton Middle School in Columbia, South Carolina. Approximately 47% of the students in the study had screened positive for AD/HD, based on rating scales completed by parents or due to a parent's report that the student had previously been clinically diagnosed with AD/HD.

This section supplies important data about participants.

       Crayton Middle School has approximately 936 students in grades 6–8. The racial distribution is 45% black, 50% white, and 6% other, with 46% of the students living at or below the poverty level. Hand Middle School has approximately 958 students in grades 6–8. The racial distribution is 50% black, 47% white, and 3% other. Nearly half of the students live at or below the poverty level. The gender distribution for the study was 70.5% male and 29.5% female. For the study, the grade distribution was 50% sixth grade, 44% seventh grade, and 6% eighth grade.

Assessing Social Skills Measurements    7

*Measures*

The measures in this study consisted of (1) the Social Activities Questionnaire, (2) the Social Skills Rating System for Parents, (3) the Social Skills Rating System for Students, (4) Grade Point Averages for the 2004–2005 school year, and (5) disciplinary referrals for the 2004–2005 school year.

*SAQ.* The Social Activities Questionnaire (SAQ) is designed to be an objective measure of adolescent social activities with peers. Question 1 asks the actual number of friends with the criteria that they be "within 2 years of the child's age, not related to the child and that they spend time with the child outside of school, at least once a month." Question 2 inquires how many children live within walking distance of the child's home; it is used for interpretive value. The following 9 questions ask about specific activities and the rate of those activities, for example: "My child invites friends over _____ times in a typical month," or "My child participated in _____ organized activities over the past year."

Other SAQ questions describe the quality of interactions during these activities, for example: "The time my child spends with friends often ends with one or both children angry" or "Some of my child's friends use alcohol, tobacco, or other prohibited substances." The final item asks about the percentage of time the child spends alone, with friends, and with family. The SAQ is an experimental measure with no published reliability or validity studies.

Details about the SAQ are provided, including sample questions.

Assessing Social Skills Measurements  8

The SSRS
questionnaire
is explained.

*SSRS.* The Social Skills Rating System (Gresham & Elliott, 1990) provides components for teachers, parents, and students to evaluate student social behaviors. These components can be used separately or together. For practical reasons related to the challenges of getting teacher data, this study used only the parent and student versions. The questionnaire is broken into five subscales that make up the total social skills score. Both the SSRS-Parent and SSRS-Student measure cooperation, assertion, and self-control. The SSRS-Parent version also measures responsibility and the SSRS-Student version also measures empathy. Research supports the reliability (.77 to .84 for parents; .52 to .66 of students) and validity for this Social Skills Rating System (Gresham & Elliott, 1990).

*Procedures*

Permission was granted through Richland One School District to administer the SSRS-Student version to the students of the Challenging Horizons Program. After the students completed the SSRS-Student version, they were given a packet to take home to be filled out by a parent or guardian. Each packet included a self-addressed stamped envelope, the SAQ, the Social Skills Rating System, and a letter explaining the forms within the packet. The participants were asked to mail the two forms back in the stamped envelope provided or to send it back with their children. Each child that filled out an SSRS-Student version received a small candy, and each child that returned a completed packet received a large candy bar of his or her choice.

Assessing Social Skills Measurements          9

*Data Analysis*

This section presents statistical details requiring technical expertise.

The hypothesis, which asks whether there might be correlations between the social skills scores, GPA, and the number of disciplinary referrals, was tested with bivariate correlations with a statistical significance level of $p = .05$ (see Tables 1 and 2). It is noteworthy that this study had low statistical power. Specifically, the power to find a small to moderate size correlation (i.e., $r = 0.20$; according to Cohen's conventions) was only .30 (with a directional alpha of .05). Given this low power, these non-significant statistical findings might be a series of Type II errors. Therefore, it is worthwhile to examine effect sizes. Because correlations with an absolute value greater than .20 were considered large enough to be interesting, these correlations are highlighted in Tables 1 and 2.

Tables appear at the end of the paper.

*Results*

While it was hypothesized that GPA and disciplinary records would correlate with both social skills scales, none were statistically significant. However, there were correlations greater than .20, which are highlighted in boldface type in Tables 1 and 2. When examining the predictive power of the SSRS and SAQ for Grade Point Average and Disciplinary Referrals, it appears that the SAQ items 9 and 10 were correlated with Grade Point Average correlations (see Table 1). In addition, the SAQ detects a positive correlation between question 10, "Some of my child's closest friends use alcohol, tobacco, or other prohibited substances" and the number of disciplinary referrals (see Table 1). Table 2 shows

Note that the results do not support the initial hypothesis.

that the SSRS does not have those same predictive features for GPA and disciplinary referrals.

## Discussion

This is a preliminary investigation into the construct validity of the Social Activities Questionnaire (SAQ), which is designed to measure important social behaviors of middle school children. While it was hypothesized that the SAQ and the SSRS rating scales would be moderately correlated, at first glance, the data support little to no convergent validity between these scales. In addition, the failure to find statistically significant correlations between these scales, GPA, and disciplinary referrals raises questions about the concurrent validity of the SAQ and the SSRS.

It is important to note that, as stated in the data analysis plan, this study was limited by low statistical power and, therefore, it may be appropriate to examine effect sizes. Indeed, examining the effect size does show some interesting results. Most notable were the positive correlations between the GPA scores and the scores on the SAQ, especially since the SSRS did not show correlations between the two. This suggests that the SAQ may be more ecologically valid than the SSRS because it is a better predictive tool for a critically important variable, GPA.

This study was limited by a small sample size, and future research should have a larger sample and a much larger and more diverse population. Despite these weaknesses, the study does provide unique information about a new social skills assessment

Assessing Social Skills Measurements     11

tool. Although the results of this study are modest, there are
indications this SAQ might be an even better tool for predictor
variables like GPA than are scales like the SSRS.

In future studies, it is recommended that the users of the
SAQ consider some modifications. For instance, it would be
helpful to have the parents indicate their level of confidence in
each question. This type of question, and other questions, might be
used to create an index of parental monitoring, which has been
shown to be an important predictor of outcomes in middle school
students. It would also improve the questionnaire to inquire about
the availability of activities for the student and to create indices
that look at the ratio of engagement in available activities. These
recommended additions might improve the overall assessment of
the SAQ.

The article concludes by suggesting future research needs and opportunities.

**Checklist 51.5 Formatting Reference Pages—APA**

Begin the References list on a separate page. Use the same formatting you used for the rest of the document, including double-spaced paragraphs, headers at the top of the page (with numbers and a shortened version of the paper's title), and 1-inch margins. But make the following adjustments:

a. **Center the title "References" at the top of the page.** If the list of entries runs over to a new page, do not repeat this title at the top.

b. **Create a one-half-inch or 5- to 7-space hanging indentation for each entry.** In other words, the first line should be aligned with the left margin, and subsequent lines in an individual entry should be indented. (You can create hanging indentations easily by adjusting the paragraph settings for this page.)

c. **List all sources referenced in the body of the paper.** See Section 51a-1 for a list of sources that don't need to appear on the References page. Don't list sources you viewed but don't reference in the body of your paper.

d. **Alphabetize the list according to the first word in each entry—** excluding articles (*A, An,* and *The*). When an individual appears first for entries as both single author and co-author, place the single-author entries first, alphabetizing subsequent entries by the second (or third, or fourth, if necessary) co-author.

e. **Proof carefully your punctuation and capitalization for each entry.** Review the guidelines for formatting individual entries. Pay close attention to the punctuation and capitalization used in the models in Section 51b-1–7.

Assessing Social Skills Measurements    12

References

Asher, S. (1978). Children's peer relations. In M. Lamb (Ed.), *Social and personality development*. New York: Holt, Rinehart, & Winston.

Asher, S. R., Oden, S. L., & Gottman, J. M. (1977). Children's friendship in school settings. In L. G. Katz (Ed.), *Current topics in early childhood education* (Vol. 1, pp. 32–61). Norwood, NJ: Ablex.

Cohen, J. (1992). A power primer. *Psychological Bulletin, 112,* 155–159.

Foster, S. L., & Ritchey, W. L. (1979). Issues in the assessment of social competence in children. *Journal of Applied Behavior Analysis, 12,* 625–638.

Gresham, F. (1998). Social skills training: Should we raze, remodel, or rebuild? *Behavioral Disorders, 24,* 19–25.

Gresham, F., & Elliott, S. (1990). *Social skills rating system manual.* Circle Pines, MN: American Guidance Service.

Gresham, F., Sugai, G., & Horner, R. (2001). Interpreting outcomes of social skills training for students with high-incidence disabilities. [Electronic version]. *Exceptional Children, 67,* 331–344.

Hartup, W. W. (1996). The company they keep: Friendships and their developmental significance. *Child Development, 67,* 1–13.

Note that volume numbers of journals are italicized, as are the surrounding commas. Page numbers are not italicized.

This source is online, but identical to the printed version. In such a case, the URL is not required.

Maleki, C., & Elliott, S. (2002). Children's social behaviors as

predictors of academic achievement: A longitudinal

analysis. *School Psychology Quarterly, 17,* 1–23.

Nagle, D., & Erdley, C. (Eds). (2001). The role of friendship in

psychological adjustment. [Special issue]. *New directions

for child and adolescent development; 2001*(91).

Parker, J., & Asher, S. (1987). Peer relations and later personal

adjustment: Are low-accepted children at risk?

*Psychological Bulletin, 102,* 357–389.

Welsh, M., Parke, R., Widaman, K., & O'Neil, R. (2001). Linkages

between children's social and academic competence: A

longitudinal analysis. *Journal of School Psychology, 39,*

463–481.

This item refers to the entire issue of a journal paginated issue-by-issue. No page numbers are given but an issue number is included within parentheses.

Table 1

*Grade Point Average and Disciplinary Referrals and Social Activities Questionnaire*

| SAQ questions | GPA | Disciplinary referrals |
|---|---|---|
| 1. Friends not related, within 2 years, spends time once a month | **0.20** | −0.06 |
| 2. # of children within 2 years of age, within walking distance | 0.03 | −0.06 |
| 3. Invites friends over X times in a month | −0.08 | 0.12 |
| 4. Spends time with friends X times in a month | 0.11 | 0.10 |
| 5. Participates in X activities in the past year | **0.30** | −0.02 |
| 6. Number of leadership roles in these activities | 0.11 | 0.08 |
| 7. Amount of time on the phone | **−0.23** | 0.15 |
| 8. Amount of time instant messaging (ICQ, AOL) | −0.10 | 0.12 |
| 9. Frequency of time spent with friends with one or both children angry | **−0.25** | 0.01 |
| 10. Frequency of friends who use alcohol, tobacco, or like substances | **−0.34** | **0.27** |
| 11. Frequency of friends who are in trouble with authority | −0.32 | 0.16 |
| Free Time Alone | **0.38** | **−0.34** |
| Free Time Friends | −0.08 | 0.11 |
| Free Time Family | −0.16 | −0.03 |

*Note.* Values are Pearson Product Moment Correlation Coefficients. All $p$ values were greater than .05 ($df = 33$). Correlations with an absolute value greater than .20 are printed in boldface type.

Table 2

*Parent and Student Social Skills Rating System and GPA and Disciplinary Referrals*

| | Parent cooper-ation | Parent assertion | Parent self-control | Parent responsi-bility | Parent standard score |
|---|---|---|---|---|---|
| DR | 0.16 | 0.00 | 0.13 | −0.15 | 0.01 |
| GPA | 0.14 | **0.20** | 0.07 | 0.17 | 0.12 |

| | Student cooper-ation | Student assertion | Student empathy | Student self-control | Student standard score |
|---|---|---|---|---|---|
| DR | 0.14 | 0.04 | 0.10 | **0.25** | 0.01 |
| GPA | 0.15 | **0.24** | 0.17 | 0.04 | 0.18 |

*Note.* Values are Pearson Product Moment Correlation Coefficients. All $p$ values were greater than .05 ($df = 33$). Correlations with an absolute value greater than .20 are printed in boldface type.

# Directory to CMS Notes—by Type

(See inside back cover for alphabetical directory.)

# 52  How Do You Use CMS Documentation?

Writers who prefer full footnotes or endnotes for their projects (rather than in-text notes) often use the humanities style of documentation recommended in *The Chicago Manual of Style* (15th ed., 2003), now also available in a searchable online version. Basic procedures for the CMS documentary-note system are spelled out in the following sections. If you encounter documentation or formatting problems not discussed here, consult the full CMS manual or *A Manual for Writers of Term Papers, Theses, and Dissertations* (6th ed., 1996) by Kate L. Turabian, which, though not updated to reflect the latest CMS citation guidelines, is still used by many colleges to set formatting requirements for formal papers.

> **e-Tips**
>
> Do you have specific questions about Chicago style or more general queries about editing? Check out the splendid Q&A page supported by the manuscript editing department at the University of Chicago Press. Go to the University of Chicago Press site <http://www.press.uchicago.edu/> and then look for the link to the *Chicago Manual of Style* site.

## 52a  How does CMS documentation work?

Whereas MLA and APA styles use *in-text notes* together with *works-cited* or *references* lists to document outside sources (see Chapters 50 and 51), CMS style uses *footnotes* or *endnotes*. Footnotes offer a fairly simple and traditional method of citation. A raised, or *superscript*, reference number (like this[2]) appears in the body of the paper where a writer quotes from, borrows from, or refers to another's work. These superscript numbers in the body of the paper then correspond to numbered notes that appear at the bottom of a page. The notes include all bibliographic information necessary to identify outside sources, as well as page numbers to direct readers to specific locations in these items. No separate bibliography page is necessary—though one may be included (see Section 52d).

Writers using CMS may have the option of using *endnotes*. Endnotes work like footnotes except notes appear at the end of the paper rather than in the footer of each page. Footnotes tend to work better for longer papers because endnotes require readers to flip to the end of the document to view details for each source. We provide guidelines that apply to both endnotes and footnotes, but Chicago style discourages endnotes. Consult with your instructor to determine whether one type of note is preferred over the other for a particular paper.

## 52b How do you use CMS footnotes and endnotes?

There are two kinds of notes: *reference notes* that acknowledge the use of outside sources and *content notes* that add supplementary material and commentary to the paper. This chapter focuses on *reference notes*, which are necessary for proper citation. (Use content notes to include information you regard as important, but that might derail the train of thought if it were run in the main text.) Whether using reference notes, content notes, or both, number them all consecutively according to their order of appearance in the body of the paper.

### ● 1 Insert a raised note number after each passage you cite.
To insert the number, use your word processor's footnote or endnote feature, which will not only format the raised number correctly (in *superscript* typestyle), but will also automatically number and renumber notes to ensure that they are ordered consecutively throughout the paper. Place the note number after the material being documented, either at the end of the sentence or at the first natural pause after the borrowed material. As you can see in the following example, note numbers appear outside end quotation marks:

> Ralph Bunche never wavered in his belief that the races in America
> had to learn to live together: "In all of his experience of racial
> discrimination Bunche never allowed himself to become bitter."[3] . . .

You may also briefly identify sources in the body of your paper, especially as you introduce quotations, paraphrased passages, or borrowed ideas. Readers will appreciate the smooth transitions between your own words and those of other writers. Consult Section 47a for more on how to introduce quotations effectively.

### ● 2 Document a source fully in the first note it is mentioned.

Whether you use endnotes or footnotes, provide full bibliographic details for a source the first time you cite it. After the full citation, give a page reference (preceded by a comma) to the relevant passage in the source:

> 3. Brian Urquhart, *Ralph Bunche: An American Life* (New York: Norton, 1993), 435.

Note: You don't always need a page reference in your note—for example, when you simply mention a source, rather than a specific passage within it. But *always* provide specific location references (as specific as possible) when you quote from or paraphrase another person's writing.

### ● 3 Shorten subsequent notes for sources you've already fully documented.

You don't need to provide all the publication details for a source already introduced to readers. Instead, simply mention the last name of the author, a shortened title (four or fewer words), and a page reference.

> 4. Helen Wilkinson, "It's Just a Matter of Time," *Utne Reader*, May/June 1995, 67.

> 5. Urquhart, *Ralph Bunche*, 177.

> 6. Wilkinson, "Matter of Time," 66.

This shortened format is sometimes used when a full bibliography is provided at the end of the paper. (See Section 52d.) Readers can use the last name and title to look up a works-cited entry that contains full citation details for a source. Consult the requirements of your paper to determine whether a bibliography is required and whether shortened notes are accepted.

Finally, you can shorten references to the same source in consecutive notes by using the Latin abbreviation *Ibid.* ("from the same place"):

> 7. Simon Singh, *The Code Book: The Science of Secrecy from Ancient Egypt to Quantum Cryptography* (New York: Anchor Books, 1999), 293.

> 8. Ibid., 303–304.

**● 4 Use in-text parenthetical notes for numerous citations of one source.** To cite multiple passages from one source, you may use a string of *Ibid.* notes. But consider using in-text parenthetical notes instead, especially when repeatedly citing well-known works (sacred texts, etc.) that are identified by standard abbreviations and numbering schemes. Simply provide full bibliographic details for the edition you're using in the first note, along with the abbreviation you will use in-text.

> 9. William Shakespeare, *Measure for Measure*, in *The Complete Works of Shakespeare*, 4th ed., ed. David Bevington (New York: Longman, 1997), act 1, sc. 3, ll. 39–43 (hereafter cited in-text as *MM* by act, scene, and line).

A subsequent parenthetical citation would look like this: The Duke exclaims, "O heavens, what stuff is here?" (*MM* 3.2.4).

## 52c How do you format CMS footnotes and endnotes?

Both footnotes and endnotes are indented, beginning with the number of the note formatted in regular typestyle (not *superscript*). Footnotes appear at the bottom of a page preceded by a 1½-inch horizontal rule (usually inserted automatically by your word processor).

> 10. Karl P. Wentersdorf, "Hamlet's Encounter with the Pirates," *Shakespeare Quarterly* 34 (1983): 434–40.

> 11. Don Graham, "Wayne's World," *Texas Monthly*, March 2000, 110–11.

Endnotes begin on a separate page titled *Notes*. Single-space each note, double-spacing between them. As for the content of the note, follow the guidelines given here.

## BASIC PARTS OF CMS FOOTNOTES AND ENDNOTES

CMS notes have five basic parts, each of which is discussed here and marked and color-coded in the sample entries that follow. Notice that all items within a note are separated by commas and that the entire citation ends with a period.

**Primary Acknowledgment (Author).** Each entry usually begins with the names of the author(s) or artist(s), but some begin with the names of other contributors (a book's editor, a movie's director, etc.). List all names in normal order: first name/last name. When four or more individuals are given for the source, list only the first person and the phrase *and others*. When giving primary acknowledgment to those not identified as the source's main author, provide an abbreviation to indicate their contribution (Dan Seward, ed.).

**Title.** Capitalize the first word and all other words in the title, except articles (*a, an*, and *the*), prepositions, and coordinating conjunctions. Place the titles of longer works in italics and enclose the titles of shorter works in quotation marks. Place all titles that appear within titles in quotation marks.

**Secondary Acknowledgments.** Some works are the result of many types of contributor: authors, editors, and translators for books; directors, performers, and scriptwriters for films; and so on. After the title of the source, list the names (in normal order) of those (besides the primary author) given credit for creating the work. Precede the names with an abbreviation indicating the form of contribution given by the individual(s).

**Publication or Production Information.** This part of a footnote can be the most complicated—especially when dealing with electronic documents—but you're always providing three key details: who published the source, where, and when. The models on the following pages provide examples of the types of publication information you should list for various kinds of sources.

**Location Reference.**    List the page number (or chapter, or section title, etc.) where the material you are citing appears in the source. This reference should be as specific as possible when citing quotations or paraphrased passages. It can be less specific or omitted when referring to the outside source as a whole.

1. Sandra Cisneros, *The House on Mango Street* (Houston: Arte Público Press, 1983), 89.

2. Kathy Lowry, "The Purple Passion of Sandra Cisneros," *Texas Monthly*, October 1997, 148–49.

3. Gregory Nava, prod., "La Casa," *American Family*, perf. Raquel Welch and others, PBS, November 23, 2003.

## CMS MODELS 52C-1 Books and book parts

1. **BOOK—BASIC ENTRY**

Author | Title

1. Andrew Feffer, *The Chicago Pragmatists and American Progressivism* (Ithaca: Cornell University Press, 1993).

**Publication information** (Place: Publisher, Year)

In addition to the basic parts of a book citation, consider these options:

- **Is the book or report a revised edition, a volume in a set or series?** Insert edition names, volume numbers, and series titles after the book title. See Models 2, 4.

- **Are editors listed first on the book's title page?** For anthologies and readers, list the editors first. Otherwise, list editors and translators after the title. See Models 3, 5.

- **Are you citing only part of a book?** List the author(s) of the part first, then the selection's title. Next, list the title of the book (preceded by *in*), acknowledgments for those named on the book's title page, the pages where the selection appears, and standard publication details for the book. For untitled parts, use a descriptive title (*preface to* . . . , etc.), omitting the word *in*. See Models 6, 7, 8.

## Footnote and Endnote Models

**2. BOOK**—
Subsequent
Edition

2. Ralph L. Pounds and James R. Bryner, *The School in American Society*, 2nd ed. (New York: Macmillan, 1967), 503.

**3. BOOK**—
Anthology

3. Tiffany M. Field and others, eds., *Review of Human Development* (New York: John Wiley, 1982).

**4. BOOK**—
One of a Series

4. Ella Flagg Young, *Ethics in the Schools*, Contributions to Education, no. 4 (Chicago: University of Chicago Press, 1902), 31–32.

**5. BOOK**—
With Editor

5. George Herbert Mead, *Play, School, and Society*, ed. Mary Jo Deegan (New York: Peter Lang, 1999), 59.

**6. BOOK
PART**—In Book
by Same
Author

6. John Dewey, "Education as Conservative and Progressive," in *Democracy and Education*, 81–93 (New York: Macmillan, 1922), 82.

**7. BOOK
PART**—
Selection from
an Anthology

7. Jane Addams, "The Arts at Hull House," in *The Work of Teachers in America: A Social History through Stories*, ed. Rosetta Maranz Cohen and Samuel Scheer, 173–80 (Mahwah, NJ: Lawrence Erlbaum, 1997), 179.

**8. BOOK
PART**—Not by
Book's Author

8. Norman Angell, introduction to *Approaches to the Great Settlement*, by Emily Greene Balch (New York: B. W. Huebsch, 1918).

## CMS MODELS 52C-2  Periodical articles

9.  **ARTICLE—NEWSPAPER**

Author | Title

9. Ashley Hassebroek, "Public Art Will Have a Place at Omaha Convention Center," *Omaha World Herald*, April 23, 2001, sunrise edition.

**Publication information** (Periodical, Issue)

List the author(s), the article's title, the periodical name, and the issue. Make the following adjustments depending on the type of periodical:

- **Is the article from a newspaper or magazine?** Identify the issue by the date on the cover or masthead. If the article is part of a regular column, such as The Talk of the Town in *New Yorker* or My Turn in *Newsweek*, list the title of the column (not in quotes) in place of or after the article title. Page references are usually omitted for newspapers, but you may list the section containing the article (before the issue date) and identify the edition used (after the date). See Models 9, 10, 11, 15.

- **Is the article from a journal?** Immediately after the periodical name list the volume number and year in parentheses. If the journal restarts pagination with each issue, list the issue number (preceded by a comma and *no.*) before the year. List page references after the year (preceded by a colon). See Models 12, 13.

- **Is the source a review, editorial, or letter to the editor?** Describe the article (*editorial, review of . . .* , etc.) immediately after the title (if any). See Models 14, 15.

## Footnote and Endnote Models

**10. ARTICLE—**
Newspaper,
Unsigned

10. "Officials Solicit Proposals for City Public Arts Projects," *St. Petersburg Times*, sec. 5, October 29, 2003, late Tampa edition.

**11. ARTICLE—**
Magazine

11. Ramiro Burr, "Los Tigres Del Norte 30th Anniversary: The Writing's on the Wall—An L.A. Mural and Los Tigres Del Norte CD Cover Depict a Vision of Struggle and Ambition," *Billboard*, November 11, 2001.

**12. ARTICLE—**
Journal, Volume
Pagination

12. Kerri N. Boutelle and others, "Using Signs, Artwork, and Music to Promote Stair Use in a Public Building," *American Journal of Public Health* 91 (2001): 2005–6.

**13. ARTICLE—**
Journal, Issue
Pagination

13. Gerald C. Cupchik, Andrew S. Winston, and Rachel S. Herz, "Judgments of Similarity and Difference between Paintings," *Visual Arts Research* 18, no. 2 (1992): 49.

**14. ARTICLE—**
Journal, Movie
Review

14. Joan M. West and Dennis West, review of *Frida*, dir. Julie Taymor, perf. Salma Hayek, *Cineaste* 28, no. 2 (2003): 39.

**15. LETTER
TO EDITOR—**
Magazine

15. Lance Cantor, letter to the editor, *Spectator*, October 26, 2002, 40.

## CMS MODELS 52C-3 Web pages, online articles, etc.

### 16. WEB PAGE

| Author | Title | Online access information |
|---|---|---|

16. Pat Schneider, "Your Boat, Your Words," *Our Words Archive*,

Amherst Writers & Artists, http://www.amherstwriters.com/Poems/

BoatWord.html (accessed November 19, 2003).

List the author (or site's sponsor if unsigned), the title of the page, the site name, the site's sponsor (if not already mentioned), the address of the page, and the date you last viewed the source. Some online sources require slight variations:

- **Is the source an article from an online periodical, news service, or database?** Cite like a print periodical article, using the name of the Web site when no other periodical is named. Insert location references (if any) before the address. If the address of the article is long and cryptic, list the address of a search page. See Models 18, 19.
- **Is the source an online version of a book or recording?** Cite typical publication or production details for the original source, then list the address of the online version. For multimedia sources, identify the format as well. See Models 20, 21, 22.

## Footnote and Endnote Models

**17. WEB PAGE**—Unsigned, with Section Reference

17. Boston Public Library, "Hyde Park Branch," *Neighborhood Branches*, "History," http://www.bpl.org/branches/hyde.htm (accessed November 21, 2003).

**18. ONLINE ARTICLE**—Review of a Book in Online Magazine

18. Melanie Rehak, "One a Day, Plus Irony," review of *The Daily Mirror*, by David Lehman, *Salon.com*, January 14, 2001, http://archive.salon.com/books/feature/2000/01/14/rehak_lehman (accessed November 22, 2003).

**19. ONLINE ARTICLE**—From Database

19. Mary Loeffelholz, "The Religion of Art in a City at War: Boston's Public Poetry and the Great Organ, 1863," *American Literary History* 13 (2001): 221, http://muse.jhu.edu/search/search.pl (accessed July 26, 2006).

**20. ONLINE BOOK**—With Section Reference

20. Emily Dickinson, *The Complete Poems of Emily Dickinson* (Boston: Little, Brown, 1924), pt. 1, poem 89, http://www.bartleby.com/113 (accessed October 31, 2003).

**21. ONLINE BOOK PART**

21. Ralph Waldo Emerson, "The Poet," in *Essays: The Second Series* (1844), http://etext.lib.virginia.edu/toc/modeng/public/EmeEssS.html (accessed October 31, 2003).

**22. ONLINE VIDEO**—Recording of Speech

22. Derek Walcott, reading of *Omeros* (Sackler Lecture Hall, Harvard University, Cambridge, MA, April 14, 2003), from WGBH, *Forum Network*, RAM, http://streams.wgbh.org/forum/ram.php?id=1147&size=hi (accessed November 19, 2003).

# CMS MODELS 52C-4 Government publications, sacred texts, etc.

### 23. SPEECH

Speaker     Title of speech

23. Vera Katz, "Let's Get Portland Back to Work,"

(mayoral address, Governor Hotel, Portland, OR, October 28, 2002).

Publication information

- **Are you citing a speech?** List the speaker, the title of the talk, and in parentheses the type of talk, the venue, city, and date. See Model 23.
- **Are you citing a government document?** Name the government agency, the title of the document, and basic publication information. For congressional documents, begin by identifying the house, committee, and session; then list the type of document, an identifying number, and other publication details. See Models 24, 25.
- **Are you citing a sacred text?** Identify the book (abbreviated, no italics) and verse. In the first note, also mention the version used (not italicized). See Model 26.
- **Are you citing a reference work?** Begin with the title, listing also other typical book details. Reference a specific entry, with the abbreviation *s.v.* (*sub verbo*, Latin for "under the word") and the phrase under which the article appears. See Model 27.
- **Is the source an audio or video recording?** List the writer or artist, the title of the recording, and production details. If citing a specific track (CDs, cassettes, etc.) or chapter (DVDs), list its title in quotes, before the title of the full recording. List secondary acknowledgments where appropriate. See Models 28, 29.

**Footnote and Endnote Models**

| | |
|---|---|
| **24. GOVERNMENT PUBLICATION**— Print, with Table Reference | 24. U.S. Census Bureau, *Statistical Abstracts of the United States: The National Data Book*, 120th ed. (Washington, DC: GPO, 2000), table no. 643. |
| **25. GOVERNMENT PUBLICATION**— Online, with Section Reference | 25. U.S. Department of Labor, "Minimum Wage and Overtime Pay," *Employment Law Guide*, "Who is covered," http://www.labor.gov/asp/programs/guide/minwage.htm (accessed May 2, 2006). |
| **26. BIBLICAL REFERENCE** | 26. Ps 104:23 (Revised Standard Version). |
| **27. ARTICLE IN REFERENCE WORK** | 27. *Dictionary of American History*, 3rd. ed., 10 vol., ed. Stanley I. Kutler (New York: Charles Scribner, 2003), s.v. "Labor Day" (by Irving Dilliard). |
| **28. VIDEO RECORDING** | 28. Nunnally Johnson, dir. and adapt., *The Man in the Gray Flannel Suit*, VHS, prod. Darryl F. Zanuck, perf. Gregory Peck and others (1956; US: 20th Century Fox, 1997). |
| **29. AUDIO RECORDING** | 29. Sting [Gordon Sumner], "Synchronicity II," perf. The Police, *Synchronicity*, CD (1983; US: A&M SP-3735, 2003). |

# 52d How do you format CMS bibliographies?

As noted earlier in the chapter, bibliographies are not always required for CMS projects. If you need to create one, use Checklist 52.3 later in this chapter to format the page and the guidelines in this section to produce individual entries. We don't offer an extensive list of models for CMS bibliographic entries because the models and guidelines for MLA works-cited entries (Section 50b) can be used with a few minor adjustments. Compare the parts of a CMS entry with those of an MLA entry:

- **Primary Acknowledgments (Author).** Follow the guidelines on page 696 of the "Basic Parts of MLA Works-cited Entries." CMS uses the same basic format.
- **Titles.** Instead of underlining the titles of long works, as MLA prefers, italicize them. Format other titles as you would in MLA (page 698), except titles within titles, which should appear within quotation marks.
- **Secondary Acknowledgments.** CMS generally uses full phrases rather than abbreviations to introduce secondary contributors. For example, replace *Trans.* with *Translated by,* *Ed.* with *Edited by,* and so on. As in MLA (page 699), list the names of secondary contributors in normal order.
- **Publication and Production Information.** Present most details just like you would in MLA, but do not use abbreviations for most items. Also give *dates* in month-day-year order, with a comma after the day: *July 1, 2001*; *November 27, 2000*; but *May 1999, December 1998,* and so forth.
- **Online Access Information.** Unlike MLA, present the address first, followed by the date of last access in parentheses. For example: http://www.dailycandy.com/home.jsp?city=4 (*accessed May 1, 2003*).

Besides the minor differences just listed, make the following adjustments for entries citing these special kinds of source:

- **For book parts, insert the word *In* before the title of the book.** And list untitled parts immediately before the title of the book, replacing MLA's stand-alone descriptive title with a full phrase: *Introduction to . . .* instead of *Introduction.*; *Preface to . . .* instead of simply *Preface.*; and so on.
- **For periodicals, insert a comma after the periodical name, before the issue date or number.** As with MLA, omit issue numbers for jour-

nals with pagination that does not restart with each issue. When listing a journal issue, however, precede it with *no.*, rather than just a period.

- **For unsigned periodical articles and Web pages, list the periodical name or site sponsor first.** In MLA, you would normally list the title of the article or Web page first. In CMS, list the periodical name or site sponsor as the primary acknowledgment.

## 52e Sample literary analysis—CMS

The sample CMS pages that follow are taken from "Diomedes as Hero of *The Iliad*," a paper written by Jeremy A. Corley, a student in Joi Chevalier's course "The Rhetoric of Epic Narratives." Jeremy wrote a short analysis of the characters Diomedes and Achilles in Homer's *Iliad*. Notice how Jeremy merges his analysis with those of his secondary sources, mostly literary critics. He uses what previous scholars have said about the epic as building blocks for presenting his own claims (supported by plenty of textual evidence and explication) about characters in Homer's *Iliad*. For more on writing a literary analysis, see Chapter 11.

Although Jeremy's paper is fairly short, the style (CMS) used to document the paper is often used for longer papers you'll write in college, especially senior theses and graduate-level term papers. The style typically divides such long documents into three parts: the front matter (title page, table of contents, preface, etc.), the main text, and the back matter (endnotes, bibliography, appendices, etc.). We don't show all the parts required for long, formal thesis papers, but we do show the basic CMS formats for presenting a title page, the main text, footnotes and endnotes, and a bibliography. (For more on using CMS paper formatting, see Kate L. Turabian, *A Manual for Writers of Term Papers, Theses, and Dissertations* (6th ed., 1996.)

---

**Checklist 52.1    Formatting Front Matter—CMS**

Short term papers usually need only a title page. Here we offer common guidelines for formatting all pages of front matter—though schools can set standards for formally submitted projects:

*(Continued)*

**Formatting Front Matter—CMS**   *(Continued)*

a. **Begin with a title page that includes basic information.** Centered, at the top of the page, list your school, the title of the paper, the course, the date, and your name. Insert blank lines to separate items clearly. Don't number this page. Repeat the title of the paper at the top of the first page of the body of the paper (*page 1*).

b. **Insert copyright, dedication, and epigraph pages when appropriate.** These pages usually only appear in formal theses. Pages are centered in alignment with no title or page number.

c. **Create a table of contents for long papers.** Place it after the title page and label it *Contents* (centered at top). List labeled pages and sections, noting the corresponding page number on the same row.

d. **Number all front matter with lowercase roman numerals.** The copyright page (if any) would be *ii*; and so forth.

---

**Checklist 52.2   Document Formatting—CMS**

Use the following settings in your word processor, but adjust them to match preferences voiced by your instructor or set by your school.

a. **Use white, 8½-by-11-inch paper with at least 1-inch margins.** For a bound manuscript, use a 1½-inch left margin.

b. **Use a 10- to 12-point readable font face throughout.** But use a slightly smaller size for footnotes.

c. **Double-space the body of the paper.** Single-space block quotations (used for material extending beyond seven lines of prose or three lines of verse). Don't enclose block quotes with quotation marks, but indent them one-half inch from the left.

d. **Indent the first word of each paragraph one-half inch.**

e. **Left-align the body of the paper.** You may also need to turn off your word processor's automatic hyphenation tool.

f. **Insert a page number at the upper right corner of every page.** The first page of the body of the main text should begin with *1*.

The University of Texas at Austin — double space

Diomedes as Hero of *The Iliad* — double space

E 309K—Topics in Writing

1 extra
line space
between
items

Division of Rhetoric and Composition

28 February 2006

by

Jeremy A. Corley

1 inch · 1/2 inch

1

Diomedes as Hero of *The Iliad*

1/2 inch → Achilles is the central character of *The Iliad*, but is his ← double space

prominence alone enough to make him the story's hero? There

are many episodes in the epic that indicate otherwise. One of the

most interesting aspects of the narrative is its use of a lesser

character, rather than the technical protagonist, as the tale's

benchmark for heroism. This lesser character is Diomedes, and

his leadership skills and maturity prove to be far superior to

those of Achilles. Book V of *The Iliad* is devoted almost entirely to

1 inch · 1 inch

Diomedes' feats, and there are many scenes in which he is

presented as a leader and hero throughout the rest of the text.

While Diomedes is singled out for his gallantry, Achilles is, by

contrast, noted for his immaturity and selfishness. Homer depicts

Diomedes in a much more positive light than Achilles, despite

the latter's obvious natural superiority as a soldier. It seems

evident that Homer is emphasizing the total *use* of one's

abilities—rather than just the *presence* of those abilities—as the

The paper → basis of heroism. Diomedes, therefore, is the actual hero of *The*
offers a
challenging *Iliad*.
thesis.

Achilles is immediately placed at the focal point of the story,

and his pride and immaturity surface almost instantaneously. In

Book I, Agamemnon embarrasses Achilles publicly, prompting

Achilles to challenge the power of the Achaians' commander:

"Khryseis / being required of me by Phoibos Appollo / . . . I myself /

will call for Briseis at your hut . . . to show you here and now who is

1 inch

2

the stronger."[1] Achilles can hardly be faulted for taking offense at this incident. As critic R. M. Frazer points out, it "threatened to invalidate . . . the whole meaning of his life."[2] But Achilles' refusal to fight afterward must be looked at from another perspective. This is the first example of Achilles' acting according to his pride, as demonstrated by his regard for himself as "peerless among Akhaians" (1.475). While it is understandable for a soldier such as Achilles, who "towers above all the other characters of *The Iliad*," to be hesitant to fight for and under the man who embarrassed him, Agamemnon,[3] it is also folly for a soldier to stop fighting because of anything as relatively unimportant as an insult, even a public one. A soldier's duty is to defend his homeland and fight in its wars, and Achilles misses this greater duty for his own selfishness. This refusal to fight is compounded by his request to his mother, Thetis, to "tell [Zeus] your good pleasure / if he will take the Trojan side / and roll the Akhaians back to the water's edge" (1.469–471). This is wholly selfish. Achilles is willing to put the fate of the entire Greek army in peril to feed his own wounded ego. Achilles is acting nothing like the leader that his divine gifts

— ← 1-1/2 inch rule

1/2 inch → [1]Homer, *The Iliad*, trans. Robert Fitzgerald (New York: Anchor Press, 1974), bk. 1, lines 211–17 (hereafter cited in-text by book and line number).

[2]R. M. Frazer, *A Reading of "The Iliad"* (Lanham, MD.: University Press of America, 1993), 12.

[3]Ibid., 11. Frazer discusses Achilles' reaction at length.

The first note identifies the edition of the classic.

Subsequent references to *The Iliad* are to book and line number. See the first footnote.

Note 3 is both a reference and content note.

The word in brackets has been added for clarity, identifying Zeus.

3

give him the power to be. Homer clearly leaves his central character open for some significant personal and psychological development.

In contrast to Achilles' infantile behavior, which is consistent throughout most of the story, Diomedes is cast in a different light. Athena makes Diomedes "bold" (5.2), and "impelled him to the center where / the greatest number fought" (5.8–9). While not Achilles' equal as a soldier, "Diomedes was extremely fierce" and proved to be a terrific leader for the Achaians.[4] Diomedes defeats a great number of Trojan warriors in Book V, acting as many hoped Achilles would, and even fighting through an injury suffered from the bow of Pandaros. Rather than back down, Diomedes prays to Athena for aid and joins the battle even more fiercely than before, assailing Trojan soldiers as well as any Greek hero (5.111–37). At this point, as W. Thomas MacCary explains it, Diomedes is

"obviously a paradigm of heroic behavior in Achilles' absence."[5] But is Diomedes merely a surrogate for Achilles, as MacCary suggests, or is he the genuine heroic figure advocated by Homer? Diomedes represents a well-behaved, properly subservient soldier in the Akhaian army who uses his courage and his honor to accomplish feats that are beyond his natural abilities.

---

[4]Scott Richardson, *The Homeric Narrator* (Nashville: Vanderbilt University Press, 1990), 159.

[5]W. Thomas MacCary, *Childlike Achilles: Ontogeny and Philogeny in "The Iliad"* (New York: Columbia University Press, 1982), 95.

4

Diomedes exhibits self-control above all else, which is the element critics note is most wanting in Achilles.[6] Diomedes' courage is further proven when he speaks against Agamemnon at the beginning of Book IX, when the Achaian commander is advocating a Greek retreat: "Sthenelos and I will fight alone / until we see the destined end of Ilion" (9.56–57). In contrast to Achilles' childish retort to Agamemnon in Book 1, this is the moment when Diomedes is confirmed as one of the Greeks' greatest leaders, as even in a time when the army is "shaken by . . . fear" (9.4), we see that "a cry went up from all Akhaians / in wonder at his words" (9.59–60). The scene underscores Diomedes' rise to greatness in the Achaian army.

A space is left before and after a slash used to divide lines of poetry.

Achilles and Diomedes finally come into direct conflict with one another in Book IX, after Agamemnon has decided to make a peace offering to Achilles in hopes of the latter's return to battle. Agamemnon makes an offer to Achilles that is outrageously generous in exchange for Achilles' return to battle. Achilles' response is far from heroic, presenting a dilemma that is characteristically self-centered on both points:

> if on the one hand I remain to fight
> around Troy town, I lose all hope of home
> but gain unfading glory; on the other,
> if I sail back to my own land my glory
> fails—but a long life lies ahead of me. (9.502–6)

1 inch

Block quotation makes the selection easier to read.

---

[6]G. S. Kirk, *"The Iliad": A Commentary*, vol. 2 (New York: Cambridge University Press, 1990), 34.

5

These words show utter selfishness on the part of the man who is
supposedly the greatest warrior in Greek history, and Achilles is
certainly not, at this point, living up to his reputation or his

Ellipses
indicate that
some lines
have been
omitted.

potential. Observing that Achilles will "fight again / . . . whenever
his blood is up / or the god rouses him" (9.853–55), Diomedes
speaks against Achilles for the first time, effectively casting
himself as something of an adversary to Achilles in the hopes of
bringing him back into the battle, an action that serves the overall
good of the Achaians. Once more, Diomedes is doing what is best
for his people and his army while Achilles thinks only of himself.
Peter Toohey observes that "Homer likes to juxtapose"[7]—here he
uses that device to highlight the stark contrast between the
protagonist of the story (Achilles) and the true hero of the story
(Diomedes).

Homer centers *The Iliad* on Achilles, whose actions are
notably selfish and immature. Homer then uses Diomedes, at first
a lesser character, as a dramatic foil. Diomedes comes across as
an example of the ideal young Greek soldier. Achilles' capacities
as a warrior are far superior to those of any man alive, yet
Diomedes betters him in both words and actions throughout most

---

[7]Peter Toohey, "Epic and Rhetoric: Speech-Making and
Persuasion in Homer and Apollonius," *Arachnion: A Journal
of Ancient Literature and History on the Web* 1 (1995): sec. 2,
http://www. cisi.unito.it/arachne/num1/toohey.html (accessed
February 21, 1996).

6

of the story. Achilles is finally brought to realize his supreme military prowess, but it is the death of his friend Patroclos that spurs his fighting spirit, still another example of Achilles' penchant for acting on emotion rather than judgment (18.88–106). Achilles is finally reconciled to Diomedes' example when he meets Priam at the end of the story and responds honorably: "I have intended . . . / to yield up Hektor to you" (24.671–72), agreeing to return the corpse of Priam's son for a proper burial. Achilles at last achieves a measure of respect that his abilities could have earned him long before. It is in that time, however, when Achilles was still selfish and immature, that Diomedes' less temperamental nature shines through as a firm example of leadership and valor, and consequently the true hero of *The Iliad*.

Conclusion brings the lines of argument together.

1 inch

1/2 inch
7

## Works Cited

Frazer, R. M. *A Reading of "The Iliad."* Lanham, MD: University
Press of America, 1993.

Homer. *The Iliad.* Translated by Robert Fitzgerald. New York:
Anchor Press, 1974.

1 line between entries

Kirk, G. S. *"The Iliad": A Commentary.* Vol. 2. New York: Cambridge
University Press, 1990.

1 inch

MacCary, W. Thomas. *Childlike Achilles: Ontogeny and Philogeny
in "The Iliad."* New York: Columbia University Press, 1982.

1 inch

single space

Richardson, Scott. *The Homeric Narrator.* Nashville: Vanderbilt
University Press, 1990.

Toohey, Peter. "Epic and Rhetoric: Speech-Making and Persuasion
1/2 inch  in Homer and Apollonius." *Arachnion: A Journal of Ancient
Literature and History on the Web* 1 (1995): secs. 1–4.
http://www.cisi.unito.it/arachne/num1/toohey.html (accessed
February 21, 1996).

---

**Checklist 52.3    Formatting Bibliography Pages—CMS**

Use the same font face and size used in the body of the paper, but make the following other adjustments to the page layout:

a. **Center the title "Works Cited" or "Bibliography" at the top of the page.** Use the title "Works Cited" for reference lists including only those works mentioned in the body of the paper or its notes. Do not repeat the title when the list of entries runs over to another page.

b. **Single-space each entry and insert a blank line between entries.**

c. **Create a one-half inch hanging indentation for each entry.** In other words, the first line of each entry should be aligned with the left margin and subsequent lines of the entry should be indented.

d. **Alphabetize the list according to the first word in each entry.** Exclude articles (*A, An*, and *The*). When the same author appears at the beginning of multiple entries, you can replace the author's name with three hyphens (---).

e. **Proof carefully your punctuation and capitalization for each entry.** Review the guidelines in Section 52c.

---

**Checklist 52.4    Formatting Endnotes and Footnotes—CMS**

The following guidelines apply to both footnote and endnote entries:

a. **Indent each note the same space (usually one-half inch) as paragraphs in the body of the paper.**

b. **Begin each note with the number corresponding to that which appears in the body of the paper.**

c. **Single-space each entry and insert a blank line between entries.**

d. **Separate multiple references in a note by semicolons.** You can also add commentary after the references, giving readers more information about each source's significance to your paper. For example:

*(Continued)*

**Formatting Endnotes and Footnotes—CMS**   *(Continued)*

4. Mary Carruthers, *The Book of Memory: A Study of Memory in Medieval Culture* (Cambridge, England: Cambridge University Press, 1990), 86; Marjorie Curry Woods, "The Teaching of Poetic Composition in the Later Middle Ages," in *A Short History of Writing Instruction: From Ancient Greece to Modern America*, 2nd ed., ed. James J. Murphy, 123–44 (Mahwah, NJ: Hermagoras Press, 2001), 143.

# Glossary of Terms and Usage

This glossary covers grammatical terms, and items of usage. Whether you require the definition of a key term (*verbals, noun*), or some advice about correct usage (What's the difference between *eminent* and *imminent*?), you'll find the information in this single, comprehensive list. For convenient review, key grammatical terms are marked by the symbol *.

**a, an.**   Indefinite articles. **A** and **an** are **indefinite articles** because they point to objects in a general way (**a** book, **a** church) while the **definite article the** refers to specific things (**the** book, **the** church). **A** is used when the word following it begins with a consonant sound: **a** *house*, **a** *year*, **a** *boat*, **a** *unique* experience. **An** is used when the word following it begins with a vowel sound: **an** *hour*, **an** *interest*, **an** *annoyance*, **an** *illusory* image.

Notice that you choose the article by the *sound* of the word following it. Not all words that begin with vowels actually begin with vowel sounds, and not all words that begin with consonants have initial consonant sounds.

* **absolute.**   A phrase that modifies an entire sentence. Absolutes are often infinitive or participial phrases. Unlike other modifying phrases, absolutes do not necessarily modify a word or phrase standing near them.

> **To put it politely**, Connie is irritating.

> She will publish the entire story, **space permitting**.

> **Scripts discarded, props disassembled, costumes locked away in trunks**, the annual Shakespeare festival concluded.

**accept/except.**   Very commonly confused. **Accept** means "to take, receive, or approve of something." **Except** means "to exclude, or not including."

> I **accepted** all the apologies **except** George's.

* **adjective.**   A word that modifies a noun or pronoun. Some adjectives describe the words they modify, explaining how many, which color, which one, and so on.

> an **unsuccessful** coach          a **green** motel
> the **lucky** one          a **sacred** icon

Such adjectives frequently have comparative and superlative forms.

> the **blacker** cat          the **happiest** people

Other adjectives limit or specify the words they modify.

**this** adventure **every** penny
**each** participant **neither** video

Proper nouns can also serve as adjectives.

**Texan** wildlife **Eisenhower** era

\* **adverb.** A word that modifies a verb, an adjective, or another adverb. Adverbs explain where, when, and how.

adverb verb
Bud **immediately** *suspected* foul play at the Hutton mansion.

adverb adjective
It seemed **extremely** *odd* to him that Mrs. Hutton should load a large burlap sack into the trunk of her Mercedes.

adverb adverb
Mrs. Hutton replied **rather** *evasively* when Bud questioned her about what she was up to.

Some adverbs modify complete sentences.

adverb
**Obviously**, Mr. Hutton had been murdered!

**adverse/averse.** Often confused. Adverse describes something hostile, unfavorable, or difficult. Averse indicates the opposition someone has to something; it is ordinarily followed by *to*.

Travis was **averse** to playing soccer under **adverse** field conditions.

**advice/advise.** These words aren't interchangeable. **Advice** is a noun meaning "an opinion" or "counsel." **Advise** is a verb meaning to "to give counsel or advice."

I'd **advise** you not to give Maggie **advice** about running her business.

**affect/effect.** A troublesome pair! Each word can be either a noun or a verb, although **affect** is ordinarily a verb and **effect** a noun. In its usual sense, **affect** is a verb meaning "to influence" or "to give the appearance of."

How will the stormy weather **affect** the plans for the outdoor concert?

The meteorologist **affected** ignorance when we asked her for a forecast.

Only rarely is **affect** a noun—as a term in psychology meaning "feeling" or "emotion." On the other hand, **effect** is usually a noun, meaning "consequence" or "result."

The **effect** of the weather may be serious.

**Effect** may, however, also be a verb, meaning "to cause" or "to bring about."

The funnel cloud **effected** a change in our plans.
Compare with: The funnel cloud **affected** our plans.

**aggravate/irritate.** Many people use both of these verbs to mean "to annoy" or "to make angry." But formal English preserves a fine—and useful—distinction between them. **Irritate** means "to annoy" while **aggravate** means "to make something worse."

It **irritated** Greta when her husband **aggravated** his allergies by smoking.

\* **agreement, pronoun and antecedent.** A grammatical principle which requires that singular pronouns stand in for singular nouns (*his* surfboard = *Richard's* surfboard) and plural pronouns stand in for plural nouns (*their* surfboard = *George and Martha's* surfboard; *everyone's* place = *his or her* place). When they do, the pronoun and its antecedent agree in **number**; when they don't you have an agreement problem.

Pronouns and their antecedent also must agree in **gender**. That is, a masculine pronoun (*he, him, his*) must refer to a masculine antecedent, and a feminine pronoun (*she, her, hers*) must refer to a feminine antecedent.

Finally, pronouns and antecedents must agree in **case**, whether objective, subjective, or possessive. For example, an antecedent in the possessive case (*Lawrence's* gym) can be replaced only by a pronoun also in the possessive case (*his* gym).

\* **agreement, subject and verb** Verbs and nouns are said to agree in number. This means that with a singular subject in the third person (for example, *he, she, it*), a verb in the present tense ordinarily adds an **-s** ending to its base form. With subjects not in the third person singular, the base form of the verb is used.

| | |
|---|---|
| **Third person, singular, present tense:** | Barney sits. |
| | He sits. |
| | She sits. |
| **First person, singular, present tense:** | I sit. |
| **Second person, singular, present tense:** | You sit. |
| **First person, plural, present tense:** | We sit. |
| **Second person, plural, present tense:** | You sit. |
| **Third person, plural, present tense:** | They sit. |

Most verbs—with the notable exception of *to be*—change their form to show agreement only in third person singular forms (*he, she, it*).

**ain't.** The word isn't appropriate in academic or professional writing.

**all ready/already.** Tricky, but not difficult. **All ready**, an adjective phrase, means "prepared and set to go."

> Rita signaled that the camera was **all ready** for shooting.

**Already**, an adverb, means "before" or "previously."

> Rita had **already** loaded the film.

**all right.** **All right** is the only acceptable spelling. **Alright** is not acceptable in standard English.

**allude/elude.** Commonly confused. **Allude** means "to refer to." **Elude** means "to escape."

> Kyle's joke **alluded** to the fact that it was easy to **elude** the portly security guard.

**allude/refer.** To **allude** is to mention something indirectly; to **refer** is to mention something directly.

> Carter **alluded** to rituals the new students didn't understand.
>
> Carter did, however, **refer** to ancient undergraduate traditions and the honor of the college.

**allusion/illusion.** These terms are often misused. An **allusion** is an indirect reference to something. An **illusion** is a false impression or a misleading appearance.

> The entire class missed Professor Sweno's **allusion** to the ghost in *Hamlet*.
>
> Professor Sweno entertained the **illusion** that everyone read Shakespeare as often as he did.

**a lot.** Often misspelled as one word. It is two. Many readers consider **a lot** inappropriate in academic writing, preferring **many, much**, or some comparable expression.

**already.** See **all ready/already**.

**alright.** See **all right**.

**among/between.** Use **between** with two objects, **among** with three or more.

> Francie had to choose **between** Richard and Kyle.
> Francie had to choose from **among** a dozen actors.

**amount/number.**   Use **amount** for quantities that can be measured but not counted. Use **number** for things that can be counted, not measured: the **amount** of water in the ocean; the **number** of fish in the sea. The distinction between these words is being lost, but it is worth preserving. Remember that **amount of** is followed by a singular noun, while **number of** is followed by a plural noun.

| | |
|---|---|
| **amount of** money | **number of** dimes |
| **amount of** paint | **number of** colors |
| **amount of** support | **number of** voters |

**an.**   See **a, an**.

**and etc.**   A redundant expression. Use **etc.** alone or **and so on**. See **etc.**

**and/or.**   A useful form in some situations, especially in business and technical writing, but some readers regard it as clumsy. Work around it if you can, especially in academic writing. **And/or** is typed with no space before or after the slash.

**angry/mad.**   The distinction between these words is rarely observed, but strictly speaking, one should use **angry** to describe displeasure, **mad** to describe insanity.

**anyone/any one.**   These expressions have different meanings. Notice the difference highlighted in these sentences.

> **Any one** of those problems could develop into a crisis.

> I doubt that **anyone** will be able to find a solution to **any one** of the equations.

**anyways.**   A nonstandard form. Use **anyway**.

| | |
|---|---|
| **WRONG** | It didn't matter **anyways**. |
| **RIGHT** | It didn't matter **anyway**. |

\* **appositive.**   A word or phrase that stands next to a noun and modifies it by restating or expanding its meaning. Note that appositives ordinarily are surrounded by commas.

> Connie Lim, **editor of the paper and a liberal**, was furious when ex-President Clinton gave his only campus interview to Sue Wesley, **chair of the Young Republicans**.

\* **articles.**   The words **the, a**, and **an** used before a noun. **The** is called a **definite article** because it points to something specific: **the** book, **the** church, **the** criminal. **A** and **an** are **indefinite articles** because they refer more generally: **a** book, **a** church, **a** criminal.

**as being.** A wordy expression. You can usually cut **being**.

> In most cases, telephone solicitors are regarded **as (being)** a nuisance.

\* **auxiliary verbs.** Verbs, usually some form of *be, do,* or *have,* that combine with other verbs to show various relations of tense, voice, mood, and so on. All the words in boldface are auxiliary verbs: **has** seen, **will be** talking, **would have been** going, **are** investigating, **did** mention, **should** prefer. Auxiliary verbs are also known as *helping verbs.*

**averse/adverse.** See **adverse/averse**.

**awful.** **Awful** is inappropriate as a synonym for **very**.

| | |
|---|---|
| INAPPROPRIATE | The findings of the two research teams were **awful** close. |
| BETTER | The findings of the two research teams were **very** close. |

**awhile/a while.** The expressions are not interchangeable. **Awhile** is an adverb; **a while** is a noun phrase. After prepositions, always use **a while**.

> Bud stood **awhile** looking at the grass.
> Bud decided that the lawn would not have to be cut for **a while**.

**bad/badly.** These words are troublesome. Remember that **bad** is an adjective describing what something is like; **badly** is an adverb explaining how something is done.

> Stanley's taste in music wasn't **bad**.
> Unfortunately, he treated his musicians **badly**.

Problems usually crop up with verbs that explain how something feels, tastes, smells, or looks. In such cases, use **bad**.

> The physicists felt **bad** about the disappearance of their satellite.
> The situation looked **bad**.

**because of/due to.** Careful writers usually prefer **because of** to **due to** in many situations.

| | |
|---|---|
| CONSIDERED AWKWARD | The investigation into Bud's sudden disappearance stalled due to Officer Bricker's concern for correct procedure. |
| REVISED | The investigation into Bud's sudden disappearance stalled **because of** Officer Bricker's concern for correct procedure. |

However, **due to** is often the better choice when it serves as a **subject complement** after a **linking verb**. The examples illustrate the point.

> subj.    l.v.    subj.comp.
> Bricker's discretion seemed **due to** <u>cowardice</u>.

> subj.    l.v.      subj. comp.
> His discretion was **due to** <u>the political and social prominence of the Huttons</u>.

**being as/being that.** Both of these expressions sound wordy and awkward when used in place of **because** or **since**. Use **because** and **since** in formal and academic writing.

| INAPPROPRIATE | **Being that** her major was astronomy, Jenny was looking forward to the eclipse. |
|---|---|
| BETTER | **Since** her major was astronomy, Jenny was looking forward to the eclipse. |

**beside/besides.** **Beside** is a preposition meaning "next to" or "alongside"; **besides** is a preposition meaning "in addition to" or "other than."

> **Besides** a sworn confession, the detectives also had the suspect's fingerprints on a gun found **beside** the body.

**Besides** can also be an adverb meaning "in addition" or "moreover."

> Professor Bellona didn't mind assisting the athletic department, and **besides**, she actually liked coaching volleyball.

**between.** See **among/between**.

**can/may.** Understand the difference between the auxiliary verbs **can** and **may**. (See also **modal auxiliary**.) Use **can** to express an ability to do something.

> Charnelle **can** work differential equations.

> According to the *Handbook of College Policies*, Dean Rack **can** lift the suspension.

Use **may** to express either possibility or permission.

> You **may** want to compare my solution to the problem to Charnelle's.

> Dean Rack **may** lift the suspension, but I wouldn't count on that happening.

**can't hardly.** A colloquial expression that is, technically, a double negative. Use **can hardly** instead when you write.

| DOUBLE NEGATIVE | I **can't hardly** see the road. |
|---|---|
| REVISED | I **can hardly** see the road. |

**censor/censure.** These words have different meanings. As verbs, **censor** mean "to cut," "to repress," or "to remove"; **censure** means "to disapprove" and "to condemn."

> The student editorial board voted to **censor** the four-letter words from Connie Lim's editorial and to **censure** her for attempting to publish the controversial piece.

**complement/complementary, compliment/complimentary.** The words are not synonyms. **Complement** and **complementary** describe things completed or compatible. **Compliment** and **complimentary** refer to things praised or given away free.

> Travis's sweater **complemented** his green eyes.
>
> The two parts of Greta's essay were **complementary**, examining the same subject from differing perspectives.
>
> Travis **complimented** Greta on her successful paper.
>
> Greta found his **compliment** sincere.
>
> She rewarded him with a **complimentary** sack of rice cakes from her health food store.

\* **conjugation.** The forms of a given verb as it appears in all numbers, tenses, voices, and moods. See Anatomy of a Verb, Section 23a.

**conjunctions, coordinating.** The words *and, or, nor, for, but, yet,* and *so* used to link words, phrases, and clauses that serve equivalent functions in a sentence. A coordinating conjunction is used to join two independent clauses or two dependent clauses; it would not link a subordinate clause to an independent clause. See also **conjunctions, subordinating**.

> Oscar **and** Marie directed the play.
> Oscar liked the story, **but** Marie did not.

\* **conjunctions, subordinating.** Words or expressions such as *although, because, if, since, before, after, when, even though, in order that,* and *while* that relate dependent (that is, subordinate) clauses to independent ones. Subordinating conjunctions introduce subordinate clauses.

> subordinate clause
>
> **Although** <u>Oscar and Marie both directed parts of the show</u>, Marie got most of the blame for its failure.

subordinate clause

Oscar liked the story **even though** no one else did.

subordinate clause

**When** the show opened, audiences stayed away.

**conscience/conscious.** Don't confuse these words. **Conscience** is a noun referring to an inner ethical sense; **conscious** is an adjective describing a state of awareness or wakefulness.

The linebacker felt a twinge of **conscience** after knocking the quarterback **unconscious**.

**consensus.** This expression is redundant when followed by **of opinion**; **consensus** by itself implies an opinion. Use **consensus** alone.

| | |
|---|---|
| REDUNDANT | The student senate reached a **consensus of opinion** on the issue of censorship. |
| REVISED | The student senate reached a **consensus** on the issue of censorship. |

\* **coordinating conjunction.** See **conjunctions, coordinating**.

\* **correlatives.** Words that work together as conjunctions: *either . . . or, neither . . . nor, whether . . . or, both . . . and, not only . . . but also.*

**Whether** Darwin **or** Travis plays makes little difference.

Brian attributed the failure of the play **not only** to a bad script **but also** to incompetent direction.

**could of/would of/should of.** Nonstandard forms when used instead of **could have, would have**, or **should have**.

| | |
|---|---|
| WRONG | Coach Rhoades imagined that his team **could of** been a contender. |
| RIGHT | Coach Rhoades imagined that his team **could have** been a contender. |

**couple of.** Casual. Avoid it in formal or academic writing.

| | |
|---|---|
| INFORMAL | The article accused the admissions office of a **couple of** major blunders. |
| REVISED | The article accused the admissions office of **several** major blunders. |

**credible/credulous.**    **Credible** means "believable"; **credulous** means "willing to believe on slim evidence." See also **incredible/incredulous**.

> Officer Bricker found Mr. Hutton's excuse for his speeding **credible**.
>
> However, Bricker was known to be a **credulous** police officer, liable to believe any story.

**criteria, criterion.**    **Criteria**, the plural form, is more familiar, but the word does have a singular form—**criterion**.

> John Maynard, age sixty-four, complained that he was often judged according to a single **criterion**, his age.
>
> Other **criteria** ought to matter in hiring.

\* **dangling modifier.**    A modifying phrase that doesn't seem connected to any word or phrase in a sentence. Dangling modifiers are usually corrected by rewriting a sentence to provide a better link between the modifier and what it modifies. See Section 30a. See also **absolute**.

> DANGLING    **After finding the courage to ask Richard out**, the evening was a disaster.
>
> IMPROVED    After finding the courage to ask Richard out, Francie had a disastrous evening.

**data/datum.**    **Data** is the plural form of *datum*. But in informal writing and speech, you will typically see *data* treated as if it were singular.

> INFORMAL    The *data* **is** not convincing.

In academic writing use **datum** when a singular form is expected. If **datum** seems awkward, rewrite the sentence to avoid the singular.

> SINGULAR    The most intriguing **datum** in the study was the rate of population decline.
>
> PLURAL    In all the **data**, no figure was more intriguing than the rate of population decline.

**different from/different than.**    In formal writing, **different from** is usually preferred to **different than**.

> INFORMAL    Ike's account of his marriage proposal was **different than** Bernice's.
>
> FORMAL    Ike's account of his marriage proposal was **different from** Bernice's.

**discreet/discrete.** **Discreet** means "tactful" or "sensitive to appearances" (*discreet* behavior); **discrete** means "individual" or "separate" (*discrete* objects).

> Joel was **discreet** about the money spent on his project.
> He had several **discrete** funds at his disposal.

**disinterested/uninterested.** These words don't mean the same thing. **Disinterested** means "neutral" or "uninvolved"; **uninterested** means "not interested" or "bored."

> Alyce and Richard sought a **disinterested** party to arbitrate their dispute.
>
> Stanley was **uninterested** in the club's management.

**don't.** Writers sometimes forget the apostrophe in this contraction and others like it; **can't, won't**.

**due to the fact that.** Wordy. Replace it with **because** whenever you can.

| | |
|---|---|
| WORDY | Coach Meyer was fired **due to the fact that** he won no games. |
| REVISED | Coach Meyer was fired **because** he won no games. |

**effect/affect.** See **affect/effect**.

**elicit/illicit.** These words have vastly different meanings. **Elicit** means to "draw out" or "bring forth"; **illicit** describes something illegal or prohibited.

> The detective tried to **elicit** an admission of **illicit** behavior from Bud.

**elude/allude.** See **allude/elude**.

**eminent/imminent.** These words are sometimes confused. **Eminent** means "distinguished" and "prominent"; **imminent** describes something about to happen.

> The arrival of the **eminent** scholar is **imminent**.

**enthused.** A colloquial expression that should not appear in academic or professional writing. Use **enthusiastic** instead.

| | |
|---|---|
| INFORMAL | Francie was **enthused** about Wilco's latest album. |
| BETTER | Francie was **enthusiastic** about Wilco's latest album. |

Never use **enthused** as a verb.

**equally as.** Redundant. Use either **equally** or **as** to express a comparison—whichever works in a particular sentence.

| REDUNDANT | Sue Ellen is **equally as** concerned as Hector about bilingual education. |
| REVISED | Sue Ellen is **as** concerned as Hector about bilingual education. |
| REVISED | Sue Ellen and Hector are **equally** concerned about bilingual education. |

**etc.** This common abbreviation for *et cetera* should be avoided in most academic and formal writing. Instead, use **and so on** or **and so forth**. Never use **and etc.**

**even though.** **Even though** is two words, not one.

**everyone/every one.** These similar expressions mean different things. **Everyone** describes a group collectively. **Every one** focuses on the individual elements within a group or collective term. Notice the difference highlighted in these sentences.

**Every one** of those problems could develop into an international crisis **everyone** would regret.

I doubt that **everyone** will be able to attend **every one** of the sessions.

**except/accept.** See **accept/except**.

**fact that, the.** Wordy. You can usually replace the entire expression with **that**.

| WORDY | Bud was aware of **the fact that** he was in a strange room. |
| REVISED | Bud was aware **that** he was in a strange room. |

**farther/further.** Although the distinction between these words is not always observed, it is useful. Use **farther** to refer to distances that can be measured.

It is **farther** from El Paso to Houston than from New York to Detroit.

Use **further**, meaning "more" or "additional," when physical distance or separation is not involved.

The detective decided that the crime warranted **further** investigation.

**fewer than/less than.** Use **fewer than** with things you can count; use **less than** with quantities that must be measured or can be considered as a whole.

The express lane was reserved for customers buying **fewer than** ten items.

Matthew had **less than** half a gallon of gasoline.

He also had **less than** ten dollars.

**flaunt/flout.** These words are confused surprisingly often. **Flaunt** means "to show off"; **flout** means "to disregard" or "to show contempt for."

> To **flaunt** his wealth, Mr. Lin bought a Van Gogh landscape.

> **Flouting** a gag order, the newspaper published its exposé of corruption in the city council.

**fun, funner, funnest.** Used as an adjective, **fun** is not appropriate in academic writing; replace it with a more formal expression.

| | |
|---|---|
| INFORMAL | Skiing is a **fun** sport. |
| FORMAL | Skiing is an **enjoyable** sport. |

The comparative and superlative forms, **funner** and **funnest**, while increasingly common in spoken English, are inappropriate in writing. In writing, use **more fun** or **most fun**.

| | |
|---|---|
| INFORMAL | Albert found tennis **funner** than squash. |
| FORMAL | Albert found tennis **more fun** than squash. |
| SPOKEN | He thought racquetball the **funnest** of the three sports. |
| WRITTEN | He thought racquetball the **most fun** of the three sports. |

* **gender.** A classification of nouns and pronouns as masculine (*actor, muscleman, he*), feminine (*actress, midwife, she*), or neuter (*tree, it*).

* **gerund.** A verb form used as a noun: *smiling, biking, walking.* (See Section 24a-3.) Most gerunds end in **-ing** and, consequently, look identical to the present participle.

| | |
|---|---|
| GERUND | **Smiling** is good for the health. |
| PARTICIPLE | A **smiling** critic is dangerous. |

The difference is that gerunds function as nouns while participles act as modifiers. Gerunds usually appear in the present tense, but they can take other forms.

> **Having been criticized** made Brian angry.
> gerund in past tense, passive voice, acting as subject of the sentence

> **Being asked** to play an encore was a compliment Otto enjoyed.
> gerund in present tense, passive voice, as subject of sentence

**get/got/gotten.** The principal parts of this verb are:

| PRESENT | PAST | PAST PARTICIPLE |
|---|---|---|
| get | got | got, gotten |

**Gotten** usually sounds more polished than **got** as the past participle in American English, but both forms are acceptable.

> Aretha **has gotten** an *A* average in microbiology.
> Aretha **has got** an *A* average in microbiology.

Many expressions, formal and informal, rely on **get**. Use the less formal ones only with appropriate audiences.

> get it together
> get straight
> get real

**good and.** Informal. Avoid it in academic writing.

| | |
|---|---|
| **INFORMAL** | The lake was **good and** cold when the sailors threw Sean in. |
| **BETTER** | The lake was **icy** cold when the sailors threw Sean in. |

**good/well.** These words cause many problems. (See Section 30c.) As a modifier, **good** is an adjective only; **well** can be either an adjective or an adverb. Consider the difference between these sentences, where each word functions as an adjective.

> Katy is **good**.
> Katy is **well**.

**Good** is often mistakenly used as an adverb.

| | |
|---|---|
| **WRONG** | Juin conducts the orchestra **good**. |
| **RIGHT** | Juin conducts the orchestra **well**. |
| **WRONG** | The bureaucracy at NASA runs **good**. |
| **RIGHT** | The bureaucracy at NASA runs **well**. |

Complications occur when writers and speakers—eager to avoid using **good** incorrectly—substitute **well** as an adjective where **good** used as an adjective may be more accurate.

| | |
|---|---|
| **WRONG** | After a shower, Coach Rhoades smells **well**. |
| **RIGHT** | After a shower, Coach Rhoades smells **good**. |
| **RIGHT** | I feel **good**. |
| **ALSO RIGHT** | I feel **well**. |

**hanged, hung.** **Hanged** has been the past participle conventionally reserved for executions; **hung** is used on other occasions. The distinction is a nice one, probably worth observing.

Connie was miffed when her disgruntled editorial staff decided she should be **hanged** in effigy.

Portraits of the faculty were **hung** in the student union.

**he/she.**   Using **he/she** (or *his/her* or *s/he*) is a way to avoid a sexist pronoun reference. Many readers find expressions with slashes clumsy and prefer *he* or *she* and *his* or *her*.

**hisself.**   A nonstandard form. Don't use it.

**hopefully.**   Some readers object to using the adverb *hopefully* as a sentence modifier. They would consider the following sentences ambiguous and incorrect.

> **Hopefully**, the stock market will grow.
> The government, **hopefully**, will not impose price controls.

*Hopefully*, they argue, should be used to mean only "with hope."

> Traders watched **hopefully** as stock prices approached yet another record.

However, English includes many adverbs like *hopefully* that function as sentence modifiers, including words such as *understandably, mercifully, predictably*, and *honestly*. By precedent and general usage, *hopefully* seems entrenched as a sentence modifier.

**illicit/elicit.**   See **elicit/illicit**.

**illusion/allusion.**   See **allusion/illusion**.

**imminent/eminent.**   See **eminent/imminent**.

**imply/infer.**   Think of these words as opposite sides of the same coin. **Imply** means "to suggest" or "to convey an idea without stating it." **Infer** is what you might do to figure out what someone else has implied: you examine evidence and draw conclusions from it.

> By joking calmly, the pilot sought to **imply** that the aircraft was out of danger. But from the crack that had opened in the wing, the passengers **inferred** that the landing would be harrowing.

**incredible/incredulous.**   **Incredible** means "unbelievable"; **incredulous** means "unwilling to believe" and "doubting." See also **credible/credulous**.

> The press found the governor's explanation for his wealth **incredible**.
> You could hardly blame them for being **incredulous** when he attributed his vast holdings to coupon savings.

**infer/imply.**   See **imply/infer**.

\* **infinitive.**   A verbal that can usually be identified by the word **to** preceding the base form of a verb: *to strive, to seek, to find, to endure*. Infinitives do take other forms to show various tenses and voices: *to be seeking, to have found, to have been found*. Infinitives can act as nouns, adjectives, adverbs, and absolutes (see Section 24a).

| | |
|---|---|
| **INFINITIVE AS NOUN** | **To capture** a market is not easy.<br>subject of the sentence |
| **INFINITIVE AS ADJECTIVE** | Greta has many posters **to redesign**.<br>modifies the noun *posters* |
| **INFINITIVE AS ADVERB** | Mr. Stavros laughed **to forget** his troubles.<br>modifies the verb *laughed* |
| **INFINITIVE AS ABSOLUTE** | **To be blunt**, the paper is plagiarized. |

\* **interjection.**   A word that expresses emotion or feeling, but that is not grammatically a part of a sentence. Interjections can be punctuated as exclamations (!) or attached to a sentence with a comma. Interjections include *oh, hey, wow*, and *well*.

**irregardless.**   A nonstandard form. Use **regardless** instead.

**irritate/aggravate.**   See **aggravate/irritate**.

**its/it's.**   Don't confuse these terms. **It's** is a contraction for *it is*. **Its** is a possessive pronoun meaning "belonging to it." See Section 28c for a discussion of this problem.

**judgment/judgement.**   The British spell this word with two *e*'s. Americans spell it with just one: **judgment**.

**kind of.**   This expression is colloquial when used to mean "rather." Avoid *kind of* in formal writing.

| | |
|---|---|
| **COLLOQUIAL** | The college trustees were **kind of** upset by the bad publicity. |
| **MORE FORMAL** | The college trustees were **rather** upset by the bad publicity. |

**less than.**   See **fewer than/less than**.

**lie/lay.**   These two verbs cause much trouble and confusion. Here are their parts.

| PRESENT | PAST | PRESENT PARTICIPLE | PAST PARTICIPLE |
|---|---|---|---|
| lie (to recline) | lay | lying | lain |
| lay (to place) | laid | laying | laid |

Notice that the past tense of **lie** is the same as the present tense of **lay**. It may help you to remember that to **lie** (meaning "to recline") is *intransitive*—that is, it doesn't take an object. You can't lie *something*.

> Travis **lies** under the cottonwood tree.
> He **lay** there all afternoon.
> He was **lying** in the hammock yesterday.
> He had **lain** there for weeks.

**To lay** (meaning "to place" or "to put") is *transitive*—it takes an object.

> Jenny **lays** a *book* on Travis's desk.
> Yesterday, she **laid** a *memo* on his desk.
> Jenny was **laying** the *memo* on Travis's desk when he returned.
> Travis had **laid** almost three *yards* of concrete that afternoon.

**like/as.**  Many readers object to **like** used to introduce clauses of comparison. **As, as if**, or **as though** are preferred in situations where a comparison involves a subject and verb.

| | |
|---|---|
| **NOT** | Mr. Butcher is self-disciplined, **like** you would expect a champion weightlifter to be. |
| **BUT** | Mr. Butcher is self-disciplined, **as** you would expect a champion weightlifter to be. |
| **NOT** | It looks **like** he will win the local competition again this year. |
| **BUT** | It looks **as if** he will win the local competition again this year. |

**Like** is acceptable when it introduces a prepositional phrase, not a clause.

> Yvonne looks **like** her mother.
> The sculpture on the mall looks **like** a rusted Edsel.

**literally.**  When you write that something is **literally** true, you mean that it is exactly as you have stated. The following sentence means that Bernice emitted heated water vapor, an unlikely event no matter how angry she was.

> Bernice **literally** steamed when Ike ordered her to marry him.

If you want to keep the image (*steamed*), omit **literally**.

> Bernice steamed when Ike ordered her to marry him.

**lose/loose.**  Be careful not to confuse these words. **Lose** is a verb, meaning "to misplace," "to be deprived of," or "to be defeated." **Loose** can be either an adjective or a verb. As an adjective, **loose** means "not tight"; as a verb, **loose** means "to let go" or "to untighten."

> Without Martin as quarterback, the team might **lose** its first game of the season.

> The strap on Martin's helmet had worked **loose**.

> It **loosened** so much that Martin **lost** his helmet.

**mad, angry.**   See **angry/mad**.

**majority/plurality.**   There is a useful difference in meaning between these two words. A **majority** is more than half of a group; a **plurality** is the largest part of a group when there is *less than a majority*. In an election, for example, a candidate who wins 50.1 percent of the vote can claim a **majority**. One who wins a race with 40 percent of the vote may claim a **plurality**, but not a majority.

**many times.**   Wordy. Use **often** instead.

**may/can.**   See **can/may**.

**media/medium.**   **Medium** is the singular of **media**.

> Connie believed that the press could be as powerful a **medium** as television.

> The visual **media** are discussed in the textbook.

The term **media** is commonly used to refer to newspapers and magazines, as well as television and radio.

> President Xiony declined to speak to the **media** about the fiscal problems facing the college.

**might of.**   A nonstandard form. Use **might have** instead.

> NOT               Ms. Rajala **might of** never admitted the truth.
>
> BUT               Ms. Rajala **might have** never admitted the truth.

\* **misplaced modifier.**   A modifying word or phrase that is ambiguous because it could modify more than one thing. See Section 30a. See also **absolute**.

> MISPLACED MODIFIER   Some of the actors won roles **without talent**.
>
> IMPROVED             Some of the actors **without talent** won roles.

\* **modal auxiliary.**   An auxiliary verb that indicates possibility, necessity, permission, desire, capability, and so on. Modal auxiliaries include *can, could, may, might, will shall, should, ought*, and *must*. See Section 32a.

Hector **can** write.
Hector **might** write.
Hector **must** write.

**moral, morale.**   Don't confuse these words. As a noun, **moral** is a lesson. **Morale** is a state of mind.

The **moral** of the fable was to avoid temptation.
The **morale** of the team was destroyed by the accident.

**must of.**   Nonstandard. Use **must have** instead.

| | |
|---|---|
| **NOT** | Someone **must of** read the book. |
| **BUT** | Someone **must have** read the book. |

**nice.**   The adjective has little impact when used to mean "pleasant": **It was a nice day; Sally is a nice person.** In many cases, **nice** is damning with faint praise. Find a more specific word or expression. **Nice** can be used effectively to mean "precise" or "fine."

There was a **nice** distinction between the two positions.

\* **noun.**   A word that names a person, place, thing, idea, or quality. In sentences, nouns can serve as subjects, objects, complements, appositives, and even modifiers. There are many classes of nouns: **common, proper, concrete, abstract, collective, noncount**, and **count**. See individual entries for details of each type.

**nowheres.**   Nonstandard version of **nowhere** or **anywhere**.

| | |
|---|---|
| **COLLOQUIAL** | The chemist couldn't locate the test tube **nowheres**. It was **nowheres** to be found. |
| **REVISED** | The chemist couldn't locate the test tube **anywhere**. It was **nowhere** to be found. |

**number/amount.**   See **amount/number**.

**off of.**   A wordy expression. **Off** is enough.

Arthur drove his Jeep **off** the road.

**O.K., OK, okay.**   Not the best choice for formal writing. But give the expression respect. It's an internationally recognized expression of approval. OK?

\* participle.   A verb form that is used as a modifier (see Section 24a). The present participle ends with -ing. For regular verbs, the past participle ends with -ed; for irregular verbs, the form of the past participle will vary. Participles have the following forms.

> **TO PERFORM (A REGULAR VERB)**
>
> **Present, active:**    performing
> **Present, passive:**   being performed
> **Past, active:**       performed
> **Past, passive:**      having been performed

Participles can serve as simple modifiers.

> **Smiling**, Officer Bricker wrote the traffic ticket.    Modifies *Officer Bricker.*

But they often take objects, complements, and modifiers of their own to form verbal phrases, which play an important role in shaping sentences.

> <u>**Writing** the ticket for speeding</u>, Bricker laughed at his own cleverness in catching Arthur.
>
> <u>**Having been ridiculed** often in the past by Arthur</u>, Bricker now had his chance for revenge.
>
> Arthur, <u>**knowing** what his friends were doing to Officer Bricker's patrol car</u>, smiled as he took the ticket.

Like an infinitive, a participle can also serve as an **absolute**—that is, a phrase that modifies an entire sentence.

> All things **considered**, the prank was worth the ticket.

* **parts of speech.**   The eight common categories by which words in a sentence are identified according to what they do, how they are formed, where they are placed, and what they mean. Those basic categories are **nouns, pronouns, adjectives, verbs, adverbs, prepositions, conjunctions**, and **interjections**.

**persecute/prosecute.**   **Persecute** means "to oppress" or "to torment"; **prosecute** is a legal term meaning "to bring charges or legal proceedings" against someone or something.

> Connie felt **persecuted** by criticisms of her political activism.
>
> She threatened to **prosecute** anyone who interfered with her First Amendment rights.

**personal/personnel.**   Notice the difference between these words. **Personal** refers to what is private, belonging to an individual. **Personnel** are the people staffing an office or institution.

> Drug testing all airline **personnel** might infringe on **personal** freedom.

**phenomena/phenomenon.** You can win friends and influence people by spelling these words correctly and using **phenomenon** as the singular form.

> The astral **phenomenon** of meteor showers is common in August.

> Many other astral **phenomena** are linked to particular seasons.

**plurality/majority.** See **majority/plurality**.

**plus.** Don't use **plus** as a conjunction or conjunctive adverb meaning "and," "moreover," "besides," or "in addition to."

| NOT | Mr. Burton admitted to cheating on his income taxes this year. **Plus** he acknowledged that he had filed false returns for the last three years. |
|---|---|
| BUT | Mr. Burton admitted to cheating on his income taxes this year. **Moreover**, he acknowledged that he had filed false returns for the last three years. |

**prejudice/prejudiced.** Many writers and speakers use **prejudice** where they need **prejudiced**. **Prejudice** is a noun; **prejudiced** is a verb form.

| WRONG | Joe Kamakura is **prejudice** against liberals. |
|---|---|
| RIGHT | Joe Kamakura is **prejudiced** against liberals. |
| WRONG | **Prejudice** people are found in every walk of life. |
| RIGHT | **Prejudiced** people are found in every walk of life. |
| COMPARE | **Prejudice** is found in every walk of life. |

\* **preposition.** A word that links a noun or pronoun to the rest of a sentence. Prepositions point out many kinds of basic relationships: *on, above, to, for, in, out, through, by,* and so on.

**principal/principle.** Two terms commonly confused because of their multiple meanings. **Principal** means "chief" or "most important." It also names the head of an elementary or secondary school (remember "The **principal** is your pal"?). Finally, it can be a sum of money lent or borrowed.

> Ike intended to be the **principal** breadwinner of the household.

> Bernice accused Ike of acting like a power-mad high school **principal**.

> She argued that they would need two incomes just to meet their mortgage payments—both interest and **principal**.

A **principle**, on the other hand, is a guiding rule or fundamental truth.

Ike declared it was against his **principles** to have his wife work.

Bernice said he would just have to be a little less **principled** on that issue.

**proceed to.** A wordy and redundant construction when it merely delays the real action of a sentence.

| WORDY | We **proceeded to** open the strongbox. |
| TIGHTER | We **opened** the strongbox. |

* **pronoun.** A word that acts like a noun but doesn't name a specific person, place, or thing—*I, you, he, she, it, they, whom, who, what, myself, oneself, this, these, that, all, both, anybody*, and so on. There are many varieties of pronouns: **personal, relative, interrogative, intensive, reflexive, demonstrative, indefinite**, and **reciprocal**. See Chapters 25–29 and individual entries for details about each type.

**real.** Often used as a colloquial version of **very**: "I was **real** scared." This usage is inappropriate in academic writing.

**really.** An adverb too vague to make much of an impression in many sentences: **It was <u>really</u> hot; I am <u>really</u> sorry.** Replace **really** with a more precise expression or delete it.

**reason is . . . because.** The expression is redundant. Use one half of the expression or the other—not both.

| REDUNDANT | The **reason** the cat is ferocious is **because** she is protecting her kittens. |
| REVISED | The **reason** the cat is ferocious is **that** she is protecting her kittens. |
| REVISED | The cat is ferocious **because** she is protecting her kittens. |

**refer/allude.** See **allude/refer**.

* **reflexive pronoun.** A pronoun form created when **-self** or **-selves** is added to personal pronouns (*myself, yourself, herself, himself, itself, oneself, ourselves, yourselves, themselves*). Use the reflexive form when both the subject and the object of an action are the same (see Section 29d).

　　　　subj.　　　　　　　　obj.
**Chunyang** had only *himself* to rely on.

　　　subj.　　　obj.
**They** took *themselves* too seriously.

**set/sit.** These two verbs can cause problems. Here are their parts.

| PRESENT | PAST | PRESENT PARTICIPLE | PAST PARTICIPLE |
|---|---|---|---|
| set (put down) | set | setting | set |
| sit (take a seat) | sat | sitting | sat |

It may help you to remember that **to sit** (meaning "to take a seat") is *intransitive*—that is, it doesn't take an object. You can't sit *something*.

> Haskell **sits** under the cottonwood tree.
> He **sat** there all afternoon.
> He was **sitting** in the hammock yesterday.
> He had **sat** there for several weeks.

**To set** (meaning "to place" or "to put") is *transitive*—it takes an object.

> Jenny **set** a *plate* on the table.
> At Christmas, we **set** a *star* atop the tree.
> Alex was **setting** the *music* on the stand when it collapsed.
> Connie discovered that Travis **had set** a *subpoena* on her desk.

**should of.** Mistaken form of **should have**. Also incorrect are **could of** and **would of**.

**sit/set.** See **set/sit**.

**so.** Vague when used as an intensifier, especially when no explanation follows **so**: *Sue Ellen was* **so** *sad*. **So** used this way can sound trite (how sad is **so** sad?) or juvenile: *Professor Sweno's play was* **so** *bad*. If you use **so**, complete your statement.

> Sue Ellen was **so** sad she cried for an hour.

> Professor Sweno's play was **so** bad that the audience cheered for the villains.

\* **split infinitive.** An infinitive interrupted by an adverb: *to* **boldly** *go; to* **really** *try*. Though correct, split infinitives offend some readers. To alter a split infinitive, simply place the adverb somewhere else in your sentence: *to go* **boldly**. See Section 24c.

**stationary/stationery.** **Stationary**, an adjective, means "immovable, fixed in place." **Stationery** is a noun meaning "writing material." The words are not interchangeable.

\* **subordinating conjunctions.** See **conjunctions, subordinating**.

**supposed to.** Many writers forget the *d* at the end of **suppose** when the word is used with auxiliary verbs.

| INCORRECT | Calina was **suppose to** check her inventory. |
|---|---|
| CORRECT | Calina was **supposed to** check her inventory. |

**than/then.**   These words are occasionally confused. **Than** is a conjunction expressing difference or comparison: **then** is an adverb expressing time.

If the film is playing tomorrow, Shannon would rather go **then than** today.

**theirselves.**   A nonstandard form. Use **themselves** instead.

| INCORRECT | All the strikers placed **theirselves** in jeopardy. |
|---|---|
| CORRECT | All the strikers placed **themselves** in jeopardy. |

**then/than.**   See **than/then**.

**thusly.**   A fussy, nonstandard form. Don't use it. **Thus** is stuffy enough without the -*ly*.

**till/until.**   **Until** is used more often in school and business writing, though the words are usually interchangeable. No apostrophe is used with **till**. You may occasionally see the poetic form **'til**, but don't use it in academic or business writing.

**toward/towards.**   **Toward** is preferred, though either form is fine.

**try and.**   An informal expression. In writing, use **try to** instead.

| INCORRECT | After its defeat, the soccer team decided to **try and** drown its sorrows. |
|---|---|
| REVISED | After its defeat, the soccer team decided to **try to** drown its sorrows. |

**type.**   You can usually delete this word.

| WORDY | Hector was a polite **type** of guy. |
|---|---|
| REVISED | Hector was polite. |

**uninterested/disinterested.**   See **disinterested/uninterested**.

**unique.**   Something **unique** is one of a kind. It can't be compared with anything else, so expressions such as *most unique, more unique,* or *very unique* don't make sense. The word **unique**, when used properly, should stand alone.

| INCORRECT | Joe Rhoade's coaching methods were **very unique**. |
|---|---|
| REVISED | Joe Rhoade's coaching methods were **unique**. |

Quite often **unique** appears where another, more specific adjective is appropriate.

| INCORRECT | The **most unique** merchant on the block was Tong-chai. |
| IMPROVED | The **most inventive** merchant on the block was Tong-chai. |

**until/till.** See **till/until**.

**used to.** Many writers forget the *d* at the end of **use**.

| INCORRECT | Leroy was use to studying after soccer practice. |
| CORRECT | Leroy was **used to** studying after soccer practice. |

**utilize.** Many readers prefer the simpler term **use**.

| INFLATED | Mr. Ringling **utilized** his gavel to regain the crowd's attention. |
| BETTER | Mr. Ringling **used** his gavel to regain the crowd's attention. |

\* **verb.** The word or phrase that establishes the action of a sentence or expresses a state of being (see Chapter 23).

verb
The music **played** on.

verb
Turning the volume down **proved** to be difficult.

A verb and all its auxiliaries, modifiers, and complements is called the **predicate** of a sentence.

complete subj.         predicate
*David's band* **would have played throughout the night**.

complete subj.                        predicate
*Turning the volume down on the band* **proved to be much more difficult than the neighbors had anticipated it might be**.

\* **verbals.** Verb form that act like nouns, adjectives, or adverbs (see Chapter 24). The three kinds of verbals are **infinitives, participles**, and **gerunds**. Like verbs, verbals can take objects to form phrases. But verbals are described as nonfinite (that is, "unfinished") verbs because they cannot alone make complete sentences. A complete sentence requires a **finite** verb—that is, a verb that changes form to indicate person, number, and tense.

| NONFINITE VERB—INFINITIVE | **To have found** security . . . |
| FINITE VERB | I **have found** security. |
| NONFINITE VERB—PARTICIPLE | The actor **performing** the scene . . . |
| FINITE VERB | The actor **performs** the scene. |

**well/good.**   See **good/well**.

**who/whom.**   Use **who** when the pronoun is a subject; use **whom** when it is an object.

> **Who** wrote the ticket?
> **To whom** was the ticket given?

See Section 28c.

**with regards to.**   Drop the **s** in regard**s**. The correct expression is **with regard to**.

**won't.**   Writers sometimes forget the apostrophe in this contraction and in others like it: **can't, don't**.

**would of.**   Mistaken form of **would have**. Also incorrect are **could of** and **should of**.

**you all.**   Southern expression for *you*, usually plural. Not used in academic writing.

**your/you're.**   Homonyms that often get switched. **You're** is the contraction for *you are*; **your** is a possessive form.

> **You're** certain Maxine has been to Iran?
> **Your** certainty on this matter may be important.

# Credits

## TEXT CREDITS

Abbey, Edward, *Desert Solitaire*. New York: McGraw-Hill, 1968.

Angelou, Maya. *I Know Why the Caged Bird Sings*. New York: Random House, 1969.

Angier, Natalie, "Mating for Life?" in *The Beauty and the Beastly*. New York: Houghton Mifflin Company, 1995.

Anzaldúa, Gloria, From "How to Tame a Wild Tongue" in *Borderlands/La Frontera: The New Mestiza*. Copyright © 1987, 1999 by Gloria Anzaldúa. Reprinted by permission of Aunt Lute Books.

Apple, RW. "A High Point in Two Decades of U.S. Might," *New York Times*, April 10, 2003. © 2003 by The New York Times Company. Reprinted by permission.

Austen, Jane. "Pride and Prejudice," 1813.

Barnett, Lincoln, *The Universe and Dr. Einstein*. New York: William Morrow and Co., 1968.

Barnett, Rosalind Shait and Caryl Rivers. "The Persistence of Gender Myths in Math." Originally appeared in *Education Week*, October 13, 2004. Reprinted by permission of the authors.

Bauknight, Lee. Two for the Road.

Bilger, Burkhard. "The Egg Men: How Breakfast Gets Served at the Flamingo Hotel in Las Vegas," *The New Yorker*, September 5, 2005.

Blackwell, Elise. "Hunger." New York & Boston: Back Bay/Little Brown & Company, 2003, p. 37.

Blake, William, "The Tyger," 1794.

Blake, William. "The Devine Image," 1789.

Boyer, Ernest L. 'Creating the New American College," *The Chronicle of Higher Education*. 1994.

Broache, Anne. "Oh Deer!" Originally published in *Smithsonian*, October, 2005.

Broder, Eric. Cleveland Free Times.

Burke, James Lee. *Black Cherry Blues*. Boston: Little, Brown and Company, 1989.

Chesler, Ellen. *Women of Valor*. Reprinted by permission of International Creative Management. © Ellen Chesler.

Churchill, Winston. From a speech to the House of Commons, January, 1952.

Codell, Esmé Raji. *From Educating Esmé: Diary of a Teacher's First Year*. Copyright © 1999 Esmé Raji Codell. Reprinted by permission of Algonquin Books of Chapel Hill, a division of Workman Publishing.

Cofer, Judith Ortiz. *Silent Dancing: A Partial Remembrance of a Puerto Rican Childhood*. Houston: Arte Publico Press-University of Houston, 1990.

Costas, Bob. "Eulogy for Mickey Mantle," August 15, 1995.

Council of Science Editors. *Scientific Style and Format: The CBE Manual for Authors, Editors, and Publishers*. Sixth Edition. Copyright © 1994 by the Council of Science Editors. Reprinted by permission.

Crouch, Stanley. "Blues for Jackie." *All American Skin Game, or the Decoy of Race: The Long and the Short of It, 1990–1994.* New York: Pantheon Books, a division of Random House, Inc., 1995.

Cummings, E.E. "anyone lived in a pretty how town." From E.E. Cummings, 100 Selected Poems by E.E. Cummings. © 1959 Grove Press. Reprinted by permission.

Deng, Alephonsion. "I Have Had to Learn to Live With Peace." From *Newsweek*, October 2005. © 2005 Newsweek, Inc. All rights reserved. Reprinted by permission.

Didion, Joan. "Georgia O'Keeffe," *The White Album.* New York: Simon & Schuster, 1979.

Ebert, Roger. *The Great Movies: Casablanca.*

Edge, John T. From "I'm Not Leaving Until I Eat This Thing." *Oxford American Magazine*, September/October 1999. Reprinted by permission of the author.

Ellis, Andy. Excerpt from Stellartone Tonestyler, *Guitar Player Magazine Online*, January 2005. <www/guitarplayer.com/story.asp>.

Engle, Gary. "What Makes Superman So Darned American?" Excerpt from Superman at Fifty. Ed. Gary Engle and Dennis Dooley. © 1987 Octavia Books.

Faulkner, William. "The Sound and the Fury." New York: Vintage, 1991.

Gerstner, Louis Jr. "High Marks for Standardized Tests," *Prism Online*, February 2001. <http://prismonline.com>.

Google Web page. Reprinted by permission.

Gosling, S.D. & O.P. John, "Personality Dimensions in Non-human Animals." Current dimensions in *Psychological Science*, 8, (3), 69–75, retrieved May 1, 2005 from Blackwell Synergy.

Gould, Stephen Jay. "The Power of Narrative" in *The Urchin in the Storm.* New York: W. W. Norton, 1987, p. 77.

Hamilton, Joan C. "Journey to the Center of the Mind." Reprinted from Business Week, April 19, 2004. © 2004 The McGraw-Hill Companies, Inc.

Hillenbrand, Laura. *Seabiscuit: An American Legend.* Hillenbrand, Laura. "Seabiscuit." © 2003 Ballantine Books. Reprinted by permission of Random House, Inc.

Hoberman, Barry. "Translating the Bible," as originally published in the February 1985 issue of *The Atlantic Monthly*, Vol. 255, No. 2. Copyright © 1985 Atlantic Monthly.

Hollandsworth, Skip, "Tyler Hollandsworth." *Texas Monthly*, Sept. 2003: 64. (<texasmonthly.com/mag/issues/2003-09-01/feature.php>)

Hughes, Robert. *Culture of Complaint: The Fraying of America.* © 1993 Oxford University Press. By permission of Oxford University Press, Inc.

Johnson, Paul. *Intellectual.* New York: Harper & Row, Inc. 1988, p. 73.

Johnson, Steve. "Watching TV Makes You Smarter." Originally appeared in *The New York Times Magazine*, April 24, 2005.

Kennedy, John F. *Inaugural Address.* January 20, 1961.

Kerouac, Jack. *On the Road.* New York: Penguin Books. © 1955, 1957 by Jack Kerouac; Copyright renewed © 1983 by Stella Kerouac, renewed © 1985 by Stella Kerouac and Jan Kerouac. Used by permission of Viking, a division of Penguin Group (USA) Inc.

King, Martin Luther Jr. Excerpt from "I Have A Dream" *A Testament of Hope: The Essential Writings and Speeches of Martin Luther King, Jr.* Ed. James M. Washington. San Francisco: HarperSanFrancisco, 1986, p. 218.

Kleine, Ted. "Living the Lansing Dream," *NEXT: Young American Writers on the New Generation*, Eric Liu, ed. New York, W. W. Norton, 1994, p. 95.

Lapham, Lewis. "Notebook," *Harper's*, October 1997. Reproduced by special permission.

Lewon, Dennis. From "Malaria's Not So Magic Bullet," *Escape*, July 1999. Reprinted by permission of the author.

Lincoln, Abraham. Excerpt from The Gettysburg Address. From *Lincoln on Democracy*. Ed. Mario M. Cuomo and Harold Holzer. New York: HarperCollins, 1990, p. 307.

McGrath, Charles. "Not Funnies," by Charles McGrath. Originally appeared in *The New York Times Magazine*, July 11, 2004 © 2004 The New York Times. Reprinted by permission.

McManus, Ray. "Split P Soup Flyer." Reprinted by permission.

Mellix, Barbara. "From Outside, In" originally appeared in *The Georgia Review*, Volume XLI, No. 2 (Summer 1987), © 1987 by The University of Georgia/© 1987 by Barbara Mellix. Reprinted by permission of Barbara Mellix and *The Georgia Review*.

The Modern Language Association Style Manual. "Rules." Reprinted by permission. Thanks to the *MLA Style Manual and Guide to Scholarly Publishing*, Second Edition. Copyright © 1998 Modern Language Association of America.

Moffett, Michael. "How College Students Choose Their Majors" from *Coming of Age in New Jersey*. New Brunswick, NJ: Rutgers University Press, 1989.

MSNBC.com-*Newsweek*, October 3, 2002. Copyright 2002 Newsweek, Inc. All rights reserved. Reprinted by permission.

*Netscape*, Netscape Communications browser window and Netscape Composer © 1999 Netscape Communications Corporation. Used with permission. Netscape Communications has not authorized, sponsored, endorsed, or approved this publication and is not responsible for its content.

*New Student Services.* Screen shot from <www.utexas.edu/depts/dos/nss> reprinted with permission of The University of Texas at Austin, Office of the Dean of Students.

*News Service.* "News Service Usenet Access," <http://www.news-service.to/>.

Nuland, Sherwin B. "Medical Fads: Bran, Midwives, and Leeches," *The New York Times*, June 25, 1995, p. E16.

Olds, Sharon. "The One Girl at the Boy's Party" from *The Dead and the Living* by Sharon Olds. Copyright © 1987 by Sharon Olds. Used by permission of Alfred A. Knopf, a division of Random House, Inc.

*The Onion*, Onionhumorgraphic, The Fast-food Lawsuit. Reprinted with permission of *The Onion*. Copyright 2002 by Onion, Inc. <www.theonion.com>.

Orphans III, Listening to Orphan Films, September 26–28, 2005. <www.sc.edu/filmsymposium/orphanfilms.html>.

Patoski, Joe Nick. "Three Cheers for High School Football." Reprinted with permission from the October 1999 issue of *Texas Monthly*.

Puentes, Robert and Bruce Katz. "Getting Real About Gas Prices." The Brookings Institution, October 10, 2005. (<www.brookings.edu/view/op-ed/20051010_puentes.htm>)

Ravitch, Diane. "Educational Insensitivity." Originally published in *The New York Times*, June 5, 2002. Copyright The New York Times. Reprinted by permission.

Santiago, Chiori. "The Fine and Friendly Art of Luis Jiménez," *Smithsonian*, 1993.

Schor, Juliet. *The Overworked American*. New York: Basic Books, 1991.

*Sigma Tau Delta Newsletter*. From the Spring 2000 issue of the *Sigma Tau Delta Newsletter*, © 2000 by Sigma Tau Delta International English Honor Society. Reprinted by permission.

Stateman, Alison. "Postcards from the Edge," *New York Times*, June 15, 2003. © 2003 The New York Times. Reprinted by permission.

Stern, Barbara Lang. "Tears Can be Crucial to Your Physical and Emotional Health," *Vogue*, June 1979, Condé Nast Publications.

Sternbergh, Adam. Got Bud All Up in the Hizzle, Yo! If it weren't for rap, our only new words would be "ideate" and "synergy." First appeared in the <u>National Post</u>, March 15, 2003. Reprinted by permission of the author.

Stevenson, Seth. "Coffeholics—A Dunkin' Donuts Ad for an Addict Nation," *Slate*, April 24, 2006. © Slate. Reprinted by permission.

*Summer Orientation 2000*. Brochure reprinted with permission from the University of Texas at Austin, Office of the Dean of Students.

Texas Business and Education Coalition. "School Gains, 1999," February 27, 2000. <http://www.tbec.org/gains>.

U.S. Unemployment rate. From *Governing* (Sourcebook 2000), p. 101; also U.S. Bureau of Labor Statistics.

*UT Library Online*. "UT Net CAT" web page reprinted by permission of The General Libraries, University of Texas at Austin.

*Utne Reader*, "homepage." <http://utne.com>.

van der Plas, Robert. *The Mountain Bike Book*. San Francisco, Bicycle Books, 1993.

Walt Whitman Web page. <www.poets.org>.

Walzer, Michael. "Feed the Face," *The New Republic*, June 9, 1997, v. 21, p. 29.

*The Weekly Standard*. "homepage." <http://weeklystandard.com>.

West, Cornel. *Race Matters*. Boston: Beacon Press, 1993.

Wilbon, Michael. <www.washingtonpost.com>, June 18, 2002, p D01.

William, Ted. "Only You Can Postpone Forest Fires," *Sierra*, July/August 1995, p. 42.

Wilson, William Julius. *The Truly Disadvantaged*. Chicago: University of Chicago Press, 1987, p. 156.

Wright, Richard. *Native Son*. New York: Harper & Brothers, 1940.

Yahoo! Web page. Reproduced with permission of Yahoo! Inc. Copyright 2000 by Yahoo! Inc. Yahoo! and the Yahoo! logo are trademarks of Yahoo! Inc.

Zinsser, William. "American Places." From *Willie and Drake: An American Profile*. New York: HarperCollins, 1992.

## PHOTO CREDITS

1 Bobby Haas/National Geographic Image Collection; 3 Myrleen Ferguson Cate/PhotoEdit Inc.; 3 Christy Friend; 3 Dan Bosler/Getty Images Inc.-Stone Allstock; 9 Shutterstock; 9 Fotosearch.Com, LLC; 9 iStock Photo International/Royalty Free; 9 David Young-Wolf/PhotoEdit Inc.; 9 SPIN; 9 David Young-Wolf/PhotoEdit Inc.; 15 Christy Friend; 16 Ulrike Welsch/PhotoEdit Inc.; 20 Christy Friend; 22 Gruber-Fashion Wire Daily/AP Wide World Photos; 33 Chuck Savage/Chuck Savage; 33 Janeart, Inc./Getty Images Inc.-Image Bank; 46 Central Pennsylvania College; 46 David Young-Wolff/PhotoEdit Inc.; 46 Mid-South Community College; 55 Library of Congress; 55 Corbis/Bettmann; 57 Getty Images, Inc-Liaison; 62 Photofest; 77 Bobby Haas/National Geographic Image Collection; 79 Getty Images/Time Life Pictures; 79 American Family Physician/Family Practice Management; 83 The University of Arizona Press/Imagination Photo Design; 83 Imagination Photo Design; 83 National Institute of Health; 97 Christy Friend; 283 CHUCK BURTON STRINGER/ASSOCIATED PRESS AP/AP Wide World Photos; 99 Mario Tama/Getty Images; 99 Louisiana State University; 102 Christy Friend; 107 Ray McManus; 111 Boston University Photo Services; 113 Christy Friend; 115 David Young-Wolff/PhotoEdit Inc.; 115 David Young-Wolff/PhotoEdit Inc.; 122 Christy Friend; 127 Scott Gries/Getty Images; 127 Imagination Photo Design; 129 Peter Hamm/The Brady Center to Prevent Gun Violence; 135 National Institute of Health; 135 National Institute of Health; 11 Lowe Worldwide, Inc./National Fluid Mil; 136 ©2006 DD IP Holder LLC; 150 Imagination Photo Design; 150 Imagination Photo Design; 157 Christy Friend; 159 Christy Friend; 160 Mike Simons/Getty Images; 163 Photofest; 163 Universal/Photofest; 168 Christy Friend; 169 Photofest; 170 The Granger Collection; 171 Christy Friend; 183 Bobby Haas/National Geographic Image Collection; 184 David Young-Wolff/PhotoEdit Inc.; 200 Jennifer Lewon/Jennifer Lewon Photography; 186 Lauren Chelec Cafritz; 190 Christy Friend; 196 Jerry Bauer; 197 John Ruszkiewicz; 197 Imagination Photo Design; 199 Ronald Reicen/Lucasfilm Ltd.; 199 Stock Montage/HultonІArchive/Getty Images Inc.-Hulton Archive Photos; 201 Boston University Photo Services; 212 Jerry Bauer; 213 Nancy Crampton/Nancy Crampton; 214 Imagination Photo Design; 218 Dominique Nabokov/Open Society Institute; 219 Ellen Domke/Library of Congress; 221 Turbo/Zefa/Corbis/Bettmann; 223 Pacha/Corbis/Bettmann; 227 Marion Ettlinger; 234 The Onion-New York; 236 Imagination Photo Design; 236 Deborah Feingold/Library of Congress; 237 Barbara Mellix; 238 Rick O'Quinn; 277 George Huey/George H. H. Huey Photography, Inc.; 282 Getty Images Inc.-Hulton Archive Photos; 282 Gordon Parks/Library of Congress; 284 Quintana Roo Dunne/Pearson Education/PH College; 284 James Wakefield/James Cahalan; 284 Globe Photos, Inc.; 288 Jeff Chiu/AP Wide World Photos; 312 Ted Kleine; 317 Bobby Haas/National Geographic Image Collection; 318 American InkMaker Magazine; 333 Xerox Corporation; 333 PH ESM; 339 (c)Warner Brothers/Photofest; 341 (c)Warner Brothers/Photofest; 341 Hellestad Rune/Corbis/Sygma; 363 John Ruszkiewicz; 364 John Ruszkiewicz; 368 Corbis Digital Stock; 369 John Ruszkiewicz; 370 John Ruszkiewicz; 372 RKO Pictures International Inc./Photofest; 376 John Ruszkiewicz; 376 John Ruszkiewicz; 382 Imagination Photo Design; 382 Imagination Photo Design; 382 Imagination Photo Design; 383 Imagination Photo Design; 383 Imagination Photo Design; 383 Imagination

# Index

*because*
  in compound and
    complex sentences,
    266
  as subordinating
    conjunction, 260,
    272, 548
*before*
  as adverb clauses, 262
  as subordinating
    conjunction, 272,
    548
Begging the question
  (circular reasoning),
  140
Beginning writing. *See*
  Draft
Biased language. *See also*
  Sexist language
  about disabled persons,
    232–33
  aged-related, 232
  avoiding, 12
  detecting, in written
    piece, 118–19
  editing, 233–34
  hostile language, 62–63
  racial and ethnic bias,
    231–32
  sexist language, 229–31
  stereotypes, 229–35
  toward sexual
    orientation, 233
Bible passages. *See also*
  Sacred books
  colons in, 568
  periods in, 533
Bibliographies, 622–23.
  *See also* Bibliography
  (CMS style);
  References (APA
  style); Works Cited
  (MLA style)

annotated, 80–81
in library, 618
listing of, 623
tracking sources, 614
types of, 622–23
Bibliography (CMS style),
  guidelines for,
  814–15. *See also*
  CMS style
Biographical information
  in literary analysis,
    170–71
  resources for, 625–26
  subjects/reference
    works, listing of,
    625–26
Biology, style guide for,
  672
Black and white thinking,
  resisting, 119
Block style paragraphs,
  322
Blogs
  parenthetical note
    (APA) for, 767
  parenthetical note
    (MLA) for, 715
  References (APA) for,
    767
  as research sources,
    629
  Works Cited (MLA)
    for, 715
Body of paper, function
  of, 33
Boldface, type style, 330
Bookmarking, of online
  texts, 114
Book reviews, guides to,
  627–28
Books
  capitalization for titles
    of, 593

Notes (CMS) for,
  806–7
parenthetical note
  (APA) for, 762–63
parenthetical note
  (MLA) for, 702–7
quotation marks
  around chapters,
  591
References (APA) for,
  762–63
Works Cited (MLA)
  for, 702–7
Boolean searching,
  630–31
*bored/boring*, ESL writers,
  489
*both . . . and*, parallelism
  and, 278
Brackets, 580–81
  around material added
    to quotations, 661
  with ellipses to show
    omitted material,
    575, 659–60
Brainstorming
  ideas used for outlines,
    40
  for topic, 13–14
Brand names, capitalizing,
  596
British conventions
  dates, 560
  for quotation marks,
    573–74
Brochures, 364–66
  denotative language
    for, 222–23
Buildings, capitalizing
  names of, 596
Business letters
  colons in salutations,
    569

## Revision Guide: Editing and Proofreading Symbols

The boldface chapter and section numbers to the right of each symbol and explanation direct you to relevant places in this book.

| Symbol | Explanation | Ref |
|---|---|---|
| abbr | Problem with an **abbr**eviation | 42a |
| adj | Problem with an **adj**ective. | 30b–d |
| adv | Problem with an **adv**erb. | 30e–f |
| agr | Problem with subject-verb or pronoun-antecedent **agr**eement. | 22, 27 |
| apos | An **apos**trophe is missing or misused. | 25b |
| art | An **art**icle is misused. | 25c, 33b |
| awk | **Awk**ward. Sentence reads poorly, but problem is difficult to identify. | 16f–i  17a–c |
| cap | A word needs to be capitalized. | 41b |
| case | A pronoun is in the wrong **case**. | 28 |
| coh | A sentence or paragraph lacks **coh**erence. | 12a,12b |
| cs | Sentence contains a comma **s**plice. | 35c |
| div | Word **div**ided in the wrong place. | 40c |
| dm (or dang) | **D**angling **m**odifier. A modifying phrase has nothing to attach itself to. | 30a |
| frag | Sentence **frag**ment. | 35a |
| ital | **Ital**ics needed. | 41a |
| lc | Use a **l**owercase instead of a capital letter. | 41b |
| mm | A **m**odifier is **m**isplaced. | 30a |
| num | Problem with the use of **num**bers. | 42b |
| p | Error in **p**unctuation. | 32  34–38 |
| pass | A **pass**ive verb is used ineffectively. | 17a, 23e |
| pl | **Pl**ural form is faulty. | 25a |
| pron | **Pron**oun is faulty in some way. | 26–28 |

| Symbol | Explanation | Ref |
|---|---|---|
| ref | Not clear what a pronoun **ref**ers to. | 26 |
| rep | Word or phrase is **rep**eated ineffectively. | 17c |
| run-on (or fs) | A **run-on** sentence or fused sentence. | 35d |
| sexist | A word or phrase is potentially offensive. | 15d1 |
| sp | A word is mis**sp**elled. | 5b |
| sub | **Sub**ordination is faulty. | 16g |
| trans | A **trans**ition is weak or absent. | 14 |
| vb | Problem with **vb**erb form. | 23, 32 |
| w (or wrdy) | A sentence is **w**ordy. | 17c |
| ww | **W**rong **w**ord in this situation. | 15 |
| ¶ | Begin a new paragraph. | 12 |
| no ¶ | Do not begin a new paragraph. | 12 |
| ⊙ | Insert a period. | 34 |
| ⋏ | Insert a comma. | 36a–c  36e |
| no ⋏ | No comma needed. | 36d |
| ⌄ | Insert an apostrophe. | 25b |
| ⦂ | Insert a colon. | 37b |
| ⦂ | Insert a semicolon. | 37a |
| ⌄⌄ | Insert quotation marks. | 38a |
| // | Make these items parallel. | 16h |
| ∧ | Insert. | |
| ↶ | Cut this word or phrase. | |
| # | Leave a space. | |
| ⌒ | Close up a space. | |
| ✕ | Problem here; find it. | |
| ∼ | Reverse these items. | |